PIONEERS OF AMERICAN LANDSCAPE DESIGN

PIONEERS OF AMERICAN LANDSCAPE DESIGN

Volume Editors

Charles A. Birnbaum, FASLA
National Park Service Historic Landscape Initiative

Robin Karson
Library of American Landscape History

A project of the
National Park Service Historic Landscape Initiative
Library of American Landscape History
CATALOG of Landscape Records in the United States at Wave Hill
Cultural Landscape Foundation

McGraw-Hill

New York   San Francisco   Washington, D.C.   Auckland   Bogotá
Caracas   Lisbon   London   Madrid   Mexico City   Milan
Montreal   New Delhi   San Juan   Singapore
Sydney   Tokyo   Toronto

Library of Congress Cataloging-in-Publication Data

Pioneers of American landscape design / edited by Charles A. Birnbaum, Robin Karson.
p.   cm.
"A project of the National Park Service Historic Landscape Initiative, Library of American Landscape History,
Catalog of Landscape Records in the United States at Wave Hill, Cultural Landscape Foundation."
ISBN 0-07-134420-9
1. Landscape architects—United States—Biography.   2. Horticulturists—United States—Biography.
3. Planners—United States—Biography.   I. Birnbaum, Charles A.
II. Karson, Robin.

SB469.9.P56   2000
712'.092'273—dc21
[B]
00-036155

McGraw-Hill

A Division of The McGraw·Hill Companies

1 2 3 4 5 6 7 8 9 0   DOC/DOC   0 6 5 4 3 2 1 0

ISBN 0-07-134420-9

The sponsoring editor for this book was Wendy Lochner, the editing supervisor was David E. Fogarty,
and the production supervisor was Sherri Souffrance. It was set in Berling Roman
by North Market Street Graphics.

Printed and bound by R. R. Donnelley & Sons Company.

McGraw-Hill books are available at special quantity discounts to use as premiums and sales promotions,
or for use in corporate training programs. For more information, please write to the Director of Special Sales,
Professional Publishing, McGraw-Hill, Two Penn Plaza, New York, NY 10121-2298.
Or contact your local bookstore.

Cover credits:
Front cover: Plan of Prospect Park, Brooklyn, 1866–1867. (National Park Service, Frederick Law Olmsted National Historic Site)
Leverett Pond from Brookline, looking toward Boston, Olmsted Park, Emerald Necklace Parks, MA, 1895. (Brookline Public
    Library)
Front flap: Annual meeting of the American Society of Landscape Architects at Stan Hywet Hall, Akron, OH, 1916. Photo by
    A. D. Taylor (Library of Congress, Manuscript Division)
Back cover, bottom: James C. Rose holding a model of his house and grounds made from scraps during World War II, Okinawa,
    Japan (James C. Rose Archives)
Back cover, top (left to right): Plan of Riverside, Illinois, 1869 (National Park Service, Frederick Law Olmsted National Historic
    Site); Maze at "Castle Hill," Crane Estate, Ipswich, MA (Smithsonian Institution, Archives of American Gardens);
    Point State Park, Pittsburgh, PA (GWSM, Inc.); "Rynwood," Samuel Savage Estate, Glen Head, NY (RMC-Cornell University
    Library); Dewey Donnell Garden, Sonoma, CA (Photograph courtesy Saxon Holt)

MISSION STATEMENTS

The National Park Service (NPS) Historic Landscape Initiative promotes responsible preservation practices that protect our nation's irreplaceable landscape legacy. In partnership with federal and state agencies, professional organizations, and colleges and universities, the HLI achieves its goal by disseminating guidelines for landscape preservation; producing innovative tools to raise awareness of the general public; organizing and conducting training symposia and workshops; and providing technical assistance for significant properties and districts.

Library of American Landscape History, a not-for-profit corporation founded in 1992, promotes conscientious land stewardship through education. The Library produces clear, engaging books about the cultural and artistic significance of North American landscapes and the people who created them. Intended for general readers as well as specialists, Library books are published in collaboration with university and trade presses. The Library organizes touring exhibitions in conjunction with its books for art museums, botanic gardens, and other cultural institutions.

The CATALOG of Landscape Records in the United States at Wave Hill, a major national research resource, gathers information about the location and content of records documenting our use of the land. Founded in 1986, the services it provides, its publications, conferences, and a newsletter, stimulate interest in American landscape and garden history. The CATALOG facilitates the exchange and collection of information vital in developing this aspect of our nation's cultural history. It invites inquiries and contributions of information to its ever-growing databank. Wave Hill is a non-profit public garden and cultural institution located on 28 acres overlooking the Hudson in the Bronx.

The Cultural Landscape Foundation (CLF), based in Washington, DC, is the only not-for-profit foundation in America dedicated to increasing the public's awareness of the irreplaceable legacy of cultural landscapes and their importance. Through education, technical assistance and outreach, the CLF aims to broaden the support and understanding of cultural landscapes nationwide in hopes of saving our priceless heritage for future generations.

CONTENTS

PREFACE

Recent, widespread efforts to unearth information about the landscape architectural past of the United States have shed new light on long-forgotten landscape architects, horticulturists, engineers, authors, teachers, park and cemetery superintendents. This encyclopedia, the first ever published about American landscape practitioners, presents this information in the form of narrative essays. The text was written by more than one hundred dedicated researchers who were inspired by the vitality, beauty, and complexity of the landscape of the United States and a desire to further appreciation of it.

While some contributors worked from voluminous archives—in a few cases, hundreds of thousands of documents—more often, scant material was available to provide information about these pioneers' stories. Some essayists had only news clippings from which to reconstruct a life. These entries represent many hours of research, many years' perspective.

The task of the Library of American Landscape History, an associate publisher in the field, was to preserve the ideas of the contributors and the cadences of their writing while shaping seven hundred manuscript pages into a cohesive whole. We hope that both specialists and general readers find the final product compelling as well as useful.

Each essay in *Pioneers of American Landscape Design* describes a practitioner's life and achievements in broad, concise strokes. Bibliographic citations, archive information, and lists of public sites where the pioneers worked are also provided, so that students, scholars, and professional researchers may delve deeper.

The illustrations in this book are, for the most part, unpeopled. Yet human beings and their relation to the land are the subjects of this project as surely as the landscapes themselves. Catha Grace Rambusch, director of the CATALOG of Landscape Records in the United States at Wave Hill, observed that one of our jobs is to *remind* people—of what we once had, what remains today, and what we are in danger of losing. We are hopeful that this book will encourage readers to become better stewards of the American landscape and that they act to preserve the extraordinary legacy that survives, before it is entirely too late.

Above all, I wish to thank the essayists who wrote this volume. They contributed vast amounts of time, energy, and goodwill to see this project through. I also thank Kay Scheuer, our copyeditor, who applied her decades of experience to ensure that the essays conformed to the highest standards of style and usage, and Kate Laliberte, our intern from the Department of Landscape Architecture and Regional Planning, University of Massachusetts, who input editing changes and resourcefully tracked down missing information. I am grateful to Wendy Lochner for sponsoring the project, David Fogarty for supervising it through production, Charles Birnbaum for imagining it and proposing that we tackle such a book together.

I am also grateful to the trustees of Library of American Landscape History—Nancy R. Turner, John Franklin Miller, Ann Douglass Wilhite, and Nesta Spink—and to Carol Betsch, our managing editor, whose sense of the power and nuance of language has benefited the text enormously.

The Viburnum Foundation provided the generous support that underwrote editing of *Pioneers of American Landscape Design*.

Robin Karson
*Executive Director, Library of
American Landscape History
Amherst, Massachusetts*

ACKNOWLEDGMENTS

A project of this magnitude could not be realized without the support, commitment, and generosity of federal agencies, university faculty, libraries, not-for-profit institutions, private collections, and hundreds of individuals including landscape architects, historians, librarians, archivists, photographers, community activists, and those who actually knew these visionaries of the designed American landscape.

To begin with, I would like to acknowledge my colleagues at the National Park Service Historic Landscape Initiative (NPS HLI), who have supported this project since its onset. Originating under the late H. Ward Jandl, who allowed me to "push the envelope" on the traditional "NPS Reading List" series, the *Pioneers* project has continued to receive full support from Charles Fisher, Jan Townsend, Antoinette J. Lee, and Sharon D. Parks over its eight-year evolution. Additionally, Kay D. Weeks and Jerry Buckbinder were invaluable in the production of the original soft-cover book editions of *Pioneers of American Landscape Design I* and *II*, published in 1993 and 1995, by the Government Printing Office. Also indispensable were Lisa E. Crowder and Julie K. Fix who served as coeditors on these two volumes and Suzanne Keith Loechl who served as a research assistant at the project's onset. It was remarkable to witness what each of these three summer interns achieved in just ten weeks' time.

Throughout this entire project, the *Pioneers* also benefited from the perfect copilot: Catha Grace Rambusch. As Director of the CATALOG of Landscape Records in the United States at Wave Hill, Catha played a key role from the project's very beginning. Her contributions, along with her colleague Chris M. Panos, have included: identifying the pioneers for inclusion, suggesting appropriate contributing authors, securing historic images, obtaining permissions to publish, identifying funding support (the Graham Foundation assisted with the photo costs on *Pioneers II*); and providing editorial suggestions which helped to mold over 100 pioneers essays prior to bringing on our managing editor Robin Karson.

Robin Karson and I first worked together when she

contributed the essay on Warren Manning to *Pioneers I* and the Percival Gallagher entry to *Pioneers II*. In 1992, the Library of American Landscape History (LALH) was founded "in the belief that clear, informative books about North American landscape design would broaden support for enlightened preservation." Recognizing this mission, the LALH was a logical choice as a participant in this project. In 1997, we began to talk about the prospect of bringing the *Pioneers* to an even wider audience. By the spring of the following year we had a publisher's agreement and in January 1999 the NPS HLI transmitted approximately 160 *Pioneers* essays to the LALH. Next the LALH took on the role normally played by the publisher; they edited and shaped all of the entries into a collection of concise narratives that were of a consistent structure and design and readied them for publication. In these final months the LALH did additional troubleshooting. This included securing a few missing historical images, writing two additional pioneer entries, providing contemporary photographs, assisting in the selection of photographic images, working directly with contributors that came late to the project, and in a period of eight months providing final copy to McGraw-Hill.

In addition to these primary sponsors, a number of institutions lent their time and resources. First, the Cultural Landscape Foundation (CLF) officers have coordinated the majority of the photo permissions and managed the project's accounting and disbursement of photo-permission-related publication costs. Working with the NPS and a very limited budget, they managed to cover most of the costs to libraries, universities, and private collections. To the CLF treasurer, Jason Hendrix, we are grateful for his time and energies.

Next, the staff at the Smithsonian Institution, Office of Horticultural Services gave us unlimited access to their rare book collection, magazines, journals, slides and clipping files. Throughout the project, the Smithsonian not only made their diverse collections accessible to us, but they also provided unlimited use of their copy machines and provided over two dozen visual images at no charge.

The dedicated staff included Kathryn Meehan, Nancy Bechtol, Susan R. Gurney, Marca L. Woodhams, and especially Paula Healy.

In addition to the Smithsonian, the Special Collections Library at the Frances Loeb Library, Harvard University, Graduate School of Design under the direction of Mary Daniels has also been an invaluable resource. The Special Collections Library has supported the project in many ways, including the writing of pioneer entries, providing detailed bibliographies, peer review, waving permission fees, and fact checking.

Likewise, the Dumbarton Oaks Garden Library gave support. Joachim Wolschke-Bulmahn, former Director of Landscape Studies, and Annie Thatcher were most generous. The American Society of Landscape Architects gave us complete access to their files of Fellows, and most importantly, the ability to copy all materials. We worked closely with Susan Cahill-Aylward and Lisa Koester. All of this work at ASLA could not have occurred without the support and endorsements of several Executive Vice Presidents including David Bohardt, James G. Dalton, and Peter Kirsch.

In addition to these major sponsors, at the project's onset, a working group was assembled to evaluate research strategies, and to identify potential pioneers for inclusion in the NPS database, and ultimately the publications that followed. This group included Sarah Boasberg, Laura Byers, Jot Carpenter, Keith Crotz, Mary Daniels, Robert E. Grese, Mac Griswold, Herbert Finch, Robert R. Harvey, Robin Karson, Susan Klaus, Michael Laurie, Arleyn Levee, Elizabeth K. Meyer, Dr. Keith Morgan, Patricia M. O'Donnell, Marion Pressley, Walter Punch, Catha Grace Rambusch, Miriam E. Rutz, Dr. David Schuyler, Julia Sniderman, David Streatfield, Dr. George Tatum, William H. Tishler, Suzanne L. Turner, Noel D. Vernon, Piera Weiss, and Dr. Cynthia Zaitzevsky.

Following the recommendations of this working group, a team of committed researchers supplemented the bibliographic findings and helped identify and confirm potential pioneers—based on their surviving written records in books, journals, newspapers, magazines, and catalogues. These responsibilities ranged from recording the full runs of period journals into the NPS database, to providing narrative descriptions for citations supplied by experts on individual practitioners. For their contributions and research efforts during the initial phase of this project we are grateful to Sarah Boasberg, Joanne Seale Lawson, Lee D'Zmura, Susan Klaus, and Piera Weiss. During the later phase in assembling the final draft for the LALH, Pam Liu, Paula Cook, Nord R. Wennerstrom,

and especially Laurie E. Hempton all assisted with final formatting, photo permissions, and troubleshooting.

A number of professional photographers also should be recognized for providing many of the black-and-white and color photographs to this project free-of-charge. To Fred Charles, Richard Cheek, John W. Gutowski, David Halpern, Saxon Holt, Catherine Joy Johnson, Barbara Purro Galasso, Alan Ward, and Carol Betsch we are very grateful.

Finally, most important have been the contributors themselves—who in some cases provided as many as five to seven entries. This group has been generous in their time, energies, and knowledge, and without their generosity this project would have never been realized. We are thankful to Charles E. Aguar, Arnold R. Alanen, Phyllis Anderson, Domenico Annese, Ania Baas, Marie Barnidge-McIntyre, Thomas E. Beaman, Jr., Robert F. Becker, Charles E. Beveridge, Amy Brown, C. Allan Brown, Frank B. Burgraff, Judy Byrd Brittenum, Malcolm D. Cairns, Dean Cardasis, Jot D. Carpenter, Lina L. Confresi, Jean Czerkas, Kurt B. Culbertson, Elizabeth Hope Cushing, Bill Dale, Mary Daniels, Tim Davis, Dennis Domer, Carolyn Etter, Don Etter, Ian W. Firth, Linda Flint McClelland, Angela W. Fowler, Paul Grebinger, Ellen Grebinger, Bradford M. Greene, Carol Greentree, Robert E. Grese, Mac Griswold, John E. Gruber, Barry Hannegan, Robert R. Harvey, Kenneth I. Helphand, Laurie E. Hempton, Gary Hilderbrand, Heidi Hohmann, Catherine M. Howett, Mary V. Hughes, Linda Jewell, Catherine Joy Johnson, Meredith Kaplan, Robin Karson, Gary B. Kesler, Joy M. Kestenbaum, Susan Klaus, Gayle Knight, Gregory Kopischke, Mary Blaine Korff, Arthur Krim, Kate Laliberte, Michael Laurie, Joanne Seale Lawson, Arleyn Levee, Valencia Libby, Blanche M. G. Linden, Eve F. W. Linn, Richard Longstreth, Virginia Lopez Begg, Eldridge Lovelace, Christine B. Lozner, E. Lynn Miller, Karen Madsen, Eleanor M. McPeck, Scott A. Mehaffey, Cydney Millstein, Keith Morgan, Daniel Nadenicek, Lance M. Neckar, Kara Hamley O'Donnell, Therese O'Malley, Jon A. Peterson, Rosetta Radtke, Reuben M. Rainey, Judith Helm Robinson, Nancy Robinson, Carol M. Roland, Miriam E. Rutz, David Schuyler, Behula Shah, Kimberly Alexander Shilland, Dean Sinclair, Stephanie S. Soell, Susan Walters Strahler, David C. Streatfield, Judith B. Tankard, William H. Tishler, Spencer Tunnell II, Christopher Vernon, Nell M. Walker, Sherda K. Williams, Deon K. Wolfenbarger, Aaron Wunch, James J. Yoch, and Cynthia Zaitzevsky.

CHARLES A. BIRNBAUM, FASLA
Coordinator, National Park Service,
Historic Landscape Initiative

A BIT OF HISTORY

In the Fall of 1989, Laura Byers, then Librarian, Studies in the History of Landscape Architecture at Dumbarton Oaks (Washington, D.C.), Charles Birnbaum, Coordinator of the National Park Service Historic Landscape Initiative (NPS HLI), and I were sitting in a coffee shop. We were bemoaning the fact that, with the sole exception of Frederick Law Olmsted, the names of those who designed America's landscapes in the last century were unknown to most people and missing in the annals of our country's cultural history; unacknowledged and yet we live surrounded by their legacy.

As an exercise, we decided to pluck from our memories the names we each knew. At the outset, there were two criteria: the individual had to be dead and we had to know a designed landscape by his or her hand. Between us, we compiled a score of names. We then decided to obviate the second criterion and to include horticulturists, writers, teachers, and others whose work influenced the subject area. Based on our collective knowledge and our new criteria, the list expanded filling not quite two columns on a legal pad. This was the genesis of the *Pioneers of American Landscape Design*, a joint project of The CATALOG of Landscape Records in the United States at Wave Hill and the Historic Landscape Initiative of the National Park Service. From this informal beginning a critical mass of information has been gathered—information that illuminates a hitherto invisible aspect of our land and its form.

How to organize our casually assembled list into a structured database? How to expand it? The search began and continues today. One of the ways was locating and reading existing sources, such as The National Union Catalog of Manuscript Collections and excerpting germane information. The CATALOG began building the database by amassing files with specific information about the location and content of collections of documents that tell us about our use of the land. These are discrete collections, like the archive of a landscape architect or an individual estate or property, and more general collections such as postcards, aerial photographs, and nursery catalogs.

Initially, our focus was the designed landscape, but quickly we realized that our cultural landscapes could not be ignored. They are the very matrix into which designed landscapes, gardens, parks, campuses, cemeteries are set. The CATALOG, therefore, began to accept and seek all such information, lest our narrower view result in the irreplaceable loss of information and in some cases real documents. The CATALOG does not hold any actual documents but has been instrumental in the placement of more than a dozen landscape archives of various sizes and description in suitable repositories.

As we gathered information, the need for the construction of a second database became evident. The first recorded the location of palpable documents. We provide our users with a list of repositories and collections in response to the subject of their research request. The second database has no connection to tangible items. It is pure information, known colloquially as "Bits and Pieces." It is just so, a gathering of data gleaned from many sources, including oral history, exhibition catalogs, academic records, obituaries, and other ephemera, as well as the vital information voluntarily reported to the CATALOG. The facts in "Bits and Pieces" seem mundane, but are essential for fundamental research, such as full name (what do those initials stand for?), birth and death dates, educational background, and academic or informal training. This database at the CATALOG is essentially a reconstruction of the lives and professional careers of people whose ideas and designs were translated into a physical reality on our land.

Operating in tandem with the Historic Landscape Initiative, the CATALOG's databases were utilized. The results of this joint national effort were made available to the public in 1993 as *The Pioneers of American Landscape Design: An Annotated Bibliography*. The fifty-eight entries in the book have a short biography, a photograph (when available), completed bibliographies, and the location of the individual's archive or a notation if none is known to exist. Following in 1995, came *Pioneers II* with the same format and fifty-one entries. In all cases, the entires were prepared, many representing years, even decades, of diligent research, by a cadre of people from around the nation who donated their time and knowledge. Together, we established American-designed landscapes as a vital element in our nation's cultural history.

On the last pages of *Pioneers II* is a Master List comprised of 641 names, all now in the database. The score of names written down in 1989 has grown and it will continue to grow. Yet there are many names on the list about whom we lack the essentials, even their full name.

There is much work to be done. We invite you to join us and participate on our course of discovery.

Gratefully noted is the continued and enthusiastic support of the Board of Directors of Wave Hill. This encouragement enables the CATALOG to provide its services to our nation.

CATHA GRACE RAMBUSCH
*Director, The CATALOG of Landscape Records
in the United States at Wave Hill*

INTRODUCTION

The *Pioneers of American Landscape Design* project was initiated because there is no singular source book or finding aid for researchers seeking information on those visionary practitioners who have had a significant impact on the designed American landscape. Begun in 1992, *Pioneers* aims to document the lives, careers, design philosophies, and in some cases, surviving landscape legacies of those people how have shaped the American landscape. To this end, the Historic Landscape Initiative of the National Park Service (NPS HLI) in cooperation with the CATALOG of Landscape Records in the United States at Wave Hill (CATALOG), and several other cosponsors started a database in 1992 to collect biographic, bibliographic, and archival information on these visionary individuals. The project seeks to document not only professional landscape architects such as Frederick Law Olmsted, Thomas D. Church, Jens Jensen, or Beatrix Jones Farrand, but all those who have played a significant role in shaping our designed landscape heritage. These visionaries are represented in assorted disciplines including: landscape gardening (John Blair, Ernest W. Bowditch, Horace W. S. Cleveland, Andrew Jackson Downing), architecture (Charles Platt, Richard Requa, Philip T. Shutze, Calvert Vaux), horticulture (Liberty Hyde Bailey, John Bartram, George Ellwanger, Kate Sessions), nursery ownership (Patrick Barry, Andre Parmentier, Peter Henderson), cemetery design (Jacob Bigelow, Henry A. S. Dearborn, John Notman, Jacob Weidenmann), planning (Harland Bartholomew, John Nolen, Henry Wright), engineering, landscape engineering (Charles W. Leavitt, Jr., Wilbur H. Simonson), education (John Brinckerhoff Jackson, Frank Waugh, Stanley White), writing (Wilhelm T. Miller, Mabel Osgood Wright, Richardson Wright), journalism (Sylvester Baxter, Mariana Griswold Van Rensselaer), conservation (Genevieve Gillette, Benton MacKaye), surveying (Benjamin Banneker, Alexander Wadsworth), farming (George Washington), sanitation (George E. Waring, Jr.), pomology, forestery (John A. Warder), and others.

A meeting of the ASLA pioneers at Colonial Williamsburg, ca. 1930. Courtesy Manuscript Division, Library of Congress.

The publication also realizes that many of these visionaries possessed a variety of skills, talents, and training. For example, the biographical entry on Chicago landscape architect Alfred Caldwell (1903–1998), also recognizes Caldwell as a "poet, civil engineer, architect, city planner, philosopher and teacher," while the earlier nineteenth century landscape gardener William Saunders (1822–1900) is also described as a "cemetery designer and author."

The *Pioneers* project grew out of the larger National Park Service (NPS) database, an evolving compendium that contains several thousand entries. This publication is one attempt to make the database available and livelier for researchers, practitioners, and homeowners. The biographical entries have been supplemented with more than 450 illustrations including historic and contemporary photographs, plans, sections, postcards, engravings, paintings, and other ephemera that in many cases are unpublished. Going beyond a traditional encyclopedia, and recognizing the power of place, another unique feature of this publication is the detailed listing of sites accessible to the public. This list, noting up to five landscapes designed or influenced by each pioneer, is presented complete with address and phone numbers, and appears as an appendix on pages 475 to 483.

Regrettably, some pioneers and their associated bibliographic records have been excluded because of insufficient information. Finally, in the interest of making *Pioneers* manageable for the reader, each pioneer entry contains a maximum of three important bibliographic citations.

(Further research requests can be made in writing to the National Park Service, Historic Landscape Initiative, 1849 C Street, NW (NC 320), Washington, DC 20240.)

The Pioneers in Context

Following the publication of the National Park Service's *Pioneers of American Landscape Design I* and *II* and the National Trust publication, *American Landscape Architecture: Designers and Places*, edited by William H. Tishler (1989), a surge of interest in landscape history and landscape architecture continues to increase. Tishler's book, part of the Building Watchers Series, contains twenty-one biographical entries. However, Tishler recognizes that a lack of information about the broader population of landscape professionals poses a challenge for historians and landscape architects when attempting to evaluate a property's significance and establish its context. In his

introduction, Tishler writes, "a better understanding of this legacy can help to shape future environments that will continue, and perhaps even strengthen, the inseparable relationship Americans have always had with their land."

Similarly, *Bulletin 18: How to Evaluate and Nominate Designed Historic Landscapes* (1987), an NPS publication of the National Register of Historic Places, states that "determining the relationship between an individual landscape and the historic development and practice of landscape architecture is an essential factor in determining significance." Collectively, these publications articulate that if our goal is to understand the significance and integrity of an individual landscape and ultimately articulate a preservation philosophy, it is critical to understand the creator's design philosophy, their body of professional work, and to understand and evaluate what survives of their legacy on the American landscape today. Following this, an historic designed landscape's context can be established.

Fortunately, an ever-increasing number of resources are available to achieve this goal. A diversity of books and monographs about landscape history, landscape types, and specific designers' works is now available with many more planned and in production. In this decade, the list of resources includes: *100 Years of Landscape Architecture: Some Patterns of A Century* by Melanie Simo (1999); *Dan Kiley: The Complete Works of America's Master Landscape Architect* by Dan Kiley and Jane Amidon (1999); *George Washington at Mt. Vernon: Landscape of the Inner Man* by Mac Griswold (1999); *Wilderness by Design: Landscape Architecture and the National Park Service* by Ethan Carr (1998); *Country, Park & City: The Architecture and Life of Calvert Vaux* by Francis R. Kowsky (1998); *Frederick Law Olmsted: Designing the American Landscape* by Charles E. Beveridge (1998); *Alfred Caldwell: The Life and Work of a Prairie School Landscape Architect* by Dennis Domer (1997); *To Live in the New World: A. J. Downing and American Landscape Gardening* by Judith K. Major (1997); *Garrett Eckbo: Modern Landscapes for Living* by Marc Treib and Dorothee Imbert (1997); *Making a Landscape of Continuity: The Practice of Innocenti and Webel* by Gary R. Hilderbrand (1997); *Pioneer of Tropical Landscape Architecture: William Lyman Phillips in Florida* by Faith R. Jackson (1997); *The Gardens of Ellen Biddle Shipman* by Judith Tankard (1996); *Apostle of Taste: Andrew Jackson Downing, 1815–1852* by David Schuyler (1996); *Beatrix: The Gardening Life of Beatrix Jones Farrand* by Jane Brown (1995); *Money, Manure and Maintenance: Marian Coffin,*

Pioneer Landscape Architect, by Nancy Fleming (1995); *Gardens of Historic Charleston* by James Cothran (1995); *California Gardens: Creating A New Eden* by David Streatfield (1994); *Presenting Nature: The Historic Landscape Design of the National Park Service* by Linda Flint McClelland (1993); *The California Garden* by Jere French (1993); *Jens Jensen: Maker of Natural Parks and Gardens* by Robert E. Grese (1992); and reprints of *Italian Gardens* by Charles Platt (1993) and *Charles Eliot, Landscape Architect* (1999) both with new introductions by Keith N. Morgan and Jens Jensen's seminal classic, *Siftings* (1990).

Additionally, The Library of American Landscape History (LALH), established in 1992, produces informative books about North American landscape design and is building a network of support for enlightened landscape preservation. In 1996, the LALH published *The Muses of Gwinn*, a monograph on a Cleveland, Ohio garden designed by Charles Platt and Warren Manning and more recently, *Landscape Architecture in the Midwest*, a collection of thirteen essays edited by William H. Tishler, that focuses on the contributions of midwestern practitioners (1999). LALH is currently undertaking a ten-volume set of reprints of classic books on American landscape architecture in celebration of the American Society of Landscape Architects' Centennial, including many originally written by the pioneers contained in this publication.

In addition to published works, a number of traveling exhibitions have focused on significant landscape architects and places, many of which have been mounted over the past five years. These exhibitions have been regional and national in scope and scale, and have focused on practitioners such as Frederick Law Olmsted, Sr., Ellen Biddle Shipman, George E. Kessler, Samuel Parsons, Jr., Calvert Vaux, Sidney and Herbert Hare, Florence Yoch, and Charles A. Platt. For example, the exhibition *A Room of One's Own: The American Woman Garden Writer, 1900–1940*, highlighted the careers and works of Martha Brookes Hutcheson, Grace Tabor, and Louisa Yeomans King. (All of these pioneers are included in this publication, and in all cases the exhibition curator has served as the author.) Other exhibitions have been mounted by the Harvard Graduate School of Design, Department of Landscape Architecture (Daniel Urban Kiley Lecture and Exhibition Fund); the University of California at Berkeley; PaineWebber; and the George Eastman Center for International Photography among many others.

Conferences on landscape history have increased in frequency and popularity. For instance, the CATALOG at Wave Hill along with the NPS HLI sponsored *The Landscape Universe: Historic Designed Landscapes in Context* (1993), *Preserving Modern Landscape Architecture* (1995), and most recently, *If Only We Knew: Landscape Preservation in Context, 1890–1950* (1999). Collectively, these conferences explored the work of a variety of pioneers contained in this encyclopedia and include: Stanley W. Abbott, Charles Eliot, Charles Freeman Gillette, Ralph Griswold, Jens Jensen, John Charles Olmsted, Frederick Law Olmsted, Jr., Andre Parmentier, Samuel Parsons Jr., James C. Rose, Arthur Shurcliff and Morley Jeffers Williams. In addition, the Garden Conservancy sponsored a series of symposia over several years titled, *Masters of American Garden Design*, that explored a variety of garden designers and types from the California gardens of Lockwood de Forest III to the modern garden designs of James C. Rose. Other groups also exploring this area include the Society of American and Regional Planning History (along with the Urban History Association), the Society of Architectural Historians, the American Society of Landscape Architects, the New England Garden History Society, the Southern Garden History Society, the National Association for Olmsted Parks, and the George Wright Society.

Public awareness has also found a more mainstream outlet with the issuance of a postage stamp by the U.S. Postal Service in September 1999 to commemorate "Frederick Law Olmsted—Landscape Architect." The stamp, designed as a montage, presents Olmsted at Vanderbilt's Biltmore Estate as portrayed in the John Singer Sargent painting, along with images from New York's Central and Prospect Parks. All this suggests that the subject area has moved from a small circle of historians, practitioners, and concerned citizenry to a much broader public who are eager to learn more about Olmsted and his contemporaries. Quite a leap since 1981, when Adele Chatfield Taylor (then director of the Design Arts program of the National Endowment for the Arts) remarked at the annual meeting of the American Society of Landscape Architects that "only now are people beginning to recognize that Central Park was not created by God—but by a man named Olmsted."

The Pioneers

The 160 pioneers included in this encyclopedia represent a broad range of skills, training and expertise. Until now, a lack of information about these practitioners has posed a challenge for landscape historians, landscape architects, and preservation professionals attempting to evaluate a property's historical significance and establish its context.

As previously noted, the need to provide a nation-wide context for evaluating designed historic landscapes or planning for their future has served as a catalyst for maintaining and expanding the NPS database and has led to the production of this expanded publication. Suzanne L. Turner, a professor of landscape architecture at Louisiana State University, encapsulated the need for more thorough research and analysis in her epilogue to *The Landscape Universe* (1993): "What is this canon of work that has preceded us, that has laid the foundation for the practice of landscape preservation? What are some of the benchmarks against which we might compare the work that is being done by landscape architects and allied professionals?"

These questions are particularly important in preservation. Our answers can determine which landscapes are preserved, rehabilitated, or restored while others may be altered or razed without any public discourse or recognition of their importance. The background events surrounding the entry on pioneer landscape architect George Elberton Burnap (1885–1938) provide an excellent example. Several years ago, historian Deon Wolfenbarger contacted NPS HLI for information about a relatively unknown landscape architect who had done some work in St. Joseph, Missouri. Wolfenbarger wanted to prepare a National Register nomination for the St. Joseph Parks and Parkways System. We sent her a copy of the working files we had on Burnap. Coincidentally, another landscape architect Ethan Carr contacted us for

background information while preparing a National Historic Landmark nomination application for Meridian Hill Park in Washington, D.C., another Burnap project. Naturally, we put Wolfenbarger and Carr in touch with one another to share information. By placing Burnap in the national context of his landscape design, both Wolfenbarger's and Carr's nominations were successful. In fact, Meridian Hill Park became a National Historic Landmark solely on the strength of its significance in the field of landscape architecture. Because of her extensive research, Wolfenbarger consented to write the narrative on Burnap that appears in her biographical essay.

Burnap (1885–1938) is representative of many of the other landscape architect pioneer entries. Born in the second half of the nineteenth century, he lived well into the twentieth century. His life spanned the crucial period that saw tremendous growth in the landscape architecture profession. Many of the pioneers, for example, presented herein were contempories of Burnap. Some, such as Alfred Caldwell (1903–1998), Marjorie Sewell Cautley (1891–1954), Thomas Dolliver Church (1902–1978), Gilmore Clarke (1892–1982), Umberto Innocenti (1895–1968), John Brinckerhoff Jackson (1909–1996), Norman Newton (1898–1992), James C. Rose (1913–1991), Margherita Tarr (1903–1990), Christopher Tunnard (1910–1979) and Harriett Wimmer (1900–1980) lived their professional lives entirely in the twentieth century. Other pioneers preceded Burnap by several decades, including: Patrick Barry (1816–1890), John Blair (1820–1906), H. W. S. Cleveland (1814–1900), Robert Morris Copeland (1830–1874), Andrew Jackson Downing (1815–1852), Hans Jacob Ehlers (1804–1858), Louis Augustus Ehlers

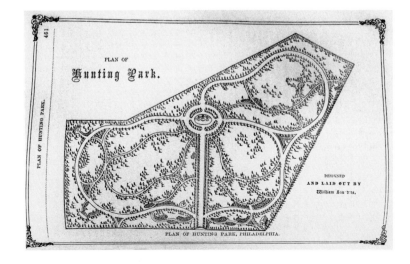

The largely forgotten landscape gardener William Saunders (1822–1900) prepared this plan for a Philadelphia Hunting Park. From *The Horticulturist*, January 1858.

(1835–1911), George Ellwanger (1816–1906), Peter Henderson (1822–1890), John Notman (1810–1865), William Saunders (1822–1900), and Alexander Wadsworth (1806–1898). Significantly, many of these important early landscape gardeners, such as Blair, Ehlers, and Saunders have been largely absent from all histories of the American landscape written to date. The entry for John Blair, for example, states that his "reputation grew as a result of a horticultural display he designed for the 1865 Chicago Sanitary Fair, an event that probably brought him into contact with Frederick Law Olmsted, Sr."

Within this earlier time period, a number of practitioners whose primary contribution was the design of rural cemeteries (which began with the design of Mount Auburn Cemetery in Cambridge, Mass., in 1831) have remained obscure, and quite often, uncelebrated. This era of professional practice from the 1830s to the turn-of-the-century included such pioneers (and projects) as Jacob Bigelow (1787–1879, Mount Auburn Cemetery), Henry A. S. Dearborn (1783–1851, Forest Hills Cemetery, Boston, Mass.), John Notman (1810–1865, Laurel Hill Cemetery, Philadelphia, Pa.); Adolph Strauch (1822–1883, Spring Grove Cemetery, Cincinnati, Ohio), Alexander Wadsworth (Woodland Cemetery, Chelsea, Mass.); Downing Vaux (1856–1926, Rose Hill Cemetery, Linden, N.J.) and Jacob Weidenmann (1829–1893, Cedar Hill Cemetery, Hartford, Conn.). Cedar Hill incidentally serves as the final resting place for Frederick Law Olmsted, Sr.

Benjamin Banneker (1731–1806) is the least-known practitioner in the encyclopedia to live and work in the eighteenth century (aside from George Washington, Thomas Jefferson, and John Bartram). He is also the only African-American. The Banneker essay suggests that he was a key contributor to the well-known Ellicott plan. Like African-Americans, women came late to the profession, and comprise thirty-one of the entries. Their contributions and careers are diverse in scope and geography. For example, Genevieve Gillette's lobbying and conservation work in Michigan, Beatrix Jones Farrand's campus work, Louise Beebe Wilder's influential garden books, and Kate Sessions as "the Mother of Balboa Park" for her years of garden-making at the site of two San Diego exhibitions.

An interesting theme emerged during preparation of *Pioneers*—the interconnectedness between members of the landscape architecture profession. For example, practitioners vying for the same projects (the Boston Park System and the Central Park competition); collaborating on designs and plans (A.J. Downing Memorial Park in Newburgh, N.Y., is the only known commission that John Charles and Frederick Law Olmsted, Sr., collaborated on with Calvert and his son Downing Vaux); working on the same landscapes at different times (Nathan F. Barrett and later Fletcher Steele at Naumkeag, Stockbridge, Mass., or Guy Lowell and later the Olmsted Brothers at the Coe Estate on Long Island); and mentoring and supporting each other professionally and academically. For example, a letter of endorsement from F. L. Olmsted, Sr., led to George E. Kessler's first professional position as the designer of a park in Merriam, Kansas.

In November 1922, James Greenleaf (far left) of the federal Commission of Fine Arts conferred with Daniel Hull (middle left) and others on the plans for the new village in Yosemite Valley. Courtesy National Park Service Historic Photography Collection.

The Palos Verdes Estates, Palos Verdes, California, 1926. The Olmsted Brothers were the Directors of Design for this 25,000-acre community. Olmsted Office staff on the project included James Frederick Dawson, George Gibbs, Edward C. Whiting, John Charles Olmsted, and Frederick Law Olmsted, Jr. Courtesy Charles A. Birnbaum.

Later, in the early 1900s, Kessler spurred young talent—by hiring Henry Wright (later of Wright and Stein) to open his St. Louis office where the young planner worked on the restoration of Forest Park and a planting plan for Washington University among other projects.

Probably the greatest illustration of this extended "family tree" can be noted by the dozens of pioneers who had close ties to the Olmsted office (and the Harvard Program that was under the direction of Frederick Law Olmsted, Jr. beginning in 1900). Olmsted office employees included Myrl E. Bottomley (1922); James Frederick Dawson (1896–1940); Alling S. DeForest (1897, 1899–1900); Charles Eliot (1883–1885, 1887–1897); Paul R. Frost (1909–1910); Percival Gallagher (1894–1934); George Gibbs, Jr. (1905–1914, 1923–1933); Henry V. Hubbard (1901–1906, 1920–1947); Warren H. Manning (1888-1896); William B. Marquis (1919–1962); Frederick Law Olmsted, Jr. (1895–1949); John Charles Olmsted (1884–1920); Bremer W. Pond (1909–1911); James S. Pray (1898–1903); Arthur A. Shurcliff (1896–1903); Edward C. Whiting (1905–1962); and Alanson P. Wyman (1899–1902).

Additionally, several pioneers graduated from the Harvard program under the direction of Frederick Law Olmsted, Jr., including Stephen Child, George Gibbs, Jr., S. Herbert Hare, Henry V. Hubbard, William Bell Marquis, William L. Phillips, Bremer W. Pond, and Arthur A. Shurcliff.

An asterisk—*—next to a name in a narrative denotes a separate biographical entry. The tree image at the beginning of each biographical entry and the serpentine image used throughout the book are from Henry V. Hubbard and Theodore Kimball, *An Introduction to the Study of Landscape Design*, New York: Macmillan, 1917.

Looking ahead, it is hoped that the *Pioneers* project will provide the spark for better informed historic preservation and design activities as well as greater research in landscape history. The National Park Service is committed to understanding these pioneers in the context of its stewardship and management of cultural landscapes nationwide. It is crucial to realize that from forests to farmyards, cities to cemeteries, roads to river corridors, parklands to private homes, these landscape pioneers have literally shaped our nation.

Finally, as I conclude this introduction on the eve of its delivery to the publishing house of McGraw-Hill on West 19th Street, I have to smile. I realize that just a stone's throw away, exactly a century ago, on January 4, 1899 in the St. James Building on Broadway at 26th Street, the American Society of Landscape Architects was founded at the offices of Samuel Parsons Jr. and Company. The interconnectedness continues and the story goes on.

CHARLES A. BIRNBAUM, FASLA
Coordinator, National Park Service,
Historic Landscape Initiative

PIONEERS OF AMERICAN
LANDSCAPE DESIGN

ABBOTT, STANLEY WILLIAM
(1908–1975)
landscape architect

Stanley William Abbott was born in Yonkers, New York. At the age of seventeen, he entered Cornell University's program in landscape architecture, concentrating on land use planning and park design. After graduating with a B.A. in 1930, Abbott took a professional position with the Finger Lakes State Parks Commission in Ithaca, New York. A year later, he left Ithaca to become Public Information Officer in charge of annual reports and photography for the Westchester County (N.Y.) Parks Commission, where he worked with two pioneers of parkway design, Jay Downer and Gilmore Clarke*. Abbott must have impressed his superiors, for in 1933, when Downer and Clarke were asked to advise the federal government on the creation of a parkway to link the Shenandoah and the Great Smoky Mountains National Parks, they recommended he be appointed as their representative on site. He was only twenty-five years old.

The new road came to be known as the Blue Ridge Parkway. Running 469 miles through the southern Appalachians, it was one of the first and most ambitious of the make-work projects initiated by the Roosevelt administration. Many people were involved in its planning, design, construction, and management, but Abbott came to play a central role. Downer and Clarke withdrew in 1934 after a disagreement over fees, and Abbott thereafter provided the vision that unified all aspects of the enormous undertaking.

Abbott emphasized the importance of scenic variety in determining the exact location of the road, and successfully advocated the acquisition of additional land for a string of recreation areas along the route. While the engineers in the Bureau of Public Roads were trying to build a modern highway with standards for grade and curvature that would provide for speed and safety, Abbott's team of landscape architects and architects was concerned to fit the road to the mountain terrain, to heal construction scars, and to develop an architectural style for bridges and other structures that reflected a sense of place. Realizing the importance of reaching out to the parkway's neighbors, particularly the farmers along the route, Abbott devised a series of programs to encourage good land management practices while preserving features associated with traditional ways of life in the mountains. He saw these

programs coming together to create a "museum of managed American countryside," a new concept in national parks.

In 1950, Abbott headed the National Park Service staff on the planning team for a proposed Mississippi River Parkway. The final report recommended a road based on the improvement of existing highways, now known as the Great River Road. In 1953, Abbott was appointed superintendent of Colonial National Historical Park in Virginia. In that capacity he oversaw the completion of the Colonial Parkway connecting Jamestown, Williamsburg, and Yorktown, and several related developments associated with the observance in 1957 of the 350th anniversary of the settlement of Jamestown. He retired from the Park Service in 1966.

Thereafter, Abbott went into private practice with his son, Carlton Sturges Abbott, forming Abbott Associates, a firm of architects and landscape architects located in Williamsburg. Among his significant projects in Virginia were the redesign of the gardens of the Governor's Mansion in Richmond, and the major site planning for Virginia Military Institute, Hollins College, Virginia Polytechnic Institute and State University, Radford College, Mary Baldwin College, and Roanoke College. Abbott also served as a consultant on the design of inter-

Stanley W. Abbott. Collection Blue Ridge Parkway. Courtesy National Park Service.

The Blue Ridge Parkway, completed road beside Rakes Mill Pond, Virginia, 1942. Photo E. H. Abbuehl. Collection Blue Ridge Parkway. Courtesy National Park Service.

Present-day view of Blue Ridge Parkway. Courtesy Robert R. Page.

state highways and planned a number of Virginia state and city parks, including Seashore State Park (Virginia Beach), James River Park (Richmond), Waller Mill Park (Williamsburg), Chippokes Plantation State Park, York River State Park, and False Cape State Park. In addition, he designed numerous residential gardens.

Abbott, Stanley W. "Historic Preservation: Perpetuation of Scenes Where History Becomes Real." *Landscape Architecture* 40 (July 1950), 153–157. Protection of historic resources with illustrated examples (e.g., battlefields, parks, historic properties).

Abbott, Stanley W. "Parkways—Past, Present, and Future." *Parks & Recreation* 31 (December 1948), 681–691. Paper given at 50th Annual Meeting of American Institute of Park Executives, Boston, October 4, 1948; illustrations.

Buxton, Barry M., and Steven M. Beatty, eds. *Blue Ridge Parkway, Agent of Transition: Proceedings of the Blue Ridge Parkway Golden Anniversary Conference.* Boone, N.C.: Appalachian Consortium Press, 1986. A collection of essays on the Blue Ridge Parkway.

Nancy Robinson and Ian Firth

ALLEN, NELLIE B. (OSBORN)
(1869–1961)
landscape architect

Nellie Beatrice Osborn was born in Cameron, Missouri, the oldest of five children. Little is known about her early years, education, and marriage to Sidney P. Allen, founder of the Louisiana Land and Exploration Company, whom she later divorced.

Between 1916 and 1919, she attended the Lowthorpe School of Landscape Architecture for Women in Groton, Massachusetts, under the name Beatrice Osborn Allen. In 1919, while living in Boston shortly after completing her studies at Lowthorpe, Allen received her first commission, from Mrs. William D. Miller of Wyndhow in Ashburnham, Massachusetts. Allen's responsibilities included the general garden layout, architectural features, and planting specifications for a steep hillside garden. The outlines of the garden exist today. Fletcher Steele*, who was also retained by the Millers and was an instructor at Lowthorpe at the time, may have provided the contact for Allen.

In 1921, Allen visited gardens in England and Italy, including Gertrude Jekyll's home at Munstead Wood, in Surrey. Jekyll's innovative planting principles, as demonstrated in her garden and in her many books, would play a decisive role in Allen's development as a landscape architect. Allen visited English gardens on several occasions until 1949.

Nellie B. Allen, 1914. Courtesy Oliver Osborn.

"A Persian Garden." Watercolor, signed and dated Beatrice O. Allen / February 17, 1919. Courtesy Rare and Manuscript Collections, Carl A. Kroch Library, Cornell University.

Between 1921 and the late 1940s, Allen maintained a landscape architectural practice based in New York City, designing residential gardens primarily in the New York–New England area, using the name Nellie B. Allen. Since no other names appear on her planting plans or office correspondence, it is likely that she had a small practice and worked alone. Allen also lectured on garden design and garden history in the area, using an extensive collection of glass lantern slides.

Like many graduates of the Lowthorpe program, Allen focused on perennials and planting design, excelling in the design of Anglo-American–style perennial borders, such as those at Dellwood, the John Henry Hammond estate in Mount Kisco, New York (1939), and Brookmeade, the Isabel Dodge Sloane estate in Locust Valley, New York (c. 1935). Allen's unusual capabilities as a planting designer can be directly linked to her familiarity with Jekyll's theories and her long personal friendship with the English designer. The attrac-

tive long double perennial borders at Brookmeade, for instance, featuring blue and white flowers, hark back to a Lowthorpe exercise involving a study of Jekyll's color borders detailed in her book *Colour in the Flower Garden* (1908).

Allen's specialties were knot gardens and geometrically hedged green gardens that incorporated traditional perennials. She took her inspiration from English cottage gardens and Elizabethan-style knot gardens she visited on her trips abroad. Allen's early interest in green gardens surfaced in her thesis project at Lowthorpe, which featured a knot garden with yew bird topiaries similar to those she had photographed at Great Dixter in East Sussex (laid out by Jekyll's collaborator, the English architect Edwin Lutyens) and in the Cotswolds. At least four of Allen's gardens included these features: the yew buttresses at Three Waters, Gloucester, Massachusetts, for Edith Notman (c. 1926); the knot garden at Thornedale, Millbrook, New York, for Mrs. Oakleigh

Gardens at Dellwood, Mount Kisco, New York, c. 1939. Courtesy Rare and Manuscript Collections, Carl A. Kroch Library, Cornell University.

Thorne (1934); the Bishop's Garden, Washington, D.C., where she was a consultant between 1927 and 1937; and the parterre garden for the 1939 New York World's Fair in Flushing, designed in collaboration with Constance Boardman.

Allen's other projects include a walled garden for Frank E. Bliss, New Rochelle, New York (1927); a pool garden for Clifford McCall at Evesdune, East Hampton, Long Island (circa 1927); a rock garden for Mrs. Evelina Ball Perkins, Riverdale, New York (1934, now Wave Hill); and the well-publicized woodland gardens at Otahnagon, the Anne Morgan and Anne Vanderbilt country estate in Mount Kisco, New York (c. 1936).

Of the sixteen gardens identified to date, Allen's most important commission was the Elizabethan-style knot garden at Thornedale which was commended by *Landscape Architecture* in 1938. The client, Mrs. Oakleigh Thorne, an influential member of the Garden Club of America (and later president), asked Marian Coffin* and Helen Page Wodell to design other areas of the garden.

Although Allen only wrote two brief articles herself, her garden designs were sometimes featured in *House Beautiful, Home and Field, Country Life in America*, and in the annual British publication *Gardens and Gardening*. She died in a New York City nursing home at the age of ninety-one.

Allen, Nellie B. "A Tulip and Geranium Garden." *House and Garden*, August 1942, 68–69. Two plans and elevations of a fragrant spring border for Morgan and Vanderbilt, plant list, and description.

"At the League Exhibit in 1938." *Landscape Architecture* 28 (July 1938), 171–173 (Thorne garden). For other projects, see *Yearbook of the Architectural League of New York and Catalogue of the Annual Exhibition* for 1928, 1937, and 1938.

Tankard, Judith B. "Women Pioneers in Landscape Design." *Radcliffe Quarterly*, March 1993, 8–11. Brief

biography of Allen and other early women landscape architects.

A small collection of photographs and plans of Nellie B. Allen's work is on deposit at the Rare and Manuscript Collections, Carl A. Kroch Library, Cornell University. An important component of the collection is Allen's Lowthorpe School projects.

———————————

Judith B. Tankard

BAILEY, LIBERTY HYDE
(1858–1954)
horticulturist, editor, author

Liberty Hyde Bailey was born on the farm his parents had built in South Haven on the shores of Lake Michigan. As a young boy, he took a keen interest in the birds, animals, and plants found near his home. His fascination with nature was lifelong. Bailey studied under the botanist William J. Beal, earning a B.S. in 1882 and an M.S. in 1886 at Michigan State Agricultural College (now Michigan State University) in East Lansing. Between his degrees, from 1882 to 1884, Bailey worked as an assistant to the botanist Asa Gray at Harvard College. Bailey stayed on at Michigan State as a professor of horticulture, organizing the Department of Horticulture and Landscape Gardening in 1885, the first of its kind in the country. In 1888, Bailey accepted a similar position at Cornell University in Ithaca, New York, where he became director of the Cornell College of Agriculture, dean of its faculty, and a professor of rural economy. During his tenure at Cornell, Bailey greatly expanded the college's programs and organized the country's first farm extension program.

In 1908, Theodore Roosevelt appointed Bailey head of his presidential commission to survey conditions of life in rural America and make recommendations for its improvement. The resulting report of the Country Life Commission provided a broad framework for agricultural education and extension work at land-grant colleges throughout the United States, including the creation of many positions in landscape architecture extension. (Bailey's editorial assistant, Wilhelm Miller*, who accepted an extension position at the University of

Illinois, was among the earliest landscape architects in that role.)

Bailey retired from the deanship of the College of

Liberty Hyde Bailey. Courtesy Rare and Manuscript Collections, Carl A. Kroch Library, Cornell University.

Illustration from Bailey's *Manual of Gardening* (New York: Macmillan, 1910). Courtesy Rare and Manuscript Collections, Carl A. Kroch Library, Cornell University.

Agriculture in 1913 to devote time to writing, editing, and lecturing on wide-ranging subjects, from practical agriculture, horticulture, and landscape design to philosophy, civics, nature study, evolution, and conservation. His book *The Holy Earth*, published in 1916, was an eloquent plea for environmental consciousness and inspired Aldo Leopold's later ideas about a land ethic. Bailey's prodigious work as an editor included the *Cyclopedia of American Horticulture* (4 volumes, 1900–1902), the *Cyclopedia of American Agriculture* (4 volumes, 1907–1909), and the magazines *American Garden* (1890–1893) and *Country Life in America* (during the early 1900s); and he did much to advance the fields of horticulture and landscape design through these popular works. Writers for the magazines and other book series he edited included many of the early practitioners of landscape architecture, including Warren Manning*, Wilhelm Miller*, Frederick Law Olmsted Jr.*, Samuel Parsons Jr.*, O. C. Simonds*, Feruccio Vitale*, and Frank Waugh*.

Bailey's extensive writings on horticulture and landscape gardening provide glimpses into his larger ideas about landscape design. In his article "What Are the Fundamental Concepts in Landscape Gardening?" which appeared in *Park and Cemetery* in December 1897, Bailey guided readers away from thinking of landscape gardening simply as a set of rules about what to plant, toward the notion of "making a picture." The garden designer should think of the place as a unit, with a central point or feature, and concentrate on the major motives—those having a "landscape effect"—before dwelling on details, the "garnishings and reliefs." Bailey urged his readers to attend to the overall framework—the lawn and mass plantings—before concentrating on the "intrinsic merits" of individual plants, and suggested keeping "the center of the place open," framing and massing the sides to avoid "scattered effects."

In his 1916 edition of the *Standard Cyclopedia of Horticulture*, Bailey wrote the entry on landscape gardening himself. In it, he noted that although the term "landscape architecture" better expressed the breadth of topics relating to the larger elements of landscape design, because his interest was in the horticultural aspects, he used the term "landscape gardening." Like other arts, it had a significant conceptual as well as practical component: "The working out of the details of the plan is to landscape gardening what building is to architecture, or what pen-work and grammar are to literature. It is the industrial or constructional part of the work." Bailey's essay provided an overview of the history of landscape gardening in the United States, describing recent trends that were changing the scope of the field: "A marked development of landscape art in recent time is the application of it to very small and plain home grounds and to secondary civic areas. Even the back yard of the tenement is within its range. This is an illustration of the extension of social democracy."

During his retirement, Bailey spent much of his time researching and collecting plants from around the world and studying the origin and adaptation of cultivated plants. From 1923 to 1949 he published over a hundred papers on the taxonomy of *Rubus, Vitis, Brassica*, the palms, and others. He also taught, both in the classroom at Cornell and on farms in his association with various extension programs. In addition he dedicated countless hours creating the Hortatorium, which he described as a "repository of things of the garden." Bailey donated the Hortatorium, which included his private herbarium of 125,000 plant specimens and a library of approximately 3,000 volumes, to Cornell in 1935.

Bailey's numerous awards and honors include the Marshall P. Wilder Bronze (1885) and Silver (1921 and 1947) medals; the Veitch Silver (1897) and Gold (1927) medals of the Royal Horticultural Society, London; the Gold Medal (1947) of the National Institute of Social Sciences; the George Robert White Gold Medal of the Massachusetts Horticultural Society (1927); and honorary membership in the American Society of Landscape Architects.

Bailey, Liberty Hyde. *The Holy Earth*. New York: Charles Scribner's Sons, 1916. Essay on humans' relationship with the earth; eloquent plea for the development of a land ethic respecting nature.

Bailey, Liberty Hyde. *The Manual of Gardening—A Practical Guide*. New York: Macmillan, 1910. Combines information from two earlier books, *Garden Making* and *The Practical Garden Book*, as a handbook for the home gardener; explains principles of design and composition and includes an extensive list of plants; line drawings, photos.

Bailey, Liberty Hyde. *Standard Cyclopedia of Horticulture*. 6 vols. New York: Macmillan, 1916 (reprinted in 3 vols., 1925). Massive compendium of information related to the horticultural arts; many individual sections were written by Bailey, including an overview of landscape gardening and its history.

Robert E. Grese

BANNEKER, BENJAMIN
(1731–1806)
surveyor, astronomer

Benjamin Banneker was born at Elkridge Landing on the Patapsco River near the present-day city of Ellicott, Maryland. Banneker's grandmother, Molly Welsh, was a white indentured servant sent to the American colonies from Great Britain for the criminal offense of accidentally spilling a bucket of milk. On completion of her period of servitude, she bought two African slaves and set them free. One of the former slaves worked on her farm; in 1696 she married the other, a son of an African prince whose name was Bannaka or Banneky. Their daughter Mary followed the same marital route; she bought a slave, set him free, and married him. He took the Christian name of Robert and assumed his wife's family name of Banneky. It was to Mary and Robert Banneky that Benjamin was born.

Benjamin Banneky's grandmother taught him to read, to write, and to assess the landscape and its elements—vegetation, wind, climate, and the like. His African grandfather passed on to him the knowledge and love of astronomy. Later, Banneky attended a Quaker school where the schoolmaster misspelled his surname as Banneker; it remained that way for the rest of his life.

The Quaker schoolmaster gave Banneker the copy of Newton's *Principia* and the pocket watch that launched him on a scientific career. After careful study of the watch, Banneker built a clock in 1753. It is considered by many historians to be the first clock built in America. (Lack of parts and of skilled craftsmen had prevented the timepieces from being manufactured or serviced in the New World.) People from all over the colonies started to seek out Banneker to repair their clocks.

In 1772 the Ellicott family, including young Andrew Ellicott, arrived in Maryland from Bucks County, Pennsylvania, and settled on land near Banneker's property. They tried to establish a grain-milling operation but were unable to assemble the pieces of their purchased mill. On advice from Quakers in the surrounding community, the Ellicotts hired Banneker, who was able to put the mill together. Banneker became friendly with the family, and they supplied him with astronomical instruments and copies of Ferguson's *Astronomy* and Flamsteed's *Lunar Tables*. In studying these classic texts, Banneker discovered that both Ferguson and Flamsteed were calculating lunar eclipses incorrectly. His astronomical study prompted him to prepare the first almanac published in America; in 1791, Goodard & Angell

of Philadelphia agreed to publish *Banneker's Almanac* for bookseller William Young.

During Banneker's work on the almanac, Andrew Ellicott, by then a well-known geographer, selected him to work with Pierre Charles L'Enfant to lay out the new capital city in Washington, D.C. Thomas Jefferson, then secretary of state and charged with overseeing the city's construction, wanted to surround the engineer-architect with able, intelligent, and sincere men because he knew of L'Enfant's reputation as intractable, hot-tempered, and determined to have his own way. Commenting on a letter he had received from L'Enfant on December 7, 1791, Jefferson wrote, "his temper must be subdued."

Jefferson was familiar with Banneker's abilities because of the stinging criticism the latter had sent to him concerning what *Notes on Virginia* said about African Americans. In this treatise Jefferson had stated that the physical, moral, and mental inferiority of "the blacks" rendered them dull, tasteless, and "anomalous." With his

Engraving of Benjamin Banneker. From *Banneker the Afro-American Astronomer*, 1921.

criticism, Banneker had sent a copy of his almanac, which Jefferson not only graciously accepted but sent on to the Academy of Sciences in Paris as an example of the intellectual ability of African Americans.

Since L'Enfant kept his plans secret, the only people who ever saw them were Ellicott and Banneker, who were responsible for surveying the land and providing him with topographic information. L'Enfant, running into difficulties with landowners and politicians, was dismissed by President George Washington and promptly left town with all his drawings. When Jefferson summoned Ellicott and Banneker to assess the damage and possibly to start over, Banneker told Jefferson that he could redraw the plans from memory in no more than two or three days.

Although the accuracy of this account cannot be completely documented, it seems that Banneker was the only one who had the mathematical mind and the photographic memory to accomplish such a stunning feat. The plan that is known today as the Ellicott plan is most likely the work of both Andrew Ellicott and Benjamin Banneker.

Following his work in the nation's capital, Banneker continued to publish annual almanacs. He died in 1806. He had never married and had no children. He bequeathed his property to the Ellicotts, but, as the last rites were being said at his grave, Banneker's house caught fire and burned to the ground, destroying the contents.

William Pitt, the leader of the British abolition movement, used Banneker's almanac as a forceful argument to further his cause and placed Benjamin Banneker's name in the records of Parliament; the Marquis de Condorcet also lauded him before the Academy of Sciences in Paris. Although only a few fragments of history record his accomplishments, Banneker was without a doubt one of the most original scientific intellects America has ever produced.

Bedini, Silvio. *The Life of Benjamin Banneker.* New York: Charles Scribner's Sons, 1972. The most detailed and comprehensive biography of Banneker, containing documents' sources, reference notes, an annotated bibliography, and 21 illustrations; Bedini disputes the idea that Banneker redrew L'Enfant's plan from memory, but he does acknowledge that the whereabouts of all Andrew Ellicott's diaries, field books, and notes concerning the design of the capital city are unknown, which makes it impossible to decide the truth of the story.

Graham, Shirley. *Your Most Humble Servant.* New York: Julian Messner, 1949. A book for young readers, which includes Banneker's proposal for a cabinet-level post for a Secretary of Peace for the United States.

Tyson, Martha. *Banneker, the Afric-American Astronomer. From the Posthumous Papers of Martha E. Tyson. Edited by Her Daughter.* Philadelphia, 1884. According to Silvio Bedini, the most authoritative of all the published accounts of Banneker's life and work; based on information collected from men and women who had known Banneker.

E. Lynn Miller

BARRETT, NATHAN FRANKLIN
(1845–1919)
landscape architect

Nathan Franklin Barrett was born on Staten Island, New York. His father was the founder of the New York Dyeing and Printing enterprise. The younger Barrett embarked as a sailor on a journey to Liverpool at the age of sixteen, but after one voyage, he returned to his parents' home, undecided about his future. In 1862, he entered the Union Army and sustained wounds at the Battle of Cedar Creek, then again returned home and worked from 1866 to 1869 in the nursery business his father had established. Under the tutelage of Daniel Reagan, an Irish gardener who served as nursery superintendent (and for whom he had great admiration), Bar-

Nathan Barrett's garden. From *Art World*, 1916.

rett learned the practical aspects of landscape architecture firsthand. He also read liberally to enhance his knowledge of the field.

In 1869, Barrett executed his first plan, a small garden in Bergen Point, New Jersey. Two years later, he began to design station grounds for the New Jersey Central Railroad. This work lasted until 1876, when he chose to pursue a wider variety of projects.

Throughout the 1870s, Barrett was closely associated with George Pullman, who retained Barrett to "study his oceanfront property at Elberon." Also at this time, Barrett began the planning of the town of Pullman, collaborating with the architect Solon Beman on the first planned industrial town in what is now part of Chicago. Beman designed the buildings, and Barrett was responsible for siting them and designing the landscapes. Pullman envisioned his town, with superior housing and community facilities, as a solution to labor problems, creating more productive workers and moderating their demands for higher wages or improved working conditions. Barrett remained close friends with Pullman until the latter's death in 1899.

Barrett's design of the Pullman community led to his involvement in other towns and suburban residential developments, including Chevy Chase, Maryland; Fort Worth, Texas; and Birmingham, Alabama. In most cases the extent of his work is unknown, or his plans were never fully executed. His design for Chevy Chase was striking. There, he worked for the Chevy Chase Land

Company in tandem with Philadelphia architect Lindley Johnson and civil engineer E. C. Reynolds on a plan featuring a broad formal avenue and street grid overlaid with picturesque curvilinear parkways. Barrett's designs included formal landscape elements based on European precedents and featured double rows of trees, boxwood parterres, and parklets. Extensive planting plans and plant species were delineated in his drawings. Although some of the more ambitious design schemes (for example, Johnson's design for Chevy Chase Circle) were not implemented, distinctive elements of the plans by this sophisticated team of professionals are extant.

In addition to his planning achievements, Barrett designed landscapes for many country places, including gardens for P. A. B. Widener in Ogontz, Pennsylvania; H. O. Havemeyer in Islip, Long Island; and Joseph H. Choate in Stockbridge, Massachusetts. Barrett's 1880s designs for Choate's estate, Naumkeag, consisted of large formal flower gardens, a topiary walk, and arbor vitae arranged in pairs. Later designs by Fletcher Steele* in the 1920s and 1930s did not affect Barrett's organizational intent for the spaces, retaining his concept of outdoor rooms. Barrett's overall axial influence on the site and paired arbor vitae are extant. Steele also retained Barrett's flower gardens, although he replanted them.

In 1895, Barrett was appointed landscape architect of the Essex County (New Jersey) Park Commission, where he designed parks and the layout of boulevards connecting them. He served as a commissioner of the

Arcade Park, Pullman, Illinois, c. 1893. Courtesy Arthur Melville Pearson.

Palisades Inter-State Parkway (located in New Jersey and New York) from 1900 to 1915. Most notably, in 1903, he was elected president of the American Society of Landscape Architects, having been one of the driving forces in its initial formation.

In his 1916 article "Fifty Years of Landscape Modeling," Barrett described the emerging field: "The art of landscape architecture was but little known in this country [at the time] Reagan presented to me the opportunity given to engage in it." He cited the work of a few early prominent professionals, and placed his own work in an interesting perspective by stating that he was the earliest exponent of the formal garden in America. Many of his designs were principally of this nature, notably his early work for the Ponce-de-Leon Hotel in Florida and the R. G. Dun estate at Narragansett Pier.

His formal designs harmonized with what Barrett termed the "general scene," or the larger setting of the house and garden, but were still distinct entities. Sensitive to the notion of house and grounds as a single unit, he used his skills to design a pleasing mix of formal gardens with wild landscape. Within the confines of formality, Barrett was admired for his creativity. He described his design philosophy as follows: "The charm of this design lies in its variety, its lack of conventionality, the absence of mass in color, the absence of shrub borders and little patches of green grass, so often called lawns . . . and while abandon is aimed at, there is a 'method in the madness,' and the wild garden and the formal play their part, each enhancing the charm of the other."

Perhaps Barrett's favorite among his own designs was Rochelle Park, New Rochelle, New York, which he

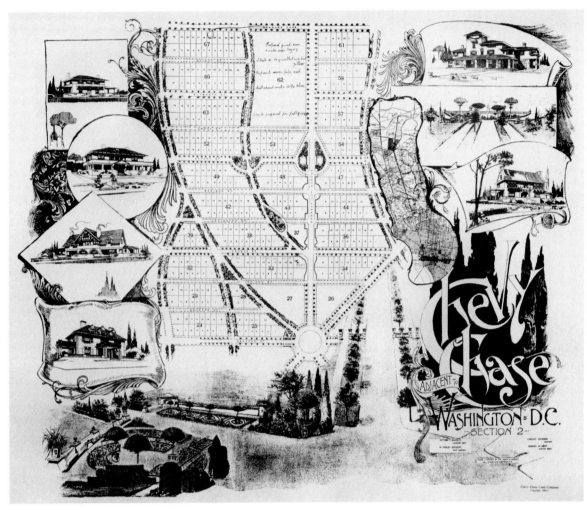

Plan for Chevy Chase, adjacent to Washington, D.C., c. 1880. Collection of the Chevy Chase Historical Society, courtesy Chevy Chase Land Company.

commenced in 1885, and where he lived from 1888 until a few years before his death. Barrett referred to the New Rochelle project as "one of the most complete resident parks. . . . Half-acre plots on a formal avenue of one-hundred feet in width, and curvilinear drives, express the two schools of landscape art." During his lifetime, however, he considered the design "ruined," through the course of natural use.

Barrett's own home in Rochelle Park was the only work over which he said he had complete control. When describing his garden, he found himself at first at a loss for words, asking, "Can I be expected to specify exactly my feelings in an atmosphere so sensuous?" In this gar-

den, Barrett illustrated what a landscape architect could create within the confines of a half-acre plot. Although professionally Barrett was a proponent of the formal garden, his own was divided into irregular sections where he instituted a variety of garden types: Colonial, English, Moorish, Roman, and Japanese. Included in his scheme was the cellar of his house, which opened at garden level and provided spaces for what Barrett described as a Normandy peasant's sitting room, a German peasant's kitchen, and a Pompeian Court. A small brook ran through the rear of the property, contributing to the picturesque appeal.

Throughout his life, Barrett was an advocate for the

field of landscape architecture, aiming to make the profession more widely understood. In a 1916 article, he wrote: "I welcome the young women and young men and their seniors, who have not grown too old to be taught something, to come and study with me, my ambition being (which is not wholly selfish) to convey by all in my power to these young people the gospel of the existence of a distinct art." At the time of his death Barrett was working on plans to beautify signs along public roads.

Barrett, Nathan F. "Fifty Years of Landscape Modeling." *Art World*, April 1916, 180–185. Barrett's only known published article, a recounting of his life and career and a detailed description of his personal garden.

Schermerhorn, Richard, Jr. "Nathan Franklin Barrett, Landscape Architect." *Landscape Architecture* 10 (April 1920), 109–113. A retrospective of Barrett's life and work, written shortly after his death, summarizing his character, prominent commissions, and design philosophy.

The archives of the Chevy Chase (Maryland) Historical Society contain several drawings either signed by or thought to be in Barrett's hand. Like other towns where he was involved in planning and designing, Chevy Chase has no correspondence from Barrett himself.

Judith Helm Robinson and Stephanie S. Foell

BARRY, PATRICK
(1816–1890)

See the joint account with Ellwanger, George.

BARTHOLOMEW, HARLAND
(1889–1989)
planner, civil engineer

Harland Bartholomew was born in Stoneham, Massachusetts, near Boston. He studied civil engineering for two years at Rutgers University but left before receiving a degree. Early in his career, Bartholomew worked for the U.S. Army Corps of Engineers and for E. P. Goodrich, a New York civil engineer. In association with architect George P. Ford, Goodrich was engaged to prepare a comprehensive city plan for Newark, New Jersey, in 1911; Bartholomew was assigned to this project. As the plan neared completion in 1914, the City of Newark hired Bartholomew as its "city plan engineer," making him one of the first public employees engaged in full-time planning in the United States. In 1916, Bartholomew accepted a similar assignment for the City of St. Louis, and in 1918 he became nonresident professor of civic design at the University of Illinois, a position he would hold until 1958. A year later he created the firm of Harland Bartholomew

Harland Bartholomew with President Eisenhower at the presentation of the Transportation Survey for the National Capital Region, July 1, 1959, at the White House. Courtesy Gelman Library, George Washington University.

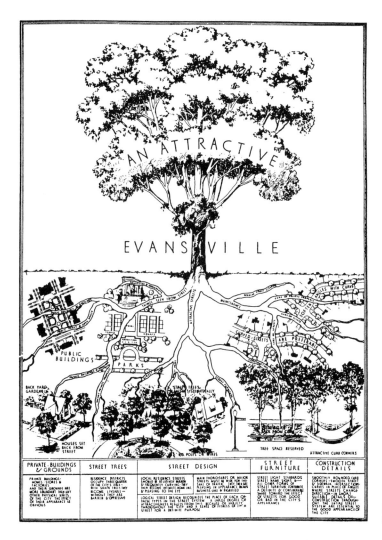

Diagram from Evansville, Indiana, Comprehensive Plan of 1922.

& Associates, City Planners, Civil Engineers, and Landscape Architects. It was one of the earliest landscape design teams in the country and was based in St. Louis.

Harland Bartholomew's astonishingly prolific career encompassed 6,000 projects, including 500 comprehensive plans for cities, counties, regions, and states; parks and park systems; subdivisions; housing projects; and highway and transportation systems. Each of the plans was characterized by human and environmental sensitivity and was prepared in the community being planned.

Bartholomew's writings also influenced his profession. *His Urban Land Policy for St. Louis*, published in 1936, was instrumental in the development of the urban renewal process. Bartholomew also discovered funda-

mental relationships between land use and zoning and in two books, *Urban Land Uses* (1932) and *Land Uses in American Cities* (1955), made his discoveries available to all practitioners. He systematized approaches to environmental planning and helped to gain acceptance for planning as a responsibility of government. Increasing governmental awareness of the need for foresight in land use, he also helped to develop planning into a rational discipline that could be studied and taught.

Bartholomew made no "paper plans." He believed that planning without the mechanisms for achieving change was worthless. To this end, he advanced zoning techniques, devised methods for encouraging public participation in planning, designed neighborhood programs, and established urban redevelopment corporations and similar institutions to carry out the comprehensive plans.

In 1940, President Franklin D. Roosevelt appointed Bartholomew a member of the Interregional Highway Committee. This committee's 1944 report, major portions of which were written by Bartholomew, was the start of the U.S. Interstate Highway System, which today reflects to a remarkable degree the plans and proposals of the report.

In 1953, President Dwight Eisenhower appointed Bartholomew chairman of the National Capital Planning Commission in Washington, D.C. During the seven years of his chairmanship he was instrumental in forming the National Capital Regional Planning Council and in preparing the 1959 transportation plan for the National Capital Region. Bartholomew realized that providing the highway capacity necessary to accommodate an all-motorized transportation system would ruin the character of the nation's capital; a rapid transit system was essential. The report led to the development of the Washington transit system, the Metro.

Bartholomew received the Distinguished Service Award from the American Institute of Planners in 1955, became an honorary member of the American Society of Landscape Architects in 1958, and was elevated to honorary membership in the American Society of Civil Engineers in 1962.

He resigned his partnership in Harland Bartholomew & Associates in 1963 but continued to operate as a consultant to the firm until his death.

—————————————

Bartholomew, Harland. *Land Uses in American Cities.* Cambridge: Harvard University Press 1955. A book that expands on the themes treated in Bartholomew's *Urban Land Uses,* considering many additional cities and introducing data for regional urban areas; 21 illustrations.

Bartholomew, Harland. *Urban Land Uses.* Harvard City Planning Studies, no. 4. Cambridge: Harvard University Press, 1932. Bartholomew's pioneer work relating to the use of land for various urban purposes, to population, and to the creation of zoning districts; 14 illustrations.

Lovelace, Eldridge. *Harland Bartholomew: His Contributions to American Urban Planning.* Urbana: University of Illinois, 1993. A full account of Bartholomew's career, including 106 illustrations and a bibliography of 244 books, articles, and speeches by Bartholomew.

—————————————

Eldridge Lovelace

BARTRAM, JOHN
(1699–1777)
plant collector, naturalist, gardener

"He was, perhaps, the first Anglo-American, who conceived the idea of establishing a botanic garden, for the reception and cultivation of the various vegetables, natives of the country, as well as of exotics, and of travelling for the discovery and acquisition of them." With these words William Bartram described his father's achievement as a pioneer botanist-explorer. William went on to describe the family's garden, which can be visited today on the banks of the Schuylkill River, at a distance of about three miles from the center of Philadelphia: "a happy situation, possessing every soil and exposure, adapted to the various nature of vegetables."

John Bartram first established his garden in 1728 and within five years was sending seeds, plants, and drawings to the most important horticulturists and naturalists in North America, Britain, and Europe. In 1738 he began to travel the forests of colonial North America, first alone and then after 1754 with his son William, in search of new plant species to bring back to his garden, where they would be planted for a period of naturalization and then disbursed through seeds and cuttings. "His various excursions," William recorded, "rewarded his labours with the possession of a great variety of new, beautiful, and useful trees, shrubs, and herbaceous plants." Bartram's unprece-

William Bartram, *Franklinia alatamaha*, c. 1781. Courtesy Natural History Museum, London.

world herbaria and physic gardens. Initially, he knew plants only in their natural environment, through farming. Later, books sent to him from Europe supplemented this almost naive approach to the study of nature. Bartram's revolutionary way of studying plants in their natural context set him apart from his European colleagues. Bartram continued to develop his unique garden in the wilderness until 1777. His achievement was appreciated by the botanist Alexander Garden of South Carolina, who observed that Bartram had substituted natural elements for traditional garden features: "He disdains to have a garden less than Pennsylvania, every den is an arbour, every run of water, a canal, and every small level spot, a parterre, where he nurses up his idol flowers and cultivates his darling productions."

Known as the Botanic Garden of America during the colonial and early national period, it was, for fifty years, regarded internationally as the greatest source of American plants. Bartram's commercial undertaking was the first of its kind and as such had a significant impact on the consumption of North American plants abroad. Although he was initially interested in medicinal plants, Bartram quickly enlarged his collection to include ornamental, economic, and simply curious species. He sent hundreds of mosses and lichen to the botanist Dillenius at Oxford which were not for cultivation but purely scientific purposes. In addition to collecting and propagating, Bartram carried on early experimentation in plant breeding through cross-pollination. According to one account, Bartram's extensive gardens "may in truth be called the *Botanical Academy of Pennsylvania*, since, being near Philadelphia, the Professor of Botany, Chemistry, and Materia Medica, attended by their youthful train of pupils, annually assemble here during the Floral season."

Through extensive exchange with botanists and collectors abroad, Bartram introduced about 200 new species into cultivation, including the *Magnolia Grandiflora*, the elusive *Franklinia alatamaha*, *Rhododendron maximum*, and *Acer pennsylvanicum*. Many of these plants played an important role in the development of the English landscape garden, which marked the beginning of the modern or natural style of garden design. Many of the plants that Bartram sent abroad can be seen today at the Chelsea Physic Garden, London, and at the newly restored Painshill Park in Surrey.

We have reports of Europeans and Americans who went to Bartram's garden to see the collection, buy seeds and plants, and to meet the humble Quaker farmer who was called by Linnaeus "the most natural botanist in the

dented success in the exportation of plants was partially due to the cultivation of plants first in his own garden before sending the specimens abroad. With this method, he was assured of several samples of healthy plants before submitting them to the dangers of transportation.

In a well-known drawing sent to Peter Collinson, the celebrated horticultural agent, who acted for Bartram in London, Bartram's garden is depicted as a rustic version of a terraced garden with three long avenues of trees leading down to the banks of the Schuylkill. This drawing, however, does not show the full extent of what Bartram called his garden, which included a 200- to 300-acre plantation outside the enclosed area. It was there that he re-created habitats or ecological niches, as similar as possible to those in which his plants had been collected in the wild.

Bartram had little contact with the tradition of old

A Draught of John Bartram's House and Garden as It Appears from the River, attributed to John or William Bartram, 1758. Courtesy Right Honorable Lord Derby, Knowsley, Prescot-Merseyside.

William Bartram, *Arethusa divaricata* (*Cleistes divaricata* [*L.*] *Ames and Isotria verticilata Raf.*), 1796 [view from Bartram Garden toward Philadelphia]. Courtesy American Philosophical Society, Philadelphia.

world" and who later became the botanist for the king of England. Various reports of memorable visitors record Bartram's stature in the world of plants and gardens. Peter Kalm, agent for Linnaeus, was always trying to goad Bartram into recording his observations and wrote in his *Travels in North America* (1753) that to Bartram we owe "the knowledge of many scarce plants." Although it was "not laid off with much taste nor was it large," George Washington described Bartram's garden nevertheless as containing one of the most valuable collection of native and imported plants he knew. J. Hector St. John de Crevecoeur devoted a chapter in his book *Letters from an American Farmer* (1782) to his visit with Bartram in the spring of 1765. This text, in itself a significant work in early American literature, has inspired an almost folk hero quality to Bartram's life and contribution.

Bartram, John. *Bartram: Travels and Other Writings*, ed. Thomas Slaughter. New York: Library of America, 1996.

Berkeley, Edmund, and Dorothy Smith Berkeley. *The Life and Travels of John Bartram: From Lake Ontatio to the River St. John*. Tallahassee: University Presses of Florida, 1982.

Fry, Joel "Bartram's Garden Catalogue of North American Plants, 1783." *Journal of Garden History* 16 (Spring 1996).

Therese O'Malley

BAXTER, SYLVESTER
(1850–1927)
journalist, activist

Sylvester Baxter was born in West Yarmouth on Cape Cod in Massachusetts, the son of a sea captain. He received his primary and secondary education at local schools. At the age of seventeen, he visited New York City and walked up Broadway to Central Park, where he explored the Ramble and, as he wrote later, became "lost in admiration for Mr. Olmsted's masterly creation." Baxter would later be one of Frederick Law Olmsted Sr.'s* most

steadfast supporters. That same year, feeling "the call of the city . . . upon him," he moved to Boston. He had hoped to study architecture at the newly established Massachusetts Institute of Technology, but family finances did not permit it. Instead, he worked at the printing office of Smith & Porter for two years, while continuing his boyhood study of piano at the New England Conservatory of Music. After leaving the printing office, he worked briefly

Sylvester Baxter. Bas-relief by Bela Pratt, 1913. Courtesy Boston Public Library.

as a rodman for a civil engineer but soon tired of "carrying a heavy theodolite about the suburbs."

In 1871, Baxter began a long and distinguished career as a journalist and author, writing on an astonishing range of topics. These included—besides architecture, landscape architecture, and city planning—painting, Japanese pottery, trains, trolleys, bicycles, public utilities, the archaeology of the American southwest, and the Zuni Indians. He was a close friend of the painter Frederic E. Church and of Francis Millet, the distinguished artist who was also his brother-in-law. Baxter was also a poet and a composer.

From 1871 through 1875, Baxter served on the staff of the *Boston Daily Advertiser*, for which he covered the Great Fire of Boston on November 9 and 10, 1872. In follow-up articles, he reported on the rebuilding of the burned area, which led him to a keen interest in city planning, a topic that became a constant theme of his career. Between 1875 and 1877, Baxter studied at the universi-

ties of Leipzig and Berlin. During the course of his study in Germany, he found a model that American city planners might follow. Among his later books and articles on this subject are *Berlin: A Study in Municipal Government in Germany* (1889) and "The German Way of Making Better Cities," published in the *Atlantic Monthly* in July 1909.

Between 1879 and 1883 and again from 1887 to 1905, Baxter was on the staff of the *Boston Herald*, for which he produced many important articles in support of the Boston municipal park system, designed by Olmsted and constructed between 1879 and 1895. He also wrote the first guide to the Boston Park System (1895).

Baxter's civic accomplishments were equally impressive. In 1879 he lobbied for the preservation of the Middlesex Fells, a wilderness reservation shared by Malden, the town in which he lived, and four adjacent towns, and gave the site its name. In 1891 he wrote a pamphlet called *Greater Boston: A Study for a Federalized Metropolis Comprising the City of Boston and Surrounding Cities and Towns*, a compilation of several articles on this subject originally published in the *Boston Herald*. Baxter coined the term "Greater Boston" seven years before New York City (Manhattan and the Bronx) united with the City of Brooklyn, Queens, and Staten Island to form "Greater New York." He actively campaigned for the goals set forth in *Greater Boston*, including the creation of more wilderness reservations, by serving on several metropolitan commissions. In 1892–1893, he was the secretary of Boston's preliminary Metropolitan Park Commission and, with Charles Eliot*, the commission's landscape architect, secured the passage of state legislation that established the commission on a permanent basis. All the reservations, including the Middlesex Fells, were also laid out by Olmsted, Olmsted & Eliot, but, in contrast to the parks in Boston's municipal system, the metropolitan reservations were kept for the most part in their natural condition; improvements to them were aimed simply at making them more accessible to the public.

In 1904, Baxter formed and became secretary of the Metropolitan Improvement League, out of which was formed the Boston Metropolitan Commission, of which he also was secretary in 1907–1909. From 1893 until 1917, Baxter was a member of the Malden Park Commission and for most of that period its chairman. He established a model park system for Malden, consisting of small neighborhood parks and playgrounds, most of which were also designed by Olmsted, Olmsted & Eliot. On September 29, 1923, Baxter published an important retrospec-

Ferryway Green, Malden, designed by Olmsted, Olmsted & Eliot in 1894, demolished 1998. Historic postcard, c. 1900s.

tive article in the *Boston Transcript*, titled "Thirty Years of Greater Boston's Metropolitan Park System."

One of Baxter's particular interests was the relationship among architecture, landscape architecture, and public art. He published several articles on this subject in *Century Magazine*, including a four-part series in 1902 and a two-part series in 1906. In 1918–1919, he wrote a series of three articles for *Architectural Record* on the innovative complexes of single- and multiple-family houses built for workers in war-related industries by the U.S. Housing Corporation toward the end of World War I. Arthur Shurcliff*, Warren Manning*, George Kessler*, and other eminent landscape architects were the town planners for the corporation's housing complexes. Baxter also published extensively in *Scribner's* and *Garden and Forest* and wrote an introduction to the 1898 edition of Edward Bellamy's *Looking Backward*.

Toward the end of his life, Baxter returned to his "early love," musical composition. He died in San Juan, Puerto Rico, where he had spent winters for the previous ten years.

Baxter, Sylvester. "Descendants of Thomas Baxter." In James Phinney Baxter, "The Baxter Family: A Collection of Genealogies." N.d. (c. 1920), 58–102. Typescript at the New England Historic Genealogical Society, Boston. Includes a 9-page account (94–102) of Baxter's own life written in the third person, which is virtually the only source of information about his early life and career.

Baxter, Sylvester. "The New New York." With drawings by Jules Guérin and photographs by Arthur Hewitt. *Outlook*, June 23, 1906, 409–424. A detailed, vivid, and thoroughly illustrated account of the architectural, engineering, and landscape changes to New York City around the turn of the century.

Baxter, Sylvester. "Report of the Secretary." In *Report of the Board of Metropolitan Park Commissioners*, Boston, January 1893, 1–81. Probably his finest public report; makes a forceful case for the metropolitanization of large forest, seashore, and riverside open spaces; also addresses the issue of local pleasure grounds, play-grounds, and breathing spots, noting that it was then a subject of worldwide interest.

There is no central archive for Sylvester Baxter, but various of his letters survive in other repositories, including the Frederick Law Olmsted Papers at the Library of Congress.

_____

Cynthia Zaitzevsky

BIGELOW, JACOB
(1787–1879)
cemetery designer, horticulturist, author

Jacob Bigelow was born in Sudbury, Massachusetts, a minister's son. He graduated from Harvard and received his M.D. from the University of Pennsylvania in 1810, then settled in Boston, where he opened a medical practice. He opposed artificial interference in nature's processes, the traditional bleedings and purgings called "heroic" treatments; yet he was one of the first doctors to use chloroform to ease the pain of childbirth.

Bigelow was a member of several Boston clubs and scholarly societies, as well as international medical and scientific groups, and he served on the committee that chose the obelisk design for the Bunker Hill monument in 1825. He published four volumes on taxonomic horticulture. At Harvard College and its new medical school, he taught botany, materia medica (medicinal use of plants), and the "application of the sciences to the useful arts"—a field he called "technology," coining the term in his book in 1829.

After a controversy threatened to close Boston's old burial grounds, Bigelow invited a dozen civic leaders to his home in 1825 to propose that they form a voluntary association to create an extramural design "of family burial lots, separated and interspersed with trees, shrubs, and flowers, in a wood or a landscape garden." Such a "picturesque" or "rural" burial landscape to double as a cultural institution was unprecedented in the United States. Bigelow believed that barren, unsightly burial grounds and tombs "in frequented parts of the city, crowded to the utmost capacity," were "resistance to the laws of nature," tainting streets with "noxious effluvia" if not endangering

public health. If "nature is permitted to take its course," he noted, the dead body "contributes its remains to the nourishment of plants around it." He also spoke about the necessity of monuments for public and private commemoration and the need to create appropriate sites for them.

Dr. Jacob Bigelow. Daguerreotype, c. 1850. Courtesy Blanche M. G. Linden.

Bigelow articulated the philosophical, aesthetic, and practical rationale for a naturalistic, multifunctional place: theoretical underpinnings for a "cemetery," a new term in American English for a landscape of the dead.

The project stalled until the Massachusetts Horticultural Society took over in 1829. The perfect site was secured, an old 72-acre estate called Stone's Woods, or Sweet Auburn, four miles west of Boston with panoramic views over the Charles River from its 125-foot central mount. Already covered with wildwood, the varied terrain had many "bold eminences, steep acclivities, dells, and deep shadowy valleys," wetlands ideal for sculpting rambling avenues, paths, and ponds to render the grounds beautiful and interesting. Flatter land at the front of the property was to be an experimental garden for developing fruit, vegetable, and ornamental hybrids, a buffer between the public road and the tranquil graves beyond a natural moraine. General Henry A. S. Dearborn* laid out Mount Auburn's initial landscape in 1831, drawing inspiration from classical design principles, eighteenth-century English gardens, and Père Lachaise Cemetery near Paris (1804). Bigelow was instrumental in the continuing expansion of the landscape, to 116 acres by 1844.

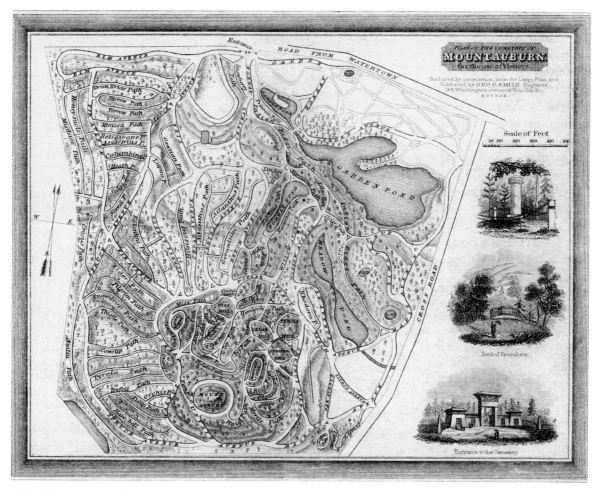

"Plan of the Cemetery of Mt. Auburn for the Use of Visitors," c. 1847. Courtesy Blanche M. G. Linden.

Consecration Dell, Mount Auburn, 1993. Photo Blanche M. G. Linden.

General view, Mount Auburn, 1995. Photo Charles A. Birnbaum.

Founders planned to embellish the picturesque with eclectic architectural structures suggesting antiquity, and Bigelow designed several of them: the 25-foot-high Egyptian gateway (1832), a surrounding massive cast iron fence with Egyptian motifs (1844), a "Protestant" Gothic chapel (1844, 1855) with Egyptian adaptations, a 62-foot "feudal" or Norman tower (1852) to honor George Washington, and a monumental granite sphinx (1871) to commemorate the Union dead.

The cemetery became so popular that it was Boston's chief antebellum tourist attraction, a "pleasure ground" in the absence of public parks, and Bigelow and the trustees limited admission in 1853 to those given tickets. Visiting gentleman horticulturists and civic leaders returned home intent on founding their own "rural" cemeteries. Guidebooks, essays, and verse spread the poetics of place. William Cullen Bryant, Andrew Jackson Downing*, and Clarence Cook observed that such cemeteries were "all the rage" and called for public parks with the same aesthetics "but without the graves."

As Mount Auburn president from 1845 to 1871, Bigelow refined the landscape, making it less naturalistic. Surveyor Alexander Wadsworth* worked into the 1850s, planting and extending avenues and paths onto peripheral farmland. From 1855 on, Bigelow altered the woodsy aesthetics by eliminating half of the dense tree canopy, to leave broad vistas and open spaces through which the works of art could be seen. He exempted some areas from burials, reserving them for floral displays, and assumed control over plantings formerly done by lot owners.

Hydrological projects transformed the landscape, draining stagnant lakes and seasonably flooded wetlands, engineering the "beautiful." From 1863 on, Bigelow transformed the "rural" into a "garden" cemetery by grading hills, lowering some by as much as 14 feet, getting in-fill to make damp areas fit for burials, laying out new avenues, and creating ornamental water features.

Bigelow boasted of his accomplishments in *A History of the Cemetery of Mount Auburn* (1860).

Aged, ill, and nearly blind, Bigelow retired in 1872. He died seven years later and was buried under the neoclassical sarcophagus topped by a severed column which he designed for his family lot in 1832.

Many period and modern publications about Mount Auburn contain errors, mistakenly attributing initial landscape design to Bigelow or to Wadsworth rather than to Dearborn.

Bigelow, Jacob. "On the Burial of the Dead and Mount Auburn Cemetery." In his *Nature in Disease, Illustrated in Various Discourses and Essays to which Are Added Miscellaneous Writings, Chiefly on Medical Subjects.* Boston, 1854. Also in his *Modern Inquiries: Classical, Professional, and Miscellaneous.* Boston, 1867. Argues for burials in a natural way and place in which return of the dead body to the elements would be facilitated.

Ellis, George E. *Memoir of Dr. Jacob Bigelow.* Cambridge, Mass., 1880. Perpetuates the belief that Bigelow designed Mount Auburn's landscape.

Linden-Ward, Blanche. *Silent City on a Hill: Landscapes of Memory and Boston's Mount Auburn Cemetery.* Columbus: Ohio State University Press, 1989. Details aspects of the cemetery's institutional and landscape development into the 1870s, focusing on Dearborn, Bigelow, and others.

Archival collections with holdings related to Bigelow include the Massachusetts Historical Society, the Massachusetts Horticultural Society, and Mount Auburn Cemetery. The bulk of his correspondence has been lost.

Blanche M. G. Linden

BIGNAULT, GEORGES H.
(1882–1959)
landscape gardener

Georges H. Bignault was born in Paris. His family summered in Brittany, where he developed an interest in plants and the landscape at an early age. Bignault studied horticultural science and landscape architecture at the University of Paris; he later conducted postgraduate studies in Algiers and Madagascar.

In 1908 the French government sent Bignault to the United States to study the cultivation of Sea Island cotton in Beaufort, South Carolina. Deciding to stay in America, he married and settled in Savannah, where he practiced as a landscape architect, artist, and gardener. As well as providing design services, he also established nurseries with his sons, the Bignault Nurseries and the Bignault Gardens.

The influence of Bignault's work in Savannah and the surrounding area can still be discerned in the landscape. Between 1910 and 1930 he designed the suburb of Chatham Crescent for millionaire Harvey Granger, president of the Chatham Land and Hotel Company. Bignault also advised Granger and other civic leaders on the design of Victory Drive, a 19.8-mile palm-lined boulevard from Savannah to Savannah Beach constructed to honor the soldiers who fought in World War I.

In the 1930s, Bignault worked as the landscape architect for the Savannah Park and Tree Commission, which was responsible for the care and beautification of the city's parks and open spaces. In this capacity Bignault produced drawings and planting plans for the redesign of most of Savannah's twenty-four squares. His drawings for this project were displayed for several years on the walls of City Hall.

Bignault's work was not limited to civic projects. He also designed private estates for vacationing northern industrialists and for Georgia and South Carolina magnates. One of his most celebrated commissions was the design of Killarney Gardens for Savannah banker William Murphy, which he began in 1935 and continued to work on through 1940. The garden survives today, having been renewed in the 1960s by the owner, Richard Stone, after suffering years of neglect and vandalism. Many of the original plantings still exist, as do Bignault's walks and open spaces. Renamed Marador Gardens, the design has been simplified. Walks and paths pass by beds of camellias, azaleas, and specimen plants; open spaces are adorned with statuary and rustic benches. The garden is an excellent example of a southern manifestation of the Country Place style.

Another important aspect of Bignault's career was his long association with local Savannah garden clubs and other civic groups. He designed a period garden for the historic Savannah headquarters of the Red Cross in 1952. Also in the 1950s he designed two important spaces for the Savannah Garden Club—the plantings at Armstrong State College and the Fragrant Garden for the Blind, one of the first of its kind in the state.

At the time of his death, Bignault was still an active practitioner. His contributions in design and plant introduction form an important part of the evolution of the public and private landscape of Savannah.

"G. H. Bignault, Landscape Architect, Dies." *Savannah Morning News*, August 3, 1959, 2A. Obituary.

Ormond, Mrs. Alex. "The Garden Club of Savannah Restores the Red Cross Garden." *Savannah Morning News*, October 10, 1954, 57. A chronicle of Bignault's design contributions to Savannah and the region, including his work for the City of Savannah Park and Tree Commission, various garden clubs, and private clients.

"The Works of George Bignault." *Savannah Morning News*, August 9, 1959, 10, 14. A tribute to Bignault's contributions to the beautification of the Savannah area.

Lina Cofresi

BLAIR, JOHN
(1820–1906)
landscape gardener

John Blair was born in Callander, Scotland, where he grew up and received early horticultural training, serving his apprenticeship at Lanrick Castle in nearby Doune. In 1851, when he was thirty-one, he and his wife decided to come to North America. They emigrated to St. Catherine's, Ontario, where he worked at general gardening.

In 1854, Blair traveled to Rockford, Illinois, to create a garden for John Holland, a successful entrepreneur who had just built a home there. Blair also laid out landscapes for the Starr residence and the homes of G. Sanford and C. Horseman in Rockford, as well as for the home of Shepard Leach southwest of the city, and several others.

Blair's exceptional skill as a garden designer was noted in newspapers of the day. Bayard Taylor, who visited Rockford in 1855, wrote in a letter to the *New York*

Portrait sketch of John Blair. Courtesy Tinker Swiss Cottage Museum, Rockford, Ill.

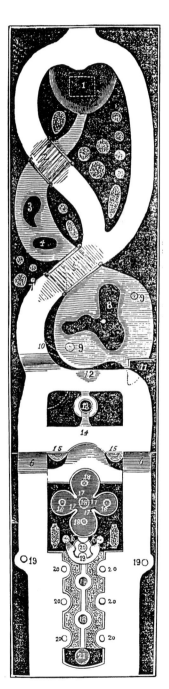

Plan of Sanitary Fair display. From *The Prairie Farmer*, June 10, 1865.

John Blair's display at the Sanitary Fair, Chicago, 1865. Courtesy David R. Phillips.

Tribune, "The residences of Mr. Holland and Mr. Starr are very fine specimens of home architecture. The grounds of the former are admirably laid out, and there is nothing better of the kind on the Hudson." Instead of following the European tradition that emphasized sweeping lawns and evergreen hedges, Blair incorporated existing trees, rocks, and water into his designs to create more natural settings. A *Chicago Evening Journal* article also praised

Blair's gardens as "some of the most tastefully arranged grounds to be found in the West," and noted that Blair had "been called to lay out many of the most beautiful grounds in Chicago and other places in the Northwest."

Among Blair's most important patrons were Mr. and Mrs. Robert Tinker, who purchased Holland's residence and retained Blair's design services to continue its development. Tinker himself was a successful landscape

Beacon Hill Bridge, Beacon Hill Park, Victoria, B.C. Photo John Blair.

designer who was instrumental in creating the Rockford park system. He and Blair became friends, and it is likely that Tinker later played a part in securing Blair work for the City of Chicago.

Blair's reputation grew as a result of a horticultural display he designed for the 1865 Chicago Sanitary Fair, an event that probably brought him into contact with Frederick Law Olmsted Sr.*, national secretary for the Sanitary Fairs. The 1865 fair in Chicago was the largest ever held. An article in the *Prairie Farmer* described Blair's display and contained a sketch and index of the many items shown. The article noted that Blair was not unknown in the area, "as some few years ago he was employed by several gentlemen to lay out their grounds."

Blair moved to the Chicago suburb of Oak Park and took a job with the city parks department. His tenure coincided with the early development of the West Parks, including Garfield, Humboldt, and Douglas, but the extent of his design contributions is not recorded. The Great Fire of 1871 put an end to his career in Chicago, as the city had other priorities to attend to and Blair found himself out of a job. An article in the *Chicago Journal* of November 25, 1871, reported that Blair was moving to Colorado "to make ground plans for the elegant and extensive improvements being constructed at Colorado Springs. A company of wealthy and enterprising gentlemen . . . has undertaken to make these celebrated springs at the base of Pikes Peak in the Rocky Mountains, a rival of Saratoga in the East." Blair laid out the area's first parks and designed a system of walking trails and bridges. In Colorado Springs, Blair also designed Evergreen Cemetery, Glen Eyrie (home of General William Palmer, the city's founder), and Briarhurst, the residence of a Dr. W. A. Bell.

Blair's work for Palmer, which spanned ten years, included a great many rustic stone features. Blair also designed a large stone bridge on the road between Colorado Springs and Denver, the first erected on public land in Colorado, and laid out a road through the Garden of the Gods between Manitou Springs and Glen Eyrie, near the famous Balanced Rock.

In 1882, Blair met members of the Dunsmuir family in San Francisco and learned of the large tract of forest land they were developing on Vancouver Island in British Columbia. He traveled north to see it and was able to purchase a parcel four miles west of the present city of Duncan. Blair had finally found the spot where he wanted to settle and build his permanent home. That same year he cleared space for a garden and an orchard and planted many exotic species of trees. A grove of trees and five outbuildings still survive. His house in Oak Park, which he did not sell until 1889, was subsequently purchased by Frank Lloyd Wright, who built a home and studio on the property. Wright later said that "the remarkable character of the foliage on the old Blair lot" was what led him to settle in Oak Park.

In 1889, at the age of sixty-nine, Blair won the competition for the design of a large park, Beacon Hill, in Victoria, British Columbia. Seven years later, he designed and laid out the 21-acre grounds of James Dunsmuir in Victoria; at the time Dunsmuir was reputed to be the wealthiest man in Canada.

Blair died in 1906 and was buried at the Mountain View Cemetery in Duncan.

Prairie Farmer, June 10, 1865. Article by Edgar Sanders on Blair's horticultural display at the Chicago Sanitary Fair.

Sprague, Marshall. *Newport in the Rockies: The Life and Good Times of Colorado Springs.* Denver: Sage Books, 1961. Contains a description of Blair's Colorado work.

Unpublished diaries of Robert Tinker kept in the Tinker Swiss Cottage Museum of Rockford, Ill., contain references to the work relationship of Tinker and John Blair.

W. A. Dale

BOTTOMLEY, MYRL E.
(1893–1956)
landscape architect, author

Myrl E. Bottomley was born in Charlotte, Michigan. He received a B.S. degree from Michigan State College in East Lansing in 1916 and, following two years of military service, studied at Cornell University, where he received a master's degree in landscape design (1922). During the summer of 1922, he worked in the office of the Olmsted Brothers* in Palos Verdes, California, and later that same year joined the faculty of the Iowa State College at Ames as assistant professor of landscape architecture. In 1925 he became associated with T. Glenn Phillips in Detroit, an arrangement that continued intermittently until 1930.

In 1926, Bottomley joined the faculty of the University of Cincinnati as head of the Department of Landscape Architecture, where he taught landscape architecture and city planning until his death. He served as campus landscape architect and during World War II worked on a master development plan for the City of Cincinnati. In 1931 he was appointed to the President's Conference on Home Building and Home Ownership, a federal agency.

Myrl E. Bottomley. Courtesy Hunt Library, Architecture Archives, Carnegie-Mellon University, Pittsburgh.

Design for "An Attractive City Back Yard." From *The Design of Small Properties,* 1926.

Bottomley's reputation rests primarily on three published books, which were highly acclaimed and widely read. *The Art of Home Landscape* (1933) was an expression of his philosophy of landscape architecture. *The Design of Small Properties* (1926) and the substantially revised *New Design of Small Properties* (1948) are more practical. These books offer many non-plant-specific plans, or "patterns," meant to be customized according to the tastes of the property owner and the local availability of materials.

Bottomley's approach to designing small residential landscapes was already established by the time he wrote his Cornell thesis in 1922. His philosophy of design advocated a rigorous and formal scheme of well-defined spaces around a dwelling which arose from salient func-

tional and visual elements of the house itself. Deriving equally from the grand notion of garden planning perfected by Charles Platt* and from the intricate, small-scale productions of Arts and Crafts garden designers, the schemes set forth in Bottomley's published works call for a tightly knit sequence of precise areas, each answering some functional or aesthetic need. His solutions were ideally suited to the suburbanite trying to infuse a 60- or 80-foot tract lot with lasting elegance and usability.

Bottomley, Myrl E. *The Art of Home Landscape.* New York: A. T. DelaMare, 1935. The most theoretical of

Bottomley's three books, with a chapter on community improvements; sketches, plans.

Bottomley, Myrl E. *The Design of Small Properties: A Book for the Home-Owner in City and Country.* Rural Science Series, edited by Liberty Hyde Bailey*. New York: Macmillan, 1926. Notable for Bottomley's ability to adapt large-scale formal planting to small suburban lots; a section on farm homes and lists of appropriate flowers and shrubs; plans.

Bottomley, Myrl E. *New Designs of Small Properties.* Rev. ed. New York: Macmillan, 1948. About half the length of Bottomley's 1926 book; illustrates his attempts to adapt to new styles of garden design; notable art deco motifs in many plans.

_____

Barry Hannegan

BOWDITCH, ERNEST W.
(1850–1918)
landscape gardener

William Ernestus Bowditch was born in Brookline, Massachusetts, and educated in the Brookline public schools. In 1865, Bowditch (who by this time had inverted his first and middle names and was known as Ernest W.) enrolled at the Massachusetts Institute of Technology, where he studied chemistry and mining. He ended his studies in June 1869, leaving without a degree, and went to Nebraska, where for several months he had a construction job with the Chicago Burlington & Quincy Railroad.

After returning to Boston, Bowditch, through family connections, was appointed assistant mineralogist with the Darien Expedition, a canal survey expedition to the Isthmus of Darien (now the Isthmus of Panama). The route Bowditch's team surveyed during the first half of 1870 proved not to be the best one for what was to become the Panama Canal. When he returned to Boston afterward, his career began to blossom. He worked in conjunction with architectural and engineering firms, as well as using his family connections to obtain independent commissions. His career is marked by associations with prominent Boston and New York architects, landscape architects, and architectural firms: Robert Morris Copeland*; McKim, Mead & Bigelow; Frederick Law Olmsted Sr.*; Bruce Price; Peabody & Stearns; H. H. Richardson; and Shedd & Sawyer.

In the fall of 1870, Bowditch was employed at the Boston office of Shedd & Sawyer, Civil Engineers. One of his first jobs for the firm was general maintenance of the grounds of Mount Auburn Cemetery in Cambridge, where he laid out driveways, paths, stone bounds for cor-

ners, curbing, and gardens. This early exposure to America's first romantic cemetery plan was a strong influence on Bowditch's future design ideas.

Ernest W. Bowditch. Courtesy MIT Archives.

Shaker Lakes Park, Shaker Heights, Ohio. Historic postcard. Courtesy Smithsonian Institution, Archives of American Gardens.

A garden path at The Breakers, Newport, Rhode Island, c. 1896. Courtesy Preservation Society.

The Italian Garden, Sonnenberg,
Canandaigua, New York, designed 1903.
Courtesy Sonnenberg Gardens.

In mid-1871, Bowditch set up his own office opposite Copeland's and did survey work for him. A year later he began to consult for Peabody & Stearns. He continued to work with the architectural firm through the mid-1880s and also collaborated with architect H. H. Richardson on several projects, notably as structural engineer for Boston's Trinity Church. From the mid-1880s through late 1890s, Bowditch shared office space with his landscape gardener brother, James H. Bowditch.

Bowditch also frequently worked with Olmsted Sr. and John Charles Olmsted*, often as a surveyor or draftsman. But despite a long professional relationship with the Olmsteds, he generally felt animosity for them because of their wide renown.

Bowditch was a talented designer, both creatively and technically, as well as an adept manager of project construction. He was involved in municipal surveys for sewer and water supply design in many eastern communities, as well as structural engineering, land surveying, cemetery design, subdivision layout, and landscape design at summer resorts of the wealthy, especially Newport, Rhode Island. His projects there included Pierre Lorillard and Cornelius Vanderbilt's Breakers, as well as the estates of Ogden Goelet, Catherine Lorillard Wolfe, and Charles Lanier, to name only a few. While much of Bowditch's residential subdivision design was carried out in a picturesque style, his designs for the estates of the wealthy often utilized a formal layout. The estate of T. W. Pierce at Topsfield, Massachusetts, showed Bowditch's mastery of a Beaux Arts approach.

Bowditch also designed many parks. Two notable surviving examples from the 1890s are Rockefeller Park and the connecting Shaker Lakes Park on Cleveland's east side. These were part of Bowditch's vision of a Lake Erie-oriented horseshoe park system, much like Boston's "Emerald Necklace."

In the late 1880s and 1890s, Bowditch executed landscape designs for several subdivisions: Tuxedo Park in New York; Newton Terraces in Waban and Allston Park in Allston, Massachusetts; and Shoreby Hill in Jamestown, Rhode Island; as well as the suburban Cleveland communities of Clifton Park and Euclid Heights.

Hamley, Kara Cathleen. "Cleveland's Park Allotment: Euclid Heights, Cleveland Heights, Ohio, and Its Designer, Ernest W. Bowditch." M.A. thesis, Cornell University, 1996. Focuses primarily on the history and development of the Bowditch-designed Euclid

Heights Allotment; includes a 63-page chapter on Bowditch and several of his other works.

Murphy, Kevin D. "Ernest W. Bowditch and the Practice of Landscape Architecture." In *The Essex Institute Historical Collections,* vol. 125 (1989), 162–176. A 15-page article based on information collected in the Ernest W. Bowditch papers at the Essex Institute.

Bowditch Family Papers, *Bowditch Reminiscences, vols. 1–2.* Ernest William Bowditch, 1850–1918. Essex Institute at Salem, Massachusetts. Bowditch's personal remembrances of his career written c. 1917, among the few of his written works available, includes information on various designs, as well as his candid opinions on the works and personalities of his contemporaries.

Kara Hamley O'Donnell

BRIGGS, LOUTREL WINSLOW
(1893–1977)
landscape architect, author

Born in New York, Loutrel W. Briggs initially visited Charleston, South Carolina, with his first wife, Emily, in 1927. In 1929 he established an office there, beginning a forty-year period of professional involvement with the city. He designed private gardens and estates for many of the wealthy northerners who were purchasing property in Charleston at that time. His private work included, for example, the William Gibbes (Roebling) garden, the gardens of the Mills Hyatt House, and Mr. and Mrs. Ben Scott Whaley's Church Street garden.

Briggs was also a prolific writer whose articles appeared in professional and popular magazines. His public

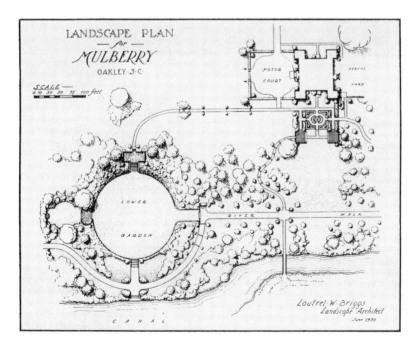

"Landscape Plan for Mulberry, Oakley, South Carolina," June 1930. Courtesy Charleston Gardens.

Mepkin Abbey, Moncks Corner, South Carolina. Courtesy Mepkin Abbey and Botanical Garden.

"Sketch for the Interment Area for Mr. and Mrs. Alfred P. Sloan, Jr.," undated plan [1956?]. Courtesy Smithsonian Institution, Archives of American Gardens.

landscapes include the Charleston World War II Memorial Garden, the 1930 Gateway Walk, and several college campuses. Briggs contributed hundreds of hours of civic pro bono work in the Charleston area. As a trustee he helped to found the Historic Charleston Foundation. In addition, Briggs was a partner in the New York City firm of Briggs & Stelling, which prepared designs for parks, subdivisions, institutional grounds, and public housing in the North.

Briggs's articles appeared in such popular magazines as *House and Garden, Country Life, Garden and Home Beautiful*, and *Garden Magazine* from the 1920s to the 1950s. He wrote about urban renewal, city beautification, parks and playgrounds, traffic congestion and circulation, parking, housing patterns, accessibility, and visibility of designed spaces. He was a proponent of respecting the original city plan and upholding its spatial and architectural integrity.

Briggs strongly believed in the necessity of documenting historic designed landscapes. He attempted to create a recorded legacy for old and new Charleston gardens as well as the gardens and landscapes of Low Country plantations. His book, *Charleston Gardens*, remains a useful resource concerning the development and evolution of the designed landscapes of the area.

Briggs, Loutrel W. *Charleston Gardens*. Columbia: University of South Carolina Press, 1951. Historical and botanical information, including photographs and measured drawings on notable seventeenth- through twentieth-century gardens in Charleston and on nearby plantations; also includes a discussion of early sources such as books on botany and natural history, a list of plants grown in North America before 1791, and the names and accounts of early nurserymen, gardeners, and landscape designers who practiced in the Charleston area.

Briggs, Loutrel W. "Charleston's Famous Gardens." *House and Garden*, March 1939. A descriptive look at Charleston's old favorites such as the Heyward-Washington House garden; includes measured drawings and photographs.

Cothran, James R. *Gardens of Historic Charleston*. Columbia: University of South Carolina Press, 1995. Discusses gardens in Charleston since the eighteenth century and includes a section on Briggs.

Rosetta Radtke

BULLARD, ELIZABETH J.
(1847–1916)
landscape architect

Elizabeth J. Bullard was one of the first women known to practice landscape architecture professionally. She began as an assistant to her father, Oliver Bullard, who worked on the U.S. Sanitary Commission with Frederick Law Olmsted Sr.* in 1862–1863, and later served as park inspector for Prospect Park in Brooklyn, New York. The Bullards moved to Bridgeport, Connecticut, in the 1880s, where Oliver Bullard served as supervisor of parks from 1885 until his death in 1890. He also designed residential gardens.

Bullard was then a painter by profession, but she had helped her father in his landscape projects in Bridgeport and was generally well acquainted with his work. Her talents were highly regarded, and so William H. Noble, president of the Bridgeport Park Commission, wrote to Olmsted to ask his opinion as to whether he thought she could take on her father's job. Olmsted replied that he could warmly recommend her, and sent Bullard a copy of his letter to Noble. In response, Bullard thanked him and suggested that her father's sudden death was due to the continuous battles over implementation of the design for Beardsley Park in Bridgeport and his attempts to protect the town parks from political exploitation. She worried that her proposed appointment might prove disastrous to the goal of completing the work, but indicated that an indirect role might be possible.

Section of preliminary plan for Beardsley Park, Bridgeport, Connecticut. Design by F. L. and J. C. Olmsted, 1884. Courtesy Visual Resources Department, Frances Loeb Library, Harvard University.

An October 1892 editorial in *Garden and Forest* magazine pointed out that Bullard (whose name was not mentioned) was the most competent person for the supervisor's post and that the Park Commission had promised her the job. Yet, they had given it to a man, declaring that local politicians would not sanction a woman in such an important position. The magazine chastised the commission, noting that women were entering the field of architecture and that, barring hard manual labor, there was no reason they should not also enter a profession that brought them into the healthy open air.

Bullard went on to develop, by her own account, a modest residential design business. Also, on at least one occasion at the turn of the century, she worked with John Charles Olmsted* on a job for Smith College, in Northampton, Massachusetts, supervising the implementation of the Olmsted firm's plan.

Although Bullard was slighted by the Bridgeport Park Commission, the American Society of Landscape

Architects recognized her early in its existence. In 1899, the year of the society's founding, she was elected a Fellow, the second woman to be so honored. She was also an active member of the American Park and Outdoor Art Association.

In 1913, toward the end of her life, she wrote Frederick Law Olmsted Jr.* about a letter she had received, asking her to join the newly forming Boston Society of Landscape Architects. Concerned that she did not see his name or his brother John's name on the list of founding members, she wondered if it was a move to secede from the ASLA. She reiterated how she valued her own membership in the ASLA and lamented that she had not been more active in it over the years, but confessed that her responsibilities had been heavy and her income always very small. Now, though in failing health, she declared her intention to remain in the society and also to continue her practice. (The Boston Society was, in fact, formed as a separate group, and both Olmsted brothers subsequently

Cove and lake view, Beardsley Park. Received March 11, 1904, from Calhoun Latham. Courtesy National Park Service, Frederick Law Olmsted National Historic Site.

joined.) Elizabeth Bullard died just three years later in 1916.

NOTE: Elizabeth Bullard is frequently confused with Helen Bullard, who worked for Olmsted Brothers from 1904 to 1928 in the running of the office, not on the design side. In addition, a Helen Elise Bullard worked as a landscape architect, first in Warren Manning's* office and then in the New York area between 1919 and 1965. Another Elizabeth Bullard (though by marriage), living in the Hartford area, was also a land-scape architect. It is possible that these Bullards are distantly related, but any connection is unknown.

———

Bullard, Elizabeth. "How a City Gained a Park." *Garden and Forest* 2 (May 8, 1889), 226. Letter to the editor; only known written work by Bullard.

———

Amy Brown

BURNAP, GEORGE ELBERTON
(1885–1938)
landscape architect

George Burnap was born in Hopkinton, Massachusetts. He entered the Massachusetts Institute of Technology (MIT) in 1902, and received his S.B. in architecture (landscape architecture option) four years later. While at MIT, Burnap had the opportunity to study with Guy Lowell*, head of the landscape architecture option between 1900 and 1910. Burnap went to Cornell University in Ithaca, New York, to do graduate work in the Rural Art program, from which he received a master's degree in 1910 (the program became the Department of Landscape Architecture a few years later). While a graduate student at Cornell, Burnap also served as a lecturer

Krug Park, St. Joseph, Missouri. Courtesy State of Missouri, Department of Natural Resources.

Design for a terrace garden, Washington, D.C. From *American Country Houses of Today*, 1924. Courtesy Smithsonian Institution, Archives of American Gardens.

St. Joseph boulevards. Historic postcard. Courtesy City of St. Joseph.

for many of the program's eleven undergraduate classes; he assisted in teaching six courses and was the sole instructor in two others. (Three of these courses were introduced in Burnap's first year of teaching, which may indicate that he was responsible for course development as well as instruction.)

During the early 1910s, Burnap served as the landscape architect for the Office of Public Buildings and Grounds in Washington, D.C. This office was responsible for the numerous public parks and monuments that would later come under the jurisdiction of the National Park Service, and he became well known for his designs (and redesigns) of many of the city's famous public outdoor spaces. While holding this public position, Burnap began accepting commissions for work around the country. He left his government post in 1916 or 1917, possibly because of the conflict that arose between his public work and private practice.

In one of his best-known public works Burnap was responsible in 1912 for lining the banks of the Tidal

Basin near the Jefferson Memorial with Japanese cherry trees and other ornamental plants. The designs for Montrose and Meridian Hill parks in Washington are also significant examples of his work. Burnap's other projects in and around the District of Columbia, some of which he prepared as a consultant, include the designs for roadways and waterside embellishment of East Potomac Park, plans for the development of the waterfront from Potomac Park to the War College, group plans for the Gallingher Hospital, plans for the Penal Reservation at Occoquan, Virginia, and designs for several school sites.

Burnap was a landscape consultant to the Office of Engineering Commissioners, as well as to the U.S. Veteran's Bureau for hospital properties throughout the country. However, he is best known as a park planner. During the late 1910s and 1920s, he designed parks in St. Joseph, Missouri; Omaha (including a redesign of Levi Carter Park), Nebraska; Council Bluffs, Iowa; Granville, New York; Hagerstown, Maryland; Petersburg, Virginia; Greenwood, South Carolina; and else-

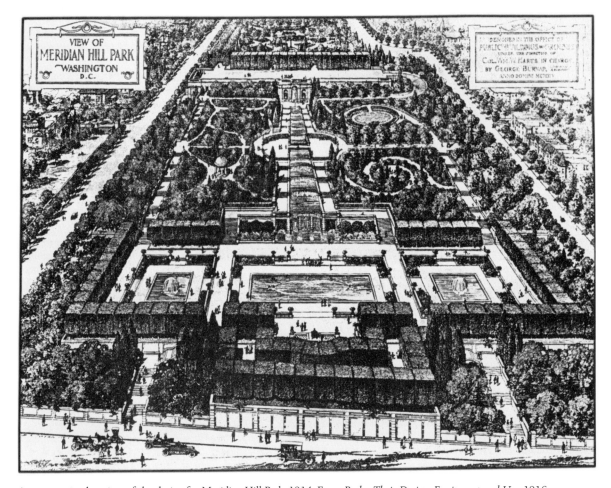

Axonometric plan view of the design for Meridian Hill Park, 1914. From *Parks: Their Design, Equipment and Use*, 1916.

where. Unfortunately, little detailed documentation is available concerning most of his park projects.

The most complete record of Burnap's involvement with park design exists in St. Joseph. Although he was the third nationally prominent landscape architect brought there to plan a city-wide park system (following Charles Mulford Robinson* and George Kessler*), Burnap is credited with the final design, and the St. Joseph park and parkway system may be the most extensive extant example of his work. It combines naturalistic treatment of landscape elements along the parkways with neoclassically inspired features such as the Children's Circus and the Refectory Building in Krug Park.

Burnap began working for the City of St. Joseph about 1917. In December 1920 he left the employ of

the parks department owing to lack of municipal funds, returning in 1924 after the city passed bonds to pay for implementing his designs. He formulated the plans for the improvements of Hyde Park, and he later received a three-year contract to supervise the park and parkway system's construction. During the latter part of his tenure in St. Joseph, Burnap worked with Jacques Gréber, a noted French architect and city planner. In 1927 staff at Gréber's Paris office prepared plans for the Civic Center around St. Joseph's new City Hall as well as for other squares and small parks in the city.

Burnap continued his education at the University of Paris, receiving a Diplome d'Urbanisme in 1923 from the university's graduate school, the Ecole des Hautes Etudes Urbaines. He was a Fellow of the American

Academy in Rome and a member of the Société des Urbanistes. He also lectured occasionally on landscape and civic design at the University of Pennsylvania, the University of Illinois, and MIT.

Burnap wrote *Parks: Their Design, Equipment, and Use,* published in 1916. He had planned to write a four-volume series about landscape architecture, covering landscape, planting, and garden design, and had already completed the chapters for the book on landscape design when he was interned on the border between France and Germany at the outbreak of World War I. His manuscript and numerous photographs were confiscated, and he was never able to recover them. Burnap was a contributing editor to both *Architectural Record* and *American Architecture and Building News* magazines.

Burnap died in Washington, D.C., and was buried in Boston.

Burnap, George. *Parks: Their Design, Equipment, and Use.* Philadelphia: J. B. Lippincott, 1916. Discussions on the relation of park design to city planning, principles of park design, various types of parks, and recommendations for certain park features such as playgrounds, monuments, water features, plants, and utilities; photographs and plans of selected Burnap designs in Washington, D.C., and photographs from Burnap's travels in Europe.

"Landscape Expert Views Omaha Parks." *Omaha World-Herald,* November 2, 1918. Article including Burnap's comments on the city's park system and development and noting his work in St. Joseph and Council Bluffs.

Who's Who in America, 1924–1925. Chicago: A. N. Marquis, 1924, 13. A brief biography of Burnap and a description of his work to date, which includes all of his known park designs.

Deon Wolfenbarger

CALDWELL, ALFRED
(1903–1998)
landscape architect, poet, civil engineer, architect, city planner, philosopher, teacher

Born in St. Louis, the third of six children, Caldwell moved with his family in 1909 to Chicago, where he grew up in poverty. Urged on by his French American mother, who insisted that he read and memorize poetry and history, Caldwell became a thinker and a dreamer early in life. He entered the University of Illinois in 1921 to study landscape architecture but never completed his studies.

In 1923 he eloped with his cousin Virginia Pullen. Shortly afterward, the couple returned to Chicago, where Caldwell took up a landscape practice in partnership with George Donoghue, who provided the capital for the business and later became superintendent of the South Chicago Park District. From offices in the Wrigley Building, Caldwell worked on small buildings and landscape projects until he decided that he had "only been trading dollars, and needed to learn something first."

A family friend suggested that he apply for work with the Prairie School landscape architect Jens Jensen*, an early ecologist who made the natural environment a

Jens Jensen and Alfred Caldwell, about 1945. Courtesy Dennis Domer.

Alfred Caldwell at Council Ring, Eagle Point Park, Dubuque, Iowa, 1991. Courtesy Dennis Domer.

Lily Pond, Lincoln Park, Chicago. Photo Robert E. Grese.

metaphor for landscape design. Jensen became his mentor, and between 1924 and 1929, Caldwell assisted him on various jobs, including landscapes for the Harley Clarke house in Evanston, Illinois (1925), the Harold Florsheim house in Ravinia, Illinois (1927), and the Edsel B. Ford house, in Grosse Pointe Shores, Michigan (1926–1932). During this period Caldwell also published his first article, "In Defense of Animals" (1931), which appeared in Jensen's journal, *Our Native Landscape*. Caldwell and Jensen became fast friends, and they carried on an extensive correspondence until Jensen's death in 1951. In a letter of reference written in 1934, Jensen described Caldwell as "an artist—a poet." Caldwell called Jensen "the great symbol of my life."

In 1927, Jensen commended Caldwell to Frank Lloyd Wright, whom Caldwell visited several times at Wright's home, Taliesin. Wright's organic ideas strongly influenced Caldwell's subsequent architecture, especially his pavilions and landscape for Eagle Point Park in

Dubuque, which won a national WPA design award in 1936. Caldwell was subsequently fired from his job (as he would be from most he held), reportedly for giving "too much attention to details," though according to Caldwell, it was because "the bastards had no dreams."

On returning to Chicago with his family, Caldwell was hired by George Donoghue as a senior draftsman in the Chicago Park District, where he worked until 1940. Caldwell, a prodigious worker, possessed masterly drawing abilities and a thorough knowledge of indigenous plants. He created large sets of landscape drawings—fully detailed with Latin and vernacular plant names—for Montrose Park, Northerly Island, Promontory Point at Burnham Park, Jackson Park, Riis Park, and the Lily Pool at Lincoln Park.

In 1938, Caldwell became acquainted with Ludwig Mies van der Rohe, Walter Peterhans, and Ludwig Hilberseimer. It was the beginning of a long relationship and a turn in his career. Mies, the most famous of the

Refectory, Eagle Point Park. Photo Robert E. Grese.

Bauhaus modernists, had come to Chicago to found the school of architecture at the Illinois Institute of Technology (IIT). Caldwell's Lily Pool, which Mies initially took to be the work of Frank Lloyd Wright, left a lasting impression on him. Mies remembered Caldwell when he graded the drawings Caldwell submitted during his architect's examination in 1940. The work was so good that Mies asked him to make drawings for Hilberseimer, who needed illustrations for his books on city planning. Caldwell's drawings appear in Hilberseimer's *The New City* (1944), *The Nature of Cities* (1955), and *Entfaltung einer Planungsidee* (1963). At the end of World War II, during which Caldwell worked as a civil engineer for the War Department, Mies hired him as the first full-time American faculty member at the architecture school of IIT. Mies granted Caldwell a Bachelor of Architecture degree in 1945, and in 1948, Caldwell completed a Master of Science in city planning under Hilberseimer. Mies assigned Caldwell to teach the second and third year of

architectural construction, the cornerstone of Mies's modern curriculum, as well as architectural history. Caldwell, who taught these courses from 1945 to 1960, became a legendary professor and had a powerful influence on the postwar generation of Chicago architects.

During this period Caldwell also completed several landscape projects that sealed his reputation. His landscape for Lafayette Park (1955–1963), an urban renewal housing project near downtown Detroit which Mies designed with the developer Herbert Greenwald, was considered a model for urbanization. (Today its owners value Lafayette Park more because of the lush landscape in an urban setting than because of the modern building design.) Caldwell also continued to publish philosophical essays on landscape and city planning. The most provocative of these, "Atomic Bombs and City Planning" (1945), in the *Journal of the American Institute of Architects*, described the problem of centralized industrial cities in the age of the bomb, and brought him national attention.

In 1960, Caldwell resigned his professorial position to protest Mies's dismissal as architect of the IIT campus. This gesture led to another significant job, as head of a special projects office at the Chicago Department of City Planning under the direction of Ira J. Bach and Lawrence Reich. Caldwell chaired a think tank composed primarily of young architects and planners who had graduated from IIT, which developed projects for Mayor Richard Daley's administration. The most dazzling of these, a grand proposal for the nation's 1976 Bicentennial, was never built. Caldwell continued his private landscape practice during this period; the most notable of his projects was the landscape for Lake Point Tower (1965–1968) in Chicago, designed by architects George Schipporeit and John Heinrich. His outside design work, as well as his unrelenting critiques of Chicago's urban renewal projects, got Caldwell fired, again.

This created an opportunity for the School of Architecture at the University of Southern California (USC) to hire Caldwell, who was well suited to bring clarity and purpose to architectural education during the turmoil and dissonance of the 1960s. He taught construction, philosophy, literature, and history in his fifth-year design studio, and most of the students gravitated to him. In contrast, Caldwell was unpopular with the faculty, although one of his supporters was Craig Ellwood, the most notable southern California architect of the Miesian School during the 1960s. Caldwell worked with Ellwood and his design architect, James Tyler, on many projects. Caldwell's most important southern California work was the Prairie School landscape for the Arts Center College of Design in Pasadena with Eric Katzmaier, whom he also advised on the design of Central Park at Huntington Beach, which was constructed according to Prairie School principles. Caldwell was retired from USC in 1972 despite strong student protest.

During his southern California period, Caldwell continued to write essays, most of which were published over the next thirty years in *The Structurist*, the art and architecture journal edited by Eli Bornstein at the University of Saskatchewan, and he took up poetry writing again.

Caldwell pursed his creative work until the end of his life. He continued to develop a superb Prairie School landscape on his farm in Bristol, Wisconsin. At the age of seventy-eight, he was re-hired at IIT in Chicago as the Ludwig Mies van der Rohe Professor of Architecture, and taught there until he died.

Blaser, Werner. *Architecture and Nature: The Work of Alfred Caldwell*. Basel: Birkhäuser, 1984. Descriptions and black-and-white photographs and color drawings of Caldwell's most important built and unbuilt work; includes one of Caldwell's essays from *The Structurist*, "Architecture: Vision of Structure."

Domer, Dennis, ed. *Alfred Caldwell: The Life and Work of a Prairie School Landscape Architect*. Baltimore: Johns Hopkins University Press, 1997. An extensive introduction to his life and work; sources include taped interviews and letters, a selection of Caldwell's essays, poetry, drawings, autobiographical writings, and correspondence.

Wilson, Richard Guy. "An Artist and a Poet, Alfred Caldwell Illuminates Nature's Ways." *Landscape Architecture* (September 1977), 407–12. A review of two of Caldwell's major landscape projects of the 1930s: Eagle Point Park in Dubuque, Iowa, and the Lily Pool in Lincoln Park in Chicago.

Dennis Domer

CAUTLEY, MARJORIE SEWELL
(1891–1954)
landscape architect

Marjorie Sewell was born into a navy family and spent part of her early years in Japan and Guam. Orphaned at age twelve, she returned to the United States, where she was raised by relatives in Brooklyn, New York, and in New Jersey. Sewell was educated at the Packer Institute for Collegiate Studies in Brooklyn, before studying landscape architecture at Cornell's College of Agriculture, where she graduated with a B.S. in 1917.

After graduation, she worked for Warren Manning* in Billerica, Massachusetts, during a period when his

Marjorie Sewell-Cautley, c. 1930. Courtesy Nell Walker.

ended shortly thereafter, and Sewell returned to New Jersey to start her own private practice.

In 1921 she began work on Roosevelt Common, a 30-acre community park in Tenafly, New Jersey, her first park project. It contained, among other landscape features, an arboretum of native plants. In 1922, Cautley wrote a series of seven articles for *Country Life in America* about the design of practical and pleasant gardens for modest homes. (She used her birth name and her married name, Cautley, during different periods in her career.)

Cautley's career took a profound turn when in 1924 she was hired by Clarence Stein and Henry Wright, philanthropist-intellectuals backing the Garden City movement, as part of a team effort to solve the East Coast "housing problem." The projects for which she served as landscape architect are, in New York City, Sunnyside Gardens, Sunnyside (1924–1928), Phipps Garden Apartments, Sunnyside (1930, 1935), and Hillside Homes (1935), and, in Fairlawn, New Jersey, Radburn (1928–1930). Among the most important features introduced by Cautley on these projects are the use of native plants in common areas, the positioning of homes and private gardens to face an interior common space, and the creation of landscape features that fostered a sense of community among residents. Years later, Stein remarked on the "rich, varied, and imaginative" landscape designs she provided.

Cautley also taught site planning and landscape de-

office was at the height of its volume of work. In 1918 she moved to Alton, Illinois, where she was employed by California architect Julia Morgan to assist in supervising construction of a hotel for war workers. World War I

Radburn, Fair Lawn, New Jersey.
Courtesy The Radburn Association.

sign as a part-time lecturer at both Columbia University and the Massachusetts Institute of Technology (1935–1937). During this same period, she published *Garden Design: The Principles of Abstract Design as Applied to Landscape Composition* (1935) and was appointed landscape consultant to the State of New Hampshire to oversee Civilian Conservation Corps projects in ten state parks. New Hampshire's Kingston and Wentworth Parks still show the fundamentals of her plans, drafted in 1935 and 1936.

In 1937, Cautley was stricken with an illness that dominated the rest of her life. She was hospitalized for several years, yet still produced articles for *House and Garden, American City, House Beautiful*, and the *Journal of the American Institute of Planners*. During a period of remission, she was able to educate herself further in city planning, earning an M.A. from the University of Pennsylvania in 1943. Her thesis, published in part as an article in *American City*, proposed renovation methods for blighted areas in Philadelphia.

Cautley, Marjorie S. *Garden Design: The Principles of Abstract Design as Applied to Landscape Composition*. New York: Dodd Mead, 1935. An eclectic text for both the "new garden woman" and site planning based on the Radburn experience; includes photos, sketches, plans, and plant lists.

Cautley, Marjorie S. "New Houses of Old Flavor." *Country Life in America*, June–December 1922. Series of seven articles; perspectives and plans; some illustrations by her sister Helen, a noted children's book illustrator.

Sewell, Marjorie. "How Blighted Areas in Philadelphia and Boston Might Be Transformed." *American City*, October 1943, 47–48. Adapted from Sewell's University of Pennsylvania master's thesis; includes sketches and photos.

Nell Walker

CHILD, STEPHEN
(1866–1936)
landscape architect

Born in Newton, Massachusetts, Stephen Child graduated from the Massachusetts Institute of Technology in 1888, and spent the next thirteen years in various engineering positions, in Buffalo, New York City, Washington, D.C., and Boston.

In 1901, Child moved to Staten Island, for a brief stint as business manager at Gordon Farms. In 1902 he embarked on a career change, by enrolling as a special student in Harvard's Lawrence Scientific School, where he studied landscape architecture and city planning under Frederick Law Olmsted Jr.* A year later, Child left the school to establish a "private practice of Landscape Architecture and Consulting Engineering." He maintained an office in Boston (1903–1914), as well as a winter office in Santa Barbara, California (1908–1914).

During this period, Child's Massachusetts work included designs for Stoneleigh Park Land Subdivision in Watertown and Montserrat Highlands in Beverly. Plans for both these projects were naturalistic in character, with topography used as the basis for the design. Child also executed designs for the Woodland Park Hotel in Auburndale, the Children's Hospital Grounds in Wellesley Hills, the grounds of the West End Thread Company in Millbury, the estate of Ivar Sjostrom in Andover, and a plan for the development of the Charles River Basin.

In the Santa Barbara area, Child's designs included the estates of Frederic L. Gould and William H. Bartlett. He also platted a subdivision, the Edwards Tract (1911), although his design was never implemented, and the property became the site of Santa Barbara High School in 1924. Child's most ambitious, though unrealized, Santa Barbara project was his 1913 plan for a 'Round the City Boulevard. Inspired by the ideas of Charles Mulford Robinson* and the City Beautiful movement, Child called for an elaborate 11-mile road around the city. Child's plan showed unusual sensitivity to natural con-

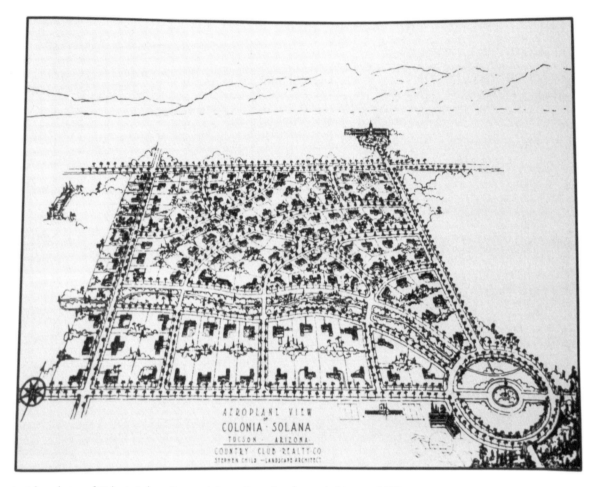

Aerial rendering of Colonia Solana, Tucson, Arizona. From *Landscape Architecture*, 1928.

ditions, changing from a broad, tree-lined boulevard in town, to rise and wind into the foothills and then become a divided road to allow for the preservation of a stand of beautiful old sycamore trees.

By 1914, Child had moved to San Francisco, where he began to focus on larger-scale projects. His work during this period included consultations on Roeding Park in Fresno and Alum Rock Park in San José. Child's monograph on Alum Rock Park calls for the exclusive use of native plants in this "wild and scenic reservation," making him one of the earliest landscape practitioners to do so. In spite of his work as a city planner, he had not abandoned his commitment to landscape architecture. He saw the detailed application of landscape architecture as having a great potential impact on planning, par-

ticularly the use of topography as a guide in the site planning of new towns.

An established professional at this point, Child served as West Coast chapter representative to the American Society of Landscape Architects (1912–1928), and also as chairman of the Professional Practice and Ethics Committee. In 1917 he was one of 52 charter members (14 of them landscape architects) of the American City Planning Institute.

In his writings, Child took the role of an advocate, almost an evangelist, for the emerging profession of landscape architecture. In nearly fifty articles directed toward engineers, architects, and other professionals as well as the general public, he explained its benefits. "Landscape Architecture: A Series of Letters," written in 1928, was an

Francis S. Gould estate, Pasadena. From P. H. Elwood Jr., ed., *American Landscape Architecture*, 1924.

imaginary correspondence between a client and a landscape architect, aimed to inform the public about the profession.

During World War I, Child designed war industry housing as a town planner with the U.S. Housing Corporation. His projects included designs at Aberdeen and Indianhead, Maryland, Ilion, New York, and Dahlgren, Virginia. The Indianhead site showed great sensitivity to topography. Curving roads gradually wound up to the bluffs overlooking the Potomac River. These bluffs, as well as a steep ravine, were heavily forested with oak, gum trees, and holly, and were to be left as natural parks. The Dahlgren site was unique in that the only access was by water; the entrance, labeled "Dock Square," was a formal cross-shape, which led to a rectilinear parade ground. The remaining roads were carefully adapted to existing topography, echoing the shape of the shoreline; consequently, nearly every house lot had a view of the water.

Child's last known, and perhaps only surviving, work is the Colonia Solana subdivision in Tucson, platted

in 1927, for which he explained his design considerations in a 1928 article for *Landscape Architecture*. He notes that "acres and acres . . . of desert had been 'gridironed' " to make Tucson, in response to the "dead flat piece of ground" that formed the Tucson valley. He describes the regional setting of Tucson, "the City of the Sunshine Climate," noting the "high mountains, incomparably beautiful, especially at morning and evening," as well as nearby social features. The designer's task, he says, is to create something "interesting."

The topographical survey revealed "one fairly important arroyo or 'wash' . . . also two other even lesser washes, flowing into the larger one." These washes, Child noted, could have been easily filled up and ignored, as usual. Instead, they were emphasized in the design, "the largest becoming the keynote of the Parkway." The most distinctive feature, Arroyo Chico Parque, a linear park along the wash, was to be "planted with native desert plants of all kinds . . . including all the important cacti, . . . native trees, . . . the surface to be covered with desert flowers." The result was to be a strip covered as thickly as possible with desert growth, so that the residents would "have the desert beauty in front of their doors."

The informal elements of Child's plan, based on topography and native vegetation, were the guiding force in the design, although he included a formal element as well—a north-south axis formed by Randolph Way, the eastern boundary of the development. The topography, of course, has not changed in sixty years, but the vegetation has considerably. The "creosote flat" vegetation of 1928 has gradually evolved into a riparian oasis in the middle of a totally urban Southwestern city. It is because of Child's design that these changes could take place. Increased runoff, from both the subdivision itself and from upstream, have nurtured the native plants, which have naturalized along Child's Arroyo Chico Parque: the evolution of a true partnership of design and nature.

Child, Stephen. "Colonia Solana: A Subdivision on the Arizona Desert." *Landscape Architecture* 19 (October 1928), 6–13. Child's design approach to the Colonia Solana neighborhood in Tucson; emphasizes topography and native plants as the basis for his design; plans, photos.

Child, Stephen. "A Plan for the Development of Alum Rock Park." 1912; revised 1916, 1929. Child's most detailed statement of his design philosophy; he recognizes the unique character of "this wild and scenic reservation" near San José and calls for the removal of all exotic plants; available at Bancroft Library, University of California, Berkeley.

Korff, Mary Blaine. "Stephen Child: Visionary Landscape Architect." Master's thesis, University of Arizona, Tucson, 1991. Documents his personal and professional life, covering his work in Boston, Santa Barbara, San Francisco, and Tucson, with special attention to Colonia Solana.

A small archive of Child's papers has been assembled at the University of Arizona College of Architecture, Planning, and Landscape Architecture, Tucson.

Mary Blaine Korff

CHURCH, THOMAS DOLLIVER
(1902–1978)
landscape architect

Born in Boston, Thomas Church spent his childhood in the Ojai Valley of southern California. There he learned to love the native landscape and to appreciate the advantages and limitations of the climate and its great potential for outdoor living. His route into landscape architecture was not clearly marked. As a student at the University of California at Berkeley, he was expected by his family to major in law. But a course in the history of garden design, offered by the fledgling division of landscape design in the College of Agriculture, intrigued him so much that he changed his direction and graduated with a B.A. degree in 1922.

To expand his skills, Church enrolled as a student of landscape architecture at Harvard University's Graduate

Thomas Church by Carolyn Caddes, 1975. Courtesy Thomas Church Collection, Documents Collection, College of Environmental Design, University of California, Berkeley.

Garden of Mr. and Mrs. Charles de Bretteville, Woodside, California (designed 1950), 1998. Photo Charles A. Birnbaum.

School of Design in 1924. Even more important to his development, however, was the opportunity to travel in Europe. As a recipient of the Sheldon Travelling Fellowship, Church spent six months in Italy and Spain. On his return to the United States in 1927, he submitted a master's thesis that drew parallels between the climates and landscapes of the Mediterranean region and California. Church interleaved pictures of houses and gardens in Santa Barbara with descriptions and photographs of the villas and gardens of Tuscany and Frascati, which he found "delightful and livable because of scale and imagination—not magnificence."

Church returned to practice in the Bay Area in 1929 and was soon at work on Pasatiempo, a planned community near Santa Cruz. His contribution was the siting of individual houses in the natural landscape and

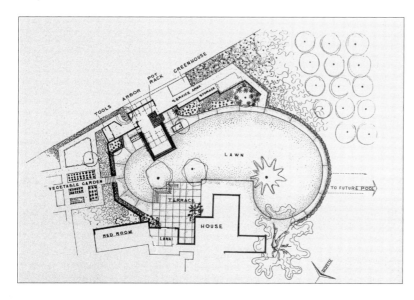

Plan for de Bretteville garden. From *Gardens Are for People*, 1955.

Donnell garden, Sonoma, California. Photo Saxon Holt.

the design of patio gardens suited to the Spanish rancho-style architecture. The climate that made outdoor living a constant and central aspect of home life was a major influence on Church's approach to garden design. The need for irrigation in summer necessitated simple plant-ing plans, small symbolic areas of lawn, and the use of native and other drought-tolerant plants. Above all, Church believed that the cultivated garden area should be compact and clearly defined.

Until the late 1930s, Church's designs could be

Stanley William Abbott.
Blue Ridge Parkway.
Courtesy Robert R. Page.

Jacob Bigelow. Mount Auburn Cemetery.
Cambridge, Massachusetts.
Photo Blanche M. G. Linden.

Jacob Bigelow. Mount Auburn Cemetery.
Cambridge, Massachusetts.
Photo Charles A. Birnbaum.

John Blair. Beacon Hill Park.
Victoria, B.C.
Photo John Blair.

Ernest Bowditch.
Shaker Lakes Park.
Shaker Heights, Ohio.
Courtesy Smithsonian Institution,
Archives of American Gardens.

Loutrel W. Briggs. Mepkin Abbey.
Moncks Corner, South Carolina.
Courtesy Mepkin Abbey
and Botanical Garden.

George Burnap.
Krug Park. St. Joseph, Missouri.
Courtesy State of Missouri,
Department of Natural Resources.

George Burnap. St. Joseph boulevards.
St. Joseph, Missouri.
Courtesy City of St. Joseph.

Alfred Caldwell. Lincoln Park.
Chicago, Illinois.
Photo Robert E. Grese.

Alfred Caldwell.
Refectory, Eagle Point Park.
Dubuque, Iowa.
Photo Robert E. Grese.

Marjorie Sewell Cautley.
Radburn. Fair Lawn, New Jersey.
Courtesy The Radburn Association.

Thomas D. Church.
Charles de Bretteville garden.
Woodside, California.
Photo Charles A. Birnbaum.

Thomas D. Church.
Donnell garden. Sonoma, California.
Photo Saxon Holt.

described as quite conservative; although not replicas of historical models, they were clearly based on traditional principles. After another European trip in 1937 to study the work of Le Corbusier and the Finnish architect and designer Alvar Aalto, as well as that of modern painters and sculptors, Church began a period of experimentation with new forms. He abandoned the central axis in favor of multiplicity of viewpoints, simple planes, and flowing lines. Texture and color, space and form were manipulated in ways reminiscent of the cubist painters, while satisfying all practical criteria. The gardens of the late 1940s indicate a continuation of this exploration: curvilinear pools, zigzags and piano curves, trompe l'oeil, and false perspective—but always with respect for context and client.

Church had arrived on the landscape scene at a time of transition. He was traditional enough to see value in the old, open enough to consider the new, and sensible enough to know that each, to be good, must be the product of a thorough knowledge of the principles on which it was based. The variety to be found in the approximately 2,000 gardens designed in forty years of practice illustrates this breadth as well as his respect for the unique qualities of every situation. In short, Church's approach to design sought direction from three major sources: the site, the architecture of the house, and the client's personality and preferences.

Regardless of their purely visual characteristics, Church's gardens typically embodied several basic concepts. These include careful siting and orientation of the house with regard to sun, views, exposure, existing trees, and topography; a distinct sequence of arrival, including entrance drive, parking area, and front door; a direct connection between house and garden, including provision for outdoor living; a defined edge for the garden, separating it and at the same time joining it to the surrounding landscape or neighbors; provision for functional spaces—parking, garage, work area, kitchen garden, doghouse, and so on—plus ease of maintenance; and a selection of plants that would reinforce the structure of the garden and the objectives of the plan.

Although garden design was always Church's chief interest and the principal source of his reputation, he is also known as the landscape architect of record for several major large-scale public and corporate projects completed in collaboration with distinguished architects. These include Valencia Public Housing (1939–1943) and Park Merced (1941–1950), both in San Francisco, and the General Motors Technical Center (1949–1959) outside Detroit.

In recognition of his contribution to modern landscape architecture, Thomas Church received the Fine Arts Medal of the American Institute of Architects (1951), the Gold Medal of the American Society of Landscape Architects (1976), the Gold Medal of the New York Architectural League (1953), the Oakleigh Thorne Medal from the Garden Club of America (1969), and a Fellowship of the American Academy of Arts and Sciences (1978).

Church's success and fame were a result of his skill in combining the rational with the romantic, his ability to produce form related to the site and to the purpose of the place, his concern for materials and details, and above all, his relationship with his clients, who were willing participants in the process.

Church, Thomas D. *Gardens Are for People: How to Plan for Outdoor Living.* 1955. Rpt. 3d ed. Ed. Grace Hall and Michael Laurie. Berkeley: University of California Press, 1995. "A garden tour with some comment in passing"; includes a discussion of design considerations, use (people and animals), views, plant materials, and characteristic elements of the California garden (e.g., terraces, swimming pools, wood decking, and garden details); profusely illustrated with large-format color and black-and-white photography, plans, sections.

Church, Thomas Dolliver. *Your Private World: A Study of Intimate Gardens.* San Francisco: Chronicle Books, 1969. Draws on forty years of practice; many photographs all credited with client name and locale; intended to inspire the homeowner to take advantage of "a whole range of new materials and techniques to stimulate our thinking and broaden our horizons."

Imbert, Dorothee. "Of Gardens and Houses as Places to Live: Thomas Church and William Wurster." In *An Everyday Modernism: The Houses of William Wurster,* ed. Marc Treib. Berkeley: San Francisco Museum of Art / University of California Press, 1995. Highlights the collaboration that began in 1930 when Wurster designed a house and studio for Thomas and Elizabeth Church; well-illustrated examples include over a dozen California projects from the 1930s–1950s; rarely seen historical photographs coupled with newly drawn as-built plans and axonometric drawings.

Michael Laurie

CLARKE, GILMORE DAVID
(1892–1982)
landscape architect

Born within sight of Vaux* and Olmsted's* Riverside Park in New York City, Gilmore Clarke was an only son. His father, with his grandfather and his uncle, ran a flourishing florist business, selling plants they grew in their nursery in the Bronx.

In 1909, Clarke enrolled in Cornell University's College of Agriculture. Initially studying ornamental horticulture, he changed course after a conversation with upperclassman Edward Lawson (subsequently the first recipient of the Rome Prize in Landscape Architecture) led him to the Department of Rural Art. Clarke graduated in 1913, the first in the family to gain a college education. He later acknowledged that Bryant Fleming*, who had developed the course in Rural Art and was already an eminent landscape designer, had influenced him most.

Oddly, when recommended for an opening in Fleming's office, Clarke did not pursue it. Instead, he returned to New York City, where he was hired by Charles Downing Lay* of Wheelwright & Lay, Landscape Architects. In 1915, he responded to a vacancy in the Hudson County Park Commission in New Jersey. Charles N. Lowrie, a landscape architect, hired Clarke even though the job described was a civil engineering position.

About the same time, Clarke met and impressed William White Niles of the Bronx River Parkway Commission, charged with cleaning up the polluted Bronx River, which flowed through Westchester County and northern New York City. By 1915 a trunk sewer had been completed and grading was under way for a linear park along the Bronx River featuring a scenic drive. Niles offered Clarke the position of Superintendent of Construction, and he accepted, a decision that set the his career path. His work was soon interrupted by service in World War I, but in June 1919 he returned to resume it.

The design of the fifteen-mile-long Bronx River Parkway was essentially the work of Herman Merkel, a landscape architect-forester trained in Germany and respected as an authority on trees and shrubs, but by superintending the rechanneling of the river, grading, aligning of the roadway, and planting, Clarke was able to infuse his ideas of landscape art into the finished work. Except for the bridges, the work was being done with minimal construction drawings by Westchester County labor forces.

While at Cornell, Clarke had formed a particular interest in bridges and their role in landscape art. By working closely with bridge engineer Arthur Hayden and the architects engaged as consultants on the parkway, he was able to exert considerable influence on the design of the bridges. He advocated native stone to clad the concrete structure, weathered wherever possible, to give a roadway bridge a feeling of age in its association with the land, trees, and water. This philosophy became basic to the design of Westchester County's parks and parkways and subsequently throughout New York State, other eastern states, and the National Park Service.

The Bronx River Parkway was open to cars only, with controlled access at interchanges and grade crossings, where Clarke developed early examples of diamond ramps and cloverleaf interchanges. Merkel had originally proposed opposing directional roadways separated by a variable width of planting, an idea that Clarke embraced and fostered. But because of the greater cost, the commission had overruled the concept; nevertheless, at least two sections were built. The design concept of the curvilinear parkway with separated roadways eventually became the model for the modern highway.

The Bronx River Parkway proved so successful that in 1922, a year before its completion, the Westchester County Park Commission was created, staffed with the personnel of the Bronx River Parkway Commission; Clarke headed the Department of Planning, Landscape, and Architectural Design. The commission was charged with preparing a plan of parks and parkways, which was completed the following year. Dictated by the county's geography, parkways were planned along the north-south valleys that paralleled the Bronx River: the Saw Mill, Hutchinson, and Grassy Sprain rivers; east-west parkways were also planned. Each was to serve large new parks with many recreational facilities along its route or at its terminus.

When the plan was authorized, Clarke moved quickly to assemble a staff of architects and landscape architects. Building on his ideas from the Bronx River Parkway, he designed 10,000 acres of parks, beaches, and golf courses, all involving original concepts in designing ingress, parking, and egress for large numbers of cars.

By 1934 the commission had completed a system of parks and parkways unparalleled in the United States, indeed in the world. Planners, engineers, and park officials (including Stephen Mather, director of the National Park Service) visited, and Clarke gained national prominence

Pedestrian timber bridge over Bronx River, Bronx River Parkway, Westchester County, New York, c. 1938. Photo John Gass.

Saw Mill River Parkway, vicinity of Woodlands Lake Park, Westchester County, New York, c. 1935. Photo John Gass.

Plan, Rye Beach Park/Playground, Westchester County, New York, March 1932. Charcoal rendering by Michael Rapuano. Courtesy Westchester County Archives.

and commissions as a result. One of these was for the Mount Vernon Memorial Parkway, completed in 1932 in commemoration of the bicentennial of George Washington's birth. When he was shown the planned location, Clarke advised the Commissioner of Public Roads (predecessor of the Federal Highway Administration) that it was not suitable for a parkway and recommended the route along the Potomac River where it was built. Clarke devoted much of his effort to the design of the stone-faced, rigid-frame bridges that grace the parkway. Subsequently, the National Park Service engaged him to advise on a parkway proposed along the Blue Ridge Mountains. In 1933 he recommended Stanley W. Abbott* from his staff to be the resident landscape architect. Following in

Bryant Park, New York, c. 1937–1940.
Photo John Gass.

the footsteps of his mentor, Abbott became the guiding genius in the development of the Blue Ridge Parkway.

In 1932, President Herbert Hoover selected Clark to be the landscape architect member of the National Fine Arts Commission in Washington, D.C.; he served as its chairman from 1937 to 1950. In 1934, Clarke left Westchester County to head the design group in the New York City Department of Parks for Commissioner Robert Moses. In 1935, Cornell University appointed Clarke to the faculty of the College of Architecture and three years later its dean, a position he held until 1950. He commuted to Ithaca weekly while maintaining a burgeoning practice in New York City in partnership with Michael Rapuano*, a landscape architect from his staff in Westchester.

Serving as consultants to Madigan-Hyland Engineers, Clarke & Rapuano designed the Henry Hudson River Parkway along Manhattan's waterfront, including in their concept abutting parts of Riverside Park designed originally by Olmsted. The parkway extended northward through Riverdale to its junction at the Westchester County line with the Saw Mill River Parkway, which Clarke had designed. Clarke, now with Rapuano, brought the same holistic design approach to the Henry Hudson which he had to the parks and parkways in Westchester, amalgamating architecture and engineering with landscape art. The two partners would play the

same role many times over in executing commissions for parks and parkways, expressways, and interstate highways in New York, New Jersey, Pennsylvania, Tennessee, and Virginia.

Clarke, Gilmore, D. "The Parkway Idea." In *The Highway and the Landscape*, ed. W. Brewster Snow. New Brunswick, N.J.: Rutgers University Press, 1959, 33–55. An overview of the issues surrounding the planning, design, and construction of parkways.

Clarke, Gilmore D. "The Relation of Architecture and Landscape Architecture." *The American Architect* 133 (March 1928), 281–286. Emphasizes landscape architecture as one of the fine arts, encouraging collaboration among architecture, landscape architecture, and other fine arts in both professional training and practice; photographs by Clarke and others.

Westchester County Park Commission. *Annual Reports.* White Plains, N.Y.: Westchester County Commission, 1924–1934. Chronicles of the planning design and construction of the parkway and associated parks along the Bronx River, including before, during, and after construction photographs.

Domenico Annese

CLEVELAND, HORACE WILLIAM SHALER
(1814–1900)
landscape gardener

Horace Cleveland was born in Lancaster, Massachusetts, and as a youth attended an innovative school there managed by his mother, Dorcas Hiller Cleveland. The school's unique curriculum emphasized landscape study and observation. Horatio Greenough, another student at the school, developed a set of aesthetic ideas in concert with Ralph Waldo Emerson, which argued for an organic approach to art. These ideas later influenced Cleveland as a landscape designer, leading him to believe that he should be as true as possible to the landscape in which he worked. As a consequence, throughout his career he advocated a starkly simple and natural style of design and maintained great disdain for superfluous decoration.

In the late 1820s, Cleveland moved with his family to Cuba, where he learned about mulching techniques on the coffee plantations and the healthful effects of tropical scenery. During the 1830s, he surveyed in the wild landscape of Illinois and other western states for railroad entrepreneurs and real estate speculators. After returning to Massachusetts in the late 1830s to stay with brother Henry in Jamaica Plain, Cleveland became involved with a literary organization called the Five of Clubs, where he met Henry Wadsworth Longfellow, whose ideas about social responsibility influenced Cleveland's entire career. In the early 1840s, Cleveland purchased Oatlands, a farm in Burlington, New Jersey, where he established himself as a scientific farmer. In that role he considered both practical and aesthetic issues of landscape design and published articles about pomological techniques in journals such as Andrew Jackson Downing's* *The Horticulturist.*

In 1854, Cleveland again moved back to Massachusetts to begin a practice in landscape and ornamental gardening with Robert Morris Copeland*. One of their first important commissions was the design of Sleepy Hollow Cemetery in Concord, for which Copeland and Cleveland were employed by Emerson and the other members of the Concord Cemetery Committee. Cleveland and Copeland designed the site to be sensitive to the existing landscape, and also as a park connected to various public open spaces in the Concord community. Their ideas about the connection of public spaces informed their suggestions for a Boston park system a year later. In 1856, as Back Bay was being filled, Cleveland and Copeland recommended that Commonwealth Avenue connect the center of Boston (the Common and Public Garden) to public spaces on the city's periphery. In the following years Cleveland contributed to a public campaign in support of a connected park system for Boston. His 1869 publication *The Public Grounds of Chicago: How to Give Them Character and Expression,* was as much about the public open space needs of Boston as it was about Chicago. Cleveland and Copeland dissolved their partnership sometime before the Civil War.

When Cleveland moved to Chicago in 1869 he used his connections with powerful railroad magnates to secure work. These men were convinced of their responsibility to help guide the advance of civilization by planning communities and planting trees in the prairie landscape. Cleveland also formed a loose partnership with William Merchant Richardson French, a civil engineer and later founding director of the Chicago Art Institute, collaborating with him on cemetery and subdivision projects. During the 1870s, Cleveland worked on

Horace William Shaler Cleveland, c. 1878. Courtesy Lancaster, Massachusetts, Public Library.

Sleepy Hollow Cemetery. Photo Lance Neckar.

Minneapolis Boulevard, 1996.
Photo Charles A. Birnbaum.

Minnehaha Falls, Minneapolis, 1996.
Photo Charles A. Birnbaum.

Chicago's Drexell Boulevard, the South Parks, and Graceland Cemetery. His office and prized library were destroyed in the Great Fire of 1871. In 1873 he published *Landscape Architecture as Applied to the Wants of the West with an Essay on Forest Planting on the Great Plains*, one of the first books to define and develop the scope of the new profession of landscape architecture.

Cleveland also corresponded extensively with colleagues such as Frederick Law Olmsted Sr.*

In 1883, Cleveland began work on the Minneapolis Park System, the crowning achievement of his long career. He laid out a system of connected lakes, parks, and parkways that were integral to the city's development over the next several decades. After moving to

Hanscom Park, Omaha, Nebraska,
1997. Photo Charles A. Birnbaum.

Minneapolis in the mid-1880s, he helped secure the area around Minnehaha Falls, known for its poetic associations with Longfellow's *Song of Hiawatha*. The Minneapolis park system is today considered one of the most significant open space systems in the United States, and it stands as a testament to Cleveland's vision.

———

Cleveland, H. W. S. *Landscape Architecture as Applied to the Wants of the West with an Essay on Forest Planting on the Great Plains*. Chicago, 1873. A seminal work on the developing profession of landscape architecture which received accolades from Olmsted Sr. and others; one of the first book-length works to clearly define the scope of the new profession.

Cleveland, H. W. S. *Social Life and Literature Fifty Years Ago*. Boston, 1888. Written ostensibly as a defense of the intellectual life of early nineteenth-century Salem, Massachusetts, which had been severely criticized by Henry James; more important, a necessary book for any understanding of the literary ideas that shaped Cleveland's world view and aesthetic vision.

Cleveland, H. W. S. *Suggestions for a System of Parks and Parkways for the City of Minneapolis*. Minneapolis, 1883. Cleveland's initial report outlining his concept for the Minneapolis park system.

———

Daniel Joseph Nadenicek, William H. Tishler, and Lance M. Neckar

COFFIN, MARIAN CRUGER
(1876–1957)
landscape architect

Among the first American women to enter the profession of landscape architecture, Marian Cruger Coffin stands out for her masterly handling of spatial composition, proportion, and plantsmanship. At the height of her career between 1910 and 1935, Coffin designed approximately fifty large estate gardens in the Northeast, primarily in New York State and Delaware. Among her more prominent clients were Childs Frick, Marshall Field, Edward F. Hutton, Frederick Frelinghuysen, and Henry Francis du Pont. Her projects were frequently written about in the

Marian C. Coffin, c. 1904. Courtesy Winterthur Library: Winterthur Archives.

magazines *Country Life in America, House and Garden, Architectural Record,* and *Home and Garden Builder.* Coffin also had institutional clients such as the University of

Delaware (1918–1940s) and the New York Botanical Garden (1942–1957), where she designed the Robert Montgomery Conifer Collection, the Havemeyer Lilac Collection, and a pavilion for the Rose Garden, an area originally designed by Beatrix Farrand*.

Marian Cruger Coffin was born in New York City and raised by her mother, Alice Church Coffin. Owing to the generosity of her maternal uncles, she grew up in the patrician world of old New York families, despite the fact that her father, Julian Ross Coffin, abandoned the family soon after her birth. During her teens, Coffin and her mother went to live in Geneva, New York, staying in the home of her uncle, John Barker Church.

As a young woman, Coffin knew that she had to earn a living to support herself and her mother. She decided on a career in "landscape gardening," one of the few fields open to women at the turn of the century. Determined to obtain an education, she was admitted to the Massachusetts Institute of Technology as a special student in 1901 and completed the program in landscape architecture in 1904. For an intensive period she studied drawing, drafting, engineering, science, math, horticulture, architectural design, and landscape architecture under the direction of Guy Lowell*. She was well trained in both formal and naturalistic styles of landscape design and toured Europe twice to study the great gardens before leaving college.

When Coffin discovered that professional design firms in New York were reluctant to hire a young

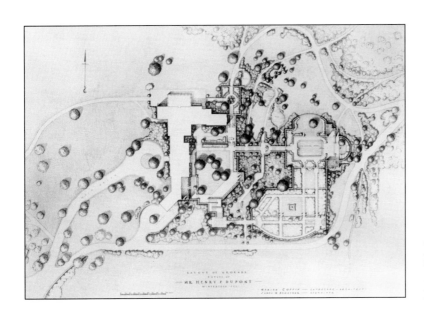

"Layout of Grounds of Estate of Henry F. du Pont, Winterthur, Del.," by Marian C. Coffin and James M. Scheiner, 1928. Courtesy Winterthur Library: Winterthur Archives.

April Garden, Winterthur, 1993. Photo Carol Betsch.

woman, she opened her own office. At first the young designer worked on flower gardens and small residential properties, but in 1912 her design for the residence of Edward Sprague in Flushing, New York, was published in *Country Life in America,* and more challenging commissions followed. Coffin received many referrals from family members and friends, but the most important source of new clients was Henry Francis du Pont, the shy millionaire from Delaware she had met while at college. The two shared a true passion for gardens and garden plants and so became lifelong friends. In 1916, du Pont was probably responsible for Coffin's receiving the commission to design the grounds of Gibraltar, Mr. and Mrs. H. Rodney Sharp's estate in Wilmington, Delaware.

Gibraltar, H. Rodney Sharp estate, Wilmington, Delaware. From P. H. Elwood Jr., ed., *American Landscape Architecture*, 1924.

(Gibraltar remains the best extant example of Coffin's residential landscapes.) In 1924, du Pont employed her to design the grounds of his summer home, Chestertown House in Southampton, Long Island, and in 1928, Winterthur near Wilmington. During a massive remodeling of the mansion at Winterthur, Coffin and her architectural associate, James M. Scheiner, laid out the walks, drives terraces, pavilions, bathhouses, swimming pool area, and several other gardens. It was the largest single commission of her career.

Coffin considered her work at Winterthur to be one of her finest achievements, along with the formal garden she designed in 1926 for Mr. and Mrs. Childs Frick at Clayton in Roslyn, New York. The Georgian Garden, as it was named, was an elegant four-part enclosed garden in keeping with the Fricks' Georgian Revival mansion designed by Ogden Codman Jr. in 1900. (Today the estate

houses the Nassau County Museum of Art). Other significant projects undertaken at the height of her career included William M. Bullitt's Oxmoor near Louisville, Kentucky (1911); Charles Sabin's Bayberry Land in Southampton, New York (1918–1919); Gordon Knox Bell's The Belfry in Katonah, New York (1920); Marshall Field's Winter Cottage Garden at Caumsett, Lloyds Neck, New York (1920–1923); Edward F. Hutton's Hillwood in Wheatley Hills, New York (1922); Stephen H. Pell's King's Garden at Fort Ticonderoga, New York (1920–1926); Edgar Bassick's The Oaks in Bridgeport, Connecticut (1928), and the swimming pool garden for Lammot du Pont Copeland's Mt. Cuba near Greenville, Delaware (1950).

Coffin joined the American Society of Landscape Architects in 1906 and was elected a Fellow in 1918. She offered young women apprenticeships in her office to help overcome the discrimination she felt persisted in the field. Landscape architect Clara Stimson Coffey trained with her before establishing her own successful firm in New York. During the Depression, when many small firms closed their doors, Coffin survived by moving her office to her home in New Haven, Connecticut, and by retaining her staff on a contract basis only. She sought out public projects and wrote *Trees and Shrubs for Landscape Effects* (1940), the only work in which she described her approach to landscape design at length. Coffin also competed in the annual exhibitions of the Architectural League of New York from 1907 to 1937, and her persistent efforts and talent were rewarded in 1930 with their Gold Medal of Honor for Landscape Design.

Coffin died in her home in New Haven at the age of eighty-one. She had been working on several landscape projects earlier that year.

Coffin, Marian. *Trees and Shrubs for Landscape Effects.* New York: Charles Scribner's Sons, 1940. Coffin's most complete expression of her theories and approaches to landscape; photographs by Mattie Edwards Hewitt, Samuel H. Gottscho, Harry G. Healy, and others.

Fleming, Nancy. *Money, Manure, and Maintenance.* Weston, Mass.: Country Place Books, 1995. Discussion of Coffin's design style, her offices in New York City and New Haven, and her largest commissions at Winterthur, Delaware College, and the Pavilion garden at Fort Ticonderoga; includes many photos, plans, etc.

Libby, Valencia. "Marian Cruger Coffin: The Landscape Architect and the Lady, 1876–1957." In *The House and Garden.* Roslyn, N.Y.: Nassau County Museum of Fine Arts, 1986. Summary of Coffin's life and career, citing major projects; plans and photos of Clayton and Winterthur.

Valencia Libby

COPELAND, ROBERT MORRIS
(1830–1874)
landscape gardener

Robert Morris Copeland was born in Roxbury, Massachusetts. After trying his luck in California during the gold rush he attended Harvard College, where he studied liberal arts and formed a lifelong association with Henry Wadsworth Longfellow. After graduating in the early 1850s, Copeland became a scientific farmer at Beaver Brook Falls near Lexington. He met Horace Cleveland* through scientific farming connections, and they established a partnership in "landscape and ornamental gardening" in 1854.

Copeland's first commission, likely prepared with Cleveland, was the State Farm at Westborough, Massachusetts. In early 1855, Copeland delivered an address in the Concord Lyceum Series titled "The Useful and the Beautiful." That address, coupled with personal connections, led to the selection of Copeland and Cleveland as designers of Sleepy Hollow Cemetery in Concord. Other notable projects they completed during the 1850s include the Samuel Colt estate in Hartford, Connecticut (today part of Colt Park), the Oak Grove Cemetery, Gloucester, and the Wyoming Cemetery, Melrose, both in Massachusetts. In 1856, Copeland used his relationship with Longfellow in a failed attempt to obtain the commission for the design of Central Park, and toward that end, he and Cleveland laid out their thoughts in a pamphlet titled "A Few Words on the Central Park." In 1857, Copeland submitted a formal entry in the Central Park design competition but won nothing (it is unclear whether he submitted the design alone or with Cleveland). Copeland also wrote a book, *Country Life: A Handbook of Agriculture, Horticulture, and Landscape Gardening* (1859), in which he offered practical and aesthetic advice to rural citizens and suggested that a managed rural landscape offered everything that might "expand the mind and ennoble the soul." Copeland and Cleve-

Copeland's home landscape. From *Country Life*, 1859.

land amicably dissolved their partnership at some point before the Civil War.

During the war, Copeland attained the rank of major in the Union Army and likely helped establish the 54th Massachusetts Regiment, the black brigade later depicted in the famous Augustus Saint-Gaudens sculpture. He was dishonorably discharged, however, in 1862, apparently for leaking disparaging information about superior officers to the press, and spent the next several years clearing his name. In the process he solicited character witnesses including Ralph Waldo Emerson and even met with President Abraham Lincoln. By the late 1860s he had established a flourishing practice in Boston with projects in New York, Pennsylvania, and several New England states. In 1869 he prepared a master plan for the Frederick Billings estate in Woodstock, Vermont, where Billings engaged in forestry study and scientific farming experiments consistent with many of the ideas presented in Copeland's *Country Life*.

Also beginning in the 1860s, Copeland began to promote his developing ideas for a Boston park system in articles and editorials published in the *Boston Daily Advertiser* (the newspaper was edited by his brother-in-law, Charles F. Dunbar). By 1872, Copeland had developed a grand plan for a system of public open spaces which he highlighted in his 1872 publication, *The Most Beautiful City in America: Essay and Plan for the Improvement of the City of Boston*. Many of his ideas foreshadowed Charles Eliot's*. Copeland designed hundreds of landscapes at all scales, including several fine community designs such as Oak Bluffs on Martha's Vineyard. He continued to refine his design philosophy and worked to position himself to design a system of parks for Boston until he died unexpectedly in 1874. After his death his apprentice Ernest Bowditch* continued to promote Copeland's concept for a connected park system in Boston. According to an obituary, likely written by Dunbar, Copeland "had done much in the way of laying out and ornamenting private grounds, but his ambition was for work on a grander scale."

Copeland, Robert Morris. *Country Life: A Handbook of Agriculture, Horticulture, and Landscape Gardening.*

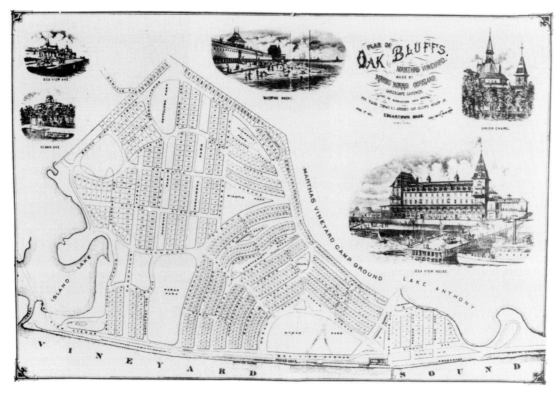

Plan of Oak Bluffs, Martha's Vineyard, 1871. From *City in the Woods.*

Boston, 1859. Practical hints arranged on a monthly basis for rural citizens, interspersed with landscape design ideas; popular book that went through several printings.

Copeland, Robert Morris. *The Most Beautiful City in America: Essay and Plan for the Improvement of the City of Boston.* Boston, 1872. An extensive plan for a system of public open spaces in the greater Boston area.

Weiss, Ellen. *City in the Woods: The Life and Design of an American Camp Meeting on Martha's Vineyard.* New York: Oxford University Press, 1987. Full development of the camp meeting story at Martha's Vineyard with part of a chapter on Copeland's design contributions.

Daniel Joseph Nadenicek, William H. Tishler,
and Lance M. Neckar

CORNELL, RALPH DALTON
(1890–1972)
landscape architect

Ralph Cornell was born in Holdrege, Nebraska. In 1908, his family moved to Long Beach, California, enticed by the booming eucalyptus industry, but that venture's sub-

sequent failure left them destitute. Enrolling in Pomona College in 1909, Cornell met his mentor, Charles Fuller Baker, and followed an independent study program. Because finances were tight, he dropped out for a year. He worked on a landscape design for Freemont Place in Beverly Hills and planted date offshoots near Thermal, California, an enterprise that led to the establishment of a booming date industry. He was able to return to Pomona College and graduated summa cum laude in 1914.

Cornell's education continued at Harvard's Graduate School of Landscape Architecture (1914–1917). Despite his Quaker upbringing, he volunteered for military duty in 1917, serving with distinction in France. Returning to Los Angeles in 1919, Cornell opened one of the city's first professional landscape architecture offices.

Cornell's first job was as Pomona College's supervising landscape architect, a relationship that continued throughout his life. One of his early projects, a master plan for Torrey Pines Park (1922), illustrates Cornell's engineering ability, his solid horticultural know-how, and his love of California's native landscape. The plan restricted alterations to the original landscape, did not permit the introduction of non-native plants or non-indigenous features, and recommended against overcultivating the Torrey pine to the exclusion of open spaces. The result: a protected microculture found nowhere else on earth.

Cornell also undertook a number of public projects, including the Administration Center for the City and County of Los Angeles. He formed a brief partnership with his friend Theodore Payne, "the greatest plantsman" he ever knew. Then, after a couple of years on his own, a new partnership was forged, Cook, Hall & Cornell (1924–1933). While a partner in that firm he designed Will Rogers Park, renowned for its wide variety of plants, and the award-

winning two-mile park that parallels Santa Monica Boulevard through Beverly Hills. In 1928 he added a second major campus to his resume, becoming supervising landscape architect for the University of Hawaii in Honolulu. On a smaller scale, he designed a garden for a blind client, utilizing textures and fragrance to appeal to senses other than the visual. At Rancho Los Cerritos, a remodeled 1844 adobe dwelling, Cornell created an estate garden preserving many of the old trees. He added flowering trees, believing that color in the garden should not be limited to the inevitable overused annuals. (Today the garden's status as a State and National Historic Landmark and a City of Long Beach museum ensures its ongoing preservation.)

From 1933 to 1955, Cornell worked in solo practice. He hosted a radio show called the Chaparral Club, sharing his passion for horticulture and the conservation of open spaces. Adding a third major campus to his credit, he became supervising landscape architect for the new University of California, Los Angeles (UCLA). Two award-winning projects there were the Franklin D. Murphy Sculpture Garden and the Sunset Canyon Recreation Center. Cornell's work at UCLA is significant not just because of the awards and the thirty-five-year time span (1937–1972); he was ultimately in control of all design and planning decisions, with engineers' and architects' powers subservient to his.

During World War II, Cornell worked with the Office of Civilian Defense lecturing on camouflaging structures and landing fields. His government contracts included the San Diego Naval Shipyard and Camp Roberts in California, and Los Alamos in New Mexico.

"Study for Campus Quad at Pomona College, Pomona, California." Watercolor rendering by Ralph D. Cornell and Theodora Payne. Courtesy UCLA Research Library.

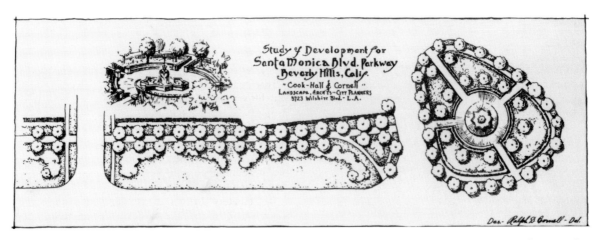

"Study for the Development for Santa Monica Boulevard Parkway, Beverly Hills, California, by Cook, Hall & Cornell." Drawn by Cornell. Courtesy UCLA Research Library.

Rose Hills Cemetery and Glen Haven Memorial are peaceful spaces where the natural beauty and the character of the land dominate.

At sixty-five, Cornell headed the new firm of Cornell, Bridgers, Troller, with Hazlett joining later. As senior partner (1955–1972) he continued to be involved in the design of such projects as the Los Angeles Civic Center Mall and Music Center. Cornell also designed cemeteries and parks; his work took him to Cairo, Baghdad, and the Philippine Islands. Throughout his career Cornell's services were sought by botanic gardens as both board member and consultant. A Fellow of the American Society of Landscape Architects, Cornell served several terms as president of the local chapter and as a trustee on the national board. Cornell was also a talented photographer whose work was widely published. Thomas Church*, one of the best known twentieth-century landscape architects, credited Cornell with inspiring him to enter the profession.

California Horticultural Journal 33 (October 1972). By The Southern California Editorial Subcommittee. A collection of memorial writings about Cornell by his friends and colleagues.

Cornell, Ralph D. *Conspicuous California Plants.* 1938. Reprint. Los Angeles: Plantin Press, 1978. A collection of Cornell's essays about California native plants with notes on their garden uses; photographs by Cornell; preface by George Marshall.

Mathias, Mildred E., ed. *Flowering Plants in the Landscape.* A compilation of series of booklets published starting in 1964, the first titled *Flowering Trees*; series also included booklets on flowering shrubs, vines, ground covers, and California native plants; Cornell's photographs make up three-quarters of the illustrations. Reissued 1982.

The Ralph D. Cornell Collection is housed at the UCLA Research Library and includes his articles, lectures, speeches, drawings, photographs, and personal papers.

Marie Barnidge-McIntyre

COUNCIL, LUCILLE
(1898–1964)

See the joint account with Yoch, Florence.

DANIELS, HOWARD
(1815–1863)
landscape gardener

Howard Daniels was born in New York City. By 1844, perhaps earlier, he was in practice as an architect in Cincinnati. In that same year, he won the design competition for the Montgomery County Courthouse in Dayton. Although for many years Daniels listed himself as an architect in various directories, the courthouse is his only known architectural work.

His career as a landscape gardener is first documented by the 1846 commission to design Cincinnati's Spring Grove Cemetery. Before preparing a plan for Spring Grove, Daniels spent four months studying and sketching the design characteristics of eastern rural cemeteries. During the early years of his career, while still in Ohio, Daniels also designed Woodland Cemetery in Xenia (1847–1848) and Green Lawn in Columbus (1849).

In 1851, Daniels moved to New York City, perhaps intending to place himself more at the center of the devel-

oping profession of landscape architecture. His 1855 advertisement in *The Horticulturist* stated that he had laid out fifteen cemeteries and an equal number of private grounds and offered his services for "Plans for Parks, Cemeteries, Country Seats, Villas, Farms, Orchards, Gardens, &c., also designs in all styles for Mansions, Villas, Cottages, Conservatories, Green-houses, Rustic Statuary, &c." In addition to the cemeteries noted above, by 1855 he had completed Erie Cemetery, Erie, Pennsylvania (1851), Dale Cemetery, Claremont, New York (1852), Woodland, Cleveland, Ohio (1852–53), Spring Forest, Binghamton, New York (1853), Brookside, Watertown, New York (1853), Riverside, Waterbury, Connecticut (1853), and Poughkeepsie Rural, Poughkeepsie, New York (1853). No designs for private grounds have yet been identified.

In 1855–1856, Daniels traveled throughout England, visiting parks and gardens. Period sources noted that his

White Sulphur Springs, Virginia, 1858. From Edward Beyer, *Album of Virginia*. Courtesy Christine B. Lozner.

trip was undertaken with the intent of improving the "taste" of his countrymen, and he offered his impressions and analysis of English landscapes in a series of seven letters published in *The Magazine of Horticulture*. These letters and his subsequent articles in *The Horticulturist* were widely read, and thus his views on landscape gardening may well have been influential among his colleagues and the general public.

On his return, in 1857, Daniels worked with Eugene A. Baumann, and perhaps with A. J. Davis, at Llewellyn

Spring Grove Cemetery, Cincinnati, Ohio, 1858. Courtesy Cincinnati Historical Society.

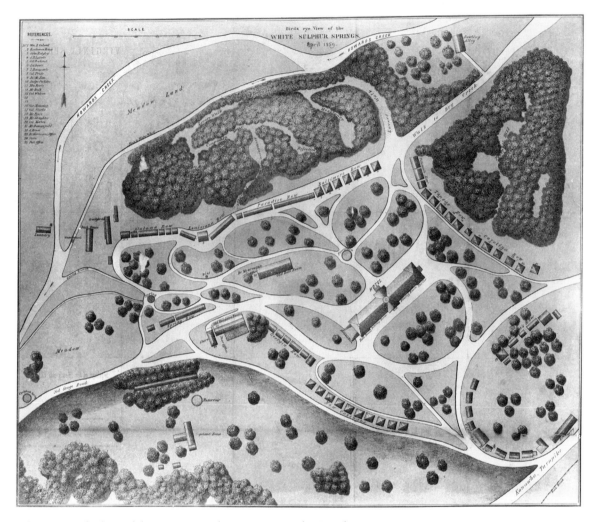

Birds-eye view of White Sulphur Springs, April 1859. Courtesy The Greenbrier.

Park, New Jersey. His influence on the design is unknown. However, in his subsequent article on villa parks published in *The Horticulturist* in 1858, Daniels defined the desirable elements of a designed suburb, clearly attempting to influence the planning of America's first suburbs.

In 1858, Daniels was awarded fourth place in the Central Park design competition for his entry titled "Manhattan." His growing stature is suggested by his 1858–1859 commission to redesign the grounds of the resort at White Sulphur Springs, Virginia (now the Greenbrier, West Virginia), then "the most resorted to of any public place of the kind in America" according to

The Horticulturist. In 1859, Daniels laid out Syracuse's Oakwood Cemetery, his last known and, arguably, his finest design for a rural cemetery. In 1860, he was hired to design Druid Hill Park in Baltimore. Despite limitations imposed by wartime conditions, Daniels planned and executed the major stages required in the conversion of Druid Hill from a private estate to a public park. His article on the park, published in *The Horticulturist* in 1860, was another of his efforts to influence public taste. Directed at the residents of cities contemplating the creation of urban parks, the article promoted public gardens as "the next great step in rural progress." While working at Druid Hill, where he served as superintendent until 1863, Daniels was commissioned to lay out the 375-acre grounds of the Sheppard Asylum (now the Sheppard and Enoch Pratt Hospital) in Towson, Maryland, where Calvert Vaux* designed the early buildings.

During 1863, Daniels provided advice for Matthew Vassar at Vassar College and competed with James Renwick for the commission to design the college grounds. Renwick's plan was chosen, and Daniels's design has been lost. Daniels died in Baltimore in late 1863.

Daniels, Howard. "European Parks, No. I." *Magazine of Horticulture* 21 (September 1855), 411–418. First of seven letters containing impressions and analyses of landscape practices evident in English parks, gardens, palaces, botanic gardens, and arboretums; includes Liverpool's Birkenhead Park, Prince's Park, and The Botanic Garden.

Daniels, Howard. "A Public Park for Baltimore." *The Horticulturist*, n.s. 10 (September 1860), 435–438. Recounting of site selected for Druid Hill Park; acknowledges link between rural cemeteries and "the next great step in rural progress . . . Parks for the people."

Schuyler, David. *The New Urban Landscape: The Redefinition of City Form in Nineteenth-Century America*. Baltimore: Johns Hopkins University Press, 1986. Analysis of origins and evolution of nineteenth-century American cemeteries, urban parks, and suburbs with discussion of Daniels's entry in Central Park competition and plan for Druid Hill Park, Baltimore.

Christine B. Lozner

DAWSON, JAMES FREDERICK
(1874–1941)
landscape architect

In 1904, John Charles Olmsted* and Frederick Law Olmsted Jr.* chose James Frederick Dawson as their first associate partner in Olmsted Brothers, Landscape Architects, the firm they formed in 1898 after the retirement of Frederick Law Olmsted Sr.* A congenial collaborator with both colleagues and clients, Dawson developed into an extraordinarily skilled and diversified designer whose output was enormous. He became a member of the American Society of Landscape Architects (ASLA) in 1905, and a Fellow in 1914. Like the Olmsted brothers, he spent his entire career (1896–1941) with the Olmsted firm. He had projects throughout the United States, and in Canada, Cuba, Bermuda, and Venezuela.

Fred Dawson, known professionally as James F. Dawson or J. Fredk. Dawson, was born in the Jamaica Plain area of Boston, where his father, Jackson Thornton Dawson, was a noted plant propagator and superintendent at the developing Arnold Arboretum (1873–1916). Dawson relatives also owned Eastern Nurseries in nearby Holliston. Dawson graduated from Roxbury Latin School in Boston (1894) and then strengthened

James Frederick Dawson at Malaga Cove Business Plaza, Palos Verdes Estates, California. Courtesy Robert Fletcher Dawson.

Cherry Walk and Azalea Way,
Washington Park Arboretum, Seattle.
Photo Catherine Joy Johnson.

his natural interest in plants by studying agriculture and horticulture at Harvard's Bussey Institution (1895–1896). In 1896 he entered Olmsted, Olmsted & Eliot* as an apprentice, and until 1903 spent extended periods in England and southern Europe studying and documenting landscapes and plant materials. His later work would show a thoughtful Olmstedian respect for the land and a clear understanding of formal, informal, and designed naturalistic landscapes. Dawson used photography to record landscapes and to reveal design faults not easily detected by the eye.

Dawson's commissions for Olmsted Brothers embraced both the public and the private sectors, and included parks and parkways, arboreta, the grounds of public buildings and expositions, land subdivisions, private residential estates, country places, resorts, golf courses, and country clubs.

In 1906, Dawson began a series of railroad trips to the Pacific coast as an assistant to his senior partner and mentor, John C. Olmsted. Their first major public pro-

jects were the park and parkway systems for Portland, Seattle, and Spokane (1903–1908); the grounds of the Alaska-Pacific-Yukon Exposition (1906–1909), where Dawson spent all of 1908 designing and supervising the grading and planting; the grounds for the San Diego Exposition (1911); and the Washington State Capitol Campus, where Olmsted drew up the plans (1911–1912) and Dawson consulted.

Olmsted Brothers built a sizable practice designing residential estates and communities as well. Making two to three trips a year, Dawson designed over 2,700 plans for the private sector in the Pacific Northwest alone (1906–1940), and he developed key relationships. By 1913, John C. Olmsted, citing ill health, cut back his long-distance travel, assigning more and more responsibility to Dawson. Dawson collaborated often with Percival Gallagher*, who had become an associate in the firm in 1906.

In 1920, John C. Olmsted died, Olmsted Jr. became senior partner, and Dawson moved his family to California

Entry pier, Rockwood Boulevard, Spokane, Washington. Photo Catherine Joy Johnson.

to open the Olmsted Western Office at Redondo Beach and participate with Olmsted in the development of Palos Verdes Estates, a 16,000-acre residential community. He was assisted by landscape architects George Gibbs* and Hammond Sadler. The Olmsted firm expanded in 1927, with Olmsted Jr., Dawson, Gallagher, Edward Clark Whiting*, and Henry Vincent Hubbard* as principals. Though Dawson moved back to the Brookline office in 1927, he continued to work on both coasts and was also active in Colorado, Kentucky, Alabama, Ohio, and Pennsylvania. Dawson was financially aware and pursued business possibilities. Through his reputation and the loyalty of past clients, he was able to bring new work to the firm. He took pride in the Olmsted name and accomplishments, as he noted in a 1931 letter: "the firm has stood in the forefront in all places of landscape architecture."

Before and during the Depression, Dawson designed major projects for Lake Wales Land Co., Lake Wales, Florida (1921–1939); Seattle Arboretum (now Washington Park Arboretum; 1936–1939); the Morris Arboretum in Philadelphia (1932–1933); and the British Pacific Properties in Canada (1931–1941). The last was probably the most ambitious and difficult undertaking of Dawson's career, involving architects, landscape architects, engineers, and capitalists. The 4,700-acre West Vancouver site was intended for residential purposes but had other amenities and required a highway through Vancouver's Stanley Park and a suspension bridge crossing the First Narrows, allowing shipping to enter Vancouver harbor. Dawson generated 574 plans and drawings for the project and helped mitigate intrusion into Stanley Park. He died in 1941 as the project was being completed.

Dawson, James Frederick. "Planting at the Alaska-Yukon-Pacific Exposition." *Landscape Architecture* 1, no. 1 (October 1910), 31–40. Plans; photos.

Johnson, Catherine Joy. *Olmsted in the Pacific Northwest: Private Estates and Residential Communities.* Friends of Seattle's Olmsted Parks, 1997. A documentary inventory of plans, correspondence, and photographs of Olmsted work for the private sector in Washington, Oregon, Idaho, and southern British Columbia, 1873–1959.

Olmsted, Frederick Law, Jr. "James Frederick Dawson: A Biographical Minute on His Professional Life and Work." *Landscape Architecture* 32, no. 1 (October 1941), 1–2. Explores Dawson's long career with the Olmsted firm.

The Frederick Law Olmsted National Site in Brookline has a large collection of plans and drawings and some photographs related to the work of James F. Dawson for Olmsted Brothers. Dawson's professional correspondence is at the Library of Congress, Olmsted Associates Collection, Washington, D.C. More material is at the University of Washington, Northwest Collections and the Manuscript Division, Seattle.

Catherine Joy Johnson

DEAN, RUTH BRAMLEY
(1889–1932)
landscape architect

Born in Wilkes-Barre, Pennsylvania, Ruth Dean briefly attended the University of Chicago (1908–1910) before finding employment in the Chicago office of Jens Jensen*, a preeminent advocate for the use of native plants. Dean opened her first New York office in 1915. After her marriage in 1923 to Aymar Embury II, a noted civic and Colonial Revival architect, she continued to maintain an independent office adjacent to the family residence. She achieved prominence in the 1920s as the demand for landscape design progressed together with the growth of country places and suburbs.

Dean was also a prolific contributor to important home and garden periodicals: *The Garden Magazine, House and Garden, House Beautiful,* and *Country Life in America.* In clear, opinionated, and witty prose, she guided homeowners through the design process, focusing on elegant planning for outdoor spaces, while always emphasizing the architectural relationship between house and garden. In the late 1920s, she was garden editor for *The Delineator,* a women's magazine published by the pattern maker Butterick.

Dean's only book, *The Livable House, Its Garden* (1917), expands the design precepts articulated in her journalism. Her designs, which showed a modernist sensibility, featured simple yet functional spatial divisions, well-chosen garden details (furniture, sculpture, paving), and a logical connection with architectural elements.

Ruth Bramley Dean. From *House and Garden,* July 1923.

Her planting palette evoked the soothing images of the Colonial Revival garden, its cool enclosures promising a nostalgic respite from the pressures of the Jazz Age. Her success was predicated on the balance between these two conflicting themes.

In 1929, Dean became the first woman awarded the Architectural League of New York's Gold Medal for three gardens she had designed in Grosse Pointe, Michigan. These gardens bore her stylistic signature: a series of private, enclosed spaces that harmoniously connected house and site, planted with a mixture of trees and shrubs, evergreen and deciduous, primarily native species, and simple color combinations to highlight the structural integrity.

Dean's own garden, designed for her summer home in Easthampton, New York, still survives, structurally

A. S. Chiren estate, Great Neck, Long Island. From *The Garden Magazine*, April 1922.

Rooftop garden of Mrs. Dodge, Sloan, New York. From *Architectural League of New York Yearbook, Work of Members, 1930.*

intact. The property is privately owned by the Embury family.

Dean, Ruth B. *The Livable House, Its Garden.* Vol. 2 of *The Livable House,* edited by Aymar Embury II. New York: Moffat Yard, 1917. One of the first landscape design primers written by a woman professional; illustrated.

Dean, Ruth B. "Solving the Intricate Problem of the Small Garden." *The Garden Magazine,* May 1922. Dean's practical approach to designing a small suburban garden.

McMullen, Frances D. "Ruth Dean, Landscape Architect." *The Woman's Journal,* June 1929. Revealing interview with Dean.

Eve F. W. Linn

DEARBORN, HENRY A. S.
(1783–1851)
cemetery designer, horticulturist

Henry A. S. Dearborn was born in Exeter, New Hampshire, son of a Revolutionary general, and spent his boyhood in Maine. He attended Williams College for two years, then entered the College of William and Mary while his father served as Jefferson's secretary of war. Graduating in 1803, he studied law for three years in Virginia and read the law for a year in Salem, Massachusetts. But Dearborn disliked the law and, following Jefferson's mandate to him to be "a loyal, useful, and contented citizen at home" rather than in a diplomatic post abroad, he devoted himself to public service. During the War of 1812, he superintended the fortification of Portland harbor, gaining significant engineering experience.

The American Academy of Arts and Sciences elected him a fellow in 1823. In 1825 he surveyed western Massachusetts in a quixotic search for a canal route to link Boston to the new Erie Canal. He was vice president of the New England Society for Promotion of Manufactures and Mechanical Arts, and he succeeded his father as collector at the Boston Custom House, a post he held until 1829. A leader of Boston's intellectual gentry, he was an extensive reader and something of a "Renaissance Man." He researched and illustrated a massive manuscript treatise on Greek architecture (1828), as well as helping found the Bunker Hill Monument Association (1823) to preserve the Revolutionary battle site overlooking Boston harbor and erect a 221-foot granite obelisk on it.

A gentleman horticulturist, Dearborn experimented extensively with plants on his Brinley Place estate in Roxbury, then a rural town just south of Boston, and was founder and first president of the Massachusetts Horticultural Society (1829). One of his goals was to remedy the lack of nurseries and develop profitable and ornamental plants in New England.

In 1831, Dearborn, aided by civil engineer and surveyor Alexander Wadsworth* and advised by a committee of horticulturists, oversaw the initial landscape design of the nation's first "rural" burial ground, 72-acre Mount Auburn Cemetery four miles west of Boston in suburban Cambridge. Dearborn relied on books ordered from France and England, especially John Evelyn's *Silva* and illustrated descriptions of the innovative Père Lachaise Cemetery (1804) in the eastern suburbs of Paris. He also applied classical design principles to make avenues, paths, and ponds responsive to the natural topography. His design preserved and accentuated the site's pano-

ramic views and dramatically varied terrain. Performing much of the labor himself, he transplanted about 1,300 indigenous trees from his own nurseries to create a woodsy, "rural" appearance. Mount Auburn quickly became the acknowledged prototype for the legions of other "rural" cemeteries that proliferated in the 1860s. It also strongly influenced the layout of the first public parks in the United States.

Dearborn envisioned cultural uses for Mount Auburn far beyond those of a traditional burial ground. He had hoped to create an experimental garden there, domesticating foreign plants and creating hybrids, "to develop the vast vegetable resources of the Union, give activity to enterprise, increase the enjoyment of all classes of citizens, advance the prosperity, and improve the general aspect of the country." Dearborn imagined Mount Auburn as an "Institution of Education of Scientific and Practical Gardeners," a school of horticulture and design, which would teach a science and an art combining "Natural History and Physics, Botany, Mineralogy, Hydraulics, Mechanics, Architecture, Chemistry, and Entomology,"

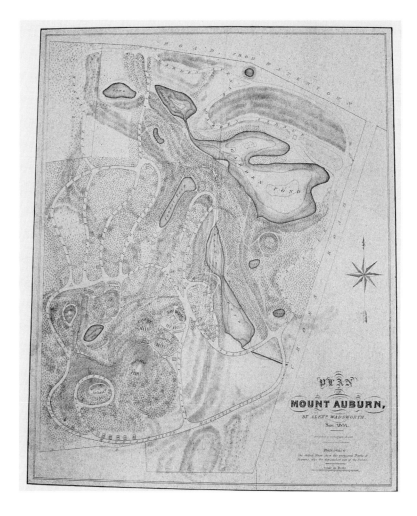

Portrait painting of General Henry A. S. Dearborn copied by Jane Stuart in the 1850s from the original by her father, Gilbert Stuart, c. 1827. Courtesy Massachusetts Horticultural Society. (*Facing page*)

First map of Mount Auburn Cemetery, engraved after General Henry A. S. Dearborn's landscape design, 1831. Courtesy Mount Auburn Cemetery.

but the funds were not available. Dearborn's affiliation with Mount Auburn ended in 1835 when the cemetery and the Horticultural Society, under whose auspices it had been developed, separated owing to irreconcilable purposes. Committees dominated by Dr. Jacob Bigelow*, the cemetery's president (1845–1871), continued landscape development and "embellished the picturesque" with structures. After Dearborn died, Bigelow and his friends claimed primary design credit.

After leaving Mount Auburn, Dearborn turned his energies to politics. He held the state offices of representative, senator, and executive councilor, spent one term in the U.S. Congress, and served as Massachusetts adjutant-general. Dearborn led a troop of militia in 1842 to suppress Dorr's Rebellion in Rhode Island, then

served four terms as mayor of Roxbury, from 1847 until his death.

As mayor, Dearborn promoted the idea of creating Forest Hills Cemetery under municipal auspices. His committee chose a 71-acre site with a varied terrain thought to be conducive to the development of a picturesque landscape, and Dearborn began design work in 1848. As at Mount Auburn, he let the lay of the land determine placement of avenues, paths, plantings, and ponds. He reserved six-foot-wide margins between lots and kept larger open spaces where no burials were permitted and discouraged tomb construction, to ensure that the cemetery would remain verdant and not become built up like Père Lachaise. By 1850, over 10,000 native and 20,000 European trees from the nurseries

Forest Hills Cemetery, Boston, 1980. Photo Blanche M. G. Linden.

Mount Auburn. Hand-tinted watercolor on lithograph by W. H. Bartlett, 1839. Courtesy Blanche M. G. Linden.

Dearborn established had been transplanted to give the cemetery the desired woodsy look. An attempt was made to introduce as many trees as would flourish in New England, including several rare varieties, to create an arboretum of the grounds.

Daniel Brims, a Scottish landscape gardener appointed superintendent, assisted in implementing the design and faithfully carried it out after Dearborn died. "The thoroughness of the work in the construction of avenues and paths, the preparation of the borders and the cultivation of trees, shrubs and plants, are in a great degree attributable to his thorough knowledge of his business, judgment and good taste," one source noted. By 1858, Forest Hills expanded to 104 acres, permitting enlargement of a lake and extension of the avenues as Dearborn had wished. He was buried there, under a marble Corinthian column on Mount Dearborn.

Dearborn's eulogist credited him with "designing and preparing" cemeteries in many towns, but few records have been discovered.

Forest Hills Cemetery: Its Establishment, Progress, Scenery, Monuments, etc. Boston, 1858. Describes establishment of Forest Hills under Dearborn, and the state of the romantic landscape after a decade, with a brief biography, copies of documents, and a list of proprietors.

Linden-Ward, Blanche. *Silent City on a Hill: Landscapes of Memory and Boston's Mount Auburn Cemetery.* Columbus: Ohio State University Press, 1989. Details aspects of institutional and landscape development of the cemetery from before its founding through the 1870s, with discussion of the roles of Dearborn and Bigelow.

[Manning, Robert, ed.] *History of the Massachusetts Horticultural Society, 1829–1878.* Boston, 1880. Putnam, George. *An Address Delivered before the City Government and Citizens of Roxbury on the Life and Character of the Late Henry A. S. Dearborn, Mayor of the City, Sept. 3rd, 1851.* Roxbury, 1851. Both credit Dearborn with initial landscape design of Mount Auburn, to counteract Bigelow's claim.

Boston Public Library Rare Books Room has some correspondence and Dearborn's two-volume illustrated folio treatise on Greek architecture. The Massachusetts Horticultural Society, Boston, has "Transactions . . . , 1829–1838" (vol. 1), orations, reports, and other documents concerning Dearborn's role in the society's founding and that of Mount Auburn under its auspices (1831–1835). Mount Auburn Cemetery has "Trustees' Minutes" in "Proprietors' and Trustees' Records," manuscript books. The New York Public Library has manuscripts and correspondence related to Dearborn's work at Mount Auburn Cemetery. Forest Hills Cemetery has documents and other records about its founding and design under Dearborn.

Blanche M. G. Linden

DEBOER, S. R.
(1883–1974)
landscape architect, planner

Saco Rienk DeBoer was born in Ureterp, Netherlands. He opened his landscape office there, after attending the Institute Poutsma and the Royal (German) Imperial School of Horticulture. DeBoer emigrated to New Mexico in 1908 for health reasons, worked briefly as an engineer for an irrigation company, and then, in 1910, succeeded Reinhard Schuetze* as Denver's Landscape Architect, a post DeBoer held until 1931. He continued thereafter to serve Denver as a planning engineer and park consultant, and his private city planning and landscape design practice, opened in 1919, continued until his death. He traveled extensively in Europe and during 1922 studied in the office of the English planner Thomas Mawson. From 1934 to 1939 he was a consultant to the National Resources Planning Board, with responsibility for major projects in Utah, New Mexico, and Wyoming.

DeBoer's career spanned seven decades, from the apogee of the City Beautiful movement to what he called the nadir of urban sprawl and impulsive automobile

Water garden, City Park, Denver, 1917. Courtesy The Denver Public Library, Western History Collection.

mobility. His projects were diverse and far-ranging, from a series of simple landscape designs for modest front yards to make Denver more attractive, to the plan for Boulder City, Nevada, the first federally sponsored model city. It was said that he "did it all": zoning and planning schemes for towns and cities, chiefly in the West; park, parkway, population, traffic, mass transit, and ring-road regional studies and plans; civic centers in the Grand Manner, as well as romantic subdivision and suburban layouts, institutional development plans, and grand estate gardens.

DeBoer's career, however, was a personal crusade that cannot be defined solely by project lists, for each project, along with his many articles, books, presentations, and proposals, promoted his lifelong commitment: to plan for beauty and thus livability; to make the city a garden by weaving public parks and parkways together with private front yards into a floral tapestry; to plant big trees; to preserve urban calm in the face of "noisy, nerve-racking,

ill-smelling, dust-raising" automobiles. DeBoer's work changed both the way the West looks and the way the West looks at itself. Indeed, the patterns he established are a significant part of the framework that informs the practice of both planning and landscape design in the region today.

At the outset of his Denver career, DeBoer collaborated closely with George Kessler* and Frederick Law Olmsted Jr.* to complete the citywide park and parkway system. Although he worked in various traditions and materials, his personal signature soon emerged. In particular, he emphasized Denver's sense of place by importing both mountain and prairie plant material into the city and arranging them in flowing, naturalistic patterns. He added variety in color, design, mood, texture, and shape and, not incidentally, promoted water conservation without detracting from the city's greenness. He was an acknowledged master of juxtaposition and transition—he could plant a picnic grove of plains cottonwoods that

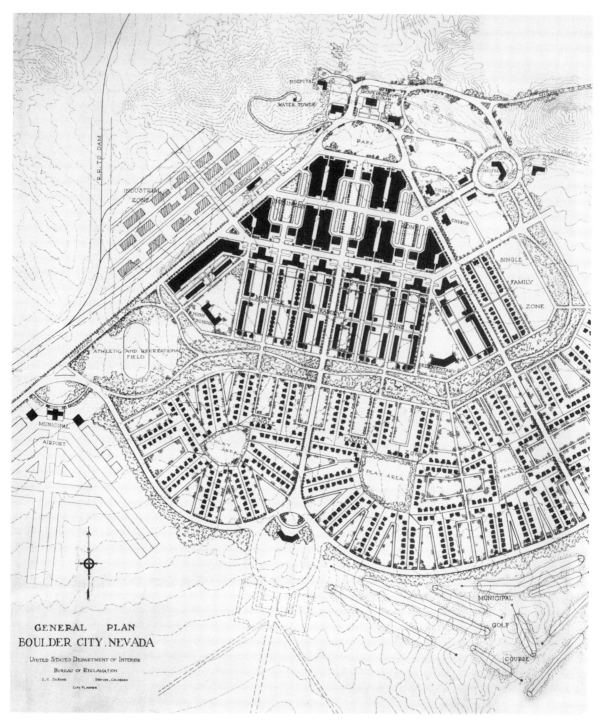

Model garden city plan for Boulder City, Nevada, 1930. Courtesy The Denver Public Library, S. R. DeBoer Collection, Western History Collection.

segued into a formal Italian garden that in turn segued into a forested English park. In addition, he reinforced the tradition of establishing viewing platforms to provide visual connections between the city and the Rocky Mountains. He also demonstrated that Denver's parks and parkways could be a year-round "flower trail," planted with hardy material in simple patterns. In this DeBoer measured his success by the extent—and it was considerable—to which his flower trail was emulated by private citizens in their own yards. And he never stopped experimenting with a wide variety of plant materials not previously thought suitable for arid urban environments.

While DeBoer was a successful plantsman and designer, it was his role as a planner that was central to his beliefs and his career. Two examples illustrate the scope of his planning work. Between 1912 and 1914, DeBoer worked closely with Olmsted Jr., not only in developing Denver's urban parks, but in planning an unprecedented circuit of mountain parks. These parks range from the high plains to the alpine tundra; they are linked with one another and with the city by a series of parkways; and they provide a carefully planned escape from the city into a world of wildlife conservation, fishing and picnicking, hiking trails and rustic lodges, and long views across the city, the prairie, and the Continental Divide.

Then in 1930, midway through his career, DeBoer received a commission from the U.S. Department of the Interior to plan Boulder City, Nevada, a harbinger of the New Deal's greenbelt towns. He drew on the earlier American experience (particularly the planned communities of Sunnyside Gardens, Radburn, and Forest Hills Gardens), but his primary inspiration came from English precedents, particularly the work of Raymond Unwin, Barry Parker, and Edwin Lutyens, and from his own certainty that he could create a garden city in the midst of the Nevada desert. His plans covered every aspect of the development, including the philosophical basis for the program; site selection; a layout that synthesized Grand Manner and Garden City; a business district of uniform Mediterranean design, arcaded to protect people from the hot sun; shaded off-street parking; superblocks and internal parks; traffic separation; and greenbelts designed to shelter the town from the desert. And he framed the whole ensemble with industrial and commercial zones, a municipal airport, and a municipal golf course.

DeBoer was a Fellow of the American Society of Landscape Architects and an honorary member of the American Institute of Architects and the American Society of Planning Officials.

Hardwick, Bonnie, ed. *S. R. DeBoer*. Denver: Western History Department, Denver Public Library, 1983. A thoughtful assessment of DeBoer and his career, an illustrated sampling of his work, and an introduction to the S. R. DeBoer Collection.

Woodward, Wes, ed. "A Tribute to S. R. DeBoer." *The Green Thumb* 29 (December 1972), 141–228. DeBoer's own illustrated memoir; partial lists of projects, articles, and major publications; and commentaries on the impact of his work.

The S. R. DeBoer Collection in the Western History Department, Denver Public Library, includes DeBoer's literary production: diaries, sketchbooks, manuscripts, and published works; office files, particularly local background materials; drawings and plans, including presentation boards; bibliographical memorabilia; and ten albums of photographs that document his work and milieu.

Don Etter

DEFOREST, ALLING STEPHEN
(1875–1957)
landscape architect

Alling DeForest spent his formative years on a farm in the village of Pittsford, outside Rochester, New York. He attended Taylor's Business College and Mechanics Institute, a forerunner of the Rochester Institute of Technology, where he completed a two-year course of freehand and mechanical drawing. In 1896, during his second year there, he was employed as a draftsman in the office of William W. Parce, a Rochester landscape architect. It was then that DeForest decided on a career in landscape architecture.

Terrace Garden, George Eastman estate, Rochester, New York, 1905. Courtesy George Eastman House International Museum of Photography and Film.

Detail design for amphitheater, Colgate Divinity School campus, Rochester, New York, 1931. Courtesy Colgate Rochester Divinity School.

Terrace Garden, George Eastman House, 1998. Photo Barbara Puorro Galasso. Courtesy George Eastman House International Museum of Photography and Film.

In the fall of 1897 he left Rochester to take a job with the Brookline, Massachusetts, office of Olmsted*, Olmsted* & Eliot*, but the following July he returned to Rochester to become a partner in the new firm of Parce & DeForest, Landscape Architects. Two of the firm's documented projects, both located in Schenectady, New York, were a housing development known as the General Electric Plot and Parkview Cemetery.

From November 1899 to December 1900, DeForest was once again employed by the Olmsted office, but again returned to Rochester and resumed his partnership with Parce. The partnership survived until the end of 1902 when Parce left Rochester because of illness and DeForest embarked on an independent practice.

Although DeForest's commissions included cemeteries, campuses, parks, housing developments, and factory grounds, the majority were private estates. Among the most notable of these were grounds for Harvey Firestone, in Akron, Ohio, and George Eastman in Rochester. For the latter, DeForest designed a garden that combined formal and naturalistic elements, and featured a sunken pool at its center. (He thought level landscapes were uninteresting.) Walled gardens also frequently appeared in his plans, offering homeowners the privacy he considered essential.

DeForest developed lasting friendships with several of his clients. His projects for George W. Olmsted of Ludlow, Pennsylvania, one of his most influential clients, spanned more than twenty-eight years and included the extensive grounds of the Olmsted estate and Wildcat Park, built on land donated by Olmsted to the city of Ludlow.

His long association with Harvey Firestone began in 1911 and continued until Firestone's death in 1938. In addition to the formal gardens of Harbel Manor, Firestone's home, he designed the 500-acre Firestone Park, a

Rock Garden, George Eastman House, 1998. Photo Barbara Puorro Galasso. Courtesy George Eastman House International Museum of Photography and Film.

housing development for the Firestone Company employees in Akron. In Columbiana, Ohio, the birthplace and childhood home of Firestone, he designed Firestone Recreation Park, additions to the Columbiana Cemetery, and the unique grounds of the Firestone Memorial which were included in the additions. At the time Firestone died, DeForest was involved in designing the landscape of a retirement home his client had planned. DeForest also designed the Akron estates of Harvey Firestone Jr., Stacey Carkhuff, secretary of the Firestone Tire and Rubber Company, and Paul Litchfield, president of the Goodyear Company. He served as special adviser to the Akron Planning Commission in 1920.

DeForest was an active member of the American Society of Landscape Architects. He was elected a Fellow in 1908, and held the offices of vice president in 1923 and secretary in 1914, 1915, and 1917. He died in 1957.

Czerkas, Jean. "Alling Stephen DeForest, Landscape Architect, 1875–1957." *Rochester History Publication*, Spring 1989. An overview of his life.

Rehmann, Elsa. *The Small Place*. New York: Knickerbocker Press, 1918. Rochester residence, photos, and plan.

"Views in Estates and Gardens Designed by Alling DeForest Landscape Architect, Rochester, New York." *Landscape Architecture*, July 1928, 293–297. Thirteen views of the gardens of the estates of George W. Olmsted, Ludlow, Pa., R. C. Watson, Rochester, N.Y., Harvey Firestone, Akron, Ohio, and George W. Todd and L. M. Todd, Rochester.

Jean Czerkas

DE FOREST, LOCKWOOD, III (LOCKWOOD DE FOREST JR.)
(1896–1949)
landscape architect

Lockwood de Forest III was born in New York City. He was the youngest of the three children of Lockwood de Forest II, a landscape painter, amateur architect, and interior designer, and a former partner of Louis Comfort Tiffany. In 1912 he was sent to Thacher School in Ojai, California, where he developed a strong love for California landscapes and painting. Leaving Williams College after one semester, he worked briefly for a landscape architect in Baltimore and took a summer class in landscape architecture at Harvard University. He served in World War I as a volunteer.

After the war, de Forest returned to California and embarked on a brief professional education that attests to unusual confidence and independence. He left the landscape architecture program at the University of California, Berkeley, after one year. In the summer of 1921 he traveled for three months in Italy, Spain, France, and England, studying historic gardens and public parks. He was especially fascinated by the gardens of Seville and the Maria Luisa Park by J. C. N. Forestier. He spent several weeks at Kew Gardens studying plants.

From 1921 to 1922 de Forest worked for Ralph Stevens, a Santa Barbara landscape architect. From 1922 until his early death in 1949, apart from war service, he practiced as a landscape architect in the affluent communities of the Santa Barbara area. The practice was largely residential, although he worked on some schools, notably Thacher, and was a consultant to several civic organizations.

From 1925 until 1942 de Forest co-edited *The Santa Barbara Gardener* with his wife, Elizabeth Kellam de Forest, also a noted landscape architect. This modest unillustrated magazine provided gardening advice for what the de Forests considered a horticulturally unique area. Although the emphasis was on horticulture, the articles clearly convey de Forest's design philosophy.

De Forest's designs show a strong architectonic feeling for space. He also possessed a strong sense of regional identity, often displayed in the careful selection of plants complementing the colors and textures of the regional landscape. His horticultural knowledge was considerable, and he played a major role in introducing and experimenting with plants from South Africa. De Forest rejected stylistic eclecticism; his designs are notable for simple detailing and bold, almost theatrical effects achieved entirely with plants. He was one of the first landscape architects in California to question the ubiquitous and excessively generous use of lawn irrigation; the small lawn at his own house has never been irrigated. De Forest's early training as a landscape painter accounts for the painterly quality of much of his work. A consistent theme in his writing is the necessity of capturing views of the regional landscape through the elimination of the middle ground.

Val Verde, the Wright Ludington estate in Montecito (1926–1949), was one of de Forest's major projects and was an important collaboration with the client. Ludington was a gifted amateur painter and collector of classical art and a pioneer collector of Cubist painting. In two major periods of development in the 1920s and 1930s, de Forest transformed the rather boxy house designed in 1915 by Bertram Goodhue into a remarkable evocation of a classical villa and garden that was an abstract and dramatic setting for classical sculpture.

His own small courtyard house and garden (1927) foreshadowed many of the qualities of modernist Californian gardens of the 1940s. The brilliant use of *sharawadgi* (the practice of placing asymmetrical elements in formal settings) expands the sense of space by completely dissolving the boundaries of the garden. At

Lockwood de Forest Jr. Courtesy Sydney Baumgartner.

West garden and house, Val Verde, Wright Ludington estate, Montecito, California, 1936. Photo Roy Flamm. Courtesy Bancroft Library, University of California, Berkeley.

the William Dickenson estate, Hope Ranch (1929–1932), one of his largest commissions, the theme of silver light unifies the garden and establishes a subtle relationship to the setting of ocean and mountains in the late afternoon.

From 1927 to 1942, de Forest provided design advice to the Santa Barbara Botanic Garden, which is devoted to the display of native plants, and later served on numerous committees and as a trustee. He laid out several trail systems to enhance visitor appreciation of the existing native plant communities with minimal disturbance; the Pritchett Trail survives as a fine example. In

the late 1930s, he disagreed strongly with Beatrix Farrand's* formalist proposals for the site, believing that the emphasis should be on a simple naturalistic character.

De Forest's practice was profoundly affected by the Depression. Commissions were smaller, and maintenance became a major design factor, which he addressed by using drought-tolerant plants and more architectonic layouts. The Mrs. George Robbins garden, Hillsborough (1932), explored the simple geometric use of colored concrete. In his writings in the 1930s, de Forest anticipated and welcomed modernist solutions. He also began to practice architecture on a small scale, designing minor

Val Verde, 1998. Photo Carol Betsch.

remodeling projects and a series of small ranch houses and beach houses at Sandyland Cove, Carpinteria. The Nicholas Ludington House (1932) and the Reese Taylor House (1936) were illustrated respectively in *House Beautiful* and *Country Life in America*. In these and other houses he experimented with unusual and highly practical details for cabinets and lighting.

From 1942 to 1944, de Forest served with the Camouflage Division of the U.S. Air Corps. This experience undoubtedly served him well in his final transformation of Val Verde, in which the formerly white walls of the house, subsidiary structures, and garden walls were skillfully painted with numerous coats to create the effect of a timeworn villa.

His postwar practice included the design of several small houses, the most notable being the Ernest Watson weekend house (1948), which was featured in *Sunset Magazine* as an innovative example of a well-planned small house. The house appears to sit *in* the landscape without a garden foreground as a result of de Forest's use of local boulders and a palette of largely native plants. The formal Sterling Morton garden (1948–1949) was one of his most striking mountain-oriented designs.

Following his unexpected death in 1949, Lutah Maria Riggs redesigned de Forest's new entry terraces to the Santa Barbara Art Museum as a public memorial to him, one of a small number of such monuments to Amer-

Costantia, Meeker estate, Montecito, California, 1997. Photo Charles A. Birnbaum.

ican landscape architects. In 1984, after her death, the museum extended the memorial to Elizabeth de Forest.

de Forest, Lockwood [III]. "In the Montecito Valley: A South African Garden in Santa Barbara," *Landscape Architecture* 30, no. 2 (January 1940), 51–55. A descriptive article that lays out an early approach to reducing garden maintenance; the design is oriented toward a spectacular mountain view.

Peters, William F. "Lockwood de Forest, Landscape Architect: Santa Barbara, California 1896–1949." Master of Landscape Architecture thesis, University of California, Berkeley, 1980. The principal work on de Forest; contains detailed analyses of several gardens, including his own.

Streatfield, David C. *California Gardens: Creating a New Eden.* New York: Abbeville Press, 1994. Descriptions of some de Forest's most important gardens; largely illustrated with color photographs taken in the late 1960s.

The Lockwood de Forest Collection in the Documents Collection of the College of Environmental Design, University of California, Berkeley, contains all the surviving drawings from de Forest's office. The William Wurster Collection in the same library contains correspondence relating to those projects on which both designers worked. Photographs of some of de Forest's projects are held by Kellam de Forest, his eldest son.

David Streatfield

DOWNING, ANDREW JACKSON
(1815–1852)
landscape gardener, horticulturist, author

A. J. Downing was born in Newburgh, New York, the fifth and youngest child of Samuel Downing, a wheelwright turned nurseryman, and Eunice Bridge Downing. On finishing schooling at the age of sixteen, Downing joined his older brother Charles in managing the family business, Botanic Garden and Nurseries. During the next decade he wrote dozens of articles for horticultural magazines and read extensively in the history and theory of landscape design.

As early as 1836, Downing had begun writing a book on the use of trees in gardening, which was published in 1841 as *A Treatise on the Theory and Practice of Landscape Gardening*. In this book Downing rejected the classical styles prevalent in landscape and architectural design and introduced American readers to the Beautiful and the Picturesque, aesthetic categories that reflected the romantic movement evident in literature and art. The *Treatise* drew heavily on previous English works, most notably by Humphry Repton and John Claudius Loudon, but consciously "adapted" those ideas to the climate and republican social conditions of the United States. Although most of the book is devoted to descriptions of trees, advice on laying out grounds, and ornamental uses of water and statuary, Downing also included a brief summary of the historical evolution of styles in landscape design, analysis of the "beauties and principles of the art," and a chapter devoted to rural architecture. Gracefully written and handsomely illustrated, the *Treatise* became an immediate success; it went through four editions during the next twelve years and sold approximately 9,000 copies.

The following year Downing published *Cottage Residences*, a series of designs for houses of modest size. This was the first of the new genre of house pattern books, which depicted the home in its landscaped setting and provided plans of the grounds and ornamental details, along with an explanatory text to assist the readers in choosing a residence appropriate to their circumstances. Several designs from *Cottage Residences* were reprinted in agricultural and horticultural periodicals in succeeding years, and numerous extant houses still testify to the popularity of the designs Downing presented in it. So great was the influence of these books, novelist Catherine Sedgwick reported, that "nobody, whether he be rich or poor, builds a house or lays out a garden without consulting Downing's works."

Downing's third book, *The Fruits and Fruit Trees of America* (1845), proved to be a landmark in the history of American pomology. Its technical information on fruit nomenclature and thoughtful advice on planting and the care of orchards attracted an enormous audience: *Fruits* sold 15,000 copies before 1853, earned its author membership in several European horticultural and scientific societies, and, periodically updated by Charles Downing, remained in print throughout the rest of the century. During the 1840s, Downing also prepared American editions of Jane Loudon's *Gardening for Ladies* (1843, 1846) and George Wightwick's *Hints to Young Architects* (1847), for whom he added an introductory chapter, "Additional Notes and Hints to Persons about Building in This Country."

Downing's final book, *The Architecture of Country Houses* (1850), is both a culmination of his own views on domestic architecture and a catalog of the works of a rising generation of architects, including A. J. Davis, Gervase Wheeler, and Richard Upjohn. In the preface Downing attributed a moral and social influence to domestic architecture and asserted that a properly designed home was "a powerful means of civilization." The text presented plans for houses in Gothic, Romanesque, Italianate, Bracketed, and other styles, and explained how each style and building type—cottage, farmhouse,

Andrew Jackson Downing. Engraving by J. Halpin after daguerreotype, c. 1852. Courtesy Shadek-Fackenthal Library, Franklin & Marshall College.

"Washington, D.C., The Projected Improvements." Lithograph by B. F. Smith Jr., 1852. Courtesy Prints and Photographs Division, Library of Congress.

villa—was appropriate to different settings and economic situations. Downing also included chapters on the treatment of interiors and furnishings.

Soon after delivering *Architecture of Country Houses* to its publisher in June 1850, Downing traveled to England. He returned to Newburgh in the fall accompanied by Calvert Vaux*, a young English architect, and shortly thereafter established a "Bureau of Architecture" in a new wing he added to his home. Downing's firm prepared designs for several buildings and the extensive grounds of Matthew Vassar's estate, Springside, in Poughkeepsie, New York; the Daniel Parish house, Newport, Rhode Island; numerous residences in the vicinity of Newburgh; and the Dodge houses in Washington, D.C.

Downing's monthly magazine, *The Horticulturist, and Journal of Rural Art and Rural Taste*, commenced publication in July 1846. In its pages Downing promoted the formation of village improvement societies and advocated sensible yet tasteful designs in rural architecture and landscape design. Rural economy was as

important as matters of aesthetics: because he realized that farmers were wastefully extracting nutrients from the soil and in older settled areas were experiencing declines in productivity, Downing became one of the earliest advocates of publicly supported agricultural education. In 1849 he was appointed one of eight commissioners to develop a plan for an agricultural college and experimental farm in New York, which was never executed because of lack of legislative support.

Living at the time when the urban population was increasing at the fastest rate in American history, Downing also recognized the need for open spaces within cities and advocated the creation of public parks. In 1848 he described parks as the "pleasant drawing-rooms" of European cities, places that promoted a more democratic social life than was the case in the United States. In succeeding years he elaborated on the role of parks as part of a reformist program that also included publicly supported libraries, galleries of art, and opportunities for social interaction.

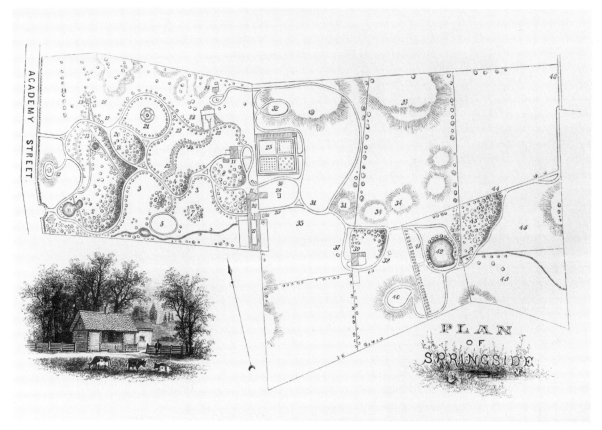

Plan of Springside. From Benson J. Lossing, *Vassar College and Its Founder,* 1867. Courtesy Special Collections, Vassar College Libraries.

In late 1850, Downing was commissioned to plan and superintend improvements to the public grounds in Washington, D.C. This 150-acre tract extended west from the foot of Capitol Hill to the site of the Washington Monument and then north to the President's House. Downing saw this as an opportunity not simply to ornament the capital but also to create the first large public park in the United States. He believed that the Washington park would encourage cities across the nation to provide healthful recreational grounds for their citizens. Although only the initial stages of construction had been completed at the time of his death, Downing's commission, as well as the influence of his writings, earned him the epithet "Father of American Parks."

Downing was also an early proponent of the suburb as a middle ground between city and country. He recognized that railroads and other transportation technologies had made possible the creation of suburban communities that combined a spacious setting for single-family homes and proximity to urban jobs and cultural institutions. In his essay "Our Country Villages," Downing rejected the rectangular plat so common in most suburban development and advocated instead the curving lines that characterized his landscape designs. He also proposed that each suburban community have a centrally located park, which would function as the "nucleus or heart of the village" and provide opportunities for communal activities.

On July 28, 1852, at the peak of his professional accomplishments, Downing died in the burning of the Hudson River steamboat *Henry Clay* near Yonkers. His death, Harvard botanist Asa Gray noted, was "a truly national loss." Downing achieved fame during his brief life as a tastemaker to the nation. He guided the prevailing taste away from geometric patterns in the garden and classical styles in architecture to less formal picturesque

The Walnut Row, Springside, 1987. Photo Charles A. Birnbaum.

The Porter's Lodge, Springside, 1987.
Photo Charles A. Birnbaum.

or romantic designs. What united his various endeavors was a recognition of the need to raise the level of "social civilization and social culture" in the United States. He considered his landscape and architectural commissions, as well as his books and the pages of *The Horticulturist*, vehicles for popularizing models of design appropriate to a middle-class society.

Thousands of cottages and farmhouses, standing amid handsome trees and gardens, still display the central gable and veranda, ornamental brackets, and other elements of residential design Downing popularized. Although few of the buildings and landscapes he himself designed have survived, these anonymous homes and landscapes are a fitting testament to his efforts to influence American taste.

Major, Judith K. *To Live in the New World: A. J. Downing and American Landscape Gardening.* Cambridge: MIT Press, 1997. Presents Downing's ideas of landscape gardening through analysis of the three editions of the *Treatise* as well as the essays he published in *The Horticulturist* between 1846 and 1852.

Schuyler, David. *Apostle of Taste: Andrew Jackson Downing, 1815–1852.* Baltimore: Johns Hopkins University Press, 1996. Contains a list of Downing's writings.

Tatum, George B., and Elisabeth B. MacDougall, eds. *Prophet with Honor: The Career of Andrew Jackson Downing, 1815–1852.* Washington, D.C.: Dumbarton Oaks / Trustees of Harvard University and the Athenaeum of Philadelphia, 1989. Scholarly papers presented at a symposium co-sponsored by the Athenaeum and the Center for Landscape Studies at Dumbarton Oaks which analyze important aspects of Downing's career.

David Schuyler

DRAPER, EARLE SUMNER
(1893–1994)
landscape architect, planner

Born in Falmouth, Massachusetts, Earle Sumner Draper graduated from the Massachusetts Agricultural College (now the University of Massachusetts) with a degree in landscape architecture. He had worked one summer with Albert Davis Taylor* and aspired to work with John Nolen*. Frank Waugh*, professor of landscape garden-

Norris Freeway. Rendering by Steven Braden based on TVA photo, c. 1930s. Courtesy Charles E. Aguar.

ing at the Massachusetts Agricultural College, recommended Draper as "the ablest man ever turned out" by the school. On the strength of Waugh's recommendation, Nolen agreed to employ Draper at his Cambridge office. After only three months Nolen dispatched him to attend to projects in Charlotte, North Carolina (including Myers Park, one of the city's suburbs), and to the new town of Kingston, Tennessee.

After two years, Nolen's practice had grown and Draper's reputation had grown with it. In 1917, Draper started his own practice in Charlotte, becoming one of the first resident planners and landscape architects in the southern United States. In 1922 he and his wife toured Europe, making sketches and taking photographs of the greatest gardens and open spaces on the continent. Draper built his own English Tudor Revival mansion in Myers Park; the estate featured a formal garden and oval pool accented by a statue he purchased in Italy, a cutting garden, a stable, and a stand of native woods.

One of Draper's earliest projects as an independent practitioner was Mayview Manor in Blowing Rock, North Carolina. The owner, W. Alexander, presented Draper with an interesting challenge: he wanted the roads on the estate, located on a mountainside, to be graded shallowly enough to trot a horse—which meant no grade over 6 percent. In his 1924 designs for Emory Wood, the High

Point Country Club, and the Farmington Country Club near Charlottesville, Virginia, Draper used the concept of extending a golf course into and around residential property.

Draper's business prospered, employing as many as a hundred people at one time with branch offices in Atlanta, Washington, D.C., and New York. In total, he planned more than three hundred subdivisions, college campuses, cemeteries, estates, and parks. Draper also prepared plans for more than a hundred new mill towns. The most famous of these is Chicopee, Georgia, built by a subsidiary of Johnson & Johnson in 1927. The master plan for Chicopee included a 4,000-acre forested greenbelt and provided for the location of all utilities underground. Draper later recalled, "I was of the old school, the Olmsted school that said that the best and finest use of the land is the most important thing and that all developments should be keyed to the land itself."

The Depression provided him with the opportunity that began his illustrious public career; Draper was appointed the first planner of the Tennessee Valley Authority (TVA). One of his first tasks was the development of Norris, Tennessee, a 2,000-acre greenbelt town designed to house construction workers. Because of the TVA board's impatience to begin construction, Draper had little more than a month to prepare a village plan. In

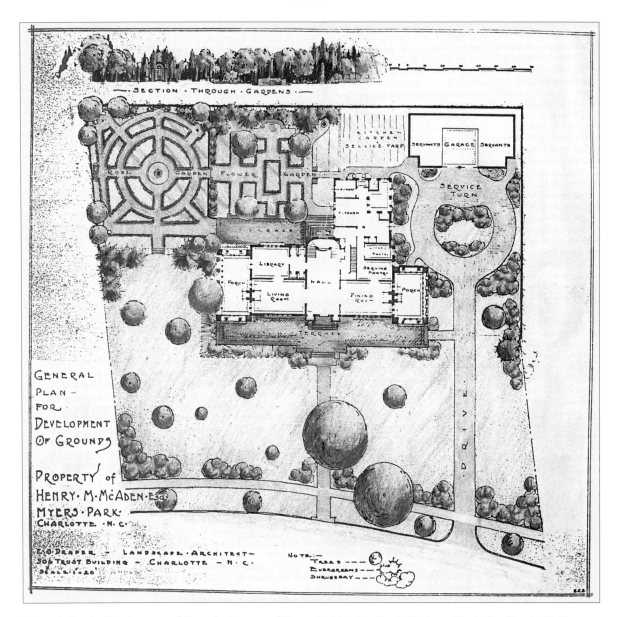

"General Plan for Development of Grounds, Property of Henry M. McAden, Esq.," Charlotte, North Carolina, 1921. Courtesy Draper Estate.

1983, at a fiftieth anniversary celebration in Norris, Draper discussed the city's design: "We put paths in the best locations for the people to reach the points they wanted to reach. We never paid any attention to lot lines; we picked the sites for the houses that seemed best. Houses were sited usually on fairly high ground; and their relationship to the street was left to the individual. In particular, we were anxious to see that the houses would fit the countryside and not be of an exotic type. I think Norris today fits the countryside and conditions just as well as it did at the time we planned it." When the government divested itself of many such con-

Horace William Shaler Cleveland. Hanscom Park. Omaha, Nebraska.
Photo Charles A. Birnbaum.

Horace William Shaler Cleveland.
Minnehaha Falls. Minneapolis, Minnesota.
Photo Charles A. Birnbaum.

Marian Cruger Coffin. Winterthur.
Winterthur, Delaware.
Photo Carol Betsch.

Howard Daniels. Spring Grove Cemetery. Cincinnati, Ohio, 1858.
Courtesy Cincinnati Historical Society.

James F. Dawson.
Washington Park Arboretum. Seattle, Washington.
Photo Catherine Joy Johnson.

James F. Dawson. Entry pier, Rockwood Boulevard.
Spokane, Washington.
Photo Catherine Joy Johnson.

Henry A. S. Dearborn.
Forest Hills Cemetery. Boston, Massachusetts.
Photo Blanche M. G. Linden.

Henry A. S. Dearborn. Mount Auburn Cemetery. Cambridge,
Massachusetts. Hand-tinted watercolor on lithograph
by W. H. Bartlett, 1839. Courtesy Blanche M. G. Linden.

Alling S. DeForest. George Eastman House.
Rochester, New York.
Photo Barbara Puorro Galasso.
Courtesy George Eastman House
International Museum of Photography and Film.

Alling S. DeForest.
George Eastman House. Rochester, New York.
Photo Barbara Puorro Galasso.
Courtesy George Eastman House
International Museum of Photography and Film.

Lockwood de Forest Jr.
Val Verde. Santa Barbara, California.
Photo Carol Betsch.

Lockwood de Forest Jr.
Costantia. Montecito, California.
Photo Charles A. Birnbaum.

Andrew Jackson Downing.
The Porter's Lodge, Springside.
Poughkeepsie, New York.
Photo Charles A. Birnbaum.

Andrew Jackson Downing.
The Walnut Row, Springside.
Poughkeepsie, New York.
Photo Charles A. Birnbaum.

Beatrix Jones Farrand. North Vista, Dumbarton Oaks.
Washington, D.C. Photo Elizabeth K. Meyer.

Beatrix Jones Farrand. Prunus allée, Dumbarton Oaks.
Washington, D.C. Photo Elizabeth K. Meyer.

struction camps at the end of World War II, Norris was the only one that returned more than its original cost.

In addition, the policy Draper initiated of acquiring the shorelines of the TVA lakes (instead of purchasing land only up to the high-water mark, the previous policy) allowed the government to impose land-use restrictions along the lakeshores; this prevented the development of slums along the waterline and controlled pollution. Water control projects throughout the United States and the rest of the world followed the TVA's successful example.

Of all his achievements, Draper was most proud of his plan for the 21-mile access road constructed between Norris and Knoxville—one of the first freeways. It had no curb cuts or access points along its length, and a 250-foot right-of-way precluded unsightly encroachments. At a 1938 national conference on state parks, held in Norris, Draper argued that "a freeway is not essentially a through express highway, nor is it solely a parkway. It embodies principles of design and aesthetic standards. . . . Above all, a freeway is safe. 'Free' from the normal traffic hazards so often attributable to engineering design (or lack of it)—intersections, steep grades, sharp curves, side roads, narrow bridges, and obstruction of vision."

President Franklin D. Roosevelt in 1940 appointed Draper as assistant administrator of the Federal Housing Authority, where he directed his experience in designing low-cost housing to the needs of war workers. Draper served as assistant commissioner, deputy commissioner, and acting commissioner of the Federal Housing Authority until 1945, when he returned to private practice as a housing consultant. He retired in 1964.

Draper joined the American Society of Landscape Architects in 1920 and served as vice president and director; he was elected a Fellow in 1927. He was also vice president and director of the American Planning and Civic Association, president of the American Institute of Planners, and a founding member and first executive director of the American Society of Planning Officials (now the American Planning Association). He died at his home in Vero Beach, Florida, at the age of one hundred.

Draper, Earle S. "Parkways and Freeways." *American Planning and Civic Annual*, Proceedings of the National Conference on National Parks, Washington, D.C., January 1938; The National Conference on State Parks, Norris, Tennessee, May 1938; and the National Conference on Planning, Minneapolis, Minnesota, June 1938, 156. Paper setting forth the concept of a freeway as realized in the road Draper designed between Norris and Knoxville.

Kratt, Mary Norton, and Thomas W. Hanchett. *Legacy: The Myers Park Story*. Charlotte, N.C.: Myers Park Foundation, 1986. An account of the development of Myers Park; details the way Draper's contributions frequently departed from Nolen's original plans.

Tennessee Valley Authority, Department of Regional Planning Studies. *The Scenic Resources of the Tennessee Valley, A Descriptive and Pictorial Inventory*. Washington, D.C.: GPO, 1938. A report Draper oversaw as director of the department; presents a thorough discussion of recreation and land use and the best ways to serve the needs of both.

Frank B. Burgraff and Charles E. Aguar

DUNCAN, FRANCES (FRANCES DUNCAN MANNING)
(1877–1972)
author, horticulturist

Frances Duncan was born in Brooklyn, New York, and was educated at the Northfield Seminary in Northfield, Massachusetts, after her family's move to that town. In a decision unusual for a young woman at that time, she chose to study horticulture and obtained a work-study position at Long Island's prestigious Parsons Nursery in 1896. There she studied the propagation and culture of woody ornamentals under the well-known nineteenth-century plantsmen Jean Rudolf Trumpy and Samuel Parsons Sr. After four years at the nursery, Duncan embarked on a career as a garden writer.

Frances Duncan wrote articles for a number of important magazines between 1901 and 1926, including *Century, Atlantic Monthly,* and *Scribner's.* She also wrote the first-ever gardening column for *Ladies' Home Journal* at the height of that magazine's influence under the legendary editor Edward Bok, and her work appeared frequently in *The Garden Magazine* and *Country Life in America.* Her subject matter included descriptions of historic gardens in the Charleston, South Carolina, area and artists' and writers' gardens in the Cornish, New Hampshire, art colony. Much of her writing, however, focused on horticulture, although she often discussed design issues when writing for an upscale audience.

Duncan was also the author of six books: two for children, *Mary's Garden and How It Grew* (1904) and *When Mother Lets Us Garden* (1909); two novels, *My Garden Doctor* (1914), in which gardening is presented as a cure for stress-related disorders, and *Roberta of Roseberry Gardens* (1916), a thinly veiled account of her experiences at Parsons; and two straightforward garden books, *The Joyous Art of Gardening* (1917) and *Home Vegetables and Small Fruits* (1918). Much of Duncan's writing was autobiographical and provides insight not only into her own life but also into some of the motivation behind the burgeoning of interest in gardens in her time. Her writing also offers a view of some important garden figures and institutions of the day.

An ardent suffragist, Duncan was an example of the "New Woman" of the early twentieth century, and one of the first women to seek a full-time, professional career as a garden writer. She was also involved with the school gardens movement at Montessori and Ethical Culture schools in both New York and California, and for several years operated the Gardencraft Toy Company, producing model gardens on the scale of doll houses, which children could use to play at landscape design and gardening.

Duncan divided her time between New York City and Cornish until 1925, when she moved to California and became garden editor of the *Los Angeles Times.* A near-fatal automobile accident in 1930 left her unable to write for several years. She later continued her work with school gardens in the Los Angeles area.

Begg, Virginia Lopez. "Charleston Gardens: A Turn of the Century View." *Magnolia, Bulletin of the Southern Garden History Society* 11 (Fall 1994).

Begg, Virginia Lopez. "Frances Duncan: The 'New Woman' in the Garden." *Journal of the New England Garden History Society* 2 (Fall 1992), 29–35. Survey of Duncan's life and work, and her place in the garden world of her day.

Duncan, Frances. *The Joyous Art of Gardening.* New York: Charles Scribner's Sons, 1917. A wide-ranging selection of Duncan's magazine articles for the middle class, emphasizing horticulture and some design.

Virginia Lopez Begg

EHLERS, HANS JACOB
(1804–1858)
landscape gardener

Hans Jacob Ehlers was born at his father's farm, Bösbyfeld, on the estate of Maasleben, near the city of Eckemförde in the Duchy of Schleswig, Denmark (a part of Germany since 1864). After finishing school, he worked for a year at Bösbyfeld farm, then spent several years as a hunting assistant to a forester named Muller. In 1828, he entered the Forestry Institute in Kiel in the neighboring Duchy of Holstein, from which he graduated in October 1830 with an excellent recommendation. Ehlers was then made responsible for the Forestry Arboretum connected with the institute. In 1833 he received a joint appointment as assistant to the Forestry Board in the Kiel office by the Pension Chamber in Copenhagen. In 1841 his employment in both positions was terminated. No landscape design projects by Ehlers in Denmark or Germany have been identified.

Ehlers emigrated to the United States about 1841, where he followed the profession of landscape gardening, working chiefly in the Hudson River Valley. Not long after his arrival, he is said to have spent more than a year traveling in the American West, studying native flora and climatological conditions. These studies be-

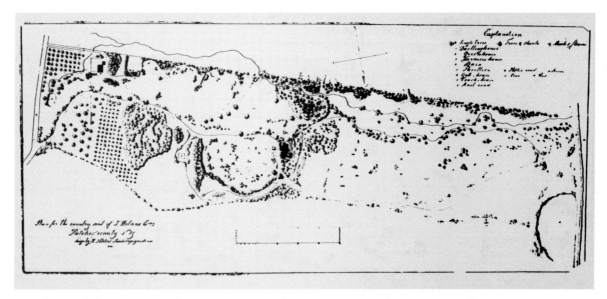

"Partial View of the Original Plan for the Country Seat of F. Delano, Esq., Dutchess Co., New York," 1848. Courtesy Rokeby Collection, Barrytown, New York.

came the basis of his 1849 booklet, *An Essay on Climate Intended Especially to Explain the Difference between the Climate of America and That of the Eastern Hemisphere.*

Only a few landscape design projects by Ehlers can be identified with certainty, but plans exist for most of these. Three of the projects date from 1849, including a plan for improving the grounds of Rokeby, the country seat of William B. Astor in Barrytown, New York. (Ehlers also prepared an undated plan for extending the grounds.) According to Astor family tradition, Ehlers was responsible for the gatehouse and the system of woodland carriage drives and bridges at Rokeby, as well as advising on ornamental tree plantings in the vicinity of the house. The other 1849 plans were for Steen Valetje (later known as Mandara, in Barrytown), the country seat of Astor's son-in-law Franklin H. Delano, great-uncle of Franklin Delano Roosevelt, and for an arboretum at Montgomery Place, in Annandale, New York. These plans appear to have been executed, although further study is needed to determine whether all details were carried out. Ehlers is also said to have designed the initial layout of Ferncliff in Rhinebeck, New York, a property purchased by William Astor, son of William B., in 1854. Later development of this estate was the work of Ehlers's son, Louis Augustus Ehlers*.

In 1851, Ehlers became involved in a dispute with Thomas Pennant Barton concerning his fee for designing the arboretum at Montgomery Place. Barton asked A. J. Downing* to arbitrate the disagreement, a situation that apparently ignited Ehlers's long-rankling resentment over an appendix, "Note on Professional Quackery," published in the second (1844) edition of Downing's *Treatise on the Theory and Practice of Landscape Gardening.* Without mentioning Ehlers by name or identifying the estate, Downing criticized him as "a foreign *soi-disant* landscape gardener," who had "completely spoiled the simply grand beauty of a fine river residence, by cutting up the breadth of a fine lawn with a ridiculous effort at what he considered a very charming arrangement of walks and groups of trees. In this case he only followed a mode sufficiently common and appropriate in a level inland country, like that of Germany, from whence he introduced it, but entirely out of keeping with the bold and lake-like features of the landscape which he thus made discordant." Although the dispute with Barton was the ostensible subject of Ehlers's 1851 booklet, *Defence Against Abuse and Slander with Some Strictures on Mr. Downing's Book on Landscape Gardening,* he also took the occasion to answer Downing's criticism of almost a decade earlier (apparently of an as yet unidentified pre-1844 design by Ehlers). Downing died a few months after Ehlers's pamphlet was published.

Hans Jacob Ehlers died in Brooklyn, New York, in 1858 and is buried at Greenwood Cemetery.

Ehlers, Hans Jacob. *Defence Against Abuse and Slander, with Some Strictures on Mr. Downing's Book on Landscape Gardening.* New York, 1852. A twelve-page pamphlet, consisting of a one-page introduction, "To the Public," and two letters from Ehlers to T. Barton, March 3, 1852, and April 1, 1852, defending his fee for the design of the Montgomery Place arboretum and objecting to A. J. Downing as an arbiter of the dispute and an authority on landscape gardening; very rare (copy in the Sidney Howard Gay Collection, New York Public Library, Astor, Lenox and Tilden Foundations).

Toole, Robert M. "Hans Jacob Ehlers: The Profession of a Landscape Gardener, Principally upon the Banks of the Hudson." *Hudson Valley Regional Review* 15 (September 1998).

The State Archives of Schleswig-Holstein in Schleswig, Germany, has official records of Hans Jacob Ehlers's life and work through 1841. No archive as such exists for either Ehlers in the United States. Plans by Hans Jacob are located in the Rokeby Collection, Barrytown, N.Y., and at Historic Hudson Valley, Tarrytown, and one plan by Louis Augustus is in the Rokeby Collection.

Cynthia Zaitzevsky

EHLERS, LOUIS AUGUSTUS
(1835–1911)
landscape gardener, architect

Louis Augustus Ehlers was born in Denmark in 1835, the son of Hans Jacob Ehlers*. He came to the United States with his father around 1842 and, after spending his early years in New York City, settled in Dutchess County, New York. The details of the younger Ehlers's education and training are unknown, although he presumably learned landscape gardening from his father and at some point acquired architectural skills. His obituary in the *Rhinebeck Gazette* describes him as an artist and art collector as well.

Ehlers traveled extensively and returned to Europe several times to study and visit gardens. In 1879 he designed the gate lodge at Ferncliff, the William Astor estate in Rhinebeck, where he was superintendent. His father is said to have done initial designs for Ferncliff, but Louis Augustus was responsible for its long-term landscape development. According to James H. Smith in his *History of Duchess [sic] County* (1882): "Mr. [Louis] Ehlers is a landscape gardener and rural architect, the results of whose handiwork and genius are to be seen at many points along the Hudson . . . and whose work has also extended to many parts of the States of New York, New Jersey, Pennsylvania, Massachusetts and Connecticut. . . . Ferncliff as it now appears is in all particulars the work of Mr. Ehlers' genius."

Ehlers has documented involvements with only a few properties other than Ferncliff. He prepared an undated plan for improving Rokeby for Mrs. William B. Astor, an estate for which his father had previously prepared plans. Ehlers married Mary Delamater, of a prominent Rhinebeck family, one other member of which commissioned a house by A. J. Davis (the Henry Delamater house, Rhinebeck, 1844, extant). In 1868, Ehlers bought Clifton Point in Rhinebeck and gradually developed its landscape. After the death of his wife in 1881, Ehlers renamed the property Marienruh. He later sold it to John Jacob Astor IV for consolidation into the adjacent Ferncliff. Louis Ehlers is said to have done work for the Delano and the Hall families. The first probably refers to Steen Valetje in Barrytown, the property belonging to Franklin H. Delano, for which Ehlers's father had also prepared a plan in 1849. The second reference is probably to Oak Terrace (also known as Oak Lawn) in Tivoli, New York, which belonged to Valentine Hall, father of Anna Hall Roosevelt and grandfather of Eleanor Roosevelt.

Louis Augustus Ehlers died at his home, Chateau de Bonair in Saugerties, New York.

"Obituary." *Rhinebeck Gazette*, February 18, 1911, 1. Fairly thorough account of Louis Augustus Ehlers's life but does not discuss his work in any detail.

See archive information under Ehlers, Hans Jacob.

Cynthia Zaitzevsky

ELIOT, CHARLES
(1859–1897)
landscape architect

Charles Eliot was born in Cambridge, Massachusetts, where he also received his education. He was a landscape architect in private practice from 1887 until his death from spinal meningitis ten years later. He also distinguished himself as a landscape historian, as an advocate for regional planning, and as a pioneer in landscape conservation. His reputation rests on two key accomplishments. First, he was the leading force in the 1891 establishment of Massachusetts' Trustees of Public Reservations, the first statewide, private-sector organization for the conservation of natural areas and the preservation of historic sites, which became a model for subsequent efforts such as the National Trust in Great Britain and, ultimately, the National Trust in the United States. Second, Eliot was a central figure in the creation of the Boston Metropolitan Park System, the first regional landscape authority in the United States.

Eliot was the son of Charles W. Eliot, who was for four decades the president of Harvard University, and Ellen Derby Peabody Eliot. In 1869, when Eliot was only ten, his mother died and his father accepted the presidency of Harvard. His mother's early death exacerbated his natural shyness, leading to a lonely and brooding adolescence. During his teenage years, Eliot developed a love of nature in his hikes through the Boston area and summers spent sailing with his family along the coast of Maine. While a student at Harvard, he formed the Champlain Society, a group of undergraduates who spent two summers camping and recording the natural history of Mount Desert Island in Maine. Eliot graduated cum laude with a bachelor of arts in 1882, but it was personal experiences with nature rather than his formal education that suggested the direction of his future career.

In October 1882, after conferring with his father about further education, Eliot enrolled at the Bussey Institution, the Department of Agriculture and Horticulture at Harvard. Faced with a dearth of graduate schools offering degrees in landscape architecture in the United States, he used the Bussey as a substitute, attending courses in agricultural chemistry, horticulture, applied zoology, applied botany, applied entomology, farm management, and topographical surveying. He interrupted his course of study in April 1883 to accept an internship in the landscape architecture office of Frederick Law Olmsted* in Brookline. With Olmsted, he worked on a wide range of projects including the Boston Municipal

Park System and the Arnold Arboretum. He returned to the Bussey briefly in 1885 to complete the interrupted courses. From the fall of 1885 through the end of 1886, Eliot traveled and studied independently in Europe, reading the literature of landscape architecture and gardening, and visiting the leading practitioners of landscape architecture, the major nurseries, and private estates and public parks, from England to Italy to Russia. He recorded his impressions in insightful letters to Olmsted and to members of his family.

On his return, Eliot established an independent practice based in Boston, after declining an invitation from Olmsted to rejoin his firm. Over the next decade he planned a range of landscapes from modest suburban gardens to expansive country estates to urban public parks and regional park systems. His important early commissions included the Longfellow Memorial Park (1887) in Cambridge and the White Park (1890) in Concord, New

Charles Eliot, c. 1895. Courtesy Family of Carola Eliot Goriansky.

View of tree-clogged notch. From
Charles Eliot, Landscape Architect.

Hampshire, where he began to work out his philosophy of landscape design and landscape conservation.

Eliot also wrote on landscape issues for the professional and the popular press. His articles prolifically encompassed horticulture, landscape preservation, landscape history, landscape literature, and professional practice. His series of articles "Six Old American Country Seats" (*Garden and Forest*, 1889) represents one of the first efforts at American landscape history. In his frequent contributions to *Garden and Forest*, he also began

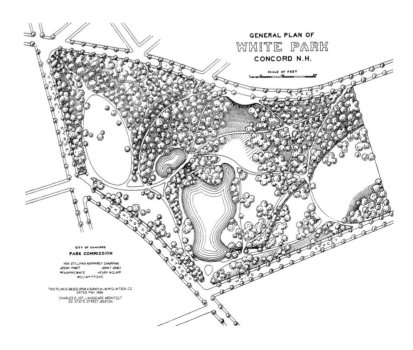

General plan of White Park, Concord,
New Hampshire, May 1888. From
Garden and Forest, August 13, 1890.

View of notch after opening. From
Charles Eliot, Landscape Architect.

to devise schemes for the preservation and management of landscapes of natural, scenic, or historic significance. In one article, "The Waverly Oaks" (March 1890), he advocated "an incorporated association, composed of citizens of all Boston towns, and empowered by the State to hold small and well-distributed parcels of land free of taxes, just as the Public Library holds books and the Art Museum pictures—for the use and enjoyment of the public." These ideas culminated in the development of The Trustees of Public Reservations in 1891 and the Boston Metropolitan Park Commission in 1893.

Early in 1893, Eliot formed a partnership with Frederick Law Olmsted Jr.* and John Charles Olmsted*. From that year until his death, he focused on the rapid advancement of the Boston Metropolitan Park System and the Cambridge Municipal Park System, while assisting in a wide range of commissions for Olmsted, Olmsted & Eliot throughout the country. For the Boston Metropolitan Park Commission he developed a regional plan that incorporated diverse landscape types such as ocean beaches, harbor islands, tidal estuaries, woodland reservations, and public playgrounds. Eliot dealt with planning as much as landscape design. During the first five years of the commission's efforts, he oversaw the acquisition of hundred of acres of new "reservations," the term that he preferred to "parks." Among the most important was his supervision of the development of Revere Beach (1896), the first public beach in the United States. Eliot's premature death in 1897 motivated the establishment of an academic program in landscape architecture at Harvard, out of which grew the profession of regional planning.

Eliot, Charles W. *Charles Eliot, Landscape Architect.* 1901. Reprint. Amherst: Library of American Landscape History / University of Massachusetts Press, 1999. A facsimile reprint with a new introduction by Keith N. Morgan of the comprehensive anthology of Eliot's writings annotated as a biography by his father; illustrated.

Eliot, Charles. *Vegetation and Scenery in the Metropolitan Reservations of Boston. A Forestry Report Written by Charles Eliot and Presented to the Metropolitan Park Commission February 15, 1897, by Olmsted, Olmsted and Eliot.* Boston, 1898. Eliot's analysis of the natural history of the park system and recommendations for maintenance and improvement of the park properties, published after his death.

Morgan, Keith N. "Held in Trust: Charles Eliot's Vision for the New England Landscape." *National Association for Olmsted Parks Workbook 1* (1991). A biographical sketch of Charles Eliot and a discussion of the forces that influenced his work.

Keith N. Morgan

ELLWANGER, GEORGE
(1816–1906)
horticulturist, nursery owner

Born in Gross-Heppach, the Kingdom of Wurtemburg, Germany, George Ellwanger grew up working in the vineyards on the southern slopes of the Remsthal. At the age of fourteen he indentured himself to a leading horticultural firm in Stuttgart to learn the nursery and florist trades. In 1835 he decided to join relatives in Tiffin, Ohio, south of Sandusky. The Erie Canal boat on which he traveled stopped in Rochester, New York, to unload freight. The city and surrounding rich vegetation impressed Ellwanger, and within a few months he returned to begin his career as nurseryman.

By the spring of 1836, Ellwanger was working for William Reynolds and Michael Bateham, co-owners of Rochester's leading nursery and seed business. When Reynolds and Bateham dissolved their partnership in the spring of 1838, Ellwanger bought their greenhouses and seed business. In 1839 he moved the greenhouses to eight acres he had purchased on Mount Hope Avenue. There he also planted an orchard of specimen fruit trees acquired from a Mr. Kennock of Newton, Massachusetts. Ellwanger and Patrick Barry, who joined the business in 1840, used this specimen orchard to perfect practical knowledge of fruit culture and to propagate stock for their nursery business.

BARRY, PATRICK
(1816–1890)
horticulturist, nursery owner

Born near Belfast, Ireland, Patrick Barry showed an early aptitude for learning. At the age of eighteen he was given charge of one of the national public schools. After two years he embarked for the United States and, in Flushing, New York, found employment as a clerk in William Prince's Linnaean Botanic Garden. Established in 1737, it was the first large commercial nursery operation in the New World and became a leader in improving horticultural methods. In 1840, Michael Bateham engaged Barry in his seed business in Rochester. There he met George Ellwanger. They entered into a partnership, and developed a friendship that endured until Barry's death.

George Ellwanger and Patrick Barry on American Pomological Society excursion to California (left to right: Mrs. Clark, Mrs. Downing, Charles Downing, Mr. Clark, Miss Clark, Mrs. Wilder, Marshall P. Wilder, Miss Wilder, Patrick Barry, George Ellwanger, Mrs. Ellwanger). Department of Rare Books and Special Collections, University of Rochester Library.

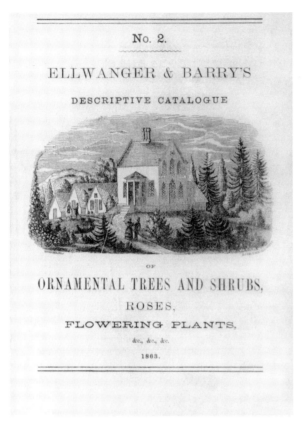

Ellwanger & Barry, *Descriptive Catalogue of Ornamental Trees and Shrubs, Roses, Flowering Plants*, 1863. Department of Rare Books and Special Collections, University of Rochester Library.

The Ellwanger and Barry Mount Hope Nurseries

Among the pioneer horticulturists of the nineteenth century, George Ellwanger and Patrick Barry were instrumental in disseminating knowledge of fruit culture and in establishing pomology as a scientific discipline. When Barry joined Ellwanger in his fledgling nursery enterprise, he brought business experience and a few hundred dollars in back pay from Prince's Linnaean Botanic Garden, which was remitted in the form of plants and trees. Barry proved a quick study in the art of growing plants and trees. During the 1840s, Ellwanger and Barry expanded the nursery and proceeded to test varieties of fruit that would grow in the local climate and soils. The grounds of the Mount Hope Nurseries became a school, and Patrick Barry the master of instruction in the propagation of fruits. Responsibilities at the nursery were divided; Barry

specialized in fruit culture and Ellwanger in ornamental plants. By 1845 both men were making regular trips to Europe in search of nursery stock.

Barry assumed editorship of the *Genesee Farmer* with the January 1845 issue, continuing through 1852. In that position he became a critic, but also a friend, of Andrew Jackson Downing*, editor of *The Horticulturist, and Journal of Rural Art and Rural Taste*. Both Ellwanger and Barry admired Downing's architectural designs, and they chose A. J. Davis to design the Mount Hope Nursery office in the Gothic Revival style Downing advocated. After Downing's tragic death by drowning in 1852, Barry was selected to replace him as editor of *The Horticulturist*. The Rochester seedsman James Vick Jr. purchased the journal and moved it there. Barry's editorial contributions to these influential journals reflected his practical experience as a nurseryman.

Barry is chiefly remembered for two other widely distributed written works. *The Fruit Garden*, which remained in print from 1851 to 1915, was a practical guide to the physiology of fruit trees, how to plant, prune, and train them, and provided instruction on laying out orchards and gardens. *Barry's Catalogue of Fruits for Cultivation in the United States and Canadas in Two Divisions* (1862) was prepared for the American Pomological Society and continued to be the authoritative source on fruit varieties throughout the nineteenth century. A much-soiled copy hung by a cord at the Mount Hope Nurseries, available for ready reference.

Both Ellwanger and Barry were important figures in the growth of pomology as a profession in the United States. In an 1886 letter to *The American Horticulturist*, Marshall P. Wilder, president of the American Pomological Society, placed George Ellwanger among the society's most distinguished members. Although Ellwanger did not have Barry's gift for the written word, his influence was felt at professional meetings, and he channeled his energy into perfecting the Mount Hope Nurseries' operations and plant collections. He took pride in seeing the new western orchards planted in trees that he had propagated, and in winning prizes for their perfect fruits.

In midlife Barry shifted his interests from the printed word to "word-of-mouth teachings" at meetings of the Western New York Horticultural Society. He served as president from 1864 until his death. In 1881 he enthusiastically endorsed plans to establish the New York Agricultural Experiment Station in Geneva, New York. He firmly believed that research into new methods would provide New York State fruit growers with a competitive advantage against western growers, who

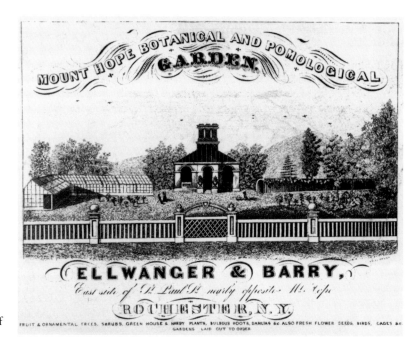

Mount Hope Nurseries, early 1840s. Courtesy Department of Rare Books and Special Collections, University of Rochester Library.

were using the new rail links to gain access to eastern markets. Barry was named to the original Board of Control and provided both expert advice and many of the grafts for the station's eighty-four varieties of apple and six varieties of crabapple set on existing trees.

In 1887, Ellwanger and Barry donated to the city twenty-two acres of their nursery land located on the highest elevation in Rochester, from which Highland Park was developed. In 1890 they provided $7,000 to support construction of a rustic open-air pavilion on The Pinnacle. At that time the City of Rochester was consulting with Frederick Law Olmsted* about the design and installation of the arboretum that still encircles The Pinnacle; Olmsted retained the architectural firm of Shepley, Rutan & Coolidge of Boston to design the pavilion, a three-story structure with open vistas in all directions. In September 1890, Ellwanger dedicated the pavilion to the children of Rochester as a joint gift with Barry (who had died the previous June) on the fiftieth anniversary of their partnership. The pavilion remained a central feature of Highland Park until 1963, when it fell victim to deferred maintenance and vandalism and was razed.

1862. Compiled under the direction of the American Pomological Society with the assistance of state and district committees; provides one of the first standardized listings of named varieties and indicates their suitability for cultivation in different localities.

Barry, Patrick. *The Fruit Garden*. New York, 1851. A complete guide for the gardener and orchardist, covering topics such as general principles of fruit tree physiology, propagation, pruning and manuring, and descriptions of selected varieties.

The Ellwanger and Barry Horticultural Library, the working library of the Mount Hope Nurseries and the real estate company that succeeded it, has been deposited in the Department of Rare Books and Special Collections, University of Rochester Library. Materials range from volumes on fruit growing, ornamentals, architecture, park development, manure, and horse doctoring, to ledgers of business operations (560 titles in 1,600 volumes).

Barry, Patrick. *A Catalogue of Fruits for Cultivation in the United States and Canadas*. Rochester, N.Y,

---

Paul Grebinger and Ellen Grebinger

ELWOOD, PHILIP HOMER
(1884–1960)
landscape architect, author, educator

Philip Homer Elwood was born at Fort Plain, New York. He studied at Michigan State College in East Lansing (1904–1906) before receiving his B.S.A. from Cornell University in 1910.

On graduation from Cornell, Elwood worked as a civil and landscape engineer in the office of Charles W. Leavitt Jr.* Civil and Landscape Engineering, in New York City, until his appointment to the Agricultural Extension Service staff at Massachusetts State College, Amherst, in 1913. In 1915 he was called to supervise the landscape architectural work at Ohio State University. In 1917–1918, Elwood served as captain in the Field Artillery and saw active service near the Argonne. After the Armistice he was appointed chief landscape engineer in charge of the engineering and landscape planning for the construction of the largest American military cemetery in Europe, the Argonne Cemetery of the American Expeditionary Forces at Romagne-sous-Montfaucon, France. Elwood then returned to Columbus, Ohio, and became a partner of the firm Elwood & Frye.

In the spring of 1923, Elwood went on to Iowa State College, and he deserves the major credit for developing its department of landscape architecture. Under his auspices, a bachelor of science degree and a one-year graduate program of the master of landscape architecture were initiated. Elwood served as head of the department from 1929 to 1950. Summer travel courses were a significant part of his method of education. He conducted tours to East Asia, to Europe, and in North America, which were open to students from other institutions as well.

In 1930, Elwood initiated the renovation of a horse barn to provide the landscape architecture department with a new home. The Landscape Studio, noted the *Christian Science Monitor*, was "probably the only building of its size and character in America occupied exclusively by an independent Department of Landscape Architecture. The building, 100 feet by 40 feet, is of brick and includes three full floors."

During his tenure at Iowa State, Elwood also made substantial contributions to the design of the college cam-

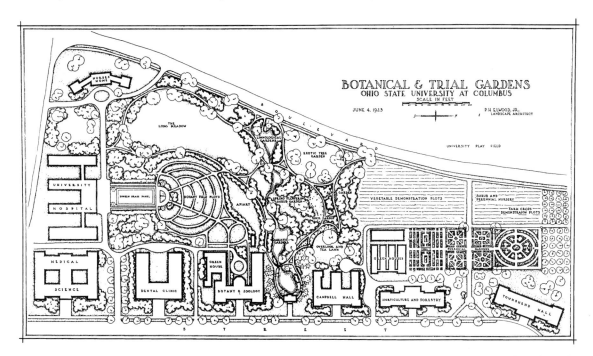

"Ohio State University, Columbus, Ohio—A Plan of the Botanical and Trial Gardens," June 4, 1923. From P. H. Elwood Jr., ed., *American Landscape Architecture*, 1924.

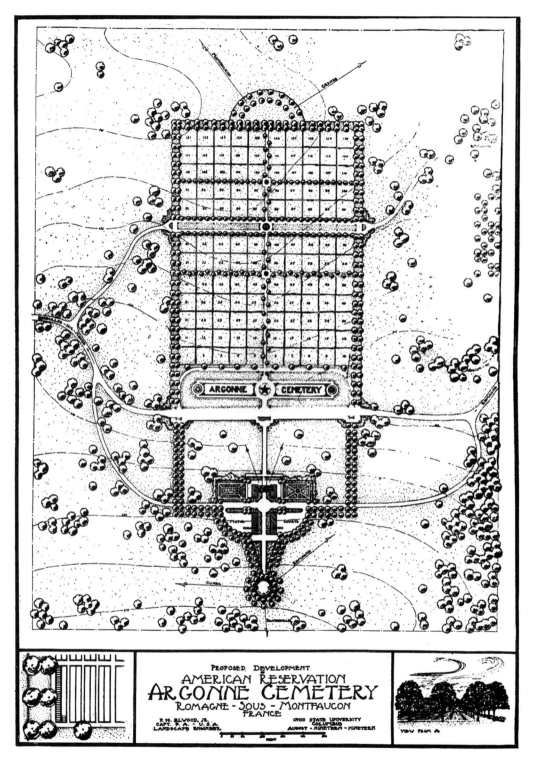

"Plan of Proposed Development of American Expeditionary Forces Reservation—Argonne Cemetery, Romagne-sous-Montfaucon," August 1919. From *Architectural Record*, June 1920. Courtesy Drawings and Archives Department, Avery Architectural and Fine Arts Library, Columbia University.

pus. He and Allen H. Kimball prepared the basic plan, known as the Twenty Year Plan, for the layout of buildings and grounds, and over the years Elwood defended it against many proposed encroachments.

By far the most significant of Elwood's many publications was *American Landscape Architecture*, which he edited in 1924. He also wrote articles for *American Architect*, *American City*, *Architectural Record*, *Landscape Architecture*, and *Parks and Recreation*, and edited the *First* and *Second Progress Report of the Iowa State Planning Board*, published in September 1934 and April 1935, respectively. Elwood was also a consultant to many national, state, and local commissions and committees, including the National Resources Planning Board, the National Park Service, the U.S. Housing Authority, the Highway Research Board, and the Mississippi River Parkway Planning Commission. In 1932 he organized and chaired the Iowa Roadside Improvement Council. He became a Fellow of the American Society of Landscape Architects in 1927, and was also president of the old Mississippi Valley chapter (1932), and of the later Missouri Valley chapter (1939–1942). He served as vice president of the ASLA in 1941, 1949, and 1950, and president of the American Society of Planning Officials in 1942–1943.

Poor health forced Elwood to leave teaching in 1952, and he and his family settled in Tucson, Arizona, where he formed the practice of Elwood & Greene. He was a member of the firm until 1955. Elwood died in Tucson in 1960.

Among Elwood's most significant commissions were the Iowa State University campus; Boys Town in Nebraska; Garrison Reservoir Townsite; the Botanical and Trial Gardens at Ohio State University at Columbus; Pi Beta Phi Settlement School, Gatlinburg, Tennessee; and a master plan for Canon City, Colorado.

Elwood, Philip Homer. "The Argonne Cemetery of the A.E.F. at Romagne-sous-Montfaucon, France." *Architectural Record* 47 (June 1920), 508–510. Recounts the 1919 construction of Argonne Cemetery, describing the process of locating and identifying the American war dead in the battle areas.

Elwood, Philip Homer. "Development beyond the City's Outer Limits: America's New Concern for the Amenities of the Countryside." *Landscape Architecture* 37 (July 1947), 142–144. Paper presented at the ASLA's 1947 meeting before the section on city and regional planning; attacks "suburban sprawl" and discusses the efforts of European countries to control developments outside their cities.

Elwood, Philip Homer, ed. *American Landscape Architecture*. New York: Architectural Book Publishing, 1924. A substantial photographic record of the work of 75 designers and 2 sculptors; entries were judged by a committee that included Frederick Law Olmsted Jr.*, Charles N. Lowrie, and Noel Chamberlain; 194 pp. of illustrations, including plans.

Robert Harvey

ELY, HELENA RUTHERFURD
(1858–1920)
author

Helena Rutherfurd was educated at Brooke Hall in Media, Pennsylvania. In 1880 she married Alfred Ely, and Meadowburn Farm near Warwick, New York, became their summer residence. Ely developed an interest in gardening but soon tired of Victorian garden design and plant material, admiring instead the hardy perennials she saw in the dooryards of neighboring farmers. She initially relied on the books of William Robinson for descriptive

information, but English cultural directions proved useless in the New York climate, so she began to experiment. Her results were so successful that she received frequent requests for information from other amateur gardeners; she responded with her first book.

Ely wrote *A Woman's Hardy Garden* in 1903. The reaction to it was swift and long-lasting. The book was widely hailed by newspapers such as the *New York Times*

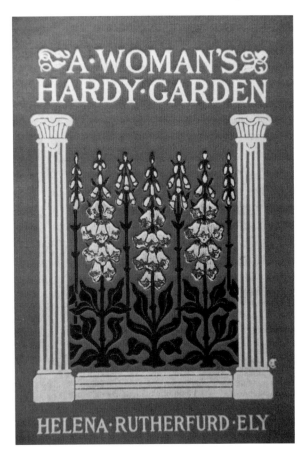

Cover of first edition of Ely's landmark book, published in 1903. Photo Virginia Lopez Begg.

A Woman's Hardy Garden and its sequels, though simple and almost naive by current standards, had a threefold impact on American gardens. First, they were the first written by an amateur with personal experience to give clear directions on how to make a perennial garden. As such, they helped to sound the death knell of Victorian garden styles, such as bedding out and displays of tropical foliage, and to create the boom in perennial gardens that lasted until World War II. Second, Ely's established social position gave many people permission to work physically in the garden themselves, behavior uncommon among the middle and upper classes in the Victorian era. This, too, abetted the tremendous growth in amateur gardening from 1900 to 1940. Finally, that Ely was a woman encouraged many other women to begin to garden, and gardening in America in that period came to be viewed as a distinctly female occupation, a phenomenon often commented on by contemporary observers.

Ely, Helena Rutherfurd. *Another Hardy Garden Book.* Illustrated by Professor Charles F. Chandler. New York: Macmillan, 1905. Sequel to *A Woman's Hardy Garden* and another simple, nonintimidating account based on Ely's practical experience, written in the same personal style; discussions of flowers, fruit, vegetables, trees, and shrubs; 49 black-and-white photographs taken in her garden.

Ely, Helena Rutherfurd. *The Practical Flower Garden.* Illustrated. New York: Macmillan, 1911. The first six chapters, based on Ely's garden, cover color schemes, raising plants from seed, fertilizers and pest remedies, and the place of the terrace in the garden; "The Wild Garden" describes a friend's garden of native plants in Connecticut; final section lists and describes plants Ely grew successfully; includes 8 color plates, 24 full-page black-and-white photographs, and 62 black-and-white illustrations.

Ely, Helena Rutherfurd. *A Woman's Hardy Garden.* Illustrated by Professor C. F. Chandler. New York: Macmillan, 1903. Ely's best-known book; how to make a flower garden, emphasizing hardy perennials but including annuals and shrubs; basic cultural directions for the beginner, illustrated with 49 black-and-white photographs of plants Ely grew and of her garden.

and the major literary magazines. After recounting the disappointing horticultural results experienced by a friend who had been reading Gertrude Jekyll, one reviewer wrote, "At last we have . . . an American book, by an American woman, about an American garden." The book went through sixteen printings in its first decade and remained in print into the 1930s. Ely extended her influence with two more books, *Another Hardy Garden Book* (1905) and *The Practical Flower Garden* (1911), several magazine articles, and her activities with the Garden Club of America, of which she was a founder and early officer. The demand for gardens increased exponentially as a result of books such as Ely's, and the growing interest in them stimulated the development of landscape architecture as a profession in the first three decades of the century.

Virginia Lopez Begg

FARRAND, BEATRIX JONES
(1872–1959)
landscape gardener

Beatrix Jones Farrand, one of the finest landscape architects of her generation, was a charter member of the American Society of Landscape Architects. Although active in the ASLA throughout her long and distinguished career, she always referred to herself as a "landscape gardener." Robert Patterson, a close professional associate, said that Farrand thought the word "architect" "should be left to the designer of buildings."

She was born in New York City, the only child of Mary Cadwalader Rawle and Frederick Rhinelander Jones, who separated in 1887 and divorced in 1896. Farrand's early life cannot have been entirely happy, but neither was it dull. Tutored at home, as many young girls of her social class were, she often traveled abroad with her mother and with her father's sister, Edith Wharton. Her mother, in response to reduced financial circumstances, acted as part-time literary agent for her sister-in-law and kept within her immediate circle of friends some of the best literary and artistic minds of the period including Brooks and Henry Adams, Henry James, and John La Farge. Farrand's uncle, John Lambert Cadwalader, a distinguished lawyer and a founder of the New York Public Library, is said to have recognized in his niece an early talent for landscape design and an "indomitable will." He later remarked, "Let her be a gardener or for that matter anything she wants to be. What she wishes to do will be well done."

Farrand first planned a career in music, but the decisive moment with respect to her ultimate choice of profession probably occurred in 1892, when by her own account "a fortunate meeting with Mary Sargent [wife of Charles Sprague Sargent*] changed the course of a young woman's life." Soon after this meeting Farrand came to live for several months at Holm Lea, the Sargents' estate at Brookline, Massachusetts. During this period, Farrand studied horticulture and the basic principles of landscape design under Sargent at the Arnold Arboretum. Although she later developed her own philosophy of design, she always followed Sargent's sound advice "to make the plan fit the ground and not twist the ground to fit the plan." It was Sargent who encouraged Farrand to become a professional.

After a European garden tour in 1895, Farrand returned to New York City and studied civil engineering with private tutors. A year later she opened a landscape architecture office in her mother's house on East 11th Street. Working initially within the immediate circle of family friends, she received her first major commission that same year from William Garrison of Tuxedo, New York. In 1899, Farrand joined ten other distinguished professionals to establish the American Society of Landscape Architects. She was the only woman among the founders.

Farrand's earliest designs were formal in character but reflected the influence of William Robinson, the English landscape architect and author of *The Wild Garden* (1881). She also shared with Gertrude Jekyll, the celebrated contemporary British landscape gardener, a subtle and harmonious approach to color based on Impressionist theory. Robert Patterson, her lifelong associate, later wrote that Farrand's work had a "freedom of scale, a subtle softness of line and an unobtrusive asymmetry." Her designs combined horticultural impressionism and the best elements of classical European gardening.

Unfortunately, none of Farrand's earliest gardens survives, although evidence of her approach may be gleaned from drawings preserved at the University of

Beatrix Jones Farrand. Courtesy Dumbarton Oaks, Trustees for Harvard University.

North Vista, Dumbarton Oaks, Washington, D.C., 1992. Photo Elizabeth K. Meyer.

California. Several major projects executed after her marriage to Max Farrand in 1913, including the country estate of Willard Straight in Old Westbury, New York, have been destroyed. However, one of Farrand's most successful gardens, designed for Abby Aldrich Rockefeller in Seal Harbor, Maine (1925–1950), is still well preserved and maintained by the Rockefeller family.

Dumbarton Oaks in Washington, D.C., is Farrand's finest surviving work. Beginning in 1921 and over the next twenty-six years, Farrand transformed for clients Mildred and Robert Woods Bliss what had been a farm into one of the most imaginative gardens in this country. The entire composition reflects her clear understanding of the topographic subtleties of the site. Lending complexity to the whole is the principle of asymmetry. The formal Georgian Revival house was placed deliberately off-axis, with its principal terraces extending to the east and descending to informal wooded areas below. Dumbarton Oaks is everywhere marked by a richness of architectural detail, an imaginative choice of materials, delicacy, and restraint—qualities associated with all of Farrand's best work.

Prunus allée, Dumbarton Oaks, Washington, D.C., 1999. Photo Elizabeth K. Meyer.

Princeton University campus, Princeton, New Jersey. Photo Alan Ward.

Among her private clients Farrand gained a reputation for thoroughness and certainty of approach. This reputation also extended to her campus work, for, unlike many of her female colleagues, Farrand secured a large number of commissions outside the residential sector. Beginning in 1916, she designed the graduate college gardens at Princeton University. At Yale, between 1922 and 1945, she designed the Memorial Quadrangle, Silliman College Quadrangle, and the Marsh Botanical Garden. Her other campus commissions include those for the University of Chicago (1919–1936) and Vassar (1926–1927), Hamilton (1924), and Oberlin (1939–1946) colleges.

Farrand devoted her final years to the creation of Reef Point Gardens in Bar Harbor, Maine, a project she and her husband had begun in 1937. Designed for both scholarly and experimental purposes, the project ultimately included an extensive library, a test garden of native flora, and a herbarium. In 1955, Farrand, concerned about the survival of Reef Point, transferred the contents of her library and the herbarium, as well as professional plans and correspondence, to the University of California at Berkeley. She died at Bar Harbor four years later.

professional achievement; emphasis on her major work including Dumbarton Oaks and the Rockefeller garden in Seal Harbor, Maine, as well as her plans for several universities including Princeton, Yale, and Chicago.

McPeck, Eleanor M. "Beatrix Jones Farrand." In *Notable American Women*, ed. Edward T. James et al. Cambridge: Harvard University Press, 1980. Concise summary of Farrand's professional career with valuable bibliography and listing of archival sources.

McPeck, Eleanor M. "Beatrix Jones Farrand, The Formative Years." In *Beatrix Farrand: Fifty Years of Landscape Architecture*, ed. Diane Kostial McGuire and Lois Fern. Washington D.C.: Dumbarton Oaks Trustees for Harvard University, 1982. Summary of Farrand's early years and education as well as account of European travel and early professional work.

The Department of Landscape Architecture, Documents Collection, at the University of California, Berkeley, holds Farrand's archive of correspondence, land surveys, and garden plans as well as her extensive private library of books on architecture and gardening. Dumbarton Oaks maintains its own collection, with the Trustees of Harvard University, of photographs, plans, and reports from Farrand's more than twenty-year relationship with the gardens.

Balmori, Diana, Diane Kostial McGuire, and Eleanor M. McPeck. *Beatrix Farrand's American Landscapes: Her Gardens and Campuses*. Sagaponack, N.Y.: Sagapress, 1985. Richly illustrated book documenting Farrand's

Eleanor M. McPeck

FLEMING, BRYANT
(1877–1946)
landscape architect

Bryant Fleming was born in Buffalo, New York. After graduating from high school, he studied at the Buffalo Botanic Gardens, his interest in landscape design strengthening as he matured. At the advice of Frederick Law Olmsted*, to whom he had written for guidance, Fleming entered Cornell University to study under Liberty Hyde Bailey*, widely respected horticulturist, naturalist, author, and educator. Cornell had no formal program in landscape architecture at that time, so Fleming mapped out his course of study with Bailey to include horticulture, architecture, architectural history, and art.

After graduating from Cornell in 1901, Fleming spent three years in the Boston office of landscape architect Warren Manning*. In 1904, Fleming and Bailey began the gradual development of the Department of Landscape Art in the College of Agriculture at Cornell. Fleming was appointed the school's first lecturer and instructor in landscape art in 1904, and he served as head of the department from 1906 until 1915.

While he was becoming increasingly involved with the landscape art department at Cornell, Fleming began private practice as a landscape designer in Buffalo with Frederic dePeyster Townsend in 1905. The firm's work included site planning, subdivision layout, and the landscape design of private residences such as the Avery Coonley house in Riverside, Illinois, designed by Frank Lloyd Wright. The firm also accepted several commissions in the Glenview, Kentucky, area. Fleming began his long association with the American Scenic and Preservation Society in the early 1900s. Through the society he helped guide the development of prominent park areas in New York State, including Letchworth State Park in western New York, the restoration of Watkins Glen at the foot of Seneca Lake, and Cascadilla Gorge, an integral green space winding through the Cornell University campus.

While maintaining his Buffalo practice, Fleming joined Manning and a team of Cornell architecture professors to develop a comprehensive campus plan for the university, one of many planning efforts for Cornell in which he would participate. He was elected a Fellow of the American Society of Landscape Architects in 1911 and served as chair of the Committee on Education. When in 1915 landscape architecture took its place as one of the allied arts at the American Academy in Rome, Fleming became a member of the jury that judged entries for the Rome Prize and was an active participant in academy affairs for several years.

In 1915, Fleming moved to the small village of Wyoming in western New York to begin his own landscape practice. After visiting for the first time in 1908, he had spent an increasing amount of time working in Wyoming for his patron Lydia Avery Coonley Ward, a wealthy social activist and writer, and her acquaintances. Fleming's young staff often included graduates of the Cornell program, several of whom won the coveted Rome Prize while under his guidance. The office was never very large but was unusually mobile, with associates crisscrossing the country by train to reach makeshift offices in cities where commissions were under way.

During the exhilarating period from 1920 to the early 1930s, Fleming and his associates designed and executed numerous schemes for the improvement or creation of residences and gardens, often acting as interior designers, architects, and landscape architects for a single commission. Fleming's knowledge of art, architectural history, and antiques equaled his command of horticulture and the technical aspects of landscape design, leading to a depth of involvement with his residential projects which

Bryant Fleming. Private collection.

"Perspective Sketch of Main Entrance Gates and Gate Lodge, at the Estate of Leslie Cheek, Esq.," July 19, 1929. Office of Bryant Fleming, Ithaca, New York. Courtesy Smithsonian Institution, Archives of American Gardens.

Lincliff estate, Louisville, Kentucky. Photo Charles A. Birnbaum.

Historic view of the Reflecting Pool, Cheekwood, Nashville, Tennessee. Courtesy Smithsonian Institution, Archives of American Gardens.

defined his style. By the mid-1920s, projects were under way in the cities of Chicago, Detroit, Cleveland, Kansas City, Memphis, and Louisville, with numerous others in small towns in New York, Pennsylvania, Ohio, Michigan, Mississippi, Florida, and southern Canada.

In 1925, Fleming's appointment as University Landscape Advisor to Cornell cast him into the thick of a new campus planning campaign and sealed his decision to move his office to Ithaca. Fleming's commitment to Cornell did not slow his prolific residential practice, however. His career as a designer of country estates reached its zenith in the late 1920s and early 1930s in Belle Meade, a burgeoning upper-class suburb of Nashville, Tennessee, where he was involved with numerous projects. One of the most comprehensive was the design of Cheekwood, a 100-acre estate for which he planned and executed the landscape, architectural, and interior design, even traveling to Europe with the Cheek family to purchase architectural details for the home. (Presently Cheekwood houses the Tennessee Botanical Gardens and Fine Arts Center.)

The Depression deprived Fleming of clients and brought his thirty-year career as a country place designer to a close. His residential design work reveals his remarkable creative ability, but Fleming is also remembered for his devotion to the profession of landscape architecture and his contribution to the education of landscape architects. His students helped shape American landscape architecture throughout the twentieth century, and his greatest impact on the profession may have been as a teacher and mentor.

Ewald, Walter, A. J. "Bryant Fleming: A Biographical Minute." *Landscape Architecture* 37 (January 1947). A brief biography.

Fleming, Bryant. *Illustrations from the Work of Bryant Fleming, Architect, Landscape Architect.* Ithaca, N.Y.: Privately printed, 1932. A collection of photographs illustrating the work of Fleming's firm; emphasis on residential commissions.

Warren, Rhoda. "Bryant Fleming: Landscape Architect." *Historical Wyoming* 31 (October 1984). Biographical information and descriptions of Fleming's commissions and clients both in Wyoming and the New York area.

Gayle Knight, Alan McCarthy,
and Charles Birnbaum

FOOTE, HARRIETT RISLEY
(1863–1951)
rosarian, author

Harriett Risley was graduated from Smith College with a bachelor's degree in 1886. After graduate study in Germany, she taught chemistry and physics. Her interest in the experimental sciences was to play a significant role in her work with roses, and she won praise from plant scientists for her observations. In 1891 she married the Rev. Henry L. Foote and soon began her extensive experiments in rose growing at the rectory garden in Marblehead, Massachusetts. Her work attracted much attention, as well as her first commissions to plan rose gardens for others.

In 1906 the Footes moved elsewhere in Marblehead and, after her husband's death in 1918, Foote expanded her rose work. She bought adjoining properties until she owned about four acres, and her collection of roses eventually included about 10,000 specimens. The effect of such a quantity of roses was intensified by her unusual growing techniques, often commented on by nationally known rosarians who visited her garden. A minimum of pruning, deep soil preparation, and heavy feeding produced plants of great height. Photographs of Foote in her garden usually show her dwarfed by closely set roses laden with blossoms.

Foote long refused to write about her own work, saying she was "too busy making rose gardens," but was often featured in contemporary garden magazines, and photographs of her gardens and references to her work made her an authority among professionals and amateurs alike. Some of her gardens were moderate in size; others were on a scale beyond grand. All of her gardens shown in the magazines are formal in design. The two examples most often cited are from the late 1920s and early 1930s: the rose garden at the Henry and Clara Ford estate in Dearborn, Michigan, and the one she created for Arthur and Harriet Curtiss James's Newport, Rhode Island, estate. On these two projects, as on many others, Foote collaborated with Herbert Kellaway, who had been trained in the office of Frederick Law Olm-

sted*. Foote also worked with Arthur Shurcliff* at the Richard and Florence Crane estate in Ipswich, Massachusetts, now owned by The Trustees of Reservations. Evidence suggests that Foote designed smaller gardens on her own.

In 1948, at the urging of Edward I. Farrington of the Massachusetts Horticultural Society, Foote published *Mrs. Foote's Rose Book,* in which she describes her meth-

Rose garden of Arthur Curtiss James and Harriet James, Newport, Rhode Island. Planned and planted by Harriett Foote and Herbert Kellaway, 1929–30. From *American Rose Annual,* 1932.

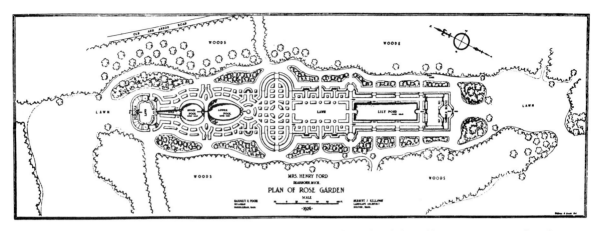

Plan of Rose Garden, Henry and Clara Ford estate, Dearborn, Michigan. Planned and planted by Harriett Foote and Herbert Kellaway, 1926. From *American Rose Annual*, 1930.

ods in detail although writes little about the gardens she planned for others.

Begg, Virginia Lopez. "Harriett Foote, 'Rose Woman of America'." *Labyrinth, Newsletter of the New England Garden History Society* 2 (Spring/Summer 1992), 10–12. A survey of Foote's career, placing her in the context of American landscape history in the 1890–1940 era.

Foote, Harriett Risley. *Mrs. Foote's Rose Book*. Introduction by Orton Loring Clark, Department of Botany, Massachusetts State College, Amherst. Boston: Charles T. Branford, 1948. Published when Foote was 84; a description of her cultural methods and an annotated list of roses she tested; foreword and first chapter give useful information on Foote's career, although she does not discuss specific gardens.

Mills, Reverend Edmund M. "A Pilgrimage to the Rose-Gardens of the Pilgrims." In *The American Rose Annual, 1924*, 134–137. Harrisburg, Pa.: American Rose Society, 1924. Includes "Mrs. Foote's Wonderful Roses" by Horace McFarland; both Mills and McFarland write about the June 1923 visit of several hundred ARS members to Foote's own garden and to several others for which she was responsible; 3 photographs, including one of the Crane estate in Ipswich, Mass.

Virginia Lopez Begg

FORDYCE, SAMUEL WESLEY
(1840–1919)
developer, conservationist, railroad builder

Samuel Wesley Fordyce was born in Senecaville, Ohio, and received his education at North Illinois University in Henry, Illinois. At age twenty, he was appointed station agent on the Central Ohio Railway, his introduction to a lifetime connection with railroads. When the Civil War broke out, he was instrumental in organizing and then enlisting in Company B, First Ohio Cavalry Volunteers, where he served throughout the war. At the close of the war he married Susan Chadick, established a banking house in Huntsville, Alabama, and became interested in political and community affairs. After ten years in Huntsville, Fordyce was forced by failing health to go to Hot Springs, Arkansas. Only six months of treatment at the then-primitive spa area returned him to health, and in 1876 he moved his family and business interests to Hot Springs.

Samuel W. Fordyce in Union Army uniform, c. 1861–62.
Courtesy Samuel W. Fordyce IV.

Fordyce recognized the city's possibilities as a national health resort and was instrumental in persuading President Ulysses S. Grant to add the mountains adjacent to the Hot Springs Creek corridor to federal park land. Under Fordyce's influence, Congress also passed a bill to construct the Army and Navy Hospital at the government reservation, the first to house both Confederate and Union soldiers. His financial support led to the development of leading hotels, one of which, the Arlington, still stands.

Fordyce developed water, gas, and electric light plants and a streetcar system in the city, constructed buildings, and later was instrumental in fostering recreational facilities to attract tourists as well as invalids. He secured the protection of the Hot Springs Creek corridor and the old-growth forests, where he initially planned hiking trails and other pedestrian ways. The golf course Fordyce established featured some of the first grass greens in the country. He was also responsible for the original design and governance guidelines for the bathhouses and services in the Spa City. (The Fordyce Bathhouse remains, today used as the interpretive center for the National Park Service.) Despite his lack of formal training, Fordyce successfully dealt with practical design problems and engineering concerns at a professional level. When the need arose, he brought well-known designers into what was essentially the American frontier.

Fordyce's influence was far-reaching, eventually garnering him the presidency of the St. Louis Southwestern Railway, known as the Cotton Belt Line. He also chaired the American Rio Grande Land and Irrigation Company of Texas, which operated the largest canal irrigation sys-

Arlington Hotel, Hot Springs, Arkansas, rebuilt 1914–15 after fire. Courtesy Samuel W. Fordyce IV.

tem in the United States. This concern offered five years of reduced land and irrigation development costs for pioneer families who moved to the Rio Grande Valley to establish farms. Fordyce knew the area well, having personally presided over construction of 10,000 miles of railway in the Southwest, spending months at a time exposed to the elements and the rigors of directing the work.

He continued to work tirelessly when he moved to St. Louis for railroad business, organizing the Laclede Light and Power Company and the Jefferson Hotel Company. His home was on Washington Terrace, one of the private streets north of Forest Park, a part of a large group of property owners whose homes represented a concentrated example of fine American domestic architecture in St. Louis during the second half of the nineteenth century.

Fordyce died in Atlantic City, New Jersey.

Brittenum, Judy Byrd. "Signposts for Determining Distinguished, Non-professional Landsmen Using Three Case Studies: Thomas Jefferson, Charlottesville, Virginia; George Washington Vanderbilt, Asheville, North Carolina; Samuel Wesley Fordyce, Hot Springs National Park, Arkansas." *Proceedings of the Council of Educators in Landscape Architecture*, Mississippi State University, Gulfport, 1994. A comparative analysis of three men, not trained as designers themselves, who significantly affected the quality and use of good design in their three historic cities.

Fordyce, Samuel Wesley. *Autobiography*. Fayetteville: University of Arkansas Special Collections, 1919. Remembrances of a remarkable life, dedicated to his son, John Rison Fordyce, the year before his death.

Paige, John C., and Laura Soulliere Harrison. *Out of the Vapors: A Social and Architectural History of Bathhouse Row*. Washington, D.C.: GPO, 1987. A definitive work about the development of Hot Springs and its bathhouses; the cultural, economic, and social history of the city with information related to the Fordyce family.

Three repositories have materials concerning Fordyce: The Hot Springs National Park Architectural / Technical Drawing and Map Collection, 1875–1900, Fordyce Bathhouse, Hot Springs, Arkansas, includes most early documentation of the hot springs and adjacent lands; the collection comprises 864 documents including plans, maps, and architectural and technical drawings. The Fordyce Papers: 1865–1922, Arkansas History Commission, Little Rock, includes a large volume of manuscripts, transcripts, photos, and other items. The Mary D. Hudgins Collection, Special Collections Division of the University of Arkansas Library, Fayetteville, holds material including scrapbooks, photographs, letters, and ephemera dealing with the Fordyce family.

Judy Byrd Brittenum

FOWLER, ROBERT LUDLOW, JR.
(1887–1973)
landscape architect

Robert Ludlow Fowler Jr. was born in New York City. Graduating from Columbia University in 1909, Fowler worked as a banker in New York and London until the outbreak of World War I. From 1919 to 1921 he attended the School of Landscape Architecture at Harvard University, subsequently opening his own practice in New York. Fowler's avocation was painting, in watercolor and oil, and drawing, in pen-and-ink and pencil, architectural and landscape details viewed during his travels abroad.

In his art, Fowler strove for a sense of balance and harmony of color. The discipline of painting and design-ing a composition provided great insight when viewing a landscape and enabled him to "see" the intended composition. In a 1938 article for *Real Gardening*, Fowler stated his belief that the raw materials available to the landscape architect provided him with the tools to create "a living picture—or rather, a series of pictures" meant to be experienced from different viewpoints. As he explained in a 1956 article for the *Patent Trader*, he believed that in both art and nature, "the simpler the decoration, the purer the form." He maintained that to achieve "maximum use and beauty with ever-changing materials the

Robert Ludlow Fowler Jr. mowing the lawn. Courtesy Angela W. Fowler.

designer must be a master of pictorial composition." The two most important influences on Fowler's design work were his love for painting and composition and his understanding of nature.

Specializing in residential planning, Fowler primarily designed private gardens during the Country Place era before World War II. Most of his projects were clustered in New York and Connecticut and include the estates of Mr. and Mrs. Geraldlyn Redmond in Bronxville, New York (c. 1924; James O'Connor, architect); Mr. and Mrs. Henry J. Whitehouse in Mt. Kisco, New York (c. 1937–1938; Mott B. Schmidt, architect); Mr. and Mrs. David Rockefeller in Tarrytown, New York (c. 1945–1955); and Averell Harriman in Arden, New York. Fowler's most impressive residential design was for his own estate in Katonah, New York (now the home of Mr. and Mrs. Ralph Lauren), which he developed over forty years. His major institutional work was the campus for the Reader's Digest Publishing Company in Pleasantville, New York (c. 1929–1930). Fowler frequently worked with such renowned architects as O'Connor, Schmidt, Delano & Aldrich, and McKim, Mead & White.

The "great lawn" at west end of Fowler residence, c. 1930. Photo Van Anda. Courtesy Angela W. Fowler.

A knowledge and understanding of the "character" of plant materials was a critical aspect of Fowler's design philosophy. It enabled him to create gardens that "look[ed] as though [they] had grown up by a natural sequence of events rather than by human direction." Fowler's gardens usually were extensions of the house or man-made element in the landscape and were intended to "harmonize with its architecture and character, so that when both are considered together (as they should be) a feeling of unity and harmony is realized." In the design for the gardens at Theodore Kiendl's residence in Bronxville, New York (c. 1927–1928), the informal aspect of the house (designed by Delano & Aldrich) dictated the overall approach he applied to the landscape, but by infusing enough formal elements into the design, Fowler also achieved a landscape of contrast, thereby giving the scheme greater depth and interest.

Fowler believed that a landscape architect should carefully seek out the design most appropriate for the architecture and site and its intended use. His approach to landscape architecture also blended the basic characteristics of the four schools of thought dominant at that time: French, Italian, English, and Japanese. The strict formality and linear qualities of the French and Italian styles suffused with the picturesque, though controlled, informality of the English gardenesque approach were frequently reflected in his design solutions. In addition, Fowler was intrigued by the Japanese ability to create in miniature landscapes that were "artificial without being affected" and to enhance and expand "on Nature's lines without being too realistic."

Fowler was a Fellow of the American Society of Landscape Architects and briefly served as its president. He died in Katonah, New York.

Fowler, Robert Ludlow, Jr. "Home and Garden in the Manner of the Colonial." *American Landscape Architect* 4, no. 4 (1931), 32–35. Article on the estate of Geraldyn Redmond, Brookville, N.Y., with photos.

Fowler, Robert Ludlow, Jr. "Mature Effects on a Difficult Site." *American Landscape Architect* 7, no. 1 (1932), 28–29. Article on the estate of Theodore Kiendl, Bronxville, N.Y., with photos, including cover.

Fowler, Robert Ludlow, Jr. "Principles of the Formal Garden." *Real Gardening* 1 (October 1938), 59–65.

Angela W. Fowler and Robert L. Fowler

FROST, PAUL RUBENS
(1883–1957)
landscape architect

Paul R. Frost was born in Cambridge, Massachusetts, the son of George Albert Frost, a noted Boston artist, and Adelia Dunham Frost. He was a graduate of Cambridge Latin School and Harvard College (A.B., 1907). In 1908 he worked in the New York office of Charles Platt*, assisting with planting at the Harold McCormick estate in Lake Forest, Illinois; the William G. Mather estate in Cleveland; and others. He was employed by Olmsted Brothers* in 1909 and again in 1910, giving most of his attention to the Boston Metropolitan Park System.

In 1912, Frost took an extended trip to Europe, where he visited gardens in the vicinity of Rome and Florence. He also completed a course on garden cities offered by London University at Hampstead Garden Suburb. The following year, he traveled to the southern United States, spending time at the plantations along the Ashley River,

including Magnolia Plantation, near Charleston, South Carolina. Frost served in a medical unit in France during World War I. (In 1930 he returned to Great Britain and visited several estates in England and Scotland.)

Frost opened an office in Harvard Square in 1914 and remained in practice in Cambridge for the rest of his life. He shared office space with a Harvard classmate, the city planner Arthur Comey. Although Frost's early interests were suburban subdivisions and garden city planning, he eventually specialized in designing gardens, especially small suburban gardens. A lifelong member of the Massachusetts Horticultural Society, Frost was highly knowledgeable about plant materials. He lectured occasionally at the Rhode Island School of Design in Providence and at the Cambridge School of Architecture and Landscape Architecture.

Paul Frost garden, Cambridge, Massachusetts. From ASLA, *Illustrations of Works of Members*, 1931.

Relatively few projects by Frost have been identified. They include the Judge Seth Gage garden in Weathersfield, Vermont (c. 1910–1912); the Mrs. George W. Pierce garden in Cambridge (c. 1914); the redesign of Longfellow Park, also in Cambridge (1915); the courtyard of the Chestnut Street Apartments in Boston (by 1922); and an herb garden for the Jeremiah Lee mansion in Marblehead, Massachusetts (c. 1938). At Shawme Farm, the George O. Dexter estate in Sandwich, Massachusetts, Frost acted as a consultant from about 1924 to 1943; his actual design work there was probably limited, and no plans have survived, but he advised his client on the rare rhododendrons that were Dexter's consuming interest. Perhaps Frost's most characteristic design was his own garden on a small cul-de-sac near Harvard Square, which he designed and cultivated between 1921 and 1953. Frost died in Boston.

Frost, Paul. "The Evolution of a Garden: Some Noteworthy Experiments for Farsighted Gardeners." *House Beautiful*, June 1924, 641–643, 693–696. Frost's description of his garden in Cambridge and his horticul-

tural "experiments"; illustrated with a plan by Frost and several photographs, probably also by him.

Scudder, Winthrop S. *The Longfellow Memorial Association, 1822–1922: An Historical Sketch.* Cambridge, Mass.: Longfellow Memorial Association / Cosmos Press, 1922. A discussion of the association and Longfellow Park in Cambridge, with reference to Charles Eliot's* initial landscape design and Frost's redesign; illustrated with two photographs by Frost.

Zaitzevsky, Cynthia. "Paul R. Frost of Cambridge: An Introduction to His Life and Work." *Journal of the New England Garden History Society* 2 (September 1992), 10–19. Discusses all the projects by Frost known to the author in 1992 in the context of his life; illustrated with photographs and plans, some previously unpublished.

No central repository exists for Paul Frost, but considerable correspondence and a few plans are located in the Olmsted Associates Records, Manuscript Division, Library of Congress, Washington, D.C.

Cynthia Zaitzevsky

GALLAGHER, PERCIVAL
(1874–1934)
landscape architect

Percival Gallagher was born in South Boston. After graduating from Boston English High School, he studied horticulture at Harvard's Bussey Institution, supplementing his education by observing plants at the Arnold Arboretum and by taking classes in the Fine Art program at Harvard, where he met Frederick Law Olmsted Jr*. After graduating from Harvard in 1894, Gallagher went to work for Olmsted's father's firm, Olmsted*, Olmsted* & Eliot*, the most prominent in the country. The senior Olmsted retired in 1895, one year after Gallagher's arrival.

For ten years Gallagher worked for the Olmsted firm on several important projects, including the restoration of the plantings on the Capitol grounds in Washington, D.C. He left the Olmsteds in 1904 to open his own firm in partnership with James Sturgis Pray*, a prominent Boston practitioner who was later chairman of the Department of Landscape Architecture at Harvard. Gallagher, however, was overwhelmed by the administration involved in running his own firm, and after two years he returned to the Olmsted operation, this time to remain. (Gallagher's former firm then changed its name to Pray, Hubbard* & White.)

Gallagher occupied a comfortable niche in the large and well-run Olmsted office, where he supervised his own projects and eventually became a full partner, in 1927, when the business expanded. Because all the Olmsted firm's design work was recorded without reference to specific individuals, several important designers operating under its name—Gallagher among them—have only recently been given recognition for their accomplishments.

Gallagher's talents were less wide ranging than those of his bosses, who excelled in park, city, and land use planning; yet he possessed, in the younger Olmsted's view, a keen artistic discrimination and a freedom from "that self-centered bias which warps the judgment of so many artists." The combination of his artistic talent, horticultural acumen, interpersonal skills, and modest, unassuming temperament served Gallagher well in dealing with his strong-minded colleagues, clients, and the architects with whom he was often asked to collaborate, men such as Bertram Goodhue, A. Stewart Walker, and Leon N. Gillette. Despite their understated qualities, Gallagher's landscape designs—particularly those done for country places—were distinctive, especially their planting designs.

Gallagher's most extensive estate work took place on Long Island, where three large and complex projects stand out from among the many he did there: Ormston, in Lattingtown, owned by John Edward Aldred (1912–1934); the George Baker estate in Glen Cove (1912–1933); and the H. H. Rogers estate in Southampton (1914–1942, completed by other members of the firm after Gallagher's death). At Ormston, Gallagher successfully subdued his clients' wishes for a more flamboyant, architecturally determined design. At the Rogers estate, where he worked with Walker and Gillette, Italian ornament proliferated unrestrainedly. Photographs by Mattie Edwards Hewitt record sumptuous, flower-filled beds, pools, a long grape-covered pergola, and an indoor swimming pool in the Pompeian style. It was Gallagher's most frequently published work, credited "Olmsted Brothers."

Gallagher's design, c. 1920, for Oldfields, the Indianapolis home of Hugh Landon, is a fine and particularly well preserved example of a more understated Country Place style, and now a part of the Indianapolis Museum

Percival Gallagher. Courtesy National Park Service, Frederick Law Olmsted National Historic Site.

of Art. There, Gallagher combined several standard features of a country estate layout, including a winding approach, broad front lawn, formal rose garden, and wild garden. Within this format, however, he created imaginative opportunities to incorporate an unusually wide array of flowers and shrubs.

Gallagher's ability to visualize planting arrangements through several seasons and from several points of view led to particularly effective planting schemes for parks and park systems, too. He worked on several in the northern counties of New Jersey—Essex, Union, and Passaic—and at League Island Park in Philadelphia. Gallagher also served as a consultant to many college campuses, where in Olmsted's words, he "solved special problems." These included Bryn Mawr, Haverford, Swarthmore, Vassar, Duke University, and Phillips Academy in Andover, Massachusetts.

During the last decade of his life, Gallagher suffered chronic ill health. He died in 1934, at the age of fifty-nine.

———————

Karson, Robin. "Report on the Life's Work of Percival Gallagher." Report for Indianapolis Museum of Art, 1993.

Chronicles Gallagher's professional activities and evaluates his design for Oldfields (part of the museum property) in the context of similar projects by him.

"The Landscape of Ormston." Olmsted office paper. A 14-page narrative, subtitled "A Brief Account of the Country Seat of Mr. J. E. Aldred in the Village of Lattingtown on Long Island"; engagingly written and sophisticated analysis of one of Gallagher's most important estate designs.

Olmsted, Frederick Law, Jr. "A Minute in the Life of Percival Gallagher." *Landscape Architecture* 24 (April 1934), 167–168. Obituary in which Olmsted pays tribute to Gallagher's "forty years of quiet, unassuming devotion to high ideals in the practice of his art."

Gallagher's work is documented by correspondence held in the Frederick Law Olmsted Papers of the Library of Congress, Washington, D.C., and by photographs, plans, drawings, and plant lists at the Frederick Law Olmsted National Historic Site (National Park Service), Brookline, Massachusetts. Jobs are listed by number rather than designer.

———————

Robin Karson

GEIFFERT, ALFRED, JR.
(1890–1957)
landscape architect

Alfred Geiffert Jr. was born in Cincinnati, Ohio. Soon after, his family moved to Jersey City, New Jersey, where he spent his childhood and young adult years. Having marshlands for a playground and outdoor classroom, Geiffert learned to appreciate the natural environment. In 1908, at age eighteen, with no formal education in landscape architecture, he went to work as an apprentice for the landscape architect Ferruccio Vitale* in New York City.

Geiffert took extension courses in horticulture and landscape design at Columbia University while apprenticing for Vitale, though to his dismay he never received a degree. He then joined Vitale as an associate and was made a partner in 1917, along with Arthur F. Brinckerhoff. The three practiced as a team until 1924, when

Brinckerhoff left to pursue his own practice. Geiffert and Vitale worked together until Vitale's premature death in 1933, after which Geiffert maintained the practice alone for another twenty-four years, still under the name of Vitale & Geiffert. In 1946 his son, Alfred III, joined him as a partner.

Geiffert was responsible for a large variety of work—from parks, town plans, subdivisions, and hundreds of residential properties, to schools and colleges, industrial and institutional projects, housing developments, hospitals, and, later in his career, shopping centers. His approach to creating natural landscapes is echoed in his 1924 essay, "The Making of a Rock Garden," for the *Bulletin of the Garden Club of America*. The secret to creating a naturalistic rock garden, he explains, is to learn from nature itself.

Landon K. Thorne country estate and summer residence, Bay Shore, New York. From *New York ASLA Yearbook and Catalog,* 1929.

Thorne country estate and summer residence. From *New York ASLA Yearbook and Catalog,* 1929.

National Gallery of Art, Washington, D.C. From *Landscape Architecture*, April 1941.

One account of his Quarry Garden at the country estate of Horatio Gates Lloyd in Philadelphia describes the planting as "hardly seem[ing] to have been designed at all."

Much of Vitale & Geiffert's work was photographed by Samuel Gottscho and William Schleisner and featured in *Landscape Architecture* and *Country Life in America*. The formal garden conceived for the new Tudor mansion house (by John Russell Pope) at Skylands, Ringwood, New Jersey, the residence of Clarence McKenzie Lewis, was completed by the firm in 1927; ten years later, the project won a place in the annual exhibit of the Architectural League of New York. The gardens were designed as a series of terraces laid out on a subordinate axis from the house to serve as the main vista to the hills beyond. In 1938, *Landscape Architecture* featured another of the firm's significant commissions, Canterbury Farms, the residence of Col. and Mrs. Albert E. Pierce at Warrenton, Virginia. Strategic placement of terraces along axial paths that project from the main house and point in the direction of great distant views had become a distinguishing characteristic of their designs.

Other extant garden projects attributed to Geiffert are the Anthony Campagna estate, Riverdale, New York (masonry drives, swimming pool complex, orangerie, and greenhouse); the Arthur V. Davis estate, Mill Neck, New York; the Clarence Dillion residence, Far Hills, New Jersey (2-mile entrance drive, indoor and outdoor tennis courts and swimming pools, brick walled gardens); the Edwin Fish estate, Locust Valley, New York; the Isaac Guggenheim estate, Villa Carola, Sands Point, New York; the G. Beekman Hoppin residence, Four Winds, Oyster Bay,

New York; the Alexandra Emery Moore McKay (Benjamin Moore) estate, Chelsea, Syosett, New York; the Carl J. Schmidlapp estate, Mill Neck, New York; the Zalmon G. Simmons residence, Greenwich, Connecticut (landscape of mature trees, stone walls, stone steps, reflecting pools built in solid granite rock); the Owen R. Skelton residence, Grosse Pointe, Michigan; the Mrs. Dodge Sloane gardens, Locust Valley, New York; and the Myron C. Taylor estate, Underhill Farm, Lattingtown, New York (6-acre lake, 65 acres of meadow and woodland).

As the landscape architect for the National Gallery of Art in Washington, Geiffert described the project in 1941 as "an interesting problem of the use of plant materials in connection with a building of such scale on a site of so superior importance." The use of a simple palette of plant materials was chosen to blend with the existing scale, form, texture, and pattern of the urban setting. Much of the original design survives today, including the grandiose cascade of wisteria along the south facade's perimeter wall.

In the postwar years, Geiffert took on more urban and planning work. Fresh Meadows, New York, a planned community, was a project for the New York Life Insurance Company (1948). In the tradition of his contemporaries Clarence Stein and Henry Wright*, Geiffert, the consulting landscape architect, was responsible for creating a new urban community with an instant sense of neighborhood. His technique was to plant hundreds of new trees in addition to preserving existing mature ones. Today Fresh Meadows is recognized by critics as an excellent example of community planning.

Geiffert was a member of the American Fine Arts Society, the Architectural League, and the Civil Service Reform Association, among other arts and civic organizations, and served on juries of the American Academy in Rome. He was president of the New York chapter of the American Society of Landscape Architects from 1928 to 1932 and secretary of the ASLA from 1937 to 1938. He practiced until his death in 1957.

———————————

"Alfred Geiffert, Jr. December 22, 1890–August 26, 1957. A Biographical Minute." *Landscape Architecture* 48 (October 1957), 48–49. A brief biography and a description of Geiffert's personal accomplishments and contributions to the profession.

MacKay, Robert B., Anthony Baker, and Carol A. Traynor, eds. *Long Island Country Houses and Their Architects,* *1860–1940.* New York: Norton, 1997. An extensive summary of residential work by architects and landscape architects during the County Place era, with brief summaries of hundreds of projects, including estate work by Vitale & Geiffert.

Newton, Norman T. *Design on the Land: The Development of Landscape Architecture.* Cambridge: Belknap Press of Harvard University Press, 1971. A historical overview of the development of landscape architecture, from ancient times to urban planning in the late nineteenth century, Newton, who worked briefly for Vitale & Geiffert, recounts the accomplishments of his two colleagues.

———————————

Laurie E. Hempton

GIBBS, GEORGE, JR.
(1878–1950)
landscape architect

George Gibbs Jr., born in Riverton, Kentucky, credited his early ambition to become a landscape architect to the influence of B. M. Watson, then head of Harvard's Bussey Institution, whom Gibbs had met when he was a child in Plymouth, Massachusetts. Gibbs received his first S.B. from the University of Illinois in 1900 and another in landscape architecture in 1904 from Harvard University, where he was a student of Frederick Law Olmsted Jr.* Armed with a letter of introduction to Edouard André, the eminent French landscape architect, Gibbs then traveled in Europe, studying notable parks and gardens. On his return in 1905, he joined the Olmsted Brothers* office in Brookline, Massachusetts, where he worked until 1914 on a range of projects across the country. During these years, in addition to work in Chicago on the Southside playground parks; in Fall River, Massachusetts; and for the Denver Mountain Park system, Gibbs was involved in planning for several educational institutions, including the Bennett School in Irvington-on-Hudson, New York; the Ypsilanti (Michigan) Normal School; and Lafayette College in Easton, Pennsylvania. Returning to his roots, he played a major role in design of the grounds for Berea College in Berea, Kentucky.

At the end of 1914, Gibbs became an expert investigator for the City Planning Board of Boston, analyzing methods to make the North End and East Boston "more habitable and more navigable"; he published his results

George Gibbs, c. 1930s. Courtesy Betsy Gibbs.

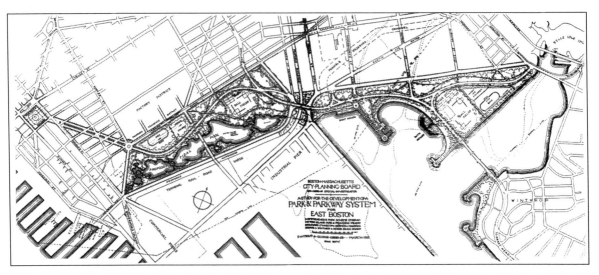

"Study for the Development of a Park and Parkway System for East Boston, March 1915." February 1915. From *East Boston: A Survey and a Comprehensive Plan, Report of the City Planning Board, Boston, Mass.*

in *East Boston: A Survey and Comprehensive Plan* (1916). Following the analytic form that Olmsted Jr. used in his many city planning reports, Gibbs examined the various neighborhoods, their ethnic and social features, their topographical, architectural, recreational, educational, and transportation amenities or disadvantages, and their economic and legal issues. His recommendations for individual districts and streets were based on plans for concentrated future occupancy of the entire area, including the still swampy waterfront, all linked by a comprehensive system of thoroughfares. His major concern, however, was "to protect both public and private property interests from injury through misplaced development." In contemporary projects for the "greening" of East Boston, some of Gibbs's park ideas are finally being achieved.

In 1917, Gibbs became an officer in the Construction Division of the U.S. Army, in charge of camp planning for Army and National Guard cantonments, which eventually housed about 400,000 men. From 1921 to 1923 he lived in France with his young family as a civilian employee of the army, overseeing the planning and

Bessemer Park, Chicago, 1907. Designed by Olmsted Brothers. Photo George Gibbs. Courtesy National Park Service, Frederick Law Olmsted National Historic Site.

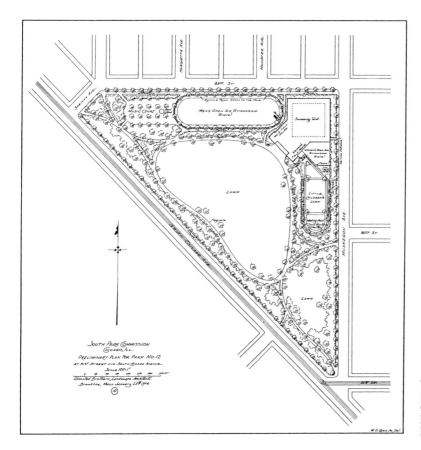

"Preliminary Plan for Park No. 12"
[Bessemer Park], January 25, 1904.
Courtesy National Park Service,
Frederick Law Olmsted National
Historic Site.

construction of American cemeteries in France, Belgium, and England for the National Commission of Fine Arts, in conjunction with the American Graves Registration Service of the Army Quartermaster Corps.

On his return to the United States, Gibbs became a chief assistant in the Olmsted office in Palos Verdes, California, supervising development in that community as well as in other Olmsted subdivision developments from California to Vancouver, British Columbia. The Palos Verdes work was particularly challenging, as it required designing for the needs and services of several different communities and a major road system on topographically complex, geologically unstable land.

When the Depression slowed design work, Gibbs was employed by the U.S. Forest Service, reporting in 1933 on the Kings River Canyon project in the Sierra Nevada. (This extraordinary wilderness area, described by John Muir in 1891, was the subject of a struggle between water power interests and conservationists in-

cluding Olmsted Jr. who wanted it for a national park, which it finally became in 1940.) In 1934, Gibbs joined the Civilian Conservation Corps, at first overseeing projects in California and then managing the Omaha office, which was in charge of camps in seven western states. Although he generally supported the work of developing national public properties, Gibbs expressed concern that there was not enough skilled planning, especially for landscape aesthetics, in advance of construction.

In 1936 he returned to California to supervise CCC projects from the San Francisco office, working on master plans for northern state parks, particularly for the Redwood Highway and Wild Cat Canyon until 1938. At that time, he moved back to Palos Verdes, opening his own office (the Olmsted western office had closed in 1937). He specialized in large-scale subdivisions in the Los Angeles area, and continued to manage some Olmsted firm work on the West Coast, such as the Beverly-Arnaz

Land Company in Los Angeles and various enterprises for F. A. Vanderlip. In conjunction with the firm, he designed a botanic garden for Susanna Bixby Bryant at Rancho Santa Ana in Long Beach. At his death, he was working on plans for projects in the greater Los Angeles area, for the Portuguese Bend Beach Club, Jordon Downs, and Marine View Housing.

Known as a pragmatic practitioner of great energy, sound judgment, and organizational ability, Gibbs did not leave much of a written legacy other than his professional reports. The plans he worked on for the Olmsted firm, many signed with his unique logo of interlocking G's, reveal his technical skill. Well respected in the field as a generous adviser and co-worker, he was elected a Fellow of the American Society of Landscape Architects in 1919.

Gibbs died in Palos Verdes at the age of seventy-one.

Gibbs, George, Jr. *East Boston: A Survey and a Comprehensive Plan.* Report of the City Planning Board, Boston, Mass., 1916. Analyzes the needs and solutions concerning streets, open space, and transportation and other municipal services for East Boston, a then rapidly growing section across the harbor from the downtown business district.

Gibbs, George, Jr. "Historical Statement Section of Advisory Engineer on Camp Planning." Engineering Division, Construction Division of the U.S. Army, 1917. Typescript report on the development of military housing with typical plans for railroad terminals, sewer systems, etc. for the Army, National Guard, and Officers Training school.

[Harvard College]. *Fiftieth Anniversary Report of the Class of 1903.* Cambridge, Mass.: Printed at the University, 1953. Retrospective on Gibbs and his work by his Olmsted colleagues Edward Clark Whiting* and Hammond Sadler.

Arleyn Levee

GILLETTE, CHARLES FREEMAN
(1886–1969)
landscape architect

Charles Freeman Gillette was born in Chippewa Falls, Wisconsin, the youngest of ten children. Gillette's family was of very modest means, and he had to work his way through high school in Madison. He never attended a college or university.

In 1909, after experimenting with several vocations, including teaching high school and nursing in a mental institution, Gillette became an apprentice in the landscape architecture firm of Warren Manning* in Boston. This decision was influenced by a love of landscape encouraged by his father, a farmer and herbalist, and by Gillette's observation while a nurse that mental patients were often aided by exposure to pastoral landscapes and gardens.

Gillette distinguished himself in the Manning firm and was chosen to supervise the construction of Man-

Charles Freeman Gillette. Courtesy Virginia State Library and Archives.

Sunken garden, Agecroft Hall, designed 1928. Photo Reuben Rainey.

ning's innovative plan for Richmond College (1911) in Westhampton, Virginia. Then, in 1912, a wealthy client sponsored Gillette's two-month tour of the major gardens and parks of Great Britain and Europe. He left the Manning office that same year and opened his own practice in Richmond, Virginia, where he lived the rest of his life.

He maintained a small professional office with one or two assistants. During his 56-year career, he designed approximately 2,500 projects, the majority of which were in Virginia and North Carolina, with a few in the Midwest and Northeast. Gillette's work as a designer of residential site plans comprised about two-thirds of his commissions; notable projects include Virginia House and Agecroft Hall in Richmond. His remaining commissions consisted of site plans for residential communities, hospitals, churches, country clubs, private colleges, secondary schools, historic garden restorations, and commercial and industrial properties.

Gillette's design vocabulary was shaped by the eclecticism prevalent in American landscape architecture at the turn of the century, which would persist in most of the profession throughout the Country Place Era. This eclecticism had many sources, ranging from A. J. Downing's* interpretation of Humphrey Repton and the theoretician John Claudius Loudon to Mariana Griswold Van Rensselaer's* essays in *Garden and Forest* and the widely influential design work of Charles Platt*. It was codified in Henry Hubbard* and Theodora Kimball's *Introduction to the Study of Landscape Design*, published in 1917, which became the standard text in the schools as well as the bible of many practitioners. Hubbard and Kimball was one of the few books on design theory in Gillette's library.

The particular form of eclecticism espoused by Gillette and most of his peers was a blend of formal design principles derived from English and European Renaissance traditions and the so-called informal aes-

Garden with statue, Agecroft Hall, designed 1928. Photo Reuben Rainey.

thetic of the eighteenth-century English landscape gardening school and Loudon's "gardenesque" vocabulary. For example, in a typical residential site plan, the grounds in the immediate vicinity of the residence would be treated in a formal fashion, with terraces axially organized along sight lines to provide a transition from the dwelling to the landscape, as well as to create functional, well-defined volumetric spaces to fulfill the particular needs of the client. This design strategy was in part a response to the predominant trend in late nineteenth-century and early twentieth-century American architecture of creating period revival buildings. Such buildings called for a formal treatment of the site—garden terraces and crisply defined outdoor spaces in harmony with the materials and design of the building. Like their architect counterparts, American landscape architects avoided the exact replication of historical styles; rather they interpreted them freely and imaginatively, using regional plants and

construction materials. The lawn of the residence provided a transition to the other component of this eclecticism, the informal vocabulary. Its soft contours and undulating lines were relegated to the fringes of the site, which frequently were treated in a parklike manner, often combined with a nineteenth-century "gardenesque" emphasis on the display of rare and exotic plant species.

Gillette's eclecticism contained strong regional overtones as well. Although French, English, and Italian Renaissance traditions continued to assert themselves in his work, they were supplemented with themes from eighteenth-century Virginia gardens. These themes included an axial organization of multilevel terraces; highly crafted masonry construction; elegant, finely detailed garden structures; and a planting design that emphasized fragrance, seasonal color, shade, and strong volumetric expression through the use of massed evergreens. Gillette was also deeply influenced by the collaborative work of

Gertrude Jekyll and Sir Edwin Lutyens; he espoused Jekyll's theory of color harmony and frequent use of the herbaceous border.

Gillette's work received national recognition, with examples of his residential site plans appearing in the annual exhibit of the Architectural League of New York in 1937 and 1938. He was elected a Fellow of the American Society of Landscape Architects in 1933, and his work was chosen on several occasions to appear in various publications of that organization. Gillette devoted his career entirely to professional practice, publishing only two short newspaper articles on planting design, two articles in *Landscape Architecture*, and a brief book review. He died in Richmond.

Lilly, Rachel M., and Reuben M. Rainey. "The Country Place Era in Virginia: The Residential Site Planning of Charles F. Gillette." *Landscape Journal* 11 (Fall 1992), 99–115. Gillette's residential site design principles accompanied by photos and analytical drawings.

Longest, George C. *Genius in the Garden: Charles F. Gillette and Landscape Architecture in Virginia*. Richmond: Virginia State Library and Archives, 1992. Definitive study of Gillette's life and work, with numerous illustrations.

The Charles F. Gillette Collection, The Virginia State Library and Archives, Richmond, contains an extensive although incomplete collection of Gillette's project drawings, client files, and family photographs.

Reuben Rainey

GILLETTE, GENEVIEVE
(1898–1986)
landscape architect, conservationist

Genevieve Gillette was instrumental in the establishment of two national lakeshores and over thirty state parks in Michigan, the preservation of several wilderness areas, and the passage of bills for parks and recreation areas. She was a highly visible lobbyist at the Michigan state capitol, pushing for protection of wilderness areas, and also ran her own private landscape architecture office in Ann Arbor, designing college campuses, parks, and residences.

Gillette was raised on a farm near Lansing, Michigan, until the death of her father, when she and her mother moved to Lansing, where she graduated from high school. In 1920 she became the first woman to graduate from Michigan Agricultural College with a major in landscape architecture. She secured a job in Jens Jensen's* office in Chicago, where her duties included

Genevieve Gillette with President Lyndon B. Johnson. Courtesy Genevieve Gillette Papers, Michigan Historical Collection, Bentley Historical Library, University of Michigan, Ann Arbor.

Sleeping Bear Dunes National Seashore, between Frankfort and Leland on shore of Lake Michigan. Photo Robert E. Grese.

helping to prepare drawings and working with the Friends of the Native Landscape, a group of conservationists headed by Jensen who were promoting state parks in Illinois. Working for Jensen, Gillette learned to appreciate the natural landscape and to design in a style less formal than the Beaux Arts tradition she learned at college. Jensen encouraged her to return to Michigan to help develop state parks, a new concept for most states in the 1920s. Gillette had graduated with P. J. Hoffmaster, who had recently been hired to develop a state park system in Michigan, and whenever she was in Lansing the two spent hours discussing ideas and inspecting landscapes they were interested in securing for the system.

After leaving Jensen's office, Gillette spent part of a year in Lakeland, Florida, working for the chamber of commerce as a consultant on city development. She was homesick for the change of seasons, however, and returned to Detroit, where she joined a florist business, assisting with landscape work generated by its nursery. She was responsible for advising developers on the landscaping of subdivision homes, and her suggestion that landscaping be done for several demonstration homes at a time to make them more appealing to buyers was considered a brilliant marketing idea. Through this job, she met many wealthy Detroit residents who later contributed to her various causes, including parks and conservation. She served as a garden instructor for the Detroit Park and Recreation Department, working with

the public school system and helping thousands of the city residents with thrift gardens during the Depression. Being a practical farmer's daughter, she taught them how to can and store their products, too.

Also during the Depression, Gillette managed the development of Westacres, a low-cost government housing project with community gardens, near Pontiac. She was responsible for the implementation of the project from the large-scale grading of the site and development of a lake to the selection of street trees. She kept this job for eight years, then served as a community consultant for the next seventeen. She also opened a private practice in the Ann Arbor area which she maintained for over thirty years, retaining such major clients as Albion College, Ferris State College, the City of Big Rapids, the sponsors of Westacres, and Star Commonwealth Schools, a nationally prominent educational center for troubled children. Her office remained small, operated out of her home with the help of one or two employees.

Gillette's major interest was always the development of state parks, and together she and Hoffmaster built a large park system in Michigan. But he died young from a heart attack, and without his guidance and ability to obtain financial support from the state, the parks began to fall into disrepair. Gillette responded by helping to form the Michigan State Parks Association, asking every organization with an interest in parks to join, including the Automobile Club, the League of Women Voters, the Fed-

erated Garden Clubs of the State of Michigan, the Federated Women's Club, the Park and Forestry Associations, the Michigan Botanical Club, and the Natural Areas Council. She served as president for ten years, lobbying the state legislature for improvements to the park system and conservation of Michigan's natural resources. In 1964, Michigan's senator Phillip Hart invited her to Washington to help lobby for a land and water bill and to establish Sleeping Bear Dunes and Pictured Rocks as National Lakeshores. The following year, President Lyndon B. Johnson invited her to serve on a citizens' advisory committee to his Council on Recreation and Natural Beauty.

At Gillette's death, the *Detroit Free Press* called her "a saving angel to Michigan's natural beauty." Her estate provided a $300,000 trust for "acquiring land exhibiting certain natural and scenic qualities" and giving the property to the public. Thompson's Harbor State Park, near Roger City in Presque Ile County, was her last gift to the people of Michigan.

President's Council on Recreation and Natural Beauty. *From Sea to Shining Sea: A Report on the American Environment—Our Natural Heritage.* Washington, D.C.: Superintendent of Documents, 1968. Report prepared by the committee that Gillette worked on with Laurance Rockefeller.

Rutz, Miriam. "Genevieve Gillette: From Thrift Gardens to National Parks." In *Landscape Architecture in the Midwest,* ed. William H. Tishler. Champaign: University of Illinois Press, in press.

The Genevieve Gillette Papers, 1883–1980, including 36 audiotapes with transcriptions, are held in the Michigan Historical Collection at the Bentley Historical Library, University of Michigan, Ann Arbor.

Miriam E. Rutz

GREELY, ROSE ISHBEL
(1887–1969)
landscape architect, architect

Rose Ishbel Greely was born in Washington, D.C. She attended the National Cathedral School for Girls in Washington, Abbott Academy in Andover, Massachusetts, and graduated from Finch School in New York City in 1905. Greely studied interior decorating at the Art Institute of Chicago, metalwork in Washington, and silver repoussé work and enameling on metal in Florence, Italy. She also studied farming at the University of Maryland and had her poetry published in the *Atlantic* and *Youth's Companion* magazines.

In 1916, Greely decided to combine her enthusiasms for design and horticulture in a program in landscape architecture at the new Cambridge School for Domestic Architecture and Landscape Architecture for Women in Cambridge, Massachusetts. She graduated in 1920 with certificates in both landscape architecture and architecture.

Greely subsequently worked in Boston as a drafts-

Rose Ishbel Greely, 1906. Courtesy Greely family.

Residence of Frances Sortwell, Washington, D.C. Photo Frances Benjamin Johnson. Courtesy Library of Congress.

man in the office of Fletcher Steele* until her return to Washington in 1923. There she worked for Horace W. Peaslee, the architect and designer of Meridian Hill Park. In 1925 she became the first licensed female architect in Washington and opened her own landscape architecture practice. She maintained a small office with a secretary, an assistant, and two draftsmen first in downtown Washington and later in her home in Georgetown until her retirement in 1960.

Greely specialized in residential design with an emphasis on the integration of house and garden. During her forty-year career, she designed over 500 landscapes as well as several architectural projects. Her commissions came from Washington, Virginia, and Maryland, and from farther afield—New England, Arkansas, Georgia, and

New Mexico, where her local clients owned second or third homes. Greely also undertook a number of large-scale public design projects in the 1940s and 1950s, including the grounds of military installations, secondary schools, suburban developments, government housing projects, embassies, and museums. Several original Greely gardens are extant in the Washington area.

Greely's work was recognized by her peers during her lifetime. She was the only woman to be a member of American Society of Landscape Architects' Advisory Committee for the Williamsburg Restoration Project (1929–1935) and was elected a Fellow of the society in 1936. Greely also published widely in *Landscape Architecture Magazine, House Beautiful, House and Garden, Country Life*, the Garden Club of America *Bulletin*, and

Residence of Ruth Hanna McCormick Simms, Washington, D.C. Photo Frances Benjamin Johnson. Courtesy Library of Congress.

newspapers including the *Washington Star*, the *Washington Post*, and the *Christian Science Monitor*.

Greely's city gardens depended on principles of strict spatial organization, which extended the architectural lines of the house into the garden. In her country house designs, Greely drew on English and Olmstedian principles, which dictated softer lines and the use of increasingly informal materials as distance from the house increased. She often borrowed from the surrounding landscape, incorporating existing landforms and plants into her design. Her use of Arts and Crafts regional styles (particularly the Spanish and Colonial Revival styles) and native plants and ornament softened the garden architecture throughout her designs.

Greely insisted on the highest quality of workmanship and an attention to detail which imbued her designs with great technical and stylistic integrity. Her projects were also exceptionally well built—a factor that has aided the survival of many.

Greely, Rose. I. "Why Should the Garden Have Design? Some of the Factors, Both Practical and Aesthetic That Influence of the Design of the Grounds." *House Beautiful*, November 1932, 100–103. The first in a series of four articles outlining Greely's design theories and her Arts and Crafts principles; subsequent articles appeared in the December 1932 (pp. 75–78), January 1933 (pp. 59–61), and February 1933 (pp. 128–129) issues.

Lawson, Joanne Seale. "Rose Ishbel Greely, A Woman's Touch." *Washington History Magazine*, Spring 1998, 46–69. An extensive bibliographical article about Greely, including an analysis of her education and work, quotations from her writings, plans and photos of her projects.

Palache, Mary. A Garden on a Narrow City Lot in Georgetown: Belonging to and Designed by Rose Greely." *House Beautiful*, November 1932, 316–317. Greely's garden; plan and photos.

Joanne Seale Lawson

GREENLEAF, JAMES L.
(1857–1933)
landscape architect

James Leal Greenleaf was born in Kortright, in New York's Delaware County. His father, who came from a New York City family of some prominence, had settled on a Catskills farm because of failing health. To have spent much of his youth in the country was, he later said, of "inestimable value" to him. It instilled in him a love for landscape which influenced the development of both his career and his public concerns, as well as his pursuit of landscape painting as an avocation.

Like many of his generation, Greenleaf came to landscape architecture from another discipline. After graduating in 1880 as a civil engineer from the School of Mines of Columbia College, he pursued that profession as both teacher and practitioner for nearly fifteen years. At the School of Mines he served as instructor for nine years before becoming adjunct professor in civil engineering. Appointed Special Agent for the Tenth Census, he prepared reports on the waterpower of the Mississippi River and the Niagara Falls and River, among others.

In 1894, Greenleaf left the Columbia faculty to open his own civil engineering practice in New York City. Before long, guided by "an unconscious feeling for the art involved," as he later described it, he began designing small-scale landscapes in the New York region. His first important commission came in the late 1890s, with James B. Duke's aspiration to convert the flat acres of his Somerville, New Jersey, estate into parkland. The project drew on Greenleaf's engineering skills while giving him an introduction to planting on a large scale.

In the years 1900–1920, Greenleaf's design work on some thirty estate projects earned him respect and admiration as one of the foremost practitioners of the Country Place era in landscape architecture. In establishing a close relationship between house and garden, he adhered

to design principles prevalent at the time. His work demonstrated meticulous care for proportion and scale—which he considered essential—and a skill at accomplishing a smooth transition from the geometric areas close to the house to the more naturalistic, parklike forms of the larger landscape. Most significant, through his approach to planting as "building up of pictures," he attained a mastery of placement and spatial composition.

Most of Greenleaf's commissions for country places came from enclaves of wealth on Long Island and in Westchester County, New Jersey, and Connecticut. With few

James L. Greenleaf by Catherine Critcher, c. 1924. Courtesy National Academy of Design, New York.

Green Garden, Killenworth, George D. Pratt residence, Glen Cove, Long Island, c. 1930. John Duer Scott, colorist. Courtesy Smithsonian Institution, Archives of the American Gardens.

exceptions (such as the Italian Garden at Frederick Van-derbilt's estate in Hyde Park, New York), these were com-prehensive projects. In accommodating his clients' desire for instant effects as well as his own goal of immediate and powerful structuring of space, Greenleaf pioneered the practice of moving large trees into newly designed landscapes. He used tall red cedars to replicate the Italian cypress effect, a technique recurrent in his estate work (best exemplified at Blairsden, C. Ledyard Blair's estate in New Jersey) and much imitated at the time.

Greenleaf's best and most influential designs for country places combined Beaux Arts precepts with a skill at the mediation of the formal and informal elements of design. Achieved through expansive plantings of ever-greens to soften rigid symmetries, as well as careful, seemingly random placement of trees to break up the rectilinearity of the plan, this legacy is most evident in his design for the Green Garden at Killenworth, George D.

Pratt's estate on Long Island. There the geometric regu-larity of a square space surrounding a central pool is moderated by the asymmetrical planting of large elms and softened by an abundant yet balanced use of ever-greens. The "green garden" concept is found in many of Greenleaf's estate designs, as is his signature technique of massing conifers to soften the harshness of masonry.

In 1921, the Architectural League of New York awarded Greenleaf the Medal of Honor in Landscape Architecture for "Blairsden and Country Places at Glen Cove, Long Island" (Killenworth and other Pratt estates). The recognition came just as he was withdrawing from estate work to concentrate on public projects, which oc-cupied him for the last dozen years of his life.

From 1918 to 1927, Greenleaf served as the land-scape architect member of the National Commission of Fine Arts and in this capacity exerted influence over the development of many sites in Washington, D.C., most

Hillside staircase, Blairsden, C. Ledyard Blair residence, Peapack, New Jersey, 1903. Wirts Brothers, frontispiece to Barr Ferree, *American Estates and Gardens*. Courtesy of Museum of the City of New York.

notably the grounds of the Lincoln Memorial. His recommendations called for a simple and stately planting about the east wall, balanced rather than symmetrical, with irregular rounded masses of evergreen foliage, the nucleus consisting of large specimens in box and yew. Greenleaf's advice was followed, as was his design concept for the west side of the memorial (implemented a decade later in conjunction with Arlington Memorial Bridge planting, which he directed as consulting landscape architect).

Although Washington and its surroundings were his primary concern, Greenleaf's service on the commission also took him to Europe to study the American war cemeteries and make recommendations for their development. In the American West, following a November 1922 conference at Yosemite, he advised national park

officials on naturalistic design of masonry for guardrails and bridges. Concerns for preservation of scenery led to his involvement with the state park movement, and to his repeated warnings against recreational development encroaching on preservation efforts.

Greenleaf took up the issue of landscape abuse, in wilderness as well as urban centers, in numerous public appearances during the 1920s. Unabashedly an idealist, he saw in spirituality the guide to the harmonious coexistence of nature and art, and therefore to human's control of nature. In this context, he emphasized simplicity as essential to good design and exhorted landscape architects to unclutter their ways and enlarge their vision.

Greenleaf was untiring in his efforts to advance the recognition of his profession and to spur the attainment of high standards in its practice. Elected a Fellow of the American Society of Landscape Architects in 1904, he served as president of the New York chapter and a trustee of the society, and as its national president from 1923 to 1927. He represented the profession as vice president of the Architectural League of New York and served on the jury of the American Academy in Rome.

In the last ten years of his life Greenleaf devoted considerable time to his avocation of landscape painting, particularly in Italy and on the Isle of Skye. His canvases were exhibited at the National Academy of Design in New York.

Greenleaf died in Stamford, Connecticut, at the age of seventy-five.

Greenleaf, James L. "Landscape—Its Use and Its Abuse." *American Magazine of Art* 13 (September 1922). A paper read at the Thirteenth Annual Convention of the American Federation of Arts at Washington, D.C., a call for awakening public opinion to the destruction of landscape in the process of civic development.

Greenleaf, James L. "Large Tree Planting." In *Transactions of the American Society of Landscape Architects, 1899–1908*. A paper sent out to Fellows of the ASLA in advance of the meeting of March 14, 1905, for discussion at that meeting; describes methods of transplanting large trees and considers their viability in a variety of circumstances.

Greenleaf, James L. "The Place, the Man, and the Garden." Address before The New York Farmers, February 16, 1915, at the New York Public Library. An 18-page speech, accompanied by slides, 16 of which are reproduced; outlines Greenleaf's design philosophy, using as examples several of his own projects as well as images of gardens in Europe and America.

Ania Bass

GRIFFIN, WALTER BURLEY
(1876–1937)
architect, landscape architect

Walter Burley Griffin was born in Maywood, Illinois, and grew up in suburban Chicago, where he attended the public schools of Oak Park and was admitted to the University of Illinois at Urbana-Champaign (1895). There Griffin was educated in both architecture and landscape gardening, and following graduation with a B.S. in architecture (1899), he embarked upon a career in both fields.

By September 1901, Griffin was at work on his first independent landscape architectural commission, a plan for the forty-acre campus of the Eastern Illinois State Normal School at Charleston. During that same year, Frank Lloyd Wright hired Griffin to work in his Oak Park studio, and, in addition to his architecturally related capacities, Griffin served as Wright's landscape architect. This relationship was an ongoing, collaborative one.

Walter Burley Griffin, c. 1912. Courtesy Donald Leslie Johnson and Mitchell Library, Sydney, Australia.

J. G. Melson Dwelling, Mason City, Iowa, 1912. Courtesy Mary and Leigh Block Museum of Art, Northwestern University, Gift of Marion Mahony Griffin, 1985.

On receipt of a commission, it is likely that Wright conceived the site design and organization and Griffin subsequently prepared detailed planting designs and specifications. His work for Wright is exemplified in his 1905 landscape design for the Darwin Martin house in Buffalo. Apparently because of a salary dispute, Griffin left the Oak Park studio later that year. Although he had executed independent commissions while in Wright's

Bryant Fleming. Lincliff estate. Louisville, Kentucky.
Photo Charles A. Birnbaum.

Bryant Fleming. Cheekwood. Nashville, Tennessee.
Courtesy Smithsonian Institution,
Archives of American Gardens.

Charles F. Gillette. Agecroft Hall. Richmond, Virginia. Photo Reuben Rainey.

Charles F. Gillette.
Agecroft Hall. Richmond, Virginia.
Photo Reuben Rainey.

Genevieve Gillette. Sleeping Bear
Dunes National Seashore.
Lake Michigan.
Photo Robert E. Grese.

James L. Greenleaf. Killenworth.
Glen Cove, Long Island.
John Duer Scott, colorist.
Courtesy Smithsonian Institution,
Archives of the American Gardens

Ralph E. Griswold.
Point State Park.
Pittsburgh, Pennsylvania.
Courtesy GWSM, Inc.

William H. Hall. Sharon Quarters, Golden Gate Park.
San Francisco, California. Photo David Streatfield.

Hare & Hare.
Country Club Plaza.
Kansas City, Missouri.
Photo John W. Gutowski.
Courtesy Cydney Millstein.

Alden Hopkins.
University of Virginia Pavilion Gardens.
Charlottesville, Virginia.
Photo Charles A. Birnbaum.

Alden Hopkins. Gunston Hall Plantation.
Mason Neck, Virginia.
Photo Charles Baptie. Courtesy Board
of Regents, Gunston Hall.

Roland Hoyt. Presidio Park. San Diego, California. Photo Carol Greentree.

employ, Griffin was now able to devote his energies solely to his own practice.

The first four years of Griffin's independent practice were dominated by commissions for more modest dwellings. Practicing under the title "architect and landscape architect," he typically prepared landscape designs as an extension of his architectural services and, less frequently, as separate commissions.

By 1913, larger-scale community and campus plans had come to dominate his landscape architectural practice. This work is best represented by his campus plan for the Northern Illinois State Normal School at DeKalb (1906), and community plans such as Trier Center Neighborhood at Winnetka, Illinois (1912–1913), and Rock Crest-Rock Glen at Mason City, Iowa (1912–1913). Ultimately, Griffin prepared designs for at least thirty-five landscape architecture commissions in the United States, including four campus and fourteen community plans.

Nature was the dominant, shaping force of Griffin's philosophy and approach to landscape design, and he saw the primary language of nature as an essentially geometric one. Consequently, in his designs, the relationship between building and site was one of architectural order. This was expressed in his characteristic synthesis of the "naturalistic" with the "formal" in landscape design.

Griffin's growing interest in the comprehensive design of environments larger in scope and scale than a single residential property motivated him to enter the 1911 Canberra Competition. He was invited to confer with Australian government representatives about his Canberra plan, and in 1913, and was offered the position of Federal Capital Director of Design and Construction. No doubt enthusiastic at the opportunity to oversee his plan's implementation, Griffin accepted and eventually relocated permanently to Australia. Despite his attempt to maintain an office in Chicago, his professional standing in the United States soon declined, and by the time of his accidental death in India (1937), he had been virtually forgotten here.

Griffin, Walter Burley. "Community and Town Planning Work of Walter Burley Griffin," *Western Architect* 19 (August 1913). A comprehensive source for Griffin's work and philosophy of landscape architecture; numerous plans and photographs.

Vernon, Christopher. "An 'Accidental' Australian: Walter Burley Griffin's Australian-American Landscape Art." In Jeff Turnbull and Peter Navaretti, eds., *The Griffins in Australia and India: The Complete Works and Projects of Walter Burley Griffin and Marion Mahony Griffin*. Melbourne: Miegunyah Press at Melbourne University Press, 1998. Focuses on the first years of Griffin's landscape architecture practice in Australia, including designs produced there for American sites.

Vernon, Christopher. "The Landscape Art of Walter Burley Griffin." In Anne Watson, ed., *Beyond Architecture: Marion Mahony and Walter Burley Griffin in America, Australia, and India*. Sydney: Powerhouse Publishing, 1998. Explores Griffin's landscape architecture, emphasizing the transference of his American-born design approach to Australia and its transformation there.

Christopher Vernon

GRISWOLD, RALPH E.
(1894–1981)
landscape architect

Ralph Griswold was born in Warren, Ohio, a small, rural town where his father ran a department store. Griswold was single-minded about pursuing a career in landscape design from the time he first encountered the profession in a novel by Robert W. Chambers, in which the hero, a landscape designer, "wore white flannels and sat on a terrace discussing garden plans with the heroine."

Griswold graduated from Cornell University with a B.S. in landscape art in 1916. His graduate work at Cornell was interrupted by service in the World War I American Expeditionary Forces. After the Armistice, he spent six months in Paris studying Beaux Arts and Parisian city planning and gardens. Returning to the United States, he resumed his graduate work at Cornell, leaving in 1919

D. B. Phillips garden, Butler, Pennsylvania, completed 1930. Lithograph by Griswold. Courtesy GWSM, Inc.

with a master of landscape design to join Bryant Fleming's* office in Buffalo.

After winning the Rome Prize in 1920, Griswold spent three years at the American Academy in Rome as the Fellow of Landscape Architecture, communicating often with Fredrick Law Olmsted Jr.*, his academic adviser in the United States. He traveled around Europe, produced measured drawings of three previously undocumented Italian Renaissance gardens, and sketched and photographed 1,500 garden details. Griswold's academy experience was to have a strong philosophical and intellectual influence on his career. Returning from Rome in 1923, he joined the large and thriving firm of A. D. Taylor* in Cleveland.

In 1927, Griswold moved to Pittsburgh to establish his own practice and acquired a strong reputation for residential design. In the deep years of the Depression, when private work steadily shrank, Griswold collaborated on the design for Chatham Village there, which is still considered an outstanding example of a successful housing project. This private row-housing development exemplified Griswold's mastery of spatial design and restrained planting.

He then turned his attention to public work, taking advantage of the federal unemployment relief programs.

Anzio-Nettuno Military Cemetery, Nettuno, Italy (completed 1955), c. 1965. Courtesy GWSM, Inc.

From 1934 to 1945, Griswold was superintendent of the Pittsburgh Bureau of Parks, the first landscape architect to be employed by the city, supplementing his salary with private commissions. In 1938 he took on a project in an area that would be a major preoccupation in his later years: historic landscape preservation. Considered the most competent landscape architect able to undertake the required historical research, Griswold was commissioned to restore the garden and the grounds of the Old Economy settlement, built 1825–1834, just outside Pittsburgh. He deemed this settlement one of the most important early nineteenth-century land planning and design achievements in the United States.

While at the Bureau of Parks, Griswold made every possible attempt to revitalize the city's parks. He lobbied the city government, drew on private funding, and encouraged increased community awareness and use of the parks by providing for innovative entertainment,

recreation, and natural science education in them. Pittsburgh lagged far behind other cites in the administration and maintenance of its parks, and Griswold attempted to set up a comprehensive system. By 1945, however, Griswold, by then a Fellow of the American Society of Landscape Architects, essentially felt that he was an artist and could spend no more time on the political maneuverings necessary to that objective.

Soon after resigning from the Bureau of Parks, Griswold became involved in a project that engaged him for over twenty-five years, and which he considered his major and most lasting work. As part of a postwar city planning initiative, he collaborated on a development study of the Point State Park, in the area in downtown Pittsburgh where the two rivers, the Allegheny and the Monongahela, merge to form the Ohio. The Point Park project spearheaded the transformation of the downtown from a smoky, dying industrial area into a clean, re-

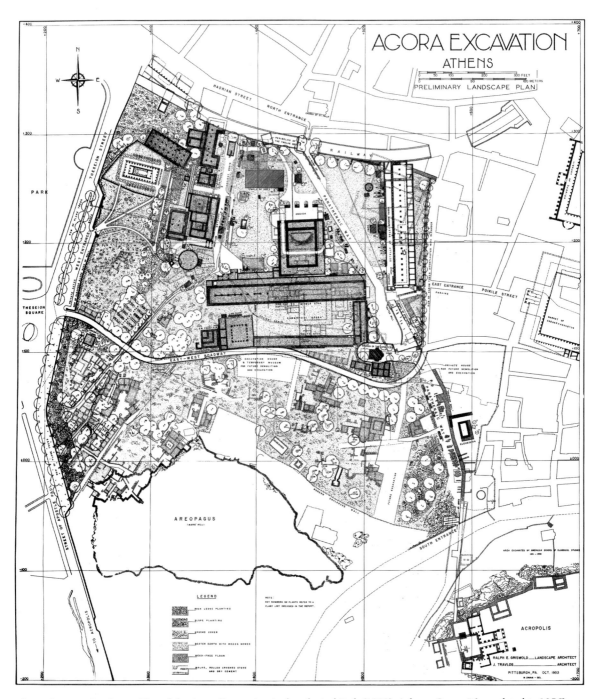

"The Preliminary Landscape Plan of the Agora Excavation Archaeological Park (1953), Athens, Greece" (completed in 1956). Courtesy GWSM, Inc.

Point State Park (designed 1946–1975), 1998. Courtesy GWSM, Inc.

vitalized "Renaissance" city. By 1953, Griswold and his team had developed the preliminary designs for what was termed the "ultra modern" Point Park. The design was based on rigorous historical research, and all its elements were aimed to convey the natural, military, and social history of the Point before 1800. Today Point Park is recognized as emblematic of the "new" Pittsburgh.

For a short period in 1949–1950, Griswold returned to the American Academy in Rome as the Landscape Architect in Residence while he developed landscape plans for the American burial ground at Anzio, the largest of the World War II cemeteries in Europe. He worked for the American Battle Monuments Commission from 1949 to 1955 and continued to visit the site until 1968, paying close attention to how the plantings were developing and being maintained.

At the age of nearly sixty, in 1953, Griswold went to Athens to work on the landscape of an archaeological park at the Agora, which had been excavated by the American School of Classical Studies. The Agora, located at the foot of the Acropolis, had served as the civic center from the sixth century B.C. to the third century C.E. Using only native plants mentioned in ancient Greek texts, Griswold's landscape plan pointed up the ancient layout of the area. For this project, which pioneered landscape architecture in Greece, he was awarded the Gold Cross of the Royal Order of George I by King Paul in 1956. While he worked on this project with the archaeologists, Griswold continually reflected

on how it would contribute to landscape architecture at a broader level: "I like to dream of the time when there will be landscape scholars who can take their place among scholars in historical research."

Griswold's passion for historical landscape research continued through his years (1956–1958) as a Research Fellow at Dumbarton Oaks (Harvard University). He worked on a "Biographical History of Garden Art," which, to his great disappointment, was never published. After his fellowship, Griswold continued his association with Dumbarton Oaks, working as a consultant to the garden and a member of the Garden Advisory committee on a redesign of the Ellipse and rehabilitation of several other garden elements.

In the early 1960s, Griswold moved to Williamsburg, Virginia, to do research on the gardens of Colonial Williamsburg. During this period, he was also the landscape consultant for the Garden Club of Virginia, leading them through four new projects, as well as the rehabilitation of the Pavilion gardens designed by Thomas Jefferson at the University of Virginia.

Throughout his career, landscape architecture remained for Griswold a high cultural art founded on rediscovery and reinvention. He died in 1981 at the age of eighty-six.

Griswold, Ralph E. "From Fort Pitt to Point Park." *Landscape Architecture* 46 (July 1956), 193–202. Written

ten years after the inception of the Point Park project and when it was one-third completed; relates the significance of the Point in Pittsburgh history and presents the conceptual and site design for Point Park which reconciled the historical and the practical engineering issues.

Griswold, Ralph E. "Landscape Architecture Pioneering in Greece." *Landscape Architecture* 47 (April 1957), 391–397. Discusses the practical problems and horticultural issues in the planting of the archaeological site at the Agora.

Nichols, Frederick Doveton, and Ralph E. Griswold. *Thomas Jefferson: Landscape Architect.* Charlottesville: University Press of Virginia, 1976. A book that Griswold co-authored with a professor of architecture at the University of Virginia and developed from his work with the Garden Club of Virginia; the first study that recognizes Jefferson as a landscape designer.

_____

Behula Shah

HALL, GEORGE DUFFIELD
(1877–1961)
landscape architect, planner

George Duffield Hall was born and raised in St. Louis. On graduation from Harvard in 1899, he spent a year traveling the world, returning with the desire to study landscape architecture. At the time no professional course in the field was offered at any university, so in the fall of 1900 he took drawing classes at the Massachusetts Institute of Technology, and the following year he studied the science and technology of farming, horticulture, and forestry at the Bussey Institution, the School of Agriculture and Horticulture of Harvard University. During this time, he also worked in the office of Charles Platt*, an architect and landscape architect so enthusiastic about Italian gardens that he convinced Hall to take a Mediterranean trip to study them.

In Platt's firm Hall met Franklin Brett, who had previously worked with Frederick Law Olmsted*. In 1903, Brett and Hall became partners, with an office first in Brookline and later in Boston. Brett oversaw design and planning work while Hall consulted with clients, architects, and contractors and supervised work on the ground. For fifteen years, the firm of Brett & Hall designed gardens, private estates, parks, subdivisions, cemeteries, and two cities—Prince Rupert and Prince George in British Colombia. For a time, the firm maintained a branch office in Montreal because it had so many Canadian commissions. In 1913, Hall and Brett were invited to join the American Society of Landscape Architects as Fellows, and Hall became active in the Boston chapter.

With American entry into World War I, the country needed planners experienced in the layout of new communities to provide temporary housing for thousands of men during training. In 1918, Brett & Hall was dissolved,

George Duffield Hall. Courtesy Orian Hallor Greene.

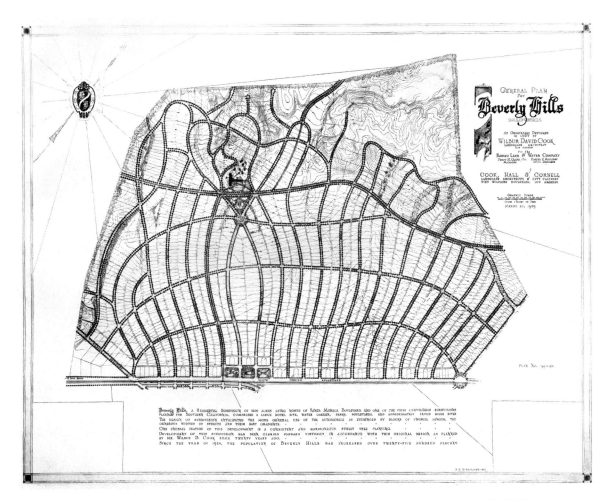

"General Plan for Beverly Hills, California" by Cook, Hall & Cornell, March 20, 1929. Courtesy Orian Hallor Hall.

and both men went to Washington, D.C. Hall served first with the War Department's Camp Planning Section and then became assistant Town Planner of Craddock, Virginia, for the U.S. Housing Corporation. In the Camp Planning Section, he met Wilbur David Cook, who had also worked in the Olmsted office. Cook had an extensive background in city, park, and campus planning in the East and, most recently, in California. There he had laid out Beverly Hills, assisted in the preliminary design for the San Diego Exposition and Palos Verde Estates with the Olmsted office, planned Exposition Park for the City of Los Angeles, and designed the grounds of many private estates, among them that of Howard E. Huntington.

After the war, Hall joined Cook in California, and in

1920 they formed the firm of Cook & Hall, Landscape Architects and City Planners. Ralph Cornell*, who joined them in 1924, later noted that Hall and Cook were the outstanding landscape architects in the Los Angeles of their day, especially in subdivision design. The firm planned private estates, Anaheim City Park, Monrovia City Park, parks in Whittier, and a 450-acre recreation park for the City of Long Beach. Subdivision plans included Eastridge in Whittier, Bird Rock in San Diego, Carthay Center on Wilshire Boulevard, Monte Mar Vista in Cheviot Hills, Montebello Park and Country Club, and Midwick View Estates in Monterey Park. The firm was employed to develop plans for a civic center in Los Angeles.

Hall became secretary of the Pacific Coast chapter of the ASLA in 1922, joining Cook, who had been one

Perspective drawing of Los Angeles Administration Center by Cook & Hall, 1925. Courtesy Orian Hallor Hall.

of the chapter's three charter members in 1919 and its first president. To publicize the profession and its importance in site planning and land management, he wrote several newspaper and journal articles. In the early 1920s, Hall served at his own expense on the Regional Planning Conference, the precursor to the Regional Planning Commission.

By 1933 the phenomenal growth of the Los Angeles region had come to a relative standstill, and Cook, Hall & Cornell was forced to dissolve. Hall and Cook initially went into government service as landscape architects, Hall with the Civilian Conservation Corps in Phoenix, Arizona. After a year or so, he returned to his home in Pasadena, where he worked for the city parks department and also for the Works Progress Administration on a landscape project at Devil's Gate Dam in the Arroyo Seco in Pasadena. He then began a private practice from his home, which he continued until his death.

Hall, George D. "The 'Freeway,' A New Thought for Subdividers." *Landscape Architecture* 21 (March 1931), 115–118. Analysis of the economic and recreational merits of a new type of artery for regional travel, the "freeway," which would reduce strip development and benefit subdivision planning.

Hall, George D. "The Future Prince Rupert as Conceived by the Landscape Architects." *Architectural Record*, August 1909, 97–106. Brett & Hall's plan to create a model city free from traffic congestion, with districts laid out—commerce, factory, wholesale, retail, business, and residential—at the terminal point of the Grand Trunk Pacific Railway.

Hall, George D. "Landscape Architecture in Los Angeles." *Southwest Builders and Contractors*, June 4, 1920, 11–12. Recommendation that Los Angeles as a metropolitan district be planned with a comprehensive boulevard system and chain of parks, urging cooperation of architects and landscape architects in the earliest stages of project development.

Meredith Kaplan

HALL, WILLIAM HAMMOND
(1846–1934)
engineer, surveyor, landscape architect, planner

William Hammond Hall was born in Hagerstown, Maryland. The family moved to San Francisco in 1850, but their losses in the fire of 1851 forced them to move on to Stockton, California, where his father reestablished his legal practice. Hall's education in a private academy was intended as a preparation for West Point, but this plan was abandoned with the outbreak of the Civil War. He therefore remained at the Stockton Academy until 1865, at which time he began a professional career as a draftsman in the U.S. Army Corps of Engineers. Hall was quickly advanced to the rank of assistant engineer and was given increasingly complex assignments of topographical surveys in Oregon and California.

In 1870, Hall was awarded the contract for the preparation of a topographic survey of Golden Gate Park in the western part of San Francisco, largely because of his army experience. An earlier proposal by Frederick Law Olmsted* observed that the cold summer fogs, accompanying strong winds, and shifting sandy soils made it an unlikely site for a large park. Olmsted instead proposed a long block-wide, depressed boulevard leading from San Francisco Bay to a small, protected park site. This proposal was rejected, however, and the platting of western San Francisco indicated a large rectangular park area clearly modeled on Central Park in New York, with a long, narrow attached panhandle.

Hall's intimate knowledge of the site gained during his surveying activities led to his subsequently obtaining the commission for preparing a plan for this 1,000-acre tract. Hall had minimal training as a designer, and his proposal attempted to replicate the pastoral character of Central Park but with the clear recognition of certain regional differences. Roads were to be paved with red granite to provide a sense of cheerfulness during the long spells of overcast gray weather, and all structures were to be surrounded by exterior porches, reflecting California's more benign climate. Hall took a scientific approach to the problem of reclaiming the sand dunes, surveying reclamation practices in Holland, Germany, Scotland, Denmark, and France and noting their dunes' physical and chemical nature and the prevailing wind patterns. His reclamation program, which was essentially a form of accelerated plant succession, was based on sand dune reclamation practices in Gascony.

Hall's plan, balancing scientific understanding with the aesthetic forms of the picturesque landscape tradi-

tion, was, according to Olmsted, the most ambitious and successful landscape reclamation project undertaken in America during the nineteenth century. Hall corresponded frequently with Olmsted, who provided advice on books in landscape theory and copies of reports of his own projects. Hall used these in his private practice, which he maintained during his tenure as park superintendent. Private projects included several subdivisions, a plan for the University of California campus at Berkeley which was partially implemented, and proposals for several estates on the San Francisco Peninsula and in Marin County. His plan for Berkeley proposed a campus of colleges arranged around a loop road and was quite unlike Olmsted's 1865 proposal for the College of California, with its integrated residential development. Apart from the subdivisions, which owe much to Olmsted's 1866 design for Riverside, none of these projects survive.

Hall served as superintendent of Golden Gate Park from 1871 to 1876, but was forced to resign as a result of dwindling financing and severe political pressure. However, he continued to serve, without compensation, as consulting engineer to the Park Commission. In this capacity, he was responsible for several buildings and projects, such as the Sharon Quarters (1888), one of the earliest playgrounds for children developed in the coun-

William Hammond Hall. Courtesy Bancroft Library, University of California, Berkeley.

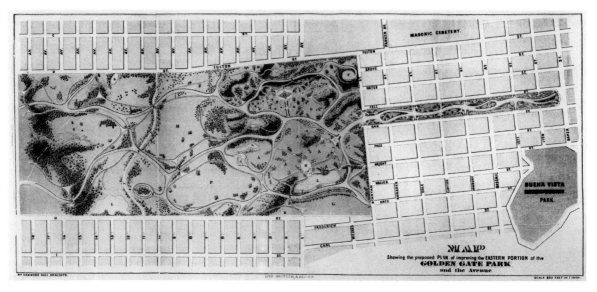

Plan of Golden Gate Park, San Francisco, 1872. Courtesy Bancroft Library, University of California, Berkeley.

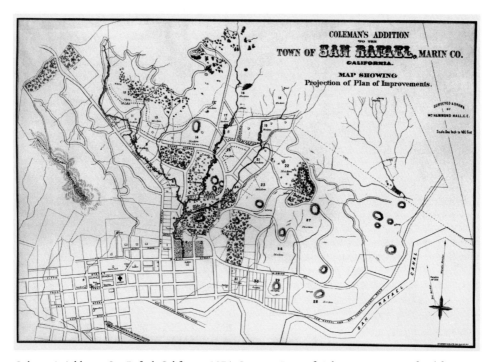

Coleman's Addition, San Rafael, California, 1874. Courtesy Bancroft Library, University of California, Berkeley.

Children's Playground, Golden Gate Park, San Francisco, 1888. Courtesy Worden Collection, Wells Fargo Bank History Room, San Francisco.

try. He also selected and trained John McLaren, a Scottish head gardener on a San Francisco Peninsula estate, to succeed him as park superintendent.

Between 1878 and 1888, Hall served as the first State Engineer of California. His major achievement during this period was to lay the groundwork for statewide water planning, water resource development, and irrigation. To this end he meticulously collected data and analyzed water legislation. Owing to political opposition, the greed of developers, and Hall's lack of tact and unwillingness to compromise, certain of his proposals were not accepted. Nevertheless, subsequent water resource planning early in the twentieth century was based

on his important and pioneering work. In recent years, he has been hailed as a "neglected prophet" of water planning.

During this time, Hall also prepared an in-depth examination of Yosemite Valley and wrote extensively on irrigation projects. In 1890 he went into private practice as a civil engineer. His work included numerous irrigation and hydroelectric projects in the United States, as well as in England, South Africa, and Russia, and a study for the Panama Canal. Despite his professional focus on engineering, he continued to fight for the preservation of Golden Gate Park as a democratic public open space, publishing at his own expense a pamphlet titled *The*

Sharon Quarters, Golden Gate Park, San Francisco. Photo David Streatfield.

Panama Pacific International Exposition Site: A Review of the Proposition to Use Part of Golden Gate Park (1911), which was intended to dissuade San Franciscan voters from holding the 1915 exposition in the park.

Hall's importance in landscape architecture is two-fold. His work as a landscape designer parallels that of Olmsted, and is a significant example of the early advocacy of regional landscape design. However, Hall went much further than Olmsted in exploring ecological principles as the basis for sand dune reclamation and the aesthetic dimensions of design. His advocacy of statewide water planning was also based on the careful use of scientific data and analysis and was an extremely enlightened early prophecy for a semi-arid region.

Starr, Kevin. *Material Dreams: Southern California through the 1920s.* New York: Oxford University Press, 1990, 7–14 and 18–19. An excellent and brief discussion of Hall's career as California State Engineer.

Streatfield, David C. "Shifting Sands," "Verdant Umbrageousness," and "The People's Park." Developments Series 1, no. 2 (1975), 15–36. A detailed analysis of Hall's various schemes for Golden Gate Park, emphasizing the proto-ecological character of his design approach; illustrated with archival plans and black-and-white photographs.

David Streatfield

HARE, SIDNEY J.
(1860–1938)
landscape architect

HARE, S. HERBERT
(1888–1960)
landscape architect

Sidney Hare was born in Louisville, Kentucky, and eight years later the family moved to Kansas City, Missouri, by riverboat. Hare received no formal landscape training, but as a high school student he studied horticulture, civil engineering, geology, surveying, and photography. From 1881 to 1896, Hare worked in the city engineer's

office, where he was introduced to George Kessler*, then a landscape engineer for Kansas City. This relationship inspired Hare's interest in landscape design.

In 1896, Hare resigned from his city job to become superintendent of Kansas City's Forest Hill Cemetery. The following year he spoke about cemetery design in

Sidney Hare, early 1920s, Kansas City, Missouri. Courtesy Western Historical Manuscript Collection, Kansas City.

S. Herbert Hare, n.d. Kansas City, Missouri. Courtesy Western Historical Manuscript Collection, Kansas City.

a national forum, the Association of American Cemetery Superintendents convention in Cleveland. At a subsequent convention in 1901, Hare discussed the cemetery as botanical garden, bird sanctuary, and arboretum—it may be the first such presentation on record in the design evolution of the modern cemetery. In accordance with his beliefs, Hare assembled at Forest Hill one of the most comprehensive collections of trees and shrubs in the Midwest.

Hare saw parallels between the landscape ideals of naturalistic parks and those of modern cemeteries. He was convinced that the large expanses of well-managed lawns with trees and shrub groups which characterized parks were also appropriate for contemporary burial grounds. For three decades he incorporated velvet lawns, groups of ornamental trees and shrubs, mirror lakes, curving roads and walks, and long vistas into the cemeteries he designed. By combining the distinctive features of parks and cemeteries, Hare helped establish precedents important in modern cemetery design.

Hare resigned his position at Forest Hill in 1902 to open his own landscape architecture office. During the first decade of the twentieth century, he established a successful business, partly owing to his 1897 article, "The Influence of Surroundings," which appeared in the widely read professional publication *Park and Cemetery*

and Landscape Gardening. Among his early projects were Cunningham Park, Joplin, Missouri, and Waterway Park and Parkwood Subdivision in Kansas City, Kansas (both 1907). He also designed grounds for institutions and cemeteries. Over twenty-five major projects in six states either had been completed or were under way by the time Hare's son joined him in partnership.

A plan for the Bethany Hospital grounds in Kansas City, dated 1910, confirms the year that the office became Hare & Hare. The new partner was fresh from studying landscape planning at Harvard University. With Frederick Law Olmsted Jr.* as his principal instructor, Herbert was among the first students in the United States to prepare formally for the new profession.

During their twenty-eight-year association, Sidney Hare continued to pursue park and cemetery projects while Herbert mastered the details of community planning and design. Herbert also worked as a consultant to city planning commissions throughout the Midwest. Early design jobs included Wagner Place, Jefferson City, Missouri (1913); Point Defiance Park, Tacoma, Washington (1914); the park and boulevard system, Kansas City, Kansas (1915); the campus of the University of Kansas, Lawrence (1913–1918); and several cemeteries, in addition to smaller private and public projects. Hare & Hare designs emphasized winding roads contoured to natural

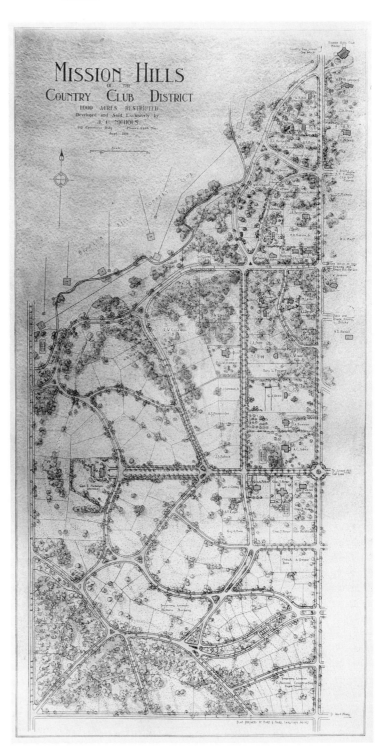

Mission Hills, Kansas, 1916. Courtesy
Western Historical Manuscript Collection,
Kansas City

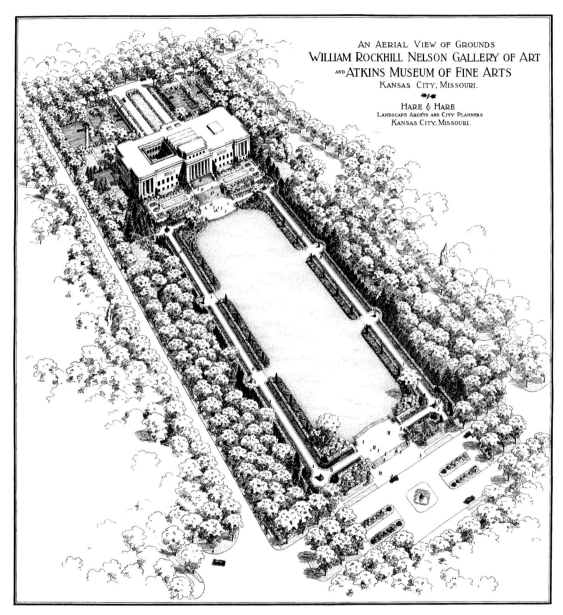

AN AERIAL VIEW OF GROUNDS
WILLIAM ROCKHILL NELSON GALLERY OF ART
AND ATKINS MUSEUM OF FINE ARTS
KANSAS CITY, MISSOURI.

HARE & HARE
LANDSCAPE ARCH'TS AND CITY PLANNERS
KANSAS CITY, MISSOURI.

William Rockhill Nelson Gallery of Art and Atkins Museum of Fine Arts, Kansas City, Missouri, 1930–1937. Courtesy Western Historical Manuscript Collection, Kansas City.

topography, the preservation of trees and valleys, and scenic vistas.

In 1913 the developer J. C. Nichols hired the Hares to work on the Country Club District in Kansas City, Missouri. In addition to laying out approximately 2,500 acres, the firm designed the grounds for many of the homes in the development, including some of the 5-acre estates that made up the original Mission Hills, across the state line in Johnson County, Kansas. Herbert was personally responsible for subdivision planning, for many of the detailed entrances and parks, and for creating appropriate settings for the sculpture that Nichols placed throughout his developments. By collaborating with Nichols on the master plan, the firm made the jump from "site scale" to "district scale" planning.

Most of Hare & Hare's private work ceased during World War I, with the exception of cemetery designs. Herbert designed military installations, including Camp Funston, Fort Riley, Kansas (1917), five camps and cantonments in the South, and projects for the U.S. Housing Corporation.

After the war, Hare & Hare collaborated with Kessler and Nichols on the plan for the new town of Longview, Washington, the largest pre-planned city of its time outside Washington, D.C. During the early 1920s, community planning and design changed appreciably in response to the needs of an increasingly industrial and technological society. Longview was created in 1922, one of the first manifestations of the new spirit. Hare & Hare received the design commission, with Kessler as landscape design consultant; Nichols was retained as realty consultant. Longview was a challenging assignment because of its scope: the plan included a central business district, three residential areas, suburban acreage, and a central manufacturing district and provided locations for two enor-

mous mills as well. It demonstrated Hare & Hare's expertise in city planning.

By the end of the 1920s, the firm's national reputation was secure. Projects including cemeteries, college campuses, subdivisions, parks, and military camps had been commissioned in twenty-eight states. Hare & Hare also collaborated with prominent Kansas City architect Edward Buehler Delk in planning the Country Club Plaza, yet another Nichols development in the city. Herbert began to spend much of his time in the public sector, as consultant to planning and parks commissions in cities such as Houston, Fort Worth, Dallas, and Oklahoma City. The Hares' appointment to finish Kessler's Kansas City commissions after his death in 1923 bore witness to Kessler's respect for and trust of the two men.

During the 1930s, the firm completed several Kansas City projects, including the Laura Conyers Smith Municipal Rose Garden in Loose Park and the setting for the Nelson Gallery of Art (1930–1937; now the Nelson-Atkins Museum of Art), as well as much work in other locations. Notable projects from this era include plans for state parks throughout Missouri, which began in 1937 and continued through the 1950s (Arrow Rock, Bennett Springs, Mark Twain, Table Rock, and Wallace); campuses for the Uni-

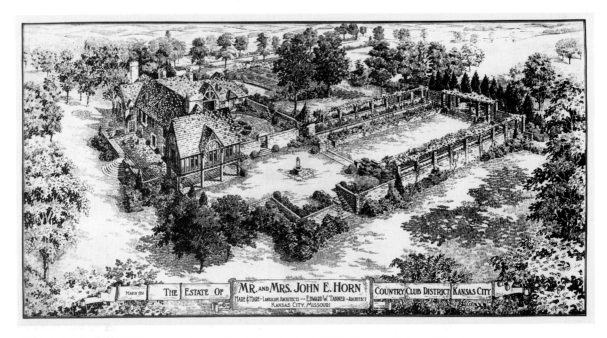

Aerial perspective of J. E. Horn estate, Kansas City, Missouri, March 1932. Courtesy Cydney Millstein.

J. C. Nichols Memorial Fountain, Country Club Plaza, Kansas City, Missouri, 1998. Photo John W. Gutowski. Courtesy Cydney Millstein.

versity of Houston (1937–1950), the University of Kansas Medical School, Kansas City (1934–1936), the University of Texas at Austin (1932–1939); and private developments in Wilmington, Delaware, and Houston.

World War II brought a change in the nature of the firm's commissions; its work in the early 1940s concentrated almost exclusively on government-subsidized projects including military housing. From 1945 through the 1950s, Hare & Hare undertook varied projects for the private sector in thirty-three states, Canada, and Costa Rica, including numerous campus plans; subdivisions in Missouri, Texas, Georgia, and Kansas; and the grounds for the Harry S. Truman Library (Independence, Missouri, 1956). In addition, planning and zoning studies became a large part of the firm's work.

Sidney Hare's national reputation as a leading authority on cemetery design led to his election as a Fellow of the American Society of Landscape Architects (1912). Herbert, also a Fellow, was active professionally too. He frequently lectured and published articles on English suburbs and European garden cities that served as models for city and regional planning. He was elected a Fellow of the American Institute of Park Executives and served as a director of the American Institute of Planners, as vice president of the ASLA in 1940, and as its president in 1944.

Hare, S. Herbert. "Planning of Industrial City of Longview, Washington." *Proceedings of the American Society of Civil Engineering* 53 (August 1927), 1177–1183. Discusses plan for the largest pre-planned city in the nation outside of Washington, D.C.

Hare, Sid J. "The Influence of Surroundings." *Park and Cemetery and Landscape Gardening*, September 1897.

Van Dyke, Bettina C. "The Evolution of 19th- and 20th-Century Cemetery Landscape Types as Exemplified by Hare & Hare's Cemetery Design." Master's thesis, Kansas State University, Manhattan, 1984. Analyzes the cemeteries that were designed by the firm during the three decades preceding the Depression; plans, drawings; extensive bibliography.

The Hare & Hare Company Papers, a collection spanning 1904–1979, are housed in the Western Historical Manuscript Collection, University of Missouri, Kansas City.

Cydney E. Millstein

HENDERSON, PETER
(1822–1890)
horticulturist, nursery owner, author

Peter Henderson was born in Pathhead, Scotland, near Edinburgh. He attended the local parish school and, at the age of sixteen, began a four-year apprenticeship at the gardens of Melville Castle. During this period, the Royal Botanical Society of Edinburgh awarded him a medal for the best herbarium collection of native and exotic plants.

In 1843, Henderson emigrated to the United States, where he found employment at a nursery owned by George Thorburn in Astoria, New York. Between 1843 and 1847 he worked for Thorburn; for Robert Buist, a prominent nurseryman, florist, and seedsman in Philadelphia; and as the estate gardener for Charles Spang of Pittsburgh. In 1847, in partnership with his brother James, Henderson started a market garden busi-

Peter Henderson. From *Garden and Farm Topics*, 1884.

Image from Henderson's seed catalogs.
Courtesy George De Vault.

ness in Jersey City, New Jersey. The partnership was dissolved after a few years, but Peter Henderson stayed in Jersey City and expanded the business to include a greenhouse florist enterprise. In 1864 he moved the business to South Bergen, New Jersey.

In 1853, as an outlet for the market garden and florist enterprise, he opened a New York City sales office, taking orders for plants and produce. In 1862 he moved the sales headquarters to the seed store owned by James Fleming and William Davidson, also in New York City, and the same year issued his first annual plant catalog. In 1865, Henderson purchased Davidson's share of the Fleming-Davidson seed store, and the firm was renamed Henderson & Fleming. After the dissolution of this partnership in 1871, he established the firm of Peter Henderson & Co. at 35-37 Cortlandt Street. About five years later, Henderson's sons, Alfred and Charles, joined him in this business, which remained in the family after his death. (In 1951 the firm merged with Stump & Walter; the merged company filed for bankruptcy in 1953.)

During Henderson's lifetime, Peter Henderson & Co. marketed flower and vegetable seeds, plants, bulbs, and garden, lawn, and landscape supplies. The company advertised that it could supply "everything for the garden." Under Henderson's leadership, the firm became a highly respected horticultural supplier, and introduced new ornamental and vegetable varieties into the trade through its widely distributed annual catalogs. Until about 1880, Henderson wrote all the material for the plant catalogs and some of the seed catalogs.

An active participant in trade associations, Henderson also helped reorganize the New York Horticultural Society and served on its executive committee. He also wrote prolifically. During the second half of the nineteenth century, he authored or co-authored six books and numerous articles for such leading agricultural and horticultural journals as *The Country Gentleman*, *Gardener's Monthly*, *The Horticulturalist*, *Hovey's Magazine of Horticulture*, *Moore's Rural New Yorker*, and *Tilton's Journal of Horticulture*. For many years he wrote a regular column as well for the monthly farm magazine *American Agriculturalist*. Two of his books, *Gardening for Profit* (1867) and *Practical Floriculture* (1869), were influential in assisting those who sought entry into commercial vegetable and flower production. He finished revising *Henderson's Handbook of Plants* just weeks before his death in 1890. Wilhelm Miller* stated in Liberty Hyde Bailey's* *Standard Cyclopedia of Horticulture* (1947 ed.): "Few men, if any, have done so much to simplify and improve methods of handling plants for commercial purposes. His greenhouses were an object lesson to many visitors, his methods were widely copied, and his business successes were the goal of ambitious market gardeners and florists, among whom he was for years the most commanding figure."

Henderson was not afraid to challenge the horticultural theory and practice of his day. He delighted in exposing charlatans who made unsubstantiated claims for horticultural products. He was an innovative experimenter and a keen scientific observer who thought in practical terms, and had a lifelong desire to pass along the knowledge he had gained, even to potential competitors.

Henderson died from pneumonia at his home in Jersey City.

Henderson, Peter. *Gardening for Pleasure: A Guide to the Amateur in the Fruit, Vegetable, and Flower Garden, with Full Directions for the Greenhouse, Conservatory, and Window Garden*. New York, 1875; rev. 1888. Advice on horticulture for the home gardener.

Henderson, Peter. *Gardening for Profit: A Guide to Successful Cultivation of the Market and Family Garden*. 1867. Rev. ed. Ed. George DeVault. Chillicothe, Ill.: American Botanist Booksellers, 1997. One of the first American books devoted to commercial production and marketing of vegetables. The revised edition includes a history of market gardening in America, special sections from Henderson's "Garden and Farm Topics," and a biography of Henderson.

An archival collection of Henderson material is housed at the Jersey City Library. It includes a 167-page manuscript about Henderson and Peter Henderson & Co. by Owen Grundy, a former city historian. Seed catalogs, magazine and newspaper articles, and correspondence are also included.

Robert F. Becker

HOPKINS, ALDEN
(1905–1960)
landscape architect

Alden Hopkins was born in Chepachet, Rhode Island, and was raised by his aunt, Elizabeth Hopkins. In 1928 he received his B.S. degree from Rhode Island State (now the University of Rhode Island). After serving briefly as a graduate assistant in the Department of Landscape

Architecture at Massachusetts Agricultural College (now the University of Massachusetts) at Amherst, he received an M.L.A. degree from the Harvard Graduate School of Design in 1934. From 1934 to 1937 he was a Garden Club of America Fellow at the American Academy in

Alden Hopkins. Courtesy Colonial Williamsburg.

Rome, where he won the prestigious Rome Prize. He then spent another year working in Italy before returning to the United States. With employment opportunities for landscape architects scarce during the Depression, Hopkins took a position in the Office of Research and Record at Mount Vernon, which gave him the opportunity to research all aspects of colonial life in Virginia.

In 1939–1941, Hopkins established his own practice in Washington, D.C., before accepting an offer from Colonial Williamsburg to become its first resident landscape architect. After only a year in this new position, he left for active duty in World War II, serving as a camouflage officer with the Marine Air Wing and using his skills to interpret aerial photographs and build terrain models. He furthered his understanding of the vernacular landscape observed in military reconnaissance by conducting intensive field investigations and making measured drawings in the same way he had recorded Italian gardens during his years in Rome. Based on material gathered in Japan, he published an article in January 1947 in *Landscape Architecture* titled "An Okinawan Farm Group: Memoranda from an Ex-Naval Officer's Notebook." (For his service, he was awarded the Bronze Star Medal with Combat "V" and Presidential Unit citation by the Marine Corps for forward combat.)

After the war, Hopkins resumed his position at Colonial Williamsburg. This was an exciting period of

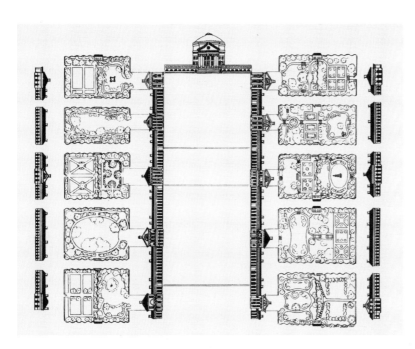

University of Virginia Pavilion Gardens by Mary Hall Betts. Courtesy Prints File, Special Collections Department, University of Virginia Library.

transition for the organization, which had initiated its restoration-reconstruction program in 1928, relying on the services of three consulting firms for design and planning: Perry, Shaw & Hepburn, Architects; Cleverdon, Varney & Pike, Engineers; and Arthur Shurcliff*, Landscape Architect. Lacking specific information about the historical layout of most of the Williamsburg town gardens, Shurcliff developed a palette of patterns, forms, and materials based on an intensive study of thirty-eight extant colonial Virginia gardens. He also relied heavily for information and inspiration on the 1782 "Frenchman's Map" of Williamsburg and eighteenth-century plans of North Carolina colonial towns and gardens drawn by French garden designer Claude Joseph Sauthier.

Following Hopkins's return to Williamsburg in 1946, the design and planning work was completed in-house by an expanding professional staff. Shurcliff remained involved in an advisory capacity, but Hopkins was the lead designer. Building on Shurcliff's methodology and period precedents, Hopkins thought of his work as garden restoration; the approach would not, however, fit the definition used in the historic preservation field today. Rather, Hopkins's and Shurcliff's designs reflected a style that later came to be called "Colonial Revival." With his own talent, scholarship, and deep familiarity with European gardens, Hopkins carried the Colonial Revival garden to new heights during these years. In Colonial Williamsburg, Hopkins's work can be seen in a series of gardens at the eastern end of the Duke of Gloucester Street: the Benjamin Powell Garden, Christiana Campbell's Tavern Garden, the David Morton Garden, and the Benjamin Waller Garden. The last is of particular note because its design is based on more site-specific documentation than was available for most of the other properties, and it therefore more authentically reflects the historical surroundings of the house. These gardens share an axial arrangement of walks and geometric parterres surrounded by boxwood edging, enlivened by a rich dis-

Perspective of Banjamin Waller Garden. Courtesy Colonial Williamsburg.

Aerial view of Gunston Hall Plantation, Mason Neck, Virginia. Photo Charles Baptie. Courtesy Board of Regents, Gunston Hall.

University of Virginia Pavilion Gardens, 1997. Photo Charles A. Birnbaum.

play of flowering shrubs, annuals, and perennials appropriate to the period but pleasing to twentieth-century tastes.

In addition to his full-time position at Colonial Williamsburg, Hopkins maintained a brisk private practice. For twelve years, he served as landscape architect for the Garden Club of Virginia, completing eight major proj204ects before his untimely death. Those projects for which he was principal designer include Woodlawn Plantation, Gunston Hall, the Adam Thoroughgood House, and the University of Virginia Pavilion Gardens. He also contributed to work at Stratford Hall, the Rolfe-Warren House, Wilton, and the Mary Washington Monument. By far the largest commission he received was the restoration of ten walled gardens on the Jeffersonian Lawn at the University of Virginia. As in his other garden projects, the only features that were actually restored to their historical appearance were the serpentine garden walls, which were reconstructed on the basis of Jefferson's drawings and

archaeological testing. The layout and planting design reflected Hopkins's taste more than Jefferson's, although the plant palette was drawn from *Thomas Jefferson's Garden Book*, a compilation of Jefferson's notes and letters edited by University of Virginia professor Edwin Betts in 1944. In 1948, Hopkins completed full construction documents and supervised construction for the West Lawn gardens, which were dedicated in 1952. Unfortunately, he died just as design of the East Lawn gardens was beginning, and the project was completed by his assistant, Donald Parker, and Ralph Griswold*.

Hopkins's practice was not limited to Virginia. He also designed the gardens at Hampton in Towson, Maryland, the Dickinson Mansion in Delaware, Governor Stephen Hopkins House in Rhode Island, and Van Cortlandt Manor in the Hudson Valley. In addition, he served as a consultant to Mildred Bliss at Dumbarton Oaks in Georgetown, where he was responsible for the design of an elliptical aerial hedge of hornbeam as a modification to the garden originally designed by Beatrix Farrand*. He engaged in over 140 private commissions during his brief career. In 1955 the Garden Club of America recognized his achievements with the Sarah Gildersleeve Fife Award, one of its highest honors, and three years later he was made a Fellow of the American Society of Landscape Architects.

Alden Hopkins was stricken with a cerebral hemorrhage while working on designs for the East Lawn gardens at the University of Virginia.

Many of Hopkins's Colonial Revival gardens are now in danger of being lost to the zeal of a new generation of historical landscape architects who embrace a narrowly focused scholarly rigor. Hopkins's works must be evaluated not as re-creations of history but as twentieth-century artifacts that merit the consideration of preservationists as a new layer in the landscape history of these sites.

Hopkins, Alden. "Cookie-Cutter Bed Graced the Garden of Last Century." *Richmond Times-Dispatch*, January 8, 1956. The designer's explanation of the historical background used as the basis for his garden plans for the White House of the Confederacy in Richmond.

Hopkins, Alden. "Early Gardens in Maryland and Virginia: Their Design and Restoration." *Garden Club of Virginia Bulletin*, September 1950, 42–52. A survey of research methods, precedents, and colonial garden patterns that inspired the garden "restorations" done by Hopkins at Colonial Williamsburg and elsewhere.

Hopkins, Alden. "The Woodlawn Garden Restorations." *Garden Club of Virginia Journal*, September/October, 1960, 8–10. An article that poignantly appears in the journal volume which also carries Hopkins's obituary notice. A description of the archaeological evidence which revealed the framework for the restoration plan of Woodlawn Plantation, and the rationale for the more conjectural reconstruction of the plantings, including the decision to convert the humble kitchen garden to an elegant rose garden.

Mary V. Hughes

HOYT, ROLAND S.
(1890–1968)
landscape architect

Roland S. Hoyt was born and raised in Iowa. He earned a B.S. from Iowa State University (1915) and then studied in the Department of Landscape Architecture at Harvard University for two years before his education was interrupted by service in World War I. From 1919 to 1922, he was vice president and manager of the landscape department of Capitol City Nurseries, and in that capacity he helped to design the grounds of Iowa's state capitol.

In 1922, Hoyt went to California as a landscape architect for the Palos Verdes project, directed by Olmsted Brothers*. Then in 1926 he moved to San Diego, where he worked for the Southland Corporation, a Point Loma development firm, before opening an independent practice two years later. His earliest commissions included Muirlands, a hilltop residential neighborhood overlooking the La Jolla coast, and Presidio Park, a privately funded preservation enterprise that encompassed the original site of California's first mission and later that of one of only four Spanish presidios, or forts. At Presidio Park, Hoyt acted as planting adviser to George Marston, the San Diego civic leader and philanthropist who had engaged John Nolen* to create a long-range plan for the city. In the park, Marston built the Serra Museum (1929; William Templeton Johnson, architect), located on a promontory overlooking the San Diego River estuary and Mission Bay, to create a monument to "the birthplace of Western civilization on the Pacific Coast." Hoyt, along with Marston and park supervisor Percy Broell, designed the park in accordance with Nolen's concepts (Nolen being involved in the project from a distance).

As he continued his work in California, Hoyt tabulated notes about the plants that he was using in his landscapes. Tapping his strong background in horticul-

Roland Hoyt (left) with Mrs. Raymond E. Smith and Dan Turner at tree planting, Salk Institute, 1966. Courtesy San Diego Historical Society, Photograph Collection.

ture, he devised an index card system for his special needs, gradually amassing a compendium of data about the cultural requirements and landscape performance of hundreds of specimens. He published this material as *Planting Lists for Southern California* in 1933. Over the next five years, he refined his reference handbook and reissued it as *Checklists for Ornamental Plants of Subtropical Regions* in 1938. Privately published, the guide is still in print today—little changed—and continues to be a valuable design tool.

Hoyt participated in the landscape design of the 1935–1936 California Pacific International Exposition, and he also worked on several other large commissions— among them State College (now San Diego State University) and navy housing projects. From 1938 through 1944, Hoyt edited *California Garden*, the long-lived magazine of the San Diego Floral Association. Afterward, he was a frequent contributor, producing illustrated articles about unusual plants, neighborhood planning, and urban ecology.

Hoyt served as a member of the San Diego Park Commission (1943–1947) and, after 1947, as consulting landscape architect for the city's largest recreation area, Mission Bay Park. In 1960, when the Salk Institute was established between the Scripps Institution of Oceanog-

Serra Museum and Presidio Park. Courtesy San Diego Historical Society, Photograph Collection.

Presidio Park, San Diego. Photo Carol Greentree.

raphy and Torrey Pines State Reserve in La Jolla, Hoyt designed the campus surrounding Louis Kahn's striking science complex with an arboretum of uncommon eucalyptus varieties. His last large commission was the 1964 downtown Civic Concourse, now a mature oasis in a hardscape of high-rise offices.

During the early 1960s, Hoyt became the nucleus of a professional group that established the San Diego chapter of the American Society of Landscape Architects, and in 1964 he was elected a Fellow of the ASLA.

Hoyt, Roland Stewart. *Checklists for Ornamental Plants of Subtropical Regions*. Anaheim, Calif.: Livingston Press, 1933; rev. 1958. A plant reference handbook for southern California landscape architects.

Hoyt, Roland Stewart. "Roland Hoyt Recommends." *California Garden*. A semi-regular series of plant portraits that appeared between 1956 and 1966 (on file at San Diego Historical Society).

Marston, George White. "Presidio Park: A Statement of George W. Marston in 1942." *Journal of San Diego History* 32 (Spring 1986), 103–115. Typeset copy of a letter from Marston describing the development of Presidio Park, which discusses the roles of Nolen, Ralph Cornell*, and Hoyt.

Carol Greentree

HUBBARD, HENRY VINCENT
(1875–1947)
landscape architect, educator, author

Henry Vincent Hubbard was born in Taunton, Massachusetts. Like five generations of Hubbards before him, he graduated from Harvard College (1897). He then went on to study at the Massachusetts Institute of Technology in 1897–1898, completing in one year the first two years of the course in architecture and hoping all the while that instruction in landscape architecture would be given. Since it was not available in any school at that time, he turned to the Harvard Graduate School, where he studied under the direction of Frederick Law

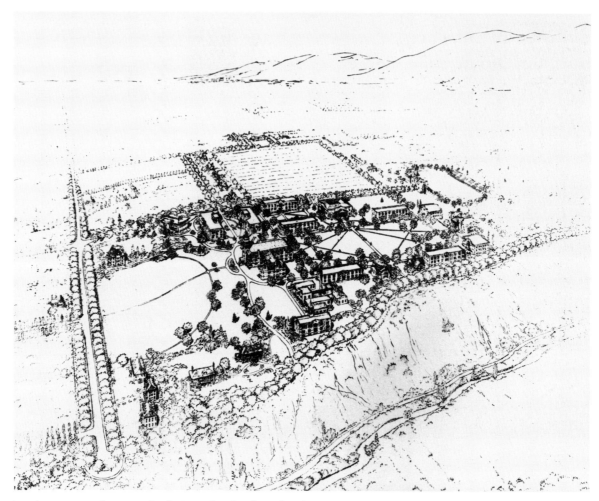

Aerial perspective of campus plan for Agricultural College of Utah at Logan, by Pray, Hubbard & White, c. 1910s. Courtesy Utah State University, Special Collections and Archives.

Olmsted Jr*. He received an A.M. in 1900 and an S.B. in 1901, both in landscape architecture, from the newly established Lawrence Scientific School of Harvard; his was the first degree conferred in landscape architecture as an independent professional course of study.

In 1901, Hubbard entered the office of Olmsted Brothers*, Landscape Architects and Site Planners, in Brookline, Massachusetts, and the following year he traveled in France and Germany for professional study with Olmsted Jr. Travel abroad has always formed part of the American landscape architect's education, and Hubbard had already been to England and the Continent in 1899. Again in 1913 he traveled to study in Italy.

In 1906, Hubbard set up an independent practice in Boston with H. P. White and James Sturgis Pray*, known as Pray, Hubbard & White. Plans and photos of estates designed by Hubbard and the firm can be found in publications such as *American Country Houses of Today* (1913) and *American Landscape Architecture* (1924), edited by P. H. Elwood*. In 1918 the firm was dissolved, its "good and interesting" practice "squelched," as Hubbard put it, by World War I.

Hubbard was called to Washington, D.C. in 1917 to serve as a designer in what became the Cantonment Branch of the Construction Division, U.S. Army. He served successively as "expert" with the Housing Com-

Cover of *An Introduction to the Study of Landscape Design*,
1917 ed., by Henry V. Hubbard and Theodora Kimball. Courtesy Charles A. Birnbaum.

pointed assistant professor in the Harvard School of Landscape Architecture in 1911 and professor in 1921. In the
wake of a conference at Columbia University in 1929 on
whether city planning should be taught in the United
States, Harvard established a program of instruction and
research in planning with funding from the Rockefeller
Foundation. Almost simultaneously, the Charles Dyer
Norton Professorship in Regional Planning was established
at Harvard and awarded to Hubbard. The Rockefeller
Foundation funding ended after seven years, however, and
to Hubbard's disappointment Harvard did not find a way
to continue instruction in the subject during his tenure
there. Hubbard retired from teaching in 1941.

In 1910, with Charles Downing Lay* and Robert
Wheelwright*, Hubbard founded *Landscape Architecture*, the (then quarterly) magazine of the American
Society of Landscape Architects. When the war years
brought financial difficulties, Wheelwright and Lay
resigned, and Hubbard remained sole editor until his
death. In the first issue Hubbard wrote: "Only within the
last two decades has there been any widespread general
realization of our need for beauty in land adapted to our
use—beauty, not merely as a luxury, but as a practical
necessity and as a matter of course." He edited thirty-
seven volumes of the publication.

In 1917, Hubbard and Theodora Kimball, the librarian of the Harvard School of Design, published *An Introduction to the Study of Landscape Design*, the first and for
a long time the standard text in landscape architecture.
The work was revised in 1929 and reprinted many times.
In 1929 the authors wrote: "We take an esthetic theory
which seems—to us at least—consistent and capable of
general application, and use it as the basis of an organization of the subject matter of the field of landscape
design." Students were counseled to go to nature for
inspiration and as training in appreciation. Among the
styles treated in the text was the "Modern American
Landscape" style, an American version of English landscape gardening distinguished the English in its emphasis
on preservation and interpretation of natural landscape
character. Natural features and native plants were incorporated into designs for residences, subdivisions, and
parks. Published one year after Congress established the
National Park Service, Hubbard and Kimball's textbook
has been acknowledged as the single most influential
source for park designers in the 1920s and 1930s.

Kimball and Hubbard also founded and edited the
journal *City Planning* (beginning 1925) and collaborated
on *Our Cities To-day and To-morrow: A Survey of Planning and Zoning Progress in the United States* (1929).

mission of the Council of National Defense; designer for
the U.S. Shipping Board; acting manager of the Town
Planning Division of the U.S. Housing Corporation; and,
finally, editor of a volume on technical design for the
report of the Housing Corporation after the Armistice.

He returned to the office of Olmsted Brothers and
in 1920 was made a partner, which he remained until his
death. He served as a planning consultant to the cities of
Boston, Baltimore, and Providence, as well as to the Federal Housing Authority, the Tennessee Valley Authority,
and the National Park Service. He was president of the
American Society of Landscape Architects from 1931 to
1934 and a member of the National Capital Park and
Planning Commission from 1932 to 1947.

Hubbard began teaching landscape architecture at
Harvard in 1906, as an instructor in what was then called
the Graduate School of Applied Science. He was ap-

Hubbard collaborated with John Nolen* on two important planning studies, *Airports* (1930) and *Parkways and Land Values* (1937). He wrote that "regional planning is based first on a recognition of the topography, the economics, the law, the political machinery, the predisposition and backgrounds of the people who are to be served, or, more properly, who are to be enabled to serve themselves." He made his contributions to the field of planning at a time when its significance was not widely recognized, and with a few other pioneers he prepared the way for its acceptance as an essential function of government. He is remembered chiefly for his teaching, his many writings, and his editing of city planning studies and professional journals.

Hubbard and Kimball married in 1924. Kimball died in 1935, and in 1937, Hubbard married Isabel F. Gerrish, who survived him. In 1953 the Hubbard Educational Trust was founded in his memory with the purpose of furthering the understanding and appreciation of landscape architecture with support for its education and history.

Hubbard, Henry V., and Theodora Kimball. *An Introduction to the Study of Landscape Design*. New York: Macmillan, 1917 (rev. 1929; rpt. 1931, 1959, and 1967). The first, and long the standard, text for landscape design and practice; bibliography; 36 plates, illustrations, plans.

Hubbard, Theodora Kimball, and Henry V. Hubbard. *Our Cities, To-day and To-morrow: A Survey of Planning and Zoning Progress in the United States*. Cambridge: Harvard University Press, 1929. Plates, maps, diagrams.

Nolen, John, and Henry V. Hubbard. *Parkways and Land Values*. Harvard City Planning Studies, no. 11. Cambridge: Harvard University Press, 1937. In-depth case studies of Westchester County, Boston, and Kansas City systems; 13 plates, illustrations, maps, diagrams.

Karen Madsen

HULL, DANIEL RAY
(1890–1964)
landscape architect, park planner

Born in Lincoln, Kansas, Daniel Ray Hull grew up in the Midwest and attended the University of Illinois at Urbana-Champaign. There he studied both horticulture and urban planning, the latter under Charles Milford Robinson*, one of the field's pioneers. After graduating in 1913, Hull entered the new landscape architecture program at Harvard where he studied with Henry Vincent Hubbard*, James Sturgis Pray*, and Fredrick Law Olmsted Jr.*

Awarded an Olmsted Fund Travel Grant, Hull spent several months in Europe before commencing his professional career in California around 1915. Working with architect Francis Underhill*, Hull designed subdivisions in Santa Barbara until he entered the army during World War I.

In 1920, Hull accepted a position as assistant to Charles Pierpont Punchard*, National Park Service chief landscape engineer. Punchard's untimely death in November of that year led to Hull's promotion to chief

landscape engineer in 1921. Faced with the monumental task of developing access and facilities in a number of new national parks, Hull concentrated his work, and that of his small staff, in three major areas: the design of park "villages" to house park administration and staff and to accommodate visitors; the development of scenic park roads; and the review and control of concessionaire work within parks.

Hull brought his background in town and subdivision planning to the work of developing the first administrative and visitor facilities in the national parks. He sought to integrate comprehensive site planning, landscape design, and architecture, always with a view to subordinating development in the parks to the natural scenic values for which they had been established. Hull's work at Yosemite, Sequoia, Grand Canyon, and Yellowstone was responsive to natural topography and minimized visual impact through sensitive siting and vegetative screening. In the design of buildings he experimented with the use

"A Hiking Shelter for Mount San Jacinto State Park," 1937. Courtesy California State Parks State Museum Resource Center.

of natural forms and native materials, refining disparate traditions of woodland and rustic architecture into a coherent, recognizable park style. Hull collaborated with Myron Hunt on the Yosemite Village plan (1923), developed a new administrative center at Sequoia (1923), and designed the Grand Canyon Village plan (1924). He also designed several important buildings that helped establish the vocabulary of the Park Rustic style. Notable among his designs are the administration buildings at Sequoia and Grand Canyon, and the lake ranger station at Yellowstone.

Roads and trails also occupied much of Hull's attention as chief landscape engineer. In dramatic scenic highways such as the Going-to-the-Sun Road in Glacier National Park, Hull and his assistant Thomas Vint* pioneered techniques to naturalize the appearance of roads, protect important roadside natural resources, and provide scenic vistas to enhance the traveler's experience of nature. They designed guardrails, bridges, turnouts, and vista points in the Park Rustic style, thus unifying road design with other park development.

Hull collaborated with concessionaires in the development of some of the national parks' most outstanding rustic hotels and lodges. His most significant and enduring collaboration was with Los Angeles architect Gilbert Stanley Underwood. In 1923, Hull moved the Park Service design office to Los Angeles, sharing office space with Underwood. Together they designed the landscape plans and buildings for the lodge and cabins at Zion (1924) and Bryce (1924), the Ahwahnee Hotel at Yosemite (1927), and the Grand Canyon Lodge (1928). They also undertook private commissions together. The unusual blending of public and private work eventually provided Hull with a transition out of the park service. He established a private practice in 1927, though it proved short-lived.

Late in 1927, Olmsted Jr. engaged Hull to supervise a statewide survey to identify scenic landscapes worthy of inclusion in the newly authorized California State Park system. Assisted by Harry W. Shepard of the University of California, Berkeley, and Emerson Knight*, a private practitioner who had worked extensively for Save-the-Redwoods League, Hull visited and evaluated hundreds of potential park sites ranging from redwood forest to Sonoran desert. This year-long study resulted in Olmsted's *California Park Survey* (1929). A seminal work on scenic landscape preservation, it not only shaped California's extensive park system, but influenced the direction of park development across the country.

Picnic Ramada, Anza Borrego Desert State Park, San Diego County, California, 1937. Courtesy California State Parks State Museum Resource Center.

Following the onset of the Depression, Hull & Underwood's practice declined, leading to the closing of their office in 1932. In 1933, Hull went to work for the National Park Service Emergency Conservation Work (ECW) program, and in 1934 he accepted a position as State Park Landscape Engineer in California, which enabled him to continue his federal ECW work. In this role, Hull assumed control over much of the development of the 28-unit California park system. Under this program, Hull established a central design office in San Francisco, partly to coordinate work with National Park Service architects and field inspectors. Although extensive in area, California's recently established state parks

lacked access, visitor facilities, and staff housing. In preparing master development plans for a large number of these often pristine areas, Hull emphasized long-term planning that integrated individual construction projects with comprehensive development schemes.

Hull's state park projects featured site-sensitive layouts, use of native materials in architectural features, and subordination of visitor facilities to natural scenery. Utilizing Civilian Conservation Corp labor, Hull oversaw the development of hundreds of miles of access roads and hiking trails enhanced with rough masonry guardrails, log bridges, and stone culverts. Campgrounds with timber-trussed picnic ramadas, masonry cook stoves, and rugged

Construction crew at Anza Borrego Desert State Park, San Diego County (Hull kneeling in first row, third from right), 1941. Courtesy California Department of Parks and Recreation, Photographic Archives.

log tables were situated in all of the parks. The ECW work also provided Hull with opportunities to design important buildings, among them the administration and concessions complex at Big Basin State Park, Santa Cruz County (1935–1938), the massive tiered granite Mountain Theater at Mount Tamalpais in Marin County (1937), and the stone masonry Lookout Building that rises from the summit of Mount Diablo northeast of San Francisco Bay (1940). Hull also experimented with historical precedent, using adobe and tile in some southern California park buildings. He was a consultant in the restorations of the Mission La Purisima and the Vallejo home and formulated policies for the treatment of historic restorations in California parks.

Beginning in 1944, Hull developed standard plans for state park administration facilities, campgrounds, signs, and entries. These simplified rustic designs became the basis of an aggressive postwar building program that extended the Park Rustic aesthetic into the 1950s in California's parks. Hull retired from state park work in 1947.

Carr, Ethan. *Wilderness by Design: Landscape Architecture and the National Park Service.* Lincoln: University of Nebraska Press, 1998. Provides a detailed description of Hull's National Park Service design work and sheds new light on his extensive collaboration with Gilbert Stanley Underwood.

McClelland, Linda Flint. *Building the National Parks: Historic Landscape Design and Construction.* Baltimore: Johns Hopkins University Press, 1998. Includes a critical discussion of Hull's career with the National Park Service, 1920–1927. Although not dealing specifically with Hull's California work, McClelland's chapter on state park development in the 1930s provides an excellent context for understanding Hull's state park work.

Hull's contribution to the development and design of the California state park system is best documented in the approximately 115 drawings (1935–1947) located in the Environmental Design Division, California Department of Parks and Recreation, Sacramento. The Correspondence and Park Commission Records of the California Division of Beaches and Parks in the California State Archives, Sacramento, provide information on Hull's role in state park administration.

The Newton Bishop Drury Papers, 1926–1966, Bancroft Library, University of California, Berkeley, document his role in the Olmsted survey of 1928, park administration, and his relationship with Drury. Correspondence and photographic records related to the 1928 State Park Survey are located at the Fredrick Law Olmsted National Historic Site (National Park Service), Brookline, Massachusetts.

Carol Roland

HUNTSMAN-TROUT, EDWARD
(1889–1974)
landscape architect

Edward Trout Huntsman was born on a small farm in Tintern, Ontario, the youngest of five children. His mother died when he was three, and at the age of six he was sent to live with his eldest sister at Gowan Hall, the Toronto estate of his uncle, Edward Trout. His rather isolated childhood there shaped many of his interests and his desire to work as a "loner." He was given responsibility for the conservatory and under his aunt's guidance developed a keen interest in and knowledge of horticulture. He spent much time on his own reading and exploring the country. His growing interest in literature was complemented in school by a burgeoning interest in languages; he was fluent in several all his life and always insisted on reading books in their original languages.

His uncle and aunt sent him to live at their winter home in Florida between 1903 and 1907 because they were concerned about his intense intellectual concentration. During this period they legally adopted him, and he became Edward Huntsman-Trout. His multilingual abilities and horticultural knowledge enabled him to obtain a job with Reasoner Brothers' Nursery, a large company doing business in many foreign countries. Rather than becoming a translator, he was advised to consider becoming a landscape architect.

In 1907 he moved with his adoptive parents to Hollywood, California, because of his sister's poor health and his uncle's business interests in Mexico. After a year at Hollywood High School making up required courses,

he entered the University of California as a science major. At that time there was no program in landscape architecture, so he enrolled in several elective courses in architecture. He later regretted not majoring in this

Edward Huntsman-Trout. Courtesy David Streatfield.

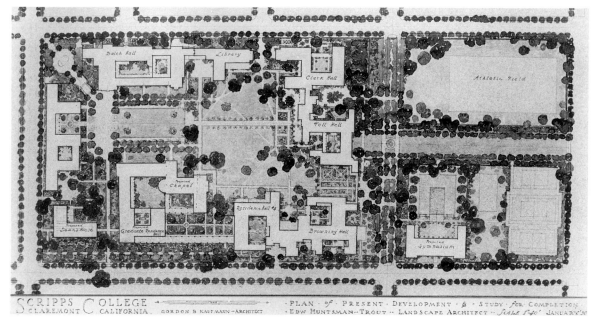

Scripps College, Claremont, California Plan, 1930. Courtesy David Streatfield.

field, believing that both fields were fundamentally concerned with the design of three-dimensional space.

He entered the graduate program in landscape architecture at Harvard in 1913. However, he was not attracted to the strong Olmstedian influence, or what he called the "spaghetti school," and he was one of very few students who took elective courses in architecture. H. Langford Warren's course in the history of architecture opened his eyes to what he saw as the strength of the Ecole des Beaux-Arts' approach. He completed the courses for the landscape architecture degree but did not take the final exams and never graduated.

After Harvard he worked for a year for Fletcher Steele*, whose enthusiastic exploration of new ideas he admired. He disliked having to work on someone else's designs, however, and in 1916 he became the head of the design department in A. D. Taylor's* office in Cleveland, where he designed large country estates until he went overseas in World War I. After the war he continued in Taylor's office until 1920, when he returned to southern California.

Huntsman-Trout worked in the design office of the Beverly Hills Nursery for two years, designing large estates in Beverly Hills. The commercial aspects this position entailed troubled him, however, and in 1922 he left to set up his own practice in Hollywood. Huntsman-

Trout maintained a small office in Hollywood from 1922 until 1941. During World War II, he worked with the architect H. Roy Kelley on camouflage projects for the Douglas Aircraft Company. From 1945 until his death, he maintained an office in Beverly Hills. His practice was almost entirely residential in the affluent communities of West Los Angeles. In the 1940s and 1950s he played an important role in the restoration of the adobe house and Queen Anne Guest Cottage at the Los Angeles County Arboretum.

Huntsman-Trout's largest and most important commission was Scripps College, a small women's college at Claremont. A series of courtyards housing dormitories, administrative offices, and classrooms is clustered around the principal communal spaces at right angles to one another. Originally, these large spaces were surfaced with rammed earth and planted with citrus trees. Unfortunately, a change in administration led to their being planted in grass. But despite this and other regrettable more recent changes, the campus still demonstrates Huntsman-Trout's regional design approach.

He saw each commission as a unique place for a particular client and site, so his designs have no signature characteristics. He believed that gardens were outdoor living rooms whose design was as important as that of a house's interior spaces. Thus, many of his designs create

Residential courtyard, Scripps College. Courtesy David Streatfield.

Service buildings, Harvey Mudd estate, Beverly Hills, California, 1929. Courtesy David Streatfield.

axially organized terraces and courtyards providing strong basic architectonic framework, with plants creating further complex spaces. An artist in his work, Huntsman-Trout spent endless hours searching for the right plant and architectural ornament and designing all the planting on a site. His designs were regionally appropriate, and he rejected the lawn as unsuitable for southern California, except for recreational places and purposes. Central to Huntsman-Trout's work was a very deep respect for the client. Clients whom he particularly liked often received a gift, a sculpture or a pot, on the completion of the job.

Huntsman-Trout's design philosophy is best summed up in a lecture he gave in 1967, in which he said: "It has always been my firm conviction that the planning which we do should seek the obvious, the straightforward answer, the least common denominator, the inevitable. . . . I like it best when what I have done seems not contrived. It was just there." This philosophy is perfectly expressed in his own home in Mandeville Canyon in West Los Angeles (1946). The T-shaped house with a large music-room loggia was built from recycled materials and carefully sited beneath a cluster of existing sycamore trees and around a large brick-paved patio. It embodies his unpretentious hopes for living appropriately in this semi-arid climate.

Eckbo, Garrett. *Urban Landscape Design*. New York: McGraw-Hill, 1964, 82–87. Detailed description of the principles underlying the design of Scripps College written by Huntsman-Trout; illustrated with a diagrammatic plan and black-and-white photographs.

Gross, Susan. "The Gardens of Edward Huntsman-Trout." Master of Landscape Architecture thesis, California State Polytechnic University, Pomona, 1976. The most complete analysis of Huntsman-Trout's work; provides a discussion of his early life, his education, his design approach, and a list of his commissions.

Huntsman-Trout, Edward. "Another Room in the Home." *Riverside Plastite Progress*, June 1928, 1–8. A clear statement of Huntsman-Trout's conception of the garden as a room designed for living and deserving the same attention from designers as a living room in a house.

_____

David Streatfield

HUTCHESON, MARTHA BROOKES (BROWN)
(1871–1959)
landscape architect, author, lecturer

Martha Brookes Brown was born in New York City. During the 1890s, she studied drafting and design at the New York School of Applied Design for Women as well as painting with artist Rhoda Holmes Nichols. In 1900, she became one of the first women to enroll in the program in landscape architecture at the Massachusetts Institute of Technology. Brown supplemented her MIT courses with studies at the Arnold Arboretum and European travel. She is among the best known of the pioneer women landscape architects.

Working under her maiden name until her 1910 marriage to William Hutcheson, she entered practice in Boston in 1902. Although Bryn Mawr and Bennington colleges engaged her for specific projects, like many other practitioners of the era, Hutcheson worked almost exclusively for residential clients. Through 1905 she designed all, or more usually part, of a number of country estates in New England, largely on Boston's North Shore. Several of these remain partially intact, and one, the Frederick and Helen Moseley place in Newburyport, Massachusetts, is now Maudslay State Park. Hutcheson worked on this project from 1901 through 1907. Other important Massachusetts commissions include Undercliff (1902–1906), a dramatically sited estate in Manchester, set into cliffs facing the Atlantic, and the Colonial Revival garden at the Longfellow House in Cambridge, now owned by the National Park Service.

In 1906, Hutcheson moved her practice to New York. There she continued her residential work on Long Island and in New Jersey and the northern suburbs. The Mr. and Mrs. Andrew Stout estate (1916–1920) in Red Bank, New Jersey, and the Harold and Harriet Pratt place (1911–1913) in Glen Cove, Long Island, are among Hutcheson's significant work in the New York area. After her marriage, she and her husband bought Merchiston Farm in Gladstone, New Jersey, which Hutcheson developed in accordance with her design philosophy. The place is now open to the public as Morris County's Bamboo Brook Outdoor Education Center.

Martha Brookes Hutcheson. Courtesy John Norton.

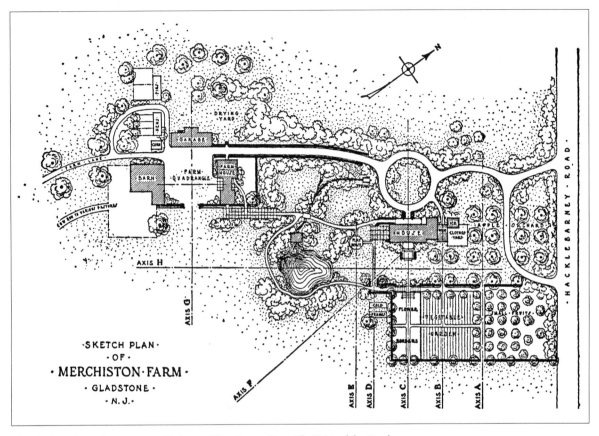

·SKETCH PLAN·
·OF·
·MERCHISTON·FARM·
·GLADSTONE·
·N.J.·

Sketch plan of Merchiston Farm, Gladstone, New Jersey. From *The Spirit of the Garden*.

European travel, especially in Italy and France, greatly influenced Hutcheson's design philosophy and practice. She visited Europe many times, but a 1905–1906 journey was especially devoted to the study of the classic examples of landscape design there. While she made no attempt to reproduce Italian gardens in a literal sense, like other landscape architects of the era Hutcheson drew important ideas from those gardens. She believed in the house and garden as an organic unity, and felt strongly that space in the immediate area of the house should be organized formally. Her designs emphasized axes and views and incorporated Italian architectural elements such as the pergola. Plant material was to be used architecturally and formal water features were often included.

Although she greatly curtailed her practice after 1920, the year she became a member of the American Society of Landscape Architects, Hutcheson remained visible in the profession for decades. She lectured, wrote for magazines, and produced a book, *The Spirit of the*

Garden, in 1923. The volume, published by Boston's respected Atlantic Monthly Press, was not the first book about landscape design by an American woman—Mariana Van Rensselaer* and Grace Tabor* are two who preceded her—but it may be described as the first account by a woman practitioner to combine a discussion of design with an extensive visual presentation of her own work.

The Spirit of the Garden contains six essays on important elements of gardens of the Country Place era, a presentation of her design philosophy through narrative and pictures. Much of the book—like her career—is devoted to the residential landscape and includes discussion of fourteen of her own projects, illustrated with photographs from her collection.

The Spirit of the Garden is addressed to an informed lay audience that did not need to be persuaded of the value of landscape design but did need information on how to judge or execute good design. It focused on subjects of interest to the many Americans moving to the

Maudsleigh. From *The Spirit of the Garden*.

Italian Garden, Maudsleigh, Frederick and Helen Moseley estate, Newburyport, Massachusetts, May 1940. Photo Charles Gattrell. Courtesy of Charles Beveridge.

suburbs in the 1920s: the flower garden; the importance of axis; the use of the hedge; arbors and gateways; greenhouses; water in the garden. Although the topics and illustrations seem to focus on costly gardens, Hutcheson's principles could be applied to modest residences as well.

Hutcheson writes clearly about her fundamental belief in the value of form and structure. She demonstrates abstract concepts with photographs of her own projects, both under construction and as built, as well as pictures of great European gardens, largely in Italy. The influence of Italian gardens on her work is apparent. She identifies the owners and locations of all her projects, not always the practice in her day but of much value to historians. The book also includes three plans of Hutcheson's designs. To publicize the book, three articles were excerpted and published in *House Beautiful:* "Use of

the Hedge" (March 1923), "Water in the Planning of the Garden" (April 1923), and "Importance of Arbors in the Garden" (May 1923).

Hutcheson, elected a Fellow of the ASLA in 1935, was also an active member of the Garden Club of America from its early days. She was forthright in speech and firm of opinion and tried to steer the club to a more public role and a more inclusive membership, but her efforts did not win support. Nonetheless, both the club and its *Bulletin* offered her an important forum for her ideas.

Davidson, Rebecca Warren. "The Spirit of the *American Garden:* Landscape and Cultural Expression in the Work of Martha Brookes Hutcheson." *Journal of the New England Garden History Society* 4 (Spring 1996).

A brief discussion of Hutcheson's book, *The Spirit of the Garden.*

Hutcheson, Martha Brookes. "The Garden of the Home of Dr. J. Henry Lancashire, Manchester, Mass., Mrs. Wm. A. Hutcheson, Landscape Architect." *House and Garden*, June 1920, 42–43. Describes one of Hutcheson's important Massachusetts commissions; photographs by noted Colonial Revival photographer Mary Northend.

Hutcheson, Martha Brookes. *The Spirit of the Garden.* Introduction by Ernest Peixotto. Boston: Atlantic Monthly Press, 1923.

The Martha Brookes Hutcheson Papers are owned by the Morris County (New Jersey) Park Commission.

———————————

Virginia Lopez Begg

INNOCENTI, UMBERTO
(1895–1968)
landscape architect

Umberto Innocenti was born outside Florence, Italy, of a family with long traditions in the Tuscan agricultural landscape. He attended the University of Florence, and in 1925 traveled to America on a scholarship for the study of landscape architecture. Shortly thereafter he began work in the office of Ferruccio Vitale* and Alfred Geiffert Jr.*, where he quickly became a primary agent of the firm on project sites. Innocenti left Vitale's firm in 1931 to form a partnership with Richard K. Webel, thereafter known as Innocenti & Webel, in Roslyn, Long Island. The firm prospered during the Depression years and continued to build significant landscape projects until long after Innocenti's death. Still operating under the same name, it continues to exist—now in its sixty-seventh year, managed by Richard C. Webel Jr. Richard K. Webel retired in the early 1990s.

The firm's major projects included the Long Island residence of Landon K. Thorne, which Innocenti personally carried forward from Vitale's office and continued for over ten years; the residences of Mrs. Evelyn Marshall Field, Howard K. Phipps, Robert J. Winthrop, and Childs Frick on Long Island, all during the 1930s; national pavilions for Italy and the Netherlands at the 1939 World's Fair in Flushing, New York; the Reader's Digest Headquarters in Pleasantville, New York; Keeneland Racecourse in Lexington, Kentucky, a project that the firm continued to service for over fifty years; the Greenbrier Hotel in White Sulphur Springs, West Virginia; the Elizabethan Gardens of Roanoke Island, North Carolina; Furman University, Greenville, North Carolina; development projects in Hobe Sound and Jupiter Island in Florida; and numerous projects for Milliken & Company in North Carolina and elsewhere.

Even if we consider only the years 1931–1968, when both partners were active, Innocenti & Webel represent exemplary endurance as a business partnership in modern times. Yet beyond longevity, the firm constitutes a unique and compelling model of practice for American landscape architecture—one based on the contrasting talents and nearly opposite working styles of the two principals. They often worked entirely separately. Webel was the erudite, Harvard-schooled designer with a passion for drawing and a deep devotion to the orthodoxy of landscape theory and practice. Innocenti was a horticultural virtuoso whose love for the work and great skill were manifested principally on site. He had little interest in plans, and he mistrusted theory. Because he did not draw, archival evidence of his role in projects is scant; yet we know from those who worked with him that what Innocenti represented in the partnership was the great tradition of garden makers, those whose handiwork raises the garden to one of our highest forms of cultural expression. Although his formal study of the discipline certainly informed his everyday work, it was his love of plants and his intimate knowledge of plant culture and practice that motivated him. From his upbringing in the social and managerial hierarchy of his family's farming and nursery enterprise, Innocenti understood the labor and organization required for successful horticultural production. From his training in Vitale & Geiffert's office, he developed a practice of managing and directing crews on job sites with author-

Umberto Innocenti at Robert Winthrop residence, Long Island, 1932. Office record photo. Courtesy Gary R. Hilderbrand.

Landon K. Thorne residence, c. 1930s. Photo Samuel Gottscho / Gottscho-Schleisner. Courtesy Gary R. Hilderbrand.

Robert J. Winthrop residence, 1930s. Photo Samuel Gottscho / Gottscho-Schleisner. Courtesy Gary R. Hilderbrand.

ity, and he knew how to get results. His manner in the field, while thoroughgoing and tough with workers, was genteel with clients; he helped establish the amicable and trusting relationships on both sides that were necessary for the long periods of time that design and construction took.

Innocenti and his partner developed a reputation on Long Island during the 1930s by insisting on a finished and mature quality in landscape installations—they called it "final planting"—with the use of large trees and abundant masses of understory vegetation. They had little use for young crops of easily acclimated trees, and no fear of moving giant specimen hardwoods. The key to this for Innocenti was the establishment of solid, long-term relationships with nursery operators. In the early years, these firms were involved in growing the plants, maintaining them during their seasons of nursery preparation, digging and transporting, and installing the plants on site. Once the trees were in the ground, under Innocenti's direction

the same crews would reduce and shape their crowns, often build protective sheds around them, and maintain them in place, sometimes for several years. These were generally family firms—such as Lewis & Valentine, or Hicks Nursery—with skilled laborers who had years of experience, working on project after project. Given these conditions of familiarity, trust, and responsibility, the chance for survival of the trees was high, and this enabled Innocenti to risk planting larger and larger specimens.

The benefits of having a principal of the firm in the field nearly all the time cannot be underestimated, especially in light of the design practices. The working drawings of Innocenti & Webel from the early decades, marvelously executed by Webel and draftsmen including Albert Shaknis and Alfred Manfre, were done with care but also speed, because of the constant work load and small staff. The office remained small—two partners and no more than three junior professionals for over thirty years. In the field, Innocenti could interpret unanticipated circumstances and settle uncertainties on the spot; when he wasn't there, he could rely on his trusted contractor to make informed judgments. Communication with the office was rapid and reliable, given his frequent site visits; mistakes of layout or execution could be corrected in reasonable time. This close proximity to the hand labor and craft of making the projects did not last forever—it was more difficult to maintain as the firm began to work on larger projects in the Carolinas, Florida, and farther reaches—but it was normal practice for the firm at least until World War II, as it had been for landscape builders in many previous generations. Indeed, it may be said that Innocenti was one of a species of professionals for whom the mastery of circumstances of the field was acquired the old way, with feet and hands in the soil. It was this reputation as gardener extraordinaire that has afforded him legendary status in the greater New York garden culture, even to this day.

Architecture and Design. "This issue devoted to the work of Umberto Innocenti and Richard K. Webel, Landscape Architects." New York: Architectural Catalog, 1937. A volume, in the format of a firm portfolio or monograph, which reproduces a large number of outstanding photographs by Samuel Gottscho of the firm's projects.

Fitch, James Marston, and F. F. Rockwell. *Treasury of American Gardens.* New York: Harper Brothers, 1956, 40–41, 57–59, 65–67, 71, 150–152. A book featuring several projects by the firm, including the residences of both Webel and Innocenti, among a broad survey of traditional and contemporary American gardens.

Hilderbrand, Gary R. *Making a Landscape of Continuity: The Practice of Innocenti & Webel.* Cambridge: Harvard Graduate School of Design and Princeton Architectural Press, 1997. A monograph on the firm; includes essays on its practices, a catalog of major projects, chronology, complete list of commissions, and bibliography.

Because the firm still practices in Locust Valley, Long Island, Innocenti & Webel retain most records of its work. However, many original drawings, photographs, and typescripts related to key projects up to the 1960s are housed in the Special Collections of the Frances Loeb Library, Harvard University Graduate School of Design. Photographs of Innocenti gardens by Samuel Gottscho, from 1931 through the mid-1950s, may also be viewed in the collections of the Avery Library, Columbia University.

Gary R. Hilderbrand

JACKSON, JOHN BRINCKERHOFF
(1909–1996)
landscape architect, educator, author

John Brinckerhoff Jackson was born of American parents in Dinard, France. His education included schooling in New England and Switzerland, the Experimental College of the University of Wisconsin in Madison, Harvard, with a major in history and literature (A.B., 1932), and brief study of architecture at the Massachusetts Institute of Technology. His equally important informal education included almost a decade of subsequent travel and writing, including reporting on the growth of fascism. In 1940 he enlisted in the U.S. Army, and his fluency in French and German led to a military career as an intelligence officer—entering a private, he left a major. This second

extended European experience, in wartime, introduced him to the work of French cultural geographers, and at war's end he wrote guidebooks for American soldiers in Europe. This set of landscapes, languages, and cultures deeply influenced his subsequent work. Here was the paradox of an American who had spent his formative years in Europe, who saw the United States with a distinct pair of eyes, an iconoclast with a firm grounding in the history and culture of Western civilization and a visceral appreciation of American differences and deviations.

Following the war, Jackson settled in New Mexico, where he had summered as boy, building his home in La

J. B. Jackson at La Cienega, New Mexico, 1986. Courtesy Marc Treib.

Cienega outside Santa Fe. With this rare perspective on the American landscape, in 1951 he founded *Landscape* magazine, which he edited, published, and wrote much of the content for. Originally focused on the human geography of the Southwest, its scope broadened until he sold the magazine in 1968.

Landscape played a significant role in publishing American landscape authors and Europeans in translation. However, it was primarily a vehicle for Jackson's developing landscape philosophy, expounded most dramatically in a series of classic essays, his preferred mode of exposition. These were later anthologized in *Landscapes: Selected Writings of J. B. Jackson*, (1970) and *Changing Rural Landscapes* (1977). Subsequent collections of his works appeared as *The Necessity for Ruins and Other Topics* (1980), *The Southern Landscape Tradition in Texas* (1980), *Discovering the Vernacular Landscape* (1984), *A Sense of Place, A Sense of Time* (1994; winner of the 1995 PEN Prize for Essays), and a posthumous volume, *Landscape in Sight: Looking at America* (1997). He also wrote *American Space: The Centennial Years* (1972), his only book-length work.

Jackson's early essays were a remarkably prescient analysis of the American scene: "Ghosts at the Door" on the meaning of the American yard; "The Westward Mov-

ing House" on the evolution of the American dwelling; "Other Directed Houses" on the highway strip and its architecture; "The Abstract World of the Hot-Rodder" on new forms of recreation and landscape appreciation; "The Almost Perfect Town" on the archetypal American community; "Jefferson, Thoreau and After" on citizenship and romanticism; and many more. Moreover, his writing laid the groundwork for a new field, Landscape Studies, which he further developed as an educator. Beginning in 1967 he taught for a decade at the University of California, Berkeley, in the School of Environmental Design and Department of Geography, and at Harvard in Landscape Architecture and Visual and Environmental Studies. His courses were on the American and European landscape, and through this direct contact with a generation of landscape architects, architects, and

J. B. Jackson house, La Cienega, 1997. Photo Charles A. Birnbaum.

Sketch of road with telegraph poles, 1947. Courtesy Helen Lefkowitz Horowitz.

geographers, he profoundly influenced design practice and scholarship.

Jackson's central theme was the landscape itself, which he saw as a human creation and artifact. He focused on how space was organized for human use, and on its meaning. Landscape, he said, "was history made visible," and his work was directed at helping people truly learn to see it and develop the tools and habits needed to read and understand its meanings. Jackson typically did not pass judgment, but challenged assumptions about what was worth looking at and cherishing in our surroundings. His bias was toward the ordinary landscape, what he called the vernacular, and his primary object of study was the American landscape (although he wrote insightfully on European landscapes as well). Steeped in a concern for regional distinctions, especially those of the Southwest and South, he nonetheless was fascinated by America's national characteristics and wrote about the grid system of land division, roads, strips, suburbs, and other national landscapes.

Jackson's "eye" sought commonalities, patterns, and consistency. His core focus was on the magnetic poles of the American experience, the pull and push of the house and the road, representing the simultaneous desire for rootedness, community, and responsibility and mobility, change, and unfettered freedom. He wrote on the meaning of houses and the associated outdoor space of the garden; and on the culture and constellation of places and vehicles associated with the American road: the

highway strip, trucking, garages, parking lots, motels, and motorcycles (his preferred mode of travel for many years). He explored the phenomena of speed and movement as landscape experience. The mobile home, not surprisingly, held a particular fascination. Allied to this were explorations of travel and tourism, especially in how they affected the perception of landscape. For Jackson both the view from the road and the aerial perspective were fundamental to understanding landscape.

Deeply felt humanistic values underlay Jackson's choice of topics and their exposition. A profoundly American scholar, he was both pragmatic and optimistic, a true democrat in the Jeffersonian tradition. Keenly aware of the virtues and vices of American individualism, he sought forces to counter its ill effects. The creation of community in a highly individualistic, private, and mobile culture was a central concern, and he wrote on the symbolic landscapes of monuments, cemeteries, parks, and recreation, of places that he deemed the public and political landscape. Jackson's sensibilities were anti-romantic and classical. He also wrote as a perceptive critic of the movements of his time: on modern architecture, urban renewal, historic preservation, and environmentalism. It is tempting to see Jackson as someone born, raised, educated, and formed by the first half of the twentieth century looking at the second half. Unlike many, he did not bemoan the transformation or posit a pastoral nostalgia for times and places past. Far from it—he had an infectious and wonderful curiosity about the changes of his lifetime.

His essays were elegant, and his writing was easily accessible. He always stressed the imperative of learning to see, but with a respect and sympathy for the dignity of those who created a landscape and had to live, work, and play within it. His writings fostered a respect and appreciation for the landscape of common experience and was a source of inspiration for designers and artists. He challenged readers to redefine the beautiful and move beyond a narrow visual concept of landscape. Jackson's aesthetic was socially and morally grounded: the function of the artistry and beauty of a landscape was to provide a meaningful setting for social life and individual fulfillment.

Jackson, John Brinkerhoff. *Landscape in Sight: Looking at America*, ed. Helen Lefkowitz Horowitz. New Haven: Yale University Press, 1997. Posthumously published representative collection from Jackson's entire oeuvre; includes most of his classic essays and insightful essay by Horowitz.

Jackson, John Brinkerhoff. *A Sense of Place, Sense of Time.* New Haven: Yale University Press, 1994. Collection of post-*Landscape* writings, continue themes of Southwest, the landscape of mobility, and the vernacular landscape.

Landscape 1–17 (1951–1968). Volumes of the magazine Jackson edited constitute the most comprehensive collection of his writings, under both his name and pseudonyms.

Zube, Ervin, ed. *Selected Writings of J. B. Jackson.* Amherst: University of Massachusetts Press, 1977. Includes "Ghosts at the Door" and other early essays.

Kenneth I. Helphand

JEFFERSON, THOMAS
(1743–1826)
architect, landscape gardener, horticulturist, author

Thomas Jefferson was born at Shadwell, his family's plantation in the piedmont of the Blue Ridge Mountains, near Charlottesville, Virginia. His father was an enterprising planter, minor public official, and professional surveyor, who, with Joshua Fry in 1751, produced the first accurately detailed map of the colony. As a youth, Jefferson likely learned the fundamentals of surveying from him.

In 1760 Jefferson left home for tidewater Williamsburg, where he entered the College of William and Mary. There he was much influenced by William Small, whom he later acknowledged as opening to him the rational universe of the Enlightenment, especially the complexities of mathematics. Finishing college in 1762, Jefferson remained in Williamsburg another five years studying law. In 1765 he purchased his first book on gar-

Thomas Jefferson, artist unknown, n.d. (probably derived from 1789 bust by Jean-Antoine Houdon). Courtesy Maryland Historical Society.

Martha Brookes Hutcheson.
Italian Garden, Maudsleigh.
Newburyport, Massachusetts, May 1940.
Photo Charles Gattrell. Courtesy of Charles Beveridge.

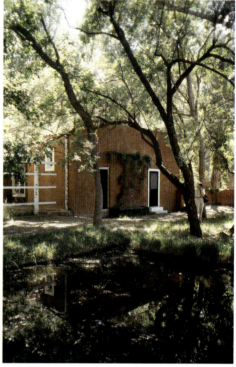

John Brinckerhoff Jackson.
J. B. Jackson house.
La Cienega, New Mexico.
Photo Charles A. Birnbaum.

Thomas Jefferson. Monticello. Charlottesville, Virginia. Photo Charles A. Birnbaum.

Thomas Jefferson. Vegetable and fruit gardens,
Monticello. Charlottesville, Virginia.
Photo Charles A. Birnbaum.

Thomas Jefferson. University of Virginia.
Charlottesville, Virginia.
Photo Charles A. Birnbaum.

Jens Jensen. Edsel and Eleanor Ford estate.
Grosse Pointe Shores, Michigan.
Photo Carol Betsch.

Jens Jensen. Prairie River, Columbus Park. Chicago, Illinois.
Photo Charles A. Birnbaum.

Jens Jensen. View from The Clearing. Ellison Bay, Wisconsin. Photo Charles A. Birnbaum.

George E. Kessler. Memphis boulevard system. Memphis, Tennessee. Photo Charles A. Birnbaum.

Emmerson Knight.
Sidney B. Cushing Mountain Theatre.
Mount Tamalpais State Park,
Marin County, California.
Courtesy Linda Jewell.

Lord & Schryver. Spring Garden, Deepwood. Salem, Oregon.
Photo Kenneth I. Helphand.

Lord & Schryver. Robinson
garden. Salem, Oregon.
Photo Kenneth I. Helphand.

Guy Lowell. Branford House landscape, glass lantern slide, c. 1902. Groton,
Connecticut. Courtesy Smithsonian Institution, Archives of American Gardens.

View of Monticello by Jane Braddick Peticolas, c. 1825. Courtesy Thomas Jefferson Memorial Foundation.

den design: John James's *Theory and Practice of Gardening*, a 1712 translation of Antoine-Joseph Dézallier d'Argenville's French treatise of 1709 which codified the principles and practical methods of making geometrically regular gardens. Jefferson's early exposure to the mathematical mode of garden design made a lasting impression; even the landscape designs that he executed late in life reflected its underlying influence.

Throughout the 1760s, Jefferson also was becoming increasingly familiar with the burgeoning literature associated with irregular or naturalistic garden design, and a set of memoranda he wrote c. 1772–1774 are some of the earliest documented musings on the picturesque from the pen of a colonial American. Jefferson specifically credited the Scottish writer Henry Home, Lord Kames, with having convinced him that garden design was one of the fine arts. Kames's widely appreciated work on aesthetic theory, *Elements of Criticism* (1762), includes one of the first methodical expositions of so-called landscape garden theory to be published in Britain. Kames recommended that the grounds immediately surrounding a house be laid out with geometric

regularity and exhibit increasing irregularity as distance from the house was gained—an arrangement characteristic of Jefferson's own site designs for his two plantation estates, Monticello and Poplar Forest.

In 1764 he inherited some 2,650 upland acres adjacent to Shadwell; eventually the property encompassed more than twice that acreage. Jefferson's selection of a mountaintop on which to establish his residence afforded a spectacular panoramic view but posed daunting practical difficulties. His initial studies for Monticello depict a series of concentric, rectangular, terraced plateaus, rounded at the lowest level by massive semicircular embankments supporting a tree-bordered road encircling the site. By late 1772, however, this idea was abandoned, and the road was laid out along an irregular course that closely followed the existing contours (eventually there were four such concentric "roundabouts" spiraling down the mountainsides). In time, his design for the uppermost rectangular terrace metamorphosed into an oval form that, although equally precise in its geometry, was more directly responsive to the natural mass of the mountain. Perhaps most significant about Jefferson's earliest studies

Monticello, Charlottesville, Virginia, 1996. Photo Charles A. Birnbaum.

is that they demonstrate that from the very outset he envisioned a logical, geometrically coordinated site arrangement.

Jefferson married Martha Wayles Skelton in 1772 and, through an inheritance from her father's estate two years later, more than doubled his wealth in land and slaves. Accordingly, he soon took a more active interest in managing plantation affairs. In 1774 he commenced a sporadic record of farming activities and compiled earlier memoranda to begin his famous garden book as well. That same year he abandoned the formal practice of law,

but already had embarked on an extraordinary career of public service, as a colonial burgess, delegate to the Continental Congress, governor of Virginia during the Revolutionary War, minister plenipotentiary to France, the new nation's first secretary of state, vice president in John Adams's administration, and two terms (1801–1809) as president; his greatest renown is as the principal author of the Declaration of Independence.

During the five years he lived in Paris (1784–1789), Jefferson visited gardens in and around the city, and in the spring of 1786, 1787, and 1788 he made extended

Vegetable and fruit gardens, Monticello, 1996. Photo Charles A. Birnbaum.

trips from Paris, to England, to northern Italy and south-ern and western France, and to the Low Countries and along the Rhine in Germany. Acknowledging that the English were regarded as preeminent in garden design, he made a methodical tour to visit all but one of the models cited by Thomas Whately in *Observations on Modern Gardening* (1770), today still considered the most authoritative contemporary source.

By the time he returned to America in late 1789, Jefferson had a sophisticated awareness of English and continental European tastes in landscape design. Much of the important literature on the subject was in his library, and he personally had visited some of the most acclaimed exemplars. Inspired by the French residential architecture that he had so admired in Paris, he radically rebuilt the house at Monticello in the 1790s and, by 1808, had laid out beside it a rather studied version of

the *jardin anglais*, comprising a serpentine walk, contin-uous adjacent borders, and an abundance of oval flower beds. As early as the 1770s, Jefferson had dreamed of improving the extended grounds of Monticello after the manner of an English park, but very little came of those ambitious proposals. He was somewhat more successful in his attempts to create an American interpretation of the *ferme ornée*, with hawthorn hedges encompassing the orchards, flowering peach trees bounding the fields, Scotch broom dotting the slopes, the novelty of weeping willows almost everywhere swaying in the breeze, and (perhaps only partly realized) small agricultural pad-docks and experimental plots lining the lower round-abouts.

In 1806 he began to build a second, smaller house as an occasional retreat, at Poplar Forest, near Lynch-burg, some ninety miles southwest of Monticello. Al-

University of Virginia, Charlottesville, 1996. Photo Charles A. Birnbaum.

though the approximately 5,000-acre plantation had come into his possession in 1774, he had visited only infrequently before retiring from the presidency in 1809. But from that date until 1823, when he gave the property to a grandson, he made numerous sojourns there and much valued its greater privacy and tranquility. No drawings by him survive for the landscape design, yet it is possible to reconstruct the basic arrangement through a synthesis of documentary evidence and existing site features. Rather than the elliptical forms suggested by the natural topography at Monticello, the rounded contours of Poplar Forest's little knoll permitted Jefferson to exploit the purer geometry of a circle. The house is octagonal, and an octagonal enclosure once surrounded it, circumscribed by a road ringed with trees. The area to the south of the house was excavated to create a rectangular sunken lawn, also bordered by rows of trees. Presumably the excess soil from digging the south lawn was used to form the matching mounds that flank the house and were linked to it by double rows of more

trees. The mounds themselves were planted in concentric geometric patterns of weeping willows and aspens. A circular carriage turnaround at the north entrance completed the biaxial composition.

Jefferson's lifelong, essentially rationalist approach to landscape design was clearly demonstrated in his evolving plans for the University of Virginia. Initially conceived about 1814 as a square composition with modular building components surrounding three sides of an open area of lawn and trees, the scheme subsequently was revised in 1817 into two linear building arrangements bounding opposite sides of three equal terraces. Gradually the ground plan was modified even further to adjust to various exigencies of the actual site, resulting in the somewhat irregularly terraced arrangement existing today. This yielding to "the law of the ground" (Jefferson's telling phrase) epitomized the transformation from the ideal to the real that was characteristic of his various site designs. Another hallmark was the physical integration of architecture and landscape, specifically the extension of lateral wings outward to embrace the site and the merging of buildings into slopes. Too, the double rows of trees that have paralleled the sides of the central lawn of the university since at least the early 1830s (and perhaps even during Jefferson's lifetime) were typical of his previous practice. And although he designed the distinctive serpentine walls that enclose the rectangular gardens behind the professors' houses, he left no indication as to how the spaces within the walls were to be arranged or planted (the gardens there today were created beginning in 1948). The very last landscape design of his life, outlined in a letter some two months before his death on July 4, 1826, was for a six-acre botanic garden and arboretum for the university, but the proposal was never implemented.

Several of Jefferson's architectural creations and at least one of his site compositions have exerted considerable subsequent influence. Especially significant has been the effect that his "academical village" concept has had on American campus planning. Of only limited success, however, was his promotion of the idea of the "chequer board" town plan in which every other square of the typical grid arrangement would be reserved as open space. More broadly, however, his advocacy of agrarianism, especially as espoused in his only published book, *Notes on the State of Virginia* (1785), has had a lasting impact on American culture, particularly in the Southern region. Also contained within the *Notes*, his celebrated descriptions of the Natural Bridge, and of the confluence of the Shenandoah and Potomac rivers near Harpers Ferry, have become canonical pieces of American nature writing.

Perhaps his most tangible imprint today results from his involvement in the 1780s in formulating federal government policy on rectilinear land division and its efficient distribution; in effect, it has geometricized the western two-thirds of the map of the United States.

Beiswanger, William L. "The Temple in the Garden: Thomas Jefferson's Vision of the Monticello Landscape." In *British and American Gardens in the Eighteenth Century*, ed. Robert P. Maccubbin and Peter Martin. Williamsburg, Va.: Colonial Williamsburg Foundation, 1984. Detailed discussion of Jefferson's interests in landscape gardening.

Brown, C. Allan. "Thomas Jefferson's Poplar Forest: The Mathematics of an Ideal Villa." *Journal of Garden History* 10 (April–June, 1990), 117–139. An account of Jefferson's development of the landscape at Poplar Forest, illustrated with a composite diagram based on documentary evidence and surviving site features.

Nichols, Frederick Doveton, and Ralph E. Griswold. *Thomas Jefferson, Landscape Architect*. Charlottesville: University Press of Virginia, 1978. Although some of the scholarship is no longer current, this survey is the only book-length study presently available.

C. Allan Brown

JENSEN, JENS
(1860–1951)
landscape architect, conservationist, educator

Born to a farm family in Dybbøl, Denmark, Jens Jensen studied in the Danish folk high schools and attended Tune Agricultural School outside Copenhagen. Much of this schooling was out-of-doors, and Jensen learned to celebrate the changes of the seasons and marveled at the legends and mysteries associated with the Danish landscape and its history. This fascination with cultural traditions and nature would later play a major role in his design work and conservation activities. After service in the German military, he immigrated to the United States in 1884 and shortly thereafter became a laborer in Chicago's West Parks.

In 1888, Jensen created his first notable design—the American Garden in Union Park, featuring common native wildflowers and shrubs from the countryside. The garden was an attempt to reconnect local people with their regional natural heritage. Like the social reformers in Chicago with whom he associated—Jane Addams and

Jens Jensen, 1921. Courtesy Lincoln Highway Collection, Special Collections Library, University of Michigan Library.

others—Jensen committed himself to promoting parks as a way of humanizing the increasingly industrial city. As a member of Chicago's Special Park Commission from about 1903, he helped to lay the groundwork for the extensive network of forest preserves, first recommended in the commission's 1904 report and established by the Illinois state legislature in 1911.

In 1905, Jensen was made superintendent and landscape architect for all of Chicago's West Parks and went to work reshaping Humboldt, Garfield, and Douglas parks. His knowledge of the native landscape clearly informed his design. Humboldt Park is a good example of his attempt at idealizing the native landscape. The woodland plantings and open meadows repeated patterns used by Frederick Law Olmsted Sr.* and Calvert Vaux* in the South Parks, but Jensen's wetland gardens here were unique; he called them "prairie rivers," celebrating native wetland plants in associations and patterns found in the wild. At Garfield Park, Jensen attempted to represent the prehistoric prairie landscape in the lush gardens in the conservatory, which at the time was the largest in the world. His work on Columbus Park, which he characterized as symbolic of the regional prairie landscape, is often regarded as the best of his designs for Chicago's West Park system. Columbus Park included a large golf course (preexisting), a large lagoon and prairie river, wooded areas and open lawns, a refectory, tennis and other playing fields, a children's

play area, and a rustic swimming pool. At the heart of the Columbus Park design was an outdoor theater space, which Jensen called a Players Green. Here the audience would sit on the gently sloped terraces of his prairie river and watch the sun set in the western sky. As the moon rose at their backs, a performance would begin on the stage area just across the prairie river. Jensen felt that outdoor performances in such settings would help to develop a culture more closely tied to the landscape.

Jensen presented "A Greater West Park System" to the West Park Commissioners in 1919 (published in 1920). This report documents his holistic vision of a city with a network of parks, playgrounds, school sites, community gardens, agricultural land, large preserves, and linear parkways along streams, canals, and boulevards. The plan provides a vision of a human-scaled and community-oriented approach to city planning which was in part a response to Daniel Burnham's earlier Chicago Plan and other City Beautiful plans of the same period.

During the same time that he was working on the parks, Jensen developed an extensive career as garden designer, creating numerous residential gardens in the area around Chicago and throughout the Midwest. He established close friendships with members of the Prairie School of architecture and occasionally collaborated with them on projects. Throughout his design career, Jensen attempted to relate forms and materials to the surrounding native landscape. Designs were not intended to be copies of nature but symbolic representations using color, texture, sunlight and shadow, seasonal change, and careful manipulation of space to evoke a deep emotional response. He saw a value in plants then thought to be common weeds and used them in ecological patterns found in the wild. One of the unique features of Jensen's parks and gardens was his use of the "council ring" for accommodating outdoor social gatherings and cultural activities. A low stone seat encircling a central fire pit, Jensen's council ring brought people together at the same level and provided a setting for storytelling, dance, drama, and simply communal gathering. His 1935 design for Lincoln Memorial Garden in Springfield, Illinois, attempted to re-create the landscape that Abraham Lincoln might have experienced and included eight council rings.

For Jensen, there was an obvious continuum between design and conservation. Through his designs, he aimed to awaken the public to the beauty and cycles of nature; through groups such as the Prairie Club and the Friends of Our Native Landscape, he sought to preserve remnants of our wild natural heritage. Often, outdoor pageantry and masques such as "The Beauty of the Wild"

Lagoon, Fair Lane, Henry and Clara Ford estate, Dearborn, Michigan. Courtesy Robert E. Grese.

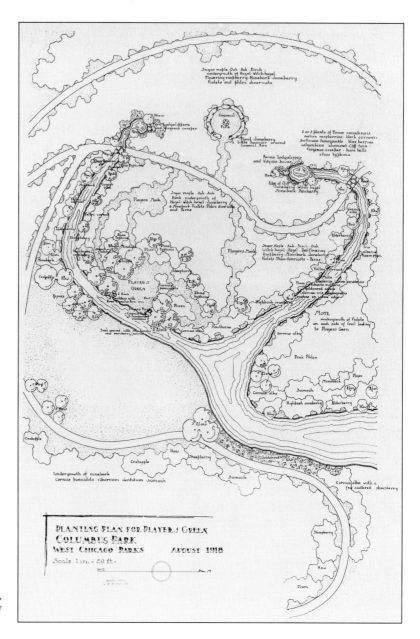

Players Green, Columbus Park, Chicago. Courtesy Jensen Collection, Bentley Historical Library, University of Michigan, Ann Arbor.

by Kenneth Sawyer Goodman were used as ways of building public support for the preservation of local natural areas. The efforts by Jensen and these conservation groups led to the preservation of many scenic, historical, and high-quality natural areas throughout Illinois, Indiana, Michigan, and Wisconsin.

After his wife died in 1934, Jensen decided he had had enough of city life and retired to what had since 1919 been the family's summer home, in Ellison Bay on Wisconsin's Door County peninsula. He was not to rest on his laurels, however. He devoted his remaining years to establishing the school he would

View from The Clearing, Ellison Bay, Wisconsin. Photo Charles A. Birnbaum.

call The Clearing. He described it as a "school of the soil" where students could get away from the hopelessly "confused" system of contemporary education and back to a simpler, more basic style of learning that combined studies of ecology, horticulture, the arts, philosophy, and a myriad of other related topics. During his lifetime, Jensen's school never attracted many students or had secure funding. After his death in 1951, his secretary, Mertha Fulkerson, continued the school with the Wisconsin Farm Bureau, and its program evolved to its present form with an emphasis on a variety of classes in nature study, arts, crafts, writing, and other topics—in the spirit Jensen intended.

Edsel and Eleanor Ford estate, Grosse Pointe Shores, Michigan, 1998. Photo Carol Betsch.

Prairie River, Columbus Park, Chicago, 1997. Photo Charles A. Birnbaum.

Grese, Robert E. *Jens Jensen: Maker of Natural Parks and Gardens*. Baltimore: Johns Hopkins University Press, 1992. Relates Jensen to his contemporaries and analyzes his contributions to landscape architecture, planning, and conservation.

Jensen, Jens. *Siftings*. 1939. Baltimore: Johns Hopkins University Press, 1990. Jensen's summary of his thoughts on design and conservation.

Miller, Wilhelm*. *The Prairie Spirit in Landscape Gardening*. University of Illinois Agricultural Experiment Station Circular No. 184. Urbana, 1915. Within dis-cussion of the Prairie style, perhaps the most in-depth analysis of Jensen's work by one of his contemporaries; features Jensen's work alongside that of O. C. Simonds* and W. B. Griffin* as the major contributors to that style.

Jensen's papers are housed in several major collections: the Bentley Historical Library at the University of Michigan, Ann Arbor, the Morton Arboretum in Lisle, Illinois, and the Chicago Historical Society.

Robert E. Grese

KERN, MAXIMILIAN G.
(late 1820s/early 1830s–c. 1915)
landscape gardener, author

Maximilian Kern was born in Tubingen, Germany, and received formal training in botany from his uncle at that city's university. He gained practical experience at the royal gardens, Stuttgart, and at the Tuileries Gardens.

Between the time he fled Paris during the revolution of 1848 and his arrival in St. Louis in 1864, Kern's whereabouts remain undocumented. At least part of this time may have been spent in Cincinnati, where he reputedly worked at Spring Grove Cemetery, which was extensively remade under the direction of Adolph Strauch* beginning in the mid-1850s. It is tempting to believe, too, that he was one and the same as G. M. Kern, a landscape gardener working in Cincinnati and author of *Practical Landscape Gardening . . .*, published locally in 1855 (interchanging Christian and middle names was a common practice among Germans in the nineteenth century). No record of Kern's presence has been found, however, in cemetery records, city directories, or other contemporary local sources.

Whatever their nature, Kern's early accomplishments in the United States gave him a reputation sufficient to be appointed superintendent of Lafayette Park, the oldest (1836) and largest park in St. Louis at that time and, under Kern's direction, the first to be extensively developed for recreational purposes. During the five years he held the post, the park was transformed into a much-acclaimed showpiece. Kern became superintendent of public parks circa 1873, devoting most of his energies to the design of Forest Park, a project of nearly unprecedented size (1,375 acres). Working with civil engineer Julius Pitzman, Kern prepared an elaborate scheme of winding roads and paths, ornamental embellishments, and a hippodrome. After its unveiling in January 1876, the basic form of Kern's plan was implemented, but Kern himself fell victim to a change in political administration. While he was credited with subsequent designs for the grounds of reservoirs at Compton Hill and Chain of Rocks, his major role in public works had ended.

Over the next decade, Kern's practice became itinerant, although he maintained a home base in St. Louis. By 1879 he was working for the Kansas Pacific Railroad and living in Topeka. In 1880, St. Louis directories listed his residence as Alton, Illinois; in 1881, Memphis. During the 1881–1882 academic year he taught horticulture at the University of Missouri. Three years later he prepared a master plan for Kansas State Agricultural College (now Kansas State University) at Manhattan, a scheme that ranked among the most fully developed of its kind in the central states. By 1887 he was an agent for the U.S. Department of Agriculture. That same year he again collaborated with Pitzman, this time on the design of the Forest Park Addition, a residential tract including what would become two of St. Louis's most elegant private streets, Portland and Westmoreland places.

Kern's greatest impact, however, may have come from his book *Rural Taste in Western Towns and Country*

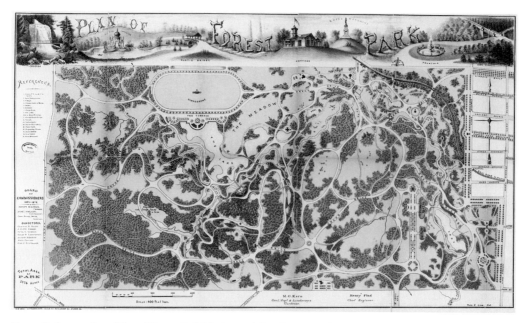

Forest Park, map from "Plan of Forest Park." Lithograph by Theo C. Link, 1875. Courtesy Missouri Historical Society Library.

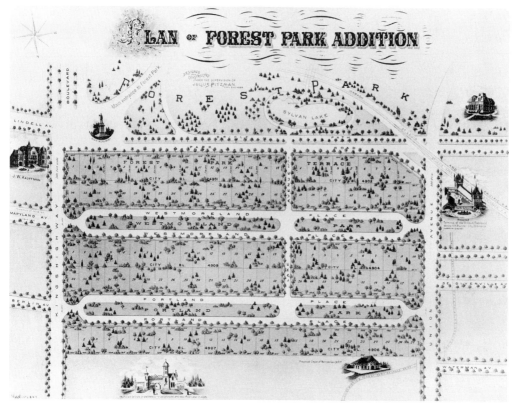

"Plan of Forest Park Addition." Lithograph by Gast after Julius Pitzman, 1887. Courtesy Missouri Historical Society Library.

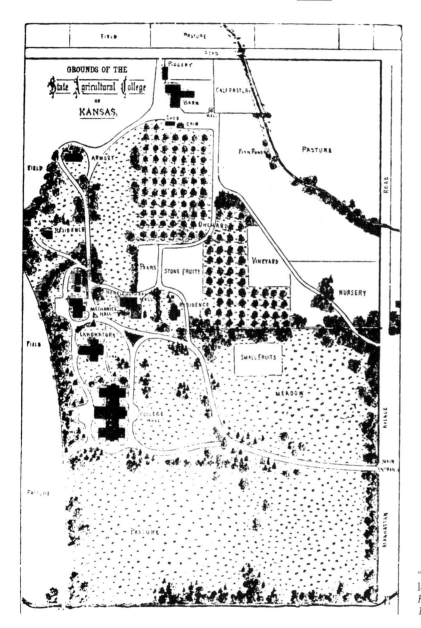

"Grounds of the State Agricultural College of Kansas." From *Catalog of the Kansas State Agricultural College, 1885–86*.

Districts (1884), which was written for a general audience and carefully tailored to conditions west of the Mississippi. Kern did not advocate a regional style of landscape design per se, but, in contrast to many advocates of naturalistic planning, he held no disdain for the standardized, geometric land subdivision patterns created by surveyors. During the nineteenth century, his treatise was perhaps unique in its use of this existing order as a basis for landscape improvements. The degree to which it set the tone for work done at the grass roots over subsequent decades deserves further exploration.

Kern lived to an advanced age (St. Louis directories list him through 1915), though by the early twentieth century he was in retirement and largely forgotten in his adopted city. The initial designs of Forest Park and other major projects were generally attributed to Pitzman.

Kern has remained in obscurity ever since, underscoring the tenuous professional stature of his field during the early decades of its existence.

Kern, Maximilian G. *Rural Taste in Western Towns and Country Districts, in Its Relation to the Principles of the Art of Landscape Gardening.* Columbia, Mo., 1884. The most extensive exposition of Kern's ideas and an unusual treatise in its acceptance of the pervasive grid matrix of communities in the central United States; a pragmatic approach, focusing on ways to improve through landscaping the standard components of settlement, including the farmstead, residential streets, courthouse square, and institutional ground.

Longstreth, Richard. "From Farm to Campus: Planning, Politics, and the Agricultural College Idea in Kansas." *Winterthur Portfolio* 20 (Summer–Autumn 1985), 149–173. Detailed historical analysis of the first half-century's development of the Kansas State Agricultural College campus, for which Kern designed the master plan in 1885; provides the most thorough coverage of what is known about Kern's career.

Report of the Commissioners of Forest Park, 1875. St. Louis, 1876. Detailed discussion of Kern's most important work; includes a lengthy description of the design by Kern himself.

Richard Longstreth

KESSLER, GEORGE EDWARD
(1862–1923)
landscape architect, planner

George Edward Kessler was born in the small village of Bad Frankenhausen, Germany. Three years later, his family emigrated to the United States, first living in Hoboken, New Jersey, then moving on to St. Louis and Hannibal, Missouri, and to Wisconsin before settling in Dallas. In 1878, Kessler returned to Germany to enter the private school for landscape gardening at the Belvedere in Weimar, studying botany, forestry, and design with Hofgartner Julius Hartwig and Garteninspector Julius Skell. Further instruction in civil engineering at the University of Jena and the Neue Garten with Hofgartner Theodore Neitner in Potsdam completed his education. In early 1882 he returned to New York, where he spent several months working for LeMoult's nursery in the Bowery.

Frederick Law Olmsted Sr.* recommended Kessler to the Kansas City, Fort Scott, & Gulf Railroad to take charge of the firm's pleasure park in Merriam, Kansas. There Kessler's work attracted the attention of the Kansas City mortgage-banking firm of Jarvis & Conklin, which hired him to prepare residential subdivision plans for Hyde Park in Kansas City, Missouri (1887), phase one of Roland Park, Baltimore (1891), Euclid Heights in Cleveland, Ohio, and a project in Ogden, Utah.

Kessler's contact with Kansas City's civic leaders led to an 1893 job designing the first park and boulevard plan for the city. This plan was likely Kessler's greatest work, in many ways as bold a vision of the City Beautiful as that articulated by the 1893 World's Columbian Exposition in Chicago. Kessler's plan preserved the

George E. Kessler. Courtesy Missouri Historical Society.

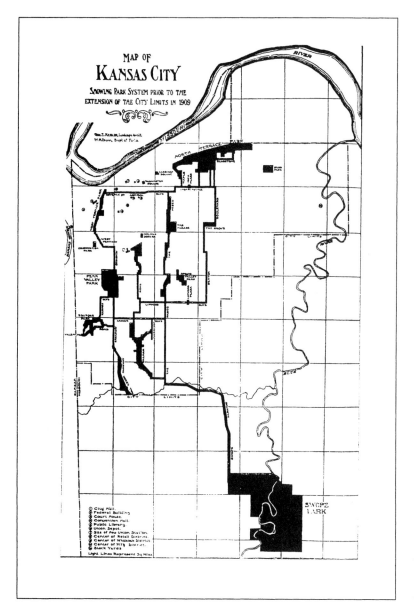

"Map of Kansas City, Showing Park System Prior to the Extension of the City Limits in 1909." Courtesy Kansas City Public Library.

stream corridors and river bluffs that separated the city into topographic units. A continuous open space system of boulevards and parkways connected the city's parks. Despite the success of this work, however, Kessler was rejected for membership in the American Society of Landscape Architects in 1899.

The Kansas City projects did lead to commissions for Fairlawn Cemetery, Oklahoma City (1892), Riverside and

Overton Park and a park system plan for Memphis, Tennessee (1900), and the landscape design of the Louisiana Purchase Exposition of 1904. The exposition project resulted in the opening of a St. Louis office, brought Eda Sutermeister and Henry Wright* into Kessler's employ, and extended Kessler's reputation throughout the region.

His roster of important projects grew rapidly. He developed the first park and boulevard plan for Indi-

Photocollage of Merriam Park, Kansas, n.d. Courtesy Kansas State Historical Society.

anapolis in 1905, thus beginning a lifelong association with that city. A park system scheme proposed for Syracuse, New York, in 1906 became the center of a heated mayoral campaign. In 1907 the groundwork for the marvelous Fort Worth park system was established, enabling the city to execute its first park and boulevard plan. Kessler's 1907 plan for Denver's parks was also brilliantly conceived. It identified high points from which distant views to the Rockies and the Great Plains could be obtained; these points were to be preserved as parks and connected by broad boulevards. However, the plan was only partially realized; Speer Boulevard and Cheesman Park are the most significant portions implemented.

In August 1906, Kessler was selected by the new park commission in Cincinnati to design a park system there. In his view, the circle of hills that surrounded the city offered more desirable locations for housing than the great plain along the Ohio River. Kessler's plan linked

the new neighborhoods with a grand central parkway. New York City Park Commissioner August Heckscher lauded Kessler's design many years later: "Here was the image of the city that did not merely contain parks, that was not merely penetrated by circuits of green, but of the city as a park in itself. The Cincinnati scheme keeps a perfect balance between the squares and malls of the central business district and the parks of the outer residential areas, between movement and stability, between neighborhood and metropolis. The open space system possesses an integrity and harmony that makes it a true work of art, surpassing in scale and complexity anything previously proposed for an American city."

In 1910, Kessler returned to Dallas, his childhood home, to begin work on a plan for the city. Published in 1911, his proposal reflects a growing awareness of the need to plan the "City Practical" as well as the City Beautiful.

Memphis boulevard system, 1997.
Photo Charles A. Birnbaum.

During World War I, Kessler worked for the U.S. Housing Corporation, responsible for the Rock Island District, with projects in Moline, East Moline, and Rock Island, Illinois. He also prepared master plans for the Camp Planning Division for cantonments in Lawton, Oklahoma (Camp Doniphan); San Antonio (Camp Travis); Little Rock (Camp Pike); and Deming, New Mexico. For two years, Kessler maintained an exhausting schedule, traveling by rail among these projects, and also to Washington and St. Louis, while continuing his involvement with private clients throughout the country. Whether Kessler, who apparently spoke with a German accent all his life, felt compelled to prove his patriotism while the United States was at war with his native land is uncertain. What is clear is that his efforts during the period were substantial. In July 1919 he was hospitalized for two months with a nervous breakdown. His health never fully recovered. There were, however, positive results from this labor. His work with other landscape architects during this period changed his relationship with his peers. In 1919 he was elected to membership in the ASLA, and three years later served as the organization's vice president.

Postwar projects designed by Kessler's office evolved as he drew on his wartime planning experiences. At the time of his death, Kessler was working on a master plan for Butler University in Indianapolis and Chapultepec Heights, a residential subdivision in Mexico City.

Dallas, Houston, Kansas City, St. Louis, Denver, Cincinnati, Indianapolis, and a score of smaller cities clearly bear the mark of Kessler's genius. They were magnificent contributions to the people and the landscape of the American Midwest.

Culbertson, Kurt. "George Edward Kessler: Landscape Architect of the American Renaissance." In *Landscape Architecture in the Midwest*, ed. William Tishler. Champaign: University of Illinois Press, in press. Documents the career canon of Kessler's work in parks, parkways, park systems, suburbs, exposition, and institutional grounds.

Wilson, William H. *The City Beautiful Movement in Kansas City*. Columbia: University of Missouri Press, 1964. Overview of Kessler's work, including his designs for suburbs and the first park and boulevard plan for the city; illustrated with many photos and plans.

The Kessler Collection, Missouri Historical Society, St. Louis, is the primary repository of Kessler's papers and records. The Kessler Society has recently been formed in Kansas City, Missouri, with the goal of preserving the works of George Kessler around the United States; their web site is at www.kessler .org.

Kurt Culbertson

KING, LOUISA YEOMANS (MRS. FRANCIS KING)
(1863–1948)
author

Louisa Yeomans was born near Washington, New Jersey, and educated in private schools. After her marriage in 1890 to Francis King and the birth of their three children, the family lived in Chicago and Elmhurst, Illinois. In Elmhurst, King developed a serious interest in gardening, an uncommon pursuit for women in the Victorian era. After a move to Alma, Michigan, in 1904, King began the gardens at her home, Orchard House, which later became famous through her books, magazine articles, and lectures. King's career wove together three themes: landscape design, horticulture, and the role of the garden in American life. Her work influenced gardens throughout the country, especially from 1910 to 1940. Many contemporaries deemed her the most influential American woman gardener, comparing her significance to Gertrude Jekyll's in England.

King studied and practiced the art of gardening as a passionate amateur for almost two decades before undertaking her professional career. Her writing first appeared in *The Garden Magazine* in 1910, and she contributed many articles thereafter to such publications as *House and Garden* and *Country Life*, including a regular column in *House Beautiful* in the 1920s. Widowed in 1927, King moved to South Hartford, New York, where she established a new garden, Kingstree.

King reached her widest audience through her nine books, most of which were compilations of her magazine articles. Her first, published in 1915, *The Well-Considered Garden*, with an introduction by Jekyll, was perhaps her most influential. It covered a variety of topics including the importance of landscape design, color in the garden as a fine art, plant combinations, and garden literature. *Pages from a Garden Note-Book* of 1921 was followed the same year by King's best-selling title, *The Little Garden*. This book spoke directly to the many new suburbanites eager to start a new life after World War I. It describes, in simple terms for the beginner, the design, planting, and maintenance of a small garden. The 1920s marked the apex of King's career as a writer, with the appearance of the collections *Variety in the Little Garden* (1923), *Chronicles of the Garden* (1925), and *The Beginner's Garden* (1927), as well as a garden diary titled *The Flower Garden Day-by-Day* (1927) and *The Gardener's Colour Book* (1929), a color planning guide adapted from a British work by John Fothergill. King's last book was *From a New Garden*, published in 1930, but she continued to write, contributing a chapter on American gardens to *The Story of the Garden* (1933) by the distinguished British author Eleanour Sinclair Rohde, introductions to other garden books, and magazine articles until 1945. In addition to her writing,

Mrs. King in her garden at Orchard House. From *Country Life in America*, March 1919.

she maintained a speaking career that extended into the 1940s and took her back and forth across North America, into Great Britain, and to the continent as well. Her influence was such that *House and Garden* declared her the "dean of American gardening" in 1940.

King was a leading figure in the garden club movement, which affected the profession of landscape architecture in a number of ways, not the least of which was in creating a market for the work of many of the period's practitioners. She was a founder, in 1911, of the Garden Club of Michigan and in 1913 of the Garden Club of America. A proselytizer for the importance of landscape design, King tirelessly promoted both the profession and individual practitioners throughout her career. The importance of design and the value of the landscape architect were two of her most frequent topics in both her writing and lecturing to garden clubs and other groups. In addition, she offered suggestions and advice to those who could not afford to hire a design professional. Arguably no other figure of this seminal period reached such a wide audience on the subject of the importance of landscape design.

King enjoyed wide-ranging friendships with many important figures of the garden world, and her role in connecting people with mutual interests was not the least important of her contributions to the field. She was a long-time friend, correspondent, and disciple of Gertrude Jekyll, and among her other friends and correspondents were Charles Sprague Sargent* of the Arnold Arboretum and the landscape architects Fletcher Steele*, Ellen Shipman*, and Martha Brookes Hutcheson*.

King believed in gardening as a force for democracy, a means of bringing people together, and, moreover, as a way for women to establish themselves professionally. An ardent suffragist, she was active in the Michigan campaign for women's suffrage, and continued her efforts for the advancement of women throughout her career. She helped found the Woman's National Farm and Garden Association in 1914, a diverse group that included several of the most prominent early women landscape architects as well as farm women seeking to support themselves. Through it, King promoted such careers for women until her death in 1948.

Begg, Virginia Lopez. "Influential Friends: Charles Sprague Sargent and Louisa Yeomans King." *Journal of the New England Garden History Society* 1 (Fall 1991). A brief survey of their separate careers and their correspondence.

Begg, Virginia Lopez. "Mrs. Francis King, 'Dean of American Gardening'." *American Horticulturist* (October 1991), 40–45. An overview of King's life and work.

Virginia Lopez Begg

KNIGHT, EMERSON
(1882–1960)
landscape architect, author, conservationist

Born in Cincinnati, Emerson Knight was the son of William Henry Knight, an author and astronomer captivated by the West, and in particular California. At the age of nine Emerson moved with his family to Los Angeles, where he lived until 1915. It is speculated that his father's lack of financial success resulted in Emerson's completing only one year of high school before becoming a stock boy at the age of thirteen.

Despite his incomplete formal education, Knight was raised in a household that valued cultural explorations—music, art, and painting—and he eagerly took advantage of every opportunity. His interests ranged from singing in a choral society to studying nature in the undeveloped mountains surrounding Los Angeles. In 1913 he spent six months in England and Western Europe, a period that included studying life drawing for two months at the Julian Academy in Paris. After returning to Los Angeles in 1916, having abandoned his job as a salesman, Knight embarked on a 300-mile journey up the coast, traveling on foot, stopping at missions, studying plants and wildlife, and experiencing the Western landscape, in pursuit of his true interests: art and nature.

Easter services at Mount Helix Nature Theatre, April 12, 1925, La Mesa, California. Courtesy San Diego Historical Society.

Knight arrived in Santa Barbara, where at the age of thirty-four, despite his lack of formal training, he supervised landscape developments for Camillo Francheschi Fenzi, who was probably a gardener rather than a landscape architect. The following year Knight was made an associate at the San Francisco office of Mark Daniels, where he managed the eighty-acre estate of J. Cheever Cowdin in Hillsborough, located on the peninsula south of the city. He continued work for Daniels until 1918, designing small gardens in San Francisco and larger country estates in the surrounding areas.

In 1918, having been left Daniels's office and equipment, Knight commenced private practice in San Francisco, initially focusing on small city gardens and estate properties. His design philosophy and approach varied greatly, resulting in a distinct lack of a stylistic trademark. He designed spaces to resemble an English meadow, a formal French lawn, or a Japanese soy tube container garden in response to the desire of the client. There is no record of his designs with which to determine the extent or breadth of his work during this period. By 1925 he began to expand his repertoire.

Knight wrote an article titled "The Four Phases of Design" in 1928 for *The Architect and Engineer*. The four design phases it outlined were the small garden for city and suburban lots; the country estate; the outdoor theater; and the park endowed by nature. His omission of commercial developments may indicate that they were not of interest to him. The article was published at a time when he had shifted his efforts away from estate gardens. The "third phase" of Knight's career had commenced in 1924, when the garden theater on the Max Cohn estate of Little Brook Farm in Los Gatos, the Woodland Theater in Hillsborough, and the inclusion of an outdoor theater

Aerial view over Mount Helix Nature Theatre, c. 1930. Courtesy San Diego Historical Society.

Sidney B. Cushing Mountain Theatre (constructed 1925–1938), Mount Tamalpais State Park, Marin County, California. Courtesy Linda Jewell.

in the proposal for Arden Wood, a planned community in San Francisco, were completed. Also in 1924, in collaboration with architects Richard Requa* and Herbert L. Jackson, he designed the Mount Helix Theater outside San Diego. Knight preserved many native trees and shrubs, and designed a planting screen to direct the view of the audience and shield people from the wind.

Over the next years Knight undertook work on the Mountain Theater on Mount Tamalpais. The site, a natural amphitheater, had been discovered by a group of conservationists hiking through the area. Designed to blend into the environment, the theater utilizes the shape of the site, taking advantage of inherent acoustic possibilities. Adaptation of indigenous stone and native plant species also helps blend the structure into the topography and the character of the mountain. Large boulders with two 90-degree angled surfaces were buried in the ground to form rustic seats; existing trees were left in place to interrupt the regularity of the boulders and show Knight's interest in conservation. The work was completed in 1938 under the supervision of landscape architect Paul J. Holloway, who adhered to Knight's design and philosophy. The theater remains integrated into the landscape of Mount Tamalpais, more than two thousand feet above sea level, with views of both the San Francisco Bay and the mountains of the Pacific coast. Knight considered the Mountain Theater his most notable contribution to the field of landscape architecture.

In the late 1920s, embarking on the fourth phase of his career, Knight went to Mexico to determine the most suitable areas to be developed into parklands and historic monuments for the Mexican National Highway Commission. During the next fifteen years, he became involved in several organizations including the Save the Redwoods League, the Monterey City Planning Commission, the California State Park Commission, and the National Park Service. Retained by the office of Frederick Law Olmsted Jr.* to analyze the potential park spaces along the California coast, Knight received endorsement from Olmsted for fellowship in the American Society of Landscape Architects.

Perhaps the largest single project of this phase was his plan for the preservation of historic Monterey, which demonstrates his thoughtful, sophisticated treatment of complex sites. It is clear from Knight's report that he was essentially a preservationist and naturalist. He outlined ways of integrating a plan with Monterey Bay, making use of the shapes and essence of the landscape. He also suggested incorporating the historic structures of the town into a small promenade to give a historical focus to the site, and shifting and redesigning the municipal wharf "to illuminate its full beauty with the bay and colorful fishing craft."

In addition to his design work, Knight wrote extensively for magazines including *Sunset, Sierra Club Bulletin, American Forests, California Arts and Architecture,* and *Landscape Architecture*, and many reports on potential park sites for the Save the Redwoods League, the California State Park Commission, and the National Park Service. One of the reports concerned the 30,000 acres north of San Francisco that today is Point Reyes National Seashore. His writings reflect the compelling subtlety of a sensitive, thoughtful man, who delighted in the scents, colors, tactile qualities, and sounds of a landscape.

In 1940, at the age of fifty-eight, Knight, after serious physical difficulties and a series of operations, became limited in his activities. However, he retained a small office, filled with books, and continued to attend all cultural events possible. He died at the age of seventy-seven.

Knight, Emerson. "Mountain Theater on Mount Tamalpais." *Landscape Architecture* 40 (October 1949), 4–7. A description of the theater that may be Knight's greatest accomplishment, as well as the evolution and history of the site; photographs.

Knight, Emerson. "Outdoor Theaters and Stadiums in the West." *The Architect and Engineer* 72 (August 1924), 53–91. Good descriptions of numerous theaters, accompanied by photographs.

Knight, Emerson. "Recent Gardens in San Francisco and the Environs." *The Architect and Engineer* 70 (July 1922), 50–64. Pictures and text communicate Knight's residential design strategy.

Linda Jewell

LAY, CHARLES DOWNING
(1877–1956)
landscape architect

Charles Downing Lay was born in Newburgh, New York, the son of portrait painter Oliver I. Lay and Hester Marion Waite. Incidentally and rather appropriately, he was named for a relative, Charles Downing, the horticulturist brother of Andrew Jackson Downing*. Lay attended Columbia University's School of Architecture from 1896 to 1900, and in 1902, became the second graduate in the landscape architecture program at Harvard University. Immediately on graduation, he began working in New York with Daniel W. Langton, a founding member of the American Society of Landscape Architects. In 1904, Lay started an independent practice that he maintained in New York for forty-four years.

Among Lay's many contributions to the profession, one of the greatest was the creation of its magazine, *Landscape Architecture*. Frustrated by the view of the American Association of Landscape Architects that the costs of publishing a professional journal would be prohibitive, Lay found a way to start one anyway. In 1910 he invited Henry Hubbard* and Robert Wheelwright* to join him in establishing and publishing *Landscape Architecture* as a quarterly magazine. Their partnership continued until 1920, during which time Lay was editor-in-chief. Then Hubbard carried on the task alone until the society officially took over publication years later.

Lay was appointed the landscape architect for New York City's Parks Department by Mayor William J. Gaynor immediately following the tenures of Samuel Parsons Jr.* and Carl Pilat, and retained the responsibility for one and a half years in 1913–1914. His private practice oversaw the design and construction of recreational parks in Troy, New York (Frear Park); Schenectady (Central Park, Pleasant Valley Park); Brooklyn (Marine Park); Stratford, Connecticut (Sterling Park), and the park system for Albany (Lincoln Park, Tivoli Park, Riverside Park, Linn Park, and Swinburne Park).

Throughout his career, Lay wrote extensively on subjects ranging from parks and urban planning to art and architecture, contributing to a variety of publications. In his *Landscape Architecture* editorials and articles early in his career, he stated his concerns for the creation and maintenance of parks and playgrounds, pointing out that parks should enhance city life as well as meet the recreational needs of the swelling population. Later, in 1930, Lay summed up his philosophy about landscape design as art: there should be more art and less nature in our work,

more thought of design and less about fancy bushes. Lay also wrote two books: *A Garden Book for Autumn and Winter* (1924) and *Freedom of the City* (1926).

Lay had a reputation as a very practical designer; although aesthetic qualities with respect to site and structures were most important to him, he always considered the maintenance aspects as well. In his natural designs he attempted to idealize the natural landscape, contending that primeval landscapes lacked interest and that evidence of human occupation was needed for full aesthetic effect. His formal gardens avoided harsh symmetry and cold formality.

Lay's list of accomplished work includes town planning studies for Albany and for the towns of Erie and Butler, Pennsylvania (for the U. S. Housing Corporation), and Arvida, Saguenay River, Canada (for the Aluminum Company of America). He prepared several studies for Nassau County, New York, which appeared in *Golf Illustrated* (1925): "A Park System for Long Island," "Jones Beach—A Great Ocean Park," and "Highways on Long Island." These writings were used as promotional materials to gain public support and entice new residents to Long Island. Lay prepared more than ten subdivision plans for communities including Pittsfield, Massachusetts; Hewlett, New York; and Westbrook, Connecticut.

Charles Downing Lay. From *Landscape Architecture*, April 1956.

Pool and gardens, J. Percy Bartram estate, Caritas Island, Stamford, Connecticut. From P. H. Elwood Jr., ed., *American Landscape Architecture*, 1924.

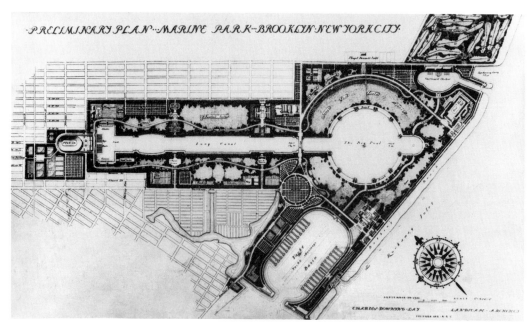

"Preliminary Plan, Marine Park, Brooklyn, New York City," September 1931. Courtesy Collections of the Municipal Archives of the City of New York.

He designed the campuses for Union College, Schenectady; the Lenox School, Lenox, Massachusetts; the Free Academy, Newburgh, New York; and the Ridgefield School, Ridgefield, Connecticut.

Lay's practice was as varied as the events of the time. He was the consulting landscape architect to the board of design for the 1939 New York World's Fair as well as for the horticultural exhibit at the fair, "Gardens on Parade," for Hortus, Inc. During World War II, Lay worked on such military projects as Fort Jay, New York, and the naval air stations at Floyd Bennett Field, New York, in Memphis, and in Wilmington, North Carolina. His consulting work after the war for the New York City and U.S. Public Housing Authorities included housing projects at Jacob Riis, Queens (1945), and Sheepshead Bay, Brooklyn (1950). In addition to his park and planning work, Lay's résumé at the time of his death in 1956 listed 30 of his most significant residential commissions by client name, most of them in the New York state and New England areas.

From 1941, Lay lived in semi-retirement at his family's residence, Wellesmere, in Stratford, Connecticut, and was concerned with public advocacy and the conservation of the Housatonic River Valley. He was instrumental in forming the Housatonic Valley Planning Association in 1948, which today continues to protect the valley from encroachment. He died in Stratford in 1956. At the time of his death, his good friend and colleague Robert Wheelwright described him as having a "truly creative mind . . . so full of ideas, it appeared that his brain had been as busy during sleep as in waking hours."

"Charles Downing Lay. September 3, 1877–February 15, 1956. A Biographical Minute." *Landscape Architecture* 46 (April 1956), 162–164. A brief biography of Lay and description of his personal accomplishments and contribution to the profession, written by Robert Wheelwright.

Lay, Charles Downing. *A Garden Book for Autumn and Winter.* New York: Duffield, 1924. Discusses the different types of gardens through the seasons and the methods by which one expresses style in the landscape; photos and plans by Lay, plus a list of useful plants.

The Lay Collection, the family's collection of Charles Downing Lay's work, including his writings, hand-colored slides, plans, and drawings, was inventoried by the Catalog of Landscape Records in the United States before donation to Cornell University's Division of Rare and Manuscript Collections.

Laurie E. Hempton

LEAVITT, CHARLES WELLFORD, JR.
(1871–1928)
landscape engineer

Charles Wellford Leavitt Jr. was born in Riverton, New Jersey, the son of a New York metal importer. The Leavitt family, with roots in Massachusetts dating to 1628, was moderately wealthy, and Leavitt was educated at two private schools, the Gunnery in Washington, Connecticut, and the Cheltenham Academy in Cheltenham, Pennsylvania. In 1891, at the age of twenty, Leavitt began his engineering career, taking his first job as the engineer in charge of construction for the Caldwell, New Jersey, Railway. He changed positions and employers numerous times in the next few years and rapidly gained experience in various aspects of civil engineering. Between 1893 and 1895 he worked for the New York Suburban Land Company. In 1895 he became the city engineer for Essex Fells, New Jersey, supervising the city's water supply, sewers and sewage disposal, and road construction. The following year, Leavitt became assistant engineer in charge of construction for the East Jersey Water Company. From these varied work experiences he gleaned a knowledge of design, construction, infrastructure planning, and subdivision layout which would serve him well in the future.

In 1897, after six years of working for others, Leavitt opened his own office in New York City, calling himself a "landscape engineer," a title he would use for the rest of

Charles Wellford Leavitt by Cecilia Beaux, 1911. Courtesy Richard York Gallery, New York.

his career. It is likely that he preferred that term to "landscape architect" because it better represented his engineering background, expertise, and interest in large-scale landscape work, civil engineering, and city planning. However, Leavitt was knowledgeable in and a member of professional organizations of both realms of practice. He also described himself as a landscape architect when it was advantageous—for example, when his articles about residential work appeared in popular magazines such as *Country Life* and *House and Garden* in the 1920s.

From its inception, Leavitt's office met with a success that would continue for the next thirty years. The projects represented a full range of landscape architectural practice, from simple suburban residences and individual cemetery plots to parks, parkways, country estates, and plans for cities and subdivisions. The large and diverse workload soon required additional staff. Among those who worked for Leavitt over the years were Anthony Morell* and Arthur Nichols*, who served on his staff in the early 1900s before establishing their own office in Minneapolis. In the early 1920s, Leavitt's son entered the practice, and the firm became known as Charles Wellford Leavitt & Son.

Leavitt's professed goal in landscape design, as one of his firm's brochures stated, was to "produce results that approach perfection . . . through matured study and skilled workmanship." These qualities were particularly apparent in his residential and estate work, which was characterized by its attention to detail, craftsmanship, and references to what the firm called the "Old World" styles of Italy, France, and Egypt. However, as critics of the time noted, Leavitt transcended both stylistic eclecticism and Beaux Arts formalism through his mastery of scale and his use of site-specific plantings. Perhaps the best example of these strengths was the gardens he designed for the estate of Charles M. Schwab in Loretto, Pennsylvania. With a huge, 14-level Italian-style water cascade, they were nevertheless praised in *Architectural Record* as "finely expressive of the landscape of the locality and of a quaint element in the Alleghanies of western Pennsylvania" and also lauded for the plantings. Other estates designed by Leavitt included those for Chester Congdon (Duluth, Minn.); George B. Post (Bernardsville, N.J.); John F. Dodge (Grosse Pointe, Mich.); Foxhall Keene (Westbury, N.Y.); and scores of others in New York, New Jersey, Delaware, Alabama, Louisiana, and Connecticut. The office also worked on less patrician projects. In the late 1920s the staff designed a series of "garden patterns" for small residential lots which were published for use by the general public in *Ladies' Home Journal*.

Leavitt's civic work was as distinguished and diverse as his residential. He designed city plans for Long Beach and Garden City on Long Island, New York; New Cape May, New Jersey; and Lakeland, Florida. He was also well known for his cemetery work, including the plan of the Cemetery of the Gate of Heaven in Mount Pleasant, New York, and others in Brooklyn, Baltimore, and Stockbridge, Massachusetts. Leavitt's park designs included Pennypack Park in Philadelphia; Monument Valley Park in Colorado Springs; and a system of parks and parkways along the Cooper River in Camden, New Jersey. He was chief engineer of the Palisades Interstate Park for twelve years, completing the original design for it, including the Storm King Highway, which opened in 1923. His park work seems to have emphasized connections to urban areas and provision of recreational facilities. For example, his 1922 design for a municipal park in Johnstown, Pennsylvania, with its 300 × 140-foot swimming pool, athletic fields, tennis courts, camping areas, and golf course, seems to foreshadow the large recreational public works projects undertaken in New York and elsewhere in the 1930s.

Leavitt also completed campus designs, including

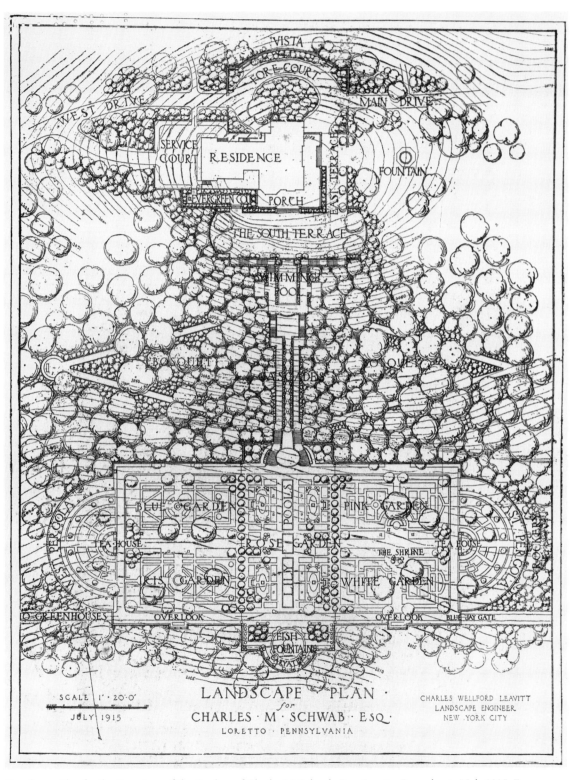

"Landscape Plan for the Core Area of the Gardens of Charles M. Schwab, Esq., Loretto, Pennsylvania," July 1915. From *Country Life in America*, June 1920. Courtesy Avery Architectural and Fine Arts Library, Columbia University, New York.

View down the Cascades toward surrounding landscape at Immergrun, Schwab estate. Photo by Gillies, from *Beauty and Gardens, A Tribute,* 1928. Courtesy Smithsonian Institution, Archives of American Gardens.

plans for the University of Georgia at Athens, Lehigh University at Bethlehem, Pennsylvania, and the University of South Carolina. Other institutional work included the Berry School in Rome, Georgia; the Tome Institute, Port Deposit, Maryland; and plans for the presidential palace in Havana, Cuba. One of the firm's specialty areas was the design of horse racing courses and their associated facilities. Its most notable track designs in the United States were the courses at Belmont and Saratoga in New York; the firm also designed courses at Toronto, Winnipeg, and Montreal in Canada and Le Havre in France. Leavitt designed sewage disposal sites, industrial housing, country clubs, and hospital grounds for numerous public and private clients. Long-term consulting positions, including Leavitt's role as consulting landscape engineer to the New York City Board of Water Supply, provided additional income for the firm.

In 1904, Leavitt became a member of the American Society of Landscape Architects. He also held memberships in the American Society of Civil Engineers and the American Institute of Consulting Engineers and was president of the latter group in 1923. He was known among his peers as a man passionately fond of the out-of-doors and enjoyed farming, camping, fishing, hunting, and sailing. In 1928, at the height of his career, Leavitt died suddenly at the age of fifty-seven. Although it seems that his son tried to continue the office after his father's death, by the early 1930s the office had been completely disbanded.

Executed Work and Drawings from the Office of Charles Wellford Leavitt & Son, Brochures I (1925) and II (1927). New York: N.p. Two advertising brochures depicting the office's work and philosophy and providing the most extensive photographic illustrations of Leavitt's work located so far; copy available at the Frances Loeb Library, Graduate School of Design, Harvard University.

Imlay, Robert. "The Gardens of Charles M. Schwab, Esq., Loretto, Pennsylvania: Charles Wellford Leavitt, Landscape Engineer." *Architectural Record* 47 (May 1920), 387–407. Contains an extensive description of the estate with very good photographic coverage.

Leavitt, Charles Wellford. "The Vista in the City Plan." *American City*, June 1928, 119–120. A brief article, written shortly before his death and published posthumously, which provides some insight into Leavitt's thinking about city planning.

Heidi Hohmann

LORD, ELIZABETH
(1887–1976)
landscape architect

Elizabeth Lord was born in Oregon, the daughter of William Paine Lord, a former Oregon governor and U.S. diplomat, and Juliette Montague Lord, who is credited with establishing the Salem Floral Society (now Salem Garden Club), the first garden club in Oregon. Lord received her education in Oregon public schools and Buenos Aires, where her father held a diplomatic post. Her mother's devotion to gardening and extensive travels to view the renowned gardens of the Far East, Europe, and South America influenced Lord's decision to pursue landscape architecture as a profession, prompting her, in 1926, to enter the Lowthorpe School of Landscape Architecture for Women at Groton, Massachusetts, becoming one of only two students from west of the Mississippi.

Elizabeth Lord met Edith Schryver*, another Lowthorpe graduate, on a European study tour sponsored by the Lowthorpe and Cambridge schools. Recognizing their similarity of tastes and philosophy in garden design, the two formed a partnership in Salem, Oregon, where they practiced from 1929 until they retired in 1970. Lord died in 1976 in Salem.

SCHRYVER, EDITH
(1901–1984)
landscape architect

Edith Schryver, known to her friends as Nina, was born in Kingston, New York. She attended the Lowthorpe School of Landscape Architecture during summers before completing high school and studied general art for one year at Brooklyn's Pratt Institute. In 1920 she enrolled full-time at Lowthorpe while working part-time in the Boston offices of landscape architects Harold Hill Blossom, Elizabeth Pattee, and Elizabeth Leonard Strang. She spent the summer of 1922 in the Cornish, New Hampshire, office of Ellen Shipman* as part of her scholarship, and on graduation she worked for the next five years in Shipman's New York office.

Schryver met Elizabeth Lord*, another Lowthorpe graduate, on a European study tour sponsored by the Lowthorpe and Cambridge schools, and the two formed a partnership (1929–1970) in Salem, Oregon, where they worked until retirement. Schryver died in 1984 in Salem.

Lord & Schryver

Lord & Schryver of Salem, Oregon, is believed to be the first firm of professional women landscape architects on the West Coast. The partners were representative of scores of Lowthorpe graduates who became pioneering professionals in their home communities. (Lowthorpe admitted only about a dozen students per year.) Their style was influenced by Gertrude Jekyll, Ellen Shipman*, and Louise Beebe Wilder*. Domesticity, intimacy, and romantic seclusion characterized the best of Shipman's designs, and the same could be said of Lord & Schryver. In the architectonic style of the time, their work was formal in character with clearly delineated landscape rooms. However, in the 1933 notes for a lecture, "The Importance of Living in a Garden," Schryver lists working, relaxing, eating, playing, and looking outdoors as garden functions. The garden, she said, is an "outdoor house." The philosophy echoes that of other West Coast landscape architects responding to the region's life style and capitalizing on the moderate climate and lush landscape. Lord & Schryver sought a quality they articulated as "charm." "Too much neatness without any careless grace will not produce charm," said Schryver.

The firm focused on garden design for private residences. Schryver was primarily responsible for design and construction drawings; Lord concentrated on planting design. Significant residential projects included Deep-wood, originally the Dr. Luke Port house, a historic site now part of the Salem Park System (the garden was designed for Alice Brown); the Robertson-Gormsen house, the Baumgartner-Caughell house; the Brown house, and their own home on Mission Street (which they called "Gaiety Hollow"), all in Salem. The firm also had commissions at Reed College (1939), the College (now University) of Puget Sound, and various Salem parks: Bush Pasture, Englewood, Pringle, Wilson, and the Marion County Courthouse. They also did historic site restoration for the Bush house in Salem and the Minthorn house in Newberg, Oregon, Herbert Hoover's boyhood home.

Lord & Schryver were active participants in Salem's Park Commission, Tree Commission, and Art Association, and the Oregon Roadside Council and Capitol Commission. Several gardens designed by the firm can be found in the National Register of Historic Places. The partners

Elizabeth Lord and Edith Schryver. Courtesy University of Oregon.

Robinson garden, Salem. Photo Kenneth I. Helphand.

Spring Garden, Deepwood, Salem, Oregon. Photo Kenneth I. Helphand.

were also involved in community education, writing articles on design for the Portland *Oregonian*, contributing to the "Home Garden House," a local radio show, and teaching briefly at Oregon State Agricultural College.

Schryver's design philosophy; illustrated with garden plan.

Duniway, David. "Lord-Schryver, Landscape Architects." *Marion County* (Oregon) *History* 14 (1983–1984), 107–120.

Helphand, Kenneth, and Nancy Rottle. "Cultivating Charm." *Garden Design*, Autumn 1988, 26–33, 88. A study of Deepwood gardens, Salem, and Lord &

Lord, Elizabeth, and Edith Schryver. *Sunday Oregonian* (Portland), March 6–May 1, 1932. A series of nine newspaper articles discussing various aspects of residential landscape design.

The archives of Lord & Schryver, with information on 238 projects, are housed at the University of Oregon Library in Eugene.

Kenneth I. Helphand

LOWELL, GUY
(1870–1927)
architect, landscape architect, educator, author

Guy Lowell was a noted New England architect and teacher of landscape architecture at the Massachusetts Institute of Technology. Educated at Harvard (1892), MIT (1894), and in the atelier Pascal and the Ecole des Beaux-Arts in Paris, he received the *diplome* in 1899. He spent time studying landscape and horticulture in Paris and at Kew Gardens. While still completing his European studies, Lowell married Henrietta Sargent in May 1898,

which brought him into closer contact with Charles Sprague Sargent*, his father-in-law and the director of the Arnold Arboretum near Boston. Returning to the United States in 1899, Lowell opened his practice on Tremont Street in Boston. Shortly thereafter, the family connection developed into a working relationship when Lowell initiated the landscape architecture program at MIT.

Although Lowell opened his office immediately on

Guy Lowell. Photo by Garo. Courtesy MIT Museum.

his return to Boston, his earliest completed project appears to be the Bayard Thayer house and gardens, c. 1903, in Lancaster, Massachusetts. Numerous residential projects quickly followed, however. This was a busy period in his life, as he was organizing the program at MIT and writing and editing *American Gardens*, a large-format photo publication (1902), in addition to setting up his practice.

Lowell designed numerous large residences, primarily in Massachusetts communities and on Long Island, New York, predominately in revival styles and classical modes. His public architecture was also significant, and among the best-known projects are the Museum of Fine Arts, Boston (1907+) and the New York County Courthouse (1913–1927).

According to Lowell's *New York Times* obituary, he designed ("fitted up") gardens for the elder J. Pierpont Morgan, Andrew Carnegie, and the Piping Rock Club. Additional specifically garden-related projects include

Branford House landscape, glass lantern slide, c. 1902. Courtesy Smithsonian Institution, Archives of American Gardens.

Italian Garden, Coe Hall, designed by Lowell & Sargent, Oyster Bay, Long Island, c. 1918. Courtesy Planting Fields Arboretum.

those of Thomas Jefferson Coolidge, Mrs. Oscar Iasigi in Stockbridge, Massachusetts, and Payne Whitney, Manhasset, Long Island. Lowell designed many of the gardens and grounds for his numerous residential commissions, but the largest and most significant project appears to have been the grounds of Clarence MacKay's Harbor Hill on Long Island, completed about 1905. This project generated substantial interest, particularly that of *Architectural Record* editor and critic Herbert Croly.

For Lowell's more formal homes, such as Harbor Hill and C. K. G. Billing's Long Island estate, Farnsworth (1905), he created a formal, structured garden close to the house, which dissolved into less rigid, natural surroundings as one moved away from the residence to stables or outbuildings. He approached the landscape of a less formal country house or gardener's cottage quite differently, allowing grass and foliage in close proximity to the dwelling, not feeling the need to separate the house from nature by so much as a terrace or a formal greenspace.

In other projects, such as George Knapp's residence near Lake George (c. 1904), he paid close attention to the topography, building the house into the hillside. In his words and in his work, Lowell demonstrated the importance of proper placement of buildings, sited to take advantage of natural landscape features and vistas.

This was an important component of Italian gardens, which he admired. However, he also advocated plantings native to America and minimal use of architectural pieces in the gardens.

Contemporary photographic views through doorways onto terraces and out into gardens reveal certain repeated elements and distinguishing qualities of Lowell's work: the vistas from inner rooms or those looking back up to the house indicate that an integrated, cohesive, simplified environment, with many native plantings, was of primary importance. He reserved the appropriate formal treatments for use closest to the house. This is supported by his introduction to *American Gardens*.

It is in the area of education that Lowell leaves his lasting mark on the profession of landscape architecture. Lowell founded the short-lived but influential landscape architecture program at MIT (1900–1910). He taught an important group of landscape architects their trade, including Mabel Babcock, George Burnap*, Marian Coffin*, and Martha Brookes Hutcheson*. Under his guidance, the program developed as a synthesis of French planning ideals and Italian garden design, with significant emphasis on horticulture and engineering. The first students graduated from the program in 1902. It was an undergraduate option from 1900 to 1904 and continued as a graduate course until 1909, with Lowell offering instruction in landscape architecture until 1912. (He did this free of charge, asking that his salary be turned over to the Architecture Department.) Lowell's program at MIT was particularly important for women because it provided educational opportunities they could not find elsewhere; many of his female students went on to become outstanding practitioners.

A great admirer of Italian gardens, Lowell believed that American landscape architecture should take the best of European traditions and evolve a discipline catering to the wide-ranging needs of the United States. He stressed a sound knowledge of horticulture so that the practitioner could use plantings appropriate to the climate, soil, and topography. Lowell believed that landscape architecture was only one of the many skills an architect could master, a philosophy made clear in *American Gardens*, in which he illustrates the work primarily of architects who were also working as landscape architects. *American Gardens* was also important in codifying the field of landscape architecture.

Lowell, Guy, ed. *American Gardens*. Boston: Bates Guild, 1902. Reveals Lowell's landscape architecture philosophy and influences and codifies the field up to that point; large-format photographs, plans.

Lowell, Guy. *Smaller Italian Villas and Farmhouses*. New York: Architectural Book Publishing, 1916. Lowell spent time in Italy with the army and had the opportunity to explore the landscape and architecture he had long enjoyed; this book is his appreciation of Italian villas and gardens.

Russell, Benjamin F. W. "On the Work of Guy Lowell." *Architectural Review* 13 (February 1906). An overview of Lowell's life and work.

No extensive repository of Lowell's work survives intact. Drawings and other materials are widely scattered. The Architectural Collections at the MIT Museum houses his thesis drawings and work relating to the teaching of the landscape architecture program.

Kimberly Alexander Shilland

MACKAYE, BENTON
(1879–1976)
planner, conservationist, forester

Benton MacKaye was born in Stamford, Connecticut, and lived in Manhattan during his early years. The majority of his life, however, was spent in the open country environment of Shirley Center, a small New England village only twenty miles from Thoreau's Concord, and he was preeminently a man of the outdoors. The blend of these environmental influences inspired Lewis Mumford to remark: "No one could have written such a clear appreciation of the respective virtues of the primeval, the rural, and the urban environments as MacKaye has done, if he were not equally familiar with all three of them."

MacKaye was a natural-born regional planner, exhibiting his perceptivity early on when he set out to map the forest of his local environment at the age of fourteen and systematically divided his survey into evergreen and deciduous communities. Without knowing it, the boy designed a crude regional survey methodology very sim-

Lewis Mumford (left) with Benton MacKaye at Hudson Guild Farm, New Jersey, 1924. Courtesy Rare and Manuscript Collections, Carl A. Kroch Library, Cornell University, Ithaca, N.Y.

ilar to what Patrick Geddes developed at the Outlook Tower in Edinburgh, Scotland. Indeed, when the two men eventually met in 1923 they instantly understood each other—so much so that they spent two days comparing activities and regional planning concepts. It was during this interchange that Geddes coined the term "geotechnics."

In 1897 the eighteen-year-old MacKaye and several other young men went on a six-week hiking trip through the primeval forests of the White Mountains in New Hampshire. MacKaye considered this experience the "toughest and greatest" adventure of his life,

and the concept of long-distance hiking trails became an obsession for him. Although he went on to earn both his B.A. and M.A. in forestry at Harvard, the direct self-education he derived from his solitary rambles and explorations always was more meaningful for him.

MacKaye completed his formal studies in 1905, the same year the U.S. Forest Service was established, and spent the first thirteen years of his professional career engaged in reclaiming and improving the nation's forests as one of Chief Forester Gifford Pinchot's young disciples. Through the process of studying the relationship

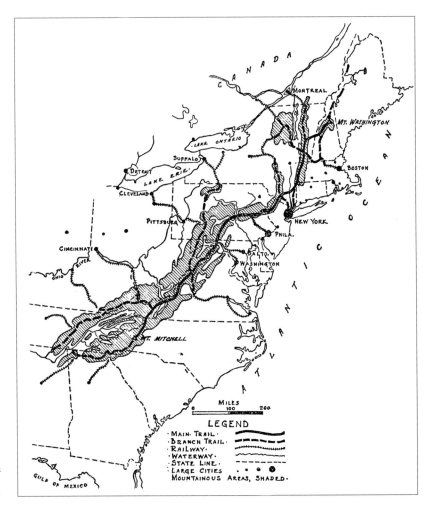

"Suggested Location of Appalachian Trail." From *Journal of the American Institute of Architects*, October 1921.

between resources and employment and the wider issues of conservation, he became interested in the need to conserve the essential resources of Alaska—then the last American frontier.

In 1918, MacKaye transferred to the Department of Labor and spent a year working on a plan to settle returning World War I soldiers on the land. His final report exhibited the most advanced thinking of the conservation movement with respect to land colonization. This scheme failed to obtain support, and the drafted bill never cleared the House committee, but it did attract the attention of President Woodrow Wilson, who personally pushed for a soldiers' colony in the White Mountains near the Maine border. (This project also failed, however, and the experimental resettlement scheme never was tested.)

During the early 1920s, MacKaye authored a series of articles recommending the public development of oil, coal, waterpower, and a marketing system that would substantially reduce the cost of living. Although MacKaye's utopian proposals did not attract widespread support, these writings were significant because they presented complex economic problems in a manner comprehensible to the layperson. During this same period, MacKaye became involved in a theoretical study that exhibited his grasp of regional planning. The study of seven northwestern states was modeled after the Garden City concepts of Ebenezer Howard while locating living and manufacturing areas close to natural resources, including raw materials and sources of power. Although this so-called Northwest Plan was never intended to be anything other than a "think piece," the concepts presented were translated into action in future years.

MacKaye's theoretical plan for the Appalachian Trail elicited much more interest than any of his other far-reaching conceptualizations, particularly after he met Clarence Stein in 1921 and followed his suggestion to write it up as an article for the *Journal of the American Institute of Architects*. The October 1921 piece, which outlined MacKaye's proposed project for a footpath between Maine and Georgia—a distance of more than 2,000 miles—has been recognized as a monument to regional planning. This footpath formed the backbone of an entire system of parks and nature preserves linked by feeder trails into a grand system that would maintain both the primeval and the rural environments at a high level—thus providing a means of land use control for the wave of population that was

then already turning the region from Boston to Washington, D.C., into what Geddes described as a formless "conurbation."

In 1923, MacKaye joined forces with Clarence Stein, Henry Wright*, Lewis Mumford, and other pioneer planners to found the Regional Planning Association of America as a means of establishing a regional approach to planning. It was because of this action that the traffic-free, new demonstration town of Radburn, New Jersey, came into being.

Perhaps MacKaye's most significant writing is his book *The New Exploration*, first published in 1929 and reprinted in 1962. Not only was it a pioneer essay in its own time; it is today still ahead of much of the thinking addressed to the problem of how best to use our natural and cultural resources. He wrote of "townless highways" and "highwayless towns," which were realized first with Radburn and then with Norris, Tennessee, and the "greenbelt" planned towns of the 1930s.

During the early years of the Tennessee Valley Authority, established in 1932, MacKaye was engaged as a farsighted regional planner. Subsequently, his work for the Rural Electrification Administration enabled him to bring his imagination to bear on the planned use of resources for social and economic benefit. When MacKaye died in 1976 at the age of ninety-six, the "Father of the Appalachian Trail" had lived to see his vision inspire the National Trails System Act of 1968 and his concepts in regional planning applied in many cities, both here and abroad.

It is fitting that the Benton MacKaye Trail Association was formed in the early 1980s and a 250-mile trail laid out in his name. This trail combines with the feeder trails that were part of the original concept to improve access to the Appalachian Trail and to connect some of the nation's finest wilderness lands in the states of Georgia, Tennessee, and North Carolina. It also links with the Great Smoky Mountain National Park, 90 percent of which is managed as wilderness.

MacKaye was co-founder and honorary president of the Wilderness Society, the primary purpose of which is to address the problem of how to use natural and cultural resources without defacing the landscape. This organization continues to further the philosophy and solutions recommended by MacKaye in an effort to make the world more habitable—which becomes ever more relevant as time passes.

MacKaye, Benton. "An Appalachian Trail, a Project in Regional Planning." *Journal of the American Institute of Planners*, October 1921. Proposal that set the stage for regional planning for an interstate trail accessible to workers wishing to escape crowded city conditions; posed the idea of food production in shelter camps near the trail to help develop community spirit.

MacKaye, Benton. *The New Exploration: A Philosophy of Regional Planning.* 1928. Reprint, with an introduction by Lewis Mumford, Urbana: University of Illinois Press, 1962. Contains a series of excellent diagrams that illustrate "industrial watersheds," the indigenous world, the metropolitan world, regional planning by watersheds, American migrations, environment as a natural resource, and "openways."

Thomas, John L. "Lewis Mumford, Benton MacKaye, and the Regional Vision." In *The American Planner: Biographies and Recollections.* 2d ed., ed. Donald A. Krueckeberg. New Brunswick, N.J.: Center for Urban Policy Research, 1994, pp. 264–300. A history of the progressive regional planning movement in the United States with the renewed momentum following World War I and the formation of the Regional Planning Association of American; contains the most detailed biography of MacKaye to date.

Charles E. Aguar

MANNING, WARREN HENRY
(1860–1938)
landscape architect, horticulturist, planner, author

Warren Manning was born in Reading, Massachusetts, the son of Jacob Warren Manning, a nurseryman, and Lydia Manning, a watercolorist. He later credited his mother with instilling in him a lifelong devotion to "making America a finer place in which to live." Manning's father, who began a thriving nursery business in 1854, helped nurture the horticultural basis for his son's distinguished career. Young Warren often traveled with his father to collect plants, to botanize, and to see other nursery operations, including that of Charles Downing, brother of Andrew Jackson Downing*. By 1884, Manning had apparently developed an interest in design, for a nursery pamphlet from that year advertises that he had become available to "make sketches and lay out grounds."

In 1888, Manning left his father's business, having secured work in the office of Frederick Law Olmsted Sr.* For the next eight years, Manning specialized in horticulture and planting design under Olmsted, gaining invaluable experience and training through contact with other talented landscape architects, primarily John Charles Olmsted*, Frederick Law Olmsted Jr.*, and Charles Eliot*. He eventually supervised about one hundred projects there.

With the Olmsted firm, Manning got his first experience with planned industrial communities, a type of work in which he later specialized and a field in which

Warren Manning. Warren H. Manning Collection, Center for Lowell History, University of Massachusetts, Lowell.

he made significant contributions. He also acquired considerable experience with planting design, particularly at Biltmore, the 125,000-acre estate of George Vanderbilt, in Asheville, North Carolina. In 1893, Manning supervised the final installation of planting at the Chicago World's Columbian Exposition. During the period, he also worked on dozens of park projects in Milwaukee, Buffalo, Rochester, Chicago, Trenton, Washington, D.C., and elsewhere.

Perhaps most important to Manning's later career was his exposure to the ideas of Charles Eliot, a partner in the Olmsted firm, who was working on the Boston Metropolitan Park System during Manning's tenure. Manning prepared sketch maps of the area's vegetation which were then overlaid with sheets detailing road layout, topography, and water features. This methodology directly influenced the development of Manning's own version of resource-based planning. Manning, no doubt, was also aware of the political side of Eliot's regional planning efforts, which had resulted in unprecedented gains in public land for Boston and a remarkable new organization, The Trustees of Reservations.

In 1896, when it became apparent that the Olmsted mantle would pass to Eliot and both Olmsted sons before it came to him, Manning decided to open his own office. One of his first projects was a report on the flora of the Boston Metropolitan Park System, produced as a consultant to the Olmsted firm. Within the year, Manning wrote to Eliot to ask his help in founding a new professional organization for landscape architects. Eliot was more interested in establishing a public organization. The American Park and Outdoor Art Association, later the American Civic Association—supported through the efforts of Manning, J. Horace McFarland*, and others—was the result. Manning continued to advocate a professional organization, and with Samuel Parsons Jr.*, convinced the younger Olmsteds to endorse the idea. In 1899, eleven charter members of the American Society of Landscape Architects, including Manning, met for the first time in New York City. (Manning served as president of the organization in 1914.)

Between 1901 and 1904, Manning's brother, J. Woodward, joined him as a partner. One of their major projects was the design and planning of a park system for Harrisburg, Pennsylvania, where they worked in close collaboration with engineers in laying out new drainage and sanitation systems. Beautiful, usable open spaces resulted from the carefully coordinated efforts, as they had from Olmsted's treatment of the Charles and Muddy rivers in

Boston. The project earned Manning's firm national attention and cemented a decades-long relationship with the city.

Some of the clients Manning found during his early years in practice would prove similarly enduring. James Tufts retained him for several jobs, including Pinehurst, a resort in North Carolina. (Manning also worked for several other members of the Tufts family.) In 1896, Manning began working for William G. Mather. Over three decades, he eventually designed 60 separate projects for Mather, among them Gwinn, Mather's Cleveland home, where he collaborated with Charles Platt* on the estate grounds and laid out a 21-acre wild garden. Manning also designed several mining towns in Michigan's Upper Peninsula for Mather, including the town of Gwinn, the first planned community on the Marquette Iron Range. Here Manning undertook an extensive site inventory to help determine the layout of community facilities, open space improvements, and worker housing. He prided himself on the variety and artistic quality of the fourteen different cottage styles he designed for the town.

In 1915, Manning moved his practice to Billerica, near his ancestral home, and began to enlarge his staff. His roster of employees reveals many talented practitioners, including A. D. Taylor*, Fletcher Steele*, Wilbur D. Cook Jr., Marjorie Sewell Cautley*, Helen Bullard, Stephen Hamblin, Charles Gillette*, and Dan Kiley. A large proportion of these assistants were women, which was unusual for the time.

Manning also undertook large regional mapping projects, one of which was done in support of the National Park Service Bill, 1915–1916. In time, Manning combined the regional data into a "National Plan." This 927-page document synthesized information about many kinds of resources—forests, animals, waterways, minerals, climate, railroads, highway systems, etc.—and made recommendations for their use and protection. A condensed version of the plan was published as a supplement to *Landscape Architecture Quarterly* in 1919. Despite the appalling racist views it expresses, the document is valuable for Manning's conception of a land classification methodology based on natural resources and systems, and the use of this methodology to attempt to control the exploitation of resources and to preserve scenic beauty.

Manning's principles of resource-based planning also informed his town planning. His plan for Birmingham, Alabama (1919), recommended a scheme of multiple neighborhood-based centers determined by available re-

Mining town of Gwinn, Michigan. Courtesy Robin Karson.

Wild Garden, Gwinn, William G. Mather estate, Cleveland, c. 1930. Courtesy Gwinn Archive, Cleveland.

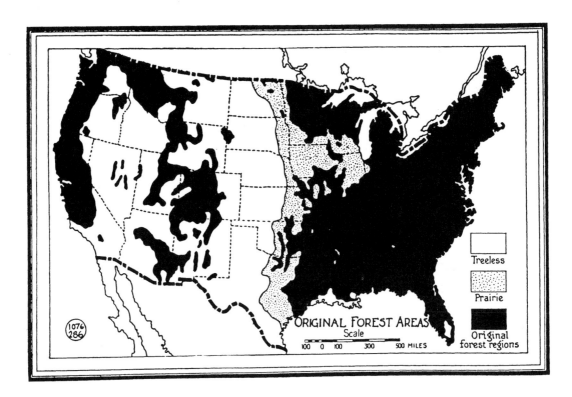

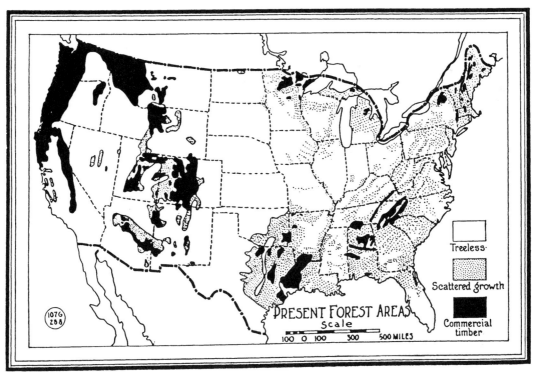

"Comparison of Original Forest Areas and Present Forest Areas (1″ = 500 miles)," from "A National Plan," 1923. From Special Supplement, *Landscape Architecture* 13, no. 4 (1919).

Birch allée, Stan Hywet Hall, F. A. Seiberling estate, Akron, Ohio, 1996. Photo Carol Betsch.

sources. The approach was revolutionary and conceived in direct opposition to the prevailing City Beautiful movement, which featured monumental civic centers and Beaux Arts public buildings.

Manning's seemingly inexhaustible energy took him to nearly every state in the nation, where he undertook almost every type of job. In general, his planting and planning skills outstripped his design ability. Manning's most successful private estates were often the product of collaborations with talented architects. Other important residential projects include estates for Gustave Pabst (Milwaukee), August and Adolphus Busch (St. Louis),

Cyrus and Harriet McCormick (Lake Forest, Ill.), J. J. Borland (Camden, Me.), and Clement Griscom (Haverford, Pa.). Manning designed parks or park systems in Milwaukee, Minneapolis, St. Paul, Providence, Wilkes-Barre, Pennsylvania, Louisville, Cincinnati, and many other cities. He also worked on college campuses, subdivisions, golf courses, institutional grounds, and projects for government and community groups. Manning was an active advocate for community participation in many of the public design projects. His client list chronicles over 1,700 jobs.

Manning was also a passionate writer. His many articles covered a wide range of topics of interest to the pro-

Amphitheater, Gwinn estate, 1993. Photo Robin Karson.

fession and the general public. Liberty Hyde Bailey* invited him to prepare several entries for Bailey's encyclopedia, including that on landscape gardening. Invariably, Manning's underlying themes echoed those of his mentor, Olmsted Sr., centering on how to improve the quality of life as civilization presented ever more problematic obstacles to healthful living and scenic enjoyment. These articles were charged with an almost Transcendentalist reverence for the wonders of nature. Manning's practice dwindled during the Depression years, and by the mid-1930s he had almost no work at all. He died from a heart attack in 1938 at the age of seventy-eight.

Karson, Robin. *The Muses of Gwinn: Art and Nature in a Garden Designed by Warren H. Manning, Charles Platt, and Ellen Biddle Shipman.* New York: Sagapress/

Abrams, 1995. A detailed narrative about one of Manning's major residential projects in Cleveland; heavily illustrated.

Manning, Warren H. "A National Plan Study Brief." *Landscape Architecture Quarterly* 8 (July 1923). A 23-page brief presenting Manning's statistical analysis of the country's resources.

Neckar, Lance. "Developing Landscape Architecture for the Twentieth Century: The Career of Warren H. Manning." *Landscape Journal* 8 (Fall 1989), 78–91. Comprehensive and detailed overview of Manning's long career.

There are two major repositories for papers relating to Warren Manning. The first is the Warren H. Manning Collection, Parks Library, Iowa State University, Ames; it consists primarily of plans, drawings, and photographs and is indexed. The second is the Warren H. Manning Collection at the University of Massachusetts, Lowell; these papers include some correspondence and photographs, copies of some office records, Manning's unpublished autobiography, and various ephemera. Plans, photographs, and correspondence relating to Stan Hywet are at Stan Hywet Hall,

Akron, Ohio; and plans, photographs, and correspondence relating to Gwinn are in the Gwinn archive, Cleveland.

_____

Robin Karson

MARQUIS, WILLIAM BELL
(1887–1978)
landscape architect, educator

William Bell Marquis was born in Rock Island, Illinois, a city situated on an island in the Mississippi River. The son of a prominent Presbyterian minister, Marquis had an early and abiding love of botany, forestry, and horticulture that would shape much of his life's work. He also had a strong belief in the prospects for the human spirit which manifested itself in his lifelong effort to aesthetically improve the world around him.

After graduation from high school in Rock Island, Marquis attended Lake Forest College, a small Presbyterian liberal arts school in a bucolic community north of Chicago. The experience of living in this planned community had a profound influence on his early philosophy of landscape architecture. Marquis graduated in 1909 and in September of that year entered Harvard University, then considered to have the leading program in the emerging field of landscape architecture. He spent the summer of 1910 traveling through Europe with his family. He visited England, Scotland, the Netherlands, Belgium, France, Germany, Switzerland, and Italy. This tour had a great impact on Marquis's concept of landscape design and likely reinforced the ideas of town planning and civic improvement that he was absorbing at Harvard. Marquis expressed his views in the 1912 edition of the Lake Forest College magazine, *The Stentor:* "It is now a universally recognized fact that, where people live and work among attractive surroundings, they accomplish better results and lead better and broader lives."

Marquis graduated from Harvard in 1912 with a master of landscape architecture. With a recommenda-

tion in hand from department chair James Sturgis Pray* he found employment as office manager and design supervisor with the P. J. Berckmans Company in Augusta, Georgia. The Berckmans family owned Fruitland Nursery, one of the largest nurseries in the country, and had been engaged in landscape architecture since the early 1900s. Marquis, however, was the first professionally trained landscape architect to work for the firm, and was among the first professional landscape architects to live and work in the South.

While working for Berckmans, Marquis engaged in numerous projects. One of the first was a plan for a 1,500-acre city to be built outside of Charleston, South Carolina. The new city of North Charleston incorporated many of the design principles of Ebenezer Howard's Garden City, including an adjacent farming area, multiple factory sites along rail lines, numerous parks and school sites, a large commercial zone, and both upper- and middle-class residential areas. Despite slight alterations to the original Marquis plan and the abandonment of many of the more innovative features of the layout such as the large public plaza, much of the original plan can be discerned in the present community. Marquis was also involved in planning other towns, subdivisions, parks, and residential estates with the Berckmans firm.

Marquis's work with Berckmans ended in December 1917 when Frederick Law Olmsted Jr.* invited him to join the Camp Planning Section of the Construction Division of the U.S. Army. During the war, Marquis

"General Map Showing Subdivision of North Charleston / P.J. Berckmans Co., Landscape Architects, Augusta, Georgia." Courtesy Dean Sinclair.

worked on hospitals and encampments in Georgia, North Carolina, Utah, and Arizona. He left the service in September 1919, and promptly joined Olmsted Brothers* of Brookline, Massachusetts, as an associate.

While with the Olmsted firm, Marquis worked on a wide variety of projects that took him all over the country, his role ranging from project leader to collaborator. In the early years he spent much time in Georgia and South Carolina. Marquis designed Charleston's first elite "automobile suburb," the Crescent, in 1926 as well

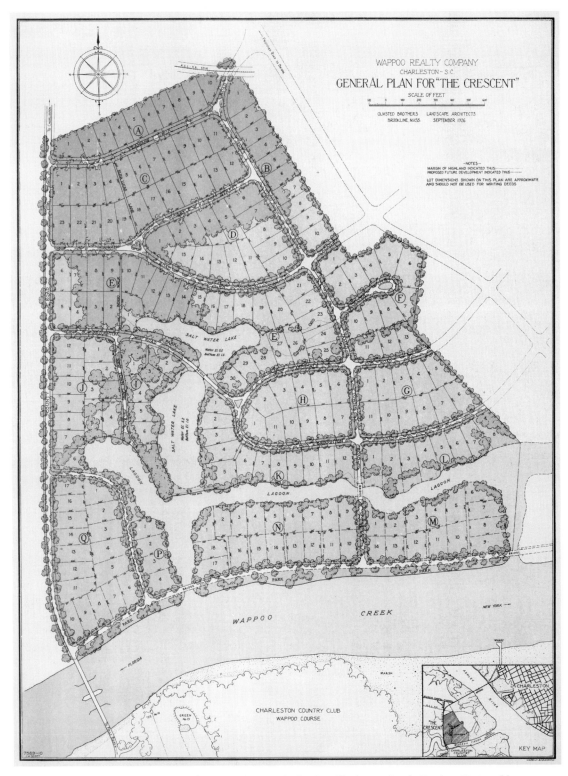

"General Plan for The Crescent," September 1926. Wappoo Realty Co., Charleston, South Carolina. Designed by Olmsted Brothers. Courtesy National Park Service, Frederick Law Olmsted National Historic Site.

The Lake at The Crescent subdivision, 1998. Photo Dean Sinclair.

as the city's first country club community (Yeaman's Hall) and the municipal golf course. These projects showcase many of his design strengths, including his use of ponds in poorly drained areas, which were both functional and aesthetically pleasing. This skill was particularly important in the South Carolina low country as well as in his many golf course designs. The most famous course he worked on was the Augusta National Golf Club, former site of Fruitland Nursery, which he designed in the 1930s in conjunction with Bobby Jones and Alexander Mackenzie. Marquis became an Olmsted partner in 1937 and retired from the firm in 1962.

An active supporter of the profession of landscape architecture, Marquis became a member of the American Society of Landscape Architects in 1920 and a Fellow in 1936, and was a member of the Boston Society of Landscape Architects. In 1953 he was a founding member of the Hubbard Educational Trust, whose purpose was to promote understanding and appreciation of

landscape architecture. In the 1940s, Marquis served as chairman of the planning board for Newton, Massachusetts. He was also as a member of the Executive Committee of the Massachusetts Forest and Park Association.

Marquis taught design and other courses at several programs in the Boston area. He was teaching at the Cambridge School of Architecture and Landscape in 1919 when he met his wife, Martha Ely. He later taught landscape construction at the Lowthorpe School of Landscape Architecture at Groton, Massachusetts, as well as at the Rhode Island School of Design during the 1940s.

Marquis was a soft-spoken man of quiet dignity who had a tremendous influence on his profession. He succinctly stated his practical and down-to-earth design philosophy in 1927: "Convenient and suitable use is always the first consideration; pleasing appearance is the second goal to be secured; and reasonable cost is a final check on the choice of any scheme." He is remembered as a man of integrity who represented his profession well throughout his long life.

Lawliss, Lucy. *Residential Work of the Olmsted Firm in Georgia, 1893–1937*. Winston-Salem, N.C.: Southern Gardens History Society, 1993. A well-illustrated publication, which details Marquis's extensive work in Georgia for Olmsted Brothers after 1920.

Marquis, W. B. "Grading the Home Grounds: What Grading Means and Why It Is Important." In *Boston Herald Book of Gardens*, ed. B. W. Pond. Boston: Boston Herald, 1929. Brief article extolling the role of landscape architecture in improving residential properties.

Marquis, W. B. "Lake Forest: An Opportunity for Observation." *The Stentor* 26, no. 26 (1912), 276–280. A brief article with photographs, providing insight into the influence of Lake Forest College on Marquis's aesthetic sensibilities.

Marquis's plans for North Charleston are available at the Charleston County Office of the Register of Mesne Conveyance, and plans for residential estates on Jekyll Island and Columbus, Georgia, are available. His work at the Olmsted firm is well documented in letter and drawing files at the Frederick Law Olmsted National Historic Site, Brookline, and at the Library of Congress in the Olmsted Associates Records in the Manuscript Division.

Dean Sinclair

MAY, CLIFF
(1908–1989)
architect/builder, author

Clifford A. May was born in San Diego, a sixth-generation San Diegan and a direct descendant of the early Estudillo and Pedrorena families. He spent his childhood summers with relatives on nearby Rancho Las Flores, a huge working ranch that traced its origins to the Spanish missionaries and their Native American charges. There he formed a deeply rooted, firsthand understanding of the true Borderlands (Mexican American) architectural vernacular and its appropriateness for modern living.

After the 1929 stock market crash, May dropped out of his college business courses to build handcrafted furniture modeled on the sturdy "Monterey" style. Soon after, he built his first suburban ranch house. His solid, comfortable furniture helped sell his early houses, and then his solid, comfortable houses began to sell themselves. In designing them, May drew heavily on his intimate acquaintance with the rambling adobe ranch of his youth. His plans featured attractive, highly functional arrangements for combining indoor-outdoor living spaces—ideal for the Southwest climate, with its mild winters, but a new notion in the 1930s suburbs.

May's earnest fervor for fusing outdoor and indoor life was firmly anchored in his boyhood awareness of the contrast between his carefree rancho summers and his more confined suburban life within a traditional boxlike house. At a precocious age, he scrutinized the factors that made his same-clime town life so different and realized that a floor plan which incorporates a garden is far more livable than the conventional Yankee layout. Therefore,

Cliff May, 1958. Courtesy San Diego Historical Society.

Warren H. Manning. Amphitheater, Gwinn. Cleveland, Ohio.
Photo Robin Karson.

Warren H. Manning.
Birch allée, Stan Hywet Hall.
Akron, Ohio.
Photo Carol Betsch.

William B. Marquis. The Lake at The Crescent subdivision. Charleston,
South Carolina. Photo Dean Sinclair.

Cliff May.
Old Town State Historic Park.
San Diego, California.
Photo Carol Greentree.

Morrell & Nichols.
Central Vista, Sunset Memorial Park.
Minneapolis, Minnesota.
Courtesy Gregory Kopischke.

Morrell & Nichols.
Residential street in Morgan Park.
Duluth, Minnesota.
Courtesy Gregory Kopischke.

Samuel Negus. D. W. Field Park.
Brockton, Massachusetts.
Courtesy Child Associates, Inc.

Samuel Negus. D. W. Field Park.
Brockton, Massachusetts.
Courtesy Child Associates, Inc.

Norman T. Newton.
Aerial view of Statue of
Liberty National Monument.
Courtesy National Park Service,
Statue of Liberty National Monument.

John Nolen.
Beaver Lake. Asheville, North Carolina.
Courtesy Charles A. Birnbaum.

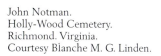

John Notman.
Holly-Wood Cemetery.
Richmond. Virginia.
Courtesy Blanche M. G. Linden.

Frederick Law Olmsted Sr.
"Plan of Prospect Park, Olmsted, Vaux & Co.,
Brooklyn, New York," 1871.
Courtesy National Park Service,
Frederick Law Olmsted National Historic Site.

Frederick Law Olmsted Sr. The Long Meadow, Prospect Park.
Brooklyn, New York. Photo Charles E. Beveridge.

Frederick Law Olmsted Jr.
Carriage road on east side of Eagle Lake,
Acadia National Park. Bar Harbor, Maine.
Photo David Halpern.

Frederick Law Olmsted Sr. Washington Park. Chicago, Illinois. Photo
Charles E. Beveridge.

Restored adobe, Old Town State Historic Park, San Diego. Photo Carol Greentree.

May built his houses around one or more patios that linked indoor-outdoor family living, cooking, and eating spaces in an arrangement typical of centuries-old Mediterranean models. His rationale sowed the ideas that were to become favorite postwar design precepts. May's patio-centered, easy-living plans became staples of domestic architecture, and garden design, for decades to come.

Earlier, in the 1920s, California's Hispanic-inspired patio garden had already been enthusiastically promoted by Pasadena landscape architect Charles Gibbs Adams. However, in most California suburbs, the patio-centered house had not yet caught the popular imagination. It took May's 1930s designs to initiate a gradual transformation of traditional ways of planning an entire property, bringing the inefficiently used yard into the house as a full-fledged garden room, and thoroughly assimilating the out-of-doors into the daily functions of the house. With their ground-hugging, unpretentious layouts, May's one-story houses were a pleasure to live in during all seasons.

May's plans called for inexpensive construction materials common in his locale: plain whitewashed stucco, hefty exposed timbers and simple tile for roofs, flooring, and decorative features. His low-slung, patio-focused houses sold well even during the Depression. These houses felt—and worked—just right in San Diego, and soon May was in demand in Los Angeles as well. There, in the 1940s, popular magazines began to embrace and promote May's practical concepts.

Meanwhile, May continued his innovations, using increasingly contemporary materials and ideas, to modernize his ranch house without compromising its relaxed, informal indoor-outdoor conveniences. In doing so, he wedded the indigenous adobe (and its semi-enclosed patio) to the then-novel "open plan," which merged living room, dining room, and kitchen into one big family room.

May's houses and patio gardens were regularly featured in *House Beautiful, Better Homes and Gardens*, and *Sunset* magazines. Thus, the California ranch house, with its integrated patio, swept into the consciousness of the entire country during an era of unprecedented residential construction activity.

The publishers of *Sunset* were so captivated by May's concepts that they produced two books featuring his work. These documented the historical origins of May's regional ideas, using archival photos, narrative descriptions, and drawings. The contemporary results were illustrated with photographs and plans of May's most up-to-date houses with landscape designs by Doug Baylis, Garrett Eckbo, and Thomas Church* among others. During the postwar period, *Sunset* published collaborations among May, his clients, and their landscape designers. Doug Baylis worked closely with *Sunset* in the production of its 1946 book, an unstinting endorsement of May's ideas. *Sunset* was so zealous in its enthusiasm for May's work that it chose him to design its Menlo Park publishing headquarters. *Sunset* also chose Thomas Church to design its demonstration gardens.

May continued his design career until his death in 1989.

May, Cliff. Interview by Marlene L. Laskey. *The California Ranch House*. Oral History Program, UCLA, Los Angeles, 1984. An informal first-person description of May's childhood and career as a trend-setting builder who collaborated with top California landscape architects of the 1940s–1980s; 355 pp. with index.

Staff of Sunset Magazine and Books in collaboration with Cliff May. *Sunset Western Ranch Houses*. Menlo Park, Calif.: Lane Books, 1946. A clear, illustrated primer to the indoor-outdoor living concepts that made May's California ranch houses so popular all over the country.

Staff of Sunset Magazine and Books in collaboration with Cliff May. *Western Ranch Houses by Cliff May*. Menlo Park, Calif.: Lane Books, 1958. An illustrated summary of May's ideas about comfortable, commonsense houses with gardens, based on the vernacular precedents of his southern California region, with residential landscapes designed by top landscape architects of the time.

May's professional papers are housed in the architecture archives at the University of California, Santa Barbara.

Carol Greentree

MCCREA, ANNETTE E.
(1858–1928)
landscape architect

Annette McCrea, who claimed to be the first woman landscape architect in the United States, was born in Cooperstown, New York. She and J. Franklin McCrea were married in the state but moved frequently in search of a climate that might improve Franklin's health. He died at age thirty-seven and was buried in Kalamazoo, Michigan, where Annette's brother, Charles Maxson, also a landscape architect, lived.

McCrea started her professional career in 1892 in Kalamazoo, taking over her husband's wholesale nursery business. There she designed the grounds of the Castle, at 1415 West Main Street, the home of Frank Henderson, a prominent resident.

McCrea and her two daughters moved in the late 1890s to Chicago, where she assumed prominent positions in civic improvement associations and worked briefly for Lincoln Park. After the park board appointed her consulting landscape architect in January 1900, she started to design tree and shrubbery plantings; but in May she had a dispute with the park superintendent and was dismissed.

About 1900, McCrea became chairman of the Committee on Railroad Grounds of the American Park and Outdoor Art Association. When it was merged into the American Civic Association in 1904, she continued her efforts for another four years as vice president of the Department of Railroad Improvements, remaining on the Civic Association's executive committee until 1913.

Her work for the Chicago, Milwaukee & St. Paul Railroad started in 1902 as the company was improving and double tracking its route in Wisconsin from Milwaukee to

Annette E. McCrea. Courtesy Barbara Neal.

La Crosse, and "expending $10,000 in the work of beautifying the garden spots around its depots," as the *Milwaukee Sentinel* reported. She would tour the rail lines with top officials, traveling in a railroad business car, visiting stations on the route, then recommend ways to "beautify" the grounds. In this way she worked for the Chicago & Alton between Chicago and St. Louis in 1904 and for the Illinois Central in 1905, who engaged her "to plan a system of improvement in the way of grass plats, shrubbery, and flowers about the principal station grounds of the system," according to the Chicago *Railway and Engineering Review.* McCrea also served as consulting landscape architect for the Chicago & North Western; Chicago, Burlington & Quincy; Duluth South Shore & Atlantic; Southern Pacific; and other lines. She kept up her efforts for station improvements with lectures in 1906.

The Chicago, Milwaukee & St. Paul Railroad effort continued in 1908 in Tomahawk, a northern Wisconsin lumber town. There, McCrea planned the station grounds, civic cleanup and improvement, and a park drive along the Wisconsin River for the Bradley Company, developer of the town. In typical fashion, she wrote about the work without personally taking credit, saying in the *Railroad Gazette* that the whole town was "transformed from ugliness to beauty."

For the most part, her railroad work was over by 1910, when profits declined as the Interstate Commerce Commission rejected company requests for higher rates. Staying in Chicago, McCrea turned her attention increasingly to civic improvement. Still active in the American Civic Association, she wrote letters to political leaders in aid of the organization's campaign to preserve Niagara Falls. ("While I'm a small woman, I know a lot of big men," she told the president of the association in 1911.)

McCrea was well acquainted with De Pere, Wisconsin, before moving there in 1917. Her first commissions came in May 1911, when she placed 2,000 shrubs in St. James Park in Green Bay and developed plans for Riverside Park in De Pere. She planned the station grounds in De Pere for the Chicago & North Western Railroads in 1916 and supervised the planting of a row of elm trees on each side of a new highway between Green Bay and De Pere. Among her later projects in the area was a plan for the grounds of Braebourne, the Frank and Emily Murphy estate in the town of Allouez, Wisconsin, completed in 1922.

McCrea died in Minneapolis. Obituaries in the *New York Times* and *Chicago Tribune*, praising her accomplishments, noted that she had been "instrumental in introducing landscape architecture into the curricula of American colleges." But in the decades when most Americans traveled by train and railroad companies were building many passenger stations, it was through her station landscape design that McCrea made her most impressive contributions.

Lawson, Victor. *Chicago Record Herald*, September 22, 1901. A column on women in horticulture that puts McCrea in context with other woman landscape architects of the early 1900s.

McCrea, Annette. "Color Harmony and Discords," *Suburban Life*, May 1907.

McCrea, Annette, Andrew Wright Crawford, and C. L. Ackiss. *Railroad Improvements*. American Civic Association, Department of Railroad Improvements, pamphlet, 1905.

John Gruber

MCFARLAND, J. HORACE
(1859–1948)
conservationist, rosarian, author

John Horace McFarland was born in McAlisterville, Pennsylvania. In 1865 his father, a returning Civil War hero, moved the family to Harrisburg and started a printing company and a nursery. At the age of twelve and with only four years of formal education, McFarland went to work in his father's printing shop. In 1878, at age nineteen, McFarland opened his own printing business and began to publish gardening and seed catalogs. Realizing that woodcuts did not adequately represent the plants, he started to explore the use of photography. By 1894 he

J. Horace McFarland inspecting a climbing rose bush at Breeze Hill. Courtesy Smithsonian Institution, Archives of American Gardens, McFarland Collection.

was experimenting with color photography, and his company had become America's premier publisher of gardening catalogs, with what may have been the first color photographs produced in the United States.

In 1900, McFarland helped launch the American League for Civic Improvement, which eventually merged with the American Park and Outdoor Art Association to form the American Civic Association. McFarland served as the organization's president from 1904 to 1924, during which time he promoted a nationwide "Crusade against Ugliness." As part of the crusade, he persuaded the City of Harrisburg to abolish billboards and to retain the professional services of landscape architect Warren Manning* to plan a metropolitan park system. Alarmed by the high typhoid death rate, he also succeeded in getting the city to provide safe drinking water and to clean up the river edges. From coast to coast, McFarland traveled with forty lantern slides preaching the "Harrisburg Story."

McFarland's vision of the future role of the American Civic Association went beyond civic improvements, focusing attention and public awareness on national and international issues. Under his leadership the control of

Niagara Falls was taken away from the State of New York and the Province of Ontario and placed under the joint authority of the International Niagara Falls Control Board. In 1908, at the White House Conference on Conservation, McFarland, together with New York governor Charles Evans Hughes, directed his listeners' attention to the preservation of natural scenery. "National parks are too few in number and extent," McFarland stated, and "ought to be held inviolate as intended by Congress. . . . The scenic value of all the national domain yet remaining should be jealously guarded as a distinctly important national resource, and not as a mere incidental increment."

McFarland went on to lobby Congress for a single agency to protect and administer the national parks. During this effort he became active, along with John Muir, Charles Sprague Sargent*, and Robert Underwood Johnson, in the fight to prevent construction of the Hetch Hetchy Dam in what is now Yosemite National Park in California. McFarland visited the Hetch Hetchy Valley and wrote a fervent letter to President Woodrow Wilson asking him to veto legislation for the dam. Although the dam was constructed, the lobbying effort culminated on August 25, 1916, with the passage of the Organic Act establishing the National Park Service. Before the House Committee on Public Lands, McFarland expressed his deep feelings about the preservation and conservation of public lands: "The national parks . . . are an American idea; it is one thing that has not been imported. . . . Each one of these national parks in America is the result of some great man's thought of service to his fellow citizens. . . . These parks did not just happen; they came about because earnest men and women became violently excited at the possibility of these great assets passing from public control." The Organic Act was a triumph for McFarland's foresight and his vision and devotion to an idea.

McFarland was widely known as "Mr. Rose." He wrote more than a dozen books on roses and transformed the American Rose Society from a trade organization to a world-renowned institution. As its president, McFarland, with the help of member Robert Pyle, established a method of rose identification and registration that is still in use today. He also was instrumental in setting up rose gardens in unusual locations such as Sing Sing and San Quentin prisons. In the days before air travel and refrigeration, he successfully sent rose bushes to Ethiopia for the coronation of Emperor Haile Selassie. At his residence in Harrisburg, Breeze Hill, designed by Warren Manning*, McFarland maintained a garden of 5,000 plants including

McFarland at Breeze Hill. Courtesy Smithsonian Institution, Archives of American Gardens, McFarland Collection.

800 varieties of roses. Three roses were named in his honor: Editor McFarland, the Doctor, and J. Horace McFarland. In recognition of his outstanding services, the American Rose Society and the Massachusetts Horticultural Society bestowed gold medals on him in 1933. In 1942 he received the Jane Righter Gold Medal from the Garden Club of America and the Dean Hole Memorial Medal from the National Rose Society of England.

Miller, E. Lynn. "The Influence of J. Horace McFarland on Parks, Riverways, and Civic Improvements in America." In *Council of Educators in Landscape Architecture Proceedings*. Washington, D.C.: Landscape Architecture Foundation, 1990. Describes McFarland's efforts to establish the National Park Service, save rivers from pollution, and clean up American towns.

Morrison, Ernest. *J. Horace McFarland: A Thorn for Beauty*. Foreword by Bruce Babbitt, U.S. Secretary of the Interior. Harrisburg: Pennsylvania Historical and Museum Commission, 1995. The definitive biography of McFarland; many photographs and supporting materials from the Pennsylvania State Archives and other sources in Harrisburg.

Wilson, William H. *The City Beautiful Movement*. Baltimore: John Hopkins University Press, 1989. An excellent description in chapter 6 of the campaign McFarland and Mira Lloyd Dock waged to combine beauty and utility in the City of Harrisburg; the notes provide information on the contents of the Dock Papers in the Pennsylvania State Archives.

E. Lynn Miller

MILLER, WILHELM TYLER
(1869–1938)
author

Wilhelm Tyler Miller was born in King William County, Virginia, and raised in Detroit. He attended the University of Michigan (A.B., 1892) and studied under the direction of the renowned horticulturist Liberty Hyde Bailey* at Cornell University, where he received both an A.M. (1897) and a Ph.D. (1899).

In 1896, while still a student, Miller was hired as Bailey's assistant at Cornell's Agricultural Experiment Station. Three years later, Bailey employed Miller as his associate editor for the monumental publication *Cyclopedia of American Horticulture* (1900–1902). In addition to editing, Miller wrote several essays for the *Cyclopedia*, and this early literary experience eventually led him to a career in horticultural writing.

In 1901, Bailey became the editor of Doubleday, Page & Company's new magazine, *Country Life in America*, and at his suggestion, Miller was retained as the periodical's horticultural editor. As with the *Cyclopedia*, Miller wrote feature articles for the magazine in addition to editing the horticultural contributions. In 1905 he became the founding editor of *Garden Magazine*. As his articles of the period reflected, Miller's attention soon shifted from horticulture to landscape design and, more specifically, to a quest for an American style of landscape gardening.

In 1908, Miller traveled to England to study its gardens, motivated by a desire to discover "the causes of English garden excellence" and to discern "methods by which the most satisfying English effects might be produced in America with American materials." Three years later, the results of his English studies were published as a book, *What England Can Teach Us about Gardening* (1911). Later that same year, Miller focused his attention on the American Midwest and the establishment of a regional style of landscape design. To this end, he published the first of a series of articles promoting the work of Chicago landscape architect Jens Jensen*.

In 1912, Miller was offered a position at the University of Illinois at Urbana–Champaign, and, seeking the opportunity to participate more actively in the development of a Midwest landscape design aesthetic, he accepted and became an assistant professor of landscape horticulture. His primary responsibility was to further the university's "Country Beautiful" programs through publications and public lectures. Though no longer serving as an editor, he continued to publish articles in both *Country Life in America* and *Garden Magazine*.

In 1914, following the passage of the Smith-Lever Act, which funded extension programs, Miller was appointed head of the university's newly created Division of Landscape Extension, and it was under these auspices that he published *The Prairie Spirit in Landscape Gardening* (1915). In this pamphlet Miller cited the work of Jensen, O. C. Simonds*, and Walter Burley Griffin* as being inspired by the "prairie spirit" and expressed in the "prairie style." The majority of Miller's text was devoted to the work of his personal friend, Jensen, who primarily manifested Miller's "prairie spirit" through the then-novel ecological use of indigenous plants in naturalistic compositions.

As a result of reduced funding, the university disbanded its Division of Landscape Extension in the summer of 1916, and Miller's employment was terminated. He then unsuccessfully attempted to establish a landscape architectural practice in Chicago, returning to Detroit in 1918 with the same goal. Unfortunately, World War I had effectively eliminated the demand for new commissions.

Wilhelm Tyler Miller, c. 1913. Courtesy Morton Arboretum.

Miller changed his name from "Wilhelm" to "William" in 1919. Shortly thereafter, he retired to Los Angeles, where he died in obscurity in 1938. By the time of his death, Miller's publications numbered in the hundreds.

Miller, Wilhelm. *The Prairie Spirit in Landscape Gardening.* University of Illinois Agricultural Experiment Station Circular No. 184. Urbana, 1915. Synthesizes and refines all of Miller's previous efforts in the development of a Midwestern landscape design aesthetic; profusely illustrated.

Miller, Wilhelm. *What England Can Teach Us about Gardening.* Garden City, N.Y.: Doubleday, 1911. Miller's only book, the results of his study in England; illustrated.

Vernon, Christopher. "Wilhelm Miller: Prairie Sprit in Landscape Gardening." In *Landscape Architecture in the Midwest,* ed. William H. Tishler. Champaign: University of Illinois Press, in press.

Christopher Vernon

MORELL, ANTHONY URBANSKI
(1875–1924)
landscape architect

Anthony Urbanski was born and educated in France. About 1902 he emigrated to the United States and changed his surname from Urbanski to Morell, his mother's maiden name.

Morell spent at least some of his early career at the New York office of Charles Leavitt Jr.* There he worked with another young landscape architect, Arthur Nichols*, on various projects including a design for the Chester Congdon estate in Duluth, Minnesota. In 1909, Morell and Nichols formed a partnership and, seeing a new market opportunity, relocated to open an office in Minneapolis.

For many years Morell worked as a consultant to the Minneapolis City Planning Department, and he also served as member and secretary of the Planning Commission. In 1922 he helped prepare plans for a new civic center development in the city. He also designed city and civic center plans for Ojibwa, Wisconsin, and Saskatoon, Saskatchewan, among others.

NICHOLS, ARTHUR RICHARDSON
(1880–1970)
landscape architect

Arthur R. Nichols was born in West Springfield, Massachusetts. In 1902 he became the first graduate of the landscape architecture program at the Massachusetts Institute of Technology. That same year, he worked very briefly in Schenectady, New York, before moving to New York City to join the firm of Charles Leavitt Jr.* While with Leavitt, Nichols was involved with such projects as Monument Valley Park in Colorado Springs; the development of Long Beach on Long Island, New York; and the estates of John D. Rockefeller Sr. in Pocantico Hills, New York, George B. Post Jr. in Bernardsville, New Jersey, and Chester Congdon in Duluth, Minnesota. In 1909, Nichols formed a partnership with Anthony Morell* and moved to Minneapolis.

One of his colleagues, Keith Wehrman, characterized Nichols as a good designer, mild-mannered, and a skilled promoter who inspired people and who saw an important synergy between civil engineering and landscape architecture. Nichols believed in large-scale plans that met the needs of the present while providing flexibility for the future. He advocated maintaining long views wherever possible and working with the land, and he cautioned against over-planning.

One of his first important commissions was the

Arthur Nichols (left) and Anthony Morell, mid- to late 1910s. Courtesy Northwest Architectural Archives, University of Minnesota Libraries.

Russell M. Bennett estate on Lake Minnetonka, Minnesota, where he created a formal plan with elements reminiscent of Versailles. Many other estate and garden plans followed, including designs for Frank Hefflefinger and Gebhard Bohn, both at Lake Minnetonka; Alexander D. McRae in Vancouver, British Columbia; Senator John Benjamin Kendrick in Sheridan, Wyoming; A. M. Chisholm and H. B. Fryberger, both in Duluth; and William O'Brian in Marine-on-St. Croix, Minnesota.

In addition, Nichols's connections in Duluth provided him with numerous projects such as the Minnesota Steel Company town plan of Morgan Park, one of the first industrial towns in the country. (In 1998, Morgan Park was approved as eligible for the National Register of Historic Places.) Other commissions in the Duluth area included parks, estates, the civic center, and portions of Skyline Drive overlooking Lake Superior.

Beginning in 1909, Nichols was a consultant to the Minnesota State Board of Control in charge of locating buildings and developing grounds for state institutions including asylums, sanitariums, hospitals, reformatories, and prisons. One noteworthy example is the site plan he prepared for Nopeming Sanatorium near Duluth; the

building is sensitively sited on a rocky, forested hillside with views overlooking a broad river valley.

Nichols and the firm were particularly sought after to plan college campuses. From 1910 to 1952, Nichols served as the consulting planner to the University of Minnesota system. Other campus plans he was involved with include the University of Washington at Pullman, the University of North Dakota at Grand Forks, and Carlton College in Northfield, Minnesota. The underlying principal in the firm's campus designs was the orderly, generous arrangement of space for human activity. They emphasized buildings sited in balance, framed with plantings, with open foregrounds and carefully planned circulation systems between them. Plans often utilized axial themes.

From 1932 to 1940 Nichols served as a consultant to the Minnesota Highway Department on statewide roadside development. During this period he published articles and gave numerous presentations concerning the need to integrate aesthetic design with utilitarian highway engineering objectives in order to maintain the natural beauty and scenic quality of the land and, therefore, to enhance the driving experience.

Nichols also became well known in the field of cemetery planning. Two important examples of his work include Sunset Memorial Park and the northeast area of Lakewood Cemetery, both in Minneapolis.

Nichols's illustrious career also involved the design of parks, park systems, country clubs, and parkways. Projects of note include part of the Minneapolis park system, a plan for the scenic St. Croix River corridor on the Minnesota-Wisconsin border, and the grounds for the Glacier Park Hotel in western Montana. In 1953, Nichols came out of retirement to work for the Minnesota State Parks Department preparing master plans and site studies for virtually every new and every existing state park. His plans showed his understanding of topography, native vegetation, natural waters, and scenic features while sensitively integrating architecture, roadways, traffic patterns, camping facilities, trails, and maintenance needs.

Nichols's 1944 site plan for the Minnesota State Capitol integrated the existing state capitol building, designed by Cass Gilbert, and proposed Veteran's Service Building, other state building expansions, roadway realignments necessitated by changing traffic patterns, and a proposed federal trunk highway (Interstate 94) into a coherent plan that essentially still exists today.

Nichols became a member of the American Society of Landscape Architects in 1906, was elected a Fellow in

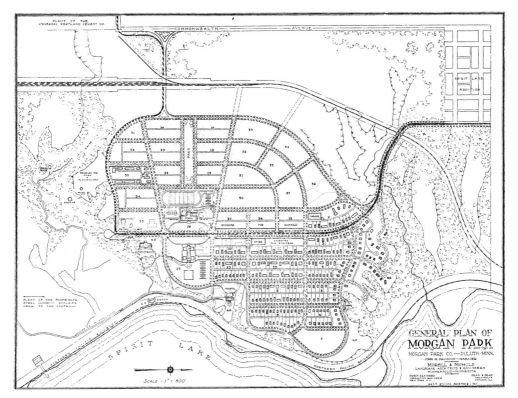

"General Plan of Morgan Park, Duluth, Minnesota," November 1, 1917. Courtesy Gregory Kopischke.

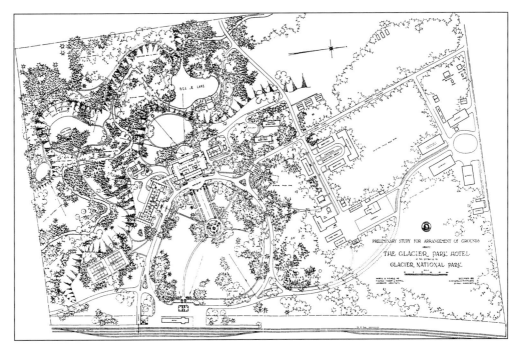

"Preliminary Study for Arrangement of Grounds around The Glacier Park Hotel at the Entrance to Glacier National Park," December 1925. Courtesy Gregory Kopischke.

Central Vista, Sunset Memorial Park, Minneapolis, 1999. Courtesy Gregory Kopischke.

Residential street in Morgan Park, Duluth, 1999. Courtesy Gregory Kopischke.

1915, and served as its vice president in 1928. He helped establish the landscape architecture program at Iowa State University in the early 1920s. He died in Rochester, Minnesota, in 1970 and was buried at Sunset Memorial Park.

Morell & Nichols, Inc.

After forming their partnership in 1909, Anthony Morell and Arthur Nichols relocated to Minneapolis to take advantage of contacts established during their work in Duluth as employees of Charles Leavitt Jr.* Morell & Nichols, Inc. became one of the first and most productive landscape architecture firms in Minnesota. The partnership blended Morell's European training and Nichols's Eastern background with both men's appreciation of the state and its regional character. The firm's broad-ranging design services included master and site plans for residential subdivisions, city and state

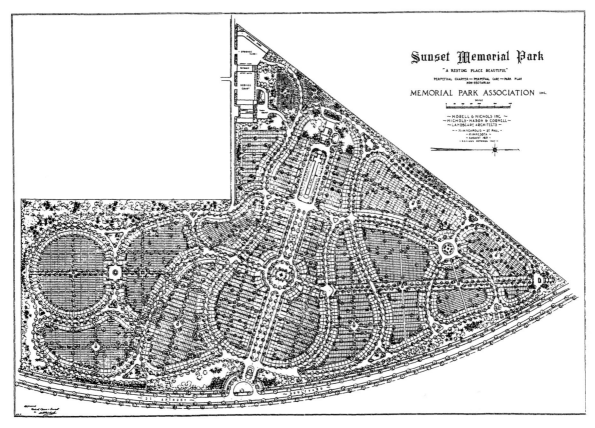

"Sunset Memorial Park, 'A Resting Place Beautiful,' " St. Anthony (Minneapolis), August 1927. Courtesy Gregory Kopischke.

parks, country clubs and cemeteries, college campuses, hospitals and sanatoriums, hotels and resort grounds, historic parks, Works Progress Administration sites, and state highways. Their projects primarily clustered in Minnesota and the adjacent five-state region, although many were located throughout the United States and Canada. After Morell's death in 1924, Morell & Nichols, Inc. continued, but in name only. Nichols went on to participate in other firms and partnerships until his retirement.

Nichols, Arthur R. "The Cemetery Design—Engineering Considerations." *The American Cemetery*, June 1933. Discusses the integration of topography, trees, water supply for irrigation, road layout, grading, and drainage in cemetery planning.

Nichols, Arthur R. "Landscape Design in Highway Development—A Coordinating Factor in the Layout of Traffic Ways." *Landscape Architecture* 30 (April 1940), 113–116.

Nichols, Arthur R. "Sunset Memorial Park." *The American Cemetery*, May 1930. Discusses Sunset Memorial Park as an example of a park plan cemetery.

The main archival collection of Morell & Nichols is held at Northwest Architectural Archives, University of Minnesota, St. Paul. It includes various plans, sketches, correspondence, and articles. Additional materials can be found at the Northeast Minnesota Historical Center on the University of Minnesota's Duluth campus.

Gregory Kopischke

NEGUS, SAMUEL PIKE
(1874–1943)
landscape architect

Samuel Pike Negus was born in New York City. He attended Hallam's School in Dresden, Germany, before entering Harvard College, where he received a B.A. in 1899. From 1899 to 1902 he studied landscape gardening and horticulture at the Bussey Institution of Harvard University and went on to receive a degree in landscape architecture from Harvard in 1906. In 1902 he began to practice landscape architecture as an office and field assistant in the offices of Manning* Brothers, James Sturgis Pray*, Stephen Child*, and Benjamin Watson.

In 1905, Negus worked briefly for the landscape architect William Punchard* as a field assistant. He reconnected with Punchard in 1908, and the two set up a partnership in Boston, billing themselves as "Landscape and Garden Architects." Their official partnership lasted only a year but the split was amicable, and they continued to collaborate on residential gardens and public projects for many years.

Samuel Negus prepared plans for sites in Brockton, Massachusetts, including a planting study for Salisbury Park (1913) and a plan for the Union Cemetery (c. 1911). He also designed plans for St. Andrews by the Sea in Hyannis Port, Massachusetts, in 1904, and for the Dayton Country Club in Dayton, Ohio. In 1921, once again teamed with Punchard, he developed "Plans for Improvement of Station Grounds, Scituate [Massachusetts] Village Improvement Society." Negus also designed many private gardens in Massachusetts, New Hampshire, and Rhode Island.

Negus and Punchard's largest joint project was prepared, again, for the City of Brockton. In 1926, Daniel Field, a wealthy Brockton industrialist and chairman of

Winter view, D. W. Field Park, Brockton, Massachusetts, 1990. Courtesy Child Associates, Inc.

Autumn view, D. W. Field Park, 1990. Courtesy Child Associates, Inc.

the Park Commissioners, who valued an earlier, unimplemented design for a Brockton park system by the Olmsteds*, hired Negus and Punchard to make a plan for a 650-acre park in the northern portion of the city. The plan they prepared had a strong Olmstedian character. Although Field, who funded the park and supervised its construction, did not implement the plan in detail, he clearly relied on it throughout the park's development.

Negus became a Fellow of the American Society of Landscape Architects in 1914. He practiced in the Boston area for his entire professional career and lived in Brookline. He retired in 1939 and died four years later in Palm Beach, Florida.

Child Associates, Inc. *D. W. Field Park, Brockton, Massachusetts. Historic Landscape Report.* Landscape Historian, Phyllis Andersen. Prepared for the Commonwealth of Massachusetts. Olmsted Historic Landscape Preservation Program, Boston, 1993. Documents Negus's work on the landscape plan for the park as well as his professional career.

Negus, Samuel. "Landscape Gardening on a Small Lot." *House Beautiful*, March 1916, 108–109. Offers advice on accommodating the automobile in the design of a small suburban garden, using a Negus project in Brookline, Massachusetts, as an example.

A collection of 52 photographs and plans of Negus's work is housed in the Special Collections division of the Frances Loeb Library, Graduate School of Design, Harvard University.

Phyllis Andersen

NEWTON, NORMAN THOMAS
(1898–1992)
landscape architect, educator, author

Norman Thomas Newton was born in Corry, Pennsylvania. A 1919 graduate of Cornell University, Newton also received a master's degree in landscape design from Cornell in 1920. In 1923, after working in the office of landscape architect Bryant Fleming* for three years, Newton was awarded a Rome Prize by the American Academy in Rome. He spent the following three years as a Fellow of the Academy, studying the gardens of Italian villas. During this period he produced meticulous measured drawings of both the Villa Chigi and the Villa Medici as well as immersing himself in disciplines—particularly music and the fine arts—which he came to view as intrinsically related to both architecture and landscape design.

On his return to the United States, Newton entered private practice in the office of Ferruccio Vitale*, designing country places. In 1932 he left Vitale to establish his own New York office. He became increasingly involved with public works projects administered by the Civilian Conservation Corps and served as an associate landscape architect for the National Park Service from 1933 to 1939. Three of Newton's most notable public projects were undertaken during this period: master plans for Bedloe's Island, the site of the Statue of Liberty in New York City; for the Salem Maritime National Historic Site in Salem, Massachusetts; and for the Saratoga Battlefield National History Park.

Returning to Italy in World War II as a lieutenant colonel in the U.S. Air Force, Newton was attached as senior monuments officer to the British Eighth Army during 1942–1946. His position entailed both surveying the condition of cultural sites and monuments and formulating recommendations for the conservation and reconstruction of war-damaged structures and sites. The multiple decorations he received from the Italian government in 1946 and 1950 testify to the importance of this work.

Newton joined the faculty of the Harvard Graduate School of Design as an assistant professor of landscape architecture in 1939 and, apart from his service during World War II, taught at the school until his retirement in 1967. He was named Charles Eliot Professor of Landscape Architecture in 1963. After leaving Harvard, Newton returned to the American Academy in Rome as resident landscape architect.

In addition to his teaching responsibilities, Newton was involved in professional activities, most notably in the American Society of Landscape Architects, which he joined in 1923. A Fellow of the society, he served as its president between 1957 and 1961. During his presidency, the society's headquarters was relocated from Boston to Washington, D.C. At the same time, through a variety of initiatives, Newton attempted to change the criteria for ASLA membership because of his strong belief in the importance of substantial experience as a practitioner.

Newton contributed to professional journals as a historian, critic, educator, and reviewer. His comprehensive book, *Design on the Land* (1971), was immediately recognized as a classic history of the discipline and has

Newton's rendering of Villa Medici at Fiesole. Courtesy Frances Loeb Library, Harvard University.

Aerial view of Statue of Liberty National Monument. Courtesy National Park Service, Statue of Liberty National Monument.

remained a standard text. The book provides keys to Newton's design approach. He asserts that "in design the role of space is primary," further arguing that "one of the best sources of positive spatial character is clarity of overall form; this occurs most convincingly when one can readily perceive the boundaries or limits of the space, the vertical planes of masonry or vegetation implied or explicit that contain it." Newton also links landscape architecture with conservation, stressing that both disciplines focus on "the desirable optimum relation between the piece of land and the proposed use: in short, wise use of the land."

Newton died in Cambridge, Massachusetts.

Newton, Norman T. *An Approach to Design.* Cambridge: Addison-Wesley, 1951. A wide-ranging analysis of design perception, philosophy, practice, and education which derived, in large part, from conversations with students and colleagues at the Harvard Graduate School of Design in the mid- to late 1940s.

Newton, Norman T. *Design on the Land: The Development of Landscape Architecture.* Cambridge: Harvard University Press, 1971. A standard reference work and overview of landscape design history; heavily illustrated with maps, plans, and photographs and including a substantial bibliography.

United States Army Headquarters Allied Commission, Subcommission for Monuments. *Final Report.* Washington, D.C.: Headquarters Allied Commission, 1945. A report to which Newton contributed, as director of the subcommission; surveys damage to architecture and historic sites in Italy and offers recommendations for postwar preservation and reconstruction projects.

Mary Daniels

NICHOLS, ARTHUR RICHARDSON
(1880–1970)
landscape architect

See the joint account with Morell, Anthony.

NICHOLS, ROSE STANDISH
(1872–1960)
landscape architect, author

Rose Nichols was the eldest of three daughters of Dr. Arthur Nichols, a prominent Boston homeopathic physician, and Elizabeth Homer. In 1889, at the instigation of her aunt and uncle, Augusta and Augustus Saint-Gaudens, the Nichols family began to spend their summers in Cornish, New Hampshire, where Saint-Gaudens had founded a colony for artists. The colony's nationally acclaimed gardens, such as those by artists Stephen Parrish, Thomas and Maria Dewing, and Charles Platt*, were formative influences on Nichols, who in 1896 laid out a walled garden at Mastlands, the family house in Cornish.

At the suggestion of her uncle, Nichols took up landscape architecture, first training informally with Platt, her Cornish neighbor, and going on to study horticulture at Harvard's Bussey Institution. She then worked in the architectural office of Thomas Hastings, of Carrère & Hastings, while taking classes in drawing at the Massachusetts Institute of Technology. Nichols completed her training in England under H. Inigo Triggs, author of *The Formal Gardens of England and Scotland* (1903), and in Paris at the Ecole des Beaux-Arts.

Nichols's style was formulated on her study of English formal gardens, influenced by American Colonial Revival gardens and Italian and Spanish ideas, the result of her extensive travels abroad. She landed her first commission in 1904 when Ellen Mason asked her to design gardens for her house in Newport, Rhode Island. In the course of her career, Nichols designed approximately thirty gardens, but little is known about her work since her planting plans and professional papers disappeared shortly after her death.

Many of Nichols's commissions were in Lake Forest, Illinois, where she collaborated with architects Howard Van Doren Shaw and David Adler, both followers of Platt. Her work there includes House of the Four Winds for Hugh McBirney, Haven Wood for Edward Ryerson, Ellsloyd for Louis Laflin, and gardens for Charles H. Schweppes and William Clow. Other commissions range from Santa Barbara and Tucson, to Georgia and the New York–New England area. Traces of extant gardens can be found at Mastlands (now the Cornish Colony Museum) and Villa Terrace Decorative Arts Museum, Milwaukee (the former Lloyd R. Smith residence). Nichols's gardens at Grey Towers National Historic Landmark in Milford, Pennsylvania, are currently undergoing restoration. They were originally designed in 1924 for Cornelia Bryce Pinchot, wife of the forestry expert Gifford Pinchot. The Nichols House Museum, Rose Nichols's longtime winter home at 55 Mount Vernon Street, Boston, was established by legacy in 1961 to preserve her collections of art, antiques, and historic needlework acquired during her travels abroad.

Like many women landscape architects of the period, Nichols specialized in the design and planting of flower gardens. She took her cue from the sunken gardens at Hampton Court, England, when she laid out the garden at Mastlands. A large space, divided into profusely planted rectangular beds with the main path on axis with the house, the garden was idyllically sited among towering pine trees and enclosed with low, rustic stone walls, with seats notched into recesses. Nichols chose as her focal point an ancient apple tree that drooped gracefully over a central pool. Author Frances Duncan* wrote enthusiastically about Mastlands, considering it one of the most delightful gardens in Cornish for its harmonious relationship with the house and its thoughtful color scheme.

Rose Standish Nichols. Drawing by Taylor Green, 1912. Courtesy Nichols House Museum.

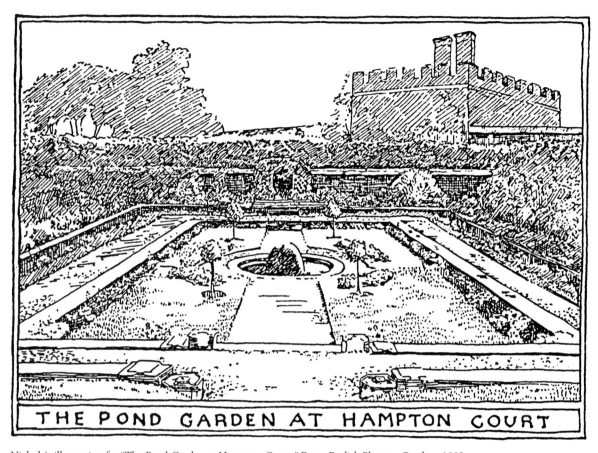

THE POND GARDEN AT HAMPTON COURT

Nichols's illustration for "The Pond Garden at Hampton Court." From *English Pleasure Gardens*, 1902.

In her collaboration with architects and other landscape architects, Nichols's responsibilities were limited to planting flower gardens. At the House of the Four Winds, for instance, her choice of plantings carefully echoed Howard Shaw's layout inspired by the Generalife gardens of the Alhambra in Spain. At Haven Wood, Nichols was part of a team that transformed twenty acres of timberland outside Chicago into consummate estate gardens. Shaw designed the architectural features, Jens Jensen* added the trees and shrubs, and Nichols designed and planted a spacious sunken walled garden. Laid out in four quarters, the garden had accents provided by pyramidal evergreens and standard heliotropes and roses. "Along with a definite color scheme," Nichols wrote, "emphasis was placed on contrasts of sunlight and shadow." For C. B. MacDonald, in Southampton, New York, Nichols designed walled gardens along Colonial Revival lines, filled with roses and perennials and surrounded by an arbor covered with grapevines to complement the Georgian-style brick house.

Nichols is better known as an author and garden scholar. She hit upon the idea for her first book, *English Pleasure Gardens*, during her travels when she was unable to find a comprehensive treatment of the history of English gardens. Nichols was a frequent contributor to *House Beautiful* and other magazines, writing about horticulture, garden design, and historic gardens as well as interior design. While much of this material was later developed into books, she also wrote individual pieces on topics such as "Futurist gardens of New Germany" and Chinese gardens.

Rose Nichols was a lively, cosmopolitan woman with many diversified interests in addition to gardens. Early on she founded reading groups in her Boston and Cornish homes, and later turned to international politics and world peace. She was a lifelong pacifist and attended

Mastlands, Nichols's garden at Cornish, New Hampshire. From Guy Lowell, *American Gardens*, 1902.

peace conferences in Europe with Jane Addams of Hull House, Chicago. Her acquaintances included Isabella Stewart Gardner, Mrs. Woodrow Wilson, Bernard Berenson, Queen Margherita of Italy, Bertrand Russell, and the English Fabians. In later years she presided over Sunday afternoon teas and lively discussion groups in her Beacon Hill home. "Tall, stately, regal in bearing," a *Boston Globe* columnist wrote, Nichols was "the embodiment of intellectual curiosity about everything."

Nichols, Rose Standish. *English Pleasure Gardens.* New York: Macmillan, 1902. Contains 300 photographs and attractive sketches drawn by the author in a style reminiscent of those in Reginald Blomfield's influential book *The Formal Garden in England* (1892).

Nichols, Rose Standish. *Italian Pleasure Gardens.* New York: Dodd, Mead, 1928. A historical study with useful appendixes and many photographs by the author.

Nichols, Rose Standish. *Spanish and Portuguese Gardens.* Boston: Houghton Mifflin, 1924. Comprehensive account ranging from historical Moorish gardens to contemporary work of C. S. N. Forestier.

Judith B. Tankard

NOLEN, JOHN
(1869–1937)
landscape architect, planner, author

John Nolen was born in Philadelphia. Accepted to the Girard School there at the age of nine, he graduated first in his class when he was fifteen years old. He went on to attend the Wharton School of the University of Pennsylvania, where he focused his studies on philosophy, economics, and public administration; he graduated with a bachelor's degree in 1893.

Although Nolen's first occupation was professor of adult education at the University of Pennsylvania, his thesis, "Municipal Mishandling of the Philadelphia Gas Works and the Steps That Should Be Taken to Correct the Corruption," and the garden work he performed on the Stephen Girard estate to pay his college tuition evinced an incipient interest in city planning and landscape de-

Ed Fletcher, George Marston, and John Nolen in San Diego Back Country, 1908. Courtesy San Diego Historic Society.

executive secretary for the Extension of University Teaching. In 1900 he did postgraduate work in Munich.

In 1903, at the age of thirty-four, with a wife and two children, Nolen decided to pursue landscape architecture as a profession. He left his University of Pennsylvania teaching position, sold his house in Ardmore to pay his expenses, and enrolled in the landscape architecture program at Harvard. There his design instructors included Frederick Law Olmsted Jr.* and Arthur Shurcliff*. He studied horticulture and herbaceous plants with B. M. Watson. Nolen opened an office on Harvard Square in Cambridge in 1905. He graduated at the head of his class the same year despite the fact that he was excused from his final examinations to undertake a commission for a new park in Charlotte, North Carolina, on the recommendation of Harvard president Charles Eliot.

Nolen continued to study planning throughout his career, making a dozen trips to European countries for this purpose. In 1931 he was awarded a grant to study city planning in Germany and attended the first all-Union Convention on City Planning in Russia open to foreign specialists.

Although many of Nolen's first commissions involved park design, he also laid out subdivisions and soon was engaged in city planning, beginning a plan for the partially developed town of Kingsport, Tennessee, in 1905. Eventually Nolen and his firm completed over 450 projects, including comprehensive plans for 29 cities and 27 new towns (7 for the federal government), and he acted

sign. He also acted as superintendent for Onteora Park, a Catskill Mountain resort, between university semesters. Between 1886 and 1891, Nolen was secretary of the Girard Trust Funds, and from 1893 to 1903 he served as

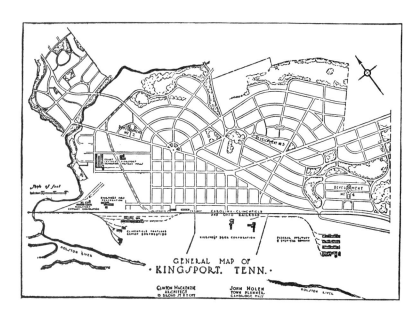

General plan for Kingsport, Tennessee. From *New Towns for Old*, 1927.

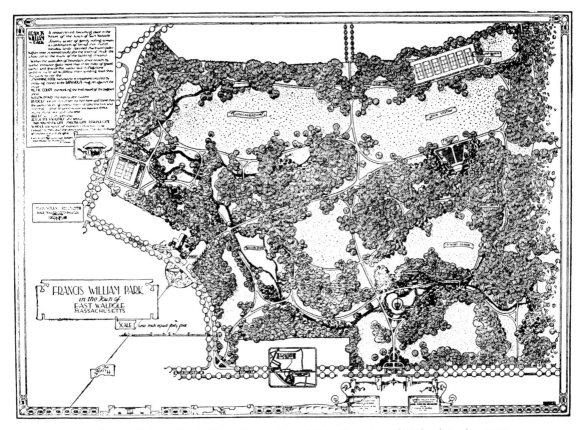

Plan for Francis William Park, East Walpole, Massachusetts. From ASLA, *Illustrations of Works of Members*, 1931.

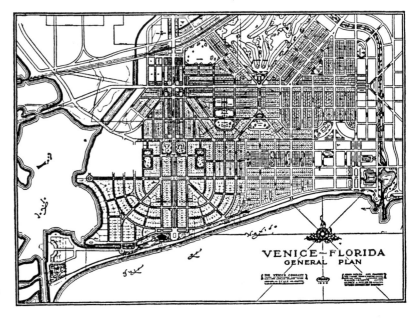

General plan for Venice, Florida. From
New Towns for Old, 1927.

Queens Road in Myers Park, 1986. Courtesy National Register of Historic Places.

as a consultant to 17 state and regional government agencies. Typically, Nolen provided planning services to a city over a period of years. For example, he prepared the first of a succession of seven reports and plans for Little Rock, Arkansas, in 1913, the last in 1930. In 1918, Nolen served on the advisory committee of the Emergency Fleet Corporation's Housing Division, a government agency created to provide housing for workers in industries vital to the war effort. He was chief of the Bureau of Housing and Town Planning for the Army Education Committee. As a consultant to the U.S. Department of the Interior he completed assignments for the National Park Service, the Natural Resources Committee, the Resettlement Administration (Greenbelt Towns), and the Housing Division of the Public Works Administration. His 1921 plan for Mariemont, Ohio, directed development of the community from the ground up. He called the Mariemont plan "an interpretation of Modern City Planning Principles ap-

plied to a small Community to produce local happiness. A National Exemplar."

Nolen believed that small towns and relatively small cities had economic and social advantages over larger municipalities, particularly if they had easy access to the larger cities via transportation networks. As early as the 1920s he recognized that the automobile and the airplane would influence the shape of future cities as much as the railroad had earlier. In his 1930 plan for Little Rock he advocated the acquisition of a square mile for a municipal airport even though the city was not yet on a federal airway.

Nolen's primary focus was town planning, but he also pioneered parkway design. He believed that major traffic routes should follow topography and that ring roads or circumferentials should be used to direct traffic around cities to avoid congestion. Parkways, he felt, sustained and increased land values sufficiently that taxes

Beaver Lake, Asheville, North Carolina, 1991. Courtesy Charles A. Birnbaum.

should pay for such improvements. He prepared a study of parkways with Henry Vincent Hubbard* which Hubbard completed after Nolen's death in 1937. A prolific writer, Nolen produced six books and numerous articles on a wide variety of subjects. He also edited and composed an introduction for the 1907 edition of Humphry Repton's *Art of Landscape Gardening.*

In addition to his writings, Nolen had a great impact on the landscape architecture profession through his influence on young city planners. Russell VanNest Black, one of the professionals who worked for a time with Nolen's firm, stated in the 1967 edition of *Planning and the Planning Profession:* "That office became an institution. From apprenticeships there many young men went out to positions of responsibility and leadership in the

planning field—among them, three presidents of the City Planning Institute. Until Harvard inaugurated its School of Planning in 1929, no better training was available than the Nolen office."

Nolen helped organize and took leading roles in the most influential planning organizations of his day. He became a Fellow of the American Society of Landscape Architects in 1910, having joined the organization in 1905. In 1909 he gave the keynote address at the first National Conference on City Planning in Washington, D.C. He was president of the National Conference on City Planning in 1926, and in 1931 he became president of the International Federation of Housing and Town Planning. He served as president of the Boston chapter of the ASLA in 1932, and he was director of the American Society of Planning Officials and the National Housing Association. Nolen was buried in Mount Auburn Cemetery in Cambridge, Massachusetts.

Nolen, John. *New Ideals in the Planning of Cities, Towns and Villages*. New York: American City Bureau, 1919. Begins with a litany of shortcomings of American cities, which Nolen attributes to unprecedented growth, the complexity of city life, and the lack of skill and experience with which they were planned; in the second part he discusses topics such as the importance of a local survey in developing a city plan, essential elements to be considered in city planning, types of plans, legislation and organization, financing, and professional training for city planning work; illustrated.

Nolen, John. *New Towns for Old: Achievements in Civic Improvement in Some American Small Towns and Neighborhoods*. Boston: Marshall Jones, 1927. Draws on a number of Nolen's most innovative projects including Kingsport, Tenn., and Mariemont, Ohio, to provide concrete illustrations of civic improvements and town planning; notes some English garden cities as historical precedents.

Nolen, John, and Henry V. Hubbard. *Parkways and Land Values*. Harvard Planning Studies, vol. 11. Cambridge: Harvard University Press, 1937. Nolen wrote the first draft of this publication, which Hubbard rewrote and published after Nolen's death; parkways in Boston, Kansas City, Mo., and Westchester County, N.Y., are examined as case studies; illustrated.

Frank B. Burgraff

NOTMAN, JOHN
(1810–1865)
landscape gardener, cemetery designer

John Notman was born in Edinburgh, Scotland, during a lively period of cultural transition, just as the Enlightenment was giving way to romanticism. Descended from a long line of stoneworkers, Notman apprenticed for four years to a builder-carpenter with country house projects in the Highlands and northern Ireland. He left Scotland for Philadelphia in 1831 and quickly applied for naturalization, going back in 1833 only to bring his mother, brother, and two sisters to America. Notman's name appeared in city directories, first as "carpenter" in 1837, then as "architect." In 1844, Notman married a widow, Martha Pullen, a painter seven years older than he.

In 1835, through work for the Library Company of Philadelphia in 1835, Notman met horticulturist John Jay Smith*, its librarian, who became a mentor, securing him many projects. Smith, China trade merchant Nathan Dunn, and other civic leaders formed a joint stock company in 1836 to found a garden cemetery on Laurel, an old estate just above the Schuylkill River Falls. Laurel Hill was designed in the gardenesque style, inspired by H. E. Kendall's Kensal Green—All Souls' Cemetery (1831)— in London, which was based on the Palladian concept of a central core with surrounding spatial units and minor irregularities. Smith planned most of the plantings, and Notman designed Laurel Hill's Norman chapel. He acquired James Thom's sculptural composition *Old Mortality with Sir Walter Scott and His Pony*, which had been exhibited in Edinburgh and London, and installed it inside the entrance in a grotto. Elsewhere in the cemetery, Notman designed several funerary monuments in diverse styles.

Notman also designed several residences during this period. His plans for Dunn's Cottage (1837–1838) in Mount Holly, New Jersey, drew recognition in Andrew Jackson Downing's* *Treatise* (1841). Its "highly elegant verandah . . . one of its striking features" opened the house to the surrounding picturesque landscape just as Downing recommended. Downing also praised Notman's Riverside Villa (1839) in Burlington, New Jersey, residence of Smith's friend George Washington Doane, an Episcopal bishop. America's first example of the Italianate, the 7-acre estate featured verandas and balustrades "picturesquely outflung to the landscape" with panoramas over the Delaware River. A glass conservatory had views

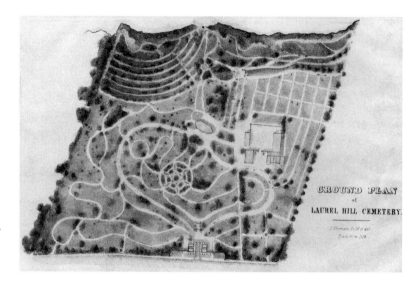

"Ground Plan of Laurel Hill Cemetery,"
Philadelphia, 1844. From *Guide to
Laurel Hill Cemetery Near Philadelphia.*
Courtesy Blanche M. G. Linden.

across back lawn "pleasure grounds." An evergreen screen concealed kitchen gardens. Downing showed a simpler, somewhat later Italian home by Notman in *Cottage Residences* (1842).

Notman also designed Henry McCall's 135-acre Italianate country seat, Ellarslie (1848–1849) near Trenton, New Jersey. It featured a formal, symmetrical carriage entrance with river views. Estates near Princeton combined Notman's architecture with landscapes by Downing: Harry Ingersoll's Medary (1847), Joshua Francis Fisher's Alverthorpe (1850) in Jenkintown, Pennsyl-

vania, and Henry Pratt McKean's Fern Hill (1851–1852) in Germantown. Other area estates by Notman placed classical, Georgian, Gothic Revival, or Tuscan houses in picturesque landscapes. The John P. Stockton House, now the residence of Princeton's president, is one example from 1848–1849; another, the Prospect, dates from the 1850s.

Gentlemen horticulturists provided many semi-public and private commissions for architects but insisted on active collaboration in "landscape gardening." In 1845 the Cincinnati Horticultural Society asked Notman

Engraving of Laurel Hill Cemetery by
A. W. Graham, after W. Croome for
Godey's Lady's Book. Courtesy Blanche
M. G. Linden.

The lawn inside the entry at Holly-Wood Cemetery, 1978. Photo Blanche M. G. Linden.

to design the 166-acre Spring Grove Cemetery. Notman's proposed design proved unsatisfactory, however, because the directors had in mind a freely flowing "rural" landscape like Boston's Mount Auburn or New York's Green-Wood. They also wanted to be part of the design process like the founders of those exemplars. Notman was enraged when they rejected his design for a "beautiful city of the dead," although he was paid $770 for his trouble. Notman's plan was criticized because it left hilly sites "inaccessible or marred by an avenue running along the summit of a fine ridge." A new scheme, by Buchanan, Ernst, and engineer Thomas Earnshaw, laid sinuous roads through low-lying areas.

In 1846, Judge Richard Stockton Field, a horticulturist and Episcopal lay leader, employed Notman to design his 40-acre Princeton estate, Fieldwood (also known as Woodlawn, Guernsey Field, or Marquand Park). Notman unified the grounds in a picturesque fashion with a system of meandering avenues, paths, plantings, woodland,

and structures, old and new, including greenhouses. It won praise in the sixth, posthumous edition of Downing's *Treatise* (1859). Half of Fieldwood remains as a municipal park.

Notman also pursued institutional commissions and received many. Field recommended him in 1846 to design Princeton's theological seminary and Ivy Hall law school. In the same year, Notman unsuccessfully entered the Smithsonian Institution competition with a Gothic design in what he termed the "collegiate style" (actually, it did not characterize campuses until much later). Through the 1840s and 1850s, commissions came from churches in the Philadelphia area, New Jersey, Delaware, Maryland, and western Pennsylvania. The New York Ecclesiological Society endorsed his work in 1853.

A Mr. Davenport recruited Notman in the fall of 1847 to "improve" the landscape of Huguenot Springs, a new spa in Midlothian, Virginia, 16 miles from Richmond. Notman aimed to create a "shady promenading ground" with a "picturesque effect" around the central hotel with its oval drive, reached after a processional through woods from the River Road. This design, however, was never completely realized. As a result of that project, Notman met Thomas T. Giles, who introduced him to founders of a new cemetery in Richmond. They had rejected as unsatisfactory a plan by William A. Pratt, the architect and subsequent superintending engineer of Baltimore's Green Mount Cemetery, who had recently moved to Richmond. In February 1848, Notman submitted a design for 42 acres of the new cemetery, which overlooked the city across the James River Falls. Inspired by large holly trees on the wooded site, he suggested the name: Holly-Wood. Sinuous gravel avenues and paths follow the natural contours of the varied terrain. The circulatory system's irregularities produced many viewing angles and corner lots for display of monuments or mausoleums. For economy and a naturalistic look, Notman prescribed indigenous plants and local materials—river granite for surface gutters and bridges of rustic white oak trunks. He promised that his landscape could be built with "little or no cutting or grading." His report, his most extensive landscape design description, emphasized function and articulated a design philosophy more picturesque than in his previous projects.

Giles and others recruited Notman in 1851 to improve Richmond's Capitol Square, designed in 1816 in a formal style by French architect Maximilian Godefroy around Jefferson's famed State House (1785–1788). They wanted Notman to create a unified, picturesque site for the neoclassical capitol, the Federal bell tower (1824), and a grand monument, an equestrian George Washington surrounded by larger-than-life statues of Virginia notables by Thomas Crawford and Randolph Rogers.

One of Notman's last structures was the arched marble Italianate gate (1856–1858) for Philadelphia's Mount Vernon Cemetery. His practice waned during the Panic of 1857 and the Civil War. Yet he had proved himself adept in both architecture and landscape design, and

in fostering their interaction and integration. He was a founding member of the American Institution of Architects (1836) and of the Pennsylvania Institute of Architects (1861). Alcoholism hastened Notman's death at age fifty-five. He lies at Laurel Hill under a simple dark gray granite shaft.

Greiff, Constance M. *John Notman, Architect.* Philadelphia: The Athenaeum, 1979. The most comprehensive survey of Notman's work, though it lacks historical context.

Morgan, Keith. "The Landscape Gardening of John Notman, 1810–1865." Master's thesis, University of Delaware, 1973.

Notman, John. "Report Accompanying the Plan of Holly-Wood Cemetery, Richmond, Virginia." *Historical Sketch of Holly-Wood Cemetery.* Richmond, 1875, 19–25. Notman's manuscript is the most detailed record of his design philosophy.

Notman left no collected correspondence, diaries, drawings, or account books. Fragmentary memoirs, legal documents, records of some clients, and newspaper accounts (from Philadelphia, Princeton, and Richmond) remain dispersed. Related materials are in the Historical Society of Pennsylvania (the Franklin Fire Insurance Company Records and the John Jay Smith Papers), the Library Company of Philadelphia, and the Princeton University Archives and Libraries. Some miscellaneous papers are at Spring Grove Cemetery, Cincinnati. Some documents about Holly-Wood and Huguenot Springs which survived Richmond's 1865 burning are in the Virginia Historical Society and the cemetery's records. Few Notman drawings remain.

Blanche M. G. Linden

OLMSTED BROTHERS

See under separate accounts of Olmsted, John Charles, and Olmsted, Frederick Law, Jr.

OLMSTED, FREDERICK LAW, JR.
(1870–1957)
landscape architect, planner, educator, conservationist

Frederick Law Olmsted Jr., born on Staten Island, New York, was the son of Frederick Law Olmsted*, the forefather of the profession of landscape architecture in the United States, and Mary Cleveland Perkins Olmsted, the widow of Olmsted's brother. From his earliest years young Olmsted was aware of his father's fervent desire, bordering on obsession, to have him carry on both the family name and profession. In a telling act, the elder Olmsted renamed the child (who had been called Henry Perkins at birth) Frederick Law Olmsted Jr., thus making his only biological son his namesake.

In the waning years of his life, the father enjoyed including his son in the culminating projects of his own career. While still a student at Harvard, young Olmsted spent a summer working in Daniel Burnham's office as the "White City" of the 1893 World's Columbian Exposition arose in Chicago. After graduating in 1894, Olmsted spent thirteen months on site at Biltmore, the 10,000-acre estate being developed for George Vanderbilt in Asheville, North Carolina. In December 1895, he entered the Olmsted firm in Brookline, Massachusetts. Following his father's formal retirement in 1897, he became a full partner with his half-brother, John Charles Olmsted*, in the family business.

As bearer of the most renowned name in landscape architecture, Olmsted was chosen for positions of prominence from the very start of his career. In 1899 he became a founding member of the American Society of Landscape Architects and served two terms as its president (1908–1909, 1919–1923). The following year he was appointed instructor in landscape architecture at Harvard, where he helped create the country's first university course in the profession.

Olmsted emerged on the national scene in 1901, when he assumed what would have been his father's place, had he been well, on the Park Improvement Commission for the District of Columbia, commonly known as the McMillan Commission. Charged with interpreting for the twentieth century Pierre Charles L'Enfant's vision of the nation's capital, Olmsted worked with his father's colleagues from the Chicago World's Fair to transform Washington into a work of civic art and to devise a comprehensive plan for its future development. For decades Olmsted steadfastly guarded and promoted the McMillan Plan, serving on the two federal oversight bodies for planning in the capital city, the Commission of Fine Arts

(1910–1918) and the National Capital Park Planning Commission (1926–1932). As adviser or designer, he worked on many prominent Washington landmarks, including the White House grounds, the Federal Triangle, the Jefferson Memorial, Roosevelt Island, Rock Creek Parkway, and the National Cathedral grounds.

The McMillan report, with its promise that the City Beautiful could be achieved through the art and science of comprehensive planning, had a galvanizing effect on municipal art societies and civic improvement associations in cities and towns around the country. Olmsted found himself in great demand to advise new quasi-official planning boards and citizen associations on civic improvement; between 1905 and 1915 he produced planning reports for Detroit, Utica, Boulder, Pittsburgh, New Haven, Rochester, and Newport. During the same period he also applied the emerging principles of comprehensive planning to suburban settings, creating master plans for new sections of Roland Park, a Baltimore suburb; Forest Hills Gardens, a model garden community outside of New York City; and the industrial town of Torrance, California (largely unrealized). Many of the features of his suburban plans have had enduring influence, including the concept of neighborhood-centered development, the differentiation of streets by function, the importance of common open and recreational spaces, and the need for continuing maintenance and aesthetic oversight to preserve the quality of the community.

In 1910, Olmsted's colleagues asked him to lead the first formal organization of the nascent planning profes-

Frederick Law Olmsted Jr., 1942. Courtesy National Commission of Fine Arts.

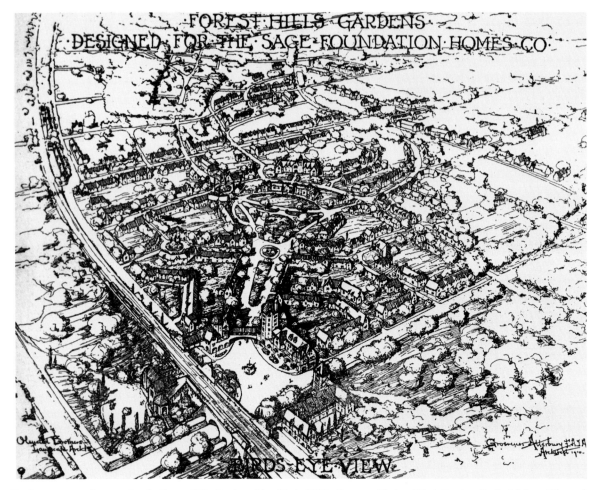

Bird's-eye view of street plan for Forest Hills Gardens, New York, 1910. Courtesy National Park Service, Frederick Law Olmsted National Historic Site.

sion, the National Conference on City Planning. One of the few planners to practice successfully in both the City Beautiful and the "City Efficient" eras, Olmsted in his presidential addresses to this body over the next nine years helped lay the theoretical foundation for the new discipline. In 1917 he was instrumental in organizing the American City Planning Institute, a professional society for planning practitioners, and he was elected its first president. As this organization's representative, he offered the planning profession's services to the government during World War I, serving as manager of the Town Planning Division of the U.S. Housing Corpora-

tion, which oversaw the first direct federal participation in building worker housing.

With his brother's death in 1920, Olmsted became the senior partner in the Olmsted firm, then the largest office of landscape architecture in the world. In 1921 he was asked to advise on the preparation of a regional plan for the New York area. His plan for Fort Tryon Park, a great urban park on the bluffs of Manhattan's northern border overlooking the Hudson River, also dates from this period. Olmsted designed two more notable suburban communities in the 1920s: Palos Verdes Estates in California and the Mountain Lake Club in Lake Wales, Florida.

"Preliminary General Plan of the Washington Cathedral Close, Washington, D.C.," March 5, 1910. Courtesy National Park Service, Frederick Law Olmsted National Historic Site.

In the latter part of his career Olmsted devoted much of his time to public service, consulting on issues of the conservation and preservation of the country's state and national park and remaining wilderness areas. The key language in the 1916 bill establishing the National Park Service, setting aside park lands for all time as places protected from development and preserved for human enjoyment, was Olmsted's. For thirty years he advised the National Park Service on issues of management and the conservation of water and scenic resources. He left his mark on national parks from coast to coast, including Maine's Acadia National Park, the Florida Everglades, and Yosemite. In 1928 he prepared a guide for the selection and acquisition of land for the California park system which became a model for other states. Olmsted also devised a master plan for saving the California redwoods.

Olmsted remained a partner in the Olmsted firm until his official retirement in 1949, eight years before his death in Malibu, California. For over a half century Olmsted had been a preeminent practitioner and spokesman for landscape architecture and comprehensive planning, both interested in the interrelationship of people and their environment. His concerns for balancing aesthetics and practicality, harmonizing use and beauty, and preserving both natural and manmade landscapes are again at the forefront of the two professions he helped guide and nourish.

Carriage road on east side of Eagle
Lake, Acadia National Park, 1994.
Photo David Halpern.

Klaus, Susan L. "All in the Family: The Olmsted Office
and the Business of Landscape Architecture." *Landscape Journal* 16 (Spring 1997), 80–93. A historical
overview of the operations of the Olmsted office,
with details on the young Olmsted's role.

Olmsted, Frederick Law, Jr. "City Planning. An Introductory Address." In *Proceedings of the Second National
Conference on City Planning* (1910), 15–32. Olmsted's presidential address expresses both awe and
apprehension for the "appalling breadth and ramifica-
tions of real city planning."

Olmsted, Frederick Law, Jr. "Landscape Architecture in
Connection with Public Buildings in Washington."
American Architect and Building News, January 19,
1901, 19–21. Olmsted's views on the treatment of
public spaces in the national capital, as well as the
need for landscape architects to deal with broad elements of the cityscape.

Susan L. Klaus

OLMSTED, FREDERICK LAW, SR.

(1822–1903)

landscape architect, author, conservationist

Frederick Law Olmsted was born in Hartford, Connecticut, a member of the eighth generation of his family to live in that city. His mother died when he was four, and from the age of seven he received his schooling mostly from ministers in outlying towns, with whom he lived. His father, a successful dry-goods merchant, was a lover of scenery, and much of Olmsted's vacation time was spent with his family on "tours in search of the picturesque" through northern New England and upstate New York. As he was about to enter Yale College in 1837, Olmsted suffered severe sumac poisoning, which weakened his eyes and kept him from the usual course of studies.

He spent the next twenty years gathering experiences and skills from a variety of endeavors that he eventually utilized in creating the profession of landscape architecture. He worked in a New York dry-goods store and took a year-long voyage in the China Trade. He studied surveying and engineering, chemistry, and scientific farming, and ran a farm on Staten Island from 1848 to 1855. In 1850 he and two friends took a six-month walking tour of Europe and the British Isles, during which he saw numerous parks and private estates, as well as scenic countryside. In 1852 he published his first book, *Walks and Talks of an American Farmer in England*. That December he began the first of two journeys through the slaveholding south as a reporter for the *New York Times*. Between 1856 and 1860 he published three volumes of travel accounts and social analysis of the South. During this period he used his literary activities to oppose the westward expansion of slavery and to argue for the abolition of slavery by the southern states. From 1855 to 1857 he was partner in a publishing firm and managing editor of *Putnam's Monthly Magazine*, a leading journal of literature and political commentary. He spent six months of this time living in London with considerable travel on the Continent, and in the process visited many public parks.

Thus it was that by the time he began work as a landscape architect, Olmsted had developed a set of social and political values that gave special purpose to his design work. From his New England heritage he drew a belief in community and the importance of public institutions of culture and education. His southern travels and friendship with exiled participants in the failed German revolutions of 1848 convinced him of the need for the United States to demonstrate the superiority of republican government and free labor. A series of influences, beginning with his father and supplemented by reading such British writers

on landscape art as Uvedale Price, Humphry Repton, William Gilpin, William Shenstone, and John Ruskin, convinced him of the importance of aesthetic sensibility as a means of moving American society away from frontier barbarism and toward what he considered a civilized condition.

In the fall of 1857, Olmsted's literary connections enabled him to secure the position of superintendent of Central Park in New York City. The following March, he and Calvert Vaux* won the design competition for the park. During the next seven years he was primarily an administrator in charge of major undertakings: first (1859–1861) as architect-in-chief of Central Park, in charge of construction of the park; then (1861–1863) as director of the U.S. Sanitary Commission, charged with overseeing the health and camp sanitation of all the volunteer soldiers of the Union Army and with creating a national system of medical supply for those troops; and finally (1863–1865) as manager of the Mariposa Estate, a vast gold-mining complex in California.

In 1865, Olmsted returned to New York to join Vaux in completing their work on Central Park and designing Prospect Park in Brooklyn. Over the next thirty years, ending with his retirement in 1895, Olmsted created examples of the many kinds of designs by which the

Olmsted Sr. in 1893. Courtesy National Park Service, Frederick Law Olmsted National Historic Site.

"Plan of Prospect Park, Olmsted, Vaux & Co., Brooklyn, New York," 1871. Courtesy National Park Service, Frederick Law Olmsted National Historic Site.

profession of landscape architecture (a term he and Vaux first used) could improve the quality of life in America. These included the large urban park, devoted primarily to the experience of scenery and designed so as to counteract the artificiality of the city and the stress of urban life; the "parkway," a wide urban greenway carrying several different modes of transportation (most important a smooth-surfaced drive reserved for private carriages) which connected parks and extended the benefits of public greenspace throughout the city; the park system, offering a wide range of public recreation facilities for all residents in a city; the scenic reservation, protecting areas

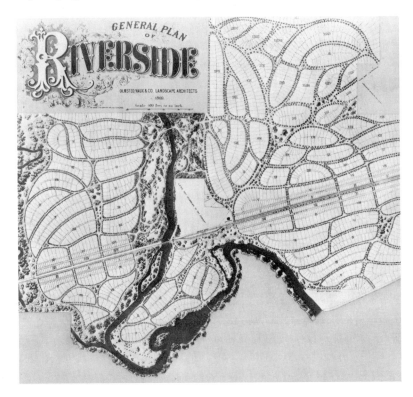

"General Plan of Riverside, Illinois, Olmsted, Vaux & Co.," 1869. Courtesy National Park Service, Frederick Law Olmsted National Historic Site.

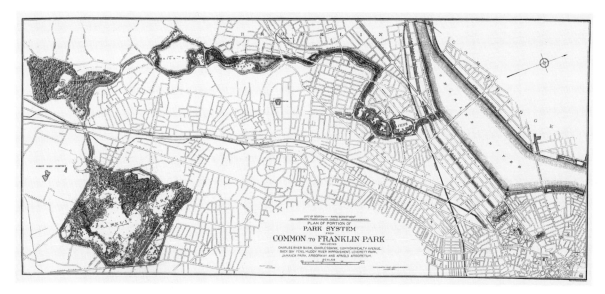

Plan of northern section of Boston's "Emerald Necklace," from Boston Common and Charlesbank to Franklin Park, by Olmsted, Olmsted & Eliot, 1894. Courtesy National Park Service, Frederick Law Olmsted National Historic Site.

of special scenic beauty from destruction and commercial exploitation; the residential suburb, separating place of work from place of residence and devoted to creating a sense of community and a setting for domestic life; the grounds of the private residence, where gardening could develop both the aesthetic awareness and the individuality of its occupants, and containing numerous "attractive open-air apartments" that permitted household activities to be moved outdoors; the campuses of residential institutions, where a domestic scale for the buildings would provide a training ground for civilized life; and the grounds of government buildings, where the function of the buildings would be made more efficient and their dignity of appearance increased by careful planning. In each of these categories, Olmsted developed a distinctive design approach that showed the comprehensiveness of

The Long Meadow, Prospect Park, 1989. Photo Charles E. Beveridge.

Washington Park, Chicago, 1990. Photo
Charles E. Beveridge.

his vision, the uniqueness of conception that he brought
to each commission, and the imagination with which he
dealt with even the smallest details.

His principal projects in each category are:

Scenic reservations. Yosemite Valley and the Mariposa
Big Tree Grove (1865) and Niagara Reservation (1887).

Major urban parks. Central Park (1858); Prospect
Park (1866); Delaware Park, Buffalo (1869); South Park
(later Washington and Jackson Parks and Midway Plai-
sance), Chicago (1871); Belle Isle, Detroit (1881);
Mount Royal, Montreal (1877); Franklin Park, Boston
(1885); Genesee Valley Park, Rochester, New York
(1890); Cherokee Park, Louisville (1891). Also notable
were Riverside Park (1875) and Morningside Park (1873
and 1887) in New York and Fort Greene Park (1868) in
Brooklyn. In smaller cities, Walnut Hill Park in New
Britain, Connecticut (1870); South (now Kennedy) Park
in Fall River, Massachusetts (1871); Beardsley Park in
Bridgeport, Connecticut (1884); Downing Park in Newburgh, New York (1887), and Cadwalader Park, Trenton,
New Jersey (1891).

Parkways. Eastern and Ocean parkways, Brooklyn
(1868); Humboldt and Lincoln, Bidwell and Chapin
Parkways, Buffalo (1870); Drexel Boulevard and Martin
Luther King Drive, Chicago (1871); the "Emerald Necklace" (1881 on), Beacon Street, and Commonwealth
Avenue extension (1886) in Boston; and Southern Parkway, Louisville (1892).

Park systems. Buffalo—Delaware Park, The Front,
The Parade, South Park and Cazenovia Park, and con-

necting parkways. Boston—the "Emerald Necklace":
Charlesbank, Back Bay Fens, Riverway, Leverett Park,
Jamaica Pond, Arnold Arboretum, Franklin Park, and
Marine Park, and connecting parkways. Rochester—
Genesee Valley, Highland, and Seneca Parks and several
city squares. Louisville—Shawnee, Cherokee, and Iro-
quois Parks, Southern Parkways, and several small city
parks and squares.

Residential Communities. Riverside, Illinois (1869);
Sudbrook, Maryland (1889); Druid Hills, Atlanta (1893).

Residential campuses. Stanford University (1886);
Lawrenceville School (1884); Buffalo State Hospital for
the Insane (1874); Hartford Retreat (1860); Blooming-
dale Asylum, White Plains, New York (1892).

Government buildings. U.S. Capitol grounds and terraces (1874); Connecticut State House (1878).

Country estates. Olmsted designed a number of large
estates, and with some of these he introduced projects
with public significance, particularly scientific forestry
and arboretums. The outstanding examples are Biltmore
Estate in Asheville, North Carolina, and Moraine Farm in
Beverly, Massachusetts.

Throughout his career, Olmsted emphasized the
importance of collaboration with professionals in other
disciplines—especially engineers, horticulturists, and architects. A prime example of such collaboration was
Olmsted's role as site planner of the World's Columbian
Exposition of 1893 in Chicago. He worked cordially
with the eastern architects of the buildings on the formal Court of Honor while creating profuse naturalistic

plantings on the Wooded Island and the shores of the lagoons, the setting for the more informal structures of Chicago architects.

Olmsted believed that it was the purpose of his art to affect the emotions. This was especially evident in his park design, where he created passages of scenery in which the visitor would become immersed, experiencing the restorative action of the landscape by what Olmsted termed an "unconscious" process. To achieve this result, he subordinated all elements of the design to the single purpose of making the landscape experience most profound. Olmsted always sought to look beyond current taste and fashion and to base his designs on fundamental principles of human psychology. In particular, he drew from the analysis of earlier British theorists of naturalistic landscape and their emphasis on the special qualities of "pastoral" and "picturesque" scenery. The epitome of pastoral landscape was the English deer park, with its sense of extended space and its gracefully modulated ground and smooth, close-cropped turf. This style he found to be a special antidote to the ill effects of urban life. The "picturesque" style he applied to steep and broken terrain, planting thickly with a variety of ground covers, shrubs, vines, and creepers in order to achieve an effect of bounteousness, profusion, and mystery. His own most intense experience of this effect was on the Isthmus of Panama during his passage to California in 1863. Both styles shared the quality of indefiniteness, of lack of individual objects for specific examination. As Olmsted expressed it, the term "scenery" does not apply to any field of vision in which all that is to be seen is clear and well defined in outline. It must contain either "considerable complexity of light and shadow near the eye, or obscurity of detail further away." These qualities were essential for the unconscious action of scenery on the psyche. They were also a crucial element of his designs as a training ground for aesthetic sensibility. The quality of "delicacy," which involved variety, intricacy, and fine gradation of texture, tint, and tone, was fundamental to Olmsted's artistic and civilizing purpose. The final test of civilization, he taught, was this delicacy, shown by "the willingness of the people to expend study and labor with reference to delicate distinctions in matters of form and color."

Although the scenery Olmsted most loved required considerable rainfall to achieve its effect, he recognized that most of the United States possessed a different climate. Accordingly, he set out to develop a separate and distinct landscape style for the South, while in the semiarid west he saw the necessity of a new water-conserving regional style. He laid the basis for this approach with a half dozen projects in the San Francisco Bay area and in Colorado, most visibly on the campus of Stanford University.

Olmsted carefully trained a handful of talented young men to carry on his design principles, but only his stepson, John C. Olmsted*, lived to serve this role. Both Henry S. Codman and Charles Eliot*, his students and then his partners, died before him.

During his career, Olmsted and his firm carried out some 500 commissions. They included 100 public parks and recreation grounds, 200 private estates, 50 residential communities and subdivisions, and campus design for 40 academic institutions. Olmsted was a prolific author, despite the difficulty he experienced in expressing his ideas in writing. Six thousand letters and reports that he wrote during his landscape architecture career have survived, dealing with 300 design commissions. Several times he paid for the publication and public distribution of important reports. The full list of his publications, including letters describing his southern journeys and various documents published by the U.S. Sanitary Commission, contains more than 300 items.

Beveridge, Charles E., and Paul Rocheleau. *Frederick Law Olmsted: Designing the American Landscape*. New York: Rizzoli International, 1995; paperbound ed., Universe Press, 1998. Comprehensive discussions of Olmsted's design concepts and career; contains many recent photographs, commissioned for this publication, of Olmsted's landscapes.

Beveridge, Charles E., et al. *The Papers of Frederick Law Olmsted*. Baltimore: Johns Hopkins University Press; 1977– (7 of 13 volumes in series published to date). A selected edition of the most significant of Olmsted's writings, with informative volume introductions and extensive annotations of documents; generously illustrated.

Roper, Laura Wood. *FLO: A Biography*. Baltimore: Johns Hopkins University Press, 1973; paperbound edition, 1983. The most fully researched and complete biography of Olmsted.

Zaitzevsky, Cynthia. *Frederick Law Olmsted and the Boston Park System*. Cambridge: Harvard University Press, 1982; paperbound ed., 1995. The best study of Olmsted's work in a single geographical area; excellent illustrations, both plans and historical photographs.

Charles E. Beveridge

OLMSTED, JOHN CHARLES
(1852–1920)
landscape architect, planner

The early life of John Charles Olmsted was filled with extraordinary and traumatic events that were important in forming his shy personality and his broad-ranging interests. He was born in Vandeuvre, near Geneva, Switzerland, the son of Dr. John Hull Olmsted and Mary Cleveland Perkins Olmsted. By the time he was five, John Charles had traversed the Atlantic twice, lost his father to tuberculosis, gained a stepfather in 1859 (his uncle, Frederick Law Olmsted*), and settled down to a more orderly life, in a house in the middle of Central Park, then under construction. The cozy stability of this situation was soon interrupted, first by the Civil War, when his stepfather transferred his new family to Washington, D.C., in 1862, and then by a move to the Mariposa Estate, a frontier gold-mining operation in the foothills of California's Sierra Nevada, which the senior Olmsted managed from 1863 until 1865. Education amid the scenic splendors of Yosemite and the giant sequoias taught John Charles to read the landscape by its flora and fauna, its fossils and minerals. These lessons were reinforced in the summers of 1869 and 1871 when he returned to the frontier, this time as a member of Clarence King's survey party in Nevada and Utah along the 40th Parallel. Here, under often dangerous conditions, he developed his visual memory to record with speed the topographical, geological, and botanical clues of the land, skills that proved invaluable in his later work.

Following his graduation from Yale's Sheffield Scientific School, Olmsted began his professional career as an apprentice in his stepfather's New York office. Early projects included work on the U.S. Capitol grounds and several park and institutional projects. Travel to Europe in 1877–1878 with concentrated architectural study in London broadened his vision and further refined his skills. By 1884, with the move of the firm to Brookline, Massachusetts, John Charles had become a full partner with his stepfather. The firm soon grew to include Henry S. Codman and Charles Eliot* as co-partners. After Frederick Law Olmsted's retirement and the deaths of Codman and Eliot, John Charles and his younger half-brother, Frederick Law Olmsted Jr.* formed Olmsted Brothers in 1898. John Charles was senior partner until his own death in 1920; the firm continued until 1950.

In addition to his extensive design and planning work, John Charles took responsibility for developing productive office and training procedures to manage a growing staff and diverse national practice. As one of the trainees, later a friend and collaborator, Arthur Shurcliff*, recalled, Olmsted was a "man of few words, fond of detail, . . . [with] a broad grasp of large scale landscape planning" who "carried to completion a vast amount of work quietly with remarkable efficiency." Other apprentices, later colleagues, praised his teaching and thoughtful advice; they admired his ability to resolve complex design problems with artistry and practicality while enhancing and protecting the natural features of a site. Like his stepfather, Olmsted was committed to the development of landscape art as a profession and to the education of communities and clients about the long-term benefits to be gained from careful, comprehensive planning. To this end he was generous with his time and skills to organizations that sought to extend the influence of sound landscape planning to beautify burgeoning cities. He was a founding member of the American Society of Landscape Architects, serving as its first president and establishing the standards of membership, while being active in other groups such as the American Park and Outdoor Art Association (later the American Civic Association) and the American Association of Park Superintendents, which brought together various professionals and civic leaders.

John Charles Olmsted, c. 1909. Courtesy National Park Service, Frederick Law Olmsted National Historic Site.

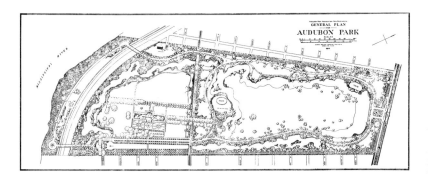

"General Plan for Audubon Park, New Orleans," 1902. Courtesy National Park Service, Frederick Law Olmsted National Historic Site.

Although Olmsted's published writings are few, his extensive professional correspondence and reports reveal his comprehensive philosophy of design, innovative yet pragmatic; reflective of the aesthetic tenets of his stepfather, yet responsive to the new social, economic, and political demands of twentieth-century cities. His advice to clients, whether for public, private, or institutional projects, was to plan for the future, to acquire as much land as possible to enable a cohesive design, protecting scenery and yet fulfilling the functional requirements. This advice was critical for municipalities for whom the firm was designing city-shaping park and parkway systems. As Olmsted noted, "the liberal provision of parks in

a city is one of the surest manifestations of the . . . degree of civilization, and progressiveness of its citizens. As in the case of almost every complex work composed of varied units, economy, efficiency, symmetry, and completeness are likely to be secured when the system as a whole is planned comprehensively and the purposes to be accomplished defined clearly in advance." On the basis of this philosophy, Olmsted continued the park planning begun by his stepfather for Boston, Buffalo, Detroit, Rochester, Atlanta, Hartford, Louisville, Brooklyn, Chicago, and other cities. He developed park systems for municipalities in diverse locations, including Portland, Maine, and Portland, Oregon, Seattle and Spokane, Dayton and Charles-

An entrance way to the Foreign Building, Alaska-Yukon-Pacific Exposition, Seattle, April 1, 1909. Courtesy National Park Service, Frederick Law Olmsted National Historic Site.

East end and south front of house at carriage drive loop, Wychwood, C. L. Hutchinson estate, Lake Geneva, Wisconsin, fall 1905. Courtesy Frances Loeb Library, Harvard University.

ton, and countywide parks and parkways for Essex County, New Jersey. In New Orleans and Watertown, New York, he designed individual parks of great originality on difficult sites. For the small parks in Chicago's densely populated industrial south side, he turned derelict land parcels into an imaginative and efficient network of playgrounds to serve immigrant families.

Park design in cities led to commissions for numerous institutions and subdivisions, often including individual residential work, large and small. Much of the fabric and amenity of cities such as Louisville, Dayton, Seattle, and northwest Washington, D.C. results from the extensive planning for residential areas which Olmsted originated, with its associated roads, greenspaces, schools, and business areas. Comprehensive planning for communities around industrial plants, as in Depew, New York, and Vandergrift, Pennsylvania, or around the National Cash Register factory in Dayton, created attractive neighborhoods instead of bleak tenements. Olmsted's abiding architectural interest was reflected in his residential work, where he took special care to accommodate building to site and vistas, often making preliminary house designs and collaborating closely with the residential architect. Likewise, plans for many park structures, particularly in the Boston system, originated with his sketches. Working cooperatively with architects was a major component of his institutional planning for school campuses, sanatoriums, state capitols, and civic buildings across the country. His landscape layout provided a remarkably perceptive guide for

future building development, retaining some degree of natural beauty in the site. Exposition planning, beginning with his work for the 1893 Chicago World's Fair and continuing with the 1906 Lewis and Clark Exposition in Portland, Oregon, and the 1909 Alaska-Yukon-Pacific Exposition, which shaped the University of Washington campus in Seattle, continued his architectural collaboration. He terminated the firm's work for the San Diego Exposition of 1915 when he felt that the architectural and business plans violated the landscape integrity of Balboa Park.

For over forty years, John Charles Olmsted was a respected leader in the landscape and early planning professions, leaving a profound mark on the land, often unrecognized today. The firm's clientele grew to more than 3,500 commissions by the time of his death, many of which he had originated. An indefatigable worker, he was slowed in his last years of practice by the cancer that eventually took his life. In his remarkable career, Olmsted bridged the centuries from the vanishing frontier to the twentieth-century urban realities, leaving a lasting legacy of public and private designs across the country which melded a picturesque aesthetic with pragmatic planning.

Olmsted Brothers [John Charles Olmsted]. "Report of Olmsted Brothers." In *First Annual Report of the Board of Park Commissioners, 1884–1904.* Seattle, 1905, 43–85. Like reports for numerous other cities where

John Charles Olmsted developed park system plans, contains an overview of his ideas concerning comprehensive park planning and its relationship to city growth and politics; it is primarily in these park reports that the main expression of his landscape ideas can be found.

Olmsted Brothers [John Charles Olmsted]. *Report of Olmsted Brothers on a Proposed Parkway System for Essex County, New Jersey.* Newark, [1915]. An exploration of the classes of parkways, with particular consideration for automobile and electric railway travel, and methods of land taking and assessment for parkways.

Olmsted, John C. "The True Purpose of a Large Public Park." In *American Park and Outdoor Art Association Proceedings, 1897–1904. First Report,* 11–17. Olmsted's justification of the reasons and special requirements for setting aside considerable acreage for parkland in urban areas.

———————————

Arleyn Levee

PARMENTIER, ANDRÉ
(1780–1830)
landscape gardener, horticulturist, nursery owner

André Parmentier was born in Enghien, Belgium, into a horticulturally prominent family. His elder brother Joseph was director of Enghien, the estate of the Duke of Arensberg, and also owned a nursery. A cousin, Antoine Augustin Parmentier, was responsible for introducing the potato as a food into France. André was educated at the University of Louvain. In his native land he practiced horticulture and landscape design as an avocation until finan-

"Euterpe Knoll, Hyde Park." Drawing by Thomas K. Wharton, 1839. Courtesy New York Public Library, Manuscripts Division.

View over deer park, Vanderbilt Mansion National Historic Site. Photo Richard Cheek for Hyde Park Historical Society.

cial reverses forced him to emigrate to the United States and pursue them professionally. No landscape design projects by Parmentier in Belgium have been identified.

Parmentier emigrated in 1824 and, the following year, established a nursery in Brooklyn, New York, which attracted the attention of numerous horticultural periodicals. His brother Joseph provided much of Parmentier's nursery stock, including grapes and pears. In the summer of 1825, Parmentier was elected a member of the New York Horticultural Society and served on its council from 1826 to 1830. He also became a member of the Massachusetts Horticultural Society. About 1826, Parmentier began receiving commissions as a landscape designer, which continued until his death four years later. His skill in landscape design was highly praised by A. J. Downing* in his *Treatise* (1841): "We consider M. Parmentier's labors and examples as having effected directly, far more landscape gardening in America than those of any individual whatever." Parmentier was especially significant as a transmitter of the European picturesque style into American landscape design.

Downing noted that, in addition to laying out numerous country seats in the vicinity of New York, Parmentier designed grounds "in various parts of the Union," including the South, and also in Canada. Only five design projects by Parmentier have thus far been documented: his own "horticultural garden" or nursery in Brooklyn (1825); the estate of Elisha W. King in Pelham Manor,

New York (1827); the estate of Dr. David Hosack, Hyde Park, New York (1828–1829); the grounds of King's College (now the University of Toronto), Toronto (1830); and Moss Park, the estate of William Allan, Toronto (1830). Of these, only the Hosack property, now the Vanderbilt Mansion National Historic Site, survives, with some alterations and overlays by three subsequent owners. The two Canadian projects are recent discoveries by Toronto scholars Stephen Otto and Pleasance Crawford. Further local research may reveal other Parmentier projects, some perhaps still extant.

Parmentier made frequent short contributions to such periodicals as the *New York Farmer and Horticultural Repository* and the *New England Farmer.* The earliest of these were written in French and translated for publication. His most important written statement is a brief essay, "Landscapes and Picturesque Gardens," in Thomas G. Fessenden's *New American Gardener* (1828).

Crawford, Pleasance, and Stephen A. Otto. "André Parmentier's Two or Three Places in Upper Canada." *Journal of the New England Garden History Society* 5 (Fall 1997), 1–8. A thorough discussion and analysis of Parmentier's two documented projects carried out in Toronto near the end of his life; includes previously unpublished photographs, details from maps, and a camera-lucida sketch.

Downing, A. J. *A Treatise on the Theory and Practice of Landscape Gardening.* New York, 1858. Downing's laudatory account of Parmentier's life and career (pp. 24–25) was also published in the first edition of the *Treatise* (1841).

O'Donnell, Patricia M., Charles Birnbaum, and Cynthia Zaitzevsky. *Cultural Landscape Report for the Vanderbilt Mansion National Historic Site.* Vol. 1: *Site History, Existing Conditions, and Analysis.* Washington, D.C.: GPO (National Park Service, United States Department of the Interior), 1993. Detailed discussion of Hosack and Parmentier and an evaluation of the significance of the Hyde Park landscape, including Parmentier's contribution within the context of the period, in chapters 2 and 9 and appendixes D and E.

No repository has been located which holds original papers and drawings by or relating to André Parmentier. However, the Saint Joseph Convent, Brentwood, N.Y., has Parmentier family portraits and records centered primarily on Adèle Parmentier Bayer and her benefactions. Additionally, the Western Historical Manuscripts Collection, University of Missouri, Columbia, holds the Charles Van Ravenswaay Collection, which includes a draft manuscript on Parmentier by the late Dr. Van Ravenswaay and extensive notes collected by him, although his research focused more on Parmentier as a horticulturist than as a landscape designer.

Cynthia Zaitzevsky

PARSONS, SAMUEL, JR.
(1844–1923)
landscape architect, author

Samuel Parsons Jr. was born in New Bedford, Massachusetts, the son of Samuel Bowne Parsons, a nurseryman, and Susan (Howland) Parsons. As did two generations of Quaker horticulturists before them, his family propagated and cultivated nursery stock. The nursery prospered until the elder Parsons's death in 1907. It brought the family international fame, international travel, and opportunities to introduce a variety of ornamental trees and shrubs to the United States.

Parsons first studied at Haverford College and later graduated from Yale Scientific School with a bachelor of philosophy in 1862. His studies emphasized agricultural chemistry, geology, botany, physics, and surveying. After college he turned to farming, spending a year on a model farm on Cayuga Lake, New York, and then six years on his own farm in southern New Jersey. This was followed by five years in the family nursery, Parsons & Sons Company, Flushing, New York, where he specialized in laying out and planting country place gardens. This period of practical experience acquainted Parsons with Frederick Law Olmsted Sr.* and Calvert Vaux*, and he joined the latter's office around 1879. (Olmsted and Vaux had dissolved their partnership seven years earlier.) In the course of a year Parsons became a partner in Vaux &

Samuel Parsons Jr., c. 1910s. From *Memories of Samuel Parsons*, 1926.

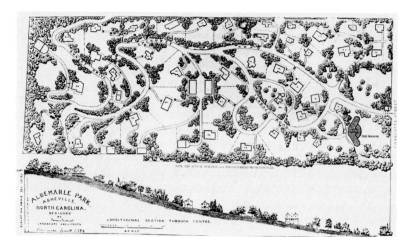

Plan of Albemarle Park, Asheville, North Carolina, designed by Parsons & Pentecost, c. 1899. Courtesy Albemarle Park and the Manor Grounds.

Canal Street Park, designed by Vaux & Parsons. Engraving by V. Perard after a photograph. From *Scribner's Monthly*, July 1892. Courtesy Charles A. Birnbaum.

Weeping beech and mansion, Inisfad, Roslyn, Long Island, grounds designed by Parsons, 1916–20. Photo Chris Faust. Courtesy Charles A. Birnbaum.

Company. During his tenure, numerous country place commissions came from around the nation.

In 1881, Vaux was offered the job of landscape architect in the New York City Department of Parks. He accepted on condition that the office of Vaux & Company also be engaged, thus bringing Parsons along with him. For Parsons, this began a thirty-year career as a public servant.

Parsons became superintendent of planting, in fact an assistant to Vaux. In this capacity he helped Vaux design city parks, with an emphasis on planting. Although Vaux resigned for two years in 1883, eventually the two worked together on every piece of park design within the city. These projects included redesign and new development in various parts of Central Park and redesign and new construction for Grant's Tomb, Bowling Green, Union and Abingdon Squares, and Jeanette, Canal Street, and Christopher Parks. After Vaux's death in 1895, Parsons assumed the position of landscape architect. He left the department briefly for four years, 1898–1902, and served as commissioner for a brief period in 1905. During this time he oversaw much of the design and planting in Central, Riverside, and Morn-

The long view from original mansion, Elmendorf Horse Farm, Lexington, Kentucky, 1993. Photo Charles A. Birnbaum.

Circular drives, Pinelawn Memorial Cemetery, Long Island, 1994. Photo Charles A. Birnbaum

ingside Parks, and the creation, design, and construction of St. Nicholas, DeWitt Clinton, Thomas Jefferson, and John Jay Parks and the Broadway Mall (59th to 125th Street). Through his responsibilities at the Parks Department, as president of the Park Board of Manhattan and Richmond (Staten Island), New York, and as landscape architect appointed to the City-Improvement Commission, Parsons exerted strong influence on the city's appearance. He played a pivotal role during the period of transition, when New York City's parks were evolving from picturesque to reform era designs.

Projects by Parsons can be found throughout the United States in the form of parks, playgrounds, estates, gardens, cemeteries, planned communities (or homestead parks, as he referred to them), public grounds, and campus plans. Parsons was the first professional landscape architect hired by the cities of Birmingham (Glen Iris Park) and San Diego (City Park, known today as Balboa Park). A sampling of career projects includes the National Capitol Grounds, Washington, D.C. (for which his design was selected under an Act of Congress; unexecuted); League Island Park, Philadelphia; Pine Lawn Cemetery, Syosset, Long Island; Evergreen Park Cemetery, Brooklyn (with Vaux); Albemarle Park, Asheville, North Carolina; the University of Alabama at Tuscaloosa; Elmendorf Horse Farm, Lexington, Kentucky; Berry Hill, Newport, Rhode Island; and Inisfad, Roslyn, New York.

Parsons was also an important force in the organization of the profession—the American Society of Landscape Architects was founded in his New York office in the St. James Building on January 4, 1899. He was one of the most persistent practitioners to argue for the need for such an organization and was elected its first vice president. Parsons helped draft its first constitution and served as president in 1902, and again in 1906–1907.

Throughout his career, Parsons wrote extensively for *Scribner's Magazine*, *Garden & Field*, *American Garden*, *The Outlook*, *American Architect*, and other periodicals. His books include *Concerning Lawn Planting*, with Vaux (1881), *Homes in City and Country* with Russel Sturgis (1893), *Landscape Gardening* (1891), *How to Plan the Home Grounds* (1899), *Landscape Gardening Studies* (1910), and *The Art of Landscape Architecture* (1915). He also edited the 1917 ASLA reprint of Prince von Pückler-Muskau's *Hints on Landscape Gardening*. His design philosophy and much of his career canon can be gleaned from these publications as well as from his significant legacy surviving on the American landscape today.

Samuel Parsons Jr. died in New York City. He is buried in the picturesque Woodlawn Cemetery in the Bronx. His daughter, Mabel, later published two books that he had started: *English Home Grounds* (1924), a photographic essay of a trip they had made to England, and *Memories of Samuel Parsons* (1926), a work he had begun several years before his death.

Birnbaum, Charles A. *Samuel Parsons Jr. and the Art of Landscape Architecture*. New York: Wave Hill, 1994. Monograph that accompanied the exhibition sponsored by the Catalog of Landscape Records in the United States at Wave Hill; overview of Parsons's influences, design philosophy, and executed works from New York City parks and Central Park to national commissions; bibliography, illustrations.

Parsons, Samuel, Jr. *The Art of Landscape Architecture.* New York: Knickerbocker Press/G. P. Putnam's Sons, 1915. Parsons's study of the development of the profession of landscape architecture and its "application to modern landscape gardening"; the culmination of his work and design philosophy.

Parsons, Samuel, Jr. *Landscape Gardening Studies.* New York: John Lane, 1910. One of the few books by Parsons to credit his own work, with project names and locations; includes many photographs and plans.

Charles A. Birnbaum

PAULEY, WILLIAM C.
(1893–1985)
landscape architect

William C. Pauley was born in Lafayette, Indiana. He received a bachelor of science degree from Purdue University in 1916 and went on to study landscape architecture at Massachusetts Agricultural College (now the University of Massachusetts), where he taught while earning his M.L.A. degree. After graduating, Pauley served in the U.S. Army during World War I and earned the rank of second lieutenant with the Officer Reserve Corps. During school and after graduation, he also worked for the Massachusetts Rural Civic Planning Commission under F. A. Cushing Smith.

In 1919, Pauley moved to Atlanta, where he worked for several local landscape firms, including E. Burton Cooke, C. A. Dahl Company, and Lakewood Nursery. In 1923 he opened his own practice in landscape architecture, initially concentrating on residential and estate design. Although architecture as a profession was well established in Atlanta, no professionally trained landscape architect had set up a practice there before Pauley. Until Pauley's arrival, Georgians who wanted professional landscape architects sought advice from nationally based firms, such as Olmsted Brothers*,

Grant Park Mall, Atlanta, c. 1960.
Courtesy Marilyn P. Beittel.

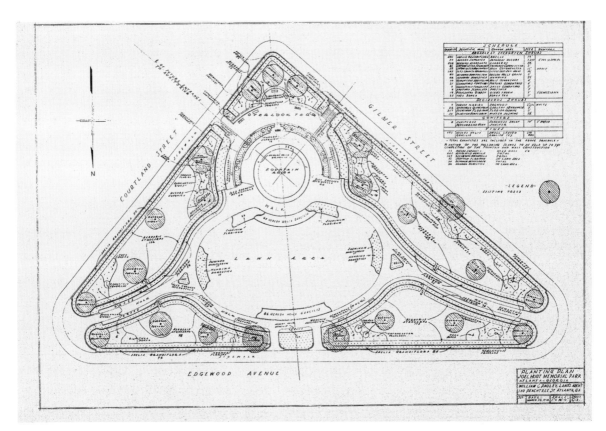

Planting plan for Joel Hurt Memorial Park, Atlanta, March 1940. Courtesy Spencer Tunnell.

or regional practices, like that of Robert Cridland of Philadelphia.

Pauley's move to Atlanta coincided with one of that city's most active periods of growth, both commercially and residentially. The neighborhoods of Druid Hills (by Frederick Law Olmsted Sr.*), Ansley Park, and Peachtree Heights were already well established, and the city's population was expanding rapidly. A managerial class was growing particularly fast, fostered by an increase in white-collar businesses. Pauley received many residential commissions in and around the city. Among the most significant was Bankshaven, the William N. Banks Sr. estate in Newnan, Georgia; work on it took place over a thirty-year period (1928–1958).

The bulk of Pauley's work, however, was nonresidential. The inventory includes 103 schools and colleges in Southeastern states, including every major college campus, both public and private, in Georgia; 35 hospitals; 18 cemeteries; and 8 children's homes. Although the South has had an ambivalent relationship with public open space, Pauley was able to participate in the planning for 50 parks ranging in size from small garden club parks to large city parks. He designed the core of what has become the Atlanta Botanical Garden and prepared a master plan for Atlanta's Piedmont Park. Among his most notable designs are those for Winn Park and Hurt Park. Winn Park includes an iris garden with naturalistic pools and waterfalls commissioned in 1933 and recently restored by the Atlanta Parks Department. Hurt Park (1940), just two blocks from the historic center of Atlanta, is bounded by Georgia State University and retains Pauley's original walks, walls, stairs, and fountain, and mature trees installed according to his planting plan.

During the Depression years, Pauley's career shifted to embrace a large number of government commissions including public housing. Pauley was involved in planning for one of the first public housing projects in the country, Atlanta's University Homes. He worked on 87 public housing projects from 1930 through 1950.

Pauley was also active in civic affairs, including the Druid Hills Civic Association, and was an adviser to Emily Harrison, steward of the Fernbank Forest, a 75-acre virgin tract six miles from the center of Atlanta. Pauley prepared a master plan for the forest to incorporate a visitors' center and education building.

Pauley became a member of the American Society of Landscape Architects in 1941 and was made a Fellow in 1965. He retired from private practice in 1968 and died in 1985, at the age of ninety-one.

Cooney, Loraine M., et al. *Garden History of Georgia, 1733–1933.* 1933. Reprint. Athens: Garden Club of Georgia, 1976. Includes a variety of Pauley projects: Pine Hill, Clark Howell garden, unattributed; Boxwood, Woodruff-Rainwater garden, unattributed; Stephenson garden, Druid Hills rose garden; and Winn Park, iris garden for the Iris Garden Club.

Mitchell, William Robert, Jr. *Gardens of Georgia.* Atlanta: Garden Club of Georgia, 1989. Includes Illges garden, 1936, Columbus; Bankshaven; Alston-Pritchett garden, 1926, Ansley Park, Atlanta; Robin-son garden, Druid Hills, Atlanta; Albert Howell garden, 1932, Atlanta; and Beaudry-Hailey garden, Buckhead, Atlanta.

Mitchell, William Robert, Jr. *Landmark Homes of Georgia, 1783–1983.* Savannah: Golden Coast, 1982. Includes Albert Howell house, 1932, Atlanta, where Pauley's work is unattributed, and Bankshaven.

William Pauley's landscape architectural drawings are stored at the Georgia Department of Archives and History and contain, partially catalogued, the vast majority of both originals and blueprints covering his entire career. A smaller collection of Pauley blueprints is housed at the Cherokee Garden Library, in the Atlanta History Center's Library and Archives building.

Significant manuscript collections for both Pauley and his wife, Frances, are kept at the Emory University Special Collections Department; Pauley's collection there includes correspondence and photographs of early work.

Spencer Tunnell

PEETS, ELBERT
(1886–1968)
landscape architect, planner, educator, critic

Elbert Peets was born in Hudson, Ohio. Educated in the Cleveland public school system, he worked as a teenager for H. U. Horvath, a landscape architect and nurseryman who served as a consultant forester to the City of Cleveland. After graduating with many academic honors from Western Reserve University (1912), Peets enrolled in the graduate program in landscape architecture at Harvard University, where he earned an M.L.A. (1915).

Peets went on to teach horticulture at Harvard and published a book, *Practical Tree Repair*, in 1916. He also worked for the Cambridge, Massachusetts, firm of Pray*, Hubbard* & White. Around 1915 or 1916, Peets met Werner Hegemann (1881–1936), a German expatriate who was then living in Milwaukee and serving as a planning consultant to many U.S. cities. Their association resulted in the preparation of proposals for numerous projects in Wisconsin, including plans for large subdivisions in Wauwatosa (Washington Highlands) and Madison (Lake Forest), and for the company town of Kohler.

Peets served as a civilian planning engineer for the U.S. Army during World War I. After the war he again collaborated with Hegemann, most notably on a plan for Wyomissing Park, a community near Reading, Pennsylvania. In 1920, Peets spent a year in Europe, utilizing funds from the Charles Eliot Travelling Fellowship that Harvard had awarded him in 1917. After his return to the United States, he once again joined Hegemann, this time to work on a book, *The American Vitruvius: An Architect's Handbook of Civic Art* (1922). The profusely illustrated volume, which was reprinted in 1972 and again in 1988, stands as one of the seminal treatises on urban design published during the twentieth century.

Returning to Cleveland in 1921 and developing a private planning practice that he maintained through the 1930s, Peets also established a reputation as one of the nation's leading critics in landscape architecture. He was the author of several insightful, albeit acerbic, articles that appeared in *American Mercury*. (His collaboration with the magazine's noted editor, H. L. Menken, is unique in the field of landscape architecture.)

During the mid-1930s, Peets joined the Resettlement Administration, a New Deal agency, to supervise the planning of Greendale, Wisconsin, one of three suburban greenbelt towns sponsored by the federal government during the Depression. In preparing the plan for Greendale, Peets drew on his familiarity with European Renaissance towns and squares, Midwestern villages and small cities, and the reconstruction of Williamsburg, Virginia. Rather than calling for the curvilinear streets and rolling lawns that were growing in popularity in many suburban areas, Peets envisioned a community "built around a line instead of a point," and developed a central boulevard that terminated at the Village Hall, a building modeled after the government buildings at Williamsburg. Also influenced by the English garden city pioneer Ebenezer Howard, Peets wanted Greendale's residents to be able to partake of the best of both country and city, and endeavored to make parks, pathways, and the open countryside easily accessible to the community's residential areas. The most noticeable garden city element implemented at Greendale was a 2,000-acre greenbelt that encircled the 1,400-acre community. As the town expanded during the 1960s and 1970s, however, the greenbelt was reduced to a parkway along the Root River.

During the latter part of his career, Peets prepared plans and reports for Puerto Rico and California's Catalina Island. His best-known project from this period is Park Forest, Illinois, one of the nation's first planned communities of the post-World War II era. With five neighborhoods adapted to the rolling terrain of the site, a centrally located shopping and recreation area, and a street system laid out in an informal ring pattern, the Park Forest plan reflected contemporary tastes in suburban design to a much greater extent than the proposal Peets had prepared for Greendale ten years earlier.

Poor health forced Peets's retirement during the early 1960s; he died in Cleveland in 1968. Outspoken, iconoclastic, articulate, and an uncommonly proficient designer and illustrator, he won praise for his ability to perceive and understand "the underlying principles of past city design and their applicability to cities of his own time," as Paul Spreiregen wrote that same year. Indeed, Elbert Peets was one of the earliest proponents of what is now identified as the "new urbanism" and "neo-traditional design," although few current practitioners possess such a clear and concise understanding of local landscape character and historical antecedents in community design.

View of Broad Street, looking at Greendale Village Hall, 1998. Photo Arnold R. Alanen.

André Parmentier.
View over deer park, Vanderbilt
Mansion National Historic Site.
Hyde Park, New York.
Photo Richard Cheek
for Hyde Park Historical Society.

Samuel Parsons Jr.
View from original mansion,
Elmendorf Horse Farm.
Lexington, Kentucky.
Photo Charles A. Birnbaum.

Samuel Parsons Jr.
Circular drives,
Pinelawn Memorial Cemetery.
Syosset, New York.
Photo Charles A. Birnbaum.

Elbert Peets.
Broad Street, looking at Greendale Village Hall.
Greendale, Wisconsin.
Photo Arnold R. Alanen.

Charles A. Platt.
Gwinn. Cleveland, Ohio.
Photo Carol Betsch.

Charles A. Platt. Faulkner Farm.
Brookline, Massachusetts.
Photo Charles A. Birnbaum.

William Punchard.
D.W. Field Park.
Brockton, Massachusetts.
Courtesy Child Associates, Inc.

Michael Rapuano.
Aerial view of
Garden State Parkway.
New Jersey.
Courtesy Clarke & Rapuano Inc.

Michael Rapuano. Model for
Cleveland Public Mall, c. 1965.
Photo Louis Checkman.
Courtesy Clarke & Rapuano Inc.

James C. Rose. James Rose residence. Ridgewood, New Jersey.
Photo Frederick Charles.

Richard Requa, Balboa Park.
San Diego, California.
Photo Carol Greentree.

James C. Rose. Rose residence. Ridgewood, New Jersey.
Photo Frederick Charles.

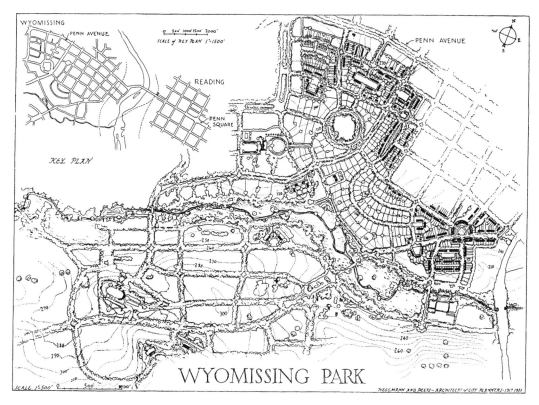

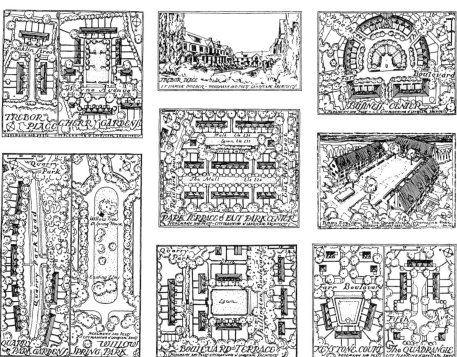

Wyomissing Park, near Reading, Pennsylvania. From *The American Vitruvius*, 1922.

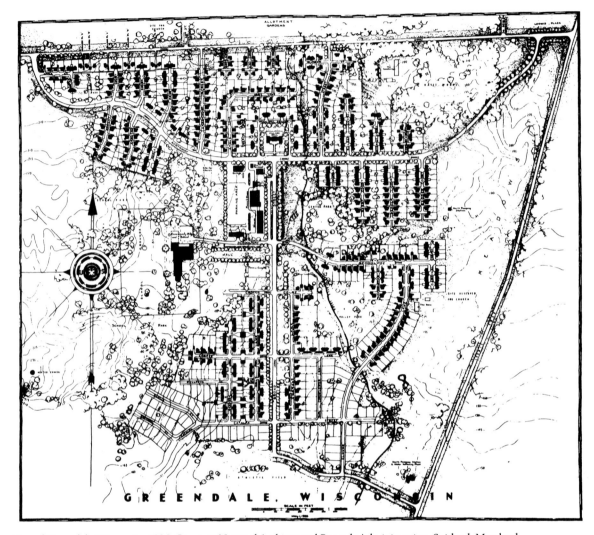

Plan of Greendale, Wisconsin, 1936. Courtesy National Archives and Records Administration, Suitland, Maryland.

Alanen, Arnold R., and Joseph A. Eden. *Main Street Ready-Made: The New Deal Community of Greendale, Wisconsin*. Madison: State Historical Society of Wisconsin, 1987. An assessment of the first fifty years of Greendale, one of three greenbelt towns developed by the federal government during the Depression.

Hegemann, Werner, and Elbert Peets. *The American Vitruvius: An Architect's Handbook of Civic Art*. New York: Architectural Book Publishing, 1922. One of the most important urban design books of the twentieth century; contains a wealth of plans, maps, and photographs from towns and cities throughout Europe and North America, many prepared by Peets.

Peets, Elbert. *On the Art of Designing Cities: Selected Essays of Elbert Peets*. Ed. Paul D. Spreiregen. Cambridge: MIT Press, 1968. A compilation of twenty-seven articles written by Peets between 1922 and 1949, including two famous essays that appeared in *American Mercury*, "Central Park" (1925) and "The Landscape Priesthood" (1927).

Arnold R. Alanen

PLATT, CHARLES A.
(1861–1933)
architect, landscape architect

Charles A. Platt was born in New York City, where he eventually established his practice as an architect and landscape architect. His father was a corporate lawyer, and his mother was member of the Cheney family, important silk mill owners from Manchester, Connecticut. Platt began his artistic education during summer vacations in Manchester, where two uncles were artists. While still in his teens, he became an early member of the Etching Revival, learning to etch from the Philadelphia artist Stephen Parrish. Platt trained briefly in painting at the National Academy of Design and the Art Students League before going to Paris in 1882 for further study at the Académie Julien. While in Paris, he met architecture students at the Ecole des Beaux-Arts and discussed with them his emerging interest in this art. In 1886, still in Europe, he married a New Yorker, Annie C. Hoe; she died the following year, losing twin daughters in childbirth. Slowly recovering from this tragedy, Platt continued to paint and spent the summer of 1890 with artist friends in Cornish, New Hampshire. He would continue to summer at the Cornish art colony, where the quality of the landscape and the collegiality of sympathetic friends remained important forces throughout his life.

In 1892 he invited his brother William, then an apprentice in the office of Frederick Law Olmsted Sr.* to accompany him on a tour of the gardens of Italy. Platt used the sketches and photographs they made of approximately twenty-five gardens from all over the Italian peninsula to illustrate two articles for *Harper's Magazine* in 1893. He expanded these articles into a book, *Italian Gardens*, published in 1894. This modest volume was one of the first illustrated publications in English depicting the gardens of Renaissance Italy, and it heavily influenced the emergence of a formal garden style in the United States.

Platt turned from this book to a career as a designer of gardens and then as an architect, both without any academic training or apprenticeship. He had begun to experiment with architecture at his own summer house and garden at Cornish in 1890, expanding and refining the gardens in accord with lessons learned from his travels in Italy. In the summer of 1893 he married Eleanor Hardy Bunker, the widow of a Paris friend. During the 1890s, his Cornish neighbors commissioned him to design informal residences and geometric gardens, influenced by what he had seen in Italy. Among these early clients was the architectural critic Herbert Croly, who

became an important promoter of Platt's architectural and landscape architectural talents in his articles for *Architectural Record*. By the late 1890s, Platt was executing significant commissions as a garden designer for patrons beyond Cornish. Most important among these early designs were his plans for Faulkner Farm, the Charles F. Sprague estate (1897–1898), and for Weld, the Larz Anderson estate (1902), both in Brookline, Massachusetts. Both these projects illustrate Platt's adaptation of the Renaissance villa garden to American conditions.

By the turn of the century, Platt had established himself as an architect, primarily producing designs for country houses and gardens. He relied in these early days on the advice of a wide circle of artistic friends in New York City and Cornish, including the architect Stanford White. Platt's associates at the Century Association, the premier club for professionals and amateurs in literature and the arts, proved invaluable as advisers and clients. Having no formal training in horticultural or engineering, he often worked in collaboration with other landscape architects, including the Olmsted Brothers*, Warren Manning*, and Ellen Biddle Shipman*, a Cornish neighbor and his most frequent collaborator. He developed a small office in New

Charles A. Platt. Courtesy Platt family.

Terrace on Lake Erie, Gwinn, William G. Mather estate, Cleveland, 1994. Photo Carol Betsch.

Faulkner Farm, Charles F. Sprague estate, Brookline, Massachusetts, 1992. Photo Charles A. Birnbaum.

York from which he executed commissions all over the country, relying on the professional expertise of junior assistants and carefully controlling the design solutions of the firm. By 1904, when Croly published a review article on Platt's work in *Architectural Record*, he had established a recognized style in planning and design of domestic architecture. Commissions for "Platt houses" and their landscapes annually grew in number and scale.

Among the most influential of Platt's estate garden plans were those for Maxwell Court, the Francis T. Maxwell house in Rockville, Connecticut (1901–1903); Gwinn, the William G. Mather place near Cleveland (1907–1908); the Manor House, the John T. Pratt estate in Glen Cove, New York (1909–1911); and Villa Turicum, the immense country estate of Harold and Edith Rockefeller McCormick in Lake Forest, Illinois (1908–1918). Platt's work was frequently illustrated and discussed in architectural and landscape magazines including *Architectural Record*, *Garden Magazine*, and *Country Life in America*. In 1913 he became the subject of the first commercially produced monograph on a living American architect or landscape architect.

Institutional designs monopolized much of Platt's time in the 1920s. He became recognized as a leading architect for art museums; his work included the Freer Gallery of Art on the Mall in Washington, D.C. (1913–1923), and an unrealized proposal for a National Gallery of Art (1924). He also gained national recognition as an architect and planner for schools and colleges, especially for the master plans he prepared for Phillips Academy in

Andover, Massachusetts, between 1922 and 1930 and the plans for the University of Illinois in Urbana, prepared between 1921 and 1933. He designed numerous buildings for both campuses and for other schools and universities throughout the country.

In all his landscape design and planning, Platt emphasized the careful integration of exterior and interior space through the use of architectonic garden components and strong vistas to provide visual and circulatory connections. He was a careful student of history and applied the lessons he learned to the needs of contemporary pleasure gardens and public spaces. Although he almost never wrote about his own work as a landscape architect, his designs were constantly published and exerted a strong influence on the emerging profession of landscape architecture.

Monograph of the Work of Charles A. Platt, with an Introduction by Royal Cortissoz. New York: Architectural Book Publishing, 1913. One of the first monographs published on the work of a contemporary American architect; established a model that was followed to record the work of many of the major practitioners of the twentieth century; photographs and drawings of Platt's buildings and landscape designs through 1913.

Morgan, Keith N. *Charles A. Platt: The Artist as Architect.* Cambridge: MIT Press/Architectural History Foundation, 1985. Thorough, well-illustrated study of

Platt's work as an architect and landscape architect; includes a catalog of his commissions.

Platt, Charles A. *Italian Gardens.* 1894. Reprint. New York: Sagapress/Timber Press, 1994. One of the first publications in English on the gardens of Italy, and the only book Platt ever wrote; illustrated with pho-

tographs, etchings, and a watercolor drawing by Platt; reprint includes additional photographs by him and an essay by Keith N. Morgan, "Al Fresco: An Overview of Charles A. Platt's 'Italian Gardens.' "

Keith N. Morgan

POND, BREMER WHIDDEN
(1884–1959)
landscape architect, educator

Bremer Whidden Pond was born in Boston. He received a B.S. degree from Dartmouth College in 1906 and studied in Germany before enrolling in Harvard's School of Landscape Architecture, where he received a master's degree in 1911. A three-year position as "secretary" to Frederick Law Olmsted Jr.* preceded the establishment of his own design office. His practice included a variety of private garden, campus, park, and recreational projects in New England; later in the decade he joined Henry Atherton Frost in a joint practice.

With the exception of a brief period in the Quartermaster Corps during World War I, Pond was associated with Harvard's program in landscape architecture from his initial appointment to the faculty in 1914 until his retirement in 1950. During that period, he served as chairman of the Council of the School of Landscape Architecture (1928–1936) and chairman of the Department of Landscape Architecture (1938–1950). He was appointed Charles Eliot Professor in 1930.

Pond's years in the nation's first formal program in landscape design encompassed both growth and turmoil. Shifting emphases in the curriculum reflected the discipline's complex relation to both architecture and planning, as well as the evolving standards and requirements of the profession. During Pond's student years and for many thereafter, the program had a broad framework of cultural reference, with traditional instruction in art history, drawing, botany, and engineering. The influence of the Olmsted office was pervasive: Pond was but one of a host of instructors trained in Brookline. Pond's education, his extensive travel, and his own tastes shaped his fidelity to the value of traditional accomplishments in both design and its presentation.

Summerhouse, Rochester, New Hampshire, c. 1910s. Courtesy Frances Loeb Library, Harvard University.

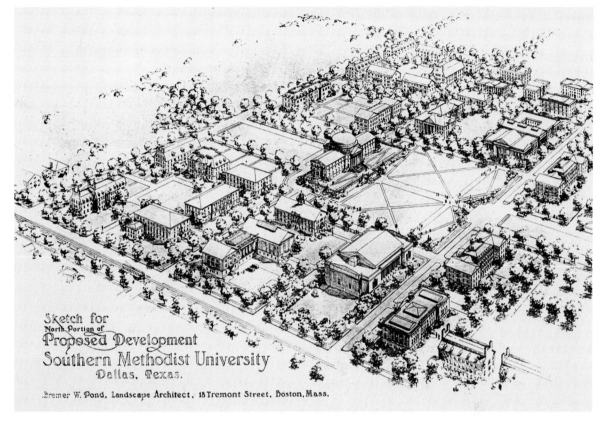

"Sketch for North Portion of Proposed Development, Southern Methodist University," Dallas, c. 1924. Courtesy Frances Loeb Library, Harvard University.

Pond was to find himself temperamentally and philosophically troubled during the mid-1930s, when the three hitherto independent programs in Architecture, Landscape Design, and City Planning were combined to form the Graduate School of Design. A variety of factors had influenced Harvard president James Conant's decision to make this change; the announced goal was to intensify the collaborative character of education among the three disciplines and to develop a curriculum less structured on Beaux Arts aesthetics and representation.

The course catalog of the landscape architecture program during the 1920s and the 1930s reveals the changes in tone as well as in the formal curriculum and program requirements. Throughout the 1920s there had indeed existed a degree of cooperation among the three disciplines; Pond himself was a quondam lecturer and

instructor in a variety of City Planning courses and maintained, in addition to his instruction in the fundamentals of drawing, site analysis, and design, active direction of landscape offerings dedicated to public parks and other large-scale projects. With the establishment of the Graduate School of Design, however, the Landscape Department no longer included in its list of suggested readings for incoming students a roll call of the classic texts that had certainly influenced Pond's own formation as a designer, critic, and educator. The appointment of Christopher Tunnard* to the Landscape Department faculty in 1937–1938 was one response to student dissatisfaction with a program still highly traditionalist in character and with apparently little concern for broad social issues or for technological advances in materials and methodology.

During this period declining enrollment necessitated a reduction in staff and other departmental economies, which also challenged Pond's administrative skill. The ideological differences were not dispelled with time. Writing to a colleague in 1945, Pond noted, "The Landscape Department is still trying to uphold the standards and type of instruction as we used to have it, with freehand and other things required; the architects look on us as old-fashioned. . . . I am quite willing to say that I am old-fashioned enough to believe most decidedly that design should be attractive to the eye as well as 'functional' if it is to survive and not become merely a form of engineering."

Pond was also associated with another significant program in landscape education, instituted by Henry Atherton Frost at the Cambridge School. At the time of the school's founding in 1916, Pond and Frost were partners in a design practice. The Harvard program in landscape architecture did not accept women students, the landscape program at the Massachusetts Institute of Technology had been discontinued, and for women with an interest in the field there were few opportunities to receive professional instruction. Harvard's James Sturgis Pray* had suggested that Frost and Pond tutor interested women, and what had initially been individual instruction became a formal program in architecture and landscape design. Although Pond's teaching responsibilities did not continue after 1921, he remained a trustee of the Cambridge School until its affiliation with Smith College in 1938.

Despite the heavy demands of both teaching and administrative responsibilities, Pond often contributed to professional journals, frequently commenting on subjects related to education and to the realities of practice and firm management. After his retirement he was active as a book reviewer, many of the titles reflecting his interests in the garden design of England, France, and Asia.

Pond's activities in the profession and allied disciplines were numerous. Having joined the American Society of Landscape Architects in 1916, he was made a Fellow in 1921 and served a substantial term (1922–1936) as secretary. He was a director of the Massachusetts Forest and Park Association, secretary of the Cambridge Historical Society, and an organizer of the Hubbard Educational Trust. In addition to his significant role in the development of the Cambridge School, Pond was a director of the Lowthorpe School of Landscape Architecture for Women, another notable independent program. His lifelong devotion to hiking, fishing, and particularly the New England rural landscape reflected not only personal enthusiasms but also vocational passions.

After retiring, Pond lived at his country place in Pittsburg, New Hampshire; he died in Hanover, New Hampshire.

Pond, Bremer W. "Fifty Years in Retrospect: [A] Brief Account of the Origins and Development of the ASLA." *Landscape Architecture* 40 (January 1950). An 8-page chronological account of the organization, leavened with humor and anecdote, examining both its membership and its activities, with some assessment of the societal and historical context in which the profession developed.

Pond, Bremer W. *Outline History of Landscape Architecture.* Cambridge: School of Landscape Architecture, Harvard University, [c. 1936]. A slim 2-volume syllabus of the course offered by the Fine Arts Department, illustrated with reduced plans; the material included is a guide to the sites and designers featured in the curriculum and to Pond's tastes.

Pond, Bremer W. *The Tuck Drive, Dartmouth College, Hanover, N.H.* [Boston], 1915. A detailed analysis of site and projected costs, and a vivid account of the difficulties imposed by a demanding terrain; illustrated with photographs. The Tuck Drive is perhaps the most notable of Pond's extant designs and, in 1913, was the impetus for his resignation from the Olmsted firm to set up an independent practice.

The Harvard University Archives is the repository of official papers relating to Pond's tenure as a member of the faculty and as a departmental chairman. The collections of the Frances Loeb Library of Harvard's Graduate School of Design include a substantial number of Pond's published works, as well as examples of professional reports (illustrated with photographs and plans) prepared by him. The Measured Drawings Collection at the Loeb includes a selection of plans and renderings (largely of Italian villas) by Pond, as well as examples of work prepared in collaboration with long-time colleagues, including Richard K. Webel. The Dartmouth College Library includes materials (drawings, plans, reports, and related correspondence) concerning his work on the Dartmouth campus. An estate report prepared as a competition entry for the Rome Prize (1915) is held by the University of Michigan Library. The records of the Cambridge School may be consulted at the Smith College Archives.

Mary F. Daniels

PRAY, JAMES STURGIS
(1871–1929)
landscape architect, educator

James Sturgis Pray was born in Boston, where he attended the Chauncy Hall School. He entered Harvard College in 1891 and completed his A.B. degree in 1898, taking two years off because of poor health. During his last two years at Harvard, he studied at the Lawrence Scientific School and the Bussey Institution, which led him to the profession of landscape architecture and a job in the preeminent Olmsted Brothers* office, where he worked until April 1903. While there Pray assisted with studies for the development of the Middlesex Fells Reservation, part of the Metropolitan Park system begun by Charles Eliot*.

Pray left Olmsted Brothers to open his own office in Boston. The firm became Pray & Gallagher* in 1905, and was known as Pray, Hubbard* & White from 1906 until 1918. Among several residential projects, the firm designed the Charles H. Schweppes garden in Lake Forest, Illinois (1914), where Fletcher Steele* later designed a theatrical swimming pool, and Rose Standish Nichols* planted the rose garden and perennial borders. Pray retired from active practice with the firm in 1918.

During World War I, Pray worked for the government designing cantonments that accommodated between 45,000 and 50,000 men. He worked on Fort Riley, Kansas, laid out the first Quartermasters' Training Camp near Jacksonville, Florida, and reorganized the base at Yaphank, Long Island, to adapt it to new army requirements. His article "Planning the Cantonments" in the October 1917 issue of *Landscape Architecture* describes this work.

Pray's major contribution to the profession of landscape architecture was as an educator. Appointed "Assistant" in Landscape Architecture at Harvard in 1902, he worked under the direction of Frederick Law Olmsted Jr.* and Arthur Shurcliff* as they developed the new landscape architecture program. In 1903 he was appointed instructor and two years later was made assistant professor. He became chairman of the department in 1908, a position that he held for twenty years. In 1909, Pray started the first course in city planning offered in the United States, which eventually led to a specialized field of study recognized by Harvard in 1923 with a special degree. When the department was made into a separate graduate school in 1913, Pray became chairman of the Council of the School of Landscape Architecture, a position he held until 1928.

Pray was also influential in the education of women in landscape architecture. In 1915, Katherine Brooks, a recent graduate of Radcliffe College, came to Pray with the request to study drafting at Harvard. (At the time women were not admitted to Harvard.) Pray assigned one of his faculty members, Henry Atherton Frost, the task of tutoring Brooks, which led to the founding of the Cambridge School of Architectural and Landscape Design for Women, a successful training ground for women for twenty-seven years. Pray and other members of the Harvard faculty were often guest lecturers, and Pray taught an intensive course in town planning and industrial housing for advanced students there beginning in October 1918. The Cambridge School closed in the 1940s when women were allowed to attend the Harvard Graduate School of Design.

Pray was an active member of the American Society of Landscape Architects, president of the Boston chapter in 1913–1914 and of the national organization from 1915 to 1920. His negotiations with the American Academy in Rome led to the establishment of its first Fellowship in Landscape Architecture while he was chairman of the Committee of Education. He died in 1929 at the age of 58.

James Sturgis Pray. Courtesy Charles A. Birnbaum.

Pray, James Sturgis. "Danger of Over-exploitation of Our National Parks" and "The American Society of Landscape Architects and Our National Parks." *Landscape Architecture* 6 (April 1915), 113–114 and 119–123. The first article, an argument for the preservation of the primeval character of the national parks and a call to educate people to respect these areas; the second, an argument that the National Park administration needs the services of the profession for four reasons.

Pray, James Sturgis. "The Survey for a City Plan." *Landscape Architecture* 5 (October 1914), 5–14. Paper presented to the Fifth Annual Conference of Mayors and Other City Officials, State of New York, at Auburn, June 4, 1914. Pray argues that planners must have not only adequate knowledge of the general principles of good planning but also a knowledge of significant local facts that will influence the plan.

Pray, James Sturgis, and Theodora Kimball. *City Planning.* Cambridge: Harvard University Press, 1913. "A comprehensive analysis of the subject arranged for the classification of books, plans, photographs, notes and other collected material, with alphabetical subject index" (according to the subtitle).

Karen Sebastian

PUNCHARD, CHARLES PIERPONT, JR.
(1885–1920)
landscape architect, conservationist

Charles Pierpont Punchard Jr. was born in Framingham, Massachusetts. After finishing high school in nearby Brookline in 1901, he entered the office of his uncle, landscape architect William H. Punchard*, where he gained experience and training in landscape design. He was associated with his uncle's firm until 1909, when he enrolled in courses in landscape architecture at Harvard University. There he met Frederick Noble Evans, with whom he opened the firm of Evans & Punchard in Cleveland in 1911. Two years later, just as his practice was expanding, Punchard became ill with tuberculosis and was forced to move to Colorado Springs to recuperate.

When he was once again able to work, he settled in Denver, where he practiced with Irvin J. McCrary from 1916 to the spring of 1917. In July 1917 he moved to the District of Columbia to assume the position of landscape architect in the Office of Public Buildings and Grounds under the Fine Arts Commission. There he oversaw the landscape development of all the public parks and reservations in the capital city. A year later he was transferred to the U.S. Department of the Interior to fill the National Park Service's newly established position of landscape engineer.

It was the responsibility of the landscape engineer to ensure that all improvements in the national parks—roads, trails, and buildings—harmonized with the natural scenery and that the scenic wonders and natural features for which the parks had been set aside were preserved for future generations. Punchard was the first of several landscape engineers (called landscape architects after 1928)

Charles Pierpont Punchard Jr. From *Landscape Architecture,* April 1921.

who shaped the policies of landscape design, planning, and development for the national parks in the early twentieth century. In an article that appeared in *Landscape Architecture*, "Landscape Design in the National Park Service," he described his work as focusing on "control," that is, maintaining a balance between the preservation of natural qualities and scenery and the provision of improvements for the comfort and the accommodation of visitors.

Punchard's first task for the Park Service was to make a comprehensive study of the existing conditions and landscape problems of each park. During his first year he visited seven national parks and four monuments, spending two and a half months in Yellowstone and seven months in Yosemite. He studied the various types of scenery and analyzed landscape problems in detail, finding immediate solutions for many of them. At Yosemite, Punchard closely studied the landscape from a historical perspective much as Charles Eliot* had studied the Massachusetts reservations. Concerned about the encroachment of trees and shrubs on the splendid meadows of Yosemite Valley, Punchard recommended that the meadows be thinned and cleared to preserve the health of the larger trees, to protect against serious fires, and to develop interesting spaces on the valley floor and open up scenic vistas.

As an adviser to National Park Service director Stephen Mather, Punchard made recommendations for improving park facilities run by both the government and the concessionaires. He gave special attention to park entrances, the location and design of park buildings, and the physical appearance of lakes and roads. Campground design occupied much of Punchard's time, and by the end of 1919 he had worked out the basic requirements for national park campgrounds. He attacked practices that disturbed the natural appearance of the parks, especially when viewed from park roads, trails, or areas frequented by visitors. He worked with park superintendents and public operators to remove unsightly conditions, to screen borrow pits, to open up scenic vistas along park roads, and to replant woodlands destroyed by fire or cutting.

Punchard believed a balance could be achieved between the preservation of nature and the development of facilities through careful planning. He endeavored to plan attractive, well-organized facilities that were harmonious with their natural surroundings as well as practicable and serviceable. By the end of 1920, he had formed development schemes for several parks. Each scheme clustered buildings together functionally and aesthetically into an "ensemble." Punchard explored the use of native materials, from volcanic rock to natural timbers, for har-

monizing park structures such as gateways, community buildings, and ranger stations. His pattern for clusters of rustic administrative and commercial buildings around three sides of a village square, with a road passing along the fourth side, would be repeated throughout the Western natural parks, including Yosemite, General Grant, and Mount Ranier.

In 1920, a strong sense of professional stewardship and advocacy for the nation's scenic treasures led Punchard to speak out against a federal power bill that proposed to remove the control and administration of national parks from Congress and place them under a commission empowered to control all federal land and to develop water resources and irrigation. In his annual report and an article he wrote for *Landscape Architecture*, Punchard unequivocally outlined the threats of water projects to parks such as Glacier, Yellowstone, and Yosemite. Recalling the earlier controversy over Yosemite's Hetch Hetchy Dam and drawing attention to the endangered scenery of Glacier National Park, he wrote, "Although this is not the first time in the history of the national parks that their beautiful valleys, lakes, streams, and scenic areas have been in danger of commercial exploitation, the movement has come at this time with a new vigor and determination to transgress upon these areas and develop them selfishly."

The length of Punchard's service was brief, amounting to less than two and a half years. His tuberculosis continued to trouble him, and he died at the age of thirty-six.

In his efforts to correct existing problems and guide future park development, Punchard established a visual standard for national parks. He drew on the naturalistic principles of landscape gardening and nineteenth-century urban parks, which dictated that vistas be carefully framed, that plantings screen unsightly views, and that roadways be laid out for the most scenic effect. As the National Park Service's first landscape designer, Punchard provided a philosophical framework for future park development and management. The twofold philosophy that he put into practice—that the natural landscape of the national parks be preserved and that all construction and development harmonize with it—has had lasting influence on the character of national, state, and metropolitan parks throughout the United States.

McClelland, Linda Flint. *Building the National Parks: Historic Landscape Design and Construction*. Baltimore: Johns Hopkins University Press, 1998. History of the policies, practices, and principles that guided the development and protection of national parks from the founding of the National Park Service to the end of the twentieth century.

Punchard, Charles P., Jr. " 'Hands Off the National Parks.' " *Landscape Architecture* 11 (January 1921), 53–57. Article published posthumously voicing Punchard's opposition to the use of national parks for livestock grazing and water projects, and particularly to several congressional bills to create reservoirs in and near Yellowstone National Park.

Punchard, Charles P., Jr. "Report of the Landscape Engineer." *Annual Report of the Director of the National Park Service.* In *Reports of the Department of the Interior, for the Fiscal Year Ending June 30, 1919 and 1921.* Washington, D.C.: GPO, 1919, 1174–1181, and 1920, 331–339. Punchard's first and second annual reports to National Park Service director Stephen Mather describing the dual challenge of landscape design in national parks: protecting the parks and improving their facilities.

Linda Flint McClelland

PUNCHARD, WILLIAM
(1868–c. late 1930s or 1940s)
landscape architect

The details of William Punchard's early life are not known. He was living in Chelsea, Massachusetts, at the time of his matriculation at the Massachusetts Institute of Technology, where he studied architecture from 1887 to 1891 (he did not receive a degree). He worked for the firm of Olmsted*, Olmsted* & Eliot* as a draftsman in 1893. During his year with the Olmsted office, he participated with Herbert Kellaway on Boston's Riverway project, primarily preparing grading plans. (He also prepared grading and building site plans for Glen Magna, the William C. Endicott estate in Danvers, Massachusetts, but these improvements were not implemented.)

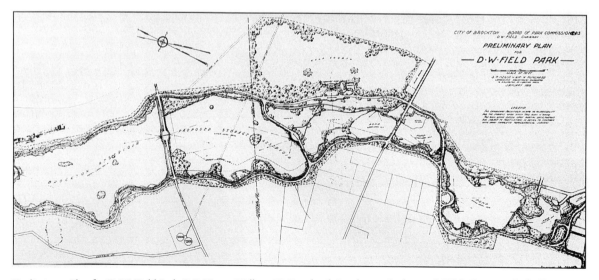

"Preliminary Plan for D. W. Field Park, S. P. Negus–William H. Punchard, Landscape Architects," 1926. Courtesy Parks Department, City of Brockton, Massachusetts.

Autumn view, D.W. Field Park, Brockton, 1990. Courtesy Child Associates, Inc.

Through his connections with the Olmsted office, Punchard found a position with landscape architect Warren Manning's* new firm in 1896. While employed by the Manning office, Punchard worked on plans for the Wisconsin Semi-Centennial project being staged in Milwaukee. At the end of 1896, he established his own independent practice in Boston as a "Landscape and Architectural Designer." His nephew, Charles Pierpont Punchard*, received his first professional training as a landscape architect in his uncle's office, where he worked for eight years. William Punchard had several partners during his professional career including Henry Dean, George Babson, Sheffield Arnold, and Samuel Negus*. All these associations were short-lived, however, and he appears to have worked as an independent designer after 1910, forming partnerships on a project-by-project basis.

Punchard joined with Negus for a number of public projects, the largest a landscape plan for the D. W. Field Park in Brockton, Massachusetts. Although the plan was not implemented in detail, it clearly guided Daniel W. Field and the city engineers, who developed the park to feature linked water bodies in a woodland setting.

Punchard joined the American Society of Landscape Architects in 1920, becoming a Fellow in 1923. In 1928 he gave a paper, "Smallest Job for Profit," at the ASLA annual meeting held in Salem, Massachusetts, where in a debate on the subject he represented the small office practitioner while Henry Hubbard* of the Olmsted office represented the large organization.

Punchard lived for many years in Belmont, Massachusetts. His name disappears from municipal and professional records in the late 1930s.

Child Associates, Inc. *D. W. Field Park, Brockton, Massachusetts. Historic Landscape Report Phase II.* Landscape Historian, Phyllis Andersen. Prepared for the Commonwealth of Massachusetts. Olmsted Historic Landscape Preservation Program, Boston, 1993. Documents Punchard's work on the landscape plan for the park as well as his professional career.

Punchard, William H. "Smallest Job for Profit." In *Proceedings of the Twenty-ninth Annual Meeting of the American Society of Landscape Architects.* Boston: Office of the Executive Secretary, 1928, 15–19. Advice on managing profit margins on small projects.

Punchard, William H. "Some Examples of Outdoor Swimming Pools." *Landscape Architecture*, October 1921, 21–27. Information on the design of public pools gathered in connection with Punchard's design of the pool at Winningham Park in Milton, Massachusetts.

Phyllis Andersen

RAPUANO, MICHAEL
(1904–1975)
landscape architect

Michael Rapuano was the son of the superintendent of parks in Syracuse, New York. Educated in the public schools of Syracuse, he entered Cornell University to study landscape architecture at the age of eighteen, and received a bachelor's degree. Rapuano won the Rome Prize in 1927; the following two years were spent at the American Academy in Rome, studying and traveling.

On his return from Italy, Rapuano found employment as a landscape architect with the Westchester County Park Commission. About the same time, he moved into an apartment on the upper east side of Manhattan, married, and set up a private practice. Several of his early clients were wealthy homeowners in New Jersey and Westchester County. In the early 1930s he began

Wesleyan University, Lawn Avenue Dormitories, Middletown, Connecticut. Completed 1966. Photo George Cserna. Courtesy Clarke & Rapuano, Inc.

Brooklyn Heights Esplanade, Brooklyn, c. 1970. Photo David Plowden. Courtesy Clarke & Rapuano, Inc.

to fill in part-time at Gilmore D. Clarke's* office, and in 1939 the firm of Clarke & Rapuano was formed. It outlived both partners and continued under the name Clarke & Rapuano, Inc., for nearly sixty years.

One of Rapuano's specialties was highway design. In the 1930s while working at Madigan-Hyland Engineers, his concept for a public esplanade to be built over the Brooklyn-Queens Expressway led to the Brooklyn Heights Esplanade Park. Also during the Robert Moses era, Rapuano provided designs for the Bronx River Parkway within the city of New York; the Saw Mill Parkway extension north; the Henry Hudson Parkway from 79th Street to the Westchester County line; and the New Jersey section of the Palisades Interstate Parkway. All were completed by 1950.

Rapuano's greatest achievement in parkway design was the Garden State Parkway, from Perth Amboy to Cape May. The roadway was laid to fit as closely as possible to the existing contours of the land. No curbs were introduced, and there were no paved shoulders. Opposing traffic lanes were kept as far apart as possible, the median being as much as 200 feet wide, and usually most of the natural woods were left intact. The parkway has long sweeping curves and very short tangents. There are no "broken-back" curves, and gradients are kept mostly below 3 percent. The Garden State Parkway is reputed to be the safest highway in America.

Rapuano's career in landscape architecture concentrated mostly on large public works. He was involved in the plans and designs for the two World's Fairs in New

Aerial view of Garden State Parkway, New Jersey. Courtesy Clarke & Rapuano, Inc.

York (1939–1940 and 1964–1965). His design for the original United Nations site in Lake Success, Long Island, was a masterpiece. (His watercolor rendering of the plan is also a work of art.) He also helped on the planning and layout of the United Nations permanent headquarters in Manhattan.

Several American cities have been greatly enhanced as a result of his planning and vision, among them are Nashville, Tennessee; Cleveland, Ohio; Bethlehem, Pennsylvania; and Middletown, Connecticut. In Nashville he produced a majestic setting for the state capitol with the Capitol Hill Redevelopment Project. He created the Cleveland Public Mall in that city on the roof of an exhibit hall and parking garages; the central feature is a reflection pool with ten illuminated bronze fountains. Bethlehem projects in which Rapuano was involved include the civic center; Historic Bethlehem; the former steel company's holdings; Lehigh University; Moravian College and Seminary; and many of the residences and parks surrounding the Saucon Valley Country Club. Middletown's redevel-

opment study in 1952, which showed how the city could be integrated with the Wesleyan University campus, was guided by Rapuano's concept and designs.

Other large-scale city planning projects include the Manhattanville Housing Study; Nashville's Central Loop General Neighborhood Redevelopment Plan and the University Center Urban Renewal Plan; Dallas's western approach; the downtown project in Scranton, Pennsylvania; the civic and business center in North Canton, Ohio; and in Pittsburgh, the "Golden Triangle," which includes Point State Park, the bridges at the point, Equitable Life Assurance's Gateway Center, and the U.S. Steel Company's headquarters building.

After World War II Rapuano designed military cemeteries for the American Battle Monuments Commission in Florence, Italy, and Margraten, Holland. He also designed the Luxembourg Memorial, the Honolulu Memorial Cemetery, and the Mexico Military Cemetery. His final military design contract was for the Calverton National Cemetery on Long Island, New York.

Model for Cleveland Public Mall, Exhibition Hall, c. 1965. Photo Louis Checkman. Courtesy Clarke & Rapuano, Inc.

Rapuano also designed several college and university campuses, including Harpur College (now the State University of New York at Binghamton), the State University of New York at Albany, and Allentown College in Pennsylvania. He executed Rutgers University's (New Jersey) campus expansion master plan and also did design work for Swarthmore College; Mohawk Valley Community College in Utica, New York; Union College in Schenectady, New York; Princeton University and the Lawrenceville School in New Jersey; and the New Columbus High School in Indiana.

"The Freeway in the City." A report to the Secretary of the Federal Department of Transportation; prepared by the Urban Advisors to the Federal Highway Administrator; Michael Rapuano, Chairman, May 1, 1968. Rapuano's report was the culmination of his work in highway design.

Rapuano, M., and G. D. Clarke. "Traffic and the Neighborhood Plan," *Architectural Forum* 79 (October 1943), 130–132.

Rapuano, M., P. P. Pirone, and Brooks E. Wigginton. *Open Space in Urban Design.* A report prepared for the Cleveland Development Foundation, sponsored by the Junior League of Cleveland, 1964.

Bradford M. Greene

REQUA, RICHARD
(1881–1941)
architect, landscape architect

Richard Requa was born in Illinois and raised in Nebraska, but in 1900, at the age of nineteen, he moved with his family to San Diego. Requa received education in electrical engineering and found work with an electrical contractor, becoming in 1907 an apprentice to an innovative local architect, Irving Gill. Following his apprenticeship, Requa opened his own architectural practice in 1910 and two years later entered into a partnership with Frank Mead, who had also worked briefly with Gill. Mead's philosophy of design, informed by extensive travel and stress-

ing the interrelationships among geography, climate, culture, and appropriate architectural adaptations, was probably a defining element of Requa's early professional development. Requa's own subsequent travels throughout Latin America and the Mediterranean increased his familiarity with Mediterranean-style architecture and gardens and led to a growing understanding of the significance of landscape elements.

Mead & Requa's practice included residential and school design projects and community planning for a

House of Hospitality courtyard, Balboa Park. Courtesy San Diego Historical Society.

Spanish-style gardens for San Diego's 1935 exposition, Balboa Park. Photo Carol Greentree.

small town that became Ojai. This partnership dissolved in 1920, and Requa formed another with Herbert Jackson. In 1922, Requa & Jackson was awarded a commission for the design of Rancho Santa Fe, a model residential village. Lilian Rice, a Berkeley-trained architect, joined the firm during this period and was ulti-

mately assigned control of the entire Rancho Santa Fe project. Requa and Jackson concentrated on the design of homes in San Diego, working primarily in the popular Spanish Revival style.

In 1934, seeking to resurrect the local economy from the Depression, the San Diego business community de-

Rancho Santa Fe, Main Street from the Inn, 1923. Courtesy San Diego Historical Society.

cided to stage a second fair (the 1935–1936 California Pacific International Exposition) on the grounds of the 1915–1916 Panama Pacific Exposition. The earlier event had left the city with well-designed avenues and greenswards and viceregal-style Spanish Colonial exhibition halls which Requa restored after being named chief architect of the exposition. In this capacity, he also expanded the area of the old fairground in Balboa Park and planned the architecture to display a broad array of then-fashionable styles. Recognizing the appeal of gardens to fair-goers, he was especially attentive to the exposition landscapes, redesigning several older garden areas—the Alcazar Gardens, the Casa del Rey Moro, and a Guadalajara patio—and modeling them on his favorite Spanish

and Mexican prototypes. Using the latest technologies for night lighting, water display, and sound projection, he also developed new areas in a style bridging Art Deco and Hollywood Moderne, which played on all the senses of the fair-goers in a manner foreshadowing Disneyland.

Requa died suddenly at the age of sixty in mid-1941, soon after bringing a new associate, Edward Morehead, into the firm. As an architect, park landscape designer, town planner, and designer of residential gardens, Requa helped define the romantic, neo-Mediterranean style of San Diego. Although the architectural and landscape fashions he helped shape were virtually forgotten during World War II, the preservation-conscious 1970s and 1980s directed new attention toward his role in establish-

Richard Requa. Courtesy San Diego Historical Society.

ing a regional vernacular that was colorful, appealing, and appropriate to San Diego's climate. Today, Requa's remaining Balboa Park gardens are among the few public examples of their genre extant in southern California; a number of his private patios and courtyards have been well maintained during the last sixty or more years.

Requa, Richard. *Architectural Details of Spain and the Mediterranean.* Cleveland: J. H. Jansen, 1927. Oversized volume of photos by Requa; became a popular visual reference for design professionals of the late 1920s and early 1930s; emphasizes importance of patios and courtyard gardens in Mediterranean design.

Requa, Richard. *Inside Lights on the Building of San Diego's Exposition: 1935.* San Diego: Published privately, 1937. First-person "insider" account of planning and rapid construction of the 1935–1936 fair; chapters on landscaping, exterior decoration, night lighting; photos of water features and plan map of expo grounds.

Requa, Richard. *Old World Inspiration for American Architecture.* Los Angeles: Monolith Portland Cement Company, 1929. Oversized volume of photos published after Requa's 1928 trip to the Western Mediterranean; emphasizes the value of regionally appropriate design and draws parallels between Spain/North Africa and southern California; illustrated.

Carol Greentree

ROBINSON, CHARLES MULFORD
(1869–1917)
planner, author

Charles Mulford Robinson was born in Ramapo, New York. Shortly after his birth his parents moved to Rochester, where Robinson lived most of his life. He graduated with a B.A., Phi Beta Kappa, from the University of Rochester in 1891. After graduation, Robinson traveled to Europe, and that trip, along with others, gave him the opportunity to study cities and provided material for his later writing on the improvement of towns and cities.

Initially drawn to a career in journalism, Robinson worked as an editor at the *Post Express* in Rochester (1891–1902), the *Philadelphia Ledger* (1904), and the *Municipal Journal* in New York City (1907). His articles for the *Post Express* on life in Rochester's third ward—sentimental accounts of the ward and its social life at the end of the century—were gathered into a book, *Third Ward Traits*, and published in 1899.

In the spring of 1899, Robinson contributed a series

of three articles, "Improvement in City Life," to the *Atlantic Monthly.* The articles attracted favorable attention, and Robinson's writing subsequently focused on civic improvement. *Harper's Monthly* hired him to go to Europe and to write a similar series on municipal developments in Europe. Robinson's prominence as a commentator grew, and he contributed articles and reviews to many other periodicals.

On his *Harper's* European trip, Robinson accumulated more information than the magazine could use, which he assembled into a book, *The Improvement of Towns and Cities; or The Practical Basis of Civic Aesthetics.* Despite Robinson's renown and a growing awareness of the importance of civic beauty (in the foreword he lists 117 organizations that concerned themselves with civic improvement), he could not find a publisher. So in May 1901 he published the book at his own expense; by November all copies had been sold. It had

Charles Mulford Robinson. From *A Plan for Civic Improvement for the City of Oakland*, 1906. Courtesy Frances Loeb Library, Harvard University.

two reprintings within a year and eleven more in Robinson's lifetime. In addition, the book was translated into several languages, and Robinson was hailed by the London *Westminster Gazette* as a "leader of a new school of prophets."

Not only was Robinson's book innovative in his own time, but many of his suggestions for improvements are still relevant. His recommendation of a pure white civic building sited on an eminence seems naive today, but his ideas of clustering civic buildings around a plaza, burying power lines, removing advertisements from buildings, and constructing urban playgrounds are still goals for city planners.

Encouraged by the book's reception, Robinson went to Boston to study the subject further and to work on a second book, *Modern Civic Art*, which was published in 1903. While in Boston, he served as acting secretary of the American Park and Outdoor Art Association, an organization composed of landscape architects, park superintendents, park commissioners, and a few citizens. In 1904 this group of professionals joined with the American League for Civic Improvement, a federation of various local improvement societies across the Mid-

west, to create the American Civic Association. Robinson served temporarily as the secretary but resigned to take up the work of city planning.

His first commission was an improvement plan for the City of Buffalo. His report was greeted with great enthusiasm, and plans for many cities across the United States followed. They include Detroit; Colorado Springs; Denver; Honolulu; Des Moines; Dubuque; Los Angeles, Oakland, and Long Beach, California; Syracuse and Watertown, New York; Columbus and Ogdenburg, Ohio; Ridgewood, New Jersey; and Raleigh, North Carolina. Most of the reports were prepared by Robinson alone, but some were collaborations.

Robinson continued to study the field, and in 1910 he went to Harvard's School of Landscape Architecture to examine the problems of residential subdivision. His research there and a trip about this time to attend the International Planning Conference in London led to his next book, *The Width and Arrangement of Streets* (1911), later rewritten, enlarged, and published under the title *City Planning; with Special Reference to the Planning of Streets and Lots* (1916). This work laid out the basic requirements for street planning, in particular, in relation to residential districts.

In 1913 the University of Illinois established a Chair of Civic Design with Robinson in mind. In that position Robinson created a course, which later became required, for the Landscape Gardening Department. It was divided into two parts: "Repair," a four-week series of lectures devoted to the historical study of city planning, its aims and general application; and in the spring, "Prepare," a program of practical experience and lectures during which he took his students to a city for firsthand study of the issues they were dealing with in the classroom. His early death at age 49 prevented his plan to put these lectures into book form.

Robinson was an active member of many organizations. He was recording secretary for the American League for Civic Improvements and organizer and first secretary of the National Alliance of Civic Organizations. He was also an honorary member of several improvement organizations and European civic societies. At home in Rochester, he was a park commissioner, a director of the Children's Playground League, member of the Rochester Art League, director of the Memorial Art Gallery, secretary of the Civic Improvement Committee, member of the Executive Committee of the Chamber of Commerce, and chairman of its City Planning Committee.

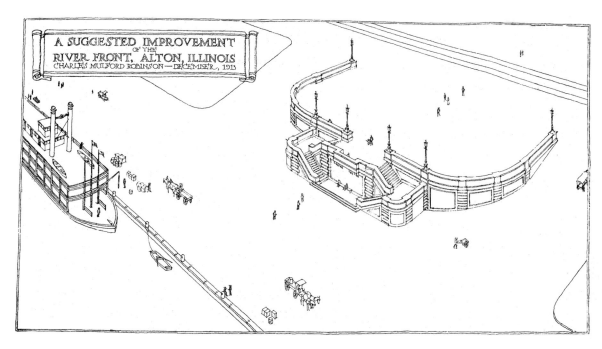

"A Suggested Improvement of the River Front." From *The Advancement of Alton, Illinois,* 1914. Courtesy Frances Loeb Library, Harvard University.

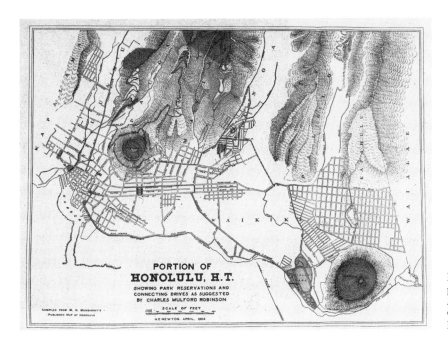

Plan for parks and connecting parkways in Honolulu. From *The Beautifying of Honolulu,* 1907. Courtesy Frances Loeb Library, Harvard University.

Robinson, Charles M. *The Improvement of Towns and Cities; or The Practical Basis of Civic Aesthetics.* New York: G. P. Putnam's Sons, 1901. Advocates civic design improvements and offers straightforward suggestions for accomplishing them; promotes the idea of the city plan. A classic, and many of its ideas are still current today.

Robinson, Charles M. *Modern Civic Art; or, The City Made Beautiful.* New York: G. P. Putnam's Sons, 1903. Robinson coined the phrase "city beautiful," and this book calls for comprehensive city plans; offers many suggestions to beautify cities but cautions against ignoring the qualities that make places individual.

Robinson, Charles M. *The Width and Arrangement of Streets: A Study in Town Planning.* 1911. Expanded, revised, and published as *City Planning; with Special Reference to the Planning of Streets and Lots.* New York: G. P. Putnam's Sons, 1916. The book's premise: good street planning promotes good housing and more efficient city planning; gives the fundamental requirements for functionally laying out streets particularly in relation to residential districts; appendix reviews the best of current practice of the town planning movement.

The Charles Mulford Robinson Collection in the Special Collections of the Frances Loeb Library, Harvard University, has books, periodicals, clippings, and city planning reports collected and written by Robinson as adviser to over thirty American cities.

Amy Brown

ROSE, JAMES C.
(1913–1991)
landscape architect, author

James C. Rose was only five years old when his father died and, with his mother and older sister, he moved to New York City from rural Pennsylvania. He never graduated from high school because he refused to take music and mechanical drafting, but nevertheless he managed to enroll in architecture courses at Cornell University, and subsequently to transfer, as a special student, to Harvard University to study landscape architecture. He was expelled from Harvard, however, in 1937 for refusing to design landscapes in a Beaux-Arts manner. Along with his fellow students, Garrett Eckbo and Dan Kiley, Rose went on to be one of the leaders of the modern movement in American landscape architecture.

The design experiments for which Rose was expelled served as the basis for a series of provocative articles expounding modernism in landscape design, published in 1938 and 1939 in *Pencil Points* (now *Progressive Architecture*). Subsequently, Rose wrote many other articles, including a series with Eckbo and Kiley, as well as four books that advance both the theory and practice of landscape architecture in the twentieth century: *Creative Gardens* (1958), *Gardens Make Me Laugh* (1965), *Modern American Gardens—Designed by James Rose* (1967, written under the pseudonym Marc Snow), and *The Heavenly Environment* (1987).

Rose was both a landscape theorist and a practitioner. In 1941 he was employed briefly in New York City as a landscape architect by Tuttle, Seelye, Place & Raymond, working on the design of a staging area to house 30,000 men at Camp Kilmer, New Jersey. For a short time Rose had a sizable practice of his own in New York City, but he quickly decided that large-scale public and corporate work would impose too many restrictions on his creative freedom, and he devoted most of his post–World War II career to the design of private gardens. (This is one of the reasons his built work is not as well known as that of his fellow modern rebels, Dan Kiley and Garrett Eckbo.)

In 1953 he built one of his most significant designs, the Rose residence (now the James Rose Center for

James C. Rose holding a model of his house made from scraps during World War II, Okinawa, Japan. Courtesy James C. Rose Archives, James Rose Center.

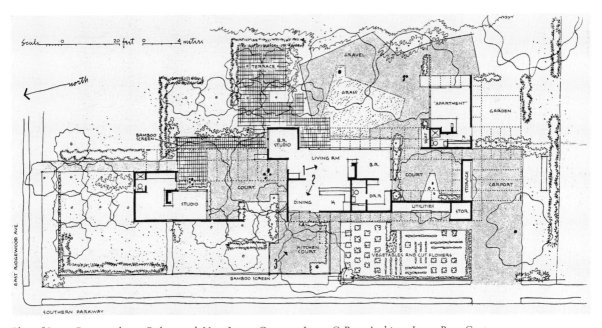

Plan of James Rose residence, Ridgewood, New Jersey. Courtesy James C. Rose Archives, James Rose Center.

View looking out, James C. Rose residence. Photo Frederick Charles.

Landscape Architectural Research and Design) in Ridgewood, New Jersey. Rose had conceived of the design while stationed in Okinawa, in 1943, and had made the first model of it from scraps found in construction battalion headquarters. The design was published in the December 1954 issue of *Progressive Architecture*, juxtaposed with the design for a traditional Japanese house built in the garden of the Museum of Modern Art in New York City; the article commends Rose's design for its spatial discipline. The house clearly expresses Rose's idea of fusion between indoor and outdoor space as well as his notion that modern design must be flexible to allow for changes in the environment as well as in the lives of its users.

From 1953 until his death, Rose based an active professional practice in his home. Like Thomas Church* and many others, Rose practiced a form of design/build because it gave him control over the finished work and allowed him to improvise in response to the sites of his

gardens. As a result, most of Rose's work is concentrated near his home in northern New Jersey and New York—although significant examples also exist in Connecticut, Florida, Maryland, California, and abroad. Besides spontaneous improvisation, several other distinct qualities characterize the gardens of James Rose. The gardens lend themselves to contemplation and self-discovery. They respond to their sites in specific ways, often recycling raw materials found therein and incorporating existing natural features such as rock outcroppings and trees as part of a designed, flexible, asymmetrical spatial geometry. Abhorring waste, Rose often reused discarded building materials and constructions originally intended for other purposes. Old doors became elegant benches, metal barbecues turned into fountains, railroad ties became walls for irregular terraces. Overall, Rose's gardens are highly ordered sculptural compositions of space meant to be experienced rather than viewed. They are like giant origami, the experience of which

Fountain and courtyard, James C. Rose residence. Photo Frederick Charles.

unfolds from the inside. While Rose's gardens exhibit little interest in color or concern for variety of horticultural species, they sensitively reveal the nature of their sites.

In 1970, Rose was invited to be a participant at the World Design Conference in Japan. This experience instilled in him a continuing appreciation for Japanese culture, reflected in many gardens that have sometimes been mislabeled "Japanese." Rose's distinctive modern American gardens, like many Japanese gardens, attempt to reflect the spirit of the place in which they exist. He made frequent trips to Japan and became a practicing Zen Buddhist, but his gardens retain their American identity almost by definition. Rose himself, in response to a query from a prospective client asking if he could design her a Japanese garden, replied, "Of course, whereabouts in Japan do you live?"

Rose was one of the most colorful figures in twentieth-century landscape design. Skeptical of most institutions, he nevertheless served as a guest lecturer and visiting critic at numerous architecture and landscape architecture schools. Before he died, he set in motion an idea that had been in his mind for forty years—the establishment of a landscape research and design study center—and created a foundation to support the transformation of his Ridgewood residence for this purpose. Rose died in his home in 1991 of cancer.

Rose, James C. *Creative Gardens.* New York: Reinhold, 1958. Rose's first book, expounding modernism in both theory and practice; includes numerous photographs and plans.

Rose, James C. *Gardens Make Me Laugh.* Norwalk, Conn.: Silvermine, 1965. Rose's second book, a humorous essay reflecting on the nature of Rose's contemporary landscape architectural practice; drawings by Osborn.

Rose, James C. *The Heavenly Environment.* Hong Kong: New City Cultural Service, 1965. Rose's last book, which he described as "a landscape drama in three acts with a backstage interlude"; expresses Rose's mature theory and practice; illustrated.

Dean Cardasis

ROWNTREE, LESTER
(1879–1979)
horticulturist, author, plant collector

Lester Rowntree was born Gertrude Ellen Lester in Penrith, England. As a young girl she immigrated with her family, and was educated at the Westtown Friends School in Pennsylvania. She married Bernard Rowntree in 1908. In the mid-1920s the Rowntrees moved to Carmel Highlands, California, where she devoted herself to the study of native plants.

In the 1930s, Rowntree became well known as an expert on both the herbaceous and woody flowering plants of California. An author, photographer, lecturer, and seed merchant, she also helped to found the California Native Plant Society. For nine months of the year she roamed the state alone in her battered station wagon and packed into the backcountry with a burro to carry her equipment. She collected seeds from a wide variety of plants, and, as an ardent conservationist, took care to leave some where she found them and to scatter others in appropriate habitats. She sold the seed to eager plant specialists in this country and abroad. Louise Beebe Wilder*, for example, was one of her customers and helped to publicize her work. Gardeners in England and on the Continent were also among her clientele.

Rowntree won permanent renown with the publication of her two books, *Hardy Californians* (1936) and *Flowering Shrubs of California* (1939), which described the state's herbaceous and woody flowering plants, respectively. In both her books and her magazine articles she emphasized the garden use of these plants, rather than their botanical characteristics. The popularity of Rowntree's books was due in large part to her colorful

Lester Rowntree, c. late 1930s. From *Flowering Shrubs of California*, 1939.

descriptions of her adventures as a plant hunter, the people she encountered, and the magnificent country she explored on her quests. She wrote in a conversational yet authoritative style, and her books were accurate, while avoiding the dryness of a botanical text.

Lester Rowntree died just days after her one hundredth birthday in 1979. She influenced the gardens of her era by introducing California's native plants to a wide audience through her writing and by making their seeds available to gardeners around the world. Perhaps most significantly, she fostered the appreciation of American native plants in her own day, as well as by later generations.

Ingram, Marie. "Lester Rowntree." *Hortus,* nos. 31, 32, 33 (Autumn 1994, Winter 1994, Spring 1995). A three-part account of Rowntree's career, published in the distinguished British garden magazine, literary and evocative rather than chronological and historical.

Rowntree, Lester. *Flowering Shrubs of California and Their Value to the Gardener.* Stanford: Stanford University Press, 1939. Includes botanical and common names, cultural requirements, Rowntree's own photographs; map on endpapers.

Rowntree, Lester. *Hardy Californians.* New York: Macmillan, 1936. Focus on herbaceous flowering California natives from many habitats and their garden use; Rowntree's adventures on the trail; her own photographs; map on endpapers.

Virginia Lopez Begg

SARGENT, CHARLES SPRAGUE
(1841–1927)
horticulturist, author, plant collector

Charles Sprague Sargent was born in Boston to a distinguished family that included Henry Winthrop Sargent, the estate owner and patron of Andrew Jackson Downing*, and John Singer Sargent, the American painter. Sargent graduated from Harvard in 1862 and served in the Union Army (1862–1865). In 1868, after touring Europe, he took over management of his father's country estate in Brookline. He used that position as his entrée into ornamental horticulture.

Sargent was in 1872 appointed director of Harvard's Botanic Garden, where he came under the influence of the noted botanist Asa Gray. In that same year, Harvard established the Arnold Arboretum in Jamaica Plain, Massachusetts, with a bequest from James Arnold, a New Bedford industrialist. Sargent was made the first director in 1873, and soon after he called on Frederick Law Olmsted Sr.* to begin laying out the grounds. When lack of funds impeded Sargent's plan for development, he and Olmsted proposed that Harvard transfer the arboretum land to the City of Boston, which would, in turn, offer Harvard a long-term, tax-free, renewable lease, development assistance, road maintenance, and police protection. After some hesitation, both sides agreed to the conditions. The agreement was signed on December 30, 1882, making the arboretum part of Boston's "Emerald Necklace" park system. By the time of Sargent's death, the plant collection, along with the extensive herbarium and library, had made the Arnold Arboretum one of the great plant study resources in North America.

Sargent was director of the arboretum for fifty-four years, and from that unique position he made far-reaching contributions to botany, horticulture, forest conservation, and landscape gardening. His writings documented native American trees, describing their physical and economic properties and promoting their conservation. His *Silva of North America* (1891–1902) and *Manual of the Trees of North America* (1905), both illustrated by Charles Faxon, catalog the diversity of native species and their geographic distribution. Sargent's plant-collecting expeditions and sponsorship of expeditions made by E. H. Wilson and Joseph Rock revealed Asiatic flora to the Western world and added valuable plants to American gardens.

Sargent also spent productive time in government service, and his advocacy of the protection of American forests shaped federal policy at the end of the nineteenth century. He produced the first comprehensive survey of American forest species, published as part of the *Tenth United States Census* (1884). In 1882 he was a member of the Northern Pacific Transcontinental Survey team that surveyed the future Glacier National Park. In 1884 he chaired a commission that developed the first conservation policy for the Adirondack region.

Sargent played an important role in the preservation of Mount Vernon, serving as a consultant to the Mount Vernon Ladies' Association from 1911 until his death in 1927. Sargent had many ties to the emerging field of landscape architecture. He established enduring professional relationships with Olmsted and with the French landscape architect Edouard André. He served as a teacher and informal adviser to a number of young practitioners, including Beatrix Farrand* and his nephews Henry and Philip Codman. Sargent's son, Andrew Robeson Sargent, became a landscape architect after serving an apprenticeship in the office of his brother-in-law, Guy Lowell*.

The Arnold Arboretum served as a field study resource for Harvard's program in landscape architecture founded in 1900. Sargent and the arboretum also played a role in Massachusetts Institute of Technology's short-lived program in landscape architecture (1900–1909), which was headed by Lowell. Sargent was the founder and "conductor" of *Garden and Forest* (1888–1897), one of the most important landscape publications of the nine-

Charles Sprague Sargent examining herbarium specimen in library of Arnold Arboretum, 1904. Photo T. E. Marr. Courtesy Arnold Arboretum of Harvard University, Photograph Archives.

Charles Sprague Sargent, Francis Skinner, and George Englemann gathering forestry data for the Tenth Census, 1880. Courtesy Arnold Arboretum of Harvard University, Photograph Archives.

View of Hickory Path, Arnold Arboretum, 1913. Photo T. E. Marr. Courtesy Arnold Arboretum of Harvard University, Photograph Archives.

teenth century. Under Sargent's direction, *Garden and Forest* published articles on ornamental horticulture, forestry, historic landscape preservation, and landscape gardening. Contributors included many of the leading landscape architects of the day: Olmsted, Charles Eliot*, H. W. S. Cleveland*, George Kessler*.

Many honors were bestowed on Sargent during his long professional life. He was awarded the first George Robert White Medal of the Massachusetts Horticultural Society (1910), and the Garden Club of America awarded him its first Medal of Honor (1920). He was a member of the National Academy of Sciences, the Linnean Society, and the Royal Society, London. Many plants were named in his honor: the genera *Sargentia* and *Sargentodoxa* and, among the many garden plants, the Sargent crab (*Malus sargentii*), the Sargent cherry (*Prunus sargentii*), and the Sargent juniper (*Juniperus chinensis sargentii*). Sargent died at his estate, Holm Lea, in Brookline.

Sargent, Charles Sprague. *Manual of the Trees of North America*. Boston: Houghton, Mifflin, 1905. An abbreviated version of the *Silva*, prepared for the general public; illustrations by C. E. Faxon.

Sargent, Charles Sprague. *The Silva of North America: A Description of the Trees Which Grow Naturally in North America Exclusive of Mexico. Illustrated with figures and analyses drawn from nature by C. E. Faxon.* 14 vols. Boston: Houghton, Mifflin, 1891–1902. The definitive catalog and description of American tree species of its time, compiled from both research and field observation.

Sutton, S. B. *Charles Sprague Sargent and the Arnold Arboretum.* Cambridge: Harvard University Press, 1970. Biography of Sargent written on the occasion of the Arnold Arboretum centennial.

Phyllis Andersen

SAUNDERS, WILLIAM
(1822–1900)
landscape gardener, cemetery designer, author

William Saunders was born in St. Andrews, Scotland, into a family of professional gardeners (and always preferred the title "landscape gardener"). In 1834 he entered Madras College in St. Andrews to study for the ministry of the Church of Scotland but soon changed to horticulture and landscape gardening. Later he moved to London and worked as an apprentice gardener on several large estates. In 1848, shortly after his marriage, he and his wife emigrated to the United States, where he became a citizen in 1857.

Saunders first settled in New Haven, Connecticut, where he worked as a gardener on the estate of William Bostwick. In the early 1850s he moved south to Baltimore. There he served as gardener and site planner on the estates of Thomas P. Winans and Johns Hopkins. In addition to designing large lakes and various flower gar-

William Saunders. From *Yearbook of the United States Department of Agriculture*, 1900.

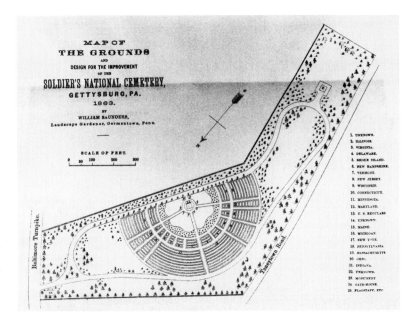

"Map of the Grounds and Design for the Improvement of the Soldiers National Cemetery, Gettysburg, Pa.," 1863. From *Revised Report Made to the Legislature of Pennsylvania . . .*

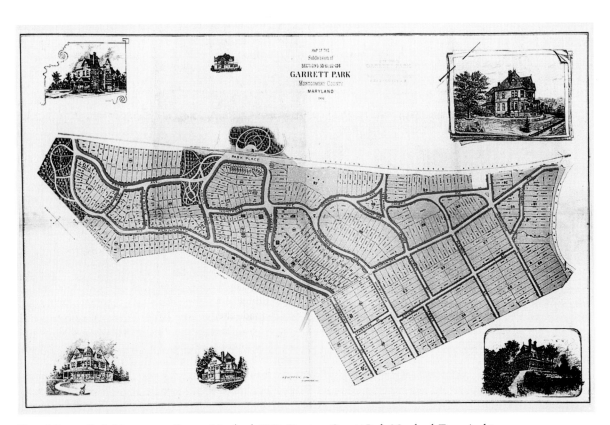

Plan of Garrett Park, Montgomery County, Maryland, 1891. Courtesy Garrett Park, Maryland, Town Archives.

View of residence, Garrett Park, 1996. Courtesy Montgomery County Department of Parks & Planning.

dens for the 400-acre Hopkins estate, Saunders served as overseer of the farm. During this period he published in the leading journals of his day, such as *The Horticulturist*, *Hovey's Magazine of Horticulture*, *Farmer and Gardener*, and *Philadelphia Florist*, most importantly on the planting and maintenance of fruit trees and grapes. Through his association with *The Horticulturist*, Saunders met A. J. Downing*, whom he admired as a theoretician though, as he noted in his autobiography, he had reservations about Downing's practical knowledge of site planning and architecture. Downing respected Saunders's horticultural knowledge and on one occasion recommended him for a job as a gardener, on the estate of Edwin Barlett in Tarrytown, New York.

In 1854, Saunders moved to Germantown, Pennsylvania, and established a partnership with the distinguished horticulturist Thomas Meehan, whom he had met in England while Meehan was working for Kew Gardens. Saunders and Meehan collaborated on a number of public park projects, cemeteries, and residential site plans. These included a planting plan and road system for Philadelphia's Fairmount Park and a site plan for that city's smaller, 46-acre Hunting Park. His cemetery designs included Rose Hill in Chicago and Oak Ridge in Springfield, Illinois. While in partnership with Meehan, Saunders also invented the "fixed roof" for greenhouses, using thinner frame members that admitted more light, which made them vastly more efficient and productive.

In 1862, Saunders was appointed superintendent of the experimental gardens of the newly created Department of Agriculture. He remained in Washington, D.C., until his death thirty-eight years later. During his long residency there he became acquainted with presidents Abraham Lincoln and Ulysses S. Grant, as well as such notables as Frederick Douglass and Walt Whitman.

In 1863 an interstate committee of Union gover-

Central Monument, Soldiers National Cemetery, Gettysburg. Photo Reuben Rainey.

nors chose Saunders to design the Soldiers National Cemetery at the Gettysburg battlefield, which was to become the site of Lincoln's famous address. Saunders's radial plan of "simple grandeur," which grouped the Union dead by states and focused on a central monument, was the single most distinguished design of his career. Saunders marked the Union graves with unadorned, curving, rectangular slabs of gray granite inscribed with the name, rank, company, and regiment of each soldier. These were contiguous and extended nine inches above the level of the sweeping lawn, delineating elegant concentric curves on its surface. Officers and enlisted men were buried alongside one another to symbolize the egalitarian nature of the Union Army. The planting plan was composed predominately of evergreen trees and shrubs, which defined the boundary and framed views. Shortly before departing for Gettysburg to deliver his address, Lincoln invited Saunders to the White House so he could study the plan; he was very impressed with it.

After Lincoln's assassination, Saunders was invited to design the grounds of a proposed monument to the president in Oak Ridge Cemetery. The Oak Ridge Board of Managers requested that he also design additional acreage adjacent to the monument in an integrated manner. His plan was characterized by large open areas of turf and irregular groupings of non-native trees; curvilinear roads and paths aligned with the contours of the hilly topography, and a living fence of osage orange defined the precinct.

Saunders was also responsible for several projects in and around Washington. In 1870 he designed the site plan for the facilities of the Department of Agriculture on the Mall, including an extensive arboretum, at the time the second most comprehensive example in North America after the Arnold Arboretum. (It was demolished in 1931 to make room for new construction on the Mall.) In 1871, Saunders, as a member of the city's Parking [sic] Commission, conceived guidelines for park design and street tree planting, which resulted in the planting of some 80,000 trees. In an 1868 article in Samuel Sloan's *Architectural Review and American Builders' Journal* he called attention to the poor site planning of the Capitol and recommended construction of a system of terraces that would be in scale with the building and properly anchor it. Saunders's suggestion attracted the attention of Senator Justin S. Morrill, who persuaded Congress to appropriate funds, and the terraces were built. Frederick Law Olmsted Sr.'s* design for the West Front later replaced them. In 1887, Saunders

created the initial plan for the town of Garrett Park, Maryland, about twelve miles north of the city.

In addition, Saunders was involved in the planning of several expositions. In 1876 he designed the site plan for the Department of Agriculture's building at the Centennial Exposition in Philadelphia. He also planned the department's exhibitions in the New Orleans Exposition of 1884 and the Paris Exposition of 1889.

Saunders profoundly influenced American ecosystems and the American farm economy while working for the Department of Agriculture by importing and distributing various foreign plants. In 1866 he introduced to California *Eucalyptus globulus* from Australia. In 1870 he imported some 300 varieties of winter hardy apple trees from Russia, which were propagated in the Northeastern states and substantially improved the region's fruit industry. He also imported the kaki, or Japanese persimmon, which was widely planted in the South. His single most significant plant introduction came in 1871, when he imported from Bahia, Brazil, what later came to be known as the Washington naval orange: it quickly became the leading commercial variety in California and stimulated the development of the citrus industry in the Southwestern states. Saunders avidly promoted the interests and economic welfare of American farmers. In 1867 he co-founded the Patrons of Husbandry, or the National Grange. He wrote the group's constitution and was elected its first Master, a position he held for six years. During his tenure he was a strong advocate of women's participation in the organization.

As did his colleague Downing, Saunders produced numerous articles, the majority of them devoted to technical matters of horticulture, and like Downing, he believed fervently in "the refining influence of the study and contemplation of the fine arts" on both individuals and society. Hence, he envisioned landscape gardening as a significant instrument for the moral improvement of the nation.

Saunders died at the age of seventy-eight in Washington, D.C.

Saunders, William. "Landscape Gardening." *The Report of the Commission of Agriculture for the Year 1869*. Washington, D.C.: GPO. An important source concerning Saunders's understanding of the history and nature of landscape gardening.

Saunders, William. "Remarks on the Design for the Soldiers National Cemetery, Gettysburg, Pennsylvania."

Revised Report Made to the Legislature of Pennsylvania Relative to the Soldiers National Cemetery at Gettysburg. Harrisburg. The definitive statement of Saunders's design concept for his most important cemetery commission.

Saunders, William. Unpublished handwritten journal. 1898. United States Department of Agriculture Li-

brary, Washington, D.C. The most detailed primary source dealing with Saunders's career with the Department of Agriculture, the background of the Soldiers National Cemetery, and his design ideas for Washington.

_____

Reuben Rainey

SCHRYVER, EDITH
(1901–1984)
landscape architect

See the joint account with Lord, Elizabeth.

SCHUETZE, REINHARD
(1860–1910)
cemetery designer, landscape architect

Reinhard Schuetze was born in Bothkamp, Holstein (Germany), and trained as a gardener, plantsman, landscape architect, and engineer at the royal gardens in Potsdam and the forestry academy at Eberswalde. His reputation on graduation led in 1889 to a commission for the design and development of the suburban grounds

Flower display in central garden, City Park, Denver. Stereograph by Keystone View Company. Private collection.

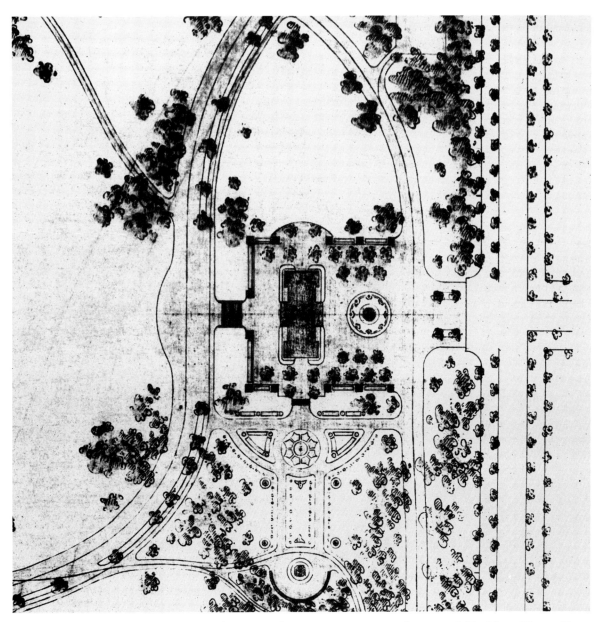

Design showing mountain viewing platform, Cheesman Park, Denver, 1898. Courtesy The Denver Public Library, Western History Collection, Denver Historic Parks Documents Collection.

of Denver's Fairmount Cemetery, and he subsequently won a competition for the design of the Colorado Capitol grounds.

Schuetze's work at Fairmount was promoted as being in the tradition of Mount Auburn, Greenwood, and Laurel Hill cemeteries. However, the Fairmount plan itself, like his later park plans, was in the more flowing, ordered, and fulsome idiom of late nineteenth-century German and Dutch parks and cemeteries. With his Fairmount design, Schuetze demonstrated convinc-

City Park at twilight from the mountain viewing platform, 1983. Photo Don Etter.

ingly, for the first time, the feasibility of creating a grand Arcadian landscape on the flat, treeless plains of the arid West. He built the necessary water works, but more important, his system also included the creation of subtle contours throughout the site so as to maximize the natural retention, absorption, and distribution of whatever water was available. He also demonstrated, again for the first time in this environment, that dense plantings of an exceptional variety of trees and shrubs would thrive in a city long used to a timid palate of sparsely planted material. Fairmount was for decades considered the finest arboretum in the West.

The quality of Schuetze's Fairmount work led the Denver Park Board to view the cemetery as a model for Denver's park system and then, in 1893, to hire Schuetze as the city's first landscape architect. Schuetze promptly embarked on a program to improve the existing infrastructure of the city's park system, including the construction and reconstruction of lakes. Within months of his appointment, a general plan for the development of a citywide park and parkway system was under discussion (1894). This plan was subsequently modified and refined by Charles Mulford Robinson* (1906) and George Kessler* (beginning in 1907). Schuetze collaborated with both. The result was a distinguished urban design framework for the city. Indeed, Denver's reputation as a premier example of the City Beautiful can in large part be credited to Schuetze. A century later, the public spaces that bear his imprint are the most notable features of the city's urban park system and a key to Denver's sylvan ambiance.

Schuetze was responsible for the design or reconstruction of virtually every turn-of-the-century public space in Denver, including parks, flower gardens, esplanades, parkways, and a zoological garden. He was equally at home designing a lake lined with copper to avoid water loss, a baroque flower bed to commemorate the end of the Spanish American War, and a rustic teahouse. On a modest site now known as Cheesman Park, he demonstrated that with judicious grading and informed planting he could both screen the surrounding city from sight and provide users with an illusion that the park is endless. At Schuetze's death, this park was acknowledged to be his masterpiece. More recently the art historian Vincent Scully called it one of the finest urban spaces in America.

Schuetze was comfortable with design traditions in the Grand Manner and employed them as counterpoint and entry (as in the City Park Esplanade) and as setting and surround (as in the Capitol grounds). However, the signature he established for Denver was in a naturalistic tradition—a rich tapestry of lakes, great meadows bordered by winding carriageways and entwined with separate walkways, forests to separate park from city, secret gardens, and well-sited viewpoints. In Schuetze's mind, the viewpoints were essential to establish a sense of place, and all his major park designs included a site or sites from which there were views, whether over water or lawn or trees, to the Rocky Mountains beyond the city. Denver citizens soon took it for granted that both urban ills and their arid climate would be ameliorated by the signature that Schuetze had established. And, once established, this example was followed by citizens in their own gardens, resulting in a significant design continuity between the city's public and private spaces.

Schuetze also worked privately, collaborating with William Lang, one of Denver's most creative architects, and designed gardens (none of which survive) for the elegant homes of Denver's newly rich. He was in addition a superb draftsman, and a substantial collection of his drawings, as elegant and sensuous as his work on the land, is in the Denver Public Library.

Denver Historic Parks Documents Collection. Western History/Genealogy Department, Denver Public Library. Includes most of Schuetze's extant work on paper: architectural and engineering plans, landscape designs, and planting schemes (also includes much of the Denver work of S. R. DeBoer*, Olmsted Brothers*, Kessler, and others).

Denver *Post* and *Sunday News-Times*, April 10, 1910. Brief obituary articles that summarize Schuetze's career and his contribution to Denver's "Legacy of Green."

Halaas, David Fridtjof. *Fairmount and Historic Colorado.* Denver: Fairmount Cemetery Association, 1976. Popular illustrated monograph on Denver's early burial grounds, focusing on the development of the cemetery and outlining the contribution Schuetze made to the effort.

Don Etter and Carolyn Etter

SCOTT, FRANK J.
(1828–1919)
landscape gardener

Frank Jesup Scott was born in Columbia, South Carolina, the son of Jesup Wakeman and Susan Scott. He attended an academy in Maumee, Ohio, and then, at some time between the fall of 1850 and the summer of 1852, studied landscape architecture in the Newburgh, New York, office of Andrew Jackson Downing*. He later testified to the importance of Downing's influence by dedicating his best-known book, *The Art of Beautifying Suburban Home Grounds of Small Extent*, to the memory of his friend and teacher.

In 1852, Scott returned to Toledo, Ohio, where his father had a prosperous real estate business. There he

"Art and Nature." From *The Art of Beautifying Suburban Home Grounds of Small Extent*, 1870.

"Neighboring Improvements." From *The Art of Beautifying Suburban Home Grounds of Small Extent,* 1870.

established an office as an architect and landscape gardener and continued to practice until 1859, when he joined his father and brother in the family's commercial activities. There are no records of Scott's practicing architecture after 1859, but he continued to think and write about the proper design of the domestic landscape.

Scott's significance in the history of landscape architecture rests on *The Art of Beautifying Suburban Home Grounds*, which was published in 1870. Scott described it as the first book "devoted entirely to the arts of suburban-home embellishment" and expressed the hope that it would "aid persons of moderate income, who know little of the arts of decorative gardening, to beautify their homes." Because the house lots of the emerging middle class were limited in extent, Scott advised readers to "make gems of home beauty on a small scale." The established principles of landscape art may have been applicable to parks, cemeteries, and large estates, but for the suburban home he advocated a type of design he termed "decorative gardening," which he defined as the "art of picture making and picture framing, by means of the varied forms of vegetable growth." Scott also called for the development of unifying plans for neighboring properties, which would not be separated by fences or hedge screens and thus would have the appearance of a large residential park.

Scott's concept of decorative gardening considered the landscape the frame of the house, and he adopted the gardenesque style that had been developed in England by John Claudius Loudon—the introduction of beds of flowering plants in the lawn and along paths, topiary, and decorative plantings at the foundation to unite house and garden. Together, he asserted, decorative gardening and competent architecture would produce homes with "an air of extent and domesticity that so many of the box-like suburban houses of the day are totally wanting in."

The first part of *Suburban Home Grounds* is filled with commonsense advice about planning gardens and contains twenty-nine plates with explanatory texts to instruct readers on how best to apply the principles of landscape taste articulated in the opening chapters. In a lengthy review, Frederick Law Olmsted Sr.* observed that Scott's advice was "copious and distinct, and may be understood by most town-bred men," while the sketches and plans were "intelligible and instructive." The second and slightly longer part of the volume presents descriptions, with numerous illustrations, of some 700 species and varieties of trees and shrubs, with a text, evocative of Downing's *Treatise on the Theory and Practice of Landscape Gardening* (1841), that describes the aesthetic qualities of trees in the landscape. "Of each part of Mr. Scott's work," Olmsted concluded, "it may be said that it is the most valuable of its class that has been published in America since Mr. Downing's 'Landscape Gardening.' "

Scott, Frank J. *The Art of Beautifying Suburban Home Grounds of Small Extent*. New York, 1870; reprinted in 1873, 1881, 1886. A major statement of the principles of domestic design in the post-Civil War years, illustrated by approximately 200 engravings.

David Schuyler

SEARS, THOMAS W.
(1880–1966)
landscape architect

Thomas Warren Sears was born in the suburban community of Brookline, Massachusetts, just a year before Frederick Law Olmsted Sr.* permanently established his home and office there. Perhaps the experience of growing up in a city and environs so transformed by Olmsted's visionary design legacy influenced Sears's decision to pursue a career in landscape architecture, at a time when the profession in this country was still emerging as an academic discipline. He had a privileged education, matriculating at Harvard in 1899 after graduation from the Volkmann School in Boston. After completing his bachelor of arts degree in 1903, he continued at Harvard

"Sketch of Garden Fountain for Miss Eliza Jenkins, Baltimore,"
by Sears & Wendell. Courtesy Smithsonian Institution,
Archives of American Gardens.

bined at least two extended European study trips with
scholarly photographic projects (John Nolen* was his
companion on a trip in 1905). His photographs consti-
tuted the entire survey for *Parish Churches of England*,
published in 1915, and in the same year, photographs of
the estate of Prince Hermann von Pückler-Muskau in
Germany were published in Samuel Parsons Jr.'s* *Art of
Landscape Architecture*. The quality of his landscape
photography undoubtedly contributed, in fact, to the
success Sears enjoyed in getting his own design work
published in books and magazine articles; twice in his
career, in 1941 and 1953, entire issues of *Architecture
and Design* were devoted to a review of his projects. This
visibility, in its turn, enhanced his national reputation as
a high-profile landscape architect with a flourishing
design practice—a perception ratified by his being made
a Fellow of the American Society of Landscape Architects in 1921.

Sears may have worked for a brief period in the
Brookline office of the Olmsted Brothers*, after which
he practiced in a partnership in Providence. There is also
evidence of a second partnership—the firm of Sears &
Wendell—whose name appears on one of the first drawings related to Sears's employment, in 1915, as designer
of formal gardens for Reynolda, the thousand-acre R. J.
Reynolds estate in Winston-Salem, North Carolina, and
also in the credits for three projects illustrated in landscape architect Ruth Dean's* *Livable House: Its Garden*
of 1917. The same volume also illustrates a residential
project attributed to Sears alone, however, and all subsequent drawings related to his work of many years at
Reynolda and elsewhere are so attributed. By 1917 he
had established the Philadelphia office in which he practiced independently for the remainder of his professional life.

During World War I, Sears, at the invitation of the
federal government, contributed his services to the war
effort. He laid out temporary quarters for troops at locations in South Carolina and Michigan, worked in association with the Detroit architect Albert Kahn on plans
for Langley Field in Hampton Roads, Virginia, and had
additional responsibilities for a housing project at the
Bethlehem Steel factory in Pennsylvania and a navy yard
in Philadelphia.

Philadelphia was the professional home of a number
of important American architects of this period, and Sears
was accorded respect by many of these influential men.
Charles Barton Keene, for example, architect for the
Reynolda project, probably recommended his Philadel-

in the Lawrence Scientific School, from which he
received a bachelor of science in landscape architecture
in 1906.

Sears's training had included courses in photography, which became a lifelong avocation. Sears was a
prize-winning member of the Harvard Camera Club,
had his work exhibited while still a student, and com-

Garden Walk, Jenkins estate, Baltimore. Courtesy Smithsonian Institution, Archives of American Gardens.

phia colleague to Mrs. Reynolds when she was looking for someone to replace the firm that had produced the master plan for her estate. This opportunity provided Sears with one of the most important commissions of his career, and one that was particularly amenable to the design strategies he favored.

Described by those who knew him as a "gentleman of the old school," a shy and reserved man whose speech and manner bore traces of his birth near Boston and his "proper" upbringing, Sears was similarly conservative in his approach to practice. Although he took advantage of opportunities to take on other kinds of projects, and although his career extended well into the period during which the modern movement influenced American landscape architecture, he was best known as a designer

of highly refined traditional gardens and grounds for wealthy clients, primarily in East Coast locations, north and south. An article published in a 1921 issue of *Garden Magazine* used a series of his photographs to illustrate the desirable qualities of "gardenesque" residential landscape design, in which plantings displaying a handsome blend of forms, colors, and textures create the illusion of artless natural beauty. In this respect Sears shared the sensibility of his contemporaries Charles Platt* and Beatrix Farrand*, although the preponderance of his residential projects were of more modest suburban scale than that of Reynolda.

In 1920, at the age of forty, Sears married and settled in suburban Ardmore, commuting to his Philadelphia office. He frequently published photographs of his

Flower garden, Reynolda, Winston-Salem, North Carolina, 1995. Photo Carol Betsch.

Reynolda House, R. J. and Katherine Reynolds estate, Winston-Salem, North Carolina. Courtesy Smithsonian Institution, Archives of American Gardens.

own domestic landscape, a work of many years in which he took keen professional pride. Many of his private clients lived in Main Line Philadelphia communities and at least two dozen others, over the course of years, in Winston-Salem, where his success at Reynolda garnered him civic projects as well. In addition to Reynolda, two other private estate gardens designed by Sears—Lammot du Pont Copeland's Mt. Cuba in Greenville, Delaware, and Mrs. Lewis R. Parsons's Appleford in Villanova, Pennsylvania—are now managed as institutions providing opportunities for public visitation.

Among the most important public commissions to which Sears contributed were the Colonial Revival gardens at Pennsbury Manor, home of William Penn; Washington Square in Philadelphia; and Pennsylvania's Valley Forge Park Chapel and Cemetery. He was a strenuous advocate for the cause of public parks, serving for many years on the Montgomery County Park Board. Sears retired from practice in 1961, in the ninth decade of his life.

American Society of Landscape Architects: Illustrations of Work of Members. New York: House of J. Hayden Twiss, 1931 and 1934. Both volumes contain photographs of landscape designs by Sears.

Architecture and Design 5 (September 1941) and 17 (November 1953). Issues "devoted to the work of Thomas W. Sears, Landscape Architect."

Mayer, Barbara. *Reynolda: A History of an American Country House.* Winston-Salem, N.C.: John F. Blair for Reynolda House Museum of American Art, 1997. A study of the evolution of the Reynolda property, including discussion of Sears's contribution in providing design services for specific areas of the estate.

Reinhard Schuetze. City Park, Denver, Colorado.
Photo Don Etter.

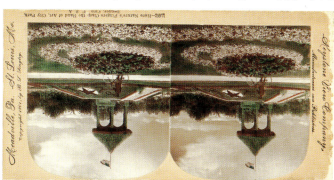

Reinhard Schuetze. Flower display in central garden, City Park, Denver, Colorado. Stereograph by Keystone View Company. Private collection.

William Saunders. Garrett Park, Montgomery County, Maryland.
Courtesy Montgomery County Department of Parks & Planning.

Ellen Biddle Shipman. English Garden, Stan Hywet Hall. Akron, Ohio.
Photo Carol Betsch.

Thomas W. Sears. Reynolda House.
Winston-Salem, North Carolina.
Photo Carol Betsch.

Philip T. Shutze. Patterson-Carr residence. Atlanta, Georgia. Photo Spencer Tunnell.

Philip T. Shutze. Swan House. Atlanta, Georgia. Photo Charles A. Birnbaum.

Ossian Cole Simonds.
Graceland Cemetery, Chicago, Illinois.
Photo Charles A. Birnbaum.

James C. Sidney. Woodlawn Cemetery, Bronx, New York.
Photo Dominick Totino. From *Woodlawn Remembers. Courtesy* The Woodlawn Cemetery.

Although his most of his office records were destroyed after Sears's death, drawings and plans for a number of specific projects have survived. The archives of the Reynolda House Museum of American Art and the Z. Smith Reynolds Library of Wake Forest University, for example, have records relating to Reynolda and other projects in Winston-Salem. In 1992, Mrs. Eleanor Tibbetts, a daughter of Thomas Sears, do-

nated to the Archives of American Gardens of the Smithsonian Institution her father's personal collection of almost 5,000 glass slides representing views of landscapes Sears visited as well as views and plans of his own design work.

_____

Catherine Howett

SESSIONS, KATE OLIVIA
(1857–1940)
horticulturist, nursery owner

Kate Sessions was born in San Francisco and raised in Oakland. While in high school, she developed an interest in collecting and pressing plants, and she enrolled in the science program of the University of California at Berkeley, where she focused on chemistry and was, reportedly, the first woman to graduate with a science degree (1881).

Sessions worked briefly as a schoolteacher in San Diego before becoming a co-owner of that city's oldest nursery. Her fifty-five-year horticulture career began with a small flower shop in the downtown district and some growing fields across the bay in Coronado. As the city grew, Sessions operated a succession of nurseries at the edges of prime urban development. Her second nursery was at the then-barren northeastern corner of the city park (later named Balboa Park), where she received free water and the title of City Gardener in return for providing free trees for parks and streets. When the city began to develop its park for the 1915–1916 Panama Pacific International Exposition, Sessions moved her nursery to what would become the suburb of Mission Hills. Then, as that neighborhood became settled, she began yet another nursery in the more distant suburb of Pacific Beach. She also co-owned a tract of palm-growing land in Lemon Grove, to supply the increasing demand for the Queen palm (*Arecastrum romanzoffianum*), which she had popularized as a street tree. In these various enterprises, Sessions sometimes worked with her father, Josiah, and her brother, Frank, and, for a short time, she hired Frank's son, Milton, as a partner. It was Sessions herself, however, who guided her business, developed civic contacts, and maintained the intellectual integrity that led to her being

awarded the Frank N. Meyer Medal in 1939, the first woman to be so honored.

During her many years as the central figure of San Diego's horticultural circles, Sessions played numerous roles in an ever-widening community of serious gardeners in southern California. She introduced many plants, including the now ubiquitous twisted juniper, a host of drought-tolerant plants, and several native specimens

Kate Sessions in Balboa Park explaining the shrubs, 1923. Courtesy San Diego Historical Society, Photograph Collection.

from the nearby chaparral. She advised local home gardeners—many of whom were new to the coastal desert climate—and wrote articles for newspapers and regional garden magazines. She corresponded with botanists, plant pathologists, experimental growers, and naturalists such as Alice Eastwood, David Fairchild, Francesco Franceschi, Hugh Evans, Bill Hertrich, Lester Rowntree*, and others. She planned and installed landscapes, using informal methods and rarely committing her designs to paper. She taught classes for children and adults and led botanical walks. She also helped establish a cut-flower trade in poinsettias and statice, and tested the performance of plants new to San Diego's many microclimates, encouraging her gardening friends to do the same. She co-founded the San Diego Floral Association with Alfred D. Robinson and others, and contributed often to the organization's magazine, *California Garden*. Sessions was also active and outspoken in city beautification efforts, and became known as the "Mother of Balboa Park," for her years of garden-making at the site of two San Diego expositions.

California Garden 44 (Autumn 1953). Special issue devoted to Sessions.

McPhail, Elizabeth. *Kate Sessions—Pioneer Horticulturist*. San Diego: San Diego Historical Society, 1976. Definitive biography of Sessions, with photographs, notes, plant list, index.

Padilla, Victoria. *Southern California Gardens*. 1961. Rpt. Berkeley: University of California Press, 1997. An illustrated history of pioneer "plantsmen" in California; includes bibliographical sketch of Sessions, photograph.

Carol Greentree

SHELTON, LOUISE
(1867–1934)
author

Louise Shelton was born in New York City but lived much of her life in Morristown, New Jersey, the ancestral home of her mother's family and the location of many significant gardens of the Country Place era. There she created a two-part career. Shelton devoted much time to the societies she founded for the protection of children and for the humane treatment of animals. She also designed a garden at her Morristown home, and then used the experience to write her first two garden books and to compile two editions of a third book, cementing her reputation as an arbiter of taste in the landscape design of a pivotal era.

Shelton's first book, *The Seasons in a Flower Garden*, initially appeared in 1906 and was revised and reprinted for two decades. It is a simple how-to manual, suited to the many new gardeners whose ranks grew steadily early in the twentieth century. *Continuous Bloom in America*, her second book, was published in 1915 and expands on the same themes. A practical work, it discusses "where, when and what to plant" in the world of annuals and perennials. It includes suggested designs for flower beds with lists of plant material, good evidence of what was popularly grown in this period. As did many advanced amateur gardeners of the time, Shelton preferred mixed groupings of plants arranged in beds of formal outline, whose designs originated in architecture or geometry.

Shelton is, however, best known for the two editions of her most important work, *Beautiful Gardens in America* (1915 and 1924). This landmark book portrays hundreds of gardens throughout the United States and constitutes an invaluable visual record of landscape design in the 1910s and 1920s. Most of the gardens depicted in the two editions belonged to wealthy families and represent the characteristic landscape styles of the Country Place era. The owners are identified, as are the names and locations of their estates. The names of photographers also appear; those of landscape architects do not. The photographs are black and white, with a small group of color illustrations in each volume.

Estate of Mr. and Mrs. Edward B. Renwick, Short Hills, New Jersey. From *Beautiful Gardens in America*, 1924.

Both editions went through several printings. The second edition added 195 new illustrations and dropped others, so it is quite different from its predecessor. One can get a good idea of the evolution of landscape design in America by comparing the photographs in the two editions. Shelton was assisted in her decision making for the second edition by Louisa Yeomans (Mrs. Francis) King*, Mrs. Edward Harding, Mrs. Banyer Clarkson, and Mrs. Percy Kennaday. Each was well known in the garden world of the day and lent the book authority.

Shelton did little writing for magazines. Her major influence was through the judgment she exercised in choosing the gardens that appeared in *Beautiful Gardens in America*.

tographs of significant American gardens, largely in the East, with brief introduction to each geographical section; second edition (1924), dropped some gardens and added others, contains over 250 photographs, and is more diverse geographically.

Shelton, Louise. *Continuous Bloom in America*. New York: Charles Scribner's Sons, 1915. A basic how-to book for the flower garden; includes flower garden photographs and some suggested plans.

Shelton, Louise. *The Seasons in a Flower Garden*. New York: Charles Scribner's Sons, 1906. Very basic how-to and very popular; some photographs and one plan in early editions; three subsequent editions.

Shelton, Louise. *Beautiful Gardens in America*. New York: Charles Scribner's Sons, 1915. Almost 200 pho-

---

Virginia Lopez Begg

SHIPMAN, ELLEN BIDDLE
(1869–1950)
landscape architect

Ellen Biddle was born in Philadelphia. Specializing in the design and planting of small residential gardens, she was one of several pioneer women landscape architects who changed the character of American gardens in the early twentieth century. In a 1938 interview, she stated: "Until women took up landscaping, gardening in this country was at its lowest ebb. The renaissance of the art was due largely to the fact that women, instead of working over their boards, used plants as if they were painting pictures as an artist." Shipman, unlike her well-known colleagues Beatrix Farrand* and Marian Coffin*, developed her own abilities in planting design through many years of hands-on gardening before she became a professional.

Ellen Biddle grew up on the American frontier, in Texas and the Arizona Territory where her father, Colonel James Biddle, was a career soldier. When she was an adolescent she returned East to attend boarding school in Baltimore, where her interests in art and architecture emerged. After briefly attending the Harvard Annex (predecessor to Radcliffe College), she left to marry Louis Shipman, a playwright who was attending Harvard. The Shipmans lived in Cornish, New Hampshire, where their friends included the sculptor Augustus Saint-Gaudens, who had founded an artists' colony there, his niece Rose Standish Nichols*, the painter Thomas Dewing, the illustrator Maxfield Parrish, and the architect Charles Platt*. Shipman's own gardens, first at Poins House and then at Brook Place, were greatly influenced by the nationally acclaimed flower gardens of the colony. She turned to landscape architecture in 1910 after a failed marriage left her with sole responsibility for three young children. Platt, who had admired her planting expertise as well as her design skills in remodeling her home, provided informal training in design and construction.

By 1912 she was collaborating with Platt on gardens across the country, from Seattle to Grosse Pointe, Cleveland, and Philadelphia. Sometimes she replanted existing gardens, but otherwise she had full design responsibility. Shipman's early independent commissions in the New England area derived more from the prevailing Colonial Revival style than from Platt's Italianate idiom. Shipman's typical walled garden formula, which varied little throughout her career, consisted of rectangular beds, axial paths, and a central sundial or fountain, enclosed by a curtain of evergreens. Small ornamental trees, espaliered fruit trees, clipped evergreens, peony or wisteria standards, and figurative statuary were some of her hallmarks. Elegant architectural features, such as dovecotes, pergolas, and arbors, served to enhance her inimitable flower borders.

In the early 1920s Shipman moved her office to Beekman Place in New York City, where she had a flourishing practice until the 1940s, designing nearly 600 gardens. She hired women only, preferring graduates of the Lowthorpe School of Landscape Architecture for Women, in Groton, Massachusetts. By the mid-1920s, when she was no longer working with Platt, Shipman was executing larger, more complex commissions that necessitated a staff of up to a dozen women. During her busiest years, her gardens were clustered on Long Island's Gold Coast and in Grosse Pointe, Greenwich, Winston-Salem, Houston, and northern Ohio.

In 1933 she was named "Dean of Women Landscape Architects" by *House and Garden* in recognition of her contribution to garden design as well as her dedication in training women in the field. Dorothy May Anderson, Edith Schryver*, and Elizabeth Leonard Strang are among the well-known landscape architects who worked with Shipman before opening their own offices. In her later years Shipman lectured widely, mainly to

Ellen Shipman. Courtesy Nancy Angell Streeter.

Brook Place, Plainfield, N.H. Courtesy
Nancy Angell Streeter.

Plan of Samuel A. Salvage estate, Glen Head, New York, 1926. Courtesy Rare and Manuscript Collections, Carl A. Kroch Library,
Cornell University, Ithaca, N.Y.

Samuel A. Salvage estate, Glen Head, New York, 1926. Courtesy Rare and Manuscript Collections, Carl A. Kroch Library, Cornell University, Ithaca, N.Y.

Samuel A. Salvage estate, Glen Head, New York, 1926. Courtesy Rare and Manuscript Collections, Carl A. Kroch Library, Cornell University, Ithaca, N.Y.

English Garden, Stan Hywet Hall, F. A. Seiberling estate, Akron, Ohio, 1997. Photo Carol Betsch.

garden club audiences who for the most part were her clientele. Unusually, Shipman never joined the American Society of Landscape Architects, finding membership unnecessary for her career. She retired in the late 1940s, at which time she made arrangements for her archives to go to Cornell University.

The basic design structure of her gardens, formulated during her training with Platt, derived from the axial relationship of the garden and the house. The gardens were laid out as a series of "outdoor rooms," each with its own character. Shipman was equally adept at laying out entire estates as well as replanting gardens designed by other landscape architects. Her professional paths frequently crossed with landscape architects Warren Manning*, James Leal Greenleaf*, Jens Jensen*, and Arthur Shurcliff*, and architects Clark & Arms, Roger Bullard, Alfred Hopkins, Mott Schmidt, William and

Geoffrey Platt, and others associated with the Country House era.

Most of the significant projects from her early career, such as the Pruyn garden (Long Island), Croft garden (Greenwich, Conn.), and Magee garden (Mount Kisco, N.Y.), are no longer extant. The best-known examples from her mature period are Rynwood, the Samuel Salvage estate (Glen Head, N.Y.); Penwood, the Carll Tucker estate (Mount Kisco); and Rose Terrace, the Mabel Dodge estate (Grosse Pointe, Mich.). Lake Shore Boulevard (Grosse Pointe) and Aetna Life (Hartford, Conn.) are rare examples of nonresidential commissions. Among Shipman's projects that are open to the public are the Grosse Pointe War Memorial (1917, the former Russell Alger estate); Chatham Manor, Fredericksburg, Virginia (1924, now a national military park); the English Garden at Stan Hywet Hall, Akron, Ohio

(1929); the Sarah P. Duke Memorial Gardens, Duke University, (1936); and Longue Vue Gardens, New Orleans (1939).

Close, Leslie Rose. "Ellen Biddle Shipman." In *American Landscape Architecture: Designers and Places*, ed. William Tishler. Washington, D.C.: Preservation Press, 1989. An illustrated overview of Shipman's career.

Tankard, Judith B. "Ellen Biddle Shipman's New England Gardens." *Arnoldia* 57, no. 1 (1997), 2–11. Discussion of several commissions in Massachusetts and Brook Place in New Hampshire.

Tankard, Judith B. *The Gardens of Ellen Biddle Shipman*. New York: Sagapress/Abrams, 1996. Detailed study of Shipman's life and career; richly illustrated with plans, drawings, historical photographs by Mattie Edwards Hewitt and others, and new photographs of two extant gardens in black-and-white and color; introduction by Leslie Rose Close sets Shipman in context of history of women in landscape architecture.

Judith B. Tankard

SHURCLIFF, ARTHUR ASAHEL (SHURTLEFF)
(1870–1957)
landscape architect, planner, educator

Arthur Asahel Shurtleff was born in Boston. He changed his name to Shurcliff in 1930 in order, he wrote, to conform to the ancient family spelling. He grew up in a loving environment where his parents both encouraged his development in the arts and in handcraft, particularly woodworking, and fostered his lifelong appreciation of nature. Early on he was deeply influenced by the writings of Emerson and Thoreau. When he graduated from the Massachusetts Institute of Technology (1894) with a degree in mechanical engineering, he was intended for the family business of inventing and producing fine surgical instruments, but Shurcliff had already decided that his love of outdoor activities and the "planning and construction for the scenes of daily life" far outweighed his interest in engineering. After a lengthy consultation with Frederick Law Olmsted Sr.* and the rising star of his Brookline, Massachusetts, office, Charles Eliot*, Shurcliff continued his education at Harvard University under Eliot's tutelage, piecing together courses at the college and the Bussey Institution, as no landscape architecture program existed at the time, and graduating with a second B.S. in 1896.

Shurcliff then began his professional career in the Olmsted offices, where he spent eight years acquiring a broad and sophisticated knowledge of landscape architecture. There, before his untimely death in 1897, Eliot

Arthur Shurtleff (Shurcliff). From *Country Life in America*, 1921.

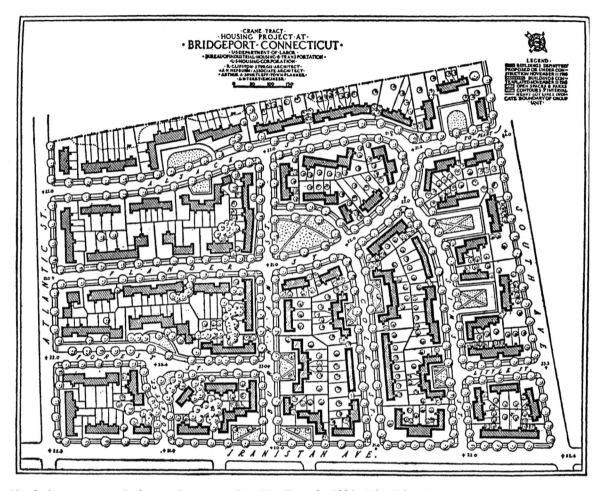

Plan for housing project, Bridgeport, Connecticut. From *New Towns for Old*, by John Nolen, 1927.

deeply influenced Shurcliff's perceptions in all areas of landscape practice. His elegant, simple, 1887 design for the Newburyport, Massachusetts, town common, left unfinished at his demise, was completed by Shurcliff, influencing his subsequent restorations of the commons in Weston, Massachusetts, and Sandwich, New Hampshire.

In 1898, Shurcliff took the first of many trips abroad, because Eliot had emphasized the necessity of studying planning in specific, significant places as essential to the education of a landscape architect. In 1899, Shurcliff assisted Frederick Law Olmsted Jr.* in founding the country's first four-year landscape program, at Harvard University, where he taught until 1906.

Upon establishing his own practice in 1904, Shurcliff initially emphasized his experience as a town planner. Within two years he had prepared groundbreaking highway studies for the Boston Metropolitan Improvement Commission and the Massachusetts State Highway Commission. During his long and prolific career, he made extensive plans for numerous towns surrounding Boston. He designed industrial communities including Bemis, Tennessee (1900–1905), for the Bemis Bag Company and sections of Hopedale, Massachusetts (1910+), for the Draper Company. His landscape design for a World War I housing project in Bridgeport, Connecticut, is cited repeatedly in planning histories as a model be-

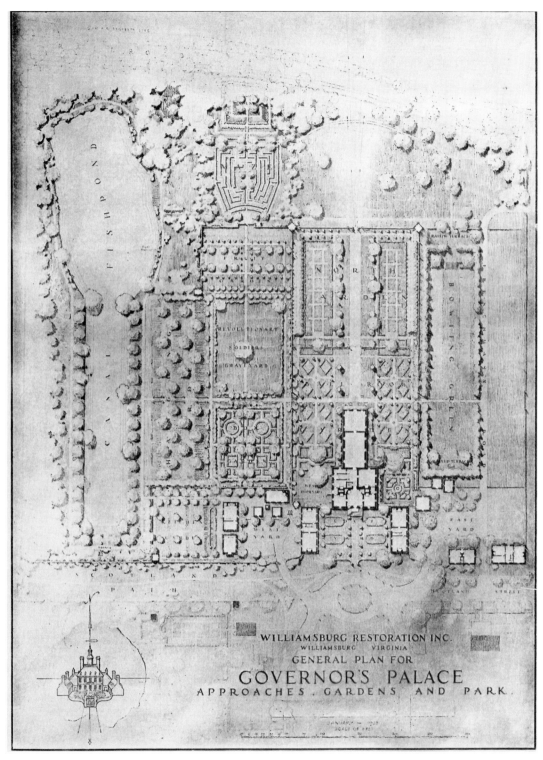

"General Plan for Governor's Palace, Approaches, Gardens and Park," Williamsburg, Virginia. From *Architectural Record*, December 1935.

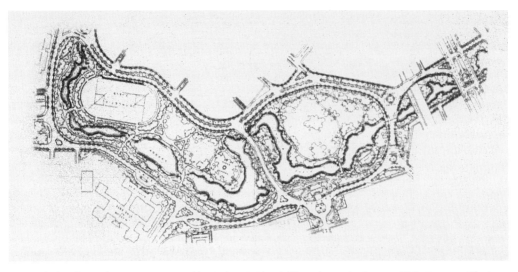

"General Plan" for Back Bay Fens, prepared by Arthur A. Shurtleff, Landscape Architect, 1926. Courtesy Charles A. Birnbaum.

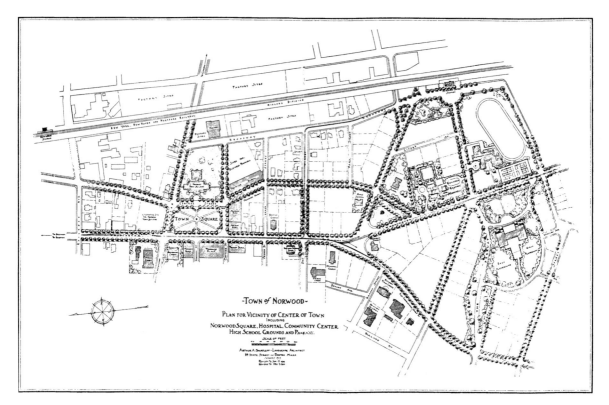

"Town of Norwood, Plan for Vicinity of Center of Town," 1917. From *Town of Norwood, Massachusetts, Report of the Planning Board to the Citizens of the Town, 1923.* Courtesy Charles A. Birnbaum.

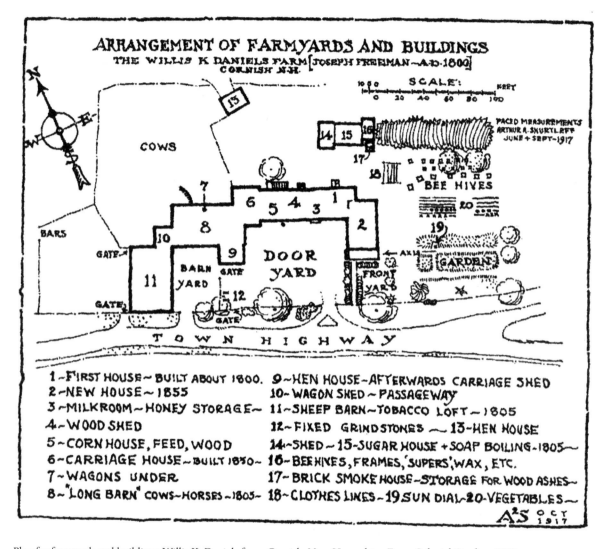

Plan for farmyards and buildings, Willis K. Daniels farm, Cornish, New Hampshire. From *Colonial Gardens*, 1929.

cause it contained "street systems following the contours of the land, the excellent spacing and placing of structures, the grouping of public and semipublic buildings, the preservation of attractive natural features, and the provision of recreational space wherever possible," according to the historian Mel Scott. Shurcliff designed planned communities, including a 46-acre tract in Fort Wayne, Indiana, and Oak Hill Village in Newton Center, Massachusetts.

For several decades Shurcliff served as a consultant to the Boston Parks Department and as chief landscape architect to the Metropolitan District Commission. His public works included dams and reservoirs. He designed hundreds of recreational spaces in and around Boston, including playgrounds and parts of the Franklin Park Zoo. His park work incorporated projects both large and small. The Paul Revere Mall in Boston's North End is an irregular urban site for which he designed a small gem of a park that serves its community as well now as it did on its construction in 1935. His large-scale Charles River Basin project, a park designed in the 1930s along the river that separates Cambridge and Boston, included a lagoon, a music shell, and curving artificial islands constructed to serve as havens for small craft. In the 1940s a second lagoon was added when he designed the contiguous Storrow Drive, still an essential means of moving traffic around the periphery of Boston. His private commissions included hundreds of gardens large and small, as well as work on college campuses, including Amherst, Brown, and Wellesley, and secondary schools such as Deerfield, St. Paul's, and Groton.

In 1928, Shurcliff undertook the largest and arguably the single most important project of his career when he was hired to assist the architectural firm of Perry, Shaw & Hepburn in John D. Rockefeller Jr.'s recreation and restoration of Williamsburg, Virginia. In his capacity as chief landscape architect for Colonial Williamsburg, from its inception until he retired in 1941, Shurcliff combined his avocational interests in American history, handcraft, and old gardens with his professional proficiency in planning and design. His pioneering restoration work was based on systematic study of Southern places and significant research into eighteenth-century landscape and horticulture in order to provide what he insisted was to be the most authentic reproduction possible. Included in that exploration were trips to England, where rural landscapes and farms, he believed, preserved the authentic looks and habits of those in eighteenth-century America. His engineering background proved invaluable in projects such as the scenic Colonial Parkway, which he convinced the National Park Service to depress, rather than run straight through the middle of town. Later he aided in laying out Old Sturbridge Village in Sturbridge, Massachusetts.

An early member of the American Society of Landscape Architects, Shurcliff was elected a Fellow in 1905, eventually serving two terms as president (1928–1932). He was a founding member of the American City Planning Institute and served on the Boston Art Commission.

Shurcliff's significance in the history of landscape architecture begins with his place among the first generation of American-trained practitioners who established the profession in the country. In his own practice he integrated his training as an engineer with the aesthetic education he had received at Harvard and during his eight years of work with the Olmsteds. In Boston he gained experience in park work and planning, and as head of the landscape segment of the Colonial Williamsburg restoration he combined all those influences with his interests in history and handcraft. Shurcliff's personal background and professional training gave him a deep sensitivity to and affinity for the natural world, which he integrated into his work.

Shurcliff, Arthur A. "Mount Vernon and Other Colonial Places in the South" and "Gardens of Old Salem and the New England Colonies." In American Society of Landscape Architects, *Colonial Gardens: The Landscape Architecture of George Washington's Time.* Washington, D.C.: George Washington Bicentennial Commission, 1932, 11–20, 45–53. Two articles reflecting Shurcliff's approach to garden restoration.

Shurcliff, Arthur A. "Municipal Improvements in Boston and Germany." In American Society of Landscape Architects, *Transactions, 1899–1908*, ed. Harold A. Caparn, James Sturgis Pray*, and Downing Vaux*. Harrisburg: Mount Pleasant Press, 1912, 111–114. An early treatise indicating Shurcliff's growing familiarity with European planning as he sought models for the rapid growth in American cities as well as his keen understanding that rigid adherence to the grid should be avoided in urban planning.

Shurcliff, Arthur A. "Park Scenery in Relation to the Fine Arts and to Physical Recreation." *American Magazine of Art*, August 1926, 391–402. An article reflecting the era's increasing demands on public spaces to provide recreational facilities and the need for planners of that time to accommodate the new requirements while endeavoring to maintain the integrity of parks as originally planned.

Elizabeth Hope Cushing

SHUTZE, PHILIP TRAMMELL
(1890–1982)
architect, landscape designer

Philip Trammell Shutze was born in Columbus, a small south Georgia town. His paternal grandfather was a German immigrant; his father was a bank officer who was shot and killed on the banking floor when Shutze was only ten years old. After this tragedy, the family moved briefly to Atlanta, then to West Point, Georgia, near the Alabama border. In 1908, Shutze, his mother, and his two sisters moved back to Atlanta, where Shutze entered the Georgia College of Technology.

Shutze graduated from Georgia Tech in 1912 with a bachelor of science in architecture. Following the advice of his part-time employers, architects Neel Reid and Hal Hentz, he enrolled at Columbia University and received his bachelor of architecture in 1913. He then returned to Atlanta, was listed as a faculty member at Georgia Tech, and worked for Hentz, Reid & Adler.

Shutze entered the competition for the Rome Prize, won, and went to the American Academy in Rome in 1915. World War I only briefly interrupted his life there. His years at the academy strikingly marked his whole career in architecture. At that time, academy Fellows were led through a rigorously structured four-year curriculum that stressed travel, archaeological research, and projects where collaboration with painters, sculptors, and landscape architects was essential. Shutze relished this association with the allied disciplines, particularly with landscape architecture.

In 1919, Shutze returned to Atlanta and rejoined Hentz, Reid & Adler. He then moved on to New York City in 1923 to work in the office of Murray Burrell Hoffman and the office of Mott Schmidt, but returned to Atlanta in 1926 to fill the void left by the death of Neel Reid. The firm was renamed Hentz, Adler & Shutze, and Shutze worked there until his retirement in 1958.

It was entirely possible for all the major events of an Atlanta citizen's life to occur in a building designed by the firm. From Emory Hospital (1917) to Patterson's Funeral Home (1927); from Boys' High School (1921) to several buildings at the University of Georgia (in Athens), and Emory University; from Rich's Department Store (1922) to the Howard Theater (1919); and from Glenn Memorial Church (1929) to the East Lake Country Club (1926), as well as downtown office buildings and branch banks, buildings by the firm populate the city and set a high standard.

The firm always had a good number of residential commissions, however, and Shutze was responsible for some of the most distinguished integrations of buildings and landscape. Throughout his career, he sought to produce designs in which the houses were intricately linked to their sites. In his early work this union was achieved through the use of devices such as the extended axis, the repetition of architectonic planes brought forward of the principal building and in the use of architectonic elements in the landscape.

Among Shutze's projects that incorporate a significant landscape element, the most famous is Swan House (1926–1928), built as the private residence of Mr. and Mrs. Edward Inman in the Atlanta suburb of Buckhead. The house and grounds were purchased by the Atlanta Historical Society in 1966 as a house museum. The

Philip Shutze in Rome, c. 1910s. Courtesy Atlanta History Center.

Boxwood garden, Swan House, Atlanta, c. 1930s. Courtesy Atlanta History Center.

house is an essay in the English Baroque Revival and incorporates the garden design ethos Shutze developed traveling in Italy. The front yard includes a series of slopes and walled terraces culminating in a five-basin cascading fountain that recalls the Villa Corsini on the Janiculum in Rome.

The 1939 amphitheater of Glenn Memorial Church is another well-known example of Shutze's work. It incorporates terracing, crosswalks and ramps; the central axis of this space is marked by an elaborate urn and cartouche that create an effective stage set and focal point.

The landscape at the Goodrum-Rushton House won Honorable Mention in the New York Architectural League 1931 competition. The original gardens included a formal boxwood garden within a serpentine wall, a camellia house, and a small garden amphitheater.

The Patterson-Carr house and garden of 1940 represents one of the most highly integrated house and garden complexes Shutze ever produced. The design is American vernacular in style, its additive forms spreading across a largely flat to gently sloping site. From the fence-lined drive to the interrelated series of courts opening from the principal rooms, Shutze achieved his goal of "a garden view from every room." The house has been frequently published and is well maintained.

Other private commissions in Atlanta where Shutze's garden design and site planning skills are evident include the Maddox-Festa, the Ben Smith, the English-Chambers, and the Hirschberg residences. Outside Atlanta, the Hightower residence in Thomaston includes significant gardens that have been widely published.

Vista, Swan House, 1998. Photo Charles A. Birnbaum.

Patterson-Carr residence, Atlanta.
Photo Spencer Tunnell.

Shutze was made a Fellow in the American Institute of Architects in 1951. Although he maintained his office until shortly before his death, he had effectively retired by 1958. In the remaining twenty-seven years of his life Shutze concentrated on collecting rare books, porcelain, and American antiques. He continued to correspond with close friends from the American Academy such as muralist Allyn Cox and Raymond Kennedy. He offered advice to friends with questions about architecture and was contacted occasionally by people interested in commissioning design work, although this he generally declined.

Dowling, Elizabeth Meredith. *American Classicist: The Architecture of Philip Trammell Shutze.* New York: Rizzoli International, 1989. Most comprehensive treatment of Shutze's career and life with excellent illustrations and photographs.

Shutze, Philip Trammell. *Memoirs of the American Academy in Rome.* New York, 1917. Discussion of archaeological restoration for the Circular Pavilion at Hadrian's Villa; one of very few examples of Shutze's academic writing.

Tunnell, Spencer, II. "Stylistic Progression versus Site Planning Methodology: An Analysis of the Residential Architecture of Philip Trammell Shutze." Masters thesis, University of Virginia, 1989. Discusses innovative site planning techniques employed by Shutze as generator of garden forms, as well as providing a historical and stylistic context for his architecture.

Shutze's architectural drawings, library, manuscript collection, and decorative arts collection are housed at the Atlanta History Center and are accessible to researchers.

Spencer Tunnell

SIDNEY, JAMES C.
(1819[?]–1881)
draftsman, mapmaker, civil engineer, landscape gardener, cemetery designer

The facts about James Sidney's childhood and adolescence remain obscure. Born in England, he had emigrated to the United States by the time he reached his mid-twenties. The earliest references to his professional life place him in Philadelphia after 1845, working as a draftsman for John Jay Smith*, Librarian of the city's Library Company. Sidney's initial work under Smith apparently included such simple tasks as tracing old maps for reproduction. Sidney was probably overqualified for these assignments, however, because Smith retrospectively categorized him as a "clever civil engineer" in this period.

In 1846, John Smith and his son Robert established a printing company geared toward the needs of "artists, architects, surveyors, and draughtsmen," a short-lived venture for which Sidney drew several maps. At the same time, he tried his hand at architecture, preparing six plates for John Smith and Thomas U. Walter's *Two Hundred Designs for Cottages and Villas* (1846), and designing a Philadelphia-area school. The following year, Sidney proved a major asset to Robert Smith's next enterprise, map publishing; the firm's first work was *Sid-*

ney's Map of Ten Miles [A]round. A detailed depiction of Philadelphia and environs, it earned Sidney recognition, and he continued to chart the area over the next two years.

Surveying also led Sidney toward landscape design. In 1849 managers of Laurel Hill, Philadelphia's first rural cemetery, hired him to lay out a southern addition to the grounds. Their decision was surely influenced by the cemetery's founder, John Jay Smith. The project required a rather rigid scheme consisting of a grid and concentric crescents. Soon after starting at Laurel Hill, he received a similar commission in Easton, Pennsylvania. Easton Cemetery's backers sought his assistance in choosing a site; he obliged, and afterward drew up plans for the road and path system, which the company adopted.

In 1850, architect James P. W. Neff joined his practice with Sidney's. Their firm displayed several residential designs in *American Cottage and Villa Architecture* (1850), a Downingesque pattern book that was Sidney's main contribution to architectural literature. Over the next few years, Sidney & Neff platted growing towns

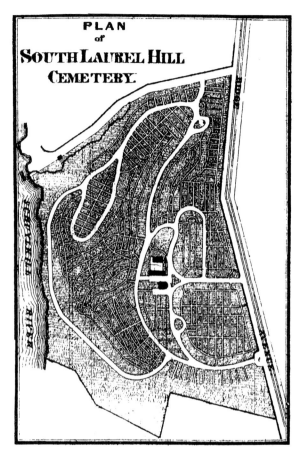

"Plan of South Laurel Hill Cemetery." From *Smedly's Atlas of the City of Philadelphia*, 1862.

tor William Saunders* had recently relocated to Philadelphia, and his arrival may have hastened Sidney's departure. But if Sidney's efforts shifted toward cartography, he did not abandon his other work. In 1857 he designed Woodlands Cemetery in Cambridge, New York. Records there identify him as both "civil engineer" and "rural architect"—a switch that may signify a turning point in his career. Previously he had supplied circulation specifications for most of his landscape projects. Now he was prepared to produce planting schemes and other accoutrements of landscape gardening.

Around 1858, Sidney teamed with architect Andrew Adams. They advertised themselves as specialists in "country seats, cemeteries, and public grounds," and

and suburbs in Pennsylvania and New York while designing houses and cemeteries for the same regions. Returning to South Laurel Hill in 1854, they relaxed Sidney's earlier design with serpentine roads while preserving large portions of the Harleigh estate. As well as reshaping old villa landscapes, the firm developed new ones. Sidney & Neff planned Chelten Hills in Montgomery County, Pennsylvania, and laid out farms as "country seats" near Jenkintown. Between 1852 and 1854, Sidney also fostered suburban Philadelphia's growth by supervising survey and construction work for the Chestnut Hill Railroad.

Sidney parted from Neff in 1855, moving to New York City to pursue his mapmaking career with Robert Smith's publishing company. County mapping had become the firm's focus, and complete coverage of New York State its goal. At the same time, Sidney's competi-

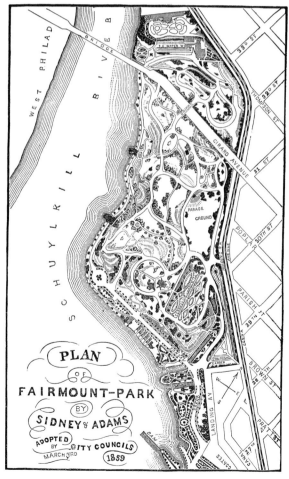

"Plan of Fairmount Park by Sidney & Adams." From *Description of Plan for Fairmount Park*, 1859.

Woodlawn Cemetery, 1988. Photo Dominick Totino. From *Woodlawn Remembers.* Courtesy The Woodlawn Cemetery.

in 1859 won a high-profile competition for the design of Philadelphia's Fairmount Park. Sidney & Adams wove together the patchwork of acquired properties with winding roads, varied plantings, and carefully controlled views, inspired in part by recent work at New York's Central Park. A Grand Avenue straightened into a linden-lined boulevard that served as the park's formal corridor. Narrower roads diverged from it, one traveling along the banks of the Schuylkill River, others leading to numerous picturesque nodes. Following Manhattan precedent, the designers depressed a major thoroughfare that cut through their scheme, crossing it with a bridge. On the park's eastern boundary, they blocked out city streets and buildings with a thick screen of deciduous trees. To the West, they broke a thinner screen at regular intervals to provide views of the Schuylkill. Individual and clumped trees adorned much of the landscape, their placement taking light, color, and seasonal change into account. Finally, Sidney & Adams integrated—even celebrated—what remained of the old estates, a treatment

that evinced a respect for Philadelphia's villa tradition, carried over, perhaps, from Laurel Hill Cemetery.

Fairmount Park was Sidney's greatest professional accomplishment, but he handled other important projects as well. Ending his partnership with Adams in 1860, he took on house and church commissions with Frederick C. Merry until 1864. He also continued his landscape efforts, designing Woodlawn Cemetery in the Bronx (1863), another professional coup. Conceived as the northern counterpart to Brooklyn's Greenwood Cemetery, it rolled across 313 acres of woods and farmland with the fluid confidence of Sidney's later work. A natural lake, brook, and old-growth deciduous trees enhanced the picturesque effect, creating a striking romantic landscape.

During the 1860s, Sidney contributed periodically to *Gardener's Monthly.* His articles ranged from building materials to plant species; frequently they underscored his interest in the relationship between architecture and landscape. So far, scholars have attributed few nonarchitectural commissions to Sidney after 1865, yet the heterogeneity of his earlier work suggests that this picture is somewhat skewed. His known projects of this era include many Philadelphia public schools, several houses, and a failed proposal for the Centennial Exposition. He joined the American Institute of Architects in 1870, and entered at least two partnerships thereafter.

Sidney died from a fall in 1881, survived by his wife and three children.

Adams, Andrew, and James C. Sidney. *Description of Plan for the Improvement of Fairmount Park, by Sidney & Adams, Printed for the Use of the Committee on City Property*. Philadelphia, 1859. A thorough explanation of the Sidney & Adams proposal, which synthesized design principles of Loudon, Downing, and Olmsted while avoiding Olmsted's democratizing rhetoric.

Gardener's Monthly and Horticulturalist 23 (June 1881). Sidney's obituary.

Moss, Roger W., and Sandra L. Tatman. *Biographical Dictionary of Philadelphia Architects: 1700–1930*. Boston: G. K. Hall, 1985. Entry on Sidney discusses the landmark events of his architectural career and lists some of his commissions (others have since come to light).

No institution has amassed a large collection of Sidney material. However, records pertaining to his cemetery commissions often survive in the holdings of those companies. The Laurel Hill Cemetery Company, for instance, owns an 1854 Sidney & Neff plan and various relevant receipt books. Michael J. Lewis of Williams College and Jefferson M. Moak of the City Archives of Philadelphia have both undertaken considerable research on Sidney, so far unpublished. Lewis has countered the long-held assumption that Sidney & Adams's Fairmount Park plan went largely unimplemented. Moak has compiled a list of Sidney's projects.

Aaron Wunsch

SIMONDS, OSSIAN COLE
(1855–1932)
landscape gardener, author

Born near Grand Rapids, Michigan, Simonds developed an early love for the native landscape of fields and forests around his father's farm. At the University of Michigan in Ann Arbor, he studied architecture and civil engineering under William Le Baron Jenney and graduated in 1878. After a short stint at surveying in western Michigan, he went to work for Jenney's office in Chicago, intending to pursue architecture as a career. Among Simonds's first projects was the design of additions to Graceland Cemetery there, and he gradually found that landscape gardening (a term he preferred to "landscape architecture") interested him more than architecture. Still, in 1880, he teamed up with one of the young architectural associates at Jenney's office to

Ossian Cole Simonds at Graceland Cemetery, Chicago. Courtesy Landscape Architecture Program, University of Michigan, Ann Arbor.

Graceland Cemetery. Courtesy Landscape Architecture Program, University of Michigan, Ann Arbor.

form the architectural firm of Holabird & Simonds, which with the addition of Martin Roche later became Holabird, Simonds & Roche. In 1881, Simonds became superintendent of Graceland and in 1883 resigned from Holabird, Simonds & Roche to devote full energy to landscape gardening and his expanding work there.

At Graceland, the young Simonds was influenced by his association with Bryan Lathrop, who, he wrote later, interested him in landscape design as an "employer, patron, and inspirer." Lathrop, who served as president of the cemetery's board of managers and was active in the parks movement in Chicago, shared his own library of books on landscape gardening with Simonds and took him to study the work of Adolph Strauch* at Spring Grove Cemetery in Cincinnati and to visit other important parks

and cemeteries in Cleveland, Buffalo, Troy, Boston, New York, Providence, and Washington. Simonds's later comments on what would constitute an ideal cemetery characterize his work at Graceland: "It would be an area of open, sunshiny places, bordered with trees, shrubs and flowers; one part would be hidden from another, enticing one to discover new charming effects; it would have water surfaces, flowers, sky, clouds, sunlight and moonlight; it would have a varied surface, with hills and valleys; it would have quietness and seclusion." At its peak, Graceland Cemetery was widely enjoyed as a quiet garden made up of a series of outdoor rooms leading one to another. Monuments did not overwhelm but were seen against a unifying backdrop of trees and shrubbery. Through his work Graceland, Simonds became widely known as a

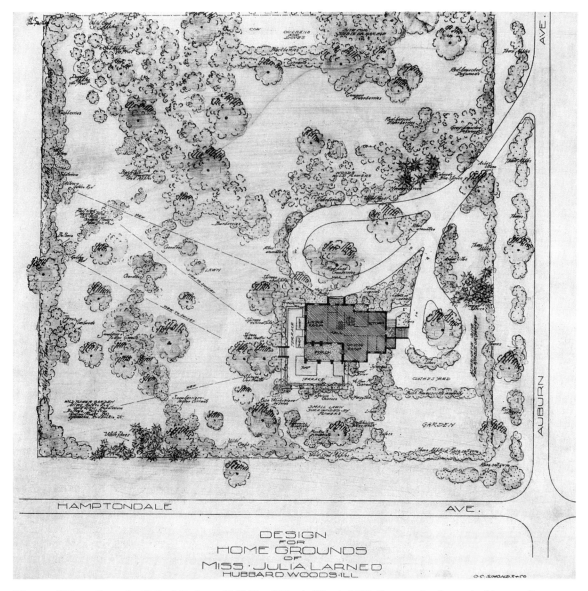

"Design of Home Grounds of Miss Julia Larned," Hubbard Woods, Illinois, 1907. Courtesy Landscape Architecture Program, University of Michigan, Ann Arbor.

landscape gardener and one of the nation's foremost authorities on "rural" cemetery design. He served as superintendent until 1898 and thereafter as a member of the board of managers and as landscape gardener for the cemetery. For his work at Graceland, Simonds was awarded a silver medal at the Paris Exposition in 1900.

Simonds advocated a style of design that emphasized local landforms and familiar plants, especially natives, formerly viewed as little more than weeds. He urged young designers to study nature "as the great teacher" and suggested that the goal of landscape design should be to help people see and respect subtle natural

E. N. Howell residence, Dixon, Illinois. From *Garden Magazine*, February 1924.

beauties. Wilhelm Miller* suggested that Simonds's work was part of an emerging regional style of landscape design which he characterized as a "prairie style." In his 1915 publication *The Prairie Spirit in Landscape Gardening*, Miller credited Simonds together with Jens Jensen* and Walter Burley Griffin* as its initiators. Simonds himself disclaimed any notion of a distinct Prairie style, suggesting instead that he simply tried to create the most beautiful effect wherever it was that he worked.

Simonds's practice included parks, residences, college campuses, and cemeteries throughout the United States, particularly the Midwest. Notable projects include the northern extension of Lincoln Park in Chicago; various parks and boulevards in Madison, Wisconsin; Fort Sheridan, Highland Park, Illinois; the Morton Arboretum in Lisle, Illinois; Frick Park in Pittsburgh; Washington Park in Springfield, Illinois; various parks in Dixon and Quincy, Illinois; Palmer Park and Subdivision in Detroit; Nichols

Arboretum in Ann Arbor and many of the city's early parks; Sinnissippi Farm, the estate of Governor Frank O. Lowden in Oregon, Illinois; and the estate of Anton G. Hodenpyl on Long Island, New York. At the time of his death in 1931, he was said to have practiced in every state of the country.

An ardent supporter of the profession of landscape architecture, Simonds was one of the founding members of the American Society of Landscape Architects and served as its president in 1913. He was also active in groups such as the American Civic Association, the Western Society of Engineers, and the Association of American Cemetery Superintendents. He actively sought to develop landscape design programs at several Midwestern universities where he had been hired to do design work, including the University of Chicago and Iowa State Agricultural College, but it was at his alma mater, the University of Michigan in Ann Arbor, where he was ultimately

Nichols Arboretum, Ann Arbor, Michigan, 1998. Photo Carol Betsch.

Graceland Cemetery, Chicago, 1993. Photo Charles A. Birnbaum.

successful in establishing a program in 1909. Most of the early professors came from Simonds's Chicago office, and Simonds himself taught at least one course a year, taking the train from Chicago to give lectures once a week or so.

Simonds wrote extensively on the art of landscape gardening; the best record of his philosophy is his book *Landscape Gardening*, published in 1920. A part of Liberty Hyde Bailey's* Rural Science series, it provided Simonds a platform for his ideas on landscape design, conservation, and management. For Simonds, landscape gardening encompassed both the small and the grand scale, from residential yards to large estates and parks to broad regional landscapes. This theme is echoed in the citation for Simonds's honorary master's degree from Michigan in 1929: "A staunch defender of the natural charm of the American landscape, sensitive to its beauty and skillful in the means of creating it, he has found joy and service in awakening civic ideals which express themselves in the development of city plans and parks. A better heritage for later days no man can leave."

Miller, Wilhelm. "The Prairie Style of Landscape Architecture." *Architectural Record* 40 (December 1916), 590–592. Response to criticism Miller received for his *Prairie Spirit in Landscape Gardening;* refers to Simonds, Jensen, and Griffin as the leaders of movement.

Simonds, Ossian Cole. *Landscape Gardening.* New York: Macmillan, 1926. Principles of landscape gardening with a City Beautiful emphasis; includes chapters on the design of residential grounds, public spaces, parks, and forests; unidentified illustrations, plans.

Simonds, Ossian Cole. "Nature as the Great Teacher in Landscape Gardening." *Landscape Architecture* 22 (January 1932), 100–108. Originally lecture delivered in 1922; advocates the study of nature as a basis of design.

Robert E. Grese

SIMONSON, WILBUR H.
(1897–1989)
landscape architect, engineer

Wilbur Herbert Simonson grew up in Lynbrook, Long Island, where his father was a builder and developer. He was awarded a Regents' scholarship to attend Cornell University, where he concentrated in landscape architecture and also took courses in architecture and engineering. He received a B.S. from Cornell's College of Agriculture and Life Sciences in 1919. Considering a career in aeronautical engineering, he worked briefly as an engineer draftsman for the Curtis Engineering Corporation. Simonson's interest in aeronautics led him to become an early proponent of the use of aerial photography in highway location and landscape design. During the early 1920s, Simonson worked in several landscape architecture, engineering, and city planning offices. He spent four years in the office of the noted landscape architect A. D. Taylor*, whom he credited as a significant influence on his career. During this period, his assignments ranged from city parks in New Britain, Connecti-

cut, to Midwestern estate designs to golf courses in Florida and the Long View Country Club in Pittsburgh.

In 1925, Gilmore Clarke* and Jay Downer invited Simonson to join the staff of the Westchester County Park Commission, then the acknowledged leader in the field of parkway design. The Bronx River Parkway's limited-access design, free-flowing curvature, and attractive landscape development created a new standard for motorway development. Westchester was in the midst of a parkway-building boom when Simonson arrived, and he gained valuable experience as a field supervisor on projects throughout the county. When the U.S. Bureau of Public Roads engaged Clarke and Downer as consultants for the development of Mount Vernon Memorial Highway in 1929, the two senior designers sent Simonson to Washington to serve as supervisory landscape architect for this high-profile project.

Mount Vernon Memorial Highway was a landmark

in American parkway and highway development. Completed in 1932, the 15-mile-long, 4-lane roadway surrounded by attractive parkland was the first of several parkways built by federal park authorities. It also garnered widespread acclaim as the most prominent commemorative landscape created as part of the nationwide celebration of the bicentennial of George Washington's birth.

The memorial highway's ostensible purposes were to preserve the Potomac shoreline, provide recreational opportunities for the national capital region, and commemorate George Washington by providing a safe and attractive roadway to his hallowed estate. Bureau of Public Roads officials and parkway promoters like Clarke, Downer, and Simonson also hoped the design would have a lasting impact on the course of American highway development. They intended it to serve as a

model motorway that would convince motorists and skeptical state highway departments that the key to the future of America's highway system lay in expanding parkway-style design principles from elite suburban recreational enclaves to mainstream arterial construction. Landscape architects had preached the virtues of parkway-style motor road development for years, but most highway engineers dismissed parkways as expensive affectations of little relevance to the serious business of utilitarian highway construction. With its prominent location and the public relations boost afforded by the George Washington bicentennial celebration, the memorial highway offered an ideal opportunity to prove that parkways were not only more attractive than ordinary highways, but safer, more efficient, and more economical as well. The project's supporters hoped it would also promote greater cooperation between high-

Mount Vernon Memorial Highway near Collingwood, Virginia, 1946. Courtesy U.S. Bureau of Public Roads Collection, Still Pictures Branch, National Archives.

ROADSIDE IMPROVEMENT

U.S. DEPARTMENT
OF AGRICULTURE

MISCELLANEOUS
PUBLICATION No. 191

Roadside Improvement. U.S. Department of Agriculture Miscellaneous Publication No. 191, Washington, D.C., 1934.
Courtesy Tim Davis.

way engineers and landscape architects, overcoming an unfortunate legacy of professional rivalry and mutual distrust.

Simonson played a vital role in ensuring the memorial highway's success, both as an outstanding designed landscape in its own right and as a compelling illustration of the practical value of parkway-style highway development. As the senior on-site landscape architect, Simonson was largely responsible for the parkway's harmonious integration of beauty, safety, and efficiency, which garnered widespread acclaim upon completion and continues to impress Mount Vernon-bound motorists. As an ardent proponent of parkway design principles, Simonson produced elaborate reports and detailed articles describing the development process, always emphasizing the practical advantages of seemingly "aesthetic" design decisions. He was widely praised for the tact and enthusiasm with which he promoted professional collaboration between landscape architects and engineers.

Simonson secured a permanent position with the Bureau of Public Roads after the completion of Mount Vernon Memorial Highway, serving as chief of the bureau's Roadside Branch until his retirement in 1965. Throughout his career, he continued to promote the integration of beauty, safety, and efficiency in highway location and design, exhorting students and colleagues, writing articles for professional journals, and drafting guidelines for the treatment of roadside landscapes in federally funded highway projects. The most widely circulated of his publications, a 1934 U.S. Department of Agriculture bulletin titled *Roadside Improvement*, so impressed Nazi highway engineer Fritz Todt that he had it translated into German to help guide the development of the *Reischsautobahnen*. Simonson also helped in the production of a U.S. Department of Agriculture film on the building of Mount Vernon Memorial Highway, which illustrated the process of parkway development in meticulous detail.

Simonson was named a Fellow of the American Society of Landscape Architects in 1940 in recognition of his contributions to the field of highway design and for his tireless efforts to promote greater collaboration between the closely aligned but frequently contentious cultures of highway engineering and landscape architecture.

Clarke, Gilmore.* "Mount Vernon Memorial Highway." *Landscape Architecture* 22 (April 1932), 179–189. The best contemporary overview of the design team's goals and methods along with detailed technical information provided by the Bureau of Public Roads Mount Vernon Memorial Highway engineers.

Simonson, Wilbur. "Notes on the Mount Vernon Memorial Highway: The Southern Terminus at Mount Vernon, Virginia." *Landscape Architecture* 22 (April 1932), 223–229, and 22 (July 1932), 313–320. Two-part essay that describes the southern terminus design of the highway and details the landscape development process, exemplifying Simonson's concern for integrating practical, aesthetic, and symbolic concerns.

U.S. Department of Agriculture. *Roadside Improvement.* U.S. Department of Agriculture Miscellaneous Publication No. 191. Washington, D.C.: GPO, 1934. The Bureau of Public Roads's primary publication on roadside development during the 1930s, drawn heavily from Simonson's official report on Mount Vernon Memorial Highway, with most illustrations taken from the extensive series of before-during-and-after photographs made of the project. *Landscape Architecture* serialized the bulletin as "Some Desirable Policies in Roadside Development," 24 (January 1934), 91–99, and "Roadside Improvement," 24 (July 1934), 198–209.

Simonson's official reports and correspondence related to Mount Vernon Memorial Highway can be found in the U.S. Bureau of Public Roads collection at the National Archives in College Park, Maryland (Record Group 30, Bureau of Public Roads Classified Central File, 1912-50; boxes 1385–1405). The extensive photographic record of the memorial highway's development is housed in the National Archives Still Pictures Branch (U.S. Bureau of Public Roads Photographs, Record Group 30-N). The Department of Transportation Library in Washington, D.C., holds an illustrated copy of Simonson's final report on the highway, along with a small collection of miscellaneous Simonson manuscripts.

Tim Davis

SMITH, JOHN JAY
(1798–1881)
cemetery designer, landscape gardener, horticulturist, author

John Jay Smith was born in Green Hill, New Jersey. His Quaker family had deep roots in the Delaware Valley, and it was there that he spent his childhood, initially preparing for a life of farming. Trips to the well-known Philadelphia estates of John Bartram*, William Hamilton, and Henry Pratt were among his favorite activities. In retrospect, he claimed that these horticultural landmarks had impressed him profoundly. After attending the Friends school in Westtown, Pennsylvania, he began a short-lived career as a pharmacist in Philadelphia. In 1821 he married Rachel Collins Pearsall of Flushing, Long Island.

An interest in literature led Smith to accept an appointment as Librarian at the Library Company of Philadelphia in 1829. Over the next five years, Smith involved himself in various publishing and editing ventures; an aspiring businessman, he also sought to emulate the gentlemen-scholars of his day. Both aims probably focused his attention on Mount Auburn Cemetery. Established in Cambridge, Massachusetts, in 1831, Mount Auburn quickly demonstrated the appeal of romantic, didactic funerary landscapes in America. Believing Philadelphians would welcome and patronize a similar institution, Smith broached plans for a cemetery company to civic and business leaders in late 1835. The following year, four of these men joined him in founding Laurel Hill Cemetery.

Laurel Hill was America's second major rural cemetery. Located on the Schuylkill River three and a half miles north of Philadelphia, it served as a professional starting point for gardener-architects John Notman* and James Sidney*. Smith also played an important design role there. At an early date he took personal charge of Notman's landscape, planting hundreds of trees and shrubs throughout the grounds. Boxwood, cedar, and rhododendron adorned a formal central node, while mountain laurel, holly, balm of Gilead, and other species appeared elsewhere in more picturesque arrangements. Like John Claudius Loudon, Smith came to consider evergreens uniquely suited for cemetery use. Accordingly, he screened the site's landward borders with pines, creating a sense of intimacy and enclosure that befitted the institution's function.

Laurel Hill's success gave Smith broad influence over the operation and appearance of rural cemeteries. His printed *Regulations* . . . (1837+) became a national model, and his consultation was a valued commodity; Joseph Perry relied on both as he founded Brooklyn's Greenwood Cemetery. During the mid 1840s, Smith marketed his newly acquired aesthetic authority in a series of design-related publications. The first was his *Guide to Laurel Hill Cemetery* (1844+), which offered visitors an orchestrated experience of the landscape, suggesting a tour route and describing the intended effect of sites along the way. Highlights included the graves of illustrious dead whose burial (or reburial) the history-minded manager encouraged. Horticulture was also a focus. Providing an extensive planting list, Smith noted his intention to make Laurel Hill an arboretum of all species capable of enduring the climate. Lavish illustrations and specific attributions promoted Notman, John Struthers, William Strickland, and Thomas U. Walter as monument designers.

Engraving of John Jay Smith. From *Gardener's Monthly*, 1881. Courtesy Library of Congress.

In 1846, Smith joined Walter in producing two pattern books. One was a collection of house plans from various sources; the other, *A Guide to Workers in Metals and Stone*, featured designs for funerary monuments and lot fences. For both, he served primarily as a compiler for these publications. Smith contributed more of his own thought to *Designs for Monuments and Mural Tablets . . . with a Preliminary Essay on the Laying Out, Planting and Managing of Cemeteries* (1846). Based overtly on Loudon, the treatise also benefited from Smith's practical experience at Laurel Hill. While repeating many of the British author's principles, Smith challenged Loudon's emphasis on formality and gave specialized advice on American burial conditions.

Cemetery horticulture brought Smith into contact with Andrew Jackson Downing*. Smith patronized Downing's Newburgh nursery in the 1840s, and the resulting friendship fostered frequent correspondence. Downing's impact on Smith's life was formidable. He introduced Smith to Henry Winthrop Sargent and other "improvers" in the Hudson River Valley—men whose estates Smith visited and scrutinized. By the time of Downing's death, Smith shared some of his credentials. He had published on architecture, edited François André Michaux's *North American Sylva* (1850–1851), and contributed articles to *The Horticulturist*. These qualifications helped him gain Downing's editorial post at the journal, filled in the interim by Patrick Barry*. As editor, Smith discussed the cultivation of certain species, offered general tips on landscape gardening, and ran a series of observations on "country places." Another series covered rural cemetery planting in detail while asserting the professional's importance in this field. Smith was interested in both the practical and the ornamental uses of trees. In an early editorial, he advocated planting trees along railroads, canals, and turnpikes to supply wood for construction.

Smith's tenure at *The Horticulturist* (1855–1859) spanned a crucial period in the development of urban public landscapes. As construction on New York's Central Park proceeded, Smith scolded Philadelphia for its negligence on this front. He routinely published articles by landscape gardener William Saunders*, both before and after Saunders secured the commission to design Hunting Park (1856). At the same time Smith lobbied for the long-awaited establishment of a larger park on the Schuylkill. Joining James Castle and Charles Keyser in raising funds for the project, he celebrated their ultimate success in print in 1857. When it came to Fairmount Park's design, Smith may have supported Saunders but

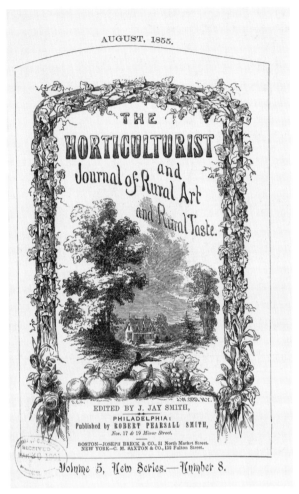

Cover of *The Horticulturist*, August 1855. Courtesy Library of Congress.

was probably pleased when Laurel Hill veteran James Sidney* won the competition (1859).

Smith's last major horticultural publication appeared in 1857 when he edited the eleventh edition of Bernard McMahon's *American Gardener's Calendar*. After 1860 he renewed his active role in the rural cemetery business. Helping to market the stock of Woodlawn Cemetery, he secured the Bronx institution's financial backing (c. 1863) and made substantial profits of his own. As ground began filling up at Laurel Hill, Smith set out to replicate his earlier success. Selling some of his interest in Woodlawn, he purchased land on the Schulylkill's west bank and established West Laurel Hill Cemetery in 1869. There he continued his planting work according to Adolph Strauch's* "landscape lawn" principles. Elsewhere in Philadelphia, his efforts helped found the Germantown Horticultural Society. At Ivy Lodge, his small Germantown estate, he created a landscape that *Gardener's Monthly* called "a singular triumph of garden art."

Gardener's Monthly and Horticulturalist 23 (December 1881), 378–380. Obituary, focusing on Smith's landscape-related achievements.

Smith, John Jay. *Guide to Laurel Hill Cemetery, Near Philadelphia*. Philadelphia, 1844. The first of many editions, the 1844 guide provided a detailed discussion of Laurel Hill's attractions.

Smith, John Jay. *Recollections of John Jay Smith*. Ed. Elizabeth Pearsall Smith. Philadelphia, 1892. Smith's

autobiographical writings, edited posthumously by his daughter, and a rich source of information on Smith's professional life, mentioning his connections to Laurel Hill, Greenwood, and Woodlawn cemeteries as well as his relationship with Downing.

Smith's papers are owned by the Library Company of Philadelphia and are accessible through the Historical Society of Pennsylvania. The collection includes letters from Downing and other members of his circle. Correspondence relating to Smith's involvement with Fairmount Park is on file at the Historical Society of Pennsylvania under the name of James H. Castle. Financial records and other materials in the possession of the Laurel Hill Cemetery Company cast light on Smith's work there.

Aaron Wunsch

STEELE, FLETCHER
(1885–1971)
landscape architect, author

Fletcher Steele was born in Rochester, New York, and grew up nearby, in the small village of Pittsford, along the Erie Canal. During his childhood, he learned to love music by listening to his mother, who was a fine pianist. Steele was also strongly influenced by the example of his aunt, a world traveler. His father, who practiced law, maintained a more aloof emotional presence in his son's life.

Steele's intelligence, outspokenness, and often raucous humor—characteristics that would serve him well later, in his practice—were much in evidence during his undergraduate education at Williams College, where he earned wildly uneven grades. On graduating in 1907, and against his father's wishes, he immediately entered the new master's degree program of landscape architecture at Harvard University. Steele later reflected that he would have gone happily into any of the visual arts, but

Fletcher Steele, c. 1925. Courtesy Robin Karson.

he wasn't a particularly good draftsman. In his second year of study, he caught the attention of Warren Manning*, who was visiting the department. Manning offered Steele a job on the spot, and Steele accepted. In Manning's office, Steele's abilities as plantsman, planner, and designer developed quickly, and he was called on to supervise several projects. Steele left Manning's office in 1913, with his mentor's blessings and partial underwriting of a grand tour of Europe. He opened his own office in Boston in 1914.

From its beginnings, Steele's practice was characterized by private work for wealthy clients with whom he maintained close social and emotional rapport. Thousands of American industrialists around the nation had recently entered the country house market, and Steele and his colleagues were eagerly developing an American style of landscape design based on an eclectic mix of European influences and a robust celebration of place. Steele differed from many of his colleagues, though, in his sense of the expressive potential of the garden as a work of art. "The chief vice in gardens," he told an interviewer in 1926, "is to be merely pretty."

Steele's early designs showed unusual assuredness. One of his first, for Charlotte Whitney Allen in Rochester, New York (c. 1915), relied on a restricted variety of plants that were used almost exclusively to architectural effect. Steele continued to refine the Whitney garden for three decades, later adding a sculpture by Gaston Lachaise and Alexander Calder's first mobile.

Through the 1910s, Steele's design reputation and practice grew, largely as a result of his writing for professional and popular magazines, his lectures, and word-of-mouth recommendations through the powerful Garden Club of America network, where he was a member-at-large. During World War I, Steele served as a photographer and ambulance driver in Russia. In 1920 his career entered its most productive and artistically successful decade.

In 1925 he traveled to Paris to visit the Exposition des Arts Decoratifs and Industriels Modernes. There Steele saw examples of new gardens by Gabriel Guevrekian and others which reflected revolutionary attitudes toward spatial layout, axial alignment, materials, and use of plants. Over the next decade Steele wrote enthusiastically about French modernist experiments such as these and their implications for American landscape design. A 1929 article in *House Beautiful* brought the topic before the general public; a more thorough

treatment appeared in *Landscape Architecture Quarterly* the following year. These and other articles by Steele influenced pivotal members of the next generation of American landscape architects, including Dan Kiley, who met Steele at Naumkeag in the 1930s, and Garrett Eckbo, who admired Steele's iconoclastic urgings.

The modernists' untraditional use of materials—such as concrete trees and revolving mirror globes—had a liberating effect on Steele's design work. Through the 1920s, his gardens became increasingly playful, expressive, and colorful. The landscape of Naumkeag, the Stockbridge, Massachusetts, summer home of Mabel Choate, was particularly enlivened by Steele's experiments. The South Lawn, a large curved form influenced by abstract modern sculpture, was revolutionary for 1934, as were the Blue Steps, completed in 1938. Steele's use of vivid color, industrial materials, and abstract plant forms was unprecedented.

During the late 1920s, Steele began to abandon strict axial alignment in his gardens. A pivotal project that reflects both his spatial investigations and an abstract approach to plant material is the garden amphitheater for the Camden Public Library, Camden, Maine, where Steele used a bent axis and white birch to dramatic effect. Steele's modernist experiments continued through the 1930s, along with more traditional designs. He considered the Helen and Robert Stoddard garden, which he laid out in Worcester, Massachusetts, in 1946, the project where his final convictions about the art of landscape architecture were "brought to fulfillment." The design interwove a series of downward spirals; Steele said the arrangement was inspired by a painting by Titian, *Bacchus and Ariadne*.

Steele was a prolific author, completing about 150 articles and two books, the more acclaimed of which was *Design in the Little Garden*, published in 1926. His ideas on suburban-scale residential layout, the subject of many of these publications, were eminently practical and geared toward middle-class incomes. Most of Steele's projects were estate-size, however. From his solo practice in Boston, he traveled throughout New England and upstate New York to Lake Forest, Illinois; Detroit; and Asheville, North Carolina, working for some of the country's wealthiest clients.

His practice dwindled during the Depression and nearly disappeared during World War II. It never resumed its previous pace, although Steele continued to design gardens. Only a relative few of the seven hun-

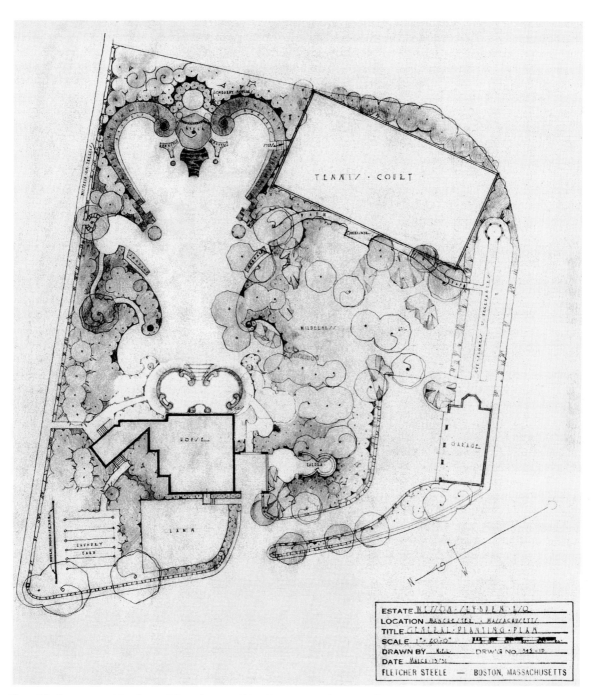

Plan of Seyburn estate, Manchester, Massachusetts, 1931. Courtesy SUNY-ESF Archives.

Blue Steps, Naumkeag, Mabel Choate estate, Stockbridge, Massachusetts, 1998. Photo Carol Betsch.

Steele and Mabel Choate painting Blue Steps, Naumkeag, 1939. Courtesy SUNY-ESF Archives.

Public Library Amphitheater, Camden, Maine, c. 1950. Photo Peter Hornbeck. Courtesy Robin Karson.

Drawing for Charlotte Whitney Allen garden, Rochester, New York, 1937. Courtesy SUNY-ESF Archives.

dred gardens Steele designed during his lifetime survive, but excellent examples remain in private hands in Pittsford, Rochester, Mount Kisco, and Garrison, New York; and Worcester, Manchester, and Gloucester, Massachusetts. Steele moved back to Pittsford in 1962, and continued to design from his home. His last work was an unusually quiescent and powerful garden for Mr. and Mrs. Richard L. Turner, a few miles from his own home. Steele died before it was completed, at age eighty-six.

Karson, Robin. *Fletcher Steele, Landscape Architect: An Account of the Gardenmaker's Life, 1885–1971.* New York: Sagapress/Abrams, 1989. Steele's biography includes background information on the period and an analysis of his major gardens; heavily illustrated; bibliography.

Steele, Fletcher. *Design in the Little Garden.* Boston: Atlantic Monthly, 1926. Written as part of Mrs. Francis King's* Little Gardens series, Steele's lightly illustrated text addresses the problem of the modest house lot with wonderfully practical insights concerning privacy, flexibility, and charm in the garden.

Steele, Fletcher. "The Effective Use of Planting in Landscape Architecture and Gardening" (Parts 1 and 2). *The Garden*, March–June, 1949. Steele's articles offer advice about the role of specific shrubs and trees in landscape design.

There are two major repositories of Steele's documents.

Visual materials, including copies of plans and drawings; some original plans and drawings; photographs; slides; glass slides; plant order books; and various other materials are at the Moon Library, College of Environmental Science and Forestry, State University of New York, Syracuse. Correspondence; interoffice memorandums; some plans and drawings; some photographs; and extensive client files with documents of many different types are held in the Fletcher Steele Papers at the Library of Congress, Washington, D.C. Photographs and documents relating to the design of Naumkeag are held by The Trustees of Reservations Western Region Management Office, Mission House, Stockbridge, Massachusetts. Client files for three important clients, Angelica Gerry, Standish Backus, and George Doubleday, are in the Fletcher Steele Papers, Rush Rhees Library, University of Rochester.

Robin Karson

STILES, EZRA CLARKE
(1891–1974)
landscape architect

Ezra Clarke Stiles was born in Painted Post, New York. Named for his illustrious forebear, a president of Yale University in the late eighteenth century, Stiles grew up in a strongly intellectual home. Through employment in a landscape nursery during his youth, he was introduced to the love of horticulture and to the vocation of landscape design. He received his professional education at Pennsylvania State University, where he majored in forestry and landscape architecture and graduated in 1914. His first position in landscape architecture was with the office of John Nolen*, of Cambridge, Massachusetts, for whom Stiles worked in Charlotte, North Carolina, on Myers Park, a vast residential development. Hired by Nolen as a temporary associate to Earl Draper* in Charlotte, Stiles assisted in a novel plan for community development, providing custom designs for every

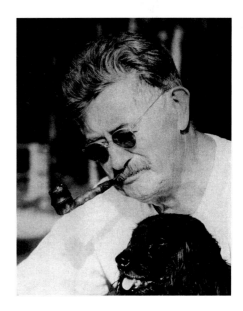

Ezra Clarke Stiles, c. 1968. Courtesy Ethel Stiles.

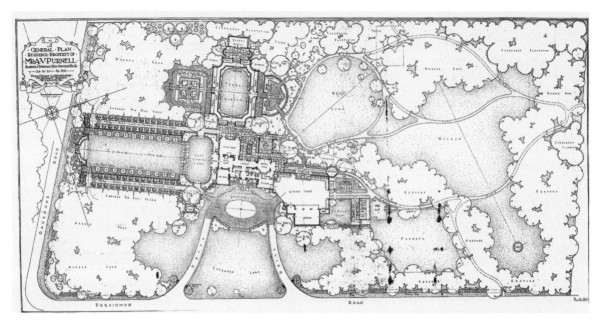

"General Plan for Mr. A. V. Purnell, Sewickley Heights, Pennsylvania," February 1938. Courtesy Pittsburgh History and Landmarks Foundation.

private garden as each property was purchased. In addition, he aided in a massive transplanting effort involving trees of substantial size.

Stiles's earliest association with Pittsburgh, the site of almost all his subsequent professional career, occurred in 1916 when he joined the A. W. Smith Company, landscape contractors and florists. He then served in the Army Corps of Engineers during World War I, leaving the service in 1919 with the rank of lieutenant and with great admiration for French landscape and horticultural practices. After returning to Charlotte for two years, this time in Draper's new independent practice, Stiles settled definitively in Pittsburgh in 1921, starting again with Smith, and then opening his own office in 1926.

The bulk of his work was residential and in the Pittsburgh area. Prominent clients included Richard K. Mellon, Alan M. Scaife, Guillum Price, and William Fownes, founder of the Oakmont Country Club. Stiles provided design consulting services to some of these clients throughout much of his career. However, he was also widely active in designing industrial parks, highways, schools, municipal parks, cemeteries, and, during the existence of the Works Progress Administration programs, public housing developments. His long association with

the Borough of Fox Chapel, an upper-class Pittsburgh suburb, as planner and garden designer, was capped by his master plan of 1955, which set forth a program that balanced growth with the preservation of the community's image of English country life. This comprehensive plan showed influences from his early involvement with Myers Park. Stiles wrote of pastoral terrain, winding scenic drives, and allocation of sufficient space defined for leisure and play purposes. He discussed the valuation impact on land resulting from park benefits when a parkway system is implemented, directly referring in this context of the Fox Chapel plan to the precedent of Myers Park.

The 1950s also saw the beginning of Stiles's involvement with a design team that included Griswold*, Winters*, Swain & Mullin, and Simonds & Simonds, which was to create the series of large parks that ring Allegheny County, of which Pittsburgh is the seat. In 1958, Stiles undertook the design of two of these regional parks, Boyce Park, which remains one of the most widely used recreation spaces in the Pittsburgh area, and Harrison Hills Park, where Stiles exploited the rich scenery along the Allegheny River to produce evocative woodland trails. He was still working on these regional parks at the time of his death.

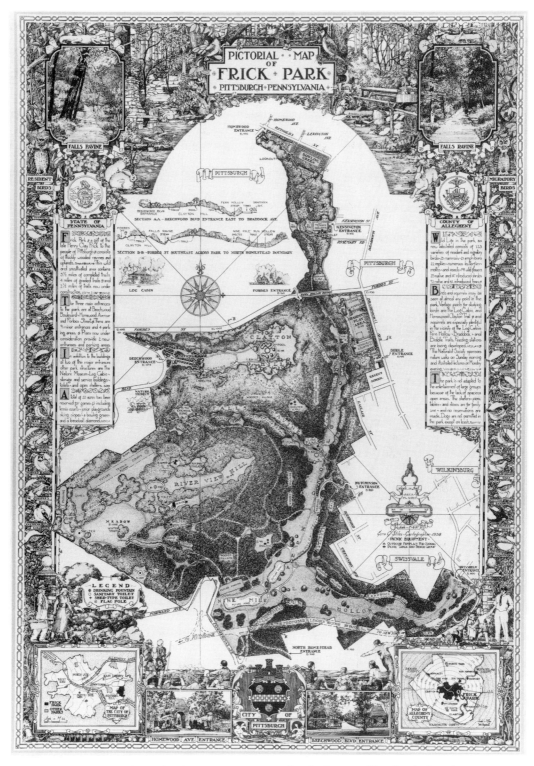

"Pictorial Map of Frick Park, Pittsburgh," 1938. Courtesy Pittsburgh History and Landmarks Foundation.

His work as a garden designer is likely his chief legacy; a considerable number of his gardens survive, either in actuality or at least in plans and drawings. From the earliest examples on, his designs exhibit a remarkable facility with a type of planning usually associated with the English Arts and Crafts aesthetic. Even when the plan covers a large area, the individual design elements are relatively small. The spatial units are tightly defined and clearly were thought of as outdoor rooms, embellished spaces for living under the open sky. The proliferation of built features in his garden designs conforms to the richly furnished nature of Arts and Crafts gardens in England, while the forms those built features took are almost always based on the vernacular styles of late Medieval and early Renaissance construction in England and, more rarely, in France. Stiles's discrimination in the choice of materials for the hardscape is still evident, while plant lists and partially surviving gardens provide testimony to a comparable fineness of taste in ornamental horticulture. A less explicit but pervasive quality in his extant gardens which also links him to the Arts and Crafts tradition is the poignant sense of their being places apart, evocative of the past or conducive to a more refined and sheltered way of life.

During the early years of his practice, Stiles was a prolific writer, producing articles, sometimes under the pseudonym Seltis Keal, for national publications such as *American City*, *Garden Magazine*, *Garden & Home Builder*, and *House and Garden*. His audience consisted of both the enlightened and the novice, as he dispensed rich design advice on subjects such as small garden design, backyard and grounds planning, garden furniture, brickwork, herb and vegetable gardening, French gardening influences, lighting, topiary, bulb planting, and pathways. Senior members of Pittsburgh's design community speak of Stiles with delight and enthusiasm as a character sui generis.

Stiles, Ezra Clarke. "Finding the Right Design to Fit the Small Garden." *Garden & Home Builder*, February 1928. Rings the changes on the theme of a small, enclosed flower garden of severely formal plan, variations of a type that occurred frequently in Stile's actual work.

Stiles, Ezra Clarke. "An Herbalogue." *Charette*, October 1926. The most direct testimony to Stiles's Arts and Crafts orientation. His delight in small, unassuming objects and works of art that bear witness to the handicraft of the artist is a clear expression of a romantic nostalgia for an Old World culture.

Stiles, Ezra Clarke. *Rock Gardening for the Small Place*. Garden City, N.Y.: Doubleday, 1935. The only book by Stiles; detailed discussion on the subject; contains his own illustrations.

Susan W. Strahler and Barry Hannegan

STRAUCH, ADOLPH
(1822–1883)
cemetery designer, landscape gardener

Born in the Prussian province of Silesia, Adolph Strauch began his training in landscape gardening at the age of sixteen in Vienna at the gardens of Schoenbrunn and Laxenburg. During his six years in Vienna working under the Hapsburg imperial gardeners, he became acquainted with Hermann Ludwig Heinrich, Prince von Pückler-Muskau. After an 1845 tour to observe landscape gardens and gardening procedures in Germany, the Netherlands, and Belgium, Strauch studied for approximately three years in Paris. He left France in 1848 for London, where he worked at the Royal Botanic Society Gardens in Regent's Park until his departure for the United States in 1851.

Strauch's stay in England was contemporaneous with the London Exhibition of 1851. Given his fluency in German, English, French, Polish, and Bohemian, he was asked to serve as a guide for visitors to the exhibition. In his role as guide at the Botanic Gardens, Strauch met Cincinnati businessman Robert A. Bowler, owner of the Mount Storm estate in Cincinnati's Clifton neighborhood.

In 1851, Strauch visited the United States. After an aborted attempt to explore the Southwest (where the

Adolph Strauch. Courtesy Collections of the Cincinnati Historical Society.

Comanches and U.S. cavalry were at war), he spent the winter in Texas with German American communities at San Antonio, Neu Braunfels, Sisterdale, Boerne, and Fredericksburg. In 1852 he decided to return to Europe after a visit to New England. When a steamer failed to arrive on time at Cincinnati, he was forced to remain overnight there. Remembering Bowler, Strauch paid him a visit and accepted his offer to remain in Cincinnati as Bowler's landscape gardener.

Strauch began developing Mount Storm in 1852 and then expanded his practice to improve the grounds of other Clifton homes. These included the estates of such notable Cincinnati citizens as Henry Probasco, George Schoenberger (whose property, Scarlet Oaks, would be purchased by John Warder*), William Neff, Robert Buchanan, and William Resor. Strauch also found other German American gardeners for some of these properties.

The general history of Spring Grove Cemetery and Strauch's involvement there is well established in several sources. The site had already been partially developed when Strauch joined the effort in the winter of 1854–1855. Strauch's "lawn plan" for Spring Grove, however, was revolutionary in that it established a unified picturesque landscape in which a few fine stone monuments and sculptures, framed by trees, would provide memorials to the dead. In his plan, traditional headstones could not exceed a height of two feet except "extra fine works of art, and by special permission from the Board." The cemetery designer would determine all site grades and create an overall planting effect. Private enclosures and plantings were discouraged. This visual unification of the landscape had been lacking in earlier "garden cemeteries." Spring Grove's character was maintained by strict rules, which sometimes caused major dissension. However, the ultimate effect is its enduring legacy.

Geyser Lake, Spring Grove Cemetery, 1984. Photo Blanche M. G. Linden.

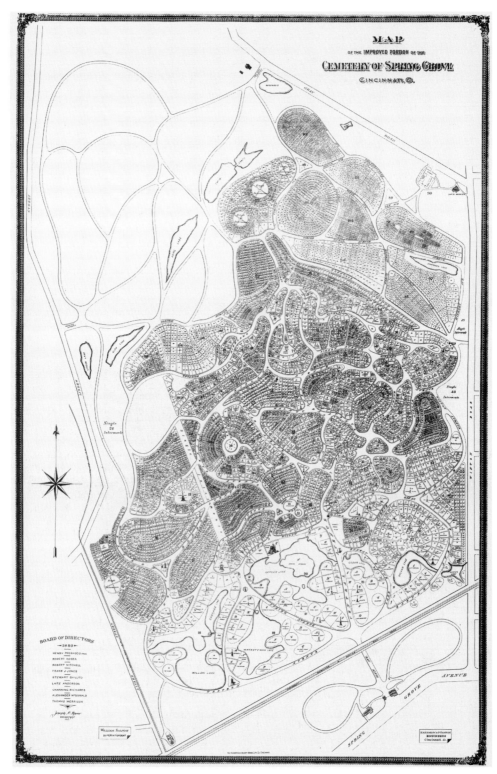

"Map of the Improved Portion of the Cemetery of Spring Grove, Cincinnati, Ohio." Private collection.

Through his public service work with Cincinnati's park system, Strauch also may have been involved with the early development of Eden Park. In addition, cemetery associations beyond Cincinnati requested his advice and design assistance, including Detroit's Woodmere Cemetery. Strauch also assisted in the creation of the Oakwoods Cemetery near Chicago in 1864. Other cemetery associations quickly made use of his ideas, some (such as New York's Woodlawn Cemetery and Philadelphia's West Laurel Hill Cemetery) specifically crediting Strauch. Sources also credit him with cemetery designs or advice for Nashville; Hartford; Chicago; Buffalo; Cleveland; and Indianapolis (Crown Hill). O. C. Simonds* noted Strauch's role in design at Chicago's Graceland Cemetery, and Strauch's biographer Heinrich A. Ratterman also recorded that he advised in the design of the Cincinnati German Catholic "Maria" Cemetery.

Strauch's relative obscurity today may be explained by the fact that he remained a Prussian citizen until 1879, four years before his death, and that he worked predominantly in a single locale. Additionally, he chose to practice in the Midwest, while the greatest professional prominence came to designers associated with the large East Coast firms such as the Olmsteds'. Frederick Law Olmsted Sr.*, however, had great respect for Strauch, and Simonds stated that "perhaps no man in the United States since A. J. Downing's* time has done more for the correction and cultivation of public taste in landscape gardening than Adolph Strauch."

The great majority of Strauch's residential work in Cincinnati appears to have been demolished. However, Spring Grove is such a seminal American landscape that by itself it firmly secures Strauch's place in our cultural landscape history.

Burnet tomb, Spring Grove Cemetery, 1979. Photo Blanche M. G. Linden.

Linden, Blanche G. M. "Spring Grove: Celebrating 150 Years." *Queen City Heritage* 53 (Spring/Summer 1995), 4–105. Extensive history of Spring Grove with solid coverage of Strauch's work there. Linden [-Ward] also covers Spring Grove in *Silent City on a Hill: Landscapes of Memory and Boston's Mount Auburn Cemetery*. Columbus: Ohio State University Press, 1989.

Ratterman, Heinrich Armin. "Spring Grove Cemetery and Its Creator." Manuscript Collection, Ratterman, Heinrich Armin. "Spring Grove Cemetery and Its Creator." Manuscript Collection, Cincinnati Historical Society, Cincinnati, 1905. Reprinted in *Spring Grove Cemetery and Its Creator: H. A. Ratterman's Biography of Adolph Strauch*. Ed. Don Heinrich Tolzman. Columbus: Ohio State University Press, 1988. The basis for much of our knowledge of Strauch's life; in his writings and through his work as editor of *Der Deutsche Pionier*, Ratterman championed the German American cause.

Strauch, Adolph. *Spring Grove Cemetery: Its History and Improvements with Observations on Ancient and Modern Places of Sepulture*. Cincinnati, 1869. Spring Grove, presented by the creator of its "lawn plan"; particularly valuable historical section, citing some of Strauch's intellectual and design sources.

Noël Dorsey Vernon

TABOR, GRACE
(c. 1873–c. 1973)
landscape architect, author

Grace Tabor, one of the first women to identify herself as a landscape architect, was born in Cuba, New York. She studied at the Art Students League in both Buffalo and New York, and at the New York School of Applied Design for Women. She acquired her horticultural training at the Arnold Arboretum.

The extent of Tabor's private design work is unknown. She expressed a strong preference for gardens for persons of average income rather than the rich, and such gardens were not recorded in magazines and books to the same extent as more lavish landscapes.

Tabor's greatest influence derived from her writing on both landscape design and horticulture. Beginning in 1905, Tabor contributed articles to such publications as *Garden Magazine* and *Country Life*. She also wrote regularly for *Woman's Home Companion*, then among the most influential women's magazines in the country, and in 1920 began a garden column for the magazine which ran until 1941.

Tabor was also the author of ten garden books, most of which were published between 1910 and 1921. Her last, *Making a Garden of Perennials*, appeared in 1951. Her most important titles include *The Landscape Gardening Book* (1911) and *Come into the Garden* (1921), both of which interpreted design principles for a general audience. Her emphasis, too, on knowledge of construction and site engineering was relatively uncommon in popular garden books, even those by other landscape architects. *Old-Fashioned Gardening* (1913) introduced readers to America's garden heritage, reflecting the popularity of the Colonial Revival. Tabor, however, emphasized design in addition to the horticultural information favored by other such writers. Her insistent use of plans is particularly noteworthy in an era when, as one publisher noted, "the public does not care for plans."

Tabor, who is occasionally confused with Gladys Taber, a country life writer from later in the century, spent most of her adult life in the New York City area. After retirement, she moved south, living in various states until the early 1970s. Her reputation rests on her position as one of the earliest woman landscape architects and as one of the first women to

Grace Tabor. From *Country Life in America*, March 1919.

attempt to persuade the public of the value of land-scape design.

Tabor, Grace. *Come into the Garden*. New York: Macmillan, 1921. A good introduction to both landscape design and horticulture for the general reader; some black-and-white photographs and a few suggested plans; bibliography.

Tabor, Grace. *The Landscape Gardening Book*. New York: McBride, Winston, 1911. An introductory-level approach to landscape design for the homeowner; em-phasizes horticultural solutions; many black-and-white photographs of residential gardens; some plans.

Tabor, Grace. *Old-Fashioned Gardening*. New York: McBride, Nast, 1913. Described as the first history of American gardens; an overview of gardens in the thirteen colonies, and Spanish and French America as well; dated but important in the Colonial Revival; instructions for reproductions; bibliography; illustrations; plans.

Virginia Lopez Begg

TAYLOR, ALBERT DAVIS
(1883–1951)
landscape architect, author

Albert Davis Taylor was born in Carlisle, Massachusetts, a twin son of Nathaniel A. and Ellen F. (Davis) Taylor. He received S.B. and A.B. degrees from the Massachusetts State Agricultural College (now the University of Massachusetts) and Boston College in 1905 and an M.L.A. from the College of Agriculture at Cornell University in 1906. After teaching at Cornell (1906–1908), he entered private practice in the office of Warren Manning*, beginning as a draftsman and four years later becoming an Associate and Superintendent of Construction and General Manager of Office and Field Work. During this time, Taylor contributed to a number of projects including Stan Hywet Hall in Akron and the Ohio State Normal Grounds, now Kent State University.

Taylor established a private practice in Cleveland in 1914. Significant projects in that area included the Van Sweringens' Daisy Hill estate in Cleveland, Julius Fleischmann's Winding Creek Farm (1926), J. J. Emery's Peterloon in Indian Hills, and the H. H. Timken estate in Canton. The office also designed the Eastern States Agricultural and Industrial Exposition in Springfield, Massachusetts, in 1915; Avondale, an Akron subdivision developed for H. H. Timken; and Nicholas Longworth's Cincinnati subdivision Rookwood, in 1922. The firm was one of the first in Ohio and served as a training ground for a generation of practitioners. Taylor also maintained a Florida office, which produced estates as well as waterfront and park developments for the cities

A. D. Taylor and John D. Rockefeller Jr. review proposed plan for Forest Hill Park, Cleveland. Courtesy Charles A. Birnbaum.

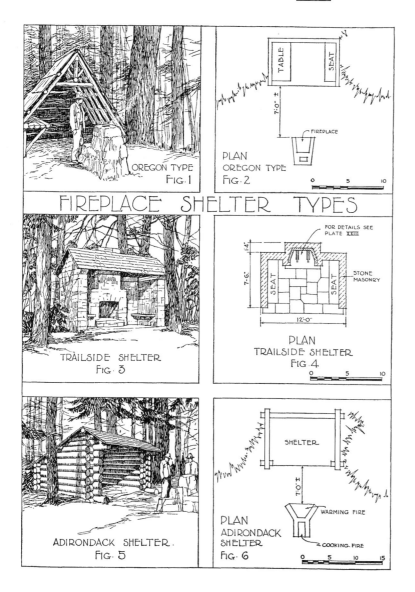

Prototype sketch Fireplace Shelter Types.
From *Camp Stoves and Fireplaces*,
U.S. Forest Service, 1936.

of Daytona Beach and Seabreeze, and resort developments in Sebring.

During the Depression, Taylor's firm worked on such Civil Works Administration projects as the Baldwin Filtration Plant Reservoir, Forest Hill Park, the U.S. Marine Hospital in Cleveland, Ault Park, the Cincinnati Art Museum's interior garden, the approach to the Cincinnati Union Terminal Station, and a campus plan for Boys Town, Nebraska. Site planning for the Cleveland Marine Hospital in 1931 led to designs for the New Orleans Marine Hospital, the Baltimore Marine Hospital, and the site plan for the Pentagon in Virginia (1942). For the National Housing Agency, he designed the Kingsford Heights Housing Project in Kingsbury, Indiana, the Erie Defense Housing Project in Erie, Pennsylvania, and the Maple Grove Park Housing Project in Windham, Ohio.

In 1936, accompanied by R. D'Arcy Bonnet, Taylor

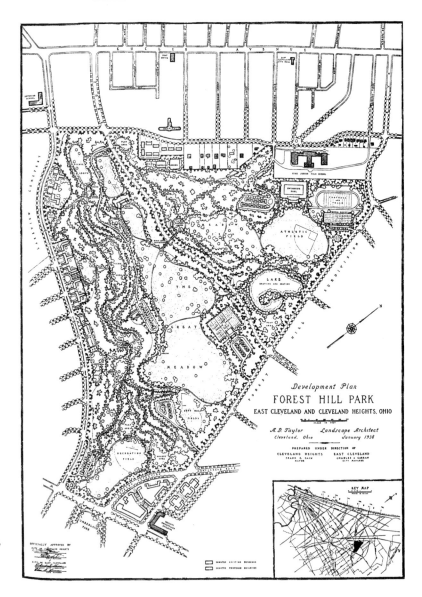

"Development Plan, Forest Hill Park, East Cleveland and Cleveland Heights, Ohio," January 1938. From *Forest Hill Park*, 1938. Courtesy Charles A. Birnbaum.

toured the national forests as a consultant to the United States Forest Service. Their report, *Problems of Landscape Architecture in the National Forests* (1936), became a major reference for recreational development in the national forests. The following year he published *Camp Stoves and Fireplaces* for the Forest Service.

Taylor wrote extensively. He prepared many important documents for the American Society of Landscape Architects as well as articles in the popular magazines of his day and some short books. From 1922 to 1936 he was a contributing editor of *Landscape Architecture*, where, assisted by associates, he wrote the majority of the "Construction Notes" columns. The "Notes," supported by meticulously detailed drawings, discussed the most up-to-date methods of landscape architectural construction. His books, such as *The Complete Garden*

Dr. Charles Briggs estate, Cleveland. Photo Mattie Edwards Hewitt. Courtesy Library of Congress.

(1920), and widely read articles in popular magazines—*Garden Magazine, Country Life,* and *Your Garden and Home*—contributed to the public's understanding of landscape architecture.

Taylor became a member of the ASLA in 1908, was later elected a Fellow, and served three consecutive terms as the organization's president (1936–1941). His volunteer work as a clearinghouse for government jobs during the Depression and World War II years was a significant contribution to the profession. In a series of six circulars and articles in *Pencil Points,* he detailed how and where to find government positions and how to participate in the planning and design of national defense construction work.

Taylor served from 1916 to 1926 as a nonresident professor in the landscape architecture program he helped establish at Ohio State University. A trustee of the Lake Forest Foundation and the Cambridge School of Architecture and Landscape Architecture, he lectured at several schools on a regular basis. He influenced several generations of professionals through his lectures, teaching, and office internships.

Taylor's work reflects both the Olmstedian tradition and the changes of the early twentieth century. The progression and changes that took place in his design approach serve as excellent examples of the blending and adaptation of ideas over time. His completed projects show a talent for integrating technical skill with aesthetic judgment in creating places of joyful quality.

Doorway, Briggs estate, Cleveland. Courtesy Smithsonian Institution, Archives of American Gardens.

Winding Creek farm, Julius Fleischmann estate, Cincinnati, c. 1956. Courtesy Smithsonian Institution, Archives of American Gardens.

"Albert Davis Taylor." *The National Cyclopaedia of American Biography*, 39:316. New York: James T. White, 1954. Entry containing biographical information and a list of projects and publications; also information on Taylor's family tree in the United States from 1635.

Hottois, JoAnn. "A. D. Taylor: His Impact on 20th-Century American Landscape Architecture Combined with a Bibliographical Compilation to Serve as a Resource to Encourage Further Research on A. D. Taylor." Master's thesis, Department of Landscape Architecture, Ohio State University, 1991. 2 vols. Has an extensive chapter on Taylor's life and professional career; also includes a database of over 2,000 records documenting the source of all existing Taylor records and drawings.

Robbins, Carle. "On the Career of a Landscape Architect." *Bystander*, March 29, 1930, 13, 14, and 64. Published on the occasion of the Third Annual Cleveland, Ohio, Garden Show. Taylor was one of a small group who established the first show and was a participant in the development of subsequent shows; he was interviewed for the article, which includes facts about his life not mentioned elsewhere.

Jot D. Carpenter

TUNNARD, CHRISTOPHER
(1910–1979)
landscape architect, planner, educator, critic, author

Christopher Tunnard was born in Victoria, British Columbia. He received his advanced education at Victoria College, University of British Columbia, and later at the College of the Royal Horticultural Society at Wisley (dipl. 1930) and the Westminster Technical Institute, where he took building construction courses in 1932. From 1932 to 1935 he worked in the London office of Percy S. Cane, one of the preeminent garden designers in the tradition of the Arts and Crafts movement. In 1936 he initiated his own practice of landscape architecture in London and Surrey. His radical modernist departure from the Arts and Crafts approach manifested itself in 1937 in the series of articles for *Architectural Review* which he gathered as his book, *Gardens in the Modern Landscape* (1938), and in the designs for the new domestic landscapes illustrated in it.

In the book, Tunnard postulated three approaches to "a new technique" for twentieth-century gardens: the functional, an overarching approach based on the concept that use determined form; the empathic, based on Japanese-inspired attitudes toward nature expressed symbolically in attention to the use of materials in asymmetrical composition; and the artistic, based on principles of modern art.

At his home and studio, St. Ann's Hill, Tunnard demonstrated his ideas of the "Garden into Landscape." His friend Raymond McGrath designed a cylindrical, white eroded-concrete addition (1936) to the house, which was set amid the larger demesne of an established eighteenth-century landscape garden designed by Charles Hamilton and once owned by Charles James Fox. To the description of the project in his book Tunnard appended a graphic history of the evolution of the site from the seventeenth century until the construction of the new building. This graphic history signified Tunnard's interest in the history of landscape design, the effects of which manifested themselves in the tentative experimental formal stance that Tunnard adopted in this period.

Other projects of the period included Galby for the Earl of Leicester, and Bentley Wood, the garden at Halland, Sussex, designed in consultation with Serge Chermayeff, the house's owner and architect. Gordon Cullen, later the editor of *Architectural Review* and the author of *Townscape*, made character sketches to illustrate these projects in *Gardens in the Modern Landscape*. In the book Tunnard also espoused an idea of "wider planning," the

principal illustration of which was the Bos Park in Amsterdam; he also included an unexecuted proposal of his own conception, a redevelopment in a Corbusian approach to the preservation of the eighteenth-century landscape garden at Claremont, Surrey. In the second edition he illustrated this larger urban planning and design agenda with citations of European projects such as Roemerstadt and Neubuehl, and one of the Farm Security Administration Camps in Texas designed by Garrett Eckbo.

In the United States, the book's appearance had a strong impact on three young American landscape architects, Dan Kiley, Eckbo, and James Rose*. In May 1939, in an article on urban landscape jointly written for *Architectural Record*, they quoted from the "English land-

Christopher Tunnard with the Monroe Planning Study. Courtesy Sterling Library, Yale University.

St. Ann's Hill, Chertsey, England, c. 1937. Private collection.

scapist," and the three persuaded Dean Joseph Hudnut to invite Tunnard to lecture at Harvard. At the time, Walter Gropius dominated an architectural curriculum that was strongly focused on the issues of planning and housing. Coming to the Department of Architecture directly from two similar projects in London—the site planning for Elizabeth Denby's "all-Europe house" for the Ideal Home Exhibition of 1939, and the "garden" architecture for the MARS Group utopian plan for the growth of London—Tunnard plunged into an architectural studio led by Gropius, with Hugh Stubbins, Martin Wagner, and himself as critics. He taught a course called "Site Planning," and a landscape history course (c. 1941). Among his students during his four years at Harvard were Lawrence Halprin, Edward Larrabee Barnes, Willo

von Moltke, and Philip Johnson. Significantly, Harvard's departments of Architecture and Landscape Architecture were fundamentally separate, the one dominated by the modernists, the other by neoclassicist devotees of Italian villa gardens.

In 1943, Tunnard was drafted into the Royal Canadian Air Force. He was married briefly during the later war years, but married again in June 1945 to Lydia Evans, his wife of nearly thirty-five years. With the help of a Wheelwright Fellowship, he returned to the United States and was briefly an editor of *The Architectural Forum*.

Tunnard began teaching at Yale in 1945, where he had been attracted by the focus on his own developing interests in city planning history and, specifically, the history of classicism in design. By 1948, with the preparation of the second edition of *Gardens in the Modern Landscape*, he had risen to the rank of associate professor of city planning. In 1958, Ian McHarg, professor of landscape architecture at the University of Pennsylvania, wrote to Tunnard and asked for references that would be "most indicative of the path toward design of open space appropriate to 20th century society." He added: "Your own book, *Gardens in the Modern Landscape*, still remain[s] the best thought on the subject."

Tunnard won a Guggenheim Fellowship in 1950. His second major published work, *The City of Man*, appeared in 1953. It is a substantial historical treatment of American urbanism that includes a didactic, anti-Radiant City analysis titled the "City of Shadows." In 1955 he co-authored *American Skyline* with his friend Henry Hope Reed, a fellow devotee of nineteenth-century American urban design history. In 1956 he won a Fulbright Fellowship, and his international perspectives seemed to broaden.

Tunnard's work in the 1950s, 1960s, and 1970s demonstrated his growing interest in history and the scenic aspects of regional genius loci. He developed teaching and research materials on the growing megalopolitan character of the Atlantic region from Boston to Washington, D.C. *Man-Made America: Chaos or Control?* (1963), written with Boris Pushkarev, won the National Book Award. He followed it with *The Modern American City* in 1968. His books and his teaching of planning and preservation courses influenced a generation of planners, especially his Yale graduates. His work also had significant repercussions for a wholly new American attitude toward historic preservation in the context of city planning. One of the progenitors of

the Venice Charter, the founding document of the International Committee on Monuments and Sites, he was also a founder of the New Haven Historic Preservation Commission. He participated in the UNESCO team that recommended preservation of cultural and natural resources of the Katmandu Valley, an approach he documented in his last book, *World with a View* (1978). Tunnard had come full circle to be identified with conservation- and preservation-oriented attitudes toward city revitalization which were antithetical to the modern movement. He died of cancer in 1979.

Neckar, Lance M. "Christopher Tunnard: The Garden in the Modern Landscape." In *Modern Landscape Architecture: A Critical Review*, ed. Marc Treib, 144–158. Cambridge: MIT Press, 1993.

Tunnard, Christopher. *Gardens in the Modern Landscape.* London: Architectural Press, 1938. An important work in which Tunnard applies theories of modernism to garden design; illustrated.

Tunnard, Christopher. *World with a View: An Inquiry into the Nature of Scenic Values.* New Haven: Yale University Press, 1978. An authoritative examination of city art and planning with a comprehensive approach to future civic design; illustrated.

Tunnard's papers are located in Manuscripts and Archives, Yale University.

Lance M. Neckar

UNDERHILL, FRANCIS TOWNSEND
(1863–1929)
landscape gardener, horticulturist

Francis Townsend Underhill was born into a rich and socially prominent family in Oyster Bay, New York. He was a seventh-generation descendant of the flamboyant Captain John Underhill, who came to the United States from Warwickshire in 1628. Underhill was educated privately and spent four years traveling in Europe with tutors, studying architecture and gardens. In 1879 he

spent six months with a tutor in Santa Barbara, California.

He maintained homes in New York City and Oyster Bay and lived the life of a typical New York "swell." He was a member of Caroline Astor's "400." He ran for Congress and was elected to represent New York City for one term. He served briefly as secretary to Union Pacific

Francis Townsend Underhill. Courtesy Santa Barbara Historical Society.

president E. H. Harriman. Underhill was a friend and Long Island neighbor of Theodore Roosevelt, with whom he served as a captain of artillery during the Spanish-American War. At one time, he owned and sailed *Mayflower* and *Mischief*, yachts that raced for the America's Cup. He was also a prominent horseman and polo player and wrote *Driving for Pleasure, or the Harness Stable and Its Appointments*, which became a standard book on horsemanship. In the 1920s, he became an expert on the scientific breeding of hogs.

Suffering from bouts of poor health, Underhill again visited Santa Barbara between 1880 and 1883 seeking a healthier climate. In 1885 he purchased the 800-acre Ontare Ranch in the Santa Ynez Valley, and in 1904 purchased the 6,000-acre El Roblar Ranch in Santa Barbara County, where he raised horses and rare plants. In 1906 he married Carmelita Dibblee, a direct descendant of Don José de la Guerra y Noriego, the Commandante of the Santa Barbara Presidio and a prosperous rancher in Santa Barbara County.

It was unusual for a man of Underhill's background to take up design, but he was a distinguished amateur residential architect and landscape architect. The extensive travel in his youth evidently served him well since he had no formal training in either discipline. He had an informal practice early in the century designing houses and gardens for close friends. From 1910 until 1917 he maintained an architecture and landscape architecture office in Montecito, which varied in size from four to six assistants and included the landscape architect Daniel Hull*. His clientele comprised socially prominent winter residents of Santa Barbara and Montecito such as George Owen Knapp, Cornelius K. G. Billings, and F. F. Peabody. In 1919 he continued work as a consultant but, partly owing to poor health, did not reopen the office. Since complete records are lacking, the total number of commissions he undertook is unknown. In a 1924 interview Underhill claimed to have designed 33 houses as well as several gardens.

Underhill did not write about his approach to design. His work, however, attests to an architectural aesthetic credo that venerated simplicity, symmetry, well-proportioned lines, the absence of elaborate detail except at carefully chosen places, and an unostentatious air of luxury. The gardens comprise large-scale circular and oval spaces created almost entirely with trees, frequently displaying a highly refined understanding of plant textures. When they occurred, walls were treated as abstract elements, devoid of historicist detail.

Until 1911, Underhill's houses stylistically fitted well into the Arts and Crafts ideology. His later designs are axially formal with classical or Mediterranean undertones. Despite this apparent paradox, all his houses were organized around rigorously rational and frequently symmetrical schemes with a strong visual and physical relation between interior and exterior space. His own house, La Chiquita, in Santa Barbara (1904), was a low pavilion-like structure subordinated to the magnificent existing oak trees and new plantings of finely textured palms, subtropical plants, and bamboo. Numerous deep bay windows, glazed doors, and large plate glass windows erased the sense of volumetric boundaries and established a unified sense of being within nature.

The later, more obviously formal house designs are often characterized by a treatment of walls as abstract, almost Cubist volumes, remarkably similar to the work of Irving Gill, which were set off by a few historicist details such as the principal entrance or an interior fireplace. Inside, the simplicity of the walls contrasted with the lavish use of rich materials such as marble and, outside, with the sculptural forms of the native oak trees and a rich palette of plant textures. Long bands of French doors opened onto interior courtyards and outer terraces.

His Francesca de La Guerra Dibblee house was a modest but refined and introverted courtyard house, classically inspired. In the 1920s, Underhill played an important role in the preservation and restoration of the Casa de la Guerra, his mother-in-law's family home, one

La Chiquita, Santa Barbara, c. 1903–4. Courtesy Documents Collection, College of Architectural Design, University of California, Berkeley.

Pool house, Arcady, George Owen Knapp estate, Montecito, California, 1916. Courtesy Kellam de Forest Collection.

of the most important surviving adobe Spanish-Mexican houses in Santa Barbara, memorialized in Richard Henry Dana's *Two Years before the Mast* (1840).

The Willis Ward estate in Montecito (1914) is Underhill's finest surviving garden, which also reveals his masterly ability to integrate broad panoramic views of the regional landscape seamlessly with his gardens. Within a large oval space formed by thick stands of red-

Willis Ward estate, Montecito. Courtesy David Streatfield.

wood trees, a series of axially arranged oval pools leads the eye down to a large unirrigated meadow with a broad panoramic vista of the Santa Ynez Mountains beyond.

Apart from a few articles in architectural magazines, Underhill's work was little known outside the small, closed social world in which he lived. Yet he was an important designer for his pioneering exploration of new solutions drawn from high style and vernacular sources. It is probable that his designs influenced Lockwood de Forest*, the Santa Barbara landscape architect.

Gebhard, David. "Francis Underhill." In *Toward a Simpler Life: The Arts and Crafts Architects of California*, ed. Robert Winter, 103–110. Berkeley: University of California Press, 1997. A sensitive essay on Underhill documenting his life and career as a designer; emphasizes his role as an Arts and Crafts designer but also brings out the paradoxical nature of his practice; illustrated with black-and-white photographs.

Saylor, Henry H. "The Best Twelve Country Houses in America, VII: La Chiquita. The Home of Francis T. Underhill, Esq., at Santa Barbara, California, Francis T. Underhill, Architect." *Country Life in America*, November 1915, 27–30. The most complete description of Underhill's own house and garden; illustrated with black-and-white photographs.

Streatfield, David C. *California Gardens: Creating a New Eden*. New York: Abbeville Press, 1994. A richly illustrated survey of gardens, containing a description of the Willis Ward estate, the finest surviving landscape design by Underhill; illustrated with color photographs.

David Streatfield

VAN RENSSELAER, MARIANA GRISWOLD (MRS. SCHUYLER VAN RENSSELAER)
(1851–1934)
author, critic

Mariana Griswold was born in New York City, the second of seven children in the wealthy George and Lydia Griswold family. The classical education she received at home from private tutors was complemented by frequent trips to Europe and summers in Connecticut and Rhode Island.

In 1868 the entire family moved to Dresden, and with the opportunity to travel more extensively in her teens, Griswold developed an interest in art and architecture, found herself particularly drawn to Corot and the Barbizon school of landscape painting, and mastered both French and German. Five years later, in 1873, she met and married Schuyler Van Rensselaer, a metallurgical engineer, and together they moved to his home in New Brunswick, New Jersey. Their only child, George, was born in 1875.

Around that time, she began a prolific and influential writing career that would span forty years, publishing both under her own name and her husband's, producing 13 books, over 200 journal and newspaper articles, and 3 exhibition catalogs. Her work included a significant book of guidelines for landscape gardening, as well as art criticism, poetry, travel journals, architectural history, environmental studies, and politics.

While her son was still a young child, Van Rensselaer spent a considerable amount of time nursing her husband, who had developed the chronic lung problems that caused his death in 1884. Her father died shortly thereafter, and she went briefly to Dresden to join her mother. The two returned to New York City permanently that year, taking a residence together with her sister Louisa. Ten years later, in 1894, her son George would die while on vacation from Harvard.

During this period, however, Van Rensselaer wrote some of her most important work in landscape gardening and art criticism, the latter published primarily in *American Architect and Building News*. Early works include the *Book of American Figure Painters* (1886), and the first monograph of its kind, *Henry Hobson Richardson and His Times* (1888). Critics noted Van Rensselaer's graceful writing style. Although based on secondary sources, her books were praised for their scholarliness and objectivity.

Van Rensselaer contributed to journals such as *Garden & Forest*, *Harper's Monthly Magazine*, and *Century Magazine*. Several series pieces eventually developed into books, most notably *English Cathedrals* and *Allegheny Mountains*, tour guides based on her own travels, and the renowned *Art Out-of-Doors: Hints on Good Taste in Gardening*. *Art Out-of-Doors* was so successful and influential in landscape gardening theory, addressing the relationship between the fitness and breadth of design and finer details such as roads, formal flower beds, and trees, that in its 1925 reprint, Van Rensselaer added three chapters and an appendix of other books on landscape architecture. Her enthusiasm for Frederick Law Olmsted Sr.*, A. J. Downing*, and Charles Sprague Sargent*, coupled with that for significant landscape designs in Europe and New England, benefited the emerging field as few other forces could. She convinced her readers that landscape architecture was a fine art.

Following her son's death, Van Rensselaer became more politically active. She became an inspector for the public schools, and then in 1899 president of the Public Education Association of New York City, a position she held for seven years. Many other journal articles concerned issues of social obligation for her class, addressing

Marianna van Rensselaer. From *Art Out-of-Doors*, 1893.

the need for improved urban environments for the less privileged and for a higher level of public education. She wrote on a variety of topics in several different media: an essay against suffrage, an exhibition catalog for the Buffalo Pan American Exposition of 1901, two collections of poetry (including one for children), and several translations. Her *History of the City of New York in the Seventeenth Century*, a two-volume work, earned her an honorary doctorate of literature from Columbia University.

In 1923, Van Rensselaer was awarded the Gold Medal from the American Academy of Arts and Letters for distinction in literature, and in 1933 she was elected a Fellow of the New York State Historical Association. She was also an honorary member of both the American Institute of Architects and the American Historical Association. She died at home in New York City.

Gebhard, David, ed. *Accents as Well as Broad Effects: Writings on Architecture, Landscape, and the Environment, 1876–1925.* Berkeley: University of California Press, 1996. Collection of journal articles by Van Rensselaer; contains a useful introduction with biographical information and thoughtful insight into her published works.

Kinnard, Cynthia D. "Mariana Griswold Van Rensselaer (1851–1934), America's First Professional Woman Art Critic." In *Women as Interpreters of the Visual Arts*, ed. Claire Richter Sherman. Westport, Conn.: Greenwood Press, 1981. Contains biographical information as well as a critical analysis of Van Rensselaer's life and times; includes black-and-white reproductions of her portrait by William Coffin and Saint-Gaudens bronze relief (1888).

Van Rensselaer, Mrs. Schuyler. *Art Out-of-Doors: Hints on Good Taste in Gardening.* New York, 1893. Celebrated work of guidelines for tasteful and artistic design of landscapes; several chapters on the aim of landscape gardening plus detailed advice on formal bed planting, trees, monuments, and similar matters.

Kate Laliberte

VAUX, CALVERT
(1824–1895)
architect, landscape architect

Calvert Vaux was born in London. He received a classical education at the Merchant Taylors' School and in 1843 became an articled pupil of Lewis Nockalls Cottingham, an architect known for his restorations of English Gothic churches. Vaux later joined the Architectural Association, Britain's first school of architecture, which had been organized in 1847. It was at the association's annual exhibition in 1850 that its secretary introduced Vaux to Andrew Jackson Downing*, the preeminent American horticulturist and landscape gardener, who asked Vaux to join him in his American practice. Vaux accompanied Downing to the latter's native city of Newburgh, New York, serving first as his assistant and, from 1851, as his partner.

Admirers of the English romantic picturesque style, Downing and Vaux designed numerous country houses and smaller cottages and their environs in the Hudson River Valley, Newport, Rhode Island, and Washington,

D.C. Vaux also assisted Downing in planning the layout of the grounds surrounding the public buildings in Washington from the Capitol to the White House. After Downing's death in 1852, Vaux continued to practice in Newburgh both alone and in partnership with Frederick Clarke Withers, an English architect who had joined the firm shortly before Downing's death. Vaux's *Villas and Cottages* (1857) documents his early work and offers house plans and views of residential buildings set in their landscapes.

Vaux moved his family and practice to New York City in 1856. A client, John A. C. Gray (who would soon become one of the Board of Commissioners of Central Park) helped Vaux obtain the job of designing and supervising the construction of the office building of the Bank of New York. In 1857 the Board of Central Park announced a public competition for the design of the new

Calvert Vaux. Courtesy Society for the Preservation of New England Antiquities.

park. Vaux, who had publicly advocated an open competition, persuaded Frederick Law Olmsted*, the superintendent of the proposed park, to join him in preparing a design. In April 1858 they were awarded the commission to execute their Greensward plan, prevailing over more than thirty other competitors. Olmsted was appointed architect-in-chief, while Vaux served first as assistant and later as consulting architect, these titles obfuscating Vaux's actual contribution as co-designer of Central Park.

Unique features of the design were the four sunken transverse roads carrying crosstown traffic, which allowed for uninterrupted landscapes and minimal disturbance to pedestrian visitors, and three distinct circulation systems within the park. Separate carriage drives, footpaths, and bridle paths provided Vaux opportunities to design numerous bridges and underpasses. He also designed a variety of rustic shelters and more substantial structures, including the Casino (1862–1863), the Mineral Springs (1869), the Dairy (1869–1870), and the Belvedere (1867–1871). The Mall, a pedestrian promenade lined with rows of overhanging elm trees, introduced a large

formally landscaped area to the park. Designed with the assistance of the English architect Jacob Wrey Mould, the Terrace (1859–1864), with its elaborate decorative and sculptural program, provides a space from which to view two of the park's principal scenic elements, the lake and the Ramble. This was the first time a terrace, primarily an architectural feature of grand country houses, was introduced into the design of a major public landscape.

In 1864, Vaux was invited to advise on the site of Prospect Park, in Brooklyn. He submitted a preliminary report in February 1865 on the rearrangement of the boundaries, recommending the acquisition of additional land. Vaux invited Olmsted, then employed in California, to return and collaborate on a design for Prospect Park. The following year they were appointed "landscape architects" and assumed responsibility for continuing to design the park and for supervising its construction. The additional land purchases that Vaux proposed permitted the broad landscape treatments of the 60-acre lake and Long Meadow in their park plan. Vaux planned a large oval plaza, later known as Grand Army Plaza, as the park's principal entryway. As at Central Park, he also designed a variety of pedestrian underpasses and numerous shelters. The Concert Grove, the formal gathering area, featured a radially planned system of walkways and terracing with plantings, elegantly carved stonework, and two major structures. Prospect Park is generally regarded as Vaux and Olmsted's finest and most mature public landscape design.

Vaux and Olmsted joined with Vaux's former partner Withers, to form the landscape partnership of Olmsted, Vaux & Company (1865–1872), which operated from the same office as the architectural firm of Vaux, Withers & Company. With his partners Vaux designed landscapes and major structures for insane asylums, campuses, estates, and residential communities, among the most important of which was Riverside, Illinois (1868–1870). Olmsted and Vaux's major public work during this period was the planning of urban parks and park systems for Brooklyn (1866–1873) and Buffalo (1868–1876), where they developed the parkway concept, as well as South Park in Chicago and its parkways (1871–1873). They also continued to work on Central Park and planned other New York City parks.

In 1873, Vaux resigned as consulting landscape architect with the Parks Department to focus on architecture. He designed major building complexes for the City of New York, collaborating with Mould on the master plans for the Metropolitan Museum of Art and the American Museum of Natural History, both planned for

The Terrace, Central Park. From *Third Annual Report of the Board of Commissioners of Central Park,* 1860. Courtesy Central Park Conservancy.

park sites. Only one wing of each museum was erected from their designs. Vaux's major independent landscape design of the decade was Parliament Square (1873), the public grounds of the Canadian government buildings in Ottawa, reminiscent of Central Park's Terrace. Vaux also designed the large country residence of Henry B. Hyde in Bay Shore, Long Island (1874–1876), with the planning of the grounds left to the Swiss-born landscape architect Jacob Weidenmann*, who had supervised the execution of Olmsted and Vaux's plan for the Hartford Retreat for the Insane in Connecticut.

In the late 1870s, Vaux resumed his earlier working method of practicing both as architect and landscape architect in two distinct but interrelated partnerships. He formed Vaux & Radford (1876–1892) and Vaux & Company (1880–1895), working with both George K. Radford, an English-born architect and engineer who had been chief engineer at the Buffalo parks, and Samuel Parsons Jr.*, a landscape gardener and horticulturist whose family owned a nursery in Flushing, New York. Later they were joined by Vaux's son, Downing. Vaux & Company prepared plans for Grace Church grounds (1881) and Trinity Cemetery (1881–1884) in New York; Cemetery of the Evergreens (1883) in Brooklyn; Bryn Mawr College (1882–1884) in Pennsylvania; Riverside

Cemetery (1887) in Macon, Georgia; and Riverview Cemetery (1888) in Trenton, New Jersey; the grounds of residences of Samuel J. Tilden, Greystone, (1879–1880) in Yonkers; G. Pierrepont Davis (1880–1881) in Hartford; Isaac Gale Johnson (1891) in Riverdale, New York; John Wisner (1889) in Summit, New Jersey (now the Reeves-Reed Arboretum), and Robert Bowne Suckley, Wilderstein (1890–1891) in Rhinebeck, New York. Other work included state-of-the-art athletic fields in the Bronx for both the Berkeley Athletic Club (1888) and the University Heights Campus of New York University (1894), neither of which has survived. In 1890, Vaux returned to Prospect Park to design Terrace Bridge.

While keeping up his private practice, Vaux resumed his public employment with the New York Department of Public Parks as landscape architect in 1881–1882 and from 1888 until his death. During his last tenure in the post, he designed Highbridge Park, north of 155th Street along the Harlem River, and continued to work on Riverside Park, executing his earlier plan for the site of President Ulysses S. Grant's tomb on Riverside Drive. He also laid out the steep, narrow hillside of Morningside Park, north of 110th Street, adapting a general plan on which he had collaborated with Olmsted in 1887. Parsons, who assisted him, believed that Morningside Park—despite the

Concert Grove, Prospect Park, Brooklyn, New York. From *Report of the Brooklyn Park Commissioners, from January, 1874, to December 31, 1879,* 1880.

limited budget and poor quality of the soil—with the careful arrangement of walks and rock work and enhancement of native plant growth—was Vaux's highest achievement as a landscape architect, "perhaps . . . the most consummate piece of art that he ever created."

As a result of the Small Parks Act of 1887, Vaux and Parsons planned many small neighborhood parks and squares. Vaux is said to have been proudest of his design for Mulberry Bend Park (1895), now called Columbus Park, which was planned for the site of a tenement district to be cleared away near New York's infamous Five Points slums. Completed after his death, the long and narrow park consisted of wide, bench-lined curvilinear walkways surrounding irregularly shaped areas of lawn. Vaux's

Morningside Park. Courtesy Collection of The New-York Historical Society.

Luna Island Bridge, New York State
Reservation at Niagara, 1895–96.
Courtesy The Local History
Department of the Niagara [New York]
Public Library.

design for it is no longer extant. His last work, approved a few months before his death, was a general plan for the new New York Botanical Garden in the newly acquired Bronx Park. Together with Parsons, he determined its siting and the location of the road system, and secured the inclusion of a restriction guaranteeing the protection of Hemlock Grove, which Vaux believed to be "the most beautiful natural spot in the entire park system."

Vaux also collaborated with Olmsted in 1887 in preparing the plans for the improvement of the New York State Reservation at Niagara, and Vaux & Company was responsible for its execution. There, in 1894, Vaux designed the Luna Island Bridge (since demolished) which connected the smaller island to Goat Island. In late 1889 he rejoined Olmsted for the last time to plan a park in Newburgh as a tribute to Downing. Andrew Jackson Downing Memorial Park combined Vaux's design for the hilly eastern section and Olmsted's design for the meadowlike western portion.

In addition to his book *Villas and Cottages*, Vaux published articles in periodicals such as *The Horticulturist*, *Harper's Weekly*, and *Harper's New Monthly Magazine*. His article "Should a Republic Encourage the Arts?" in *The Horticulturist* in 1852 outlined his belief that it was the government's responsibility to promote quality in public architecture. He co-authored with Olmsted numerous

park reports, providing cogently composed narratives to accompany their attractive color-lithographed plans. With Parsons he wrote *Concerning Lawn Planting* (1881). Letters and articles by Vaux often appeared in the *New York Times*, *New York Evening Post*, and other daily papers offering proposals or defending the city's parklands from insensitive intrusions. He also wrote the article on landscape gardening for the supplement to the ninth edition of *Encyclopaedia Britannica* (1886).

Vaux established important ties with artists, often accompanying his brother-in-law, Jervis McEntee, a Hudson River School painter, and others on sketching trips to the Catskills. He was a member of the Century Club (from 1859), of the Greater New York Commission (from 1890), and a founding member of the National Sculpture Society (1893). Vaux was also a member of the American Institute of Architects (1857–1869), and exhibited his architectural designs at the National Academy of Design (1863–1880).

The term "landscape architect," a title that Vaux favored, was first used in the early 1860s in connection with Vaux and Olmsted's appointment to the Central Park Commission. On numerous occasions Vaux fought to preserve the integrity of Central Park and other public landscapes. Recent scholarship has recognized Vaux's important contributions to this field, as well as his pro-

Bethesda Terrace, Central Park, 1995.
Photo Charles A. Birnbaum.

found influence on Olmsted, encouraging him to pursue landscape architecture and joining him in the designing of their two most important works, Central and Prospect parks.

Alex, William, and George B. Tatum. *Calvert Vaux, Architect and Planner.* New York: Ink, Inc., 1994. Well-illustrated compendium with an introductory overview of Vaux's career.

Kowsky, Francis. *Country, Park, and City: The Architecture and Life of Calvert Vaux.* New York: Oxford University Press, 1998. First full-length scholarly monograph on Vaux's life and work.

Vaux, Calvert. *Villas and Cottages.* New York, 1857; rev. ed., 1864. Vaux's major book, issued in two editions and reprinted through 1874, with text and accompanying plans and views documenting his early approach to design and independent and collaborative works with Downing and Withers.

Joy Kestenbaum

VAUX, DOWNING
(1856–1926)
landscape architect, architect, educator

Downing Vaux was born in New York City, a few months after his father, Calvert Vaux*, had moved his architectural practice and his family there from Newburgh, New York. The second of four children, Downing was named after his father's mentor and former partner, Andrew Jackson Downing*, the respected landscape gardener, horticulturist, and author, who had died four years earlier. About a year after Downing Vaux's birth, Calvert Vaux and Frederick Law Olmsted Sr.* began to collaborate on their plan for the competition to design New York's Central Park. Downing Vaux grew up well aware of the profound influence of his father, A. J. Downing, and Olmsted on the development of landscape architecture as a profession in America.

Downing Vaux, c. 1901. From *Universities and Their Sons.*
Courtesy New York University Archives.

Vaux attended schools in New York City and board-ing school in Plymouth, Massachusetts, where his friends and classmates included his older brother, Calvert Bowyer Vaux, as well as John Charles Olmsted* and Owen Olm-sted, Frederick Law Olmsted's stepsons. His professional education consisted of one year at the School of Mines of Columbia College, which he entered in 1874. This was followed by three years of training with his father and one year with the New York City engineering firm of McClay & Davies. In the mid-1880s he rejoined his father's office (which housed both the architecture and engineering firm of Vaux & Radford and the landscape architecture firm of Vaux & Company), working alongside his father and his partners, architect and engineer George K. Rad-ford and landscape architect and plant specialist Samuel Parsons Jr.* After his father was reappointed landscape architect to the Department of Public Parks in late 1887, Vaux became a senior member of the firm of Vaux & Company. In this capacity, among other responsibilities, he prepared the survey and plan for Wilderstein, the grounds of Robert Suckley in Rhinebeck, New York, and collaborated with his old friend John Charles Olmsted on the design for the estate of Adrian Iselin in New Rochelle, New York. He also oversaw the construction of Ohio Field, an athletic field that Vaux & Company had planned

in 1894 in connection with the firm's proposed layout for the grounds of the new University Heights Campus of New York University.

Before his father's death in 1895, the younger Vaux had already begun to practice in his own name, from the office of Vaux & Company. Among his partners were the architects Nicholas Gillesheimer in 1893, and from 1895 to the early 1900s, Marshall L. Emery. Like his father, Vaux practiced as an architect and as a landscape archi-tect. He maintained a small office, designing parks and park structures, cemeteries, and institutional, recreational and residential grounds. For about twenty years after his father's death, Vaux continued to prepare plans according his philosophy of design. He combined picturesque and pastoral landscape treatments with an increased attention to a variety of more active recreational requirements. After the dissolution of Vaux & Company, he inherited some of his father's clients, many of whom resided in the Hudson River Valley. His obituaries also credit him with laying out Riverside Drive in New York City.

In Newburgh, Downing Vaux, along with John Charles Olmsted, finalized the last collaborative plan by the senior Vaux and Olmsted: Andrew Jackson Downing Memorial Park. Later, he prepared plans for the small LeRoy and Broadway Parks, also in Newburgh, and in 1898 developed the plan for College Hill Park, the prin-cipal pleasure ground of Poughkeepsie. Influenced by his father's principles of design, the compact plan separated the drives and paths and combined pastoral and woody areas, adding a more formal section for the museum building and gardens at the park's summit. During this period the younger Vaux designed Kingston Point Park and Orange Lake Park, both privately owned, Victorian-era amusement parks that served as popular destinations for local residents and passengers on the Hudson River day liners. Kingston Point Park featured winding paths, gardens, summerhouses, a merry-go-round, dance hall, and shooting gallery, and a bandstand on a man-made island in a lagoon. (The latter recalled a design that Calvert Vaux and Olmsted Sr. had prepared some thirty years earlier for Brooklyn's Prospect.)

From 1906 to 1907, Vaux's clients included Carl F. Baker in Seabright, Abraham Isaacs Elkins in Red Bank, and Rosehill Cemetery in Linden, all in New Jersey. He was the landscape architect for the estate of James A. P. Ramsdell in Balmville, near Newburgh. Vaux also collab-orated with John Charles Olmsted on Shinnecock Hills, a subdivision in Southampton, New York, which was only partially executed. In 1902, he prepared a subdivi-

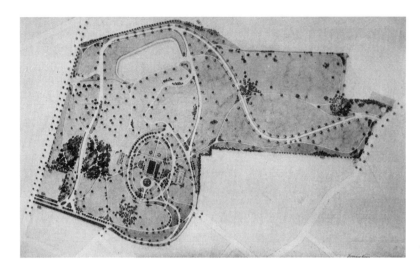

Plan of College Hill Park,
Poughkeepsie, 1898 *From Catalogue of
the Fifteenth Annual Exhibition of the
Architectural League of New York.*
Courtesy David Schuyler.

sion for the property of William Whitlock in the Todt
Hill area of Staten Island, New York. Also in the early
1900s he executed designs for the grounds of the Home
for the Friendless in Scranton, Pennsylvania, the Rest for
Convalescents in White Plains, New York, and the Grand
Hotel in the Catskills, and also laid out the athletic field
of the Hackley School in Tarrytown, New York.

From 1893 to 1911, Vaux was a lecturer on landscape architecture in the School of Engineering at the
University Heights Campus of New York University, and
also briefly taught the subject at Rensselaer Polytechnic
Institute in Troy, New York. One of eleven charter members of the American Society of Landscape Architects,
founded in 1899, Vaux was elected first chairman of the

Bandstand at Kingston Point Park,
Kingston, New York. Courtesy
Collection of John F. Matthews.

The Mountain and Lake, Rockwood Park, St. John, New Brunswick, Canada. Courtesy New Brunswick Museum, St. John.

executive committee. From 1900 to 1910 he served as secretary, and, in that capacity, wrote letters to editors defending the integrity of Central Park and New York City's other parks. (Calvert Vaux had done the same, but without his son's advantage of the backing of a professional organization.) In this era, which saw the dominance of the Beaux-Arts–trained architect, Vaux advocated full cooperation and collaboration among the architect, engineer, and landscape architect and the participation of the landscape architect from the outset of the design process. He was also a member of the National Arts Club, the Society for the Preservation of Scenic and Historic Places and Objects (later known as the American Scenic and Historical Preservation Society), and the Architectural League of New York, where he showed his work in the League's annual exhibitions.

Around 1913, Vaux retired to Kingston, New York, where his mother's family originated. After a long illness, he succumbed to a tragic death, which, like his father's, has been interpreted by some as a suicide. He fell from the roof of Kingston's Central YMCA, where he had been living.

"Landscape Architect Dies in Fall off Roof." *New York Times*, May 16, 1926, 28. Short obituary; notes a few of his major works.

Vaux, Downing. "Historical Notes." In *Transactions of the American Society of Landscape Architects from Its Inception in 1899 to the end of 1908*, ed. Harold A. Caparn, James Sturgis Pray*, and Downing Vaux. Harrisburg, Pa.: J. H. McFarland*, 1912. A three-page summary of the background of the profession of landscape architecture and its development.

Vaux, Downing. Entry in *Universities and Their Sons*. Boston: R. Herndon, 1901, p. 180. Written at the peak of his career, a brief autobiographical entry, including information on his training and professional affiliations.

Joy Kestenbaum

VINT, THOMAS CHALMERS
(1894–1967)
landscape architect, park planner, conservationist

Thomas Chalmers Vint was born in Salt Lake City, and grew up in Los Angeles, where he attended Polytechnic High School. Having decided on a career in landscape architecture, he enrolled at the University of California, Berkeley. While in school, Vint worked in the offices of several Los Angeles landscape architects, architects, and builders, including A. S. Falconer, who was designing bungalows for the Southern California Home Builders and Standard Building Investment Company, and W. J. Dodd, a residential architect. For nearly a year he served as an assistant to Lloyd Wright, a landscape architect and the son of Frank Lloyd Wright, who was designing the grounds of large residences and laying out residential subdivisions. The following summer, he returned to work for Wright and his new partner, Paul G. Thiene, who were preparing landscape designs for several Pasadena suburbs. Years later Vint recalled that in Wright's office he had the opportunity to deal with "every problem from many angles" and received "thorough" training and exposure to the landscape profession. Vint graduated from Berkeley with a B.S. in landscape architecture in 1920, having spent a semester studying at the Ecole des Beaux-Arts after serving in Europe during World War I.

In 1921 he studied city planning at the University of California, Los Angeles, and then worked a variety of short jobs while intermittently accepting contracts to grade and plant residential grounds and supervise construction. While working for a Los Angeles construction company, he learned about the large-scale planting of trees and shrubs, and as an employee of the architectural firm of Mayberry & Jones, he observed firsthand the use of concrete for the construction of hotels, garages, and hospitals. He briefly headed the landscape office for Armstrong Nurseries of Ontario, California, advising on planting designs and supervising planting projects. Vint also conducted experimental nursery work for the California Walnut Growers Association at the state's experiment station at Riverside. Vint's early work experience equipped him with a variety of practical skills that prepared him well for his long career with the National Park Service.

In November 1922, Vint became an architectural draftsman in the office of Daniel Ray Hull*, the National Park Service's chief landscape engineer, in Yosemite National Park. In 1923 the office moved to Los Angeles,

where Hull and Vint shared the offices of architect Gilbert Stanley Underwood, who was designing park lodges for concessionaires. Vint became an assistant landscape engineer in the National Park Service in 1923 and an associate landscape engineer in 1926. When the office moved to San Francisco in 1927, he took charge of the landscape program and soon after was made chief landscape architect with responsibility for the location, character, and quality of construction and planning in all the parks in the system.

Under Vint, the landscape program of the National Park Service expanded into a single, fully orchestrated process of park planning and development based on naturalistic principles of design and an ethic of landscape preservation. Vint developed a highly successful program to train his staff, assembled from several fields of study and areas of expertise: architects, landscape architect, engineers, and draftsmen. He coordinated a service-wide program of landscape preservation and harmonization to meet the park service's difficult twofold mission, that parks be both accessible to the public and preserved unimpaired for future generations. His standards for locating and designing park roads have had substantial influence on highway construction outside the National Park Service.

By July 1929, Vint had transformed the Landscape

Thomas Vint (middle left) in the Western Field Office, 1928–33. Photo George A. Grant. Courtesy National Park Service Historic Photography Collection.

The Loop at Sunrise Ridge, Mount Rainier National Park, designed by Ernest Davidson of Vint's office, developed 1929–30. Courtesy National Park Service Historic Photography Collection.

Division into a design office with an increasing emphasis on general planning. The division prepared the architectural and landscape plans for government projects under the direction of the park superintendents, reviewed the plans for tourist facilities to be built by the concessionaires and the plans for roads, and prepared the architectural plans for bridges constructed by the Bureau of Public Roads. In a 1930 annual report, Vint remarked that the San Francisco office operated much like the usual professional landscape office except that it had "the ideal condition of having park superintendents for clients."

In the late 1920s, plans were under way for many of the larger parks; by the end of 1931, as a result of the Economic Stabilization Act, Vint and his staff, in conjunction with park superintendents, had begun plans of proposed improvements for all parks. Dubbed "master plans" by National Park Service director Horace Albright in 1932, they quickly became the essential tool for all park planning and development. Updated annually, they guided national park development for many years.

During the 1930s, under the leadership of Vint and his staff, the National Park Service developed an increasing number of parks from historic sites, the monuments and parkways of Washington, D.C., many other national monuments, and national parkways such as the Blue Ridge Parkway. The Historic American Building Survey was launched under Vint's supervision. As a member of the editorial committee for *Park Structures and Facilities* (1935) and *Park and Recreation Structures* (1938), Vint communicated many of his ideas on park planning and

Scenic promenade for rim of Crater Lake, designed by Merel Sager of Vint's office, c. 1930. Photo George A. Grant. Courtesy National Park Service Historic Photography Collection.

development to state park designers. In 1938 he became chief of Planning, supervising 150 to 200 architects, landscape architects, and planners in four regional offices and two field divisions.

World War II brought a rapid end to the CCC and PWA allocations. Planning, design, and construction in national parks virtually ceased for the duration of the war. In 1946 master plans were once again revived and updated; however, there was little money for construction and development.

By the mid-1950s, burgeoning numbers of park visitors coupled with inadequate and outdated facilities raised public concern about the condition of national parks. The National Park Service successfully argued for new appropriations, and Congress approved a ten-year program of park development and improvements called "Mission 66." Vint was a member of the steering committee and headed the initial planning stage; in 1961 he was made assistant director for Design and Construction. Shortly thereafter, Vint retired after almost forty years of federal service.

Vint was a Fellow of the American Society of Landscape Architects, a Fellow of the American Institute of Architects, and a recipient of the Distinguished Service Award, the highest civilian honor conferred by the United States.

Civilian Conservation Corps enrollees shaping the steep slopes of the North Rim Road, Grand Canyon National Park, 1930s. Courtesy National Archives, Record Group 79.

Carr, Ethan. *Wilderness by Design: Landscape Architecture and the National Park Service.* Lincoln: University of Nebraska Press, 1998. A compilation of case studies highlighting the accomplishments of the landscape architects of the National Park Service and their contributions to American landscape history; a chapter documents the role of Vint and his staff in coordinating a master plan and designing facilities for Mount Rainier National Park.

Hubbard, Henry V*. "Landscape Development Based on Conservation." *Landscape Architecture* 29 (April 1939), 105–121. A comprehensive view of the work of the National Park Service's Branch of Planning headed by Vint and the process of planning and construction that he had spearheaded since the late 1920s.

McClelland, Linda Flint. *Building the National Parks: Historic Landscape Design and Construction.* Baltimore: Johns Hopkins University Press, 1998. History of the policies, principles, and practices of landscape design which guided the development and protection of the national parks from the founding of the National Park Service to the end of the twentieth century; several chapters trace the leading role that Vint played in shaping the design services and planning process from 1928 to 1961.

Linda Flint McClelland

VITALE, FERRUCCIO
(1875–1933)
landscape architect

Ferruccio Vitale was born in Florence, Italy, the son of Lazzaro and the Countess Giuseppina Barbaro Vitale. In 1898, Vitale came to the United States as a military attaché to the Italian embassy in Washington, D.C. While on a return trip from an assignment in the Philippines, he met landscape architect George F. Pentecost Jr. Having been trained as an engineer at the Royal Military Academy of Modena and worked as a young man in his father's architectural practice, Vitale decided, after conversing with Pentecost, that the profession of landscape architecture was the place for his many interests and talents. In 1902 he resigned from the military, and by 1904 he was working with Samuel Parsons Jr.* and Pentecost in New York City; his professional career took off quickly and continued steadily until his death.

Vitale joined the American Society of Landscape Architects in 1904 and was elected a Fellow in 1908. This was also the year that he established his own practice, and over the course of the next nine years he and Alfred Geiffert Jr.* worked together as associates. In 1914 the New York Chapter of the ASLA was organized in Vitale's office at 101 Park Avenue. James L. Greenleaf* was elected its first president, and Vitale followed him for a one-year term in 1916.

In 1917 the partnership of Vitale, Brinckerhoff & Geiffert was formed. The firm received the Architectural League of New York's first Gold Medal award in landscape architecture in 1920. In 1924, Arthur F. Brinckerhoff withdrew to resume a practice under his own name, and Vitale & Geiffert continued to practice together until Vitale's death in 1933. It was only in 1932 that they dropped Brinckerhoff's name from the firm's. Alfred Geiffert Jr. carried on the practice under the name of Vitale & Geiffert for another twenty-four years.

Throughout his career, Vitale was active in promoting the profession to the arts community as well as the general public. As a member of the board of trustees and executive committee of the American Academy in Rome, Vitale was instrumental in establishing the first fellowship in landscape architecture in 1915; the second and third fellowships were also a result of his efforts. He was a founder and trustee of the Foundation for Architecture and Landscape Architecture at Lake Forest, Illinois, and is credited with establishing its scholarship program.

Vitale's professional practice was extensive; his rep-utation was based primarily on the design of numerous private estates in the wealthy suburbs of New York, Chicago, Philadelphia, and Pittsburgh. His impressive client list included Percy Rockefeller, Owenoke Farm (Greenwich, Conn.; formal gardens); Richard B. Mellon (Pittsburgh; walled Renaissance garden); William Hall Walker, Brookside, originally built for William Stanley (Great Barrington, Mass.; rose garden reminiscent of a Tuscan villa with brick walls, a loggia with 67 marble pillars and specially designed lighting and irrigation systems); Myron C. Taylor, Underhill Farm (Lattingtown, N.Y.; Vitale & Geiffert with then-apprentice Annette Hoyt Flanders designed the estate setting to overlook a 6-acre lake and 65 acres of meadow and woodland); Horace Schmidlapp, Ca Sole (Walnut Hills, Ohio; 4-tiered garden terraces and hexagonal walled garden room, designed by Vitale with apprentice Umberto Innocenti*); Isaac Guggenheim, Villa Carola (Middle Neck Road, Sands Point, N.Y.); Clarence McKenzie Lewis, Skylands (Ringwood, N.J.); Landon K. Thorne (Bay Shore, N.Y.); Alexandra Emery Moore McKay (Benjamin Moore), Chelsea (East Norwich, N.Y.; gardens); Donald G. Geddes (Glen Cove, N.Y.; sunken

Ferruccio Vitale. From *Landscape Architecture*, July 1933.

Skylands, Clarence McKenzie Lewis estate, Ringwood, New Jersey. Italian Garden designed by Vitale & Geiffert. Courtesy The Architectural League of New York.

walled gardens); and Carl J. Schmidlapp (Mill Neck, N.Y.; pool complex).

Vitale's project superintendent, Larry Linnard, provided written accounts of several projects constructed during 1926–1933. The Anthony Campagna estate in Riverdale, New York, included a sequence of masonry drives, a swimming pool complex, and a greenhouse with an orangerie. The residence of Clarence Dillion in Far Hills, New Jersey, was built on several thousand acres with a two-mile entrance drive, indoor and outdoor tennis courts, swimming pools, and extensive brick walled gardens. The Zalmon G. Simmons residence, in Greenwich, Connecticut, comprised great stone walls, flights of stone steps, vast reflecting pools, and dozens of mature trees planted in trenches excavated of solid granite rock eight to ten feet deep. Col. Albert E. Pearce's residence, Canterbury Farms, in Warrenton, Virginia, was developed on 14,000 acres, including stables for 75 hunters and jumpers, one race track, miles of roadways, a swimming pool built into the slope of the mountain,

over 600 feet of holly hedges, a large boxwood garden, and hundreds of feet of serpentine brick walls.

During World War I, Vitale played an active role in the Town Planning Division of the U.S. Housing Corporation. He worked on developments in Dayton, Ohio, and Watertown, New York, and prepared plans for towns including Scarsdale and Pleasantville, New York. Vitale was the landscape architect for many public projects. He is credited with contributing to the planting plan at Meridian Hill Park in Washington, D.C., where he designed the oak groves at the upper terrace and the hillside juniper gardens (no longer extant). He was also a participating member of the Architectural Commission for the Chicago Fair of 1933, "A Century of Progress."

Vitale devoted his energy throughout his career to strengthening the importance of landscape architecture as one of the fine arts and worked hard to foster collaboration among the arts generally. He organized lectures for garden clubs and other groups to increase the public's knowledge of the fundamental principles of the art, its

The Oasis, F. E. Drury residence, Cleveland, Ohio, designed by Vitale, Geiffert & Brinckerhoff, 1916–17. From P. H. Elwood Jr.*, ed., *American Landscape Architecture*, 1924.

history, and the methods by which a landscape architect's scheme is conceived and executed. In 1927, President Calvin Coolidge appointed Vitale to the Fine Arts Commission for a four-year term, the same year the American Institute of Architects elected him as an honorary member. Health problems forced Vitale to resign from the commission in 1931. After an extended period of illness, he died of pneumonia at his home in New York City.

"Ferruccio Vitale—A Minute on His Life and Service." *Landscape Architecture* 23 (July 1933), 219–220. A brief biography and a description of Vitale's personal accomplishments and contributions to the profession of landscape architecture.

Mace, Robert B., Anthony Baker, and Carol A. Trainer, eds. *Long Island Country Houses and Their Architects, 1860–1940.* New York: Norton, 1997. An extensive summary of residential work by architects and landscape architects during the Country Place era, with brief summaries of hundreds of projects, including estate work by Vitale & Geiffert.

Newton, Norman T.* *Design on the Land: The Development of Landscape Architecture.* Cambridge: Belknap Press of Harvard University Press, 1971. A historical overview of the development of landscape architecture, from ancient times to urban planning in the late nineteenth century; Newton, who worked briefly for Vitale & Geiffert, accounts for the accomplishments of his two colleagues.

Laurie E. Hempton

WADSWORTH, ALEXANDER
(1806–1898)
surveyor, civil engineer

Alexander Wadsworth was born in Hiram, Maine, the eighth of eleven children to Charles and Ruth Wadsworth. He was first cousin to Henry Wadsworth Longfellow, the American poet, whom he knew as a childhood playmate. Wadsworth attended nearby Fryeburgh Academy, transferring in 1823 to the Gardiner Lyceum, where

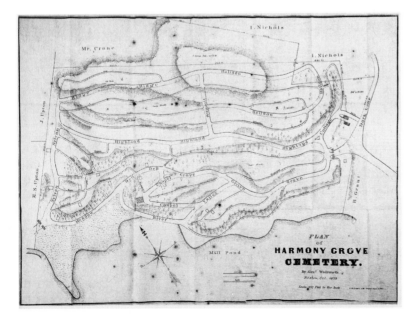

"Plan of Harmony Grove Cemetery," October 1839. Courtesy Peabody Essex Museum.

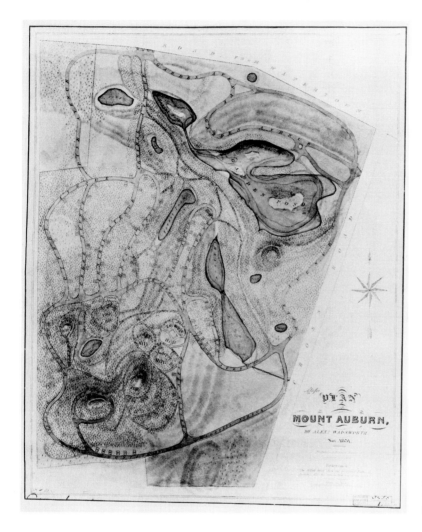

"Plan of Mount Auburn," November 1831. Courtesy Cambridge Historical Commission.

he studied civil engineering. In 1825 he moved to Boston, where he obtained a position as a surveyor through William Minot, a family friend. Within four years he had joined the Boston Athenaeum and the West Church, where he later became a deacon.

During the summer of 1831, Wadsworth received two notable commissions that established his reputation as the leading landscape surveyor in Boston. The first was for Washington Square in nearby Lowell, a formal park for the fashionable Belvidere Village owned by the Nesmith brothers. The second was for Mount Auburn Cemetery in Cambridge. Wadsworth was hired, likely through family connections, as civil engineer by the Garden and Cemetery Committee, with members including

General Henry A. S. Dearborn*, also from Maine, and Jacob Bigelow* of Harvard College.

Wadsworth worked with Dearborn on an innovative survey plan of Mount Auburn Cemetery during September and October 1831. It was the first picturesque topographic design of its type in the United States. They traced out the path and roadway system following the natural contours of the hilly site along the Charles River, originally the Stone Farm in Watertown. The inspiration for such topographic naturalism was Dearborn's reading about English picturesque garden design and knowledge of the French contoured plan for Père la Chaise Cemetery in Paris (1804). The final *Plan of Mount Auburn by Alex. Wadsworth* was published in November 1831 as an advertisement for burial lots, which included depiction of trees and shrubs on the site. The Wadsworth plan achieved national attention in the *American Magazine of Useful Knowledge* for June 1835, and served as a design model for other New England rural garden cemeteries including Mount Hope in Bangor, Maine (1835), and Mount Pleasant in Taunton, Massachusetts (1836).

Wadsworth executed picturesque cemetery plans for a rocky site at Harmony Grove in Salem in 1839 (assisted by local architect Francis Peabody) and for a gentle slope in Chelsea at Woodland Cemetery in 1850 (assisted by Henry Wald Fuller). In 1835, Wadsworth won the commission for Pemberton Square, a residential park on Beacon Hill in Boston which received considerable publicity. Wadsworth also laid out suburban residential parks along the Boston & Worcester Railroad—Walnut, Kenrick, and Auburn Parks—in Newton, during 1844–1847. Wadsworth was also active with picturesque plans for other Boston suburbs including Belmont, Roxbury, and Malden Highlands. All of these hilly sites are covered with contoured streets, prefiguring naturalistic designs such as Alexander Jackson Davis's at Llewellyn Park, New Jersey.

In his later years Wadsworth devoted himself to civic concerns as a member of the Boston City Council and Cochituate Water Board. He died in Boston and was buried in the family plot at Mount Auburn.

Dall, Caroline H. *Alexander Wadsworth, 1806–1898*. Washington, D.C., 1898. Biography of Wadsworth, including brief references to such projects as Mount Auburn Cemetery and Pemberton Square.

Krim, Arthur. "The Diffusion of Garden Cemeteries in New England." In *New England-St. Lawrence Valley Geographical Society Proceedings* 13 (1983). Regional review of Mount Auburn–inspired designs.

Linden-Ward, Blanche. *Silent City on a Hill: Landscapes of Memory and Boston's Mount Auburn Cemetery*. Columbus: Ohio State University Press, 1989. Extensive history of funereal landscape design and early planning of Mount Auburn Cemetery with Wadsworth plan.

Arthur Krim

WARDER, JOHN ASTON
(1812–1883)
forester, conservationist, horticulturist, pomologist, author

The eldest son of Philadelphia Quakers, John Aston Warder was educated at Jefferson Medical College. In 1836 he married Elizabeth Bowen Haines, daughter of a prominent member of Philadelphia's botanical community. Warder followed his family when they emigrated to the Miami Purchase of Ohio, and practiced medicine in Cincinnati, from 1837 to 1851, before becoming influential in the fields of horticulture, landscape gardening, and forest conservation.

Cincinnati and the Miami River valleys were centers of interest and experimentation in horticulture and landscape gardening, and through various horticultural, agricultural, and scientific societies Warder associated with other prominent Cincinnatians. These included Nicholas Longworth, grower and promoter of the Catawba grape and other small fruits, Robert Buchanan and F. R. Elliott, small fruit growers, and Andrew H. Ernst, involved in the design of Spring Grove Cemetery.

Warder and his family lived in the fashionable neighborhood of Clifton at Scarlet Oaks, whose grounds were originally designed by Adolph Strauch*.

Warder became more heavily involved with horticulture as he approached retirement. He created and edited two publications, *Western Horticultural Review* (1850–1853) and *The Horticultural Review and Botanical Magazine* (1854), which were influential in the Ohio River Valley and the Midwest. Warder himself was influenced by the work of A. J. Downing* and used his editorials, along with excerpts from Downing's writings, to promote landscape gardening design principles in the region.

Warder's understanding of Downing's ideas was directly reflected in the landscape of his estate, Aston, on the Ohio River bluffs to the west of Cincinnati at North Bend. Around 1851, Warder built and moved his family into a frame cottage very similar to one designed by

John Warder. Courtesy American Forests.

A. J. Downing and Calvert Vaux* for the Springside estate in Poughkeepsie, New York.

By 1872, Warder had built a larger, more elaborate house. The house and adjacent smokehouse (both still intact) are constructed of rough limestone in a rustic Tudor Gothic style and are visually framed by picturesque groupings of trees. Of the trees Warder planted close to the main house, a ginkgo is now an Ohio State Champion and an English oak is listed as a National Champion. Other planted trees include large American elms, Japanese maples, Catalpa (three species), Eastern hemlocks, Empress trees, magnolias, larch, scarlet oak, and various spruces. Warder introduced *Catalpa speciosa*, Western Catalpa, to the public through his *Western Horticultural Review*. His designed landscape was fairly intact until the late 1980s, when the property was developed for single-family residences and condominiums. The house is listed on the National Register of Historic Places.

Warder designed the entire 200-plus-acre estate of Aston in the *ferme ornée*, or ornamental farm style described by Downing in his *Treatise on the Theory and Practice of Landscape Gardening*. The historic agricultural fields were irregularly shaped and lined by tree hedges (Warder was an advocate of living fences, particularly Osage orange fencing). The fields adjacent to the

entrance road contained irregularly scattered clumps of trees, emulating a pastoral scene. The layout of the entrance road was a precise application of Downing's design ideas: "it curves in easy lines through certain portions of the park or lawn, until it reaches that object," the main house. The gently curving road set up an approach sequence that gradually allowed the visitor intriguing glimpses of the house, before it became obvious that the house was the principal destination.

Aston was also developed as a working farm and as an experiment station to test Warder's ideas for suitable hedge material, apple varieties, and forest conservation species. Warder had published a classic text on apples, *American Pomology* (1867), and regularly contributed articles on new apple varieties to other publications. He exhibited 109 varieties at an Ohio Horticultural Society meeting in 1873. He helped organize and served as president of the Ohio Pomology Society and was a member of the American Horticultural Society. His influence on landscape design in the Midwest continued through the work of his son, Reuben Haines Warder, who became superintendent of Lincoln Park in Chicago in 1900.

Around 1872, Warder's interests shifted more exclusively into the culminating work of his career—forest conservation. He had published a manual, *Hedges and Evergreens*, for the Midwest as early as 1858, but also planted some 2,000 evergreens of various sorts on the Aston estate. Concerned by the severe erosion occurring in the lower Midwest, he made his most lasting contribution to the developing forest conservation movement by working to establish the American Forestry Association in 1875. Today the association is the largest lay group devoted to forest conservation. Warder was selected as a U.S. Commissioner attending the Vienna International Exhibition of 1873, and produced a report on European forestry practices for the government. Ten years later, President Rutherford B. Hayes appointed him as an agent for the Department of Agriculture to report on forest issues, but Warder died in July of that same year.

Although Warder's Downingesque landscape is no longer intact at the Aston estate, his influence remains broadly evident in the fields of horticulture, pomology, and forestry.

Warder, John Aston. *Rural Cemeteries and Landscape Gardening*. Columbus, Ohio, 1881. Warder's rendition of Downing's design principles applied to the Midwest.

Warder, John Aston, ed. *Western Horticultural Review.* 3 vols. (1850–1853). General horticultural and landscape gardening information adapted to the Ohio River region and the Midwest. Includes excepts from Andrew Jackson Downing's writings; continued in 1854 as *The Horticultural Review and Botanical Magazine.*

Warder, John Aston, and Jas. W. Ward, eds. *The Horticultural Review and Botanical Magazine* (1854). General horticultural and botanical information for the Ohio River Valley.

Sherda K. Williams

WARING, GEORGE EDWIN, JR.
(1833–1898)
scientific agriculturist, civil engineer, sanitarian, author

George Edwin Waring Jr. was born in Poundridge, New York. His father manufactured stoves and agricultural tools in Stamford, Connecticut, where Waring grew up and attended public and private schools. He completed his early education at Bartlett's School (College Hill) in Poughkeepsie, New York.

Waring wasted little time starting a career. In the spring of 1853, at age nineteen, he became a pupil of Professor James Jay Mapes, an eminent inventor, chemist, author, and practitioner of scientific agriculture, who owned a model farm near Newark, New Jersey. That same year Waring began writing the first of fourteen books, *The Elements of Agriculture*, and made farm-lecture tours of Vermont and Maine.

Waring's managerial and agricultural acumen quickly attracted notice in high circles. Horace Greeley, the oracular founder-editor of the *New York Tribune*, was a friend of Mapes and a scientific agriculture enthusiast. He persuaded Waring to manage his newly acquired 54-acre farm at Chappaqua, New York, beginning in the spring of 1855, for two years. Then, early in 1857, Waring began renting the Staten Island farm of Frederick Law Olmsted Sr.* In August, the Board of Commissioners of Central Park appointed him agricultural engineer for the new park.

Over the next four years, Waring designed and installed subsoil drainage throughout Central Park, working first for the board, then directly for Olmsted, who became superintendent and then architect-in-chief of the park. Waring's grasp of this procedure and its effects on the soil as well as his knowledge of small-diameter drain pipes would underpin his later contributions to household and city sanitation. Waring also oversaw planting of the four rows of elm trees that framed the Central Park Mall. His long friendship with Olmsted dates from this period.

In May 1861, Waring rode off to the Civil War on his beloved, highbred mare, Vix—originally rescued from oblivion as a wagon horse for use in inspecting the park.

George E. Waring Jr. From *Street Cleaning and the Disposal of a City's Wastes,* 1898. Courtesy Special Collections, The New York Public Library, Research Library.

He returned to farm management in 1867, taking full charge of a run-down, 60-acre tract in Newport, Rhode Island, called Ogden Farm and nicknamed "poverty farm." To improve its wet soil and meager output, Waring underdrained the entire holding, using tile pipes as in Central Park. He also resumed agricultural writing, now emphasizing land draining and its bearings on crop yields and health, especially in reducing malaria. Interested in cattle breeding, he organized the American Jersey Cattle Club, served as its secretary, and edited its *Herd Book*. He is credited with popularizing the tomato as a luxury food by introducing the trophy tomato.

From 1868 to 1870, Waring was a strong promoter of earth closets, an English alternative to water closets, as the best means of farmhouse and town sanitation. He emphasized fecal waste as the cause of typhoid and other zymotic fevers as well as the key to boosting farm fertility. The near death of one of his children from typhoid gave edge to his efforts. Waring and Olmsted conferred about the use of earth closets for Riverside, a suburb then

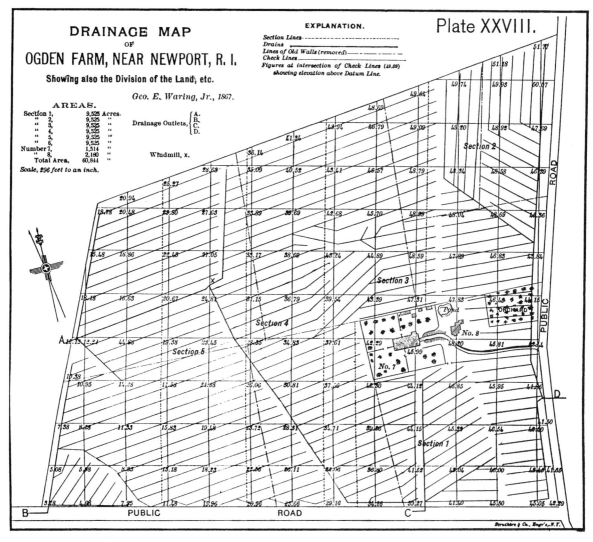

"Drainage Map of Ogden Farm, Near Newport, R.I.," 1867. From *Sewerage and Land-Drainage*, 1889.

under design by Olmsted*, Vaux* & Company on the western edge of Chicago. Sewerage adapted to such low-density places did not yet exist in America and would not until Waring himself took up the matter ten years later.

Waring's ambitions began to outstrip Ogden Farm. In August and September 1873 he made the first of several tours of northern and central Europe which resulted in essays for *Atlantic Monthly* and *Scribner's*, later reissued as three travel books. In the meantime, his Newport neighbors and others who knew his reputation sought his advice on sanitary matters, especially the newfangled plumbing devices being built into their homes. Working for a fee and tapping deep public anxieties about typhoid, diphtheria, and other "filth diseases," Waring stepped up his attacks on shoddy plumbing, outdoor privies, and leaching cesspools and made the healthfulness of isolated homes and small towns his special concern.

The nation was gradually abandoning the age-old regime of private lot waste removal in which kitchen slops and dirty water were pitched onto the ground and into cesspools while bodily wastes were consigned to privy vaults, all within the vicinity of the lot owner. But the new era of water-carriage sanitation, with its water closets, soil pipes, vents, traps, and sewer hookups, brought its own nightmares, especially sewer gas. Waring, working from an agricultural drainage perspective and unencumbered by mainstream civil engineering ideas, built a towering reputation as an independent, outspoken expert in house and town sanitation, especially after publishing *The Sanitary Drainage of Houses and Towns* (1876), probably the most widely read sanitary treatise of the period.

In 1878 a yellow fever epidemic devastated the lower Mississippi River Valley, leaving 5,150 dead in Memphis. The catastrophe became a turning point for Waring. Invited in 1879 by the American Public Health Association to propose an ideal water-carriage sewerage scheme for a city, Waring imagined a system designed solely to remove household wastes. (Conventional urban sewerage then mingled household water with rainwater in what were called combined sewers.)

Separate sewerage, as Waring's idea was known, had originated in the 1840s with Edwin Chadwick, the great British sanitarian. It had never been tried in America (although Waring had approximated it at Lenox, Massachusetts, in 1875 and 1876), nor had it been fully implemented in England, where building regulations required backyard and roof water to enter household sewers to flush them out. The exclusion of rainwater enabled Waring to recommend sewer pipes as small as six inches in diameter and relegate storm water removal mostly to surface arrangements rather than much larger and more costly underground conduits. Waring's method thus slashed sewerage construction costs by at least 60 percent, giving his idea instant appeal to Memphis.

The Memphis system, built in 1880, worked well enough and offered sufficient savings so that by 1899 at least thirty small American cities and towns had adopted it. Waring patented its special features, including automatic flush tanks, and profited from all installations. Thanks to Waring, the separate system, sometimes known as sanitary sewerage, gained an early foothold in the United States—but only after heated opposition from civil engineers. During the uproar, Waring was accused in professional journals such as the *Sanitary Engineer*, and *American Architect and Building News* of "sanitary shrieking" and flawed engineering judgment; he fought back in an article published in the *Sanitary Engineer* in October 1883 repudiating combined sewers as "relics of barbarism." Too big to be self-flushing, he argued, they collected debris that festered.

Waring's engineering firm, Waring, Chapman & Farquahar, with offices in Newport and New York, conducted a sizable business. He surveyed much of it in *Sewerage and Land Drainage* (1889), the magnum opus of his professional life.

Waring's career came to a spectacular climax. In 1895, William L. Strong, elected as reform mayor of New York, invited him to serve as street cleaning commissioner. Taking charge of a notoriously inefficient, deeply politicized department that rarely cleaned more than the main thoroughfares, he reorganized it from top to bottom. He ran it almost like a cavalry unit, put all street sweepers into white duck uniforms, banished party politics as a basis of employment, instituted labor arbitration, upgraded all gear and apparatus, fostered both juvenile cleanup clubs and a civic advisory board, and, for the first time in living memory, got all New York City streets clean. The sweepers, known as the White Wings, became the toast of the city. Many other cities adopted White Wings in the next two decades. Historians have judged his reforms a turning point in the history of the American municipal administration. However, Tammany Hall returned to power in 1897 and terminated his service.

Waring's life ended abruptly. In 1898, with his reputation still growing, President William McKinley sent him to Cuba to deal with what was still seen as the king of the dirt diseases, yellow fever. After a two-week study of camp sanitation and conditions in Havana, he returned to New York, took ill upon arrival, and within four days succumbed to the disease he had been sent to conquer. Within months, he was apotheosized as the "Apostle of Cleanliness."

Melosi, Martin V. *Garbage in the Cities: Refuse, Reform, and the Environment, 1880–1890.* Environmental History Series, no. 4. College Station: Texas A&M Press, 1981. Provides an excellent, well-documented chapter on Waring's career; views his achievements as street cleaning commissioner as a turning point in the history of urban refuse management.

Peterson, Jon A. "The Impact of Sanitary Reform upon American Urban Planning, 1840–1890." *Journal of Social History* 13 (September 1979), 83–103. Discusses the sanitary reform context out of which Waring, Olmsted, and others addressed issues of waste removal, townside layout, and sanitary survey planning.

Tarr, Joel A. *The Search for the Ultimate Sink: Urban Pollution in Historical Perspective.* Akron, Ohio: University of Akron Press, 1996. A sophisticated reworking of the late nineteenth-century civil engineering critique of Waring and his separate sewerage idea, faulting his preoccupation with sewer gas and his financial interest in his own system.

Jon A. Peterson

WASHINGTON, GEORGE
(1732–1799)
general, farmer, surveyor, president of the United States, landscape designer

George Washington was born into a modest planter family of fourth-generation Virginia colonists. His father died when he was eleven, and his formal education ended at fifteen when he was apprenticed as a surveyor. It was a skill he used all his life to describe landscape and to design and plan.

Washington joined the top ranks of Virginia gentry thanks to his own industry and intelligence, and to his marriage (1759) to a rich widow, Martha Dandridge Custis. In 1761 he inherited Mount Vernon, then 2,126 acres, the property he had been leasing as a planter since 1754. In 1775 he took command of the colonies' Continental Army and carried the American Revolution through to a successful conclusion in 1783. He then retired to Mount Vernon. From 1789 through 1797, he served as president of the United States. During his two terms, he went home only fifteen times, but there probably wasn't a day that he didn't think of improving Mount Vernon, as is amply borne out in his private papers.

During his forty-five-year tenure, Washington twice extensively remodeled the house (which now again stands as he finished it). Having at first completed the original outbuildings and rectangular gardens that were partly in place when he moved to Mount Vernon, he then completely redesigned them, beginning in the 1770s, just as he rode off to war. The lines of the curved bowling green and the two brick-walled gardens, so familiar today, were in place by the time he became president, although he continued to plan and make changes until the day before his death.

The work was carried out by slaves and by a series of hired and indentured servants and craftsmen. Washington's domestic correspondence during his long absences give a fairly complete picture of what he wanted the place to be. That picture changed over time, from a local and conventional vision of a handsome slave-run plantation machine (like Westover, Shirley, Stratford Hall, or Carter's Grove) to something that could be called a national vision. Washington saw good agriculture as the basis of a strong and self-sufficient nation, and Mount Vernon as the model, even as he dealt with insurmountable problems of bad soil and slave labor. From the time that he returned from war until his death, he struggled with the problem of slavery, feeling a personal repugnance for it but finally accepting its inconsistency with the freedoms offered by his new nation. Yet for political and financial reasons, he found himself unable to act in his lifetime as he did by the terms of his

East front overlooking the Potomac, Mount Vernon, Virginia. courtesy The Mount Vernon Ladies Association of the Union.

will in freeing his slaves, the only founding father to do so.

Washington designed his house, gardens, and landscape himself, creating a highly sophisticated composition and one that is unusually well integrated owing to two unique features: the open hyphens connecting the house block with the kitchen and the visitors' hall, and the famous double-story piazza. Washington was the first to open both sides of such a connecting hyphen, and the flashing slices of the view of the Potomac River framed by the arches are practically cinematic. He was the best horseman of his age, said Thomas Jefferson*, and this love of rhythmic movement and successive views is one of the hallmarks of Mount Vernon. The old main drive, now no longer used, was once equally kinetic as well as theatrical in this sense, with strong contrasts of darkness and light, enclosure and openness. The much-copied piazza directly links an otherwise enclosed house

with the outdoors. It cools and shades, as so many of Washington's visitors admiringly remarked. It mediates the difference between the vast river and the comparatively small house. Seen from the river, the principal viewpoint of the house, the piazza transforms the building into that ideal landscape ornament: the temple in the distance, seen in so many classical landscape paintings.

What enabled Washington to envision and create such an outstanding work of landscape art? More extensively than any of the other figures that shaped the young nation, he traveled in the thirteen colonies that would form the union. He was also vastly more familiar than they with the frontier, fighting in the French and Indian War (1756–1759), traveling as a surveyor and land speculator throughout his life. He described the landscapes he saw in his diaries. He rode through the Virginia woods hunting with equal interest foxes and young flowering trees to transplant.

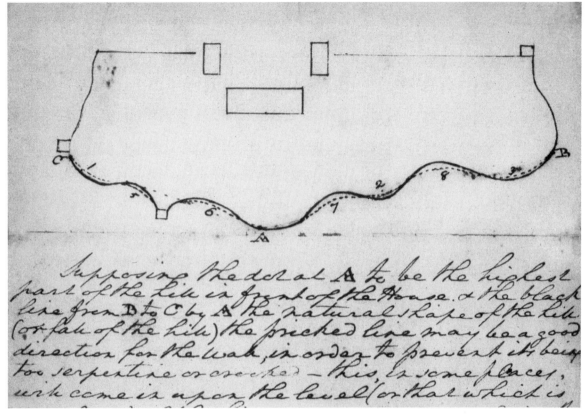

Deer park wall, Mount Vernon. Sketch by Washington. Courtesy The Mount Vernon Ladies Association of the Union.

His design training can be said to depend on these experiences, as well as on an ingrained habit of military efficiency, an obsessive interest in detail, and what seems to have been a very good visual memory. That visual lexicon would have included gardens, townhouses, and plantations observed from his service as a colonial burgess in Williamsburg, Virginia, during the Revolutionary War and on his presidential tours. He once described himself quite truthfully as a man who used "no other guide but his eye to direct his choice."

He owned only three books that dealt with landscape and garden: Batty Langley's *New Principles of Gardening: The Laying out and Planting of Parterres, Groves, Wildernesses, Labyrinths, Avenues, parks, etc., after a more Grand and Rural Manner than has been done before* (London, 1728), the one-volume abridgement of Philip Miller's *Gardener's Dictionary* (London, 1771), and Miller's *Gardeners Kalender* (London, 1762). He must

also have read Joseph Addison's thoughts on "the pleasures of the imagination" and "the beautiful wildness of Nature" (*The Spectator*, London, 1711–1712) since Addison's collected essays stood on his shelves.

This said, a broader index of what "landscape" meant to him is found in part in his large battery of books on "the New Husbandry"—Enlightenment agricultural improvement—and in his diaries and correspondence, which are filled with directives that deal equally with aesthetics on the farm and function in the garden. (It goes without saying that he was not the only American colonial of his class and era to create a beautiful and efficient domestic ensemble; it was the age of the confident and often gifted amateur landscape designer.)

The larger landscape of the five farms (7,600 acres) no longer exists and is now a series of suburban developments and a riverine park. Washington treated the farms as five separate work units but united them as a whole

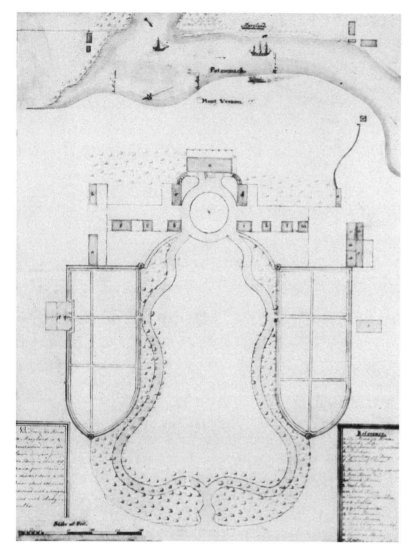

Detail of engraving after the plan of
Mount Vernon. Drawn by Samuel
Vaughan, 1787. Courtesy The Mount
Vernon Ladies Association of the
Union.

by placing the barns and roads strategically for visual
effect as well as for efficiency. He had vistas cut through
the woods from the house and from various approaches.
Not until much later in American landscape history
(during the Country Place era, 1890–1940) would one
find such large scale, topographically determined patterns again used so successfully.

Washington's widest influence on landscape design
is indirect. As president, he commissioned Pierre-
Charles L'Enfant, the French military engineer, who in
1791 created the radial plan for Washington, D.C., and
supported him in the face of considerable opposition
from Jefferson and others just long enough for the
designer to produce the plan before being fired early in
1792.

Washington's understanding of landscape, well-
honed at Mount Vernon, was deeply symbolic, almost
defying translation into language. From his work at
Mount Vernon, it is also clear that he understood the
power of design especially when it is strongly determined by topography. The heroic scale of the capital
city's plan (11 square miles, at a time when other

founding fathers were thinking in terms of 1,500 acres) spoke to Washington's firm hopes for the eventual wealth and stability of the nation. The design embodied the structure of the new government, with its "President's House" and "Congress House" linked symbolically by the Mall, representing the Constitution. Hills capped with buildings and sight lines that linked the parts of the city would have been familiar to him from his own beautifully placed farm structures and his prized "Vistos" at Mount Vernon, waving with amber fields of grain.

Greenberg, Allan. *George Washington, Architect*. New York: Andreas Papadakis Publisher, 1999. Plans and section drawings illustrate Washington's design of the larger landscape.

Griswold, Mac. *Washington's Gardens at Mount Vernon: Landscape of the Inner Man*. Boston: Houghton Mifflin, 1998. A character sketch thinly disguised as a garden book.

Washington, George. *The Diaries of George Washington*. Ed. Donald Jackson and Dorothy Twohig. 6 vols. Charlottesville: University Press of Virginia, 1976–1979. The annotated diaries give the best continuous picture of Washington's development of Mount Vernon.

Mac Griswold

WATERMAN, HAZEL WOOD
(1865–1948)
architect, landscape architect

Hazel Wood was born in Tuskeegee, Alabama, but her family moved to northern California when she was three years old. Her parents prized education for all ten of their children and made it possible for her to attend the University of California at Berkeley as an art student. In 1889, after completing only one year of college, Wood married Waldo Waterman, a fellow student, a mining engineer, and the son of California governor Robert Waterman. As a bride, Hazel moved to Julian, a tiny mountain town east of San Diego, where Waldo managed a family-owned gold mine; there the Watermans began their family of three children.

In 1894, after a nationwide depression forced the sale of the family mining interests, the Watermans moved to San Diego. The young couple hired architect Irving Gill to help them plan a house overlooking San Diego's harbor. The process of designing the house shaped Waterman's future career.

In 1900, Gill was beginning to establish his reputation as an innovative, regionally sensitive architect. Working with him, Waterman was able to put her own artistic talents and commonsense instincts to practical use. After finishing her modest, functional "granite cottage," Waterman recorded her design philosophy in a

Hazel Wood Waterman. Courtesy San Diego Historical Society, Photograph Collection.

Casa de Estudillo, "Ramona's Marriage Place," San Diego, restored by Waterman, 1909. Courtesy San Diego Historical Society, Photograph Collection.

March 1902 article for *House Beautiful*. She advocated creating a place for family living that incorporated "an open-air life" in which the "veranda and garden are a kind of out-of-door rooms which seem to form a part of the arrangement of the house itself." Although this is a popular concept in modern California architecture, it was considered avant-garde at the turn of the century.

Other articles followed as Waterman developed her interest in interrelationships among the architecture, landscapes, and histories of geoclimatically similar regions of the Mediterranean and southern California. As she refined her architectural awareness, she also integrated the companion landscape roles of patios and livable gardens into her design consciousness.

In 1903, Waterman's husband died, leaving her and their children with a limited income. At Gill's suggestion, she pursued correspondence studies in architecture and then took on drafting and rendering assignments in her home for Gill's firm. At the age of forty-one, after a three-year apprenticeship, she began designing houses for her own clients under her mentor's supervision.

Waterman's clientele and reputation expanded quickly in San Diego. In 1909 sugar magnate John D. Spreckles commissioned her to restore one of San Diego's period landmarks: the aged, disintegrating, adobe town home of a family of notable early settlers, the Estudillos. Waterman's thorough historical research and authentic methods of reconstruction—using early Mexican building techniques—were so successful that for decades the Casa de Estudillo was acclaimed as a prototype for similar preservation projects.

Although most of Waterman's reconstruction of the rambling old adobe structure was true to its regional style, the design of its inner courtyard was not. Her landscape layout for the large patio and utility yard deviated widely from its original use as a chore-centered outdoor workplace. The courtyard was ornamented with plants fashionable in Waterman's time and with decorative, but inauthentic, features such as a plain concrete central fountain. These fanciful additions enhanced the commercial value of the Casa de Estudillo for the development of a cluster of souvenir and curio shops. The Casa

Casa de Estudillo, Old Town State Historic Park, San Diego. Photo Carol Greentree.

de Estudillo became a prime tourist attraction in southern California.

Popularly dubbed "Ramona's Marriage Place" because it called up the sentimental images prevalent in such novels as Helen Hunt Jackson's *Ramona*, the rebuilt adobe structure romanticized California's short-lived Mexican rancho era. The layout of the courtyard helped shape the myth of the nineteenth-century picturesque garden that became popular in Waterman's day and contributed to the rise of tourism and real estate enterprises in southern California.

Waterman's other landscape designs were few, but choice. Her first love was architecture, but in siting her houses she was ever mindful of the advantages of incorporating gardens and vistas into her plans. Waterman's most brilliant landscape design was a striking, large town garden commissioned in 1917 by Julius Wangenheim, a prominent San Diego businessman. Highly architectural in concept, this walled landscape featured formal stepped terraces, a series of broad lily pools linked to tiled fountains, and a three-sided tea pavilion open to intimate vistas within the densely planted enclosure. Kate Sessions*, a famed local nurserywoman, installed the plants. The colors and shadows of foliage on buttressed brick walls softened the bold masses of masonry, and the richly textured effect was doubled by reflections in the tiered pools. Hints of interesting spaces beyond the confines of the garden were given through pierced-wall brickwork panels and by the placement of heavily carved, spindled gates. Featured in the August 1920 issue of *House and Garden*, this roomy city garden won a 1930 award "for design and execution" from the San Diego chapter of the American Institute of Architects. The garden was demolished during the 1960s.

Until 1929, Waterman continued to design houses in San Diego's garden neighborhoods near Balboa Park, the site of the 1915–1916 Panama Pacific Exposition. After she retired at age sixty-four, she moved to Berkeley, where she continued to write and travel until her death in 1948 at age eighty-two. Most of the buildings she designed are still in use today, but her gardens have been obscured by three-quarters of a century of change.

Thornton, Sally Bullard. *Daring to Dream: The Life of Hazel Wood Waterman*. San Diego: San Diego Historical Society, 1987. Illustrated biography discusses Waterman's professional contributions and her influence on the romantic garden image of southern California.

Waterman, Hazel W. "A Granite Cottage in California." *House Beautiful*, March 1902. Illustrated description of the San Diego house the author and her husband co-designed with architect Gill; focuses on planning that favors indoor/outdoor living in the mild coastal California clime.

Waterman, Hazel W. "The Influence of an Olden Time." *House Beautiful*, June 1903. General illustrated summary of the garden history of southern California, with special emphasis on the era of adobe buildings and their courtyards; written at the apogee of the Mission Revival era.

Carol Greentree

WAUGH, FRANK ALBERT
(1869–1943)
landscape architect, educator, author

Frank A. Waugh was born in Sheboygan Falls, Wisconsin, and was raised in rural McPherson, Kansas. He studied horticulture at Kansas State Agricultural College at Manhattan, earning an undergraduate degree in 1891 and a graduate degree in 1894. From 1893 to 1895 he taught at the Oklahoma Agricultural and Mechanic Arts College at Stillwater, where the design of the school's campus became the subject of his master's thesis.

In 1895, Waugh moved to New England to take a post teaching horticulture at the University of Vermont at Burlington. Shortly thereafter he began to contribute articles on pomology and fruit culture to the *Country Gentleman*, a rural journal for which he later served as horticultural editor for many years.

In 1902, Waugh moved to Amherst, Massachusetts, to head the Division of Horticulture at Massachusetts Agricultural College. By 1908 he had established the school's Department of Landscape Gardening (later renamed the Department of Landscape Architecture). There he authored several textbooks that exerted substantial influence on higher education in landscape architecture throughout the United States.

Waugh's first book, *Book of Landscape Gardening*,

Frank Waugh. Courtesy Special Collections and Archives, W.E.B. Du Bois Library, University of Massachusetts Amherst.

was published in 1899 and went through several major revisions and three editions, the last being introduced in 1926 as a comprehensive text for professional practice. Other texts treated specialized topics and included *Landscape Beautiful* (1910), *The Natural Style of Landscape Gardening* (1917), *Formal Design in Landscape Architecture* (1927), and *Outdoor Theaters: The Design, Construction and Use of Open-Air Auditoriums* (1917). Waugh's *Textbook of Landscape Gardening Designed for Non-Professional Students* (1922) demonstrated his strong belief that principles of landscape design should be the concern of the common citizen and not just the professional designer.

Waugh's teaching and writings remained rooted in the principles of naturalistic nineteenth-century landscape gardening, while his practice sought modern applications in campus design, orchard management, rural improvements, road and trail design, and landscape engineering for natural areas. In 1911 he edited English landscape theorist Edward Kemp's writings in *Landscape Gardening Revised and Adapted to North America: How to Lay Out a Garden*. Waugh's admiration for Andrew Jackson Downing* inspired his own writings and led him to edit in 1921 a tenth edition of Downing's *Theory and Practice of Landscape Gardening* with selected rural essays from *The Horticulturalist*.

Waugh maintained close ties to the Midwestern practitioners of the Prairie style, Jens Jensen* and Wilhelm Miller*, sharing their interest in the native landscape and use of indigenous plants in naturalistic compositions. The native landscape, particularly the varied New England landscape that extended from coastal waters and salt ponds to mountain peaks and lakes, inspired Waugh's theories and appeared as the subject of his writing as early as 1910 when he published *The Landscape Beautiful*. Influenced by the writings of German theorist Willy Lange and the horticultural work he observed at the Koeniglische Gaertner-Lehronstaldt, at Dahlen in Berlin, Waugh became interested in the emerging field of ecology and began exploring the practical applications of planting native species in association with other commonly occurring plants and under natural conditions of soil, climate, and moisture. This theory first appeared in 1917 in *The Natural Style of Landscape Gardening*, was expanded in the 1926 edition of *Book of Landscape Gardening*, and matured in the early 1930s in a trilogy of articles in *Landscape Architecture* on the ecology of the roadside, physiography of lakes and ponds, and natural plant groups.

After the passage of the Smith-Lever Act of 1914 (designed to link the research and educational programs of the land grant colleges with practical applications in agriculture and other rural arts), Waugh established a program of cooperative extension work in landscape architecture for Massachusetts. For Waugh, extension work was an opportunity to foster a sense of artistic design as well as practical horticultural knowledge among homeowners, farmers, and civic leaders who could directly influence the beautification of the rural communities where they lived. He consulted on projects in rural communities and public reservations and published *Rural Improvement: Principles of Civic Art in Rural Conditions* in 1914 and a variety of pamphlets on designing town commons, school grounds, and country roadsides.

In 1917, Waugh began consulting on the recreational development of national forests and the following year published *Recreational Uses of the National Forests* and a plan for Grand Canyon Village for the U.S. Forest Service. As a seasonal consultant, Waugh continued to work on developing national forests in many areas of the West including Bryce Canyon and Wasatch in Utah, Kings River Canyon in California, the Black Hills in South Dakota, and Mount Hood in Oregon.

During the New Deal, Waugh wrote a handbook to be used by the Civilian Conservation Corps working in national and state parks and forests, *Landscape Conservation: Planning for the Restoration, Conservation, and Utilization of Wild Lands for Parks and Forests*. Originally distributed in typescript, the work was republished as a training manual in 1937 under the CCC's Project Training Series.

The campus of the Massachusetts Agricultural College, now the University of Massachusetts, became a design laboratory for the school's department of landscape architecture. Waugh studied the recommendations made historically for the campus design by Frederick Law Olmsted Sr.* and Warren Manning*, many of which were never carried out. Waugh's own work is evident in the naturalistic design of the campus pond, the hillside beyond Morrill Hall, and the Rhododendron Garden. Waugh also drew up a fifty-year master plan for Kansas State College in 1914. An accomplished photographer, printmaker, and flutist, Waugh traveled extensively in the United States, Germany, and Japan.

Waugh was a Fellow of the American Society of Landscape Architects and received the George Roberts White Gold Medal of Honor from the Massachusetts Horticultural Society. In his obituary A. D. Taylor* wrote: "No single individual has done more to inspire the layman to live a richer life by bringing to his home surroundings the orderly and attractive elements of landscape architecture."

Steiner, Frederick R., and Brooks, Kenneth R. "Agricultural Education and Landscape Architecture." *Landscape Journal* 5 (Spring 1986), 19–32. Scholarly article examining the relationship between land grant colleges and the professional training of landscape architects and horticulturists in the United States.

Waugh, Frank Albert. *Book of Landscape Gardening: Treatise on the General Principles Governing Outdoor Art; With Sundry Suggestions for their Application in the Commoner Problems of Gardening.* [1899.] 3d rev. ed. New York: Orange Judd, 1926. Waugh's most comprehensive text for professional practice, including general principles of unity, variety, motive, character, propriety, and finish with instructions for what he called the "architectural," "natural," and "picturesque" styles.

Waugh, Frank Albert. "Ecology of the Roadside." *Landscape Architecture* 21 (January 1931), 81–92; "Natural Plant Groups." *Landscape Architecture* 21 (April 1931), 169–179; and "The Physiography of Lakes and Ponds." *Landscape Architecture* 22 (January 1932), 89–92. A trilogy of articles setting forth the practical applications of an ecological theory for planting of native trees, shrubs, and other plants according to natural conditions of climate, moisture, and soil and in association with other naturally occurring species; theory based on observations of nature and aimed at the replication of natural conditions to enhance the beauty of the country roadside, the shores of manmade lakes and ponds, and the restoration of woodlands.

Linda Flint McClelland

NELVA MARGARET WEBER
(1908–1990)
landscape architect, author

Nelva Margaret Weber was born in Arrowsmith, in central Illinois. One of three daughters of a farm family, Weber was plowing the fields with a six-horse tandem team at the age of eleven. She knew she wanted to become a landscape architect from the moment when, as a sophomore in a four-room high school, she read a description of the profession that cited three essentials: artistic ability, love of nature, and imagination. That it was also described as a good field for women was amazing to her in the 1920s, she later recalled.

Weber took a B.A. majoring in English at Illinois Wesleyan University, and followed that with a B.F.A. in Landscape Architecture at the University of Illinois. In 1935, she completed her M.A. in plant ecology there with a thesis titled "Prairie Borders and Their Application in Landscape Architecture."

Weber's career was firmly grounded in public practice. Her first ten years' experience (1935–1945) included

Nelva Weber. Courtesy Mac Griswold.

HOW TO PLAN YOUR OWN HOME LANDSCAPE

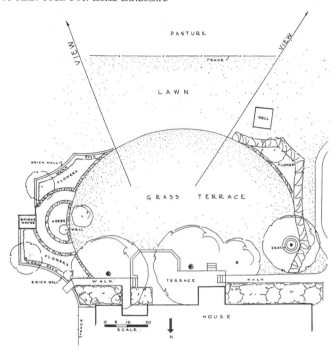

Plan for "Redesigning the Outdoor
Space," c. 1960s. Courtesy Mac
Griswold.

designing cloverleaves and interchanges for the Palisades
Parkway along the Hudson River, with the New York City
landscape architectural firm of C. C. Combs; site planning
and circulation layout at the Bermuda Air Base for the
architectural firm of Shaw, Maess & Murphy; and five
years with the New York City Parks Department, where
she took on all areas of landscape work, from grading and
planting design to the supervision of five draftsmen.

These experiences focused elements of her approach
which she brought to her later projects: from the Palisades
Parkway, a desire always to understand the geology of the
site; from the air base, a preoccupation with elegant, efficient circulation and grading; and from the park work, an
interest in shifting shadow patterns as they are dispersed
over large areas. Where many other practitioners of the
day, especially women, came to the field from the arts,
Weber came to landscape architecture from the sciences.
She was never "painting a picture" but rather was driven
by an interest in process—the soil chemistry, the angle of
the sun or of slope, the annual rainfall.

Weber's plantings were informed by a profound
horticultural curiosity, to judge from voluminous notes
made during years of nursery visits. She preferred to use
indigenous species but was no native plant extremist. She
was especially fond of deciduous woodland understory
shrubs and small trees, such as sourwood, shadblow, and
summersweet, species that are now ubiquitous but were
unusual in designed landscapes at the time.

After the birth of her two children, Weber set up
her own office in 1945 in the New York City apartment
she shared with her husband, Joseph M. Sammataro. In
1970, when he retired as a project architect with
Edward Durrell Stone, he joined her as a drafting,
administrative, and planning associate. Today, Sammataro's impact on Weber's practice can be seen mainly
in the plans he drew to illustrate her book, *How to Plan
Your Own Home Landscape*. One of Weber's signature
designs stands out in this text: an elliptically curved and
graded terrace in brick, turf, or bluestone which is as
much a part of sinuously curved fifties' design as the
famous bias-cut wraparound skirt created by Claire
McCardell. A number of the projects Weber reworked
illustrate the power of this sweep: they had been cast in
the strict rectilinear patterns of the Beaux Arts, which

View from the Lowell Thomas Terrace, 1961. Photo N. M. Weber.

included the straight-shot vista; Weber often managed the transit to modernism by broadening not only their terraces but also the sweep of their viewsheds.

In the sixties and seventies, as modernism lost its allure, Weber accommodated herself to other influences and sometimes to the more elaborately traditional ideas of her clients. However, whenever she found the chance—whether in design or in horticulture—she went for the simplest plan, the most irregular plant silhouette. Other signatures are her stacked forest plantings, which again echo her thesis training; sitting areas carefully shaded both by simply built forms and by deciduous foliage; and the adroit separation of vehicular traffic from pedestrian and recreational areas.

Well-known private clients included Mary Rocke-feller, Oscar de la Renta, comedian Gary Moore, and dancer Arthur Murray. A large body of Weber's residential work exists in Litchfield, Connecticut, where she and Sammataro maintained a home, and in the Bernardsville–Far Hills section of New Jersey.

Public work in later life included parts of the Illinois Wesleyan University and Bard College campuses; the site planning and landscape architecture of Purnell School, Pottersville, New Jersey; and the landscape of the First Congregational Church, Litchfield, Connecticut. In 1974 she designed the Tree of Life Arboretum around the visitors' center at Hancock Shaker Village in Pittsfield, Massachusetts, which is in good condition today. She published nearly a hundred articles in major news publications such as the *New York Times* and in professional magazines such as *Landscape Architecture*. She left an unpublished book manuscript, "One Hundred and One Little Landscapes," which remains with her papers.

Weber belongs to the generation that formed a bridge between the Country Place era and the postwar suburban years. Her designs reflected the simplification of the elaborate pattern of country life that by the 1920s had evolved at the summer and weekend residences of America's elite. Her best residential projects throughout her career can be called modernist in the sense that they

Fletcher Steele.
Blue Steps, Naumkeag.
Stockbridge, Massachusetts.
Photo Carol Betsch.

Fletcher Steele.
Public Library Amphitheater,
Camden, Maine, c. 1950.
Photo Peter Hornbeck.
Courtesy Robin Karson.

Adolph Strauch.
Burnet tomb, Spring Grove Cemetery.
Cincinnati, Ohio.
Photo Blanche M. G. Linden.

Adolph Strauch.
Geyser Lake, Spring Grove Cemetery.
Cincinnati, Ohio.
Photo Blanche M. G. Linden.

Albert D. Taylor.
Charles Briggs estate.
Cleveland, Ohio.
Courtesy Smithsonian Institution,
Archives of American Gardens.

George Washington.
East front overlooking the Potomac,
Mount Vernon, Virginia.
Courtesy The Mount Vernon Ladies
Association of the Union.

Hazel Wood Waterman.
Casa de Estudillo,
Old Town State Historic Park.
San Diego, California.
Photo Carol Greentree.

Nelva Weber.
View from the Lowell Thomas Terrace.
Pawling, New York.
Photo N. M. Weber.

Robert Wheelright.
Allée of magnolias, Goodstay.
Wilmington, Delaware.
Courtesy Smithsonian Institution,
Archives of American Gardens.

Morley J. Williams.
Tryon Palace State Historic Site.
New Bern, North Carolina.
Photo Thomas Beaman.

Harriet Barnhart Wimmer.
Sea World.
San Diego, California.
Photo Carol Greentree.

Margaret Winters.
Garden plan for
Mr. and Mrs. James Fisher.
Pittsburgh, Pennsylvania.
Private collection.

Florence Yoch and Lucille Council.
Il Brolino. Santa Barbara, California.
Photo Robin Karson.

rigorously return garden and landscape to their elemental purposes. In her designs, as in her considerable writings, Weber was always asking how design serves function. That spirit of inquiry into the working practicalities of design produced a body of work that achieved purity and an almost tensile elegance.

Weber, Nelva Margaret. "Prairie-Forest Borders and Their Application in Landscape Architecture." Master's thesis, Department of Botany, University of Illinois, Urbana, 1935. Analyses of soil and climate conditions and of prairie border plants, different types of prairie borders in nature (including one on Long Island: Hither Woods), and ways to use them in highways, parks, and gardens; appendix of prairie plants suitable for landscape planting; illustrated with photographs, plans, and sketches.

Weber, Nelva Margaret. *How to Plan Your Own Home Landscape: How to Organize Your Outdoor Space and How to Utilize It for Maximum Pleasure and Minimum Maintenance All Year Round.* 1976. Reprint. Indianapolis: Bobbs-Merrill, 1982. Guides reader to look first at geomorphology and solar positioning of a residential site, then continues on to the landscape planning of all areas; illustrated with photographs by Molly Adams (mostly unidentified and undated) and plan drawings by Joseph Sammataro.

An archive of Weber's papers consisting of five boxes, one map case of drawings, and one oversize box of rolls of drawings is in the Rare and Manuscript Collections, Carl A. Kroch Library, Cornell University (Nelva Margaret Weber, 1908–1990. Papers, 1933–1986).

Mac Griswold

WEIDENMANN, JACOB
(1829–1893)
landscape gardener, cemetery designer, author

Jacob Weidenmann was born in Winterthur, Switzerland. He studied architecture and fine art at the Akademie der Bildenden Kunste in Munich before emigrating to the United States in 1856. Shortly thereafter he adopted landscape architecture as a profession and in 1859 designed and became superintendent of City Park (later named Bushnell Park) in Hartford, Connecticut. Over the next ten years Weidenmann also designed that city's South Common (Barnard Park), Cedar Hill Cemetery, and the grounds of several private homes. He superintended construction of plans prepared by Frederick Law Olmsted* and Calvert Vaux* for the grounds of the Hartford Retreat for the Insane, now the Institute for Living. Weidenmann's first book, *Beautifying Country Homes* (1870), documents the major commissions he executed during the Hartford phase of his career; it also contains the best surviving evidence of his technical skill in site engineering as well as his taste in landscape design. On publication of the book, *The Horticulturist* praised Weidenmann for "excellent service to the public in his superb work." Olmsted later described it as a "standard work," and Mariana Griswold Van Rensselaer* included *Beauti-*

Jacob Weidenmann. Courtesy Miriam and Ira D. Wallach Division of Art, Prints, and Photographs, The New York Public Library, Astor, Lenox and Tilden Foundations.

"Ocean-view from the Terrace," Weidenmann's watercolor drawing showing improvements to Masquetux, Babylon, N.Y. Courtesy Miriam and Ira D. Wallach Division of Art, Prints, and Photographs, The New York Public Library, Astor, Lenox and Tilden Foundations.

fying Country Homes in a select list of the best books on landscape gardening published since 1820.

In 1870, Weidenmann traveled to Europe, and the following year resumed his association with Olmsted and Vaux as a landscape architect at Prospect Park in Brooklyn. After Olmsted and Vaux dissolved their partnership in 1872, Olmsted increasingly relied on Weidenmann for professional assistance, an arrangement that became a partnership two years later. Weidenmann assisted his more famous partner with plans for the Buffalo park system, Mount Royal Park in Montreal, and the grounds of the U.S. Capitol, as well as the design of several private residences. Together they prepared plans for the Schuylkill Arsenal, and Olmsted praised as "first rate" Weidenmann's contributions to a design that met the complex needs of a military installation. Weidenmann also assumed primary responsibility for the design of Congress Park in Saratoga Springs, New York. Olmsted found his associate "well informed, capable and efficient" and testified that in their various collaborations Weidenmann conducted his responsibilities in a highly skilled and professional manner.

During these years Weidenmann also enjoyed several commissions independent of Olmsted, including designs for the Cornell University campus; at least five private estates; a Staten Island subdivision, Hill Park Estate; and preparation of plans for Stewart Hartshorne's

new suburban community at Short Hills, New Jersey. Weidenmann's growing professional standing was recognized by the medal and citation he received from the U.S. Centennial Commission in 1876 for his designs for Masquetux, the Henry B. Hyde estate at Babylon, New York. He then began preparing a handbook, *American Garden Architecture*, which he intended as a showcase for his designs for ornamental garden structures, gatehouses, and cottages. Weidenmann apparently expected to publish the book in monthly installments—the first number appeared in January 1878—but perhaps because of poor sales he left the bulk of the project uncompleted, and subsequent issues are fragmentary.

In 1884, Weidenmann accepted a major commission to design the grounds of the state capitol in Des Moines, Iowa. The plans for the capitol, he informed Olmsted, "are the most detailed work I ever prepared. I had to embrace everything connected with the grounds, including a flight of eighty steps 40 feet wide [and] ornamented with architectural embellishments, fountains, seats and statues." There he also designed the grounds of the Iowa State Agricultural Fair and a 45-acre residential subdivision for the firm of Polk & Hubbell. While he was overseeing these commissions, Weidenmann retained an office in New York City. But the absence of commissions in the East and the amount of time spent traveling to Iowa led him in January 1886 to accept a five-year contract for the

Weidenmann's cover for first issue of *American Garden Architecture,* January 1877. Courtesy Miriam and Ira D. Wallach Division of Art, Prints, and Photographs, The New York Public Library, Astor, Lenox and Tilden

superintendence of Mount Hope Cemetery in Chicago. His relationship with the cemetery's directors was acrimonious and short-lived, however. While in Chicago, Weidenmann began writing a series of essays on cemetery design for *Building Budget,* a local architectural publication, which formed the basis for his book *Modern Cemeteries* (1888). On his return to New York, Weidenmann began preparing a site plan for Brooklyn College. His last known work was a design for Pope Park in Hartford, but Weidenmann died before it could be completed.

Weidenmann was highly regarded for his cemetery designs. He championed the "lawn plan," first advocated by Adolph Strauch* at Cincinnati's Spring Grove Cemetery, which prohibited enclosing individual or family plots with railings. Olmsted considered Weidenmann the "highest authority on the subject" of cemetery design and described him as the most skilled practitioner "in this department of our profession." Perhaps appropriately, the man who once remarked "my destiny is to work for the grave diggers" was buried in Cedar Hill Cemetery, Hartford, one of his first important landscape designs.

Weidenmann was devoted to landscape architecture, which he considered "this noblest of all Art professions." He was appalled that individuals without adequate training could practice landscape architecture, and attempted to increase the stature of practitioners by advocating the establishment of a "school in which all branches of our profession are taught." Thorough knowledge of horticulture, engineering, architecture, and the fine arts would, he hoped, "purify the so maltreated profession and elevate it in the minds of the people to proper standing in science and art."

Weidenmann, Jacob. *American Garden Architecture, 1877–1878.* A fragmentary edition, with numerous finished drawings and sketches, in the Miriam and Ira D. Wallach Division of Art, Prints and Photographs, New York Public Library, New York City.

Weidenmann, Jacob. *Modern Cemeteries: An Essay upon the Improvements and Proper Management of Rural Cemeteries.* Chicago, 1888. Weidenmann's most complete statement of the history and principles of cemetery design, and an articulate plea for simplicity and breadth of scenery in burial grounds.

Weidenmann, Jacob. *Victorian Landscape Gardening: A Facsimile of Jacob Weidenmann's "Beautifying Country Homes,"* with a new introduction by David Schuyler. Watkins Glen, N.Y.: American Life Foundation, 1978. Weidenmann's best-known work, originally published 1870, and his most comprehensive statement of his principles of landscape design; plans and descriptive texts for several of his important designs.

David Schuyler

WELCH, ADONIJAH STRONG
(1821–1889)
landscape gardener

Adonijah Strong Welch was born in East Hampton, Connecticut. At the age of eighteen he moved to Michigan, where he prepared for college at the academy at Romeo. He was admitted to the University of Michigan in 1843, receiving a B.A. in 1846 and an M.A. in 1852. He studied law in 1846–1847 and was admitted to the bar, but chose not to practice.

In 1847, Welch was elected principal of the first union or graded school in Michigan, at Jonesville. He served for two years and then joined the gold rush to California, where he remained for over a year. Because of his success in the conduct of the school at Jonesville, in 1851 he was offered, and accepted, the principalship of the State Normal School at Ypsilanti, Michigan, where he remained for fifteen years. In 1865, because of impaired health, Welch left the Normal School, moving to Florida, where he was elected to the U.S. Senate, serving from 1867 to 1869. He then resigned to become the first president of the Iowa State Agricultural College.

The new president's inaugural address provides insight into his philosophy of education and his character: "The plan of organization which we have adopted commits our College to the promotion of two great and

Adonijah Strong Welch. Courtesy Iowa State University, University Archives.

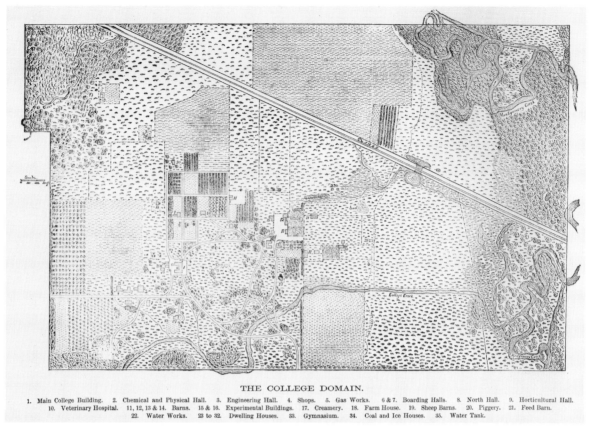

THE COLLEGE DOMAIN.

1. Main College Building.   2. Chemical and Physical Hall.   3. Engineering Hall.   4. Shops.   5. Gas Works.   6 & 7. Boarding Halls.   8. North Hall.   9. Horticultural Hall.
10. Veterinary Hospital.   11, 12, 13 & 14. Barns.   15 & 16. Experimental Buildings.   17. Creamery.   18. Farm House.   19. Sheep Barns.   20. Piggery.   21. Feed Barn.
22. Water Works.   23 to 32. Dwelling Houses.   33. Gymnasium.   34. Coal and Ice Houses.   35. Water Tank.

Plan of Iowa State Agricultural College, c. 1883. From *Tenth Biennial Report of the Board of Trustees of the Iowa State Agricultural College and Farm, Made to the Governor of Iowa, for the Years 1882 and 1883.*

Landscape plantings and central lawn southeast of Old Main, c. 1880s. Courtesy Iowa State University, University Archives.

salutary educational reforms. One of these is the withdrawal of the ancient classics from the place of honor which they have largely held in our college curricula, and the liberal substitution of those branches of natural science which underlie the industries of this beautiful state. The other is the free admission of young women on equal terms with young men to all the privileges and honors which the institution can bestow."

Welch found at Iowa State a splendid opportunity and a wealth of raw material with which to practice the thing he liked best to do, landscape gardening. On a bleak windswept prairie farm, he laid out the college campus, locating buildings, drives, walks, groups of trees, and shrubbery. In addition to his administrative work, he lectured on landscape gardening, using Andrew Jackson Downing's* *Treatise on the Theory and Practice of Landscape Gardening* as a text for his nine-week course. Early reports of the board of trustees indicate that Iowa State was among the earliest institutions in the United States to offer a landscape gardening course. With the help of 35 to 40 students, who were required to work three hours daily for the institution, Welch put his teaching on landscape gardening into practice. Having very little to guide him in selection of plants, he depended largely on native American species. O. C. Simonds*, later brought to Ames to continue work on the campus, deemed Welch's plan admirable.

Welch served as president from 1869 until failing health obliged him to resign in 1883. After resigning he accepted a commission from the United States government to report on the organization and management of the leading agricultural schools of Europe. He visited Germany, England, and Belgium, and his report was published in 1885. He then returned to the college, where he accepted the chair of history of civilization and practical psychology. The duties of this professorship and the writing of several books occupied him until his death at his winter home in Pasadena, California.

Budd, J. L. "Condition of the Department of Horticulture and Forestry for the Year 1877; The Lawn and Drives." *Seventh Biennial Report of the Board of Trustees of the Iowa State Agricultural College and Farm, made to The Governor of Iowa for the Years 1876 and 1877.* Des Moines, 1877. A description of the laying out and planting of the grounds of the college.

Chamberlain, W. I., and Benjamin F. Gue. "At Rest. Exgovernor Gue's Address." *The Aurora of the Iowa Agricultural College, Ames, Iowa* 18, no. 1 (1889). Issue dedicated to the memorial address on Welch's death; contains biographical information on Welch: how he came to be selected as the first president of Iowa State Agricultural College, his plan of organization of the college, and his academic career as "a scholar, a scientist, a metaphysician, an artist, a statesman, and an educator."

Welch, Adonijah Strong. *Report on the Organization and Management of Seven Agricultural Schools in Germany, Belgium, and England, made to Hon. George B. Loring, U.S. Commissioner of Agriculture, by A. S. Welch, LL. D.* [Department of Agriculture Report No. 36.] Washington, D.C., 1885. Results of Welch's inspection of foreign agricultural schools and stations; 107 pages.

Robert R. Harvey

WHEELWRIGHT, ROBERT
(1884–1965)
landscape architect, educator, author

Robert Wheelwright was born in Jamaica Plain, near Boston. He graduated from high school in Pottstown, Pennsylvania in 1902, received an A.B. from Harvard College in 1906, and earned an M.L.A. from Harvard University in 1908. After graduating, Wheelwright worked briefly for the Philadelphia architect Wilson Eyre. In 1910 he entered the office of Charles Downing Lay*, a landscape architect who was one of the founders of the American Society of Landscape Architects.

Wheelwright's association with Lay prompted him

Robert Wheelwright by Gardner Cox. Courtesy Mrs. Austin Lamont.

to found, with Henry Vincent Hubbard*, then an instructor at Harvard, the quarterly journal *Landscape Architecture,* the "Official Organ of the American Soci-

ety of Landscape Architects." The first issue (1910) carried Wheelwright's article, "The Attacks on Central Park," decrying proposed modifications to Olmsted's park, as well as a letter from Charles W. Eliot, president emeritus of Harvard, offering a definition of the newly founded profession.

Wheelwright continued as editor of *Landscape Architecture* until 1920, although this work was interrupted in 1917 when he entered the service. During World War I, he worked as a camp planner, laying out Camp Dodge in Des Moines, Iowa, and Camp Merritt in Tenafly, New Jersey. Discharged from the military in January 1919, he practiced alone for a year in New York City and in Philadelphia from 1920 to 1923. In 1924 he founded the Department of Landscape Architecture at the University of Pennsylvania and taught there until 1941.

In 1926, Wheelwright established the firm of Wheelwright & Stevenson in partnership with Markley Stevenson, with offices in Philadelphia. During the early 1930s, Wheelwright designed two well-known private country estates near Wilmington, Goodstay and the Valley Garden. The former became Wheelwright's home after his marriage to Ellen Coleman Dupont Meeds in 1937. The 102-acre Valley Garden was bequeathed to the City of Wilmington in 1943 as a public park. Although Wheelwright's work was primarily private, in the mid-1930s he designed a public housing project under the Federal Emergency Relief Administration at Wayne, Pennsylvania,

Garden and grounds of Spite House, Dodge summer home, Rockport, Maine, c. 1930. Courtesy Mr. And Mrs. Charles Dodge.

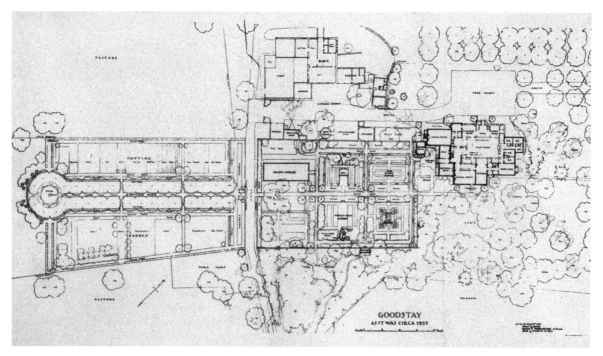

Plan of Goodstay, Wilmington, Delaware, reflecting alterations and additions since 1924 by Wheelwright & Stevenson. From *Landscape Architecture Quarterly*, 1929.

Allée of magnolias at Goodstay. Courtesy Smithsonian Institution, Archives of American Gardens.

which included extensive park and playground space. The firm also, in 1937, designed Fort Christina Park, a memorial to the first Swedish immigrants in Wilmington, on a 2-acre site overlooking the Christina River. After World War II, Wheelwright designed St. Laurent Cemetery on Omaha Beach in Normandy, France.

Although Wheelwright maintained his principal office in Philadelphia, he also had an office on the island of North Haven, Maine, where he summered. Beginning in 1925, he planned several gardens on the mainland. The first of these was in the Colonial Revival style for Mrs. William J. Curtis at Portlaw, her Camden summer home. Also in 1925, Wheelwright began work on two other Colonial Revival-style gardens: for Donald D. Dodge's Spite House at Rockport and the Pierce House garden at West Baldwin. His plans for both reflect a thorough grasp of New England Colonial architecture and garden design. Here, as in other gardens, he included carefully crafted fences, gates, granite steps, and retaining walls based on Colonial models. Wheelwright shared with Fiske Kimball and others a firm belief in the authority of Colonial tradition as a rich visual resource for architectural and landscape design. In this sense he

may be thought of as a pioneer in the now emerging field of historic landscape restoration.

McPeck, Eleanor M. "Robert Wheelwright, 1884–1965." In *A Biographical Dictionary of Architects in Maine*, vol. 7. Maine Citizens for Historic Preservation, 1995. Illustrated summary of Wheelwright's contribution to landscape architecture with emphasis on his Maine work.

Wheelwright, Robert. "The Garden at 'Goodstay'." *Landscape Architecture* 20 (October 1929), 5–11. Contains recommendations for the design of small urban playgrounds; illustrated.

Wheelwright, Robert. "Notes on a Colonial Garden." *Landscape Architecture* 4 (October 1913), 13–20. Account of typical Dutch Colonial architectural and garden details including fences, arbors, etc.; well illustrated.

Eleanor M. McPeck

WHITE, STANLEY HART
(1891–1979)
landscape architect, educator

Stanley Hart White is recognized by many as one of the most influential educators in the history of landscape architecture. White was born in Brooklyn in 1891. That same year his parents, Samuel T. and Jessie White, moved to Mount Vernon, New York. Jessie's father, William Hart, was one of the early residents of Mount Vernon and a landscape painter prominent in art circles in the 1890s. Stanley was the fourth of six children. His younger brother, author E. B. White, wrote of him: "Although eight years older than me, Stan latched onto me because he liked to have someone to instruct. He was a born teacher. . . . He imparted information as casually as a tree drops its leaves in the fall. He resembled Grandfather Hart, and, like his grandfather, he liked to draw and paint."

Stanley White was graduated from Cornell University in 1912 with a B.S. in agriculture. In the summer of 1912 he worked for Hydes Nursery on Long Island. That fall he entered Harvard and graduated with the master of landscape architecture degree in 1915. For the following several months White worked for Fletcher Steele*, John Nolen*, and Harris Reynolds, until early 1916, when he became the landscape architect for the Lake Placid Club. His stay at Lake Placid was short. Later in 1916 he went to work for the Olmsted* office in Brookline, Massachusetts, and remained there until 1920. An attempt at his own practice in 1920–1922 was, in his word, a "fizzle." His second-place submission (to Ralph Griswold*) for the Rome Prize in 1922, he concluded, was his most cherished "fizzle." During his tenure with the Olmsteds

Stanley White. Courtesy Department of Landscape Architecture Archives, University of Illinois.

and for two years after, he was "exposed to the teaching fever" at the Lowthorpe School. He left Boston in 1922 to become assistant professor of landscape architecture at the University of Illinois.

White taught at Illinois for 37 years, from 1922 to 1959. His students, numbering in the hundreds, include some of today's most respected designers and educators, such as Hideo Sasaki, Peter Walker, Charles Harris, Stuart Dawson, Richard Haag, Philip Lewis, and Lawrence Zuelke. Universally regarded as an extraordinarily talented teacher, White was an inspiration to a generation of students. He possessed something of an actor's personality, and he used his talents as musician, artist, and poet not only to impart knowledge but to affect students' lives. His methods were unconventional and often humorous. The emphasis was always on the idea, which he described as "something between magic and philosophy." Throughout his teaching career he refrained from promoting a particular style or form of design, preferring to engage students in exploring new ideas. White taught landscape architecture as a high art, requiring a well-rounded education in humanities and the natural sciences and a generalist's impartial view of site and context.

White's contributions not only to teaching but to the allied institutions that support the field of landscape architectural education were substantial. He was very active in the National Conference on Instruction in Landscape Architecture (NCILA), now Council of Educators in Landscape Architecture (CELA), from his early years to his retirement. White's most noteworthy contribution in support of this forum was the development and administration of the Landscape Exchange program. The Landscape Exchange began in 1924 as a result of recommendations of the NCILA meeting at the University of Michigan that year. Initial organizers were White and W. R. Sears of Ohio State University. White continued as secretary and director of the nationwide program until 1953.

White's efforts in the creation of the Landscape Exchange led to other associations as well. In the summer of 1925, Ferruccio Vitale*, then chair of the American Society of Landscape Architects Committee on Education, asked White to become involved in the Lake Forest Graduate Institute of Architecture and Landscape Architecture. The institute, supported by the ASLA and funded by the Foundation for Architecture and Landscape Architecture and the Garden Club of Lake Forest, offered summer courses in postgraduate design study from 1926 to 1931. White served as director of the institute for those years.

White wrote extensively, but little of his writing was ever formally published. Included among his unpublished manuscripts are the "Primer of Landscape Architecture," the "Teaching of Landscape Architecture," and his 52-year collection of professional diaries—referred to by White as the Commonplace Books—which constitute an insightful collection of sketches, notes, and comments on the practice and teaching of landscape architecture. In the "Primer," White defines landscape architecture as "the superb handling of the land by the creative artist who engraves upon the face of nature those expressions of the culture we need to set the stage of our ordinary lives."

Perhaps the most significant record of his approach to the art and theory of landscape architecture are White's renowned "Ten Slides on the Teaching of Landscape Architecture," beautifully illustrated images that he executed with colored chalk and a blackboard in the basement of his house in the mid-1950s. The slides illuminate White's fascination with design process. The process he espoused was timeless: the "right" solution was one that enhanced the character of the site and form that fit the land. The slides guide the reader sequentially through this process and conclude with commentary on qualities of light, form, and materials. As White notes in his diaries, "Landscape is not appreciated for everything that it is; it has a tremendously broad spread. It is one of the most misunderstood of the arts. . . . It is called simply landscape architecture . . . awfully hard to do well and very costly to be without."

White retired from full-time teaching in 1959, yet continued to be active as an observer, writer, and guest instructor for many years. In 1972, at the ASLA annual meeting in Philadelphia, the Council of Education presented him with its first commendation for his "long years of service, for his sensitivity and ability in producing graduates who have changed, moved, and expanded the profession of landscape architecture." White died five days before his eighty-ninth birthday, in Denver, Colorado.

Cairns, Malcolm, and G. Kesler. "Stanley White, Teacher." *Landscape Architecture* 75 (January/February 1985), 87–91. An overview of White's life and teaching career, including passages from his diaries and quotes from students.

Walker, Peter, and M. Simo. *Invisible Gardens: The Search for Modernism in the American Landscape.* Cambridge: MIT Press, 1994. Chapter 7, "The Moderniza-tion of the Schools," discusses two educators, White and Sasaki, comparing their approaches to teaching and impact on education in landscape architecture.

White, Stanley. *A Primer of Landscape Architecture.* Urbana-Champaign: University of Illinois Department of Landscape Architecture, June 1956. 38 pages; a short treatise on the principles and techniques of landscape architecture.

White, Stanley, ed. *The Teaching of Landscape Architecture with Special Reference to the Teaching of Design.* Assembled and published by Samuel Peaslee Snow. 99 pages; a report to the National Conference on Instruction in Landscape Architecture, East Lansing, Mich., June 1953, by a committee of writers and editors under the general direction of White.

Materials related to White may be found in the University of Illinois Library and the Department of Landscape Architecture Archives, Urbana-Champaign. Included in the collection are his Commonplace Books, manuscripts, course materials, audio tapes, and personal slides.

Gary Kesler and Malcolm Cairns

WHITING, EDWARD CLARK
(1881–1962)
landscape architect

Edward Clark Whiting was born in Brooklyn, New York. He spent his entire professional career with the firm of Olmsted Brothers*, joining them in 1905 following his graduate study in landscape architecture at Harvard University, where he had also received an undergraduate degree in 1903.

Whiting began as a draftsman and assistant engineer, became a general designer, and eventually progressed to partnership in 1920. He spent 1918 in Washington, D.C., working under Olmsted colleague George Gibbs Jr.* on the design of cantonments for the Construction Division of the Army. In the postwar world, Whiting observed, the profession of landscape architecture had to reorient its thinking to contend with increased public uncertainty over the future and greater governmental controls on public projects.

Whiting's several articles and his extensive professional correspondence are articulate and thoughtful. He served as the firm's spokesman on many projects, public and private, in which he participated, including Fort Tryon Park in Manhattan, the Hartford Arboretum, and Ormston, J. E. Aldred's estate on Long Island, New York. His writings consistently express the principle that landscape design must integrate the compositional tenets of a fine art—unity, balance, harmony, and rhythm—with the ever-changing palette of nature, climate, topography, and

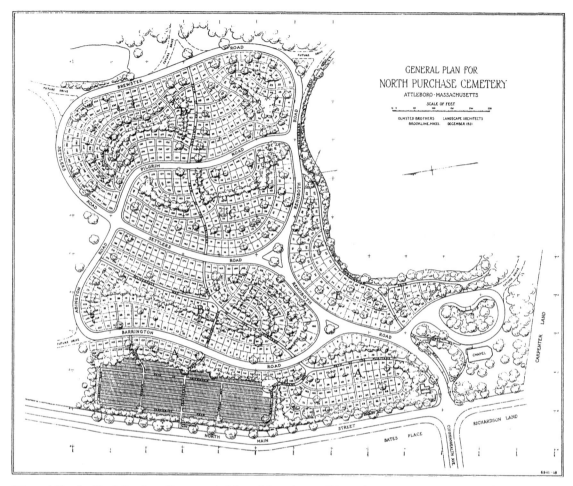

"General Plan for North Purchase Cemetery, Attleboro, Massachusetts." December 1921. Courtesy National Park Service, Frederick Law Olmsted National Historic Site.

living materials, to create environments of beauty and function. Whiting followed Frederick Law Olmsted's* example, expressing the belief that park planning should serve the public's needs, providing recreational spaces of various types and sizes near population clusters. He was a strong proponent of "real landscape parks in which the preservation of scenery is the basic function," with athletic fields relegated to peripheral areas. Beautiful landscape could also function as a learning laboratory, as in the Hartford Arboretum, where the plantings were planned not only to show botanical relationships but to create aesthetic compositions that would spur public appreciation of the value of plants as components of beauty.

Whiting's written works also evidence a strong sense of mission regarding the professional practice of landscape architecture, striving to maintain high standards in the creation of public amenities. Toward that end, he chaired the American Society of Landscape Architects' Committee on Membership Qualifications for many years, served as president of the Boston Society of Landscape Architects, and as director, later president, of the Hubbard Educational Trust. He was elected a Fellow of the ASLA in 1930.

Whiting listed his specialties as subdivision design and land planning for industrial and institutional development, although his work on private residential design for large estates is also significant. Among the projects

Garden of George A. Cluett,
Williamstown, Massachusetts, c. 1922.
Courtesy National Park Service,
Frederick Law Olmsted National
Historic Site.

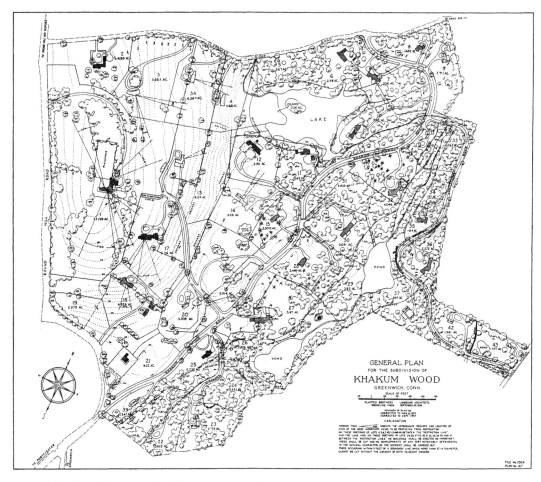

General plan for Khakum Wood subdivision, Greenwich, Connecticut, c. 1925. Courtesy National Park Service, Frederick Law Olmsted National Historic Site.

Shrub and heather garden for Edward K. Davis, Marstons Mills, Massachusetts, fall 1951. Courtesy National Park Service, Frederick Law Olmsted National Historic Site.

that he considered most noteworthy were the subdivision plans for Oyster Harbor in Osterville, Massachusetts (600 acres with golf course); for Khakum Wood in Greenwich, Connecticut (175 acres of exclusive properties); for Munsey Gardens in Manhasset, New York; for the Whippoorwill development near Chappaqua, New York; and for several Louisville, Kentucky, communities (Indian Hills, Cherokee Gardens). In anticipation of the creation of Babson College in Wellesley Hills, Massachusetts, he designed a compact residential neighborhood, the Uplands, on land belonging to some of his relatives, naming streets Clark Road and Whiting Road. Notable among his estate designs are those for Mrs. Edward V. Hartford at the Wando Plantation in Charleston, South Carolina; for George Cluett in Williamstown, Massachusetts; and for H. G. Lapham in Brookline, Massachusetts. He also had considerable design responsibility for the Aldred estate (with Percival Gallagher*) and for Warren

Bicknell's estate in Cleveland. In his extensive work for E. K. Davis in Marstons Mills, Massachusetts, he graced the Tudor mansion with specialized areas, such as the heather garden, well suited to the Cape Cod climate. He subsequently expanded his planning for Davis when the latter decided to turn some of his land holdings into the golf community of Seapuit.

Whiting's institutional work included the Burr Memorial for the capitol grounds in Hartford; campus design for Southern Baptist Theological Seminary in Louisville, for Catholic University and Trinity College in Washington, D.C., for Phillips Academy, Andover, Massachusetts, and for the Taft School in Watertown, Connecticut, among many others. He designed cemeteries for Attleboro, Massachusetts (North Purchase), for Torrington, Connecticut (Hillside), and for Ann Arbor, Michigan (Washtenong Memorial Park). In conjunction with John C. Olmsted* he worked on park systems for Essex and

Union counties in New Jersey, and for Louisville; and with F. L. Olmsted Jr.* on the New Haven, Connecticut, parks, Fort Tryon Park, and Rock Creek Park in Washington, D.C. With the latter, Whiting also worked on city planning projects for Pittsburgh and Newport.

Whiting never retired and was still an active partner of Olmsted Associates when he died, in Boston. All his work, whether reports, plans, or projects carried through construction, was characterized by his philosophy that lasting landscape design must transcend a set time, place, or circumstance.

Whiting, Edward Clark. "Garden Design: Some Influences and Opportunities." *Architectural Forum* 36 (June 1922), 211–216. Observations on the balance of art and nature in the design of gardens, using Ormston as one example.

Whiting, Edward Clark. "Guiding Motives in the Design of a Modern Park." *Parks & Recreation* 17 (March 1934), 221–230. Discussion of the design considerations for a park for active recreation while retaining some landscape value.

Whiting, Edward Clark, and William Phillips. "Frederick Law Olmsted—1870–1957: An Appreciation of the Man and His Achievements." *Landscape Architecture* 48 (April 1958), 145–157. Articulate and thoughtful tribute to a colleague and teacher.

Arleyn Levee

WILDER, LOUISE BEEBE
(1878–1938)
author

Born in Baltimore and educated privately, Louise Beebe married architect Walter Robb Wilder in 1902 and had two children. The couple purchased a country place, Balderbrae, near Suffern, New York, and Wilder described her garden there in articles for such publications as *Garden Magazine, Country Life,* and *Good Housekeeping,* and in two books, *My Garden* (1916) and *Colour in My Garden* (1918). These established her reputation as a talented horticulturist and author. Her early articles and books also helped further the growing interest in the design of perennial gardens.

Soon after World War I, Wilder moved with her children to a new home in suburban Bronxville, New York. There she concentrated on the rock plants that had increasingly attracted her attention. Most of her writing after 1920 concerned rock plants and rock gardens, and she both benefited from and stimulated the burgeoning interest in those subjects, which characterized the horticulture and landscape design of the period. Wilder defined "rock plant" broadly, so much of her subject matter was applicable to the larger garden picture. She was arguably the nation's leading authority on rock gardens, then enjoying a peak of popularity.

In 1925, Wilder began a column in *House and Garden* which she continued until her death. Her magazine work was then largely confined to *House and Garden.* The column gave her a distinguished platform from which to share her extensive knowledge of plants, and many of these articles were gathered together as books. She published a total of eleven books, although one, *The Rock Garden* (1933), was excerpted from the earlier *Adventures in My Garden and Rock Garden* (1923), and another was not a garden title, so nine constitute her relevant body of work.

Wilder's influence resulted from her literary ability as well as her knowledge of plants. Her plant descriptions, precise and alluring, popularized many little-known species and played a significant role in the choice of plant material in the gardens of her era. Her writing also served to encourage the good design of rock gardens, a difficult achievement. Wilder was recognized as one of the country's finest garden writers in her day, and many of her books have been reprinted.

Wilder, Louise Beebe. *Colour in My Garden.* New York: Doubleday, Page, 1918. A lavish exploration of color

Louise Beebe Wilder's rock garden, Bronxville, New York. From *Pleasures and Problems of a Rock Garden*, 1928.

through the seasons in Wilder's perennial garden; illustrations from Anna Winegar's paintings are in color, unusual in American garden books of this period; reprinted in 1990 by Atlantic Monthly Press with a brief critical and biographical introduction by Lynden Miller.

Wilder, Louise Beebe. *My Garden*. Garden City, N.Y.: Doubleday, Page, 1916. An account of her first garden, Balderbrae, and its plants through the seasons.

Wilder, Louise Beebe. *Pleasures and Problems of a Rock Garden*. Garden City, N.Y.: Doubleday, Doran, 1928. Her largest and possibly most important book on rock gardens and their plant material.

Virginia Lopez Begg

WILLIAMS, MORLEY JEFFERS
(1886–1977)
landscape architect

Morley Jeffers Williams was born in Tillsenburg, Ontario, Canada. His early training was in civil engineering, at the Engineering School of the University of Toronto, in 1910–1911. Williams left Toronto for employment as a bridge construction inspector with the Canadian Pacific Railroad and was hired in 1912 by the Montreal–Port Arthur District of the Canadian Northern Railway as the acting engineer of bridge site surveys and bridge construction inspector. He eventually became the resident engineer in charge of roadbed grading and track laying.

Williams moved to Kingsville, Ontario, in 1914, where he acquired half ownership in a grain elevator and began operating 300 acres of cropland specializing in seed grades of corn, small grains, and grasses. In 1922, Williams took over the farm operations of Vincent Massey (then president of Massey–Harris Farm Machinery) in Port Hope. As part of his duties, he consulted on the buildings and layouts of private farms: this was probably his first experience with landscape design.

In 1925, at the age of thirty-eight, Williams received a B.S.A. in horticulture from the Ontario Agricultural College in Guelph. He immediately enrolled in Harvard's School of Design, where, in 1928, he received his M.L.A. in city planning; his thesis illustrated how to introduce gardens and greenery into an urban landscape. Williams was awarded a year-long Sheldon Travelling Fellowship in 1929, which he spent studying landscape design in Europe and North Africa. He officially joined the faculty of the School of Design in 1930.

The following year Williams received a grant from the Clark Fund for Research in Landscape Design to investigate "American Landscape Design as Exemplified by the Plantation Estates of Maryland and Virginia, 1750 to 1860." He traveled throughout Virginia and Maryland making topographical surveys of historic plantations, including Gunston Hall, Woodlawn, and Mount Vernon. His 1931 survey of Mount Vernon was significant because of the discovery of four early outbuilding foundations near the main house; it was the first time that Williams used archaeological evidence to formulate ideas about the development of historical landscapes. The results of this survey also prompted his suggestion that the Mount Vernon landscape was consciously designed to resemble the shield in Washington's coat of arms.

In 1932 the Garden Club of Virginia asked Williams to complete earlier research begun by Arthur Shurcliff on the landscape of Stratford Hall. Using data from Shurcliff's investigations and from new archaeological

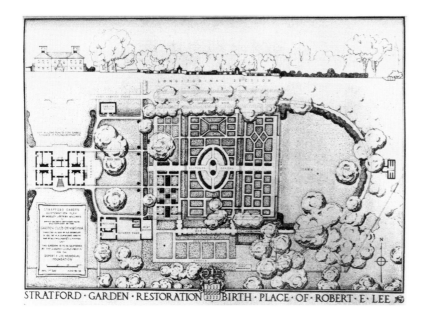

Plan for reconstruction of East Garden, Stratford Hall, 1932. Courtesy Jessie Ball duPont Memorial Library, Stratford Hall Plantation.

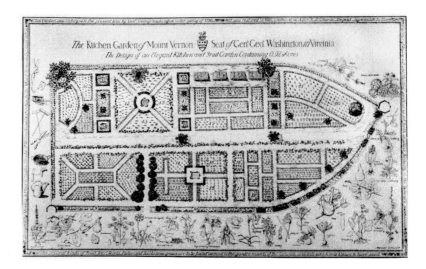

Williams's restoration plan for kitchen garden, Mount Vernon, drawn by Nathalia Uhlman, 1935. Courtesy Mount Vernon Ladies' Association.

excavations supervised by Charles Pinkney, Williams identified the layout, walls, and terraces of the East Garden. He was also able to document the original approach to the mansion and the historical view from the mansion to the Potomac River. Williams was asked to draw up plans for the restoration of the East Garden, which were implemented the next year. Also during the summer of 1932, Williams conducted a landscape survey of Monticello, in which he located the serpentine walk and several planting beds on the West Lawn.

Williams and Pinkney conducted further archaeological investigations at Stratford Hall in 1934 to determine the extent of westward development from the main house. They also oversaw the restoration of "God's Acre" in Harvard Square. Williams also continued the exploration of the four foundations he had discovered at Mount Vernon, and in 1935 he returned there to oversee the restoration of the kitchen garden. Also in 1935, Olmsted Brothers* asked him to research the history of the White House grounds to inform a possible redesign of that landscape.

Williams resigned from the Harvard faculty in 1936 to be the director of research and restoration at Mount Vernon. Over the next three years, he supervised the continued investigation of archaeological features and documentary research necessary to begin the restoration of the property as depicted in Samuel Vaughan's 1787 drawing. His research focused on identifying when buildings and landscape features were built, an integral part of interpreting the historic landscape. He left Mount Vernon in 1939, when the coveted appointment of director was given to someone else.

From 1941 until 1947, Williams operated a joint practice with his wife, Nathalia Ulman, an architect, in Bluemont, Virginia. Williams joined the faculty of North Carolina State College (now University) School of Design as a professor of landscape architecture in 1947, and the following year became head of the department.

In early 1952, Williams left academia to pursue the development of Tryon Palace State Historic Site, the opulent pre-Revolutionary, Palladian-style home of loyalist governors William Tryon and Josiah Martin in New Bern, North Carolina, which was planned for reconstruction. From 1952 until 1955, he directed excavations to uncover the floor plan and interior details of the main house and kitchen. In 1955, with the majority of the physical research completed, he was hired as landscape architect to design the gardens and supervise their construction. No archaeological evidence of the formal or kitchen gardens was found, so Williams chose designs based on eighteenth-century English landscapes. By 1962 the association between the Tryon Palace Commission and Williams had dissolved because of almost continual disagreements.

Never fully retiring, Williams continued researching and restoring historic houses and gardens, such as the Samuel Smallwood House in New Bern. He died in Lottsburg, Virginia.

Tryon Palace State Historic Site, New Bern, North Carolina. Photo Thomas Beaman.

Beaman, Thomas E., Jr. "Fables of the Reconstruction: Morley Jeffers Williams and the Excavation of Tryon Palace, 1952–1962." *North Carolina Archaeology* 48 (in press 1999). An account of Williams's involvement with the restoration, with specific attention to information gained from the archaeological investigations and how it was integrated into the reconstruction.

Pogue, Dennis J. *Archaeology at George Washington's Mount Vernon, 1931–1987.* Mount Vernon Ladies' Association Archaeology Department, File Report no. 1. Mount Vernon, Va., 1988. Summary of Williams's excavations; classifies them into three categories: to identify past garden and landscape designs, in conjunction with the planned restoration of buildings, and to confirm buildings shown on Samuel Vaughan's 1787 plan of Mount Vernon; also considers Williams's findings in light of subsequent research.

Williams, Morley Jeffers. "Washington's Changes at Mount Vernon Plantation." *Landscape Architecture* 28 (January 1938). Summarizes his research at Mount Vernon; discusses changes Washington made to the landscape after his marriage in 1759; primary focus is evidence contained in historical documents, but also makes reference to the use of excavation to confirm the 1787 Vaughan plan; concludes with a brief comments on the restoration of the kitchen garden.

Thomas E. Beaman Jr.

WIMMER, HARRIETT BARNHART
(1900–1980)
landscape architect

Harriett Barnhart was born in Corning, Iowa, and lived there until 1912 when her family moved to San Diego. She earned her bachelor's degree at Stanford University in 1922, and married a fellow student, John Wimmer, in 1925. Her husband was to be her lifelong supporter in garden design ventures, many of which they undertook as a team. The young couple enjoyed extended travels in Europe before financial reverses caused by the Depression curtailed such activities.

Wimmer attended the California School of Fine Arts in 1930 and, in tandem with her husband, went on to pursue graduate studies in landscape architecture at Oregon State University. In 1932 the couple returned to San Diego, where they spent the remainder of their lives. They had no children; both taught in public schools while developing their shared avocation of garden design.

In 1950, having established a strong local reputation as a designer of residential gardens, Wimmer opened a landscape design firm. In 1954 she obtained a license and became San Diego's first woman landscape architect in commercial practice. She joined the American Society of Landscape Architects and the following year became a founding member of San Diego's

Harriett Wimmer and business partner Joe Yamada. Courtesy Wimmer, Yamada & Associates, San Diego.

Sea World. Photo Carol Greentree.

Urey Hall, Library Court, University of California at San Diego. Courtesy San Diego Historical Society.

own chapter; she chaired the fledgling group through 1956.

Wimmer had hired a young graduate of the University of California at Berkeley, formally trained as a landscape architect, to join her practice in 1954. This apprentice, Joe Yamada, became her full business partner in 1960. Over nearly a decade, Wimmer & Yamada won many design awards, and together they helped shape the postwar urban aesthetic of a rapidly growing southern California metropolis. Among the most notable and enduring planning achievements of the firm are the designs for the Revelle campus—the first among several at the multicampus complex of the University of California at San Diego—and the much-visited theme park gardens at Sea World, which are widely admired for their diversity and attractiveness.

In 1961, Wimmer was suddenly widowed, losing her lifetime background-collaborator in garden design. She continued her active involvement in landscape planning, however, until 1967. Even after Wimmer's formal retirement, Yamada kept her name together with his on the firm they had helped each other to establish. In her post-retirement years, Wimmer continued to design a limited number of private gardens for her friends. In 1976, she became a Fellow of the American Society of Landscape Architects.

Greentree, Carol. "Harriett Barnhart Wimmer: A Pioneer San Diego Woman Landscape Architect." *Journal of San Diego History* 34 (June 1988), 223–239. A career biography, with photographs, of Harriett Wimmer—her schooling, community activities, private freelance practice, and later partnership with Joe Yamada, ASLA involvement, and honors.

Hagberg, Marilyn. "Wimmer and Yamada—Part of the Landscape." *San Diego Magazine*, February 1969, 26–33. An illustrated profile of the professional partnership of Harriett Wimmer and Joe Yamada, written in the tenth-anniversary year of their collaboration.

"In Memoriam—Harriett Wimmer, FASLA 1899–1980." *Land*, August 1980, 10. A half-page synopsis of Wimmer's design career and the firm she established with Yamada; lists award projects and honors.

Carol Greentree

WINTERS, MARGARET
(1907–1979)
landscape architect

Margaret Winters was born in Pittsburgh. She was broadly educated, with a B.A. from Wellesley College in 1928, a B.S. in architecture from the Carnegie Institute of Technology in 1929, and a bachelor of landscape architecture from Cornell University in 1936. Cornell, where women were never excluded from enrolling, began its first landscape program in 1903 and soon became very successful. Nonetheless, Winters later recalled that she was the only woman out of sixty in the program.

Winters's career centered in Pittsburgh, where she remains highly regarded more than twenty years after her death. Her life's work encompassed every aspect of landscape architecture. Her first job was as the director of the Pittsburgh Garden Center. From 1939 to 1942 she turned to the planning of private and public housing, for Theodore Kohankie. Between 1942 and 1944, she worked for the U.S. Army Corps of Engineers in Philadelphia, on drainage plans, site engineering, and development for the barracks and military airfields that the army was building at the time. She then spent 1944–1946 in the office of Clarke* & Rapuano*, New York, during the period when they were designing many early parkways.

Winters made her earliest known drawings for her next employer, Rose Greely*, who practiced in Washington, D.C. Drawings from 1948 of gardens for the townhouses of William R. Hearst and Senator and Mrs. Cabot Lodge were typical of her work for Greely, which was almost entirely concerned with private residences.

Winters was a founding member of the prominent Pittsburgh firm GWSM (Griswold, Winters, Swain, & Mullen), Inc., Landscape Architects, where she became partners first with the nationally known Ralph Griswold* and later with William G. Swain. As part of her work there, Winters designed and supervised an impressive number of private gardens for prominent families. "I started out with big projects and then found out that I actually enjoyed doing the small ones better," she recalled. Winters contributed to all aspects of the office's work. She produced designs for parking lots and for Pittsburgh's West End Overlook. In 1961–1965 she collaborated with architect and antiquarian Charles Stotz on the restoration of the gardens at Old Economy, Ambler, Pennsylvania. She also supplied drawings for projects that were primarily the responsibility of colleagues, as in the case of the Bastion at Point Park, work undertaken by Griswold in the 1940s. Remembered by associates and clients alike for her horticultural expertise, she reviewed the planting schemes of every project in the office. Colleagues also respected her knowledge of the engineering side of landscape architecture.

Her final garden, built for Mr. and Mrs. James A. Fisher in Squirrel Hill, was designed and carried out over more than a decade. The Fishers bought the property in 1958, and Winters designed the first garden in 1960; ten years later, the Fishers acquired the site next door, demolishing the house, and in 1970–1971, Winters planned a second and larger garden. This garden is the masterpiece of her career and the best extant example of her work. It includes several changes in level, a service area, swimming pool, terrace, lily pond, and perennial border, along with many trees and a shade garden. Incorporated into one-and-a-half city lots are many of the elements found on far more extensive grounds.

Margaret Winters. Courtesy GWSM, Inc.

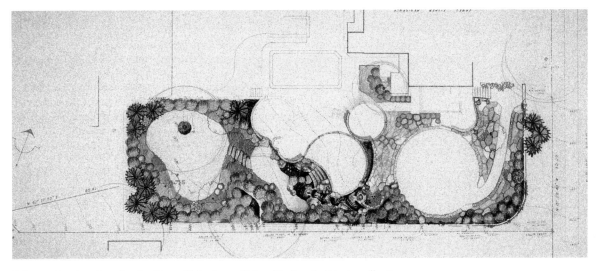

Color-rendered garden plan for Mr. and Mrs. James Fisher, Pittsburgh. Private collection.

Hull, Judith S. *A Century of Women Landscape Architects and Gardeners in Pittsburgh*. Exhibition catalog. Heinz Architectural Center, Carnegie Museum of Art. Pittsburgh: Carnegie Museum of Art, 1996. Contains an overview of Winters's career.

Winters, Margaret. Interview by Donna Palmer, North Carolina State University, April 7, 1976. Transcript in archives of GWSM, Inc.

Papers and drawings of Margaret Winters remain with GWSM, Inc., Pittsburgh. Additional materials may also be found in the possession of her clients.

Judith S. Hull and Behula Shah

WRIGHT, HENRY
(1878–1936)
planner, architect, landscape architect, engineer

Henry Wright was born in Lawrence, Kansas. After high school, he apprenticed to Walter C. Root and George Siemens in their prominent Kansas City, Missouri, architectural firm from 1896 to 1899. He then enrolled in a special two-year course in architecture at the University of Pennsylvania, graduating in 1901.

Returning to Kansas City, Wright established a professional relationship with landscape architect George Kessler*, and went on to open an office for him in St. Louis. There he assisted Kessler on the overall design for the Louisiana Purchase Exposition, the restoration of Forest Park, and the planting plan for Washington University. Wright remained in St. Louis after he left Kessler's employ in 1909 to launch his own practice in landscape architecture, urban design, and architecture. According to city directories of the period, he referred to himself as landscape architect, architect, landscape gardener, and engineer.

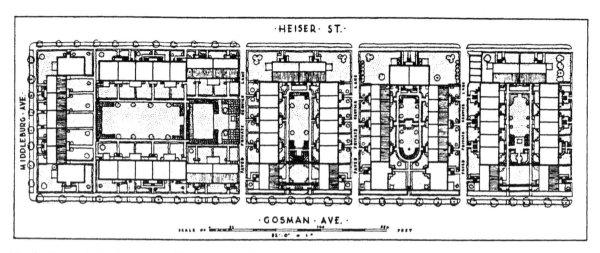

Plan for Sunnyside Gardens, designed by Stein & Wright, 1927. From Clarence S. Stein, *Toward New Town for America*.

Wright designed his later and more acclaimed projects according to general principles he established while completing his first independent commissions, the housing developments of Brentmoor Park, Brentmoor, and Forest Ridge, platted in 1910, 1911, and 1913 respectively. These exclusive subdivisions of Clayton, Missouri, share such characteristics as limited access from surrounding thoroughfares, curving interior drives, lot sizes from one to two acres, and large houses of eclectic design. Wright designed all three projects to face inward

An inner court at Sunnyside, 1946. Constructed 1926. From *Toward New Town for America*.

"Car Shelter" at Brentmoor, Clayton, Missouri. Courtesy National Register of Historic Places.

toward their own common grounds, away from the noise and congestion of the surrounding environment.

Wright continued his St. Louis practice until 1923, planning subdivisions and designing residences. As architect for the St. Louis City Planning Commission he prepared and administered rules for land subdivision control and wrote a report on the economics of land subdivision that, according to his later collaborator, architect Clarence S. Stein, "contained the seed of much of his future thinking, writing, and work."

Wright left St. Louis for New York in 1923 when he was asked to join Stein in planning two new communities for the City Housing Corporation. One of these was Sunnyside, today considered an important model in town planning. Together with Stein and landscape architect Marjorie Cautley*, Wright also conceived the 1928 design for Radburn, New Jersey. He discussed Radburn in an article in the *Western Architect* in 1930: "The Garden City Plan (1898) fitted into the old condition of its day, but Radburn (1928) had to meet an entirely new set of con-

Aerial view of Radburn, c. 1950s. Private collection.

ditions. City Planning had been engrossed in the solution of traffic movement, adjusting old time street systems to new demands of the motor car, but no completely new town had recognized the necessity of meeting the human problems of danger, noise, and nuisance accompanying the convenience of the new vehicle. The 'Radburn Idea' attacked the problem as a related whole." Although the Depression prevented Radburn from being completed, Wright's "Radburn Idea" significantly influenced the town planning movement. Wright and Stein also codesigned Chatham Village in Pittsburgh in 1931.

In 1933, Wright was appointed consultant to the housing division of the Public Works Administration and one year later was chosen (with Albert Mayer, Henry Churchill, Carol Aronovici, and William Lescase) by the National Housing Association to observe and report on existing housing conditions nationwide. He was also city planning consultant to the New York State Commission on Housing and Regional Planning. In addition, Wright was appointed head of the School of Architecture at Columbia University in 1935 when the school established its four-year program of town planning and housing studies. Before his death in 1936, Wright was elected to the committee of architects established to prepare a general plan for the 1939 New York World's Fair.

Clarence Stein wrote of Wright shortly after his death: "Most architects have many unrelated jobs; from the time Henry came to see clearly what he wanted to attain, he had one job. This was the building of better communities—the re-housing of urban Americans in more desirable communities in a practical way. It was all one job—the planning of Sunnyside, Radburn and Chatham Village; his ceaseless analytic writing; his reports on city and state planning; his teaching at various universities."

Churchill, Henry. "Henry Wright: 1878–1936." *Journal of the American Institute of Planners* 26 (November 1960). Wright remembered by his friend and colleague; recounts his contributions to planning, specifically mentioning Sunnyside, Chatham Village, Greenbrook, and Radburn; also includes a list of references by or about Wright; illustrated.

Mather, Alan. "Henry Wright." *Pencil Points* 21 (January 1940), 3–14. Discusses Wright's involvement with the City Planning Commission of St. Louis and his subsequent influence on the planning and design of multi-family housing; highlights Radburn and Chatham Village; also includes a brief biography.

Wright, Henry. *Rehousing Urban America*. New York: Columbia University Press, 1935. Notes on the subject using a variety of project examples from his work.

Cydney Millstein

WRIGHT, MABEL OSGOOD
(1859–1934)
author, conservationist, activist

Mabel Osgood was born in New York City but is most closely identified with Fairfield, Connecticut, where her family had a summer house and where she eventually lived permanently. She received a thorough education at Number One Fifth Avenue, a New York girls' school, and studied nature with her father, a prominent clergyman who had many friends among the city's literary elite. After her 1884 marriage to James O. Wright, she began to write nature essays for the *New York Times* and other papers. In 1894 these were collected in her first book, *The Friendship of Nature*. She then published a book every year through 1911. At her death, she had written more than twenty-five.

Wright's essays focused on four topics, which she often interwove: native plants, birds, gardens, and sociological comment on the rapidly changing American culture and landscape. Her books about native plants and birds, such as *Birdcraft* (1895) and *Flowers and Ferns in Their Haunts* (1901) used a conversational tone to transmit scientific information. Wright's science was accurate for her time. Not all nature writers of the era were so scrupulous, and Theodore Roosevelt led the charge

"A Fern Haunt." Photo by Mabel Osgood Wright. Frontispiece to *Flowers and Ferns in Their Haunts*, 1901. Courtesy Virginia Lopez Begg.

Like other garden writers of the period, Wright sometimes turned to fiction to present her themes. She used the pseudonym "Barbara" so that she might speak more freely. It was as Barbara, the wife of a landscape architect, that Wright wrote her best-seller, *The Garden of a Commuter's Wife* (1901), and its sequels, *The People of the Whirlpool* (1903), *The Garden, You, and I* (1906), and others. Barbara lives and gardens in a small New England village that is rapidly being transformed into an exclusive suburb (a thinly disguised Fairfield). The first novel, in print for decades, addresses issues of interest to landscape historians—suburbanization, women's increasing role in the garden, popular plants, and in particular, the reasons behind the burgeoning interest in gardens around 1900. In these books, Wright combines horticultural instruction and design description with revealing commentary on the socioeconomic and psychological role of the garden in early twentieth-century America, particularly for women. Her novels often contrast the simplicity and honesty of the old-fashioned garden with the lavish and soulless gardens of the nouveaux riches who were rapidly transforming the rural landscapes surrounding the nation's cities. Wright proposes the intimate, personal garden space as a refuge from the stunning rate of change experienced by her generation.

Wright also influenced the landscape through her role as an environmental activist. She was a founder and long-time board member of both the Connecticut and the National Audubon societies and was instrumental in the creation of Birdcraft Sanctuary, a Fairfield preserve she helped design. The sanctuary, with its Arts and Crafts–style museum and caretaker's cottage, is today a National Historic Landmark, open to the public. Her writing about the design and construction of Birdcraft Sanctuary influenced many other such preserves, especially through *Bird-Lore*, now *Audubon*, magazine. Visitors involved in planning sanctuaries elsewhere often came to study the design of Birdcraft, notable for its emphasis on the needs of birds rather than the entertainment of casual observers. In addition, Wright served on the committee that planned the Theodore Roosevelt Bird Sanctuary on Long Island.

Wright also wrote pamphlets and devised publicity campaigns to promote the use native plants through the Fairfield Garden Club, of which she was founder and first president. Although many women and men also wrote about nature topics, the number of Wright's books, her Audubon work on a national level, and the length of her career place her in the front rank. Indeed, a 1902 article

against such "nature fakirs." Such books created great interest in nature among Americans of the late Victorian era, many of whom turned increasingly to garden making to bring nature into their lives.

Books about wildflowers and ferns appearing from 1890 to World War I formed the preamble of the influential garden literature of the 1890–1940 era. They also stimulated the growth of the profession of landscape design in that era by helping to create a market of consumers for the young profession's services. In *Flowers and Ferns in Their Haunts*, Wright provides accurate information about such plants in their habitats, using the storytelling style and vivid anecdotes that made her books widely read. Wright was also a talented photographer, and included many examples of her work in her texts.

Wright's garden, Fairfield, Connecticut. From *The Critic*, April 1906. Courtesy Virginia Lopez Begg.

in the *Review of Reviews* included Wright in such company as John Burroughs and John Muir. In her career as an author and as an activist, Wright both reflected and affected a rapidly changing American landscape.

Begg, Virginia Lopez. "Mabel Osgood Wright, The Friendship of Nature and the Commuter's Wife." *Journal of the New England Garden History Society* 5 (Fall 1997). A brief biography of Wright, as well as a discussion of her work and some of her most important cultural themes as they affect landscape history.

[Wright, Mabel Osgood.] *The Garden, You, and I*. New York: Macmillan, 1906. A sequel to *The Garden of a Commuter's Wife*, covering many of the same themes, in the form of letters between an experienced gardener (Barbara) and a beginner (Mary Penrose); the most horticultural of Wright's books and an interest-

ing snapshot of the transition between Victorian flower gardens and the Jekyll-inspired perennial gardens of the early twentieth century; illustrated.

[Wright, Mabel Osgood.] *People of the Whirlpool*. New York: Macmillan, 1903. Another sequel to *The Garden of a Commuter's Wife*, emphasizing two themes: the negative social effects of suburbanization on a small New England community and the rise of a new millionaire class in this country, with its materialistic values and aggressive display of wealth.

Although there is no archive of Wright's papers, the Fairfield Historical Society, the Fairfield Public Library, and Birdcraft Sanctuary have files or other material related to her.

Virginia Lopez Begg

WRIGHT, RICHARDSON
(1886–1961)
author, editor

Richardson Wright was born in Philadelphia. After his 1910 graduation from Trinity College, Hartford, he worked briefly as a newspaper editor in Albany and then spent a year as a foreign correspondent in Russia. Returning to New York City, he became a literary and theater critic for the *New York Times* and *Smart Styles* from 1911 until his 1914 appointment as editor of *House and Garden*. During his tenure at this magazine he became one of the most influential tastemakers of his time.

Wright came to *House and Garden* just as the interest of many Americans in both house and garden making was reaching a peak. He was well suited to the position. Wright's intellect, wide-ranging mind, and intuitive sense of the cultural pulse of his upper-middle-class audience led him to publish top-quality material of interest to legions of readers. *House and Garden* quickly became one of the most influential design periodicals of the day. Articles by many important landscape designers and horticulturists offered a variety of information about American residential landscapes in this period.

Richardson Wright also encouraged the writing careers of many authorities, including plant hunter E. H. Wilson and Louise Beebe Wilder*, both of whom wrote regularly for *House and Garden*. He provided a forum for many women garden writers at a time when women were struggling to enter the professions, but also sought to coax men into the garden with arguments as creative as describing gardening as a sport.

Wright's running editorial commentary in *House and Garden* on the state of America's houses and gardens, and on a wide variety of related issues, make thoughtful and intelligent reading even today. Wright stated that he wrote or edited forty books; of these, thirteen focused on gardens and gardening. They demonstrate extensive knowledge and experience, as well as a sense of humor.

Wright edited two collections of garden photographs and text from the magazine to create *House and Garden's Book of Gardens* (1921) and *House and Garden's Second Book of Gardens* (1927). Both are useful to landscape historians for their depiction of the work of a number of landscape architects of the period. Wright himself enjoyed landscape history and produced a creditable history of gardening for the popular reader titled *The Story of Gardening* (1934). *The Winter Diversions of a Gardener* (1934) and *Gardener's Tribute* (1949) are interesting collections of essays about figures and events from landscape history. In addition to his roles as author and editor,

Richardson Wright. From *The American Rose Annual*, 1933. Courtesy Smithsonian Institution, Archives of American Gardens.

Wright was a strong political force in the garden world, serving as chairman of the International Flower Show in New York, president of the American Rose Society, director of the New York Horticultural Society, and in countless other such positions.

Wright died in 1961, survived by his widow and two foster sons.

Wright, Richardson. *The Gardener's Bed-Book*. Philadelphia: J. B. Lippincott, 1929. A collection of brief gardening bits—how-to, garden history, folklore, plant description, and so on—for each day of the year.

Wright, Richardson. *The Practical Book of Outdoor Flowers*. Philadelphia: J. B. Lippincott, 1924. A thorough treatment of flower gardening in all its aspects; very popular for years.

Wright, Richardson, ed. *House and Garden's Book of Gardens*. New York: Condé Nast, 1921. Useful collection of plans, photographs, and articles about American gardens, written by a variety of early twentieth-century landscape architects, including many women; a sequel was published in 1927.

Virginia Lopez Begg

WYMAN, ALANSON PHELPS
(1870–1947)
landscape architect

Phelps Wyman was born and raised in Manchester, Vermont, and attended college preparatory school at the Burr & Burton Seminary in Manchester Center. He received a B.S. in agriculture from Cornell University in 1897. After graduating, Wyman worked briefly for Warren Manning*, then moved to Chicago and a job as a draftsman for O. C. Simonds*. He then moved to New York, where he worked for D. W. Langdon (1898). From 1899 to 1902 the Olmsted Brothers*, in Brookline, Massachusetts, employed him. For the two years following, Wyman was enrolled as a special student at the Massachusetts Institute of Technology, where he took courses in architecture, engineering, and landscape design. During the summers of 1902 and 1903 he worked in the New York office of Charles Platt*. Wyman spent the summer of 1904 touring Europe, returning that fall to teach landscape gardening at the University of Illinois, Urbana.

In 1905, Wyman's teaching position was elevated to full-time status, he gained the title of Assistant Professor, and he opened an office in Chicago. Over the next seven years, he lived and practiced in Chicago while commuting to downstate Urbana to teach. He also began writing about landscape planning and design, a practice that he continued throughout his career. In 1909 the University of Illinois Agricultural Experiment Station published a circular he had written titled "Small Home Yard," followed in 1910 with his "Arrangement and Planting of School Grounds." During this time Wyman was also an active member of the Illinois Outdoor Improvement Association, contributing to and editing a volume titled *Street Tree Planting for Illinois* published by the organization.

The Pool, Mount Curve Triangle Park, Minneapolis. *American Landscape Architect*, November 1931.

In 1911, Wyman stopped teaching and moved his practice to Minneapolis, where he became active in civic affairs, including the development of the Minneapolis park system. He served on the Minneapolis Park Board from 1916 to 1924, and was a member of the Minneapolis Planning Commission from 1921 to 1924. In 1912, Wyman was made a Fellow in the American Society of Landscape Architects, later serving on the board of trustees (1919–1921) and as secretary of the Minnesota chapter. He was also a frequent contributor to *Horizons*, a publication of the Mississippi Valley ASLA chapter. An active member of other professional and civic organizations, Wyman also completed several residential commissions in addition to park designs.

In 1924, Wyman moved to Milwaukee, where he became the landscape architect for the Milwaukee County Regional Planning Department. He was specifically charged to develop a park and parkway system as well as planting plans for arterial roads and parks. During this time, Wyman became active in the American Institute of Park Executives, and soon began contributing articles to the journal *Parks and Recreation*. In 1926 he resigned from his county position and returned to private practice, advertising himself as both landscape architect and engineer. He continued to complete both larger-scale public improvement projects and residential designs throughout the Midwest, and his work was frequently featured in *American Landscape Architect*, of whose editorial advisory

B. J. Denman garden, Wilmette, Illinois. ASLA, *Illustrations of Works of Members*, 1934.

board he was a member. In 1935, Wyman prepared an innovative plan for improving Milwaukee's Lake Michigan shoreline, encouraging the city to purchase the industrial site for parkland and expand it with landfill. He became one of the founding members of the Milwaukee Citizens' Lakefront Committee, which was instrumental in establishing a publicly accessible lakefront.

By the late 1920s, Wyman had become a recognized leader in the planning and design of parks and public lands, and in 1929 he was commissioned by the Greater North Dakota Association to study a section of the Badlands region to determine its feasibility as a national park. The Wyman report was instrumental in building support in Congress and from the National Park Service. Wyman's work in the Dakotas included the Yankton College Garden Theatre in Yankton, South Dakota, as well as the state capitol grounds in Pierre. He was also responsible for the site selection and landscape development for the Custer State Park Game Lodge, located in the Black Hills near Custer, South Dakota, which was later used as a summer White House by President Calvin Coolidge.

Throughout his life, Wyman preferred working alone or with a small number of assistants. His 1948 obituary in *Landscape Architecture* credits his attention to detail and his dedication to every aspect of a project. At the time of his death, the seventy-seven-year-old was working on a

road-widening project in Wisconsin Rapids. Wyman's professional library was given to the University of Illinois, where students may still find his books on the library shelves—made discernible by the imprint of his name in gold on the cover.

Wyman, Phelps. "A Preliminary Park Study of the Bad Lands of Western North Dakota." *Landscape Architecture* 20 (April 1930), 178–86. Describes the content of the park suitability report submitted in 1929 to North Dakota governor George F. Shafer.

Wyman, Phelps. "Why Beauty In Parks?" *Parks and Recreation* 8 (January/February 1924), 232–233. First in a series of essays; attributes the need for parks to an innate human desire for beauty.

Wyman, Phelps, "New York's Central Park as Seen by a Western Landscape Architect." *Parks and Recreation* 8 (July/August 1925), 513–15. A "superficial study" of Central Park with limited suggestions for restoration and modernization.

Scott Mehaffey

YOCH, FLORENCE
(1890–1972)
landscape architect

COUNCIL, LUCILLE
(1898–1964)
landscape architect

The sixth and last daughter of a family which had immigrated to California from Illinois in 1883, Florence Yoch grew up among complex landscapes and communities. At her childhood home in Santa Ana, orange groves and grape arbors provided backdrops for amateur theatricals. At the Yoch Hotel in Laguna Beach, summer evenings included Shakespearean readings and exhibitions of California plein air paintings. Experienced in banking and mining, Yoch's father invested in coal and was on the boards of many businesses, while her mother pursued interests in politics

and social issues. The atmosphere in their home was one of educated country leisure.

Yoch studied at the University of California, Berkeley, then moved to Cornell, and completed her bachelor of science in landscape gardening at the University of Illinois at Urbana-Champaign in 1915. Later in her career she prescribed studying Greek and Latin, subjects her eldest sister taught, as the first step for a young woman who wished to enter landscape architecture.

Yoch's practice extended from 1918 to 1971 and included 250 projects. These ranged widely in location

Lucille Council (left) and Florence Yoch in their garden for Mrs. C. Pardee Erdman, Pasadena, California, c. 1940. Private collection.

and kind: estates in Pasadena and Santa Barbara, the faculty club and undergraduate housing at the California Institute of Technology, the grounds of several clubs including the Women's Athletic Club in Los Angeles, mansions for movie moguls, as well as Robinson's Department Store in Beverly Hills, historic adobes in San Gabriel and Monterey, parks in Orange County and Idaho, a botanical garden in Mexico, and sets for five movies.

Yoch began on her own in 1918, and her ambition and talent immediately brought her prestigious commissions including the residence of Mrs. Howard Huntington in Pasadena, the Wilshire Country Club, and the national park at Shoshone Falls. Lucille Council, after studying at the Cambridge School in Massachusetts and starting as an apprentice in 1921, became Yoch's partner in 1925 and concentrated on locating plants and keeping track of the business aspects of their practice. They lived and worked together until Council's death in 1964.

Yoch & Council

During the 1920s and 1930s, the firm successfully adapted for American lifestyles the elegance of aristocratic garden motifs and the ingenuity of peasant designs. They worked with the most fashionable architects (Myron Hunt, Reginald Johnson, Gordon Kaufmann, and Roland Coate). Many of their landscapes were pictured in *California Art and Architecture* and national magazines

Garden for George Cukor, 1936. Private collection.

Yoch and Council's home, Pasadena, c. 1942. Photo George de Gennaro. Private collection.

including *House Beautiful;* they earned more pages than any other firm in Winifred Dobyns's influential *California Gardens* (1931). While living in San Marino, the esteemed Beatrix Farrand complained that they had tied up all the best work.

An important commission in 1932 from the first woman movie director, Dorothy Arzner, led to a decade of residential gardens for Hollywood notables including David Selznick and Jack Warner as well as movie sets for several studios. Producers wanted the "outstanding landscape artist" as Selznick labeled Yoch, whose set for Tara in *Gone With the Wind* (1939) daringly mixed splendid oaks, rough hummocks, and clambering vines to suggest the beauty of a real farm, far from conventional subur-

ban glamour. In addition to Selznick's *The Garden of Allah* (1936), her cinema work included the Capulet garden in *Romeo and Juliet* (1936), the terraces for *The Good Earth* (1937), and the meadow of 10,000 daffodils for *How Green Was My Valley* (1941).

Travel supported Yoch & Council designs. Both partners kept careful journals of their annual European journeys with photographs of places they admired. Yoch took slides and sketched architecture and details. From these materials, they invented new American gardens. In 1935, David Selznick commissioned Yoch to research scenes in North Africa for use in *The Garden of Allah.* Her trips, Yoch said, were the principal cause of the special character of her work. In even the sim-

Pool Garden, Mrs. G. P. Griffith residence, Hancock Park, California, 1929. Drawing by Harrison Clarke. Private collection.

plest garden, Yoch & Council compacted diverse scenic experiences of sun and shade, parterre and grove, and walk and arbor along an efficient route of exploration. As Yoch wrote, "Let traffic carry the bonework of the design."

When the outbreak of World War II led to the loss of their crews, Yoch and Council ceased working and moved to a new home, emphatically American in its combination of Midwestern farm and Monterey Custom House. After the war, when they resumed working, they began giving natural scenery a much larger role in design. After Council's death, Yoch continued to work on several projects, including a forested modern villa in Pasadena and a Monterey house engulfed in antique roses.

Yoch led California garden thinking from plant collecting and flower beds to a more serious, all-encompassing vision of the landscape. Indeed, the garden as a unified place of learning and working became a design principle. Particularly in Pasadena, where Yoch & Council executed about half of their commissions, women were often the clients and had the lead in maintaining the garden. Plans usually included potting sheds, lath houses, and service areas. With the installation of a garden, Yoch & Council provided an individualized set of

Il Brolino, Mary Stewart estate, Santa Barbara, 1991. Photo Robin Karson.

"Garden Maintenance Directions," which set the owner's specific garden tasks within large contexts of climate, history, and horticulture. The sacred black book, as the office staff labeled it, laid out planting schedules, listed plants by season for sun and shade, and gave rules for making compost. Yoch customarily took clients on excursions to learn more about plants and gave numerous lectures on gardens. Despite the hurry she recognized in Californian life, Yoch appreciated the test of time and study. She once wrote, "Marcus Aurelius' motto, 'make haste slowly,' was the truest thing ever said when applied to growing a hedge or even developing a whole garden."

Beyond instructions on caring for plants, Yoch's and Council's writings were brief. Their 1928 article in *Garden and Home Builder*, "The Little Garden of Gaiety," reveals their approach: "Given simple, satisfying lines worked out in substantial materials and interesting shapes and leaf texture, we have the framework on which to apply the ever changing element of color."

In her last twenty years, Yoch set down in a few pages her principles of landscaping and developed several chapters on the characteristics of admired plants and the rules for caring for them. Consistency eluded her, for her exemplary skill was flexibility in addressing specific scenes. Indeed, she admonished herself to "break shackles, however bejeweled."

Yoch & Council gardens join formal geometry with informal, even wild planting. Often they embody the unexpected: a dramatic turn in a walk, a rogue tree out of bounds, or a dynamic mix of local and imported plants.

Changing from the adaptation of European motifs as America asserted its powers in the 1930s and 1940s, Yoch & Council gave the new emblems of status, including automobiles and swimming pools, central roles in the landscape. These yielded to the dominion of rambling roses, fields of barley, wild meadows, and oak forests in the final decades of their lives.

Phillips, Michael J. "New Garden of Eden Laid out in Great Mexican Estate." *Western Florist and Nurseryman* 24 (December 1930), 4–6, 17. Description of the B. F. Johnston 60-acre botanical garden in Los Mochis, Sinaloa, Mexico, with extensive quotes from Florence Yoch about the savage vigor for which she aimed.

Yoch, Florence. "Fitting the Land for Human Use, an Art Closely Allied to Architecture." *California Arts and Architecture* 38 (1930), 19, 20, 72. Article with sketches and pictures, on Mrs. Richard Fudger's garden, which won an AIA award for the handling of an unusual lot.

Yoch, James J. *Landscaping the American Dream: The Gardens and Film Sets of Florence Yoch, 1890–1972.* New York: Sagapress/Abrams, 1989. Full-length study focusing on Florence Yoch's and Yoch & Council's landscapes; more than 200 illustrations including travel sketches and gardens for Pasadena and Hollywood, for movies, for institutions, and for their homes.

James J. Yoch

SITES ACCESSIBLE TO THE PUBLIC

Following is a selected list of landscapes open to the public (or by appointment) for each practitioner. Addresses of small and discrete sites have been included, and, where possible, streets, directions, and phone numbers have been provided.

NOTE: Many regional, city, and park plans are credited here to more than one practitioner, a reflection of various layers of design. Conversely, although some are credited to an individual practitioner, often more than one designer was involved. Most of these sites have changed considerably over time.

(+) by appointment only

ABBOTT, STANLEY WILLIAM

Blue Ridge Parkway, along the crest of the southern Appalachians, linking the Shenandoah and Great Smoky Mountains National Parks, Virginia and North Carolina. (828) 298.0398

Chippokes Plantation State Park, 695 Chippokes Park Road, Surry, Virginia. (757) 294.5148

Roanoke College, Salem (five miles west of Roanoke), Virginia. (540) 375.2500

Virginia Military Institute, intersection of I-81 and I-64 (Exit 191), Lexington, Virginia

York River State Park, 5526 Riverview Road, Williamsburg, Virginia. (757) 566.3036

BAILEY, LIBERTY HYDE

Cornell Plantations, One Plantations Road, Ithaca, New York. (607) 255.3020

BANNECKER, BENJAMIN

Washington, D.C.: plan. Best views of the overall plan are from the west side of the U.S. Capitol (across the Mall and up Pennsylvania Avenue) and from the front steps of Arlington House, Arlington, Virginia (looking back across the Potomac River).

BARRETT, NATHAN FRANKLIN

Naumkeag, Stockbridge, Massachusetts. (413) 298.3239

Branch Brook Park, Southern Division at Clifton Avenue, Newark, New Jersey

BARTHOLOMEW, HARLAND

Babler Park, St. Louis County, Missouri

Civic Center and Mall from Old Court House to Union Station, St. Louis

Glendale, Ohio, residential suburb of Cincinnati

Interstate highway system of Memphis, Shelby County, Tennessee

Ladue, Missouri, residential suburb of St. Louis

BARTRAM, JOHN

Bartram Trail: routes taken by John and William Bartram through North and South Carolina, Georgia, Alabama, and Florida. Information about the trail network can be found via the Internet (search for Bartram Trail).

Chelsea Physic Garden, 66 Royal Hospital Road, London SW4. 0171 352 5646

Historic Bartram's Garden, 54th Street and Lindbergh Boulevard, Philadelphia, Pennsylvania. (215) 729.5281

Painshill Park, Cobham, Surrey, England. (01932) 868113 or 864674

BAXTER, SYLVESTER

Bell Rock Park, Malden, Massachusetts

Boston Metropolitan Park System (except reservations and parks not mentioned in 1893 report)

Cradock Field (now Devir Park), Malden, Massachusetts

Fellsmere Park, Malden, Massachusetts

BIGELOW, JACOB

Mount Auburn Cemetery, 580 Mount Auburn Street, Cambridge, Massachusetts. (617) 547.7105

BIGNAULT, GEORGES H.

Forsyth Park: Fragrant Garden, intersection of Bull and Gaston Streets, Savannah, Georgia

BLAIR, JOHN

Beacon Hill Park: Goodacre Lake and the stone bridge, Victoria, B.C., Canada

(+) Glen Eyrie Castle, Blair Bridge, and Garden of the Gods, Colorado Springs. Start at visitor center, Rock Ledge

Ranch, 1805 North 30th Street, Colorado Springs (719) 578.6777 and (719) 598.1212

Tinker Swiss Cottage Museum, 411 Kent Street, Rockford, Illinois. (815) 964.2424

BOWDITCH, ERNEST W.

Euclid Heights Allotment, Cleveland Heights, Ohio

Newton Terraces, Waban, Massachusetts

Rockefeller Park, Cleveland

Shaker Lakes Park, Cleveland, Shaker Heights, and Cleveland Heights, Ohio

Sonnenberg Gardens, 151 Charlotte Street, Canandaigua, New York. (716) 394.4922

BRIGGS, LOUTREL WINSLOW

Mepkin Abbey grounds, 1098 Mepkin Abbey Road, Moncks Corner, South Carolina. (843) 761.8509

Mills-Hyatt House Hotel, 11 Meeting Street, Charleston, South Carolina. (843) 577.2400

Nathaniel Russell House, 51 Meeting Street, Charleston, South Carolina. (843) 724.8481

(+)Whaley garden, 58 Church Street, Charleston, South Carolina 29401

BURNAP, GEORGE ELBERTON

Krug Park and parks and boulevards system, St. Joseph, Missouri

Meridian Hill Park, Washington, D.C.

Montrose Park, Washington, D.C.

Tidal Basin, Jefferson Memorial, Washington, D.C.

CALDWELL, ALFRED

Burnham Park: Promontory Point, Chicago

Eagle Point Park, Dubuque, Iowa

Lafayette Park, Detroit

Lake Point Tower, Chicago

Lincoln Park: Lily Pool, Chicago

CAUTLEY, MARJORIE SEWELL

Kingston State Park, 124 Main Street, Kingston, New Hampshire

Phipps Garden Apartments, between 50th and 52nd Streets at 39th Avenue, Long Island City, New York

Radburn, 2920 Fairlawn Avenue, Fairlawn, New Jersey

Sunnyside Gardens, between Skillman and Middleburg Avenues at Barnett Avenue, Long Island City, New York

Wentworth State Park, 297 Governer Wentworth Highway, Wolfeboro, New Hampshire

CHURCH, THOMAS DOLLIVER

Center for Advanced Studies in the Behavioral Sciences, 75 Alta Road, Stanford, California. (650) 321.2052

Fay garden, 2366 Leavenworth Street, San Francisco

Lakewold Gardens: entry drive, herb knot garden, and quatrefoil-shaped swimming pool, 12317 Gravelly Lake Drive, S.W., Lakewood, Washington. (253) 584.4106

Park Merced (Metropolitan Life), San Francisco

Sunset Magazine display gardens, 80 Willow Road, Menlo Park, California. (650) 321.3600

CLARKE, GILMORE DAVID

Bronx River Parkway, from Bronxville to Kensico Dam in Valhalla, Westchester County, New York

Bryant Park, between West 40th and 42nd Streets, Avenue of the Americas

Central Park Conservatory Garden, Fifth Avenue north of 86th Street, New York City

Rye Beach Park and Playland, Rye, New York

Sprain Brook Parkway, from Mt. Vernon to I-287 interchange, Westchester County, New York

CLEVELAND, HORACE WILLIAM SHALER

Minneapolis park system (including Minnehaha Park), Minneapolis, Minnesota

Omaha park system, Omaha, Nebraska

Roger Williams Park, Providence, Rhode Island

Sleepy Hollow Cemetery, Bedford Street, Concord, Massachusetts. (978) 371.6299

Washburn Park development (subdivision at 50th Street and Nicollet Avenue), Minneapolis, Minnesota

COFFIN, MARIAN CRUGER

C. W. Post College, 720 Northern Boulevard, Brookville, New York. (516) 299.2413

Ft. Ticonderoga Park: Kings Garden, Route 87, Ft. Ticonderoga, New York. (518) 585.2821

Gibraltar, Greenhill and Pennsylvania Avenues (Rt. 52), Wilmington, Deleware. (302) 651.9617

Nassau County Museum of Art, One Museum Drive, Roslyn Harbor, New York. (516) 484.9338

Winterthur Garden, Rt. 52, Winterthur, Deleware. (302) 888.4600

COPELAND, ROBERT MORRIS

Oak Bluffs, Martha's Vineyard, Massachusetts

Oak Grove Cemetery, Washington Street, Gloucester, Massachusetts

Marsh-Billings National Park, Route 12, Woodstock, Vermont. (802) 457.3368

Sleepy Hollow Cemetery, Bedford Street, Concord, Massachusetts. (978) 371.6299

CORNELL, RALPH DALTON

Beverly Hills Parkway (portions), Beverly Hills, California

Torrey Pines Reserve, between La Jolla and Del Mar, north of San Diego. (619) 755.2063

Rancho Los Cerritos, Historic site, 4600 Virginia Road, Long Beach, California

Franklin D. Murphy Sculpture Garden and Sunset Canyon Recreation Center, UCLA, Westwood, California

DANIELS, HOWARD

Druid Hill Park, Baltimore. (410) 396.7931

Oakwood Cemetery, 940 Comstock Avenue, Syracuse, New York

Poughkeepsie Rural Cemetery, 342 South Avenue, Poughkeepsie, New York

DAWSON, JAMES FREDERICK

Lake Washington Boulevard, from the Arboretum to Seward Park, Seattle

Palos Verdes Estates, south of Los Angeles

Planting Fields Arboretum State Historic Park, Planting Fields Road, Oyster Bay, New York. (516) 922.9200

Rockwood Boulevard, near Highland Drive, South Hill, Spokane, Washington

Seward Park: south entry and three-mile road system, Seattle

DEARBORN, HENRY A. S.

Forest Hills Cemetery, 95 Forest Hills Avenue, Jamaica Plain, Massachusetts. (617) 524.0128

Mount Auburn Cemetery, 580 Mount Auburn Street, Cambridge, Massachusetts. (617) 547.7105

DEBOER, S. R.

Alamo Placita Park, Speer Boulevard at Ogden Street, Denver

Boulder City Historic District, Boulder City, Nevada

Denver Mountain Parks, from Lariat Trail entrance at 19th Street and U.S. Hwy. 6, Golden, Colorado

East 6th Avenue Parkway, between Colorado Boulevard and Monaco Street Parkway, Denver

Washington Park: north end including Marion Street Parkway entrance, Evergreen Hill, and lily pond, Denver

DEFOREST, ALLING STEPHEN

George Eastman House, 900 East Avenue, Rochester, New York. (716) 244.9023

Warner Castle: Sunken Garden, 5 Castle Park, Rochester, New York. (716) 244.9023

LOCKWOOD DE FOREST III

Casa del Herrero: motor court and south lawn, 1387 East Valley Road, Montecito, California. (805) 565.5653

Santa Barbara Botanical Garden: information kiosk, Pritchett Trail, Pritchett Memorial Bench, and Wildflower Meadow, 1212 Mission Canyon, Santa Barbara. (805) 682.4726

Santa Barbara Museum of Art: entrance terrace and memorial bench, 1130 State Street, Santa Barbara. (805) 963.4364

(+) Val Verde, Montecito, California. (805) 965.3639

DOWNING, ANDREW JACKSON

Springside, east side of Academy Street, Poughkeepsie, New York. (914) 454.2060

DRAPER, EARLE SUMNER

Chicopee, Georgia: town plan

Myers Park, Route 16, East and West Queens Road, and Lillington Avenue, Charlotte, North Carolina

Norris, Tennessee: town plan

Norris Freeway, Norris, Tennessee

ELIOT, CHARLES

Copps Hill Terrace, Boston

Longfellow Park, Mt. Auburn Street, Cambridge, Massachusetts

Revere Beach, Ocean Avenue, Revere, Massachusetts

Waverly Oaks Reservation, Trapelo Road, Belmont and Waltham, Massachusetts

White Park, Concord, New Hampshire

ELLWANGER, GEORGE, AND PATRICK BARRY

Barry House, 692 Mount Hope Avenue, Rochester, New York

(+) Ellwanger garden, 625 Mount Hope Avenue, Rochester, New York. (716) 546.7029

Gothic cottages designed for nursery workmen at 548, 554, 560, and 566 Mount Hope Avenue (between Linden and Cypress Streets), Rochester, New York

Highland Park and the Pinnacle, Rochester, New York

Mount Hope Nurseries office building, 668 Mount Hope Avenue, Rochester, New York

ELWOOD, PHILIP HOMER

Argonne Cemetery, Romagne-sous-Montfaucon, France

FARRAND, BEATRIX JONES

Dumbarton Oaks, 1703 32nd Street, N.W., Washington, D.C. (202) 339.6401

Dumbarton Oaks Park, R Street at 31st Street, Washington, D.C. (202) 282.7603

Harkness Memorial State Park: Italian Garden and Oriental Garden, 275 Great Neck Road, Waterford, Connecticut

Princeton University: Graduate College, Princeton, N.J.

Yale University: Harkness Quandrangle, Branford and Silliman College, New Haven

FLEMING, BRYANT

Cheekwood, Tennessee Botanical Gardens and Fine Arts Center, 1200 Forrest Park Drive, Nashville. (615) 356.8000

Warner Park, Nashville

FOOTE, HARRIETT RISLEY

Crane Beach, Argilla Road, Ipswich, Massachusetts. (978) 356.4354

FORDYCE, SAMUEL WESLEY

Arlington Hotel, Bathhouse Row grounds, and Fordyce Bathhouse, Central Avenue, Hot Springs National Park, Arkansas

FOWLER, ROBERT LUDLOW, JR.

Reader's Digest Corporate Headquarters, Reader's Digest Road, Pleasantville, New York

FROST, PAUL RUBENS

(+)Frost garden, 12 Ash Street Place, Cambridge, Massachusetts

Heritage Plantation: rhododendron plantings, 67 Grove Street, Sandwich, Massachusetts. (508) 888.3300

Jeremiah Lee Mansion: herb garden, 161 Washington Street, Marblehead, Massachusetts

GALLAGHER, PERCIVAL

Essex, Passaic, and Union County Parks (sections), New Jersey

Gardencourt, Louisville Presbyterian Seminary, Louisville, Kentucky

Indiana University/Purdue University: Ball Nurses' Sunken Garden and Convalescent Park, Indianapolis

Oldfields, Indianapolis Museum of Art, 1200 West 38th Street, Indianapolis. (317) 923.1331

GEIFFERT, ALFRED, JR.

Fresh Meadows Housing Development, Fresh Meadows Lane and Nassau Boulevard, Queens County, New York

National Gallery of Art, West Building, Constitution Avenue, N.W., between 3rd and 7th Streets, Washington, D.C.

New Jersey Botanical Garden: formal gardens, Morris Road, Ringwood, New Jersey. (973) 962.9534

GIBBS, GEORGE, JR.

Berea College campus, Berea, Kentucky

Hamilton, Palmer, and Mark White Parks, Chicago

Kennedy Park, Fall River, Massachusetts

GILLETTE, CHARLES FREEMAN

Agecroft Hall, 4305 Sulgrave Road, Richmond, Virginia. (804) 353.4241

Kenmore Plantation and Gardens, 1201 Washington Avenue, Fredericksburg, Virginia. (540) 373.3381

Virginia House Museum, 4301 Sulgrave Road, Richmond, Virginia. (804) 353.4251

GILLETTE, GENEVIEVE

Albion College, Albion, Michigan

Genevieve Gillette Visitor Center, Hoffmaster State Park, Muskegon, Michigan

Hartwick Pines State Park, between Grayling and Gaylord on Highway 75, Michigan

Sleeping Bear Dunes National Seashore, between Frankfort and Leland on the shore of Lake Michigan

Westacres Housing Development, both sides of Commerce Road, 9 miles west of Pontiac, Michigan

GREELY, ROSE ISHBEL

Commandants House, Marine Corps Barracks, 8th and I Streets, Washington, D.C.

National Presbyerian Center, Van Ness and Nebraska Avenues, Washington, D.C.

Textile Museum, 2310–20 S Street, Washington, D.C.

GREENLEAF, JAMES L.

Bronx Zoo: north end of Astor Court, Bronx, New York

Lincoln Memorial plantings, Washington, D.C.

Planting Fields Arboretum: Green Garden, Planting Fields Road, Oyster Bay, New York. (516) 922.9200

Vanderbilt Mansion National Historic Site: Italian Garden, Route 9, Hyde Park, New York. (914) 229.7770

GRIFFIN, WALTER BURLEY

(+) Darwin D. Martin House, 125 Jewett Parkway, Buffalo

Northern Illinois University campus, DeKalb, Illinois

Rock Crest/Rock Glen Suburban Community, Mason City, Iowa

(+) Ward Willitts House, 1445 Sheridan Road, Highland Park, Illinois

GRISWOLD, RALPH E.

Chatham Village, off Bigham Street, Mount Washington, Pittsburgh

Mary Washington House, 1200 Charles Street, Fredericksburgh, Virginia. (540) 373.1569

Old Economy Village Restoration, 1401 Church Street, Ambridge, Pennsylvania. (724) 266.4500

Point State Park, Pittsburgh

St. John Mews, 23rd and 24th Streets, Richmond, Virginia

HALL, GEORGE DUFFIELD

Beverly Hills, California: plan and tree plantings

Carthay Center, Los Angeles: plan

Midwick View Estates, Los Angeles: fountain

Marine Stadium, Long Beach, California

Prince Rupert, Canada: plan and tree plantings

HARE, SIDNEY J., AND S. HERBERT HARE

Country Club District, Kansas City, Missouri

Forest Hill Cemetery, Kansas City, Missouri

Jacob L. Loose Memorial Park and Laura Conyers Rose Garden, Kansas City, Missouri

Mission Hills, Kansas

Philbrook Museum of Art, 2727 South Rockford Road, Tulsa, Oklahoma. (918) 749.7941

HUBBARD, HENRY VINCENT

Colony Hills, Springfield, Massachusetts
Longfellow Park, Mt. Auburn Street, Cambridge, Massachusetts

HUNTSMAN-TROUT, EDWARD

Hugo Reid Adobe and Queen Anne Cottage, Los Angeles County Arboretum, Baldwin Avenue, Arcadia, California. (818) 821.3222
Scripps College, Claremont, California

HUTCHESON, MARTHA BROOKES

Bamboo Brook Outdoor Education Center, 170 Longview Road, Chester Township, New Jersey. (908) 234.0061
Longfellow House: Colonial Revival Garden, Brattle Street, Cambridge, Massachusetts. (617) 876.4491
Marsh-Billings-Rockefeller National Historical Park: entry drive, Route 12, Woodstock, Vermont. (802) 457.3368
Maudsley State Park: entry drive and formal garden, Curzon's Mill Road, Newburyport, Massachusetts. (508) 465.7223

INNOCENTI, UMBERTO

Elizabethan Gardens, 1411 Highway 64 and 264, Roanoke Island, North Carolina. (252) 473.3234
Furman University, Greenville, South Carolina
Greenbrier Hotel, 300 West Main Street, White Sulphur Springs, West Virginia. (304) 536.1110
Greenville-Spartanburg Airport, Greer, South Carolina
Keeneland Race Course, 4201 Versailles Road, Lexington, Kentucky. (800) 456.3412

JEFFERSON, THOMAS

Monticello, Charlottesville, Virginia. (804) 984.9822
Poplar Forest, Lynchburg, Virginia. (804) 525.1806
University of Virginia, Charlottesville, Virginia. (804) 982.5407

JENSEN, JENS

The Clearing, 12171 Garrett Bay Road, Ellison Bay, Wisconsin. (920) 854.4088
Edsel and Eleanor Ford House, 1100 Lake Shore Road, Grosse Pointe Shores, Michigan. (313) 884.4222
Fairlane, Henry and Clara Ford Estate, Dearborn, Michigan. (313) 593.5590
Lincoln Memorial Garden, 2301 East Lake Drive, Springfield, Illinois. (217) 529.1111
West Parks, notably Columbus Park and Garfield Park Conservatory, Chicago

KERN, MAXIMILIAN G.

Forest Park, St. Louis, Missouri
Kansas State University, Manhattan, Kansas

KESSLER, GEORGE E.

Cincinnati park system, notably Eden Park, Madison and Montgomery Road, Cincinnati
Forest Park, St. Louis, Missouri
Hermann Park, Hermann Boulevard at Main Street, Houston
Indianapolis park system, notably the Garfield Park Sunken Gardens, Raymond and Shelby Streets, Indianapolis
Kansas City, Missouri: parks and boulevards system, notably Kessler Park, Penn Valley Park, and Paseo Boulevard

KNIGHT, EMERSON

Mount Helix Nature Theatre, La Mesa, California
Sidney B. Cushing Mountain Theatre, Mt. Tamalpais State Park, Marin County, California

LAY, CHARLES DOWNING

Frear Park, Oakwood Avenue, Troy, New York
Lincoln Park, Delaware Avenue, Albany, New York
Sterling House Community Center, 2238 Main Street, Stratford, Connecticut. (203) 378.2606
Swinburne Park and Bleecker Stadium, Albany, New York

LEAVITT, CHARLES WELLFORD, JR.

Chester Congdon Estate, 3300 London Road, Duluth, Minnesota. (888) 454.GLEN
Congress Hall Park, Saratoga Springs, New York
Gate of Heaven Cemetery, Bradhurst Avenue, Valhalla, New York
St. Francis College, Mt. Assisi Monastery, Loretto, Pennsylvania
Untermeyer Park, 919 North Broadway, Yonkers, New York

LORD, ELIZABETH, AND EDITH SCHRYVER

Bush Pasture Park, Salem, Oregon
Deepwood Estate, 1116 Mission Street S.E., Salem, Oregon. (503) 363.1825
(+) Lord and Schryver House. Contact Sylvia Strand, 545 Mission Street S.E., Salem, Oregon 97302

LOWELL, GUY

Boston Museum of Fine Arts: plantings at Fenway facade, Boston
Planting Fields Arboretum: Italian Garden, Planting Fields Road, Oyster Bay, New York. (516) 922.9200
The Fens: entrance at Westland Avenue Gate and adjacent Fensgate at 56 Hemenway Street, Boston
Frick Park, Pittsburgh

MACKAYE, BENTON

Appalachian National Scenic Trail. (304) 535.6331

MANNING, WARREN HENRY

(+) Gwinn, 12407 Lake Shore Boulevard, Cleveland. Contact Cleveland Botanic Garden (216) 721.1600 regarding tours

Gwinn, Michigan: town plan
Harrisburg park system, Harrisburg, Pennsylvania
Stan Hywet Hall and Gardens, 714 North Portage Path, Akron,
   Ohio. (216) 836.5533

MARQUIS, WILLIAM BELL

Bok Tower Gardens: reflecting pool, 1151 Tower Boulevard,
   Mountain Lake, Florida. (941) 676.9412
The Crescent (subdivision), Charleston, South Carolina
Fairfax Mill Village, Valley, Alabama
North Charleston, South Carolina: town plan

MAY, CLIFF

Casa de Estudillo, Old Town State Historic Park, San Diego.
   (619) 237.6770
Sunset Magazine office, 80 Willow Road, Menlo Park, California. (650) 321.3600

MCFARLAND, J. HORACE

Front Street, Harrisburg, Pennsylvania

MORELL, ANTHONY URBANSKI, AND ARTHUR RICHARDSON NICHOLS

Carlton College, First Street and College Avenue, Northfield,
   Minnesota
Minnesota State Capitol grounds, Wabasha Avenue, St. Paul
Morgan Park, Hwy. 23 south of I-35, Duluth, Minnesota
Rolling Green, Interlachen Boulevard, Edina, Minnesota
Sunset Memorial Park, St. Anthony Boulevard, St. Anthony
   (Minneapolis), Minnesota

NEGUS, SAMUEL PIKE

D. W. Field Park, Pleasant Street, Brockton, Massachusetts

NEWTON, NORMAN THOMAS

Statue of Liberty National Monument and Ellis Island, New
   York. (212) 316.3200

NICHOLS, ROSE STANDISH

Cornish Colony Gallery and Museum, Route 12A, Cornish,
   New Hampshire. (603) 675.6000
Grey Towers National Historic Landmark, Old Owego Turn-
   pike, Milford, Pennsylvania. (717) 296.9630
Villa Terrace Decorative Arts Museum, 2220 North Terrace
   Avenue, Milwaukee. (414) 271.3656

NOLEN, JOHN

Madison, Wisconsin: city plan
Kingsport, Tennessee: town center
Little Rock, Arkansas: town plan

Mariemont, Ohio: town center and Dogwood Park
San Diego: city plan, including Presidio Park

NOTMAN, JOHN

Capitol Square, Richmond, Virginia
Holly-Wood Cemetery, 412 South Cherry, Richmond, Virginia.
   (804) 648.8501
Laurel Hill Cemetery, 3822 Ridge Avenue, Philadelphia, Penn-
   sylvania. (215) 228.8200
Marquand Park, Stockton Street and Lover's Lane, Princeton,
   New Jersey

OLMSTED, FREDERICK LAW, JR.

Acadia National Park, Hulls Cove Visitor Center, Route 233,
   Eagle Lake Road, Bar Harbor, Maine. (207) 288.3338
Baltimore: park system, notably Clifton Park, Wyman Park, and
   Wyman Park Dell
Palos Verdes Estates, Los Angeles
Forest Hills Gardens, Forest Hills, Queens, New York
Fort Tryon Park, New York City

OLMSTED, FREDERICK LAW, SR.

Biltmore, Asheville, North Carolina. (704) 274.6230
Central Park, New York City
Druid Hills, Ponce de Leon Avenue, Atlanta
Fairsted, F. L. Olmsted National Historic Site, 99 Warren Street,
   Brookline, Massachusetts. (617) 566.1689
Prospect Park, Brooklyn
Riverside, Illinois. Visitor information at Riverside Historical
   Commission, 27 Riverside Road.
U.S. Capitol Grounds, Washington, D.C.

OLMSTED, JOHN CHARLES

Alta Vista and Braeview (subdivisions), Alta Vista Avenue,
   Louisville, Kentucky
Audubon Park, New Orleans
Louisville, Kentucky: parks and boulevard system
Seattle: parks and boulevard system
University of Washington, Seattle: fountain and Mt. Rainier vista

PARMENTIER, ANDRÉ

Vanderbilt Mansion National Historic Site, Route 9, Hyde Park,
   New York. (914) 229.7770

PARSONS, SAMUEL, JR.

Albemarle Park, Charlotte Street, Asheville, North Carolina
Glen Iris Park, Birmingham, Alabama
New Jersey Botanical Garden, Morris Road, Ringwood, New
   Jersey. (973) 962.9534
Pinelawn Memorial Park Cemetery, Pinelawn Road, Hunting-
   ton, Long Island. (516) 249.6100
St. Nicholas Park, New York City

PAULEY, WILLIAM C.

Hurt Park, at Gilmer Street, Edgewood Avenue, and Courtland Street, Atlanta

Winn Park, at Westminster Drive and Peachtree Circle, Atlanta

PEETS, ELBERT

Greendale, Wisconsin: town plan

Lincoln Circle, Kohler, Wisconsin

Park Forest, Illinois: town plan

Washington Highlands, Wauwatosa, Wisconsin

Wyomissing Park, Reading, Pennsylvania

PLATT, CHARLES A.

Freer Gallery of Art: courtyard, Washington, D.C.

(+) Gwinn, 12407 Lake Shore Boulevard, Cleveland. Contact Cleveland Botanic Garden (216) 721.1600 regarding tours.

Harrison House Conference Center, Dosoris Lane and Old Tappen Road, Glen Cove, New York

Francis T. Maxwell House: Maxwell Court, Rockville, Connecticut

Phillips Academy, Andover, Massachusetts

POND, BREMER WHIDDEN

Dartmouth College: Tuck Drive, Hanover, New Hampshire

PUNCHARD, WILLIAM

D. W. Field Park, Pleasant Street, Brockton, Massachusetts

RAPUANO, MICHAEL

Capitol Hill, Nashville

Cleveland Public Mall/Exhibition Hall, Cleveland

Eisenhower Park, East Meadow, New York

Orchard Beach, Pelham Bay Park, Bronx, New York

Point State Park, Pittsburgh

REQUA, RICHARD

Balboa Park public gardens including the Alcazar Gardens at House of Charm, the House of Hospitality courtyard, and the Cafe del Rey Moro at House of Hospitality, San Diego, California

Ojai, California: town plan

Rancho Santa Fe, San Diego County, California: town plan

ROSE, JAMES C.

James Rose Center, 506 East Ridgewood Avenue, Ridgewood, New Jersey. (201) 444.2559

SARGENT, CHARLES SPRAGUE

Arnold Arboretum, 125 Arborway, Jamaica Plain, Massachusetts. (617) 524.1718

SAUNDERS, WILLIAM

Garrett Park Historic District, Garrett Park, Maryland

Oak Ridge Cemetery, Springfield, Illinois

Soldiers National Cemetery, Gettysburg, Pennsylvania

SCHUETZE, REINHARD

Colorado State Capitol Grounds, Lincoln Street at East Colfax Avenue, Denver

Cheesman Park, Denver

City Park Esplanade and City Park, East Colfax Avenue at Elizabeth Street, Denver

Washington Park, Denver

SEARS, THOMAS W.

Ballmuckey, Baltimore

Pennsbury Manor (home of William Penn), 400 Pennsbury Memorial Road, Morrisville, Pennsylvania. (215) 946.0400

Reynolda Gardens, Wake Forest University, Winston-Salem, North Carolina. (910) 759.5593

SESSIONS, KATE OLIVIA

Former site of Sessions' nursery at Sixth and Upas Streets; Ladies Annex (of the Chamber of Commerce); and tree plantings at west entrance, Balboa Park, San Diego

SHIPMAN, ELLEN BIDDLE

Chatham Manor, Fredericksburg and Spotsylvania National Military Park, 120 Chatham Lane, Fredericksburg, Virginia. (540) 371.0802

Grosse Pointe War Memorial, 32 Lake Shore Drive, Grosse Pointe, Michigan. (313) 881.7511

Longue Vue Gardens, 7 Bamboo Road, New Orleans. (504) 488.5488

Sarah P. Duke Memorial Gardens, Duke University, West Campus, Durham, North Carolina. (919) 684.3698

Stan Hywet Hall: English Garden, 714 North Portage Path, Akron, Ohio. (330) 836.5535

SHURCLIFF, ARTHUR ASAHEL

Carter's Grove Plantation, "restoration" (now the property of Colonial Williamsburg)

Charles River Basin, park and esplanade along Storrow Drive, Boston

Colonial Williamsburg: landscape and planting, notably Governor's Palace gardens, Williamsburg, Virginia. (800) 447.8679

Fuller Gardens, 10 Willow Avenue, North Hampton, New Hampshire. (603) 964.5414

SHUTZE, PHILIP TRAMMELL

Swan House, Atlanta History Center, 130 West Paces Ferry Road, Atlanta. (404) 814.4000

SIDNEY, JAMES C.

Easton Cemetery (eastern portion): circulation system, 401 North 7th Street, Easton, Pennsylvania. (610) 252.1741

Fairmount Park (portion south of Thompson Street), Philadelphia

Laurel Hill Cemetery (portion south of Hunting Park Avenue): circulation system, 3822 Ridge Avenue, Philadelphia (215) 228.8200

Oakwood Cemetery (portion west of Oakwood Avenue [Route 40]): circulation system, Troy, New York. (518) 272.7520

Woodlawn Cemetery, Webster Avenue and East 233rd Street, Bronx, New York. (718) 920.0500

SIMONDS, OSSIAN COLE

Brucemore, 222 Collins Road N.E., Cedar Rapids, Iowa. (319) 373.9638

Graceland Cemetery, 4001 North Clark Street, Chicago. (319) 373.9638

Indian Mounds Park, Gardner Park, Parker Heights Memorial Park, and South Park, Quincy, Illinois

Lincoln Park, from Diversey to Devon Avenue, Chicago

Nichols Arboretum, Ann Arbor, Michigan. (734) 998.9540

SIMONSON, WILBUR H.

George Washington Memorial Parkway, between Alexandria and Mount Vernon, Virginia

SMITH, JOHN JAY

Laurel Hill Cemetery: portions of mature tree canopy, 3822 Ridge Avenue, Philadelphia. (215) 228.8200

West Laurel Hill Cemetery: mature trees, 227 Belmont Avenue, Bala Cynwyd, Pennsylvania. (610) 664.1591

STEELE, FLETCHER

Camden Public Library Amphitheater, Atlantic Avenue, Camden, Maine

Mission House, Stockbridge, Massachusetts. (413) 298.3239

Naumkeag, Stockbridge, Massachusetts. (413) 298.3239

Williams College: Hopkins Memorial Steps, Williamstown, Massachusetts

STILES, EZRA CLARKE

Boyce Park: entrance area, Route 380, Monroeville, Allegheny County, Pennsylvania

STRAUCH, ADOLPH

Oak Woods Cemetery, 1035 East 67th Street, Chicago. (773) 288.3800

Mt. Storm Park: Temple of Love and associated landscape, Lafayette Avenue, Cincinnati

Spring Grove Cemetery, 4521 Spring Grove Avenue, Cincinnati, Ohio. (513) 681.6680

TAYLOR, ALBERT DAVIS

Beltsville Agricultural Research Center Center, Powder Mill Road, Beltsville, Maryland. (301) 504.8483

Forest Hills Park, Cleveland

Mt. Airy Arboretum, 5083 Colerain Avenue, Cincinnati. (513) 352.4080

UNDERHILL, FRANCIS TOWNSEND

Santa Barbara Biltmore Hotel: main lawn, La Chiquita Bungalow, Santa Barbara

Casa del Herrero: south lawn, 1387 East Valley Road, Montecito. (805) 565.5653

VAUX, CALVERT

Central Park, New York City

Eastern and Ocean Parkways, Brooklyn, New York

Mills-Norrie State Park, including former estate of Lydig M. Hoyt, Staatsburg, New York. (914) 889.4100

Prospect Park, Brooklyn, New York

Riverside Park and Drive, north of 72nd Street, New York City

VAUX, DOWNING

College Hill Park: North Clinton Street entrance and remnants of circulation system including the drive to summit, Poughkeepsie, New York

Downing Park, Newburgh, New York

Kingston Point Park, Kingston, New York

Rockwood Park, City of St. John, New Brunswick, Canada. (506) 658.2829

Wilderstein Preservation, Morton Road, Rhinebeck, New York. (914) 876.4818

VINT, THOMAS CHALMERS

Bandelier National Monument, Los Alamos, New Mexico. (503) 672.0343

Going-to-the-Sun Highway, Glacier National Park, West Glacier, Montana. (406) 888.7800

Mount Rainier National Park: roads, trails, and park villages, Ashford, Washington. (360) 569.2211

Skyline Drive, Shenandoah National Park, Luray, Virginia. (540) 999-3500

Yosemite National Park: road to Glacier Point and associated landscape, Yosemite, California. (209) 372.0200

VITALE, FERRUCCIO

Admiralty Town House Community, Harbour Lane, Bay Shore, New York

Chelsea Center, Nassau County Office of Cultural Development, Route 25A, East Norwich, New York. (516) 571.8550

Glen Cove Golf Club: sunken gardens, 109 Lattingtown Road, Glen Cove, New York. (516) 671.0033

New Jersey Botanical Garden: formal gardens, Morris Road, Ringwood, New Jersey. (973) 962.9534

Village Club of Sands Point, Middle Neck Road, Sands Point, New York. (516) 944.7400

WADSWORTH, ALEXANDER

Auburn Park, Islington Road, Newton, Massachusetts
Harmony Grove Cemetery, 30 Grove Street, Salem, Massachusetts. (508) 744.0554
Kenrick Park, Park Street, Newton, Massachusetts
Mount Auburn Cemetery, 580 Mount Auburn Street, Cambridge, Massachusetts. (617) 547.7105
Woodland Cemetery, 302 Elm Street, Malden, Massachusetts

WASHINGTON, GEORGE

Mount Vernon, Virginia. (703) 780.2000

WATERMAN, HAZEL WOOD

Casa de Estudillo: courtyard, Old Town State Historic Park, Mason Street at San Diego Avenue, San Diego. (858) 220.5423

WAUGH, FRANK ALBERT

Mount Hood Road, Mount Hood National Forest, Oregon

WEBER, NELVA MARGARET

Bard College: President's House garden; redesign of main campus mall; red oak planting along campus road, Annandale-on-Hudson, New York. (914) 758.6822
Hancock Shaker Village: Tree of Life Arboretum at Visitors' Center, Pittsfield, Massachusetts
(+) Hildegarde Plehn/Oneglia Garden. Contact Litchfield Historical Society, 7 South Street, Litchfield, Connecticut 06759
Illinois Wesleyan University: tree plantings from 1960s, notably on Eckley Quad, Bloomington. (309) 556.1000
Purnell School: plan and plantings, 51 Pottersville Road, Pottersville, New Jersey

WEIDENMANN, JACOB

Bushnell Park, Hartford
Cedar Hill Cemetery, 453 Fairfield Avenue, Hartford. (860) 956.3311
Congress Hall Park, Saratoga Springs, New York

WELCH, ADONIJAH STRONG

Iowa State University campus, Ames

WHEELWRIGHT, ROBERT

Fort Christina Park, Wilmington, Delaware
Goodstay (now part of the University of Delaware campus), 2700 Pennsylvania Avenue, Wilmington
Valley Garden, north of intersection Routes 82 and 52, Wilmington, Deleware

WHITING, EDWARD CLARK

Cherokee Gardens and Indian Hills (subdivisions), Louisville, Kentucky
Fort Tryon Park, New York City

WILLIAMS, MORLEY JEFFERS

George Washington's Mount Vernon, restoration, Mount Vernon, Virginia. (703) 780.2000
Monticello: west lawn, Charlottesville, Virginia. (804) 984.9822
Samuel Smallwood House and Garden, 520 East Front Street, New Bern, North Carolina. (252) 633.2931
Stratford Hall Plantation, Stratford, Virginia. (804) 493.8038
Tryon Palace Historic Sites and Gardens, New Bern, North Carolina. (252) 514.4900

WIMMER, HARRIETT BARNHART

Revelle Campus, University of California, Torrey Pines Road, La Jolla. (858) 534-2230
Sea World, Mission Bay Park, 500 Sea World Drive, San Diego. (858) 226-3901

WRIGHT, HENRY

Brentmoor, Brentmoor Park, and Forest Ridge (subdivisions), at Big Bend and Wydown Boulevards, Clayton, Missouri
Chatham Village, Bigham Street, Mount Washington, Pittsburgh
Colonial Village, 1702 North Troy Street, Arlington, Virginia
Kessler Park: colonnade and pergola, Galdstone Boulevard and St. John Avenue, Kansas City, Missouri
Radburn, 2920 Fairlawn Avenue, Fairlawn, New Jersey
Sunnyside Gardens, between Skillman and Middleburg Avenues at Barnett Avenue, Long Island City, New York

WYMAN, ALANSON PHELPS

Custer State Park, U.S. Hwy. 16A, Custer, South Dakota
Parklawn Public Housing Project, Lincoln Creek Parkway, Milwaukee
South Dakota State Capitol, Capitol Avenue, Pierre
Thomas Lowry Park, Minneapolis
Wisconsin Rapids Parkway (now part of Veteran's Parkway), between Jackson Street Bridge and West Grand Avenue Bridge, Wisconsin Rapids, Michigan

YOCH, FLORENCE AND COUNCIL, LUCILLE

The Athenaeum, California Institute of Technology, Pasadena
Gone With the Wind (1939), set design of Tara
The Good Earth (1937), set design of rice fields and countryside
How Green Was My Valley (1941), set design of field of daffodils
Romeo and Juliet (1936), set design of the Capulet Garden

CONTRIBUTORS

CHARLES E. AGUAR is a professor emeritus in the School of Environmental Design of the University of Georgia, Athens.

ARNOLD R. ALANEN is a professor in the Department of Landscape Architecture at the University of Wisconsin, Madison.

PHYLLIS ANDERSEN is director of the Institute for Cultural Landscape Studies of the Arnold Arboretum of Harvard University in Jamaica Plain, Massachusetts.

DOMENICO ANNESE, FASLA, is former vice president (retired) of Clarke & Rapuano, New York, consulting engineers and landscape architects.

ANIA BAAS is a garden designer in Peapack, New Jersey.

THOMAS E. BEAMAN JR. is a historical archaeologist with North Carolina State Historic Sites and a graduate student in anthropology at East Carolina University, Greenville, North Carolina.

ROBERT F. BECKER (deceased) was with the New York State Agricultural Experiment Station, Department of Horticultural Sciences, Geneva, New York, Campus, Cornell University.

VIRGINIA LOPEZ BEGG is a landscape historian, lecturer and designer, based in Andover, Massachusetts.

CHARLES E. BEVERIDGE, Ph.D., is the series editor of the Frederick Law Olmsted Papers editorial project and research professor in the Department of History at the American University, Washington, D.C.

CHARLES A. BIRNBAUM, FASLA, is coordinator of the Historic Landscape Initiative of the National Park Service, Washington, D.C.

JUDY BYRD BRITTENUM is an associate professor of landscape architecture at the University of Arkansas, Fayetteville.

AMY BROWN is a Ph.D. candidate in the Department of Urban Studies and Planning at MIT.

C. ALLAN BROWN is a landscape architect and historian in Charlottesville, Virginia.

FRANK B. BURGRAFF, FASLA, is a professor emeritus of landscape architecture at the University of Arkansas, Fayetteville, the University of Georgia, Athens, and Penn State University, University Park.

MALCOLM D. CAIRNS, ASLA, is an associate professor of landscape architecture at Ball State University, Muncie, Indiana.

DEAN CARDASIS, ASLA, is a landscape architect, an associate professor in the Department of Landscape Architecture and Regional Planning, University of Massachusetts, Amherst, and director of the James Rose Center for Landscape Architectural Research and Design, Ridgewood, New Jersey.

JOT D. CARPENTER, FASLA, (deceased) was a professor of landscape architecture at the Ohio State University, Columbus, Ohio, and a past president of the ASLA.

LINA L. COFRESI, Ph.D., is a principal of CR Landscape Design, a landscape historian, and writer based in Savannah, Georgia.

KURT B. CULBERTSON, FASLA, is president of The Design Workshop, Aspen, Colorado.

ELIZABETH HOPE CUSHING is a landscape historian, and Ph.D. candidate in the American and New England Studies Program at Boston University, and a former editor of the *Journal of the New England Garden History Society*.

JEAN CZERKAS is a landscape historian and preservation advocate in Rochester, New York.

W. A. DALE is an independent historian in Victoria, B.C.

MARY F. DANIELS is director of Special Collections at the Frances Loeb Library, Graduate School of Design, Harvard University.

TIM DAVIS is a historian with the Historic American Engineering Record of the National Park Service in Washington, D.C.

DENNIS DOMER is a professor emeritus in the School of Architecture and Urban Design at the University of Kansas, Lawrence.

CAROLYN ETTER and DON ETTER are historians and former managers of the Denver Park and Recreation Department, and honorary members of the ASLA.

IAN FIRTH, ASLA, is a professor of landscape architecture and historic preservation at the University of Georgia, Athens.

STEPHANIE S. FOELL is a senior associate with Robinson & Associates, Inc., a Washington, D.C., private firm specializing in architectural and landscape history.

ANGELA W. FOWLER, ASLA, is a landscape architect based in New York City and the granddaughter of Robert L. Fowler Jr.

ELLEN GREBINGER and PAUL GREBINGER are with the Warren Hunting Smith Library at Hobart and William Smith Colleges in Geneva, New York, and the College of Liberal Arts of the Rochester Institute of Technology, respectively.

BRADFORD M. GREENE, FASLA, is a former member (retired) of Clarke & Rapuano, New York, consulting engineers and landscape architects.

CAROL GREENTREE is a horticultural journalist and landscape historian, based in La Jolla, California.

ROBERT E. GRESE, ASLA, is an associate professor of landscape architecture at the School of Natural Resources and Environment and director of Nichols Arboretum at the University of Michigan, Ann Arbor.

MAC GRISWOLD is a garden historian who writes frequently for the *New York Times* and the *Wall Street Journal*.

JOHN GRUBER is an independent historian and photographer in Madison, Wisconsin.

BARRY HANNEGAN, Ph.D., is director of the Department of Historic Landscape Preservation at the Pittsburgh History & Landmarks Foundation.

ROBERT R. HARVEY, FASLA, is a professor emeritus in the Department of Landscape Architecture, College of Design, Iowa State University, Ames.

KENNETH I. HELPHAND, FASLA, is a professor of landscape architecture at the University of Oregon and editor of *Landscape Journal*.

LAURIE E. HEMPTON is a historical landscape architect with the Historic Landscape Initiative of the National Park Service, Washington, D.C.

GARY R. HILDERBRAND, ASLA, is an associate professor of landscape architecture at the Graduate School of Design, Harvard University, and a principal with Douglas Reed Landscape Architecture, Cambridge, Massachusetts.

HEIDI HOHMANN, ASLA, is a landscape architect with BRW, Minneapolis, Minnesota.

CATHERINE HOWETT is a professor emerita in the School of Environmental Design at the University of Georgia, Athens, and a senior fellow in the Studies in Landscape Architecture Program of Dumbarton Oaks, Washington, D.C.

MARY V. HUGHES, ASLA, is university landscape architect at the University of Virginia, Charlottesville.

LINDA JEWELL is a professor of landscape architecture at the University of California, Berkeley, a partner in Freeman & Jewell, Berkeley, and a consulting partner in Reynolds & Jewell, Raleigh, North Carolina.

CATHERINE JOY JOHNSON is a landscape historian and photographer in Seattle.

MEREDITH KAPLAN is a landscape architect and planner with the National Park Service in San Francisco and superintendent of the Juan Bautista de Anza National Historic Trail.

ROBIN KARSON is executive director of the Library of American Landscape History, Inc., Amherst, and adjunct faculty at the University of Massachusetts, Amherst.

GARY KESLER, FASLA, is associate head of the Landscape Architecture Department at the University of Illinois, Urbana-Champaign.

JOY KESTENBAUM is an art and architecture librarian and an assistant professor at Pratt Institute, Brooklyn, New York.

SUSAN L. KLAUS is an urban historian in Washington, D.C.

GAYLE KNIGHT is a graduate of the University of Georgia, Athens.

GREGORY KOPISCHKE is a principal landscape architect/planner with Westwood Professional Services, Inc., Minneapolis, and adjunct faculty with the College of Architecture and Landscape Architecture at the University of Minnesota.

MARY BLAINE KORFF is a graduate of the Department of Landscape Architecture at the University of Arizona, Tucson.

ARTHUR KRIM, Ph.D., is a geographer and the principal of Slide Survey Systems, a Cambridge, Massachusetts, survey consulting firm specializing in historic preservation.

KATE LALIBERTE is a master's candidate in the Department of Landscape Architecture and Regional Planning at the University of Massachusetts, Amherst.

MICHAEL LAURIE is a professor emeritus in the College of Environmental Design, Department of Landscape Architecture and Environmental Planning, University of California, Berkeley.

JOANNE SEALE LAWSON is founding principal of Lawson Carter Epstein Landscape Architects, Washington, D.C., and a landscape historian.

ARLEYN LEVEE is a landscape historian, designer, and landscape preservation advocate in Belmont, Massachusetts.

VALENCIA LIBBY is an associate professor in the Department of Landscape Architecture, Temple University, Ambler, Pennsylvania.

BLANCHE M. G. LINDEN, Ph.D., is a historian and principal of Voices & Visions, Fort Lauderdale, Florida.

EVE F. W. LINN is a freelance writer based in Carlisle, Massachusetts.

RICHARD LONGSTRETH is a professor of American civilization and director of the Graduate Program in Historic Preservation at George Washington University, Washington, D.C.

ELDRIDGE LOVELACE, FASLA, FASCE, AICP, was chairman of the board (retired) of Harland Bartholomew & Associates, St. Louis, Missouri.

CHRISTINE B. LOZNER is a historic preservation consultant in Manlius, New York.

KAREN MADSEN is editor of *Arnoldia* and teaches landscape history at Radcliffe Seminars, Radcliffe Institute for Advanced Study, Harvard University.

LINDA FLINT MCCLELLAND is a historian with the National Register of Historic Places Program of the National Park Service, Washington, D.C.

MARIE BARNIDGE-MCINTYRE is horticulturist at Rancho Los Cerritos Historic Site in Long Beach, California, and a garden writer and designer.

ELEANOR M. MCPECK is a landscape historian and instructor at Radcliffe Institute for Advanced Study, Harvard University.

SCOTT A. MEHAFFEY, ASLA, is landscape architect for the Morton Arboretum in Lisle, Illinois.

E. LYNN MILLER is a professor emeritus of landscape architecture at Pennsylvania State University and a member of the Business Faculty with the University of Phoenix.

CYDNEY E. MILLSTEIN is principal of Architectural and Historical Research, Kansas City, Missouri.

KEITH N. MORGAN, Ph.D., is a professor of art history at Boston University.

DANIEL JOSEPH NADENICEK, ASLA, is an associate professor of landscape architecture and director of the Center for Studies in Landscape History at Pennsylvania State University, University Park.

LANCE M. NECKAR, ASLA, is associate dean of the College of Architecture and Landscape Architecture at the University of Minnesota, Minneapolis.

KARA HAMLEY O'DONNELL is historic preservation planner for the City of Cleveland Heights, Ohio.

THERESE O'MALLEY, Ph.D., is associate dean for the Center for Advanced Study in the Visual Arts at the National Gallery of Art, Washington, D.C.

JON A. PETERSON, Ph.D., is an associate professor of history at Queens College of the City University of New York.

ROSETTA RADTKE is landscape coordinator for the City of Savannah, Georgia, Park and Tree Department.

REUBEN RAINEY, Ph.D., is a professor in the Department of Landscape Architecture at the University of Virginia, Charlottesville.

JUDITH HELM ROBINSON is principal of Robinson & Associates, Inc., Washington, D.C., a private firm specializing in architectural and landscape history.

NANCY ROBINSON is a landscape architect in Kansas.

CAROL ROLAND is a historian with the State of California Department of General Services.

MIRIAM E. RUTZ, ASLA, is an associate professor in the Landscape Architecture and Urban and Regional Planning Programs, Department of Geography, Michigan State University, East Lansing.

DAVID SCHUYLER, Ph.D., is a professor of American studies at Franklin & Marshall College, Lancaster, Pennsylvania.

KAREN SEBASTIAN is a graduate of the Department of Landscape Architecture and Regional Planning, University of Massachusetts, Amherst.

BEHULA SHAH is director of Landscape Studies at Chatham College, Pittsburgh.

KIMBERLY ALEXANDER SHILLAND is curator of the Architecture and Design Collections at The MIT Museum, Cambridge, Massachusetts.

DEAN SINCLAIR is an assistant professor of geography at Northwestern State University, Natchitoches, Louisiana.

SUSAN W. STRAHLER is a landscape designer in Pittsburgh and a graduate student in the Landscape Studies Program at Chatham College, Pittsburgh.

DAVID STREATFIELD is an associate professor of landscape architecture at the University of Washington, Seattle.

JUDITH TANKARD is a landscape historian based in Newton, Massachusetts, and the editor of the *Journal of the New England Garden History Society.*

WILLIAM H. TISHLER, FASLA, is a professor of landscape architecture at the University of Wisconsin, Madison.

SPENCER TUNNELL, ASLA, is principal of Tunnell & Tunnell Landscape Architecture, Atlanta.

CHRISTOPHER VERNON is a senior lecturer in landscape architecture in The School of Architecture and Fine Arts at the University of Western Australia, Nedlands, Perth, Western Australia.

NOEL DORSEY VERNON, ASLA, is associate dean of the College of Environmental Design, and a professor of landscape architecture at California State Polytechnic University, Pomona.

NELL WALKER is a landscape designer and principal of a design build firm in Lexington, Massachusetts.

SHERDA K. WILLIAMS is the leader of the Cultural Landscapes Program for the Midwest Region of the National Park Service, in Omaha, Nebraska.

DEON WOLFENBARGER is a historic preservation consultant and principal of Three Gables Preservation, Kansas City, Missouri.

AARON WUNSCH is a Ph.D. candidate at the University of California, Berkeley, and served as a historian with the Historic American Buildings Survey in Washington, D.C.

JAMES J. YOCH is a professor of English at the University of Oklahoma, Norman, and nephew of Florence Yoch.

CYNTHIA ZAITZEVSKY, Ph.D., is a historian of architecture and landscape architecture.